The Art of Equanimity: A Study on the Theological Hermeneutics of Saint Anselm of Canterbury

European University Studies

Europäische Hochschulschriften
Publications Universitaires Européennes

Series XXIII
Theology

Reihe XXIII   Série XXIII
Theologie
Théologie

Vol./Bd. 750

PETER LANG

Frankfurt am Main · Berlin · Bern · Bruxelles · New York · Oxford · Wien

Emery de Gaál Gyulai

The Art of Equanimity: A Study on the Theological Hermeneutics of Saint Anselm of Canterbury

PETER LANG
Europäischer Verlag der Wissenschaften

BR
754
.A56
G33
2002

Die Deutsche Bibliothek - CIP-Einheitsaufnahme

Gaál Gyulai, Emery / de :

The art of equanimity: a study on the theological hermeneutics
of Saint Anselm of Canterbury / Emery de Gaál Gyulai. -
Frankfurt am Main ; Berlin ; Bern ; Bruxelles ; New York ;
Oxford ; Wien : Lang, 2002
   (European university studies ; Ser. 23, Theology ; Vol. 750)
   Zugl.: Pittsburgh, Univ., Habil.-Schr., 2000
   ISBN 3-631-39811-5

On the cover: the End of Anselm's *Monologion* and Beginning
of his *Proslogion*
  – As a visualisation of human thinking's tension-filled
  constitution and bridging function. –
Prague, The University Library (National Library)
MS XIII F 20, f. 240v

ISSN 0721-3409
ISBN 3-631-39811-5
US-ISBN 0-8204-6010-9

© Peter Lang GmbH
Europäischer Verlag der Wissenschaften
Frankfurt am Main 2002
All rights reserved.

Printed in Germany 1 2   4 5 6 7

www.peterlang.de

Gratefully dedicated to
my parents, sister and brother.

Preface

This paper is not a thorough presentation, still less a meticulous analysis of the Anselmian mind. It aims rather at showing some of the main currents and attitudes of a saint's thoughts and the channels through which they flowed. Many in the past have confined themselves to presenting the system, logical structure or certain aspects of Anselm's manifold intellectual contributions. This book – an anbridged form of the dissertation I defended at Duquesne University's theology department in the Spring of 2000 - is an endeavour to present Anselm's philosophy and theology as a unit and as a direct continuation of Greek and Latin thought, colored through its Medieval surroundings, ennobled by Christian purpose, service and teaching and embedded thoroughly in the singular beauty of monastic life.

Having passed the threshold to the second millennium, Europe's mind blended in the eleventh century the bygone ten centuries already into one, little differentiated whole. The ruptures of dissent and lines of division between Christian creed and pagan achievements were no longer that well defined. The task of the monastery is to praise God and to meditate on Him (*opus Dei*). This is not accomplished by participation in liturgy and labor alone. The monastery was the precious vessel (*depositum*) preserving and handing down to future generations what were considered valuable contributions of previous ages: the *scriptorium*. The monks' mind brought this heritage in disputations to life within the all-encompassing context of the praise of God, thereby edifying the immediate monastic community, the greater church and society in general. Reading Anselm, one detects that a conscious blending of different lines of thought occurs - Gadamer calls this process "Horizontverschmelzung" – "tradition" is the more fitting term.

It is this paper's first concern to shed some light on this development and define some vectors involved therein: ancient philosophy - represented by Platonism and particularly by its Neo-Platonic exponent Plotinus and the monastic life-context as existence in the Lord's presence (*domus Dei*) (Chapters 1-3). The peace of mind the monastery afforded, granted Anselm singular equanimity and thereby the ability to build an intellectual edifice marked by symmetry and balance (Chapters 4-11). The discussion of this intellectual achievement is the second and central concern.

The reviews of Guardini's, Barth's and Balthasar's contributions to Anselm research (Chapters 12 and 13) serve the paper's third concern: to rekindle interest for an imagined dialogue with Anselm as Christianity enters its third millennium. Could it serve as an invitation to rediscover God as inalienably and inextricably present in every human mind?

It is fitting that I should express my gratitude to Dr. William M. Thompson. It is he who had sufficient confidence in my capabilites to suggest this topic. It is he who as dissertation director deserves my thanks for his patience and generosity in allowing me to apportion my matter as I thought best. With unfailing pertinancity he indefatigably scoured the draft.

Words of special gratitude are also due to Dr. Michael Slusser, whose magnanimous hospitality was the starting point of this intellectual adventure. His home provided the proper ambience to formulate the dissertation proposal and is the place where the paper took on its first contours. As first reader, he thoroughly examined the drafts twice with unrivalled attention to detail. In the process he brought to bear his wide experience as scholar. Also to Dr. Anne Clifford and to Dr. James P. Hanigan - as second and third readers - do I express my gratitude. Their helpful and crucial suggestions greatly improved the paper. I owe a great debt to Duquesne University's theology department. It graciously lent support to my studies.

During the long period of writing I received help and encouragement from many scholars and friends. It is impossible to thank them all, but I must mention a few. The numerous discussions with Leo Card. Scheffczyk and Professor Manfred Hauke have been a constant stimulus and corrective. The same applies to meetings with Univ.Prof.Dr.habil. Joseph Schumacher. My friends from Munich's Protestant theology department clarified certain biographical and systematic points concerning Karl Barth. Dr. Karla Mertens provided invaluable insights into the life and thoughts of Hans Urs von Balthasar. Participation in Professor Michael Seybold's "Oberseminar" at Eichstätt University shed additional light on this theologian's thoughts. My thanks go out also to Professor Ulrich Horst for permitting me to use the facilities of the Grabmann Institute for Medieval Studies at Munich's Catholic theology department.

H. Ex. Dr. Walter Mixa, Bishop of Eichstätt, kindly encouraged this book. Rector Lic.theol. Willibald Harrer gave me the necessary liberty to defend this paper. Dean Isidor Vollnhals, Pastor of the magnificent Münster-Church in Ingolstadt, generously provided office space. Interesting theological discourses with Prelate Wilhelm Reitzer enriched my stay there.

Last but not least I wish to record my deeply felt gratitude to the Munich-based "Dr. Olbrich Stiftung zur Förderung der Geisteswissenschaften." This foundation's magnanimous grant made this publication possible in the first place.

Despite the generous help of all the above mentioned and many others any remaining errors or weaknesses must be imputed to me alone.

E. G.

Munich, April 21, 2002, Feast of St. Anselm of Canterbury

Table of Content

The art of hermeneutics is the art of letting oneself be told something.
Hans-Georg Gadamer

Tomorrow's Christian will either be a mystic or nothing.
Karl Rahner

CHAPTER ONE

1.0 Introduction

Instead of conducting a yet further philosophical and theological exegesis of the Anselmian corpus and adding perhaps further critiques from a logician's perspective, this paper attempts to determine Anselm's central intuition and to suggest its possible sources.

An examination of Anselm's writings reveals that it is the human mind wherein insight into divine matters is being granted to the thinker. This cognitional event is neither by chance nor automatic nor let alone the result of preceding, purely human efforts. The numinous as the "fascinosum et tremendum" takes the initiative and appears. Thinking's subject and object cooperate in such a way that the subject (i.e. the thinking human being) becomes cognizant of this "joint" effort. As a consequence, the previously enterprising mind assumes an attitude of grateful awe.

To establish this claim, the monastic life context and aspects of the intellectual heritage current to Anselm's day are considered to some extent. Plotinus seems to express in greater detail - but nota bene outside a Christian context - the very same central Anselmian intuition: the mind as the locale of an encounter with the divine.[1] No doubt Anselm was influenced by both Aristotelianism and Neoplatonism. In order to accommodate the salient features of Plotinian thought some aspects of monastic life receive in the final edition less attention.

The "explicandum" of Anselmic thought is based primarily on the available textual evidence. Yet, it receives adumbrating confirmation from the concrete monastic context from within which it originated and the historical perspective in which it legitimately can be situated. These two factors relieve the author from the unattractive task of providing merely an additional Anselm-immanent exegesis. The two crucial vectors: 1. his Christian monastic setting and 2. the history of ideas to which he is indebted give life and contours to his

---

[1] Not more than a Neo-Platonic/Plotinian affinity in this limited sense is being maintained. Boethius' commentaries on Aristotle and Porphyry of Tyre's *Isagoge* and their influence on Medieval thinking should not be trivialized. They do, however, serve not that well to illustrate what Anselm actually intended to achieve. Plotinus is in this regard more helpful.

disciplined and restrained language. It was his central concern that not he, but the monastic community - and therefore more precisely the Church Catholic - should be speaking in his, the Benedictine archbishop's writings.

At the beginning (chapter 1.0) and at the end (14.0) the topicality of the thinker and monk Anselm for the new century and millennium is suggested. Chapter 2.0 prepares the ground for what Anselm had in mind when referring to the "id quo maius cogitari nequit." In details paralleling Anselm, Plotinus elaborated on God as the central agent of metaphysical insight. The unity and mutual interrelatedness of philosophy and theology as reciprocally immanent to both disciplines are discussed at the beginning of that chapter. Thus the oftentimes recurring question when Anselm is writing as a philosopher and when as a theologian is laid to rest. This frees the examination to apprehend in Anselm - as in all of pre-Scholatic theology - an underlying unity between philosophy and theology.[2] The subsequent chapter (3.0) outlines the monastic context from within which Anselm unfolded his reflections. The philosophical-theological exegesis (chapters 4.0 - 10.0) is opened with a discussion of Anselm's understanding of the "Unum." Thereby an arch is spanned through time back to Plotinus. Thereupon a chronological investigation into Anselm's writings is conducted.[3] The result leaves the reader impressed by the inner unity, stringency and clarity of the "via Anselmi." More than once one feels not merely confronted with the honest, but albeit subjective conjectures of an individual human being, but rather touched by truth itself.

In an effort to illustrate the arduous process of retrieving Anselm for current philosophy and theology Guardini's, Barth's and Balthasar's contributions to ongoing Anselm research are presented and discussed on the canvas of the insights gained in chapters 4.0 through 10.0. Thereby an effort is being undertaken to demonstrate Anselm as central and crucial to their respective "theologies." In the final chapter neither rationalism nor fideism pass as viable alternatives to describe the "via Anselmi." In fact, the mere proposition of such a question is a challenge to state: in Anselm's thinking "analogia entis" and "analogia fidei" operate jointly and - seen from today's perspective - in "ecumenical" harmony.

1.1 The Challenge of Globalization to Theology

Sir Richard Southern's recent book *Scholastic Humanism and the Unification of Europe* contains the legacy of the doyen of English Medievalists. In a number of publications he influenced this century's Anselm studies in a

---

[2] Therein an answer is given to what relationship there exists between nature and grace. However, this significant aspect cannot be discussed in greater detail in the present study.

[3] For the chronological sequence of Anselm's writings see Franciscus Salesius Schmitt, S. Anselmi Cantuariensis Archiepiscopi Opera Omnia, Vol. I - VI (Stuttgart-Bad Cannstatt: Frommann, 1968) at Vol. I, Prolegomena 41-63.

decisive manner. In this book he develops a picture of Scholastic Humanism as a model worthy of emulation for a future united Europe.[4] By so doing, the author, however, makes a more modest assertion than the claim actually implies. The topicality of the Medieval mind for modernity - and accordingly for human culture per se - is laid claim on.[5]

Throughout the world a civilization is spreading that defintely augurs the end of a Euro-centric view. A pluralistic and multicultural situation asserts itself. Simultaneously a sense of urgency to assume collective responsibility for the whole globe is increasingly viewed as important. Around such terms as world economy, globalization, peace, justice and ecology a global awareness evolves. A sense of solidarity, of having a common purpose and destiny, however vaguely perceived and circumscribed, asserts itself. Yet more than these palpable phenomena, the corresponding erosion of certainties carries with it also a sense of alienation which has become the carrying note of the global society.[6] This alienation possesses neither a religious-moral (Augustinian) nor economic (Marx) undertone. Rather, it is a sense of human existence's pointlessness in a cosmos without center and without aim.

As Waldenfels states, theology has not yet properly addressed this epochal, new situation.[7] Heidegger had formulated something similar to this in a much too principled perhaps even dogmatic way. In Rahner's writings one senses premonitions of the world to come. The loss of categories such as the "One", "nature", "God" or "substance" are usually mentioned. In Germany Eugen Biser, Eugen Drewermann and Hans Küng express this new situation in their more recent publications. New world ethics, therapeutic sensibilisation and new experiences should offer solutions. Needless to say, the pluralistic world order poses a challenge for every culture and every religion. How are nations to deal with a loss of sovereignty and the attendent loss of national identity in a

---

[4] Richard Southern, <u>Scholastic Humanism and the Unification of Europe</u> (Oxford: Blackwell, 1995).

[5] Without such clarity also the following contributions postulate the current relevance of the Middle Ages: Kurt Flasch, "Wozu erforschen wir die Philosophie des Mittelalters?" in: Wilhelm Vossenkuhl, Rolf Schönberger (eds.), <u>Die Gegenwart Ockhams</u> (Weinheim: Acta Humaniora, 1990) 393-409; see also i.a. Emmerich Coreth, Honnefelder, Wieland, in: <u>Theologische Quartalschrift</u> (3. Heft, 1992) - the entirety of this issue is dedicated to the current value of Medieval Studies.

[6] Cf. Erich Fromm, <u>The Art of Loving</u>, 2nd impr. ed. (London: Allen & Unwin, 1976); Morris Kline, <u>Mathematics in Western Culture</u> (London: Allen & Unwin, 1954); Karl Löwith, <u>Wissen, Glaube und Skepsis</u>, 3rd ed. (Göttingen: Vandenhoeck & Ruprecht, 1962).

[7] "Diese Gesellschaft wird in der theologischen Analyse weithin nicht eingeholt. ... Zwar wird der Verlust des Einen - des Seins oder Gottes oder der Natur und Substanz -, nicht aber die Vielgestaltigkeit der Gesichter und Erfahrungen in der einen Welt zum Ausdruck gebracht." Hans Waldenfels, "Die vielen Gesichter der einen Welt," <u>Christ in der Gegenwart</u> (No. 19, 1997) 157. cf. also Joseph Ratzinger, <u>Wesen und Auftrag der Theologie, Versuche zu ihrer Ortsbestimmung</u> (Einsiedeln: Johannes, 1993) 7, where theology is placed in the fulcrum of the described global development.

global world? Moreover, the binding character of religious precepts is questioned. Apparently this opens a scenario for a period of prolonged insecurity and of constant flux. The challenge will be to find an orientation that responds both to the Christian vision and to the more immediate needs of humanity: i.e. provide it sustenance and harmony with humanity's need for self-transcendence.[8] As history demonstrates, humankind has excelled in the liberal arts whenever a strong sense of an inspiring origin of humanity lying beyond itself was very present in society.[9] Equally the individual from a purely psychological perspective seems mature and stable if he serves a purpose lying outside his own person.[10]

While one readily agrees with Küng when he views the 21st century as a "Weltjahrhundert," one cannot fail to consider the project "Weltethos" unsuccessful if it is but the lowest common denominator of what religions, cultures and civilizations esteem.[11] Here one cannot help but detect in Küng's writings "sich in ihm eine untergründige Vorherrschaft des westlich-säkularistischen Weltverständnisses mit einem asiatisch-harmonisierenden Einheitsgefühl verbindet."[12]

While lamenting the rampant spread of crime and consumerism, he mentions no means or criteria by which one can remedy this malcondition.

The "struggle of cultures" - thus Samuel P. Huntington - cannot be avoided by relativizing the seriousness of religions' contents. Undeniably, such an intention might on the contrary provoke conflict. The contents of the various religions convey a sense of respect for the human person and its existence; no scientific discipline, ideology or Weltanschauung was ever able to match this in its evocative strength.[13] Only upon a religious background, i.e. a definition of the finite human person grounded in an infinite origin, respect, sympathy and tolerance for different cultures, faiths and viewpoints can cultures find their

---

[8] The question to what degree such a culture formed and transformed by the mass media is still able to raise questions commensurate to humanity's inner teleology must remain unanswered.

[9] Cf. examplarily Otto v. Simson, Die gotische Kathedrale (an improved version of the 2nd. English edition of 1962) 3rd edition (Darmstadt: Wissenschaftliche Buchgesellschaft, 1979) 1-10.

[10] Cf. examplarily Viktor Frankl, Der Mensch vor der Frage nach dem Sinn. 3rd ed. (München: Piper, 1988); see by the same author also Im Anfang war der Sinn (Wien: Deutilke, 1982).

[11] Cf. his recent book on this topic: Hans Küng Weltethos für Weltpolitik und Weltwirtschaft (Piper, München, 1997).

[12] Küng, Weltethos.

[13] More than any other, this century bears witness to the failures of non-religious world-views, ideologies,and pursuasions: Ausschwitz, Gulag, Pol Pot, Cultural Revolution etc. cf. Stéphane Courtois, Le livre noir du communisme - Crimes, terreur, répression (Paris: Robert Laffont (publ.), 1997).

justification and be promoted. Without the anthropological phenomenon of religion a sense of absolute respect for the human person is intellectually and existentially difficult to sustain. As a consequence cynicism and totalitarianism may rule unchecked. What is called for is the clear respect for the different and alien religions and worldviews in their being different. On the one hand the Middle Ages may offer a paradigm for bringing different cultures, positions and religions into a mutually beneficial dialogue. On the other hand it and history in general demonstrate that to possess such generosity one also needs to have a clear and unambigious understanding of one's own worldview.

This calls for a reconsideration of the specificity of each religion. To move beyond mere tactical accommodation to the present exegencies, the question must be raised as to whether Christianity has unwittingly contributed to the current sense of loss and whether it possesses from within itself the means to overcome this temper. In modern theology it was particularly the contribution of the Russian universal scholar and priest Pawel Florenski[14] to perceive Christianitiy as the most sublime articulation of a relational worldview. He chides the late Middle Ages, Renaissance and modernity as having succumbed to an analytic world description which invariably inaugurated the destruction of the unity and comprehensive interrelationality of the universe. Not only are products of art some kind of sign of a hereafter reality, of a meaning undergirding the palpable reality. Rather such art can be identical with this meaning and indeed constitutes it here and now: in the present life-context. There is a Platonic unity of life and art, of science and faith which allows every element to retain its proper nature and role. The finite and infinite are distinct and yet not unrelated or separate. This perspective permits one to behold the essential of life. There is a principal and central interrelationality and, therefore, interactivity of all occurrences and phenomena in life which does not justify a choristic difference between subject and object. It is Anselm´s achievement to unfold in his writings such an understanding. In cogitation an interactivity of subject and object occurs.

---

[14] Pawel Florenski, Raum und Zeit, ed. and transl. by Radetzkaja and Werner (Berlin: Ed. Kontext, 1997). It is his vision of the universal understanding of life, of his vision of a comprehensive totality of life, that compelled him to decide to become an Orthodox priest. In this book he rejects in no uncertain terms the central perspective prevalent in Western art since the days of Giotto as condemning the beholder to a passive role in which art is but a theater. Accidental aspects of existence are stylized to high art. This he contrasts to Antiquity´s and the early Medieval understanding of art as a crucial manifestation of the interrelationality of all things. There is an essential content to all of life. The modern central perspective in art makes the artist project a vision unto life in which the beholder is but an accidental spectator. This he defines as the Cartesian-Kantian-Euclidian "Weltanschauung." The beholding I is inactive and uncreative in this situation. Florenski, arguing very much from the Eastern understanding of the role and mission of the icon, pleads for active passivity. There is a creative interactivity of passivity and activity in every concrete life context.

Christians can play a meaningful part in such a pluralistic global community only if they bear witness to the unifying vision of the Gospel. It is incumbent upon them to relate what in their view is necessary to give life meaning, what gives existence fulfillment and salvation. What graces life here and thereafter with its particular and unique glistening must be central topoi of their contributions.

1.2 An "Anamnesis" of Modernity

For our present purpose it suggests itself to know what valence the word "modern" contains. Modernity - as every epoch - cannot define itself. Such a task requires points of contrast. These are acquired through a historical perspective. Contrasting and comparing various epochs, the pre-history of an idea and the formation of structures suggest an image, a bird's eye view of the enduring characteristics of human existence. Southern points out that the intellectual insecurity prevailing towards the end of the 19th century had brought forth already once before a rediscovery of Medieval thinking. This is paralleled today by the current resurgence of popular interest in medieval studies amidst a postmodern temper equally insecure of its bearings and in search of a compass.[15]

This said, it appears that the singular most striking feature of modernity is on the one hand the heightening of the individual's consciousness and on the other the collapse of the possibility of communal life within a self-evident order. Individual and communitarian aims seem to mutually exclude one another in civil life. Individuals no longer experience themselves as members of a greater whole: such as humanity, nation, religion, ethnic group or even the most basic social entity: family and themselves as a living articulation of the same. Indeed, persons find themselves torn between conflicting allegiances. Autonomy and authenticity, self-definition by orientation toward a public sense of justice and self-realization by way of orientation to the subjectively defined good assume the character of oxymorons. The feeling of the presence of a split personality is so pervasive, it barely is reflected upon. This presence thereby also acquires a tragic quality, for modernity had claimed to liberate the human race from the most varied restraints: social, religious, political, cultural, etc., yet it achieved something of a "self-enslaved slavery." The guiding principle is the "sovereignty of the subject." This principle has produced a situation of irreconcilable tensions and conflicts. Modern lifestyles frequently take on the character of being inextricably without a solution.

In comparison to past eras of history this striking feature of the individual's "unrelatedness" exhibits an additional salient feature: a conscious relationship to the Divine which can no longer be assumed for the majority

---

[15] Umberto Eco, Der Name der Rose (München: DTV, 1987); Jacques LeGoff, Le Moyen Age d´aujourd´hui (Paris: Léopard d´Or, 1998); Georges Duby; Le Moyen Age (Paris: Hachette, 1987); etc.

living in Western society. This temper seems by no means geographically limited.[16] After millennia of religious experiences and metaphysics, modern philosophy has coined the phrase "the end of metaphysics." Philosophy frequently experiences itself as "post-metaphysical thought." The thinking subject's object is altered as it finds itself within this process of more recent "Wirkungsgeschichte"[17] re-defined as an autonomous entity. Evidently it is oftentime not borne in mind that only in recourse to previous ages can such a definition be arrived at. The inability to relate to previous centuries renders the present increasingly unable to behold its own situation. Thus the precarious relativity of a presumedly autonomous thought as independent reflection is evidenced.

The assertion is that in view of globalization as the present epochality, this "split personality" increasingly is the carrying note not only for modern Occidental facticity but for all of humanity. The distance between the individual's and society's cultural identity[18] and current, prevailing intellectual vectors and economic exigencies grows exponentially daily at a rapid pace world-wide.

The claim made here is that[19] choices, tensions and conflicts belong inherently to the "conditio humana." It is only within such a matrix that one experiences oneself called to "do the right and to accomplish the good." Life's positivity, its "worthwhile-ness" beyond any utility[20] is experienced in the struggle to overcome seemingly insurmountable adversities, assist others materially or morally, preserve some meaning or dignity in one's life, etc. The singular factor that renders the modern situation and vital consciousness ("Lebensgefühl") seemingly inextricable is the inability to behold life as containing a transcending and also ethical challenge - for the purpose of something or someone else. Attendant to this is the increasing inability to build relationships. Only if one beholds in a person an absolute, inalienable value can one take him or her seriously. It is this feature in turn which indeed translates into a sense of being thrown into hopelessly inextricable situations. Only if one does not countenance the ethical quality of life, does all of existence take on the character of being inextricably tragic, as the Hegel-scholar Menke holds.[21]

How is one to know of generally binding ethical principles if these take on the character of but the ephemeral articulation of a volition which is the mere

---

[16] See already Mircea Eliade's introduction to Le sacré et le profane (Paris: Gallimard, 1965).

[17] I.e. from about the Renaissance onward. "Wirkungsgeschichte" means history of the reception and of the effects of an idea, etc.

[18] Which in Europe, North America and Japan remains almost exclusively evident in outward manifestations such as architecture, performed music and past art.

[19] Contrary to Christoph Menke, Tragödie im Sittlichen. Gerechtigkeit und Freiheit nach Hegel (Frankfurt am Main: Suhrkamp, 1996).

[20] I.e. "Werthaftigkeit" in the sense of possessing its own value and dignity which is not at somebody's disposition.

[21] Cf. Menke, Tragödie im Sittlichen.

mirror of a fleeting judgment of the subject of an ethical act? Do not ethical criteria evaporate into whimsical conjectures and egoistic, personal preferences if there is no point of reference lying outside individuals? How can one sustain life as an ethical effort if life does not contain irrevocably a personal dimension that is not yet again merely ephemeral in character? Is the absolutely compelling nature of ethics sustainable without a supra-individual personal presence endowed with an obliging appellative character not yet again subject to contingent, accidental circumstances?

1.3 The "Kairos" of Medieval Hermeneutics

Because of a lack of metaphysics in modern consciousness, philosophical discourse evolves around questions of hermeneutics.[22] Gadamer's hermeneutics apprehends a continuum in the "Wirkungsgeschichte" which - not in spite of but due to additions and adumbrations -constitutes a unity. To comprehend something means to Gadamer always making it present as a moment of "Wirkungsgeschichte." The presence of meaning appears justifiable only as tradition. This presence of tradition carries the understanding process and continues underwriting the understanding process.

Nietzsche's works may be interpreted as perspectival integration. In this sense truth is not thought to be written but exclusively the understanding process itself.[23] The process of making tradition present brings the past with it and performs thereby a heightening of present life that interprets itself.

Figal opposes an unreflected, mere commemoration of the past and an undirected progression from one point in time to the next - which he apparently divines as the peril per se of contemporary existence. This point of continuous appropriation is well illustrated by his judgment on the role of art in society. The meditation on a piece of art renders the alien past present in a way that the alien remains alien irretrievably. Yet precisely therefore it enables one to gain deeper knowledge of the self and its very own epochality. History is experienced herein as unrepeatable. To him modernity in such a situation is no longer defined as being unavoidably at the mercy of time, but as the struggle to master the conflict of time and presence.[24]

As a result of such a state of affairs, theology is frequently dismissed as incapable of dealing with truth questions.[25] Fodor holds:

---

[22] Cf. Günter Figal, Der Sinn des Verstehens (Stuttgart: Reclam,1996).

[23] This begs the obvious question: how can there be understanding if there does not exist an object to be understood? An epistemological endeavor without truth as at least a theoretical possibilty is doomed to fail.

[24] Cf. Figal, Der Sinn der Verstehens.

[25] The historic low esteem which pastors, theologians, etc., commonly enjoy in the Western hemisphere may well be caused by this situation.

21

"(t)he woeful lack of credence accorded to theology in our time is due, at least in part, to theology's devaluing of the referential import of its own discourse."[26]

Theology is called also by (post-) modernity to be more than an incommensurable language game and requires more than intratextual meaning. It must give an account of a reality beyond linguistic strategems and plays.

Contrary to structuralism's reduction of the text to the text, Ricoeur demonstrates how language, particularly in metaphor and narrative, operates centrifugally, developing indirect references. This mere reference evolves in the overarching process of tradition into refiguration. To Ricoeur refiguration is the more felicitous term because it conveys a sense of the innovative effect texts possess. This comes to light when the text experiences an appropriation in lived life: in action. Theology as the fourth step, after text, reading and appropriative action, is telling the reality of the narrative, of truth as testimony, initiative and guidance to master life.[27]

To continue this train of thought, hermeneutics may not so much lead to an emancipation (of the individual) but to humanity's greater authenticity. The thesis is that henology, as the scientifically critical and responsible reflection on the ontologically prior one and the all being underlying unity, is the consistent feature of Occidental thought well into the modern era. It is at the same time a felicitous key with which to unravel in a scientifically - and insofar also hermeneutically - responsible manner the thoughts of Anselm. Henology - see below - is a constitutive element of the Occident's "Wirkungsgeschichte." Its hermeneutic retrieval permits the present to discover its very own authenticity. Tradition's refiguration of incarnation is found consonant with extrabiblical, philosophical refigurations (aspects of Platonism).

The present reflections also wish to contribute to a discovery of the "quidditas" of the Medieval disposition as an articulation of humankind's "quidditas" throughout intellectual history.[28] It is also the unifying theme of the Middle Ages. It anticipates in many small mosaic-stones the whole of reality.

---

[26] James Fodor, Christian Hermeneutics: Paul Ricoeur and the Refiguring of Thelogy New York: Oxford/Clarendon, 1995) 332.

[27] Particularly: Paul Ricoeur, Du texte à l'action (Paris: Edition du Seuil, 1986). In the book's scope, theology is the refiguration of historical and non-historical referentiality of biblical narratives - not of the Church (= tradition) as salvation history.

[28] The Swiss mediavalist Ruedi Imbach notes: "Das Thema der historischen Bedingtheit dessen, was m.E. durchaus Scholastik genannt werden kann, ist noch nicht mit der erforderlichen Umsicht und der notwendigen Präzision erforscht worden." "Notabilia V," Freiburger Zeitschrift für Philosophie und Theologie 42 (1995) 186-207, at 195. Scholasticism's historicity has yet to be analyzed in a thorough and consistent manner. While Anselm is counted as a member of the Middle Ages, he is not a Scholastic. However, he did contribute to Scholasticism. Literature in general subsumes him still under the Scholastics. This is, alas, also the case in the cited article.

The totality of divine salvation and its interpretation are the themes.[29] The ability to live and think in such an ambience of unity and totality and yet to refrain from defining it constitutes the era's greatness.[30] Nowhere - in contrast to Neo-Scholastic tendencies - does one find references to a closed system. Discourse is open to an unthinkable number of participants. No subject, argument or opponent is barred. The discourse rarely leads to a definitive conclusion. An exhaustive presentation is not presumed. The way of insight opens the view to infinity. This tolerant, cosmopolitan openness is possible due to the underlying confidence in the unity of the cosmos.

Consequently the Medieval mind contains a message relevant well beyond the geographic confines of Medieval Europe. It may well contribute to a future global community, indeed to a "global scientific community" as unified, cosmopolitan and pluralistic as that of Medieval Europe.

Already Medieval disputations teach the usefulness of presenting and discussing diverse, contradictory and alien positions. Rémi Brague goes one step further in his essay and suggests a paradigmatic feature of that era of utmost relevance. Medieval thinkers were in command of "the art to borrow" and advises present-day Europe:"Es ist gut daran zu erinnern, woher Europa die nährenden Säfte hat, durch die es fett wurde."[31] Europe of the Middle Ages, but also that of today can only be understood properly if one sees it as the continent where different cultures met and meet. Gothic art could only come about due to the Greek, Roman, Arab and Byzantine influences upon it. This renders the Middle Ages worthy of imitation.

Die Menschen des Mittelalters haben fremde Elemente zu sich holen können, und zwar ein Fremdes, das entweder außerhalb ihrer unmittelbaren Erfahrung lag - in der Antike - oder gar außerhalb ihrer eigenen Tradition - in der jüdischen oder in der arabischen Welt. Diese Elemente haben sie bearbeitet, fortgeführt und weiterentwickelt.[32]

Here the alien is blended into the already inherited to achieve a new, meaningful synthesis.

This relevance becomes all the more evident if one bears in mind that it was a prominent feature of Medieval intellectual life to distinguish clearly between science and faith.[33] Inspite of the century's rationalistic temptations,

---

[29] "Und das macht tatsächlich einen weiteren Wesenszug der Scholastik aus: daß sie in einem ungemein energischen Denkimpuls schlechterdings aufs Ganze ging." Josef Pieper, "Die Aktualität der Scholastik," Die Aktualität der Scholastik Joseph Ratzinger ed. (Regensburg: Pustet, 1975) 110.
[30] The first lines of the Summa Theologica affirm: "We know not what God is."
[31] Andreas Speer, Philosophie und geistiges Erbe des Mittelalters mit Beiträgen von Jan A. Aersten, Klaus Jacobi, Georg Wieland und Rémi Brague (Köln: U Köln, 1994) 62.
[32] Speer, Philosophie 64f.
[33] S.Th. I.q.1.a.1.

both Pope Leo XIII[34] in the encyclical "Aeterni Patris"[35] and Pierre Mandonnet in his sizable study "Siger de Brabant et l'averroïsme latin au XIIIe siècle"[36] detect at the close of the 19th century this characteristic of Medieval philosophy as well.[37]

Gilson's interpretation of Christian philosophy arises from his preoccupation with that of the Middle Ages. He is certain that this distinction between science and faith also influenced some of modernity's principles.[38] The ontological ground of existence and its unity in pre-Christian times already previously discovered by humanity is not contradicted but amplified and directed by faith to the personal relationship between God and humanity, in the Middle Ages. The correlation and tension between faith and reason stand now in the foreground.

J'appelle donc philosophie chrétienne et toute philosophie qui, bien que distinguant formellement les deux orders, considère la révélation comme un auxiliaire indispensable de la raison.

A few pages thereafter he adds:

En choississant l'homme dans son rapport à Dieu comme centre de perspective, le philosophe chrétien se donne un centre de référence fixe, qui lui permet d'introduire dans sa pensée l'ordre et l'unité.[39]

In this sense Medieval philosophy takes on a character all its own and yet it is not an idiosyncratic, alien, forced, artificial entity in the flow of the history of philosophy. It is the Christian form of human reason's self-execution: "l'exercice chrétien de la raison" which is beheld as consonant with the extra-Christian experiences of this same human intellect.[40] This peculiar feature of the Medieval mind is not the gradual product of that age, but rather finds itself thus defined at its very beginning by the "Father of Scholasticism," Anselm of Canterbury: "Fides quaerens intellectum, voilà le principe de toute spéculation médiévale."[41]

---

[34] Cf. no. 23 of the encyclical.

[35] ASS 12 (1879) 275; for the high estimation of Thomistic philosophy during the Second Vatican Council cf. OT 16.

[36] Pierre Mandonnet, Siger de Brabant et l'averroïsme latin au XIIIe siècle, 1899 (Louvain: Institut de l'Université, 1909-1911) LXV.

[37] Cf. Contemporary philosophy. A new survey, edited by Guttrom Flöistad, Volume 6, Philosophy and Science in the Middle Ages, parts 1 and 2 (The Hague: Nijhoff, 1990).

[38] Etienne Gilson, L'Esprit de la philosophie médiévale, 2nd. ed. (Paris: Vrin, 1969) 11.

[39] Gilson, L'Esprit 33.35 respectively.

[40] Gilson, L'Esprit 11.

[41] Gilson, L'Esprit 5. Compare Jean Leclercq's observation in The Love of Learning and The Desire for God. A Study of Monastic Culture (New York: Fordham UP, 1961) 272 "Through many aspects of his work, St. Anselm belongs to Scholasticism; but an authentic monastic

Maritain arrives at a similar verdict from a systematic perspective. Not only do Christian philosophers exist, as Mandonnet postulated at the conference of Juvisy in 1931, but philosophy can and must be also Christian. He distinguishes between the nature of philosophy and its condition. The adjective "Christian" does not define the essence of philosophy. Philosophy is defined by its formal object. As such philosophy is by no means dependent on faith. Yet in its concrete execution it may be Christian.

L'expression de philosophie chrétienne désigne non pas une essence prise en elle-même, mais un complexe: une essence prise sous son état, sous des conditions d'exercice, d'existence et de vie, pour ou contre lesquelles à vrai dire l'homme est tenu d'opter.[42]

1.4 The Symbolic Nature of Philosophy and Theology - A Recovery[43]

Negligentia mihi esse videtur, si, postquam confirmati sumus in fide, non studemus quod credimus intelligere.[44]

Thereby Anselm describes the significant relationship between faith and reason. Seen from a modern perspective, to bring theology and philosophy into dialogue was his unreflected constant mission

While referring to Varro's book offering 288 possible philosophies, Augustine takes for granted that this means there are 288 different ways to the "beata vita", or blessed life, desired by all of mankind.[45] Philosophy's purpose is to enable a life commensurate and conducive to this end: participation in a "visio beatifica."

For early Christians the relationship between philosophy and Christian faith was by no means an abstract one. Christian faith was seen as the response

---

doctrine can also be found in his work." This is puzzling as he previously admits Anselm to have a "mystical vocabulary" not to be be found readily elsewhere in scholastic literature: at 243: cf. for example the end of the *Proslogion:* "to elevate his spirit unto God." A definition of the terms "scholasticism" or of "doctrine" cannot be found in Leclercq's book.

[42] Jacques Maritain, Science et sagesse, suivi d´éclairissements sur la philosophie morale (Paris: Labergerie, 1935) 140.

[43] For a concise and succinct presentation of the relationship of the two disciplines in the Middle Ages cf. Gillian R. Evans, Philosophy and Theology in the Middle Ages (London: Routledge, 1993) particularly at 3-47. Jörg Splett's book Denken vor Gott, Philosophie als Wahrheitsliebe (Knecht, Frankfurt am Main, 1996) is symptomatic of a recovery of philosophy as an overarching discipline concerned with truth, the thinking subject's relationship to a personal, perceived absolute principle and therefore not unrelated to theology.

[44] Cu I 1: 48,17.

[45] De Civ. Dei XIX.i.2.

to the perennial questions of philosophy.[46] The earliest known Christian pieces of plastic art date back to the third century. On such sarcophagi the canon of motifs comprises three figures: shepherds, prayers and philosophers. This relationship of the three is of import. It demonstrates that these three together provide answers to the perennial questions which the phenomenon of death inevitably invites. It is the philosopher, not in search of hypotheses but who wrestles with life's finality, with death's gravity and the meaning of life who holds the Gospel in his hands. In early Christian art not images of Scripture or of the lives of saints stand in the center of attention, but the philosopher as archetype of the homo christianus, who is granted by the Gospel revelation of the true meaning of life and certitude of paradise.[47]

The blending of philosophy and Christendom is central to the later part of antiquity. The philosopher is transposed into an image of Christ. The disposition of the true philosopher is the life according to and with the Logos.[48]

---

[46] The mutual relevance of philosophy and theology hardly finds treatment in current literature. Particularly via a philosophical grasp of reality can the various - seemingly disparate theological disciplines, such as biblical exegesis, systematic theology and liturgical studies - be brought into relationship to one another. This philosophical "overview" permits an intellectual maturity with independent opinions. Without such a basis hermeneutics is at the mercy of taste. Homilies follow the changing tempers of the Zeitgeist. Wilfried Härle in Systematische Philosophie, Eine Einführung für Theologiestudenten (Göttingen: Vandenhoeck und Ruprecht, 1982) treats questions of logic, epistemology and metaphysics but does not consider the relationship between theology and philosophy. Pannenberg is the first to dedicate a book to this topic: Wolfhart Pannenberg, Theologie und Philosophie: Ihr Verhältnis im Lichte ihrer gemeinsamen Geschichte (Göttingen: Vandenhoeck und Ruprecht, 1996). The attempt is one from the Reformation's understanding of nature and grace.

The philosophical treatment of the question of God has all but evaporated (Henri Bergson and Alfred North Whitehead are exceptions confirming the rule). In its wake also the universe's unity is placed in jeapordy. The present deliberation is in part the attempt to uncover a, if not the, central strain of the history of philosophy: "henosis." Perhaps it is theology's kairos today to recover this forgotten feature of the history of philosophy and to articulate thereby again the fruitful tension between philosophy and theology. This could not only be beneficial for both disciplines but offer in addition a comprehesive orientation for reality.

[47] Friedrich Gerke, Christus in der spätantiken Plastik, 3rd edition, (Mainz: Kupferberg, 1948) 5-8; cf. Frederick van der Meer, Die Ursprünge christlicher Kunst (Freiburg i. Br.: Herder, 1982) 51ff.

[48] Otto Michel, „Philosophia," Theologisches Wörterbuch zum Neuen Testament IX, at 185. Michel notes that gnostics avoid using the term „philosophia." They considered the term "gnosis" as higher. While philosophy poses questions and always awaits answers as its proper habitus, gnosticism claims to provide power and clear knowledge of the ways in this life and the one hereafter. In this sense philosophy fends off the peril of controlling and manipulating life and the divine. The truth apprehended remains veiled in unutterable secrecy; however, it reveals itself precisely as such. Early Christan art confirms the relevance of Wittgenstein's words "Wovon man nicht sprechen kann, darüber muß man schweigen." Ludwig Wittgenstein, Tractatus logico-philosophico, 6.522 (Frankfurt am Main: Suhrkamp, 1960). Cf.

The single most important material argument for Christians in finding such kinship between their faith and philosophy was the teaching of Jesus as the Christ: as the one and true God of all people and of the universe.[49]

Little wonder then that theology did not consider itself a distinct and separate discipline until well after Anselm's time. The later Archbishop of Canterbury treats the area of philosophy and theology under the terms "ratio" and "fides." Boethius explicitly defines "theologia" as a branch of philosophy or as "speculativa."[50] Theology ponders what is wholly free of matter and motion. It is the meditation on divine substance, in agreement with previous Platonic thought.[51] To Boethius the burning questions of his day - the nature of God as well as Trinity and God's relationship to the created order - occur to the philosopher-Christian, not to the pure theologian.[52] Only when addressing issues such as humanity's fall, incarnation and redemption - which are uniquely Christian - does he use the title "De Fide Catholica."

Theology is introduced in the thirteenth century as defining a scientific articulation of revealed truth. Asked "whether any further doctrine is required, except for philosophy" Thomas responds that revelation contains things necessary to salvation but which reason alone could never gain insight into.[53]

This does not convey the impression that Christianity is accidental to philosophy. The synergy of philosophical inquiry and faith, as realized in Christian philosophy, has altered philosophy and enriched it. It found its proper self, for philosophy approached and approaches rationally what is revealed in veiled form in faith. Christian faith contributed in an objective manner to philosophy.[54] Philosophical existence is not being suppressed but transformed. Christianity has made in Maritain's judgment particularly profound

---

also Hans Urs von Balthasar, Sponsa Verbi. Skizzen zur Theologie II (Einsiedeln: Johannes, 1961) 349-387.

[49] Already to Greek philosophy there must have been one God. As the cosmos was perceived as one, it must call one origin its own, namely the one God. Only one God could have brought forth the universe's unity. As a result, philosophers inquired into the true form of that God. Pre-Socratic philosophers offered a broad tablet of variations on this central theme. Their concern was always to demonstrate something as the one origin of all: water, the infinite, air, reason, etc. cf. for this complex area Uvo Hölscher, "Anaximander und die Anfänge der Philosophie" (1953)reprinted in: Hans-Georg Gadamer (ed.), Um die Begriffswelt der Vorsokratiker (Darmstadt: Wissenschaftliche Buchgesellschaft, 1968) pp. 95-176; Werner Wilhelm Jaeger, The Theology of the Early Greek Philosophers (Oxford: Clarendon P, 1960)

[50] De Trinitate, II.

[51] Henry Chadwick, Boethius. The Consolations of Music, Logic, Theology and Philosophy (Oxford: Clarendon P, 1981) 110.

[52] A term well into the Middle Ages not applied in the systematic and academic sense to Christian cogitation.

[53] S.Th. I.q.1.a.1.

[54] Chadwick, Boethius 138.

contributions in the areas of metaphysics[55] and ethics. A purely natural ethics is a task impossible after the fall in paradise:

> Une philosophie morale purement naturelle et adéquate à l'agir humain aurait pu exister comme l'état de nature pure aurait pu exister, elle n'existe pas plus que celui-ci.[56]

Consequently practical philosophy depends on faith in order to glean necessary insights: not only into the pragmatic contents of right and wrong but also into the ethical challenge of good and bad.[57]

Pannenberg[58] calls for a new appreciation of the relationship between philosophy and theology. This can occur in the dialogue of the two terms "world" and "God." Here philosophy is called upon to recover the unity of the cosmos. Theologians again should increasingly use philosophy, for no singular discipline, such as sociology or psychology, is capable of posing overarching questions, to which theology offers responses in a guarded manner: guarding the secret that is the numinous.[59]

> Philosophie und Theologie haben ein gemeinsames Thema im Bemühen um ein Verständnis der Wirklichkeit des Menschen und der Welt im Ganzen. Man kann freilich Theologie als auch Philosophie betreiben in mancherlei Weisen, die hinter dieser Aufgabe zurückbleiben. Doch die Philosophie entspricht nur dann ihrer großen Tradition, wenn sie sich ihrer Aufgabe stellt, und nur so nimmt sie eine Funktion wahr, in der sie von keiner der Einzelwissenschaften ersetzt werden kann. Die Theologie umgekehrt kann nur dann sachgerecht von Gott und seiner Offenbarung sprechen, wenn sie dabei von dem Schöpfer der Welt und des Menschen handelt und also ihr Reden auf ein Gesamtverständnis der Wirklichkeit des Menschen und der Welt bezieht.[60]

He unequivocally postulates a reciprocal relatedness of one discipline to the other. The philosopher is impelled by philosophical inquiry towards God, whereas the theologian - as a central part of his or her proper self-execution - speaks of God. Only in pursuance of this aim do the two sciences do justice to their own formal object. Theology does justice to her call when choosing God

---

[55] Jacques Maritain, "De la notion de philosophie chrétienne," Revue Neo-Scholastique de Philosophie 34 (1932): 153-186, at 174.

[56] Maritain, "De la notion" 185.

[57] Maritain, "De la notion" 178.

[58] It is noteworthy that a prominent Protestant theologian addresses this issue head on. Underlying the relationship between philosophy and theology is the relationship of the created order to grace. There was in the last centuries the opinion that there exists a tension between the two disciplines, mirroring the hiatus between nature and grace.

[59] "quia inter creatorem et creaturam non potest tanta similitudo notari, quin inter eos maior sit dissimilitudo notanda." in Cap. 2. "De errore Abbatis Ioachim," IV. Lateran Council, 1215, DH 806.

[60] Pannenberg, Theologie und Philosophie 367.

and His revelation as topics of a reflection aiming at the overarching meaning of life.

With unmistakable clarity Gallus Manser asserts the legitimacy of Christian philosophy. To him philosophy is a purely rational science. This strict rationalism is constitutive for philosophy and explains that discipline's autonomy. Such rationality determines both its aim and its unity.

Das, was der unendlichen Vielheit der Probleme die Einheit gibt, daß sie philosophisch sind, ist die reine Vernunftevidenz, durch die sie erkennbar sind.[61]

Pure rationality permits the clear distinction of faith and theology, from which it is set apart through its epistemological origin, its principles and its method.[62] Correctly Manser points out that Thomas drew a sharp and formal line between divinely revealed truth and human insight. Christian philosophy must be set apart from credal contents lest it be reduced to an unscientific subjective "Weltanschauung" or lifestyle.[63]

This clear distinction should not, however, lead to a separation. Christianity in the Middle Ages prevented philosophy from becoming sterile, brittle, static and geometric-logical to such an extent that it would not have related to life.[64] Also the surgical separation of philosophy and theology - as frequently proposed today by some parties[65] - fails to appreciate the philosophical fecundity of theological rationality during the Middle Ages.[66] In Medieval studies - be they theologically or philosophically motivated - one cannot ignore their reciprocally beneficial relationship.

Still influenced by the significant role Thomism played in Catholic theology, Martin Grabmann defined the main thrust of Medieval thinking in his seminal book *Geschichte der scholastischen Methode* as closely aligned to Christian faith:

---

[61] Gallus M. Manser, "Gibt es eine christliche Philosophie?," Divus Thomas 14 (1936): 19-51.123-141, at 29.

[62] Manser, "Gibt es eine christliche Philosophie?" 30.

[63] Manser, "Gibt es eine christliche Philosophie?" 129.

[64] Ruedi Imbach, Laien in der Philosophie des Mittelalters (Amsterdam: Gruner, 1989).

[65] See Fernand van Steenberghen, Introduction à l'étude de la philosophie médiévale (Löwen-Paris: Nauwelaerts, 1974).

[66] It should be noted, however, that inevitably the scholastic method did introduce some degree of secularisation by perceiving the human intellect as distinct and separate from grace and God. This process can be traced back to Albert the Great and Thomas. Nevertheless the perfectability of the human intellect by virtue of humanity's possession of the divine image was upheld quite naturally. Ludwig Hödl, "Die 'Entdivinisierung' des menschlichen Intellekts in der mittelalterlichen Philosophie und Theologie," Zusammenhänge, Einflüße, Wirkungen - Kongreßakten zum ersten Symposium des Mediavistenverbands in Tübingen, 1984 (Berlin: de Gruyter, 1986): 57-70.

Die scholastische Methode will durch Anwendung der Vernunft, der Philosophie auf die Offenbarungswahrheiten möglichste Einsicht in den Glaubensinhalt gewinnen, um so die übernatürliche Wahrheit dem denkenden Menschengeiste inhaltlich näher zu bringen, eine systematische, organisch zusammenfassende Gesamtdarstellung der Heilswahrheit zu ermöglichen und die gegen den Offenbarungsinhalt vom Vernunftstandpunkte aus erhobenen Einwände lösen zu können. In allmählicher Entwicklung hat die scholastische Methode sich eine bestimmte äußere Technik, eine äußere Form geschaffen, sich gleichsam versinnlicht und verleiblicht.[67]

Therein Grabmann implies the notion of unity as a singular outstanding feature of that era. The intelligibility of Christian faith makes the position of a strict separation of faith and philosophy impractical. In order to enable a better comprehension of Scripture's teachings, philosophy was used to demonstrate the correctness of credal precepts to the intellectual mindframe of the Middle Ages. This was important since insight into truth was understood as the key to salvation. In the course of time a methodology developed. Pieper,[68] who is much indebted to this position, however, stresses less methodology and places greater emphasis on the credal aspect.

M.-D. Chenu,[69] W. Kluxen[70] and L.-M. De Rijk[71] reflect much less the credal content and to a greater extent the methodology which gave the medieval era its particular identity. As Lawn well documents, in the Middle Ages the "Questio disputata" was a form of discourse and a vehicle to advance knowledge in all fields. He observes the Scholastic quaestio to have been "the chief method of instruction in all the disciplines in the schools and universities," to have formed the way of Europe's thinking over centuries and even to have influenced indirectly Galilei's kinematics.[72]

---

[67] Martin Grabmann, Geschichte der scholastischen Methode. Bd. 1 Die scholastische Methode von ihren ersten Anfängen in der Väterliteratur bis zum Beginn des 12 Jahrhunderts (Freiburg i. Br.: Herder, 1909) 36.

[68] His preferences are motivated by the times he lived and worked in. During the Third Reich Thomism supplied the arguments to oppose National Socialism. After World War II there existed in parts of the general public in Germany the opinion that to ward off a repetition of totalitarian rule, society should be well informed in matters of religion and ethics.

[69] "Scholastik," Handbuch theologischer Grundbegriffe. Band II. ed. Heinrich Fries (München: Kösel, 1963) 488:
"Mit dem Wort `scholastisch´ ist zunächst nicht ein besonderes Lehrgut gekennzeichnet, sondern eine Methode, eine Gesamtheit von Verfahrensweisen, durch die der Glaube ein Verstehen des ihm Vorgegebenen zu erreichen sucht."

[70] "Thomas von Aquin," Grundprobleme der großen Philosophen, ed. J. Speck, Band I (Göttingen: Vandenhoeck und Ruprecht, 1972) 181: "Scholastik besagt primär die mittelalterliche Gestalt von `Wissenschaft´ schlechthin."

[71] Lambert.-M. De Rijk, La philosophie au moyen âge (Leiden: Brill, 1985) 20. He describes scholasticism primarily as a method distinguished by the use of terms, distinctions, types of argumentation, rules of discussion and analysis of sentences.

[72] Brian Lawn, The Rise and Decline of the Scholastic "Quaestio disputata," With special Emphasis on its Use in the Teaching of Medicine and Science (Leiden: Brill, 1993) 145-7.

Schönberger has dedicated a book to the exclusive purpose of finding out the meaning of the term "Scholasticism."[73] The survey of previous discussions of this difficult question has him conclude: "(ein) einheitlicher Begriff von Scholastik weder logisch möglich noch historisch wünschenswert..."[74]

Nevertheless, he does not want to dismiss the term. It is helpful as an encapsulation of a complex structure of descriptions. Common to these diverse phenomena is their "de-subjectivizing of thinking."[75] This is the case because the "magistri" understood their task as handing down a truth they had inherited. Isolated by itself, one cannot comprehend the Middle Ages. The "theoretical context" as well as matrix of basic dispositions must be taken into consideration.[76] The Middle Ages perceived itself as a continuation of Western civilization and of Christianity. Terms such as "quaestio," "written text," "commentary," "auctoritas" and its relationship to language play significant roles. The complexity of the dimensions suggests the author's conclusion: the recourse to Scholasticism calls into question a univocal understanding of rationality:

> Die Geschichte des Denkens dokumentiert gerade in seiner mittelalterlichen Phase, daß es verschiedene Arten von dem gibt, was als ein Grund gelten kann. Wenn dem aber so ist, dann bedarf der Begriff der Rationalität einer Differenzierung, welche jeden univoken Rationalitätsbegriff als ein ungeschichtliches Konstrukt zu destruieren imstande ist.[77]

Rationality had been defined in all ages in a variety of ways. This applies also to the days of Anselm and Thomas. The seeming homogeneity at first sight of the Medieval mind in the sense of a monlithic religiosity does not stand up to a closer scrutiny.

1.5 The abiding Relevance of Medieval Studies to Theology

The significance of Medieval studies for theology arises not only from a historian's curiosity, nor from a postmodern, eclectic playful jest to put various positions into interaction with one another. Assuming themselves as being in the uninterrupted continuation of the tradition of Occidental thought, Medieval

---

Exclusively for the 12th Century cf. Paola Feltrin, M. Rossini (eds.), Verità in quaestione, Il problema del metodo in diritto e teologia nel XII secolo (Bergamo: Pierluigi Lubrina, 1992). This book is a compilation of various essays. The two by Jacques Jolivet and particularly that of Henryk Kantorowicz are seminal treatises for the understanding of the culture of disputation.

[73] Rolf Schönberger, Was ist Scholastik? Mit einem Geleitwort von Peter Koslowski (Hildesheim: Bernward,1991).

[74] Schönberger, Was ist Scholastik? 41.

[75] Schönberger, Was ist Scholastik? 46.

[76] Schönberger, Was ist Scholastik? 49: "Geflecht basaler Einstellungen."

[77] Schönberger, Was ist Scholastik? 118.

thinkers' interest was "to state what is the case" from within a Christian horizon. As Christians, it was their assumption that it was equally their, quasi, connatural task to live as witnesses to the incarnation of the Word.[78] Due to the presence of the Crucified during the eucharist[79] for the vast majority of Christians and the guidance afforded the Church by the Holy Spirit,[80] church history - regardless of the human failings that occurred therein - is experienced as salvation history. Arguably, Christian faith never had permeated society to such an extent before and after as in the time from 900 to 1500 A.D. Upon this background the reflection on the intellectual contributions of that era takes on special significance for faith and theology.

A theology purely pragmatic in orientation, i.e. utilitarian in the sense of serving predefined goals, will hesitate to reflect further upon the first causes. The insight of the things via their causes is not re-considered "sub specie divinitatis." In this context to think God as creator and cause of all causes - the oneness, truth and goodness of all things - remains unthinkable.[81] In contrast to Medieval theologians, present-day system- and theory-oriented theology is little inclined to conduct its studies under the consideration of God as "deus est maxime unus."[82] God, not considered as the One, can no longer serve as the "unifying" principle, as "causa prima." The admission of God as "causa prima" corresponds with the indivisibility of all things. This entails a congruence between insight and "res" in the identity of the creator's plenitude and His truthfulness which receives its articulation, e.g., in Anselm's central concept of "rectitudo."[83] Moreover, frequently it is not appreciated sufficiently that the being of the diverse objects refers to the divine creative intellect. The transcendental definition of Being as "unum, verum et bonum"[84] does not describe so much a state of utter power but rather of a threefold ability, which one can only ascribe to the individual being objects insofar as one recognizes a God-creator first. Only by virtue of the creative act of God is a content deposited in the created order and can the human intellect correspond to this Word as it is affected by the same. Thanks to their relationship to the divine

---

[78] Anselm's *Cur Deus Homo* is a central Medieval topos for precisely this reason.

[79] Cf. Vatican Council II.: LG 7.11; SC 7; PO 5 with SC 35.

[80] LG 4,7, 44 along with 39f.; DV 8.

[81] The problematic relationship of grace and nature comes to the fore: if there is no relationship between God and fallen nature, then one cannot "divine" from nature a divine will (= natural law). Such a Reformation point of departure renders now, in the secularized life-context, all of nature at the subjective disposition of humanity. There does not exist an objective criterion for judging human action vis-à-vis nature.

[82] Thomas Aquinas, S.Th. 1,11,4.

[83] V 7:186,1.

[84] Cf. Oeing-Hanhoff, Ludger, Ens et verum convertuntur, Stellung und Gehalt des Grundsatzes in der Philosophie des hl. Thomas von Aquin (Münster: Aschendorff, 1953).

origin, where intellect and will are one, created things possess the ability to be one, true and good and acknowledge God´s resonance in the world.[85]

Medieval ontology is one of unity. It repeatedly uses terms such as "ordo," "providentia," "ordinatio" and relates these time and again to "gubernatio (Divina)." "Ordo" becomes the outside expression in this unified world-view of the "providentia et gubernatio Dei." This harmony in turn can be documented in "numeri" and "mensura."[86] All is in relation to everything, striving towards its own "finis proximus." Hence the "ordo" is experienced as "veraciter" and "singulariter." God is the ground of being and, therefore, the ground for the condition of the possibility of all particular things. The underlying ontic premises are the "creatio ex nihilo" and the "similitudo Dei".[87]

In addition, currents of present transcendental theology are susceptible to the danger not to articulate the metaphysical contents attendant to Medieval thought. It seems to have proven itself repeatedly - just as liberal arts in general - less inclined to discuss the contents, but rather mainly the formal structures of philosophical thought. This structure-oriented approach, however, does yield a high degree of appreciation for the hermeneutical process and the situated conditioning of insight. This granted, it also could better consider the matter itself, which is already very much present in the insight into structures. Equally, the pitfall of reducing the historical to what may be perceived as of primary contemporary concern and useful for a particular situation useful needs to be avoided. By allowing "die Sache selbst," the object itself, to speak, i.e. the content and the concern behind a thought, one provides a basis for gaining an insight into present reality which one had not anticipated before. Such a transcendence beyond the merely momentary is the opportunity to apprehend the value of the present yet at the same time to perceive something possibly contained also in it but not necessarily obvious prima facie.

Such a position agrees that a difference exists between the "Für-uns-Sein" and the "An-sich-Sein" of the object of insight. It is upon this reality that transcendental reflexion can investigate the causes for the possibility of scientific insight into an object.[88] The discoveries of these transcendental

---

[85] Hödl uses the term "mitklingt," = something "resonates" or "swings" along. Cf. Ludwig Hödl, "Welt-Wissen und Gottes-Glaube in der Synthese des Thomas von Aquin," Welt-Wissen und Gottes-Glaube in der Geschichte und Gegenwart, FS for Ludwig Hödl, Ausgewählte Aufsätze, Gesammelte Forschungen, Manfred Gerwing ed. (St. Ottilien: EOS, 1990): 11-17, at 16.
[86] Cf. Heinz Meyer, Rudolf Suntrup, Lexikon der mittelalterlichen Zahlenbedeutungen (München: Fink, 1987). This book treats exhaustively the use of numbers during the Middle Ages up to and including 200,000,000. Unfortunately Anselm´s have not been considered.
[87] Cf. Herrmann Krings, "Das Sein und die Ordnung, Eine Skizze zur Ontologie des Mittelalters" Deutsche Vierteljahreszeitschrift für Literaturwissenschaft, 18 (1940): 233-249; the terms "ordo" and its derivatives appear 167 times in the Anselmic Opera.
[88] Cf. for the definition of "transcendental:" "Ich nenne alle Erkenntnis transzendental, die sich nicht sowohl mit Gegenständen, sondern mit unserer Erkenntnisart von Gegenständen, sofern

structures are by no means by themselves a-religious in character and propagated exclusively by protagonists of the subject's autonomy. Quite the contrary, owing to Maréchal's "transposition du Kantisme," Rahner's transcendental philosophical point of departure becomes possible. The structures of insight evidence human existence always as an anticipation of an all-encompassing being towards the one God.[89]

It has repeatedly been mentioned that such a transcendental position may be prone to "privatization," "Praxisentfremdung" and "de-politicization." Besides Metz, Neuhaus, and Moltmann, also Dalferth raised such concerns. Frequently the structures enjoy so much attention in deliberations that the references within and between them go altogether unnoticed. Moreover, the particularities of history and personal biographies are disregarded, although these are the ones anticipating Being.[90] Both Schelling and Heidegger had attempted to combine transcendental philosophy with historical reflection. The Tübingen School of Catholic theology endeavored to a certain degree to continue Schelling's position.

Gottlieb Söhngen defined incarnation as the "Heilstatsache der Heilstatsachen," as the salvific basis for all the subsequent acts in salvation history. The utmost significance the Christ mystery receives, is due to its historic uniqueness and the personal character this event takes on in the decisions of every individual's life. This is the single most important decision in personal life, which irrevocably comes to a head in the moment of death. Every theological design not taking seriously historicity in this meaning must countenance the danger of contravening the historicity the Christian message contains.[91]

It is a significant contribution of the historical-critical method to heighten the awareness of the process-character of Scripture. Both its development and the understanding gained are subject to a historical process.[92] When speaking in

---

diese a priori möglich sein soll beschäftigt." Immanuel Kant, _Kritik der reinen Vernunft_, B 25.

[89] Karl Rahner, Grundkurs des Glaubens 4th ed. (Freiburg, Basel, Wien: Herder, 1976) 54-96. Cf. Joseph Maréchal, Le point de départ de la métaphysique, Cahiers I-V (Bruxelles, Paris: Alcan, 1922-1947).

[90] Ingolf U. Dalferth, Kombinatorische Theologie. Probleme theologischer Rationalität, (Freiburg i. Br., Basel, Wien: Herder, 1991) (QD 130); Jürgen Moltmann, Was ist heute Theologie? (Freiburg, Basel, Wien: Herder, 1988) 83ff; Gerd Neuhaus, Transzendentale Erfahrung als Geschichtsverlust? Der Vorwurf der Subjektlosigkeit an Rahners Begriff geschichtlicher Existenz und eine weiterführende Perspektive transzendentaler Theologie (Düsseldorf: Patmos, 1982).

[91] Gottlieb Söhngen, Die Einheit in der Theologie. Die Einheit von natürlicher und übernatürlicher, historischer und systematischer Theologie in christlicher und humaner Existenz. Gesammelte Abhandlungen, Aufsätze, Vorträge (München: Karl Zink, 1952) 350f.

[92] Heinrich Schlier, "Kurze Rechenschaft," Bekenntnis zur katholischen Kirche, Karl Hardtz (ed.), 4th edition. (Würzburg: Echter, 1956) 171-195, at 178. Cf. Reinhard von Bendemann,

a qualified manner of "sacra doctrina" and the Christ mystery, the "veritas facti" appears inseparable from divine revelation and ecclesial attention in history. Only such credal truth is attested truth, living from the past's living "traditio," confirming a promise for the future and calling for a decision ever anew in the present.[93]

The incarnation of the Logos as "the mysterious wisdom of God" (1Cor. 2,7) manifests itself in history as "traditio divina" and "actio divina." Since this is a unique and irrepeatable historical fact theology must show particular sensitivity to tradition's historicity. With such an attitude theology is able to appreciate the variability and wealth of structure-enabling insights. Via such a perspective one is further capable to reflect critically the validity of present positions.

Mindful of history as salvation history - aside from the fact that history is a fact for everyone - theology and particularly research into the Middle Ages can contribute to a comprehension of the "renovation" and "change of thought" Paul speaks of:

> Do not model your behaviour on the contemporary world, but let the renewing of your minds transform you, so that you may discern for yourselves what is the will of God - what is good and acceptable and mature. (Rom. 12:2;)

It does not suffice to investigate the validity of the word of faith for the present situation; rather the task is to make it critically present in its historical meaning's fullness. There is no gainsaying that such an effort must go beyond the alibi-function it is often accorded in order to find a common terminology, derived perhaps from Augustine, Anselm, Thomas, etc. by members of the same church who frequently held diametrically opposed opinions.[94] Without the intellectual effort to repeat previously made thinking processes theology faces the prospect of degenerating into an ideology. Lacking a critical appropriation of past contents, it becomes stale. In this context Gerwing remarks:

> Ohne, wie Hegel sagen würde(n), die "Arbeit des Begriffes" zu leisten, verliert die Theologie den historischen Boden unter ihren Füßen und droht zur rechtfertigenden Ideologie des gerade Faktischen oder gar zur weltfremden und realitätsfernen Utopie zu verkommen.[95]

Heinrich Schlier, Eine kritische Analyse seiner Interpretationen paulinischer Texte (Gütersloh: Gütersloher Verlag, 1995).

[93] Söhngen, Die Einheit 350f.

[94] Bernhard Georg Langenmeyer, "Leitideen und Zielsetzungen theologischer Mittelalterforschung aus der Sicht der systematischen Theologie," Renovatio et Reformatio. Wider das Bild vom "finsteren" Mittelalter, FS Ludwig Hödl zum 60. Geburtstag, Manfred Gerwing, Godehard Ruppert (eds.). (Münster: Aschendorff, 1985): 3-13. Under this consideration also the German title of Barbara Tuchman's book - translated into German as - Der ferne Spiegel is infelicitous.

[95] Manfred Gerwing, "Zur Bedeutung der Mediavistik für die systematische Theologie," Freiburger Zeitschrift für Philosophie und Theologie 43 (1996): 65-83, at 74.

By engagement with divine matters one becomes worthy of this similarity.[12] Much like the gods who are unalterable by nature and "nourish" this state by beholding eternal ideas, also human beings attain a similar state by virtue.[13] To ward off evil mortals ought to strive to achieve this similarity by being just, insightful and pious.[14] Augustine takes up this thought. God is good and all things strive to be good to be united with the good. Therefore, Augustine can fully support Plato when the Greek thinker defines philosophizing as loving God.[15]

In the concept of "homoiosis Theô" ancient Christianity not only discovered the Christian ideal for conducting life. One beheld the Platonic ideal, realized and confirmed in Jesus Christ's path. Human life's consummation in the God-man Jesus Christ has repeatedly been interpreted as the model "homoiosis Theô." Jesus' judiciousness and virtuousness were so great that he attained a state of imperturbability in the good while being therein one with the immutable God. This is evidenced by His resurrection from the dead and His participation in eternal life.[16] In the process He manifests Himself as God's Son.

The full force of the concept "homoiosis Theô" for early Christian theology is only shown when bearing in mind that the Greek version of the Old Testament, the Septuagint, renders "make man in our own image, in the likeness of ourselves" (Gen 1:26) "kath' eikona kai homoiosin theou." The translation of the Hebrew word "demuth" as "homoiosis" along with the Hebrew word "zelem" as "eikon" endowed Scripture with an irresistably Platonic coloring. This implied that humanity is not only made in the mere image of the divine original but destined for a progressive alignment to God in the Platonic meaning of "homoiosis theô" (cf. Col 18-22:27; Eph 2:19-22; 4:15f.).[17]

2.2 Reflect(x)ion and Unification - Mysticism as a Philosophical Attitude - Plotinus

Eines zu sein mit allem, das ist Leben der Gottheit, das ist der Himmel des Menschen. Eines zu sein mit allem, was lebt, in seliger Selbstvergessenheit wiederzukehren ins All der Natur, das ist der Gipfel der Gedanken und Freuden, das ist die heilige Bergeshöhe, der Ort der ewigen Ruhe, wo der Mittag seine Schwüle und der Donner seine Stimme verliert und das kochende Meer der Woge des Kornfelds gleicht.   Hölderlin[18]

---

[12] Politics 500c 9f.

[13] Phaidrus 247d 3f.

[14] Theaetetus 176a5-b2.

[15] De civitate Dei VIII, 8.

[16] This has often been asserted in Patristic literature: Origen, Paul of Samosata and Theodore of Mopsuestia. Cf. Wolfhart Pannenberg, Grundzüge der Christologie, 6th ed. (Gütersloh: Mohn, 1964) at 118f and 202.

[17] Pannenberg, Systematische Theologie II 238ff.

[18] Hölderlin, Sämtliche Werke, III, 8f (ed. F. Beißner).

40

The way of liberation in Hölderlin´s novel *Hyperion* begins with a description of heaven and the ocean. The world is lost in the poet's opinion in many ephemeral distractions and will again be reprieved only through unity. In his judgment humanity's aim is to achieve a unity of nature and the I - of Being and the I.

What was present in early Church history to all of Christendom, has been retained in the concept of "henosis" as a central notion of Christian existence in Eastern Christianity. [19] Eastern theology differentiates, however, between divine properties: "doxa," "glory," "goodness," "beauty," "luminosity," etc., and divine "ousia": essence. There always remains a qualitative difference between creator and creature. The perfection of humanity in the meaning of fulfilling nature's design means becoming similar to the one God in the sense of "homoiosis Theô". [20]

Not only is union with the divine a feature of Christian existence, its possibility is the underlying presumption of philosophy in general: in the Occident, India and China. [21] In Thales' reduction of multifarious things to a common beginning one detects a general attempt by civilizations throughout the world to reduce being to one common denominator. In his early writings *Die Philosophie im tragischen Zeitalter der Griechen*, Nietzsche divines in Thales' thoughts the first steps of philosophy. All things possess a unity which precedes them and endows them with being. He considers this "ungeheure Verallgemeinerung" as not an empirical statement based on rational principles and insight but a "metaphysischer Glaubenssatz." [22] For him philosophy is the reflexion upon the unity of all of reality. It is beheld exclusively in a vision. [23] Such an intuition is prior to any formal verbalization. Heraclitus observed already that "all is one." [24]

Early on this one seems to acquire personal features. Fränkel considers the term "unio mystica" a justified description of Parmenides´ thought:

Daß dem Parmenides solches in der Tat widerfahren und geschickt ist, läßt sich weder dokumentarisch beweisen noch zwingend widerlegen. Wohl aber gibt es gewichtige Argumente zu Gunsten unserer Annahme, daß Parmenides die "unio mystica" mit dem

---

[19] Cf. as example Irenaeus, Adv. Haer. IV, 38,3.

[20] Sergius Heitz, Christus in Euch: Hoffnung auf Herrlichkeit, Orthodoxes Glaubensbuch für erwachsene und heranwachsende Gläubige (Göttingen: Vandenhoeck und Ruprecht, 1994) 253f.

[21] Cf. Albert Keller, Einführung in die philosophische Mystik, (Darmstadt: Wissenschaftliche Buchgesellschaft, 1996); see also articles "Philosophie" and "Mystik" Historisches Wörterbuch der Philosophie, Vol. 7, Basel, 1989, rubrics 572-797; vol. 6, Basel 1984, rubrics 268-279 respectively.

[22] KSA I 813.

[23] KSA I 817.

[24] Fragment B 50.

wahren Sein persönlich erfahren hat. Wäre das nicht geschehen, so hätte er die Einheit und Einigkeit des reinen Seins immer nur postuliert aber nie eigentlich gedacht.[25]

Such considerations are not accidental products of Western thought but appear characteristic of every genuine philosophical endeavor. For instance, the forty second chapter of Lao tse's *Tao-te-ching* begins with the observation "Tao generates unity."

Aristotle's Categories were not known directly to Anselm. In the context of the "universalia," "substantia," "differentia," "corpus," "vivens," "animal," the "homo" as "species specialissima" and finally the single "individuum" were perceived as constituents of one reality. His world was rather embedded in Augustinian categories. Accordingly Anselm and his environment shared in a qualified sense in the Platonic worldview. As Plotinus, Augustine and Boethius had been formed by Platonism, Platonism is a helpful, if not essential reflexive moment when pondering Anselmic concept of the mind's pondering divine matters.[26] For this reason, for example, one reads in the critical treatise *Proslogion*: "to elevate his spirit unto God."[27]

McEvoy marvels at the unity of Medieval philosophy and theology and perceives in this connection its indebtedness to Greek thinking.[28] To the present author's mind this Platonic "leitmotiv," consistent through the centuries, is articulated in a succinct manner by Plotinus. His thoughts constitute a summary collection of Platonic and - albeit to a far lesser degree - Aristotelian philosophies, in the present case particularly (mystic) metaphysics in an intellectually responsible variant.[29] Mutatis mutandis he bundles and focuses it as a central insight of ancient Occidental thought one final time and transmits it

---

[25] Herrmann Fränkel, Dichtung und Philosophie des frühen Christentums, 2. ed. (München: Beck, 1962) 418f. One might want to add that this attitude of Hellenic thought remains much alive to this very day. When the Greek author Kazantzakis confesses his inability to believe, the hermit monk Makarios explains this as the direct result of the emergence of reason and of the I. At the beginning everything had been one in the One: God. This unity is paradise. For this reason the monk blesses death, for it means the return to this primordial unity. Cf. Nikos Kazantzakis, Rechenschaft vor El Greco. 3rd ed. (München, Berlin: Herbig, 1980) 193.

[26] Enders in Wahrheit und Notwendigkeit establishes the broader intellectual linkages between Anselm and antiquity. For the purpose of this study the Plotinian component figures prominently, as it is the mind where the individual experiences the divine to both Plotinus and Anselm.

[27] For the profound influence of (Neo-)Platonism via Augustine on Anselm see Franciscus Salesius Schmitt, "Anselm und der (Neu-)Platonismus" 39-71. It is Schmitt's expressed concern to prove the notion of "participatio" as a cardinal term in Monologion, De Grammatico, De Veritate and Cur Deus Homo.

[28] George McEvoy, "La philosophie du Moyen Age, la civilisation médiévale et la culture du médiéviste," Jacques Follon et George McEvoy (ed.), Actualité de la pensée médiévale, Receuil d'articles (Louvain-la-Neuve, Paris: Ed. Peeters, 1994): 69-78.

[29] Plotinus' biographer and editor Porphyry observed an essential underlying harmony between Plato and Aristotle as expressed in the works of Plotinus. Cf. Chadwick, Boethius 16.

- albeit often covertly and unidentifiably - as antiquity's legacy to the yet to come, but already nascent Medieval era and well beyond.

"Plotinus finds employment for what we should call the whole personality in a union of knowledge and love with One ineffably present to the soul."[30] The influence of this kind of Plotinian thinking is all the more foundational to Augustine, Boethius and later to monastic theology because his universe is wholly spiritual. The "regressus animae" is the most important notion philosophy can offer well into Christian thought.[31] All reality is spiritual - even that of sense. Senses and spirit are not separable but correlates of one same reality. Disregarding the unrecorded Platonic writings, reception history had perceived a rupture, an unbridgeable dualism between the intelligible and the visible world. By having the One communicate in the mystic ascent of the soul, the most sublime philosophical achievement becomes reality.

By regarding all reality "a parte Dei," and no longer as Plato did "a parte nostra," he gives it a unity and completeness previously unknown. He constructs a system surpassing in its completeness and logical cohesion the work of his predecessors. His overall presentations are apt and rarely digress from the intended aim. He thereby offers a more profound and satisfying answer to philosophy's perennial topic. As a result, Plotinus created a system and an order which had the potential to be and indeed was adopted and transformed. This transformation occurred also in the Middle Ages.

Plotinus' imprint on Western thinkers such as Augustine, Pseudo-Dionysius Areopagita, Boethius, Bonaventure, Meister Eckhart, Nicolas of Cusa, Marsilio Ficino, Pico della Mirandola, Hegel and Camus is particularly noteworthy and already well established.[32]

The basis for parallelling Anselm and Plotinus may appear fragile indeed at first glance. In a footnote Roques even concluded: "Il va sans dire que la `raison´ et la `preuve´ anselmiennes ne sont pas celles de Platon."[33] However,

---

[30] David Knowles, The Evolution of Medieval Thought (Baltimore: Helicon P, 1962) 23.

[31] Arthur Hilary Armstrong, Plotinian and Christian Studies (London: Viviorum Reprints, 1979).

[32] Beierwaltes, Denken des Einen 13; Albert Keller, Einführung in die philosophische Mystik 27f and 112ff.; Knowles, The Evolution of Medieval Thought 16-31, represents a very general but insightful treatment of the first part of this transmission. By common consent Plotinus is upon first sight difficult to understand. This circumstance and Gibbons' marking the decline of the Roman Empire to begin with the end of the age of the Antonines (180 A.D) perhaps explain the obscurity Plotinus (205-270 A.D.) suffers to this day.

[33] René Roques, Structures Théologiques de la Gnose à Richard de Saint Victor (Paris: Presses Universitaires de France, 1962) 290, footnote 1. One might note that Roques' approach deduces only from the inner textual evidence. It is, however, a characteristic trait of Anselm rarely to make references to outside sources. Armstrong sees on the same textual basis no connection between Plotinus and Anselm, except to observe a similarity in the teaching methods of Anselm, Plotinus and Porphyry. A(rthur) Hilary Armstrong, Plotinian and Christian Studies (London: Viviorum Reprints, 1979) at 107. There is even a little evidence that Anselm had read one of Plato´s dialogues, the Timaeus, which in part at least

both Plotinus and Anselm assumed human reason to be sustained by the object of its thinking. At the same time this object propels the human mind towards itself (called by Plotinus the "One" and by Anselm "God").[34] And yet this is not achieved without an intellectual and ethical effort on the human being's part. The Plotinian notion of "epibole" is in Anselm's thought the indispensable element of not having human reason arrive at the formula "id quo maius cogitari nequit" without "rectitudo." Without "epibole" for Plotinus - for Anselm this will be prayer - the One is perceived merely as an undetermined: "aoristia."[35] At this point philosophy as a purely human, intellectual effort - lacking a prayerful and ethical component - would have come to an impasse in both Plotinus' and Anselm's judgments.[36] With the aid of "epibole," however, human consciousness is transposed into contemplation.[37]

The Plotinian call to prayer prior to speaking on divine matters[38] is echoed by Augustine when he engages the reader of the *Soliloquia* first in prayer before proceding to discuss the nature of God. Inspired by Augustine and thus indirectly by Plotinus, Anselm starts his reflections in the *Proslogion* likewise with a prayer. All three see an intimate connection between prayer and philosophical discourse. Whether via Augustine alone or directly indebted to Plotinus, Anselm is also influenced by Plotinian thought.[39]

There do exist significant differences between the two. Plotinus held that there exists something in the human soul which is both divine and eternal (prior to the individual's existence on earth). Christian Platonism never accepted this concept. The Christian God is charitable and shows empathy with the human condition. Plotinus taught that the ideas are universals and could not be of particulars. Plotinus held the One to emanate the "nous" - much like the Christian Logos - but it could never have become incarnate to redeem humanity. A *Cur Deus Homo* would likely have been utterly impossible for Plotinus to write.[40]

Both Plotinus and Anselm do not subscribe to some naive form of rationalism nor to passive fideism. Rather, it is precisely the human intellect itself which calls for a letting lose of oneself for divine initiative to take over. Divine transcendence is experienced as transcendence and not as a determinable entity. While Plotinus did perhaps seek indeed the self-dissolution of the self,[41]

---

was widely available in Latin and which Lanfranc knew well. Cf. Southern, Saint Anselm. Portrait in a Landscape 447.

[34] Enn., VI, 7,35,19ff.

[35] Enn., II, 4,10.

[36] Enn., VI, 9,35ff.

[37] Enn., VI, 9,3,1ff.

[38] Enn., V, 1,6ff.

[39] Klaus Kienzler, Gott ist größer. Studien zu Anselm von Canterbury (Würzburg: Echter, 1997) at 13f.

[40] Rogers, The Neoplatonic Metaphysics at 4f.55.

[41] Enn., VI, 6,1,1-3.

this is certainly not the case with Anselm. Nor did Anselm share in Platonism's negative appreciation of matter. Much like Gregory of Nyssa in another vein, Anselm holds that after the insight into the "id quo maius cogitari nequit" had been granted human beings remain unambiguously and distinctly creatures.

After outlining these general lines of agreement and divergence, it is justified to investigate possible actual parallels between the two. Chapter 18 of the *Monologion* attempts to demonstrate that the "summa natura" possesses neither a beginning nor an end by showing the impossibility of its indebtedness to some causality.[42] This "summa natura" is neither mortal nor destructible.[43] This insight adds somewhat a parenthesis to the discovery that the "summa natura" could not possibly perish voluntarily or involuntarily. Voluntary self-destruction contains an element of internal difference. However, the absolute and simple Good lacks such an internal difference. Involuntary self-destruction on the other hand runs counter to the omnipotence proper to the "summa natura."[44] This confirms the "vera aeternitas" of the highest nature:

> Si summa illa natura principium vel finem habet, non est vera aeternitas, quod esse supra inexpugnabiliter inventum est.[45]

Remarkably, Plotinus had made similar observations when reflecting on eternity and time. Also he defines eternity and divine boundlessness.

> It must be at once something akin to unity and diversity ... Eternity ... announces an identity in the Divine. ... That what never (merely) was nor (merely) will be but always has being ... is eternity. ... a life which belongs to what truly is out of itself. This is the object of our inquiry (and) is eternity.[46]

Eternity and boundlessness are perceived by both as exclusively divine predicates:

> Et quidem solus es aeternus, quia solus omnium sicut non desinis, sic non incipis esse ... Incircumscriptum vero, quod simul est ubique totum; quod de te solo intelligitur.[47]

When defining in *De Veritate* the essential understanding of "veritas" as "rectitudo" he observes that all temporal entities are contained in the "summa

---

[42] M 18: 32,9-20.

[43] Cf. M 15 and 16.

[44] M 18: 33,5-7.

[45] M 18: 33,9f.

[46] Enn., III 7, 3,16f.36-38. Beierwaltes detects a link between Plotinus and his reception in the Middle Ages in Boethius: "aeternitas igitur est interminabilis vitae tota simul et perfecta possessio." Cf. Boethius, De Consolatione Philosophiae V 6,4 (CCSL XCIV) 101,8f. Walter Beierwaltes, Plotin. Über Ewigkeit und Zeit. 3rd ed. (Frankfurt am Main: Klostermann 1981) 198-200.

[47] P 13: 110,17f.21f.

veritas." All created things are encapsulated in God. This view - held among others by Neo-Platonists - has up to now not been recognized in Anselm research but is of no small significance. Apodictically he claims: "An putas aliquid esse aliquando aut alicubi quod non sit in summa veritate, ... Non est putandum."[48] Everything that had come forth from God is destined also to be traceable back to its origin. Whatever is bound to the categories of space and time is contained in the immanence of God.[49] Anselm´s term "continere" in chapter 19 of the *Proslogion* matches precisely Plotinus´ notion of "synechein." Both convey the meanings "to contain" and "to hold together."

> tu autem, licet nihil sit sine te, non es tamen in loco aut tempore, sed omnia sunt in te. Nihil enim te continet, sed tu contines omnia.[50]

"Continere" as well as "synechein" seem to have been used in the sense of termini technici to denote humanity´s radical dependence on God. These moments of "containing" and "encompassing" go to such an extent that this dependence effects concrete everyday life. By no means is an identity of God and humanity stipulated. Rather it implies that the created (or nota bene *emanated* for Plotinus) order has its existence sustained "in" God.[51] To Anselm´s mind it follows from this that the "summa natura´s" utter ubiquity[52] is constitutive for everything created. All created things are permeated by the "summa natura."[53]

> At quoniam absurdum est, ut scilicet, quaemadmodum nullatenus aliquid creatum potest exire creantis et foventis immensitatem, sic creans et fovens nequaquam valeat

---

[48] V 7: 185,11-14.

[49] The fact that this assumption is contained in a heading is remarkable: "Quod non sit in loco aut tempore, sed omnia sint in illo." P 19: 115,6.

[50] P 19: 115,14f. Cf. Enn., VI, 8,18,2f. V, 5,9,8-12.

[51] Enn., V, 5,9,1-4. The tangible effects are contained in their cause.

[52] "Quod sit ita est, immo quia ex necessitate sic est consequitur ut, ubi ipsa non est, nihil sit. Ubique igitur est per omnia et in omnibus." M 14: 27,19f.

[53] Kremer notes in this context that there exists a "unilateralen Dependenzverhältnis des Niederen vom Höheren" Some pages further he asserts: "Enthalten (continere) entpuppt sich als eine Tätigkeit, die das enthaltende Prinzip immer als von höherem Seins-, Wert- und Mächtigkeitsrang gegenüber dem enthaltenden Prinzipiat ausweist. Umgekehrt deutet das Insein stets auf irgendeine Bedürftigkeit des enthaltenden Prinzipiats hin. Gott ist aber nun in jeder Hinsicht Unbedürftige, das aufgrund seiner Natur allein restlos für sich Autarke. Welt und Kreatur dagegen sind das in jeder Hinsicht Bedürftige, das aufgrund ihrer Natur restlos auf ein anderes Angewiesene. Also ist nicht Gott in der Welt, sondern die Welt in Gott, vermag nicht die Welt Gott, sondern Gott allein die Welt enthalten." Klaus Kremer, Gott und Welt in der klassischen Metaphysik. Vom "Sein der Dinge" in Gott (Stuttgart, Berlin, Köln, Mainz: W. Kohlhammeer, 1969) at 55 and 81f.

aliquomodo excedere factorum universitatem: liquet quoniam ipsa est, *quae cuncta alia portat et superat, claudit et penetrat.*[54]

His lifelong endeavor was to render this foundational circumstance conscious to his readers.

Something similar was the concern of the Plotinian project. "Mystic" is an appropriate description of Plotinus[55] inasmuch as mysticism in the sense of the subject's existential involvement and encounter is the cognitional endeavor to come into union with the principle or origin of the whole of being.[56] He concerns himself with the rational comprehension of the commonly obligatory nature of metaphysical truth; particularly that of the principle of origin and comprehensive causation. At the end of this process the rationality of the comprehending act is not evidenced as dissipating into a not obliging, individual-psychic, purely emotional or even irrational act.[57] Rather, Plotinus apprehends understanding, discursive and dialectical thinking as necessary exercises in their own elimination (in the Hegelian meaning of "Aufhebung"); thereby it fulfills itself in unification, by transcending itself. Reflection denotes understanding, i.e. discursive and dialectical thinking. Philosophy is thus a mystical experience between the two poles of reflection and unification. All philosophizing tends as its intrinsically proper telos towards unification; in this unification, in turn, it tends back to thinking as its fulfilling-promising and consequently forward-propelling stimulus.

Hence reflection relates the unfolding of an existential principle. Since this principle is the one, the unfolding act is (= brings forth) unity. This springs forth from the graduated multitude of being. Since per definitionem the one is

---

[54] M 14: 27,20-24. Italics added.
[55] Cf. Renatus Arnou, Le désire de dieu dans la philosophie de Plotin, 2nd ed. (Rome: Gregorian UP, 1967) 231ff; Beierwaltes, Denken des Einen 127ff; Pierre Hadot, Plotin ou la simplicité du regard, 2nd ed. (Paris: Plon, 1973).
[56] Thus a purely philosophic definition of the term.
[57] In Plotinus' opinion, to acquire the necessary faculties to undertake such an intellectual advance towards metaphysics and theology, one first must become proficient in music and mathematics. This inclines the mind to abstract thought and familiarizes the student with the underlying harmony and beauty of the intellectual world. Upon this dialectics builds. Aspiring philosophy is only thus prepared able to ascend to truth and reality (Plato's influence is evident: Republic, 532a ff. and Theaeteus 189e-190a. There Plato speaks of thinking as the inward dialogue within the soul. Dialectics gives order to this introspection.). Dialectics in Plotinus' judgment trains the mind for the vision of transcendent truth (Enneads I,3). By parting from the realm of senses and differences (Enneads V 8,11,10ff.17; VI 9,7,17f) one achieves inward awareness and becomes an interior human being (Enneads I 10,10). To the early Christian mind this constitutes an anticipation of and preparation for Christianity; more precisely for Christian philosophy, theology, asceticism and spirituality (cf. Bierwaltes, Denken des Einen 147-154). The biblical basis for such congeniality is Gal 2:19f.: "I can be alive to God. I have been crucified with Christ and yet I am alive; yet it is no longer I, but Christ living in me."

the universal basis and source as the most valuable ("agathon"), everything that originates therein must be of lesser value. The many-diverse (thing) intromits the "dynamis" of the singular one in itself: as what it is (qua being) but also in its difference to the primordial unity. It bears this primordial unity merely as a more or less powerful trace in itself. In the unfolding process (i.e. the emanation from the One), the One remains free of the category of temporality: for the source remains inalienably source.

The unfolding of unity occurs on three levels. They are graduated in different beings and are thus different essences: the One, the Spirit (absolute and primarily non-human) and the Soul. Philosophical reflection investigates these three as regards their respective beings. The cognitional passing through these levels of beings (= things that are) is of utmost anthropological relevance, for this reflection upon the unfolding of unity is at the same time the return of the thinking subject to this unity. As a consequence, thinking is not an abstract process isolated and apart from the concrete life-context of the thinking subject. Rather it transforms the thinking subject. Ethical perfection - as the realisation of virtue - is thus always co-implied in the cognitional process; for it wants to identify itself with the principle itself. The critical nexus between thinking and existential self-execution, between rational apprehension and existential appropriation, is evident. This recurs last but not least in Anselm's ontological argument.

At its beginning the thinking-through of these levels is the return of the thinking subject into itself ("epistrophe"). While this dialectic process implies in Plato's *Symposion* and *The Republic* primarily a return, it also co-implies an ascent ("anagoge") in Plotinus´ thought. It constitutes liberation from the entanglement with the world of senses, of temporality and finality. There is an important caveat to bear in mind, insofar as this entanglement is characterized by an unreflexive existence.[58] If, however, human beings are able to give the world of senses their proper and fitting value by having beheld the source of all being, namely the One, Being itself, worldly existence no longer can be termed negatively as an entanglement.[59] The logical term "Apheresis" of Aristotle is transformed by Plotinus into an ethical imperative: "Aphele panta."[60] One must remove all alien and covering ("apheresis allotrion pantos")[61] in order to penetrate to the essence of being; similarly, a sculptor must chisel away the alien and covering parts of stone in order to allow the hidden picture to appear.

---

[58] Cf. page 57, footnote 99: Pondering the import of being is a constitutive element of human existence; therefore the use of the term *reflexion* rather than *reflection.*

[59] The Christian tension of grace and postlapsarian nature encounters herein a pre-figuration. Creation per se possesses a pejorative quality. It is humanity's relationship with the creator and thus also with creation that is no longer on an even keel and must be straightened out. By thinking the One this malcondition is overcome.

[60] Enn., V 3,17,38.

[61] Enn., I 2,4,6.

The cognitional movement of abstraction is thus perceived as one of Platonic purification ("katharsis") from superficial and multitudinous things in order to liberate the soul for the Interior and One.[62] This recourse of the thinking subject into the Interior does not yield solipsistic introvertedness. On the contrary, it intends the making-conscious of the as yet unconscious cause within oneself: the soul experiences in this process that it is rooted in an area transcending itself.

According to Plotinus, this is an ascertaining act of one´s own proper and true Self; an awakening of the pure corporality by which it liberates itself from the irritations of external matters and thereby becomes interior.[63] To live life without knowing the being-indebtedness (= contingency) of the cosmos and of its constituent parts is unworthy of the human being. It is incumbent upon the animated and spirited human being qua homo to realize the ontological difference of the particular objects and the One. This knowledge of the difference beween the finite and the infinite in finitude grants one the opportunity to allot the contingent order its proper value - to grace it: to endow it with a poetic quality neither artificial nor forced nor alien to it.[64]

Plotinus attempts to explain a priori the structure of human insight in acquiring cognition. This arises from the context of the Platonic anamnesis-teaching, which illumines the ontological relationship of the insight-yearning soul to the idea, and the Aristotelian concept of the active reason. The common ground for the a priori explanation is Plato's concept of the soul: it is the centerpiece between the intelligible ("nous") and the sensual ("aisthesis"). It is directed towards both, placing in order and comprehending the sensual and receiving and comprehending the intelligible, which constitutes the soul. When asserting "everyone of us is an intelligible world," Plotinus does not claim that the human soul is identical with the spirit. Therein he implies, in spite of its interwovenness in temporality, its innate capability of performing permanently an absolute act. He affirms strongly that the spirit is the soul's constituting cause. The soul does participate immediately in the spirit's realm as a chronologically preceding and causing entity, towards which it must transcend itself. It possesses spirit as its very own property, "oikeion." This determination

---

[62] Cf. Plato, Phaidon 83a, where he calls upon the soul to collect itself, thereby faciliating a unification of the personality's diversity.

[63] Enn., IV 8,1,1f. Plotinus postulates a non-identity of the self with its temporal appearance. The soul is properly understood as the substantial center of sensual awareness and pure thinking (cf. V 3.3,37ff. with IV 7,1,22 "kup....anthropos," IV 4,18,14). This "Self", the "interior" (cf. V 1,10,10) or "true" human being (cf. I 1,7,20) is the ontological reason for the historically, thus corporeally being human being (II 3,9,31) but also the reason for the ethical decision in freedom (III 1,4,24ff.). The return of thinking in the self-realisation becomes an ascertainment of the rational and ethical capacities of the soul (V 3,4,7ff).

[64] "Poetic" ("poietikos") is meant here in its original etymological meaning (in Greek). To fashion reality in such a manner that its (to it already always veiled immanent) true form becomes transparent.

of the soul's essence has as consequence for the determination of the human being that it actuates the "true" human being. The human being who liberates himself from the "lower," retracing the self and recognizing the self, actuates thinking as a thinking on and from the origin: the "kata noun" living human being in the interior human being ("endon" or "eiso anthropos") actuates the ontologically preceding injunction (= order), that "this", i.e. terrestial human being is rooted in "that" according to his being (in the order of being). The spirit in us, or to put it more precisely, the three hypostases in us do not occlude the explaining to the explained; do not reduce it to a mere factuality of a determined consciousness. Rather they keep awake and present the thought of a transcendent Whence: the absolute Spirit and the One. Thus the human soul is inalienably characterized by a dialectic relationship of an "in" and an "above."

The aforementioned sentence "everyone of us is an intelligible world" neither intends to affirm the identity of the human soul and the absolute spirit nor the separation of the two: "ou gar nous hemeis" - we are not spirit; humans possess, however, this spirit as an essential constituent of the created order insofar as it is created: it is ours and is not ours under the same consideration and at the same time: "hemeteros kai ouch hemeteros." It is our possession insofar as we think it and ascertain its effects upon us. It is not our possession insofar as we experience it as that transcending the soul - experiencing it thus hypostatically as the being-causation.[65]

This dialectics of "in" and "above," i.e. the fact that the human soul is thus constituted in its immanent structure because it is grounded in the transcendent "nous" and reflects on the same, is explained by the sentence: "Our soul did not sink completely." What remains of it permanently continues to effect. The human being owns as his very nature the task to turn his preceding consciousness ("to antilambanomenon") inward, in order to render conscious the unconscious - the one intelligible - and thus to transcend itself in this process of self-reflection towards that which grounds the presence of the intelligible in one. This "re-member-ing"[66] - rendering conscious of his "true self" - implies also the insight that this process is proper ("idion") to our self and, however, must also be common ("koinon") to all. In this manner we participate on the basis of this in the other through commonality's being and effect. The ascertaining (in the sense of verifying) turn to the interior of the inward or true human being opens the individual both to the other person in the comprehending act of the common uniting all, as well as to the dimension of the transcending "nous," and through it to the One itself. Self-ascertainment is

---

[65] For the two last paragraphs cf. Enn., III 4,3,21-27 and IV 8,8,2-6.

[66] The English etymology of the word is helpful in the Plotinian context: the process entails a re-assembly of members to one complete whole, while the world of phenomena renders one oblivious to it. Thereby the world of sense-impressions is not negated, but receives its proper valence, priority and context.

thereby listening to "the voices from above": "We must retain the soul's capacity for perception, pure and willing to hear the voices from above."[67]

It is Plotinus' intention to supply an a priori explanation of the soul's ability to gain insight and of its self-reflecting return in its self and its ground. Prior to Augustine's reflecting I-consciousness and his understanding of "personality," Plotinus' reflection upon the soul's essence is already a supreme accomplishment of genuine metaphysics, which attempts to explain the possibility of human thinking, neither determined purely by the senses nor primarily related to and constituted by the same.[68]

The making-conscious of one's own reason, i.e. the self-ascertaining retracing into oneself , is to Plotinus' mind identical with the ascent to the higher, causing level: "He who knows himself, knows also his whence."[69] Knowing, however, is the transforming act into the acknowledged and recognized known. Therefore, the soul by turning to itself, or to its true self, not only acquires consciousness concerning its own origin, it becomes the origin, i.e. it becomes spirit.[70] If the soul is purely in the spiritual realm, then it is that entity which also the Spirit is. The soul comes to a unity, a unison, without passing. Both are One and Two at the same time. The soul then does not alter as long as this state is being preserved and the soul's attention remains focused on the thinking process. Since the soul has become one with the thought object, it possesses simultaneously consciousness of itself.[71]

As the discussion of the conscious-making-process illustrates, spirit is to the soul at the same time both transcendent and immanent. As transcendent or absolute spirit, the soul is vis-à-vis the One,[72] as the universal origin, the first multitude or the first, differing entity. While the One self remains without reflection in itself, it is the self-reflecting spirit, which determines and self-executes - through reflecting (as reflexion) on being per se and its own existence - its own constitution. The thinking recourse on that originating process in the One does not thus lose the original One, does not permit a total apostasis into pure otherness, but rather performs precisely through the Otherness the recourse onto its origin. The self-relationality of the spirit in the

---

[67] "akouein phdoggon ton ano," Enn., V 1,12,18-20.

[68] For the evolution of the imago-Dei teaching from late antiquity to the early Middle Ages: Ludwig Hödl, "Zur Entwicklung der frühscholastischen Lehre von der Gottesebenbildlichkeit des Menschen," L'Homme et son Destin, Actes general du Congrès international de Philosophie Médiévale (Louvain, Paris: Nauwelaerts, 1960): 347-359.

[69] Cf. Enn., VI 9,7,33f.

[70] "noothenai," Enn., VI 7,35,4f.

[71] Cf. Enn., IV 4,2,24-32.

[72] Plotinus, as other Neo-Platonists, has as axiom that nothing can be superior to its own cause (cf. Enn., V, 4,1; also Porphyry, Sententiae 13; Proclus, El.Th. 7). In addition, the supreme beatitude and the highest good are identical, for the definition of perfection precludes even the theoretical possibility for two or more contenders for the perfect position in the hierarchy of being.

thinking process implies the thinking of the primordial origin as the constituting One in the ontological difference from it. Although intending the origin, self-reflection does not eliminate again the difference to the One, but rather preserves and limits it. For this reason spirit is a limited multitude or relative, by virtue of difference, relational unity. The spirit thinks being or the intelligible ideas which are the spirit's being. If, therefore, the spirit thinks itself, it thinks being or ideas; if, however, the ideas or being are to be thought, it thinks itself. It is, therefore, the unity of thinking and of being in the thinking act itself. Also when this thinking act is directed unto itself, one should imagine this self as a point of reference first directed to the other, as the object of the thinking act. Only via being different is the self as such identifiable to the thinking process. In a certain way the "nous" eliminates the otherness of itself through its unity. Spirit is unity only insofar as it apprehends the other as its own or as its self.

This act of the spirit's thinking itself is its very life. Already Aristotle had introduced in his Book "Lambda" of *Metaphysics* the notion of life as the destiny of pure, divine self-thinking.[73] Plotinus adopts this determination as the primary feature of the absolute spirit. Life thereby becomes being's self-thinking reality. These three elements, which determine the spirit - being, thinking and life - constitute also its relational or dynamic identity: being is living and thinking. Spirit is perceived as a triadic unity of being, thinking and life. The spirit is able to actualize this unity through the unity's effective energy in it, i.e. by retracing within its generation its origin, the One. Reflexion hence constitutes both the spirit's being and its essence. At the same time it is the condition of the possibility for preserving its identity as a timeless one. The one is accordingly the immanent - coming forth (= emanation) in the "nous" - and transcendent - remaining in spite of its coming forth itself, the point of reference, of reflection and therefore the sole reason of this second unity.

If the spirit's thinking (reflective) unity in the multitude is at the same time the origin (not torn asunder by temporality) of the temporally being soul, this unity constitutes - becoming through self-reflecting Spirit - a more intensive form of unity. It fulfills thereby the requirement of being able to be simple ("haplosis") and thus becomes similar to the first origin, as well as of being able to be similar ("homoiousios"), in order, thus collected by asceticism and reflection, to actualize unification with the One.[74] As everything springs forth through difference (be it as pure being different or as the distance between object and subject) and as everything is marked through the spirit's being and temporality, the describing movement of abstraction is to be apprehended both

---

[73] Metaphysics, 1074 b 34.

[74] The notion of "Henosis" has as Medieval pendant "unio mystica;" cf. for instance Meister Eckhart, sermo 29; LW IV 270, 5ff. or Pred. 2; DW I 31,7f., 43,2ff. While Anselm's terminology does not use the term "unio mystica," "consubstantialis" and its derivatives have entered his writings. Quite tellingly they occur exclusively in the Monologion, such as at 29: 48, 4; 30: 48, 10 and 37: 55, 16 i.a.

as de-differentiation (= liberation from being different) and as de-temporalization (= return to the timeless cause of temporal beings). Unification, however, is the incommunicable climax and aim of this movement.[75]

Through the soul's transcending in the spirit its historic concrete precondition, it is created to "behold," to "touch" and to "become one" with the One. This process is ontologically enabled by the preliminary and preceding nature of the One.[76] If indeed we are "grounded"[77] in the One, i.e. our cause is similar to the absolute or universal cause and origin - which in turn entails that immanence is a transcendent "trace" - then an access to the One is opened in spite of all essential differences. The self-enactment or better perhaps execution (as actualization or consummation) of this possibility is the conversion and ascending return of self-ascertaining thinking to itself; guided as it is by the eros to "a great light."[78] This great light, however, is the aim-cause/ground; the One. This light's attracting energy lies in that through which it appears: in the infinite plenitude of the One. Precisely therein the aporia or paradoxicality of mystical philosophy is evidenced. The aim of the reflective process, namely to eliminate the irritating multitude, cannot be verbalized. Negative dialectics can merely demarcate or delimit (i.e. demonstrate the boundary of) it. One can rather state what it is not than what it is. However, it can sufficiently be affirmed if one apprehends the One as the solely sufficing ground and cause or constitutive ontic strength or hinge for all.

"All being things are being by the grace of the One."[79] Herein a principle of Neo-Platonic thought is present. If all being things are through the One, then it follows that they are only insofar as they are one. The being one of the One is sufficient reason for the being one of the being things. The effect of the being one (whole) of the One shows itself as identification: the One causes the being things to be in fact something. Plotinus negates the illusion that by stating the One as cause or origin anything is already said as regards the One's per se being. We only state what the One is in relation to us: we are caused, and this again by Him.[80] By virtue of its very structure language is already insufficient for an adequate statement concerning the One. Language is applicable in the realm of multitude; the unity of subject and predicate is merely a unity in the

---

[75] Plotinus listed ten categories that apply exclusively to the realm of sensible things and not to the supra-sensible one. God cannot be predicated with relation. Equally the One transcends the category of substance. Likewise one cannot state God is everywhere. Every place is present to the One in a way that it is contained in God, yet no place contains the One (Plotinus, Enn. V, 5,9f; VI, 4,3; cf. Augustine, Conf. I,3,3; VI,16,28f.; Porphyry, Sent. 31).

[76] For Christianity the "imago Dei" teaching is the decisive cord through which to relate humanity to God. Greek Philosophy defined the human being as "zoon noetikon," a creature gifted with reason.

[77] Plotinus: "enidrumeda," cf. Enn., V 1,11,14.

[78] Enn., VI 7,33,29f.

[79] Enn., VI 9,1.

[80] Cf. Enn., VI 9,3,49ff.

multitude and, therefore, characterized by difference. However, an entity determined by difference or by relations is not capable of making an adequate statement regarding what is without difference or relations. Therefore, if one wishes to make an observation regarding the One, negative dialectics is the most adequate form of expression. This de-limits the One from what can be stated legitimately and sufficiently of all other things. It defines the One as the one over and above all categories par excellence: it is strictly speaking the not-many ("a-pollon"), without difference, without time and without distance. The qualitative difference of the One from all categories of being is to such a degree radically beyond comprehension and grasp that in relationship to the multitude it is nothing: it is neither being, nor essence nor life.[81]

Here Plotinus is faithful to Plato, who asserts the absolute transcendence of the One in *Republic* [82] as being also radically beyond (= "epekeina") all being which it constitutes.[83] Were not the One some thing rather than nothing, it could not be the absolute beginning and (exhaustive and comprehensive) cause for all that is. Only since it is without form is it capable of conveying form to all things. As the nothing of all that is, by virtue of its absolute transcendence, Plotinus thinks the One as the one different from all ("eteron panton"). He sharply distinguishes this transcendent primal Good from all concrete and particular objects to which goodness is only an accidental, adjectival quality. This goes so far, that Plotinus claims that the term "good" when applied to the primal One is used in a radically different sense than when applied to inferior things.[84] There is an unfathomable distinction between goodness as the first "hypostasis" and goodness as an accidental possession of a given entity.[85] This demarcation receives its parallel in the antithesis of "ousia", Being, and "ta onta", actual existing.[86] Likewise "above" and "beyond" are negative statements. These are the most general observations concerning the fact that the One effects being in all, yet is set apart from all. According to Plotinus it is everywhere and nowhere.[87] Irretrievably the One is far from the being things. It remains present only as the one from which being things abandoned unity and became the multi-unity. As absolute transcendence, it is therefore also absolute difference, and this in such a manner that there is no difference within itself. It is characterized as the non-difference par excellence, and hence this marks its most outstanding difference to all that is.[88]

---

[81] Enn., III 8,10,26-31.

[82] Republic, 509c.

[83] Cf. for example Plotinus, Enn., V 4,2,39.

[84] Enn., VI 2,17.

[85] Enn., VI, 6,10, 27-33.

[86] Enn., VI, 6,10, 44f. Simplicius demonstrates (In Categ. 45, 24ff.) this to have been generally accepted school doctrine.

[87] Enn., III 9,4,1-9.

[88] Also to Anselm things are contingent upon the principle through which they are:

This demarcation of the One through negative dialectics follows Plato's intention: via abstraction from the wide field of varied appearances to the one cause of all appearances; to arrive at the proper idea, which appears in varied refractions. This negative demarcation of the One does not rotate around an empty term, but rather affirms acutely the little that can be said of the One's reality: universally responsible for all being things, yet not identical with these - their sublimely elevated cause. Such a cognitional concentration is to Plotinus the highest form of life: "zoen aristein energein".[89]

This negative predication of the One, i.e. its demarcation from the being things, has relevant consequences for the ascent of thought to the One and its unification with it. This movement of abstraction must further be described, on the basis of the negativity of the One, as a liberation from relations, difference and form. Thought must overcome ("aufheben") its own structure characterized by something, form, difference and relation through demarcation and self-transcending. Thereby language becomes mute. Accordingly, unification becomes the transforming act into the totally different, into the in itself difference-less difference (vis-à-vis all being things). With great urgency and intensity Plotinus delineates this process in the last part of the *Enneades* VI 9.

One should bear in mind that the One is identical with the Good, in whose plenitude it partakes without envy; at the same time it is God.[90] In keeping with Stoic tradition, Plotinus introduces the universally causing cause as "Father." The One can never be thought of in antiquity without the category of personality. In spite of alienation the soul is related by virtue of "eros" to the origin. "Eros" frees or actuates the essential feature of the soul: to be mediation, as its intention towards the origin. "Eros" is the moving and transcending element in the soul's return from the realm of otherness to the "fatherland" ("phenomenon de philen es patrida").[91] Particularly therein a religious moment in Plotinus' thinking is evidenced: his salvation or failure depends on whether

---

"Restat igitur unam et solam aliquam naturam esse, quae sic est aliis superior ut nullo sit inferior. Sed quod tale est maximum et optimum est omnium quae sunt. Hoc autem esse non potest, nisi ipsa sit per se quod est et cuncta quae sunt sint per ipsam id quod sunt." (M 4:17,24-29)

He also empatically negates that the One (or highest) may be thought of as the conclusion of an ascending order. As the truly highest, it is at the same time completely different from the other things. It is constituted by its very own essence, whereas all members of the ascending chain are caused by it. Contrary to some criticism leveled against Anselm, he does not hold fast to the notion of a graduated cosmos. Whilst there is a graduated order in the created world, God is not merely the highest one can think (P 15). Divine greatness is beyond human insight: "non potest intellectus meus ad illam." (P 16:112,24). For this reason Nicolas of Cusa can cite Anselm centuries later to claim every insight into God is "docta ignorantia" (cf. Nicolas of Cusa, De veneratione sapientiae, cap. 26 Par. 77).

[89] Enn., IV 8,1,4.
[90] Cf. also Enn., V 8,11,5; VI 9,9,59.
[91] Enn., I 6,8,16: this metaphor occurs already in Homer B 140. V.18ff.

the human being plods the way of purifying ascent. In this way and in the unification - be it merely as stimulating memory - human existence finds its fulfillment in the here and now and in the thereafter .

The manner of the unification - thought of as being an immediate one - can, in a statement, (which remains inextricably bound to the difference-structure of thinking) be merely demarcated from common forms of thinking and seeing: unification "is an other way of seeing." This beholding act neither differentiates something outside and thereby causes the beholding subject to become one with the beheld object, nor possesses any kind of difference within itself, because it reflects in a different manner. Hence, the foundational problem lies in the at least momentary sublation (= "Aufhebung") of difference and relation in the thinking act. If there is, however, no difference, then the non-different must be proximate. This One, which is above, is to Plotinus always next to us. We, however, are only next to it if we have no difference-ness within us. The One does not long for us (to be next to us), yet we yearn to be next to it. We are always around it (the One), but we do not always look upon it.[92] The non-separation from the One is the ontological prerequisite for unification. The real act of being together or being one requires a seeing without difference between the beholding subject and the beheld object.[93] Indirectly Plotinus admits readily the paradoxicality of this state of affairs:

> In our self-seeing ... the self is seen as belonging to that order ... It is a knowing of the self restored to its purity. ... In the seeing, we neither hold an object nor trace distinction; there is no two. The man is ... merged with the Supreme ... Centre coincides with centre.[94]

This beholding act is "ekstasis":[95] stepping beyond the common relations of being and thinking. Becoming definitively simple as abolition of every two-foldness and thereby sublation of relationality or the cognitional subject-object-relationship. Plotinus means an intuitive self-entrusting without theoretic distance and unmediated reception of the per se immediate. Accordingly ecstasis is the identity of "hen," "agathon" and "theos," of the absolute one, good and God, a being in God, "Enthusiasmos."[96] The human being is in God, the One, because the One does not incline towards the human being. The human being becomes God-loved, by becoming close to the fulfilling aim of the thinking ascent. Ek-stasis becomes the "stasis" of thinking; transcending movement towards the elimination of any movedness,[97] because that presupposes and simultaneously causes difference. Although the intending is

---

[92] Cf. Enn.,VI 9,8,33ff.
[93] Enn., VI 4,14,17ff; VI 9,9,7ff.
[94] Enn.,VI 9,10,13ff; Stephen MacKenna, trans. by, Plotinus, The Enneads (London: Penguin, 1991) 547.
[95] Enn., VI 9,11,23.
[96] Enn., VI 11,13.
[97] Enn., VI 6,52; 11,11.

capable of actuating this other kind of seeing, nothing is present to it.[98] The rule that only the non-thinking can pass into the non-thinking principle does not imply that thinking sinks in the act of self-overcoming into irrational darkness. Rather it reached its pre-reflexive cause, the illumination and intelligibility constituting primordial light. This causes in the medium of the "nous" in the soul, the reflexive[99] ascent and permits the thinking of the thinking process.

For the characterization of the realized unity, which has overcome every distance-implying relationality and difference - the circle and its center is a telling metaphor.[100] If at the end of the above-mentioned text it reads, "the seeing is one, by touching central point with central point,"[101] then our central point, the one in us, is the moment of unification in the center of the whole. This requires that the soul performs a circular motion, moving in a circular way towards its own center and thereby to the universal center, in which it is grounded and caused and that it reduce the distance between the center and the periphery and finally completely negate this distance.[102] This integrating or touching of centers does not, however, imply that individuality or the beholder's self are being completely eradicated. Rather they are abolished in the unity with the One or God in the timeless "Nous" and thereby lifted to their highest perfection. This means their mode of existence has been altered. He has been "grabbed" by God and taken in possession. Human freedom is not annihilated in unification. In the present (contingent) state man must ever anew free himself to but also from unification.[103] Plotinus does not so much consider the intention as rather the reality of human interwovenness, which does not permit another possibility. Unification succeeds only for a few conspicuous moments.

A further characteristic metaphor - like circle and center - is light. The abstracting movement, the purification of the self as it becomes similar with the principle, is also to be understood as illumination ("ellampsis"):[104] as an exercise preparing thinking for the luminosity of the different levels of reality, first of the spirit and finally of the One. Light is an index of reflexive unity: the reciprocal penetration of the intelligible meaning-structure, but also of the relation-free, voluntary one-ness of the principle. Therefore, the higher or the more intensive an object, the more luminous it is. The thinking elevation into the respectively more intensive and, therefore, more luminous being must be equated with the self-rendering-luminous which makes one aware of one's

---

[98] Enn., VI 11,26.

[99] Nota bene: "reflexive" and not "reflective."

[100] The simile of the circle and sphere has also been well received into Christian thinking via Augustine. He speaks of God as the "supreme hub of causes" (= "summus causarum cardo;" De Trin. III,9,16).

[101] Cf. Enn. VI 8,4f and 8,20 - also II,2,1; III,2,3; VI, 8,18,23.

[102] This is a recurring motif: Plato's Phaidros; Dante, Div.Com., Parad. 30 and 31.

[103] Enn., VI 3,4ff.

[104] Enn., VI 7,16.

causation. This process has its telos in the indiscriminate (= obliterating all differences) fusion of the light proper to the soul with the primordial light.[105] A preceding text conveys yet more powerfully the difference-less melting of the lights as an intensive unification: the transcending one

> is torn away by the spirit's surge and carried high by its torrent: there it beholds the One with a stroke. He does not see, rather the seeing act fills his eyes with light and permits nothing else to become visible, except the light itself. The beheld was not by itself and per se its light, likewise not the thinking subject by itself and the thought, rather it is one single radiance, which gives birth retroactively and grants it to be a beholding.[106]

The beholding is one with the beheld, it is thus not actually a "beheld" but rather a "unified."[107] The light of the One and the through "epistrophe" light made conscious of the One becomes in us the One Light. The beholding act is abolished in the unity of the One, it appears in that light without difference as that very light itself.[108]

The circumstance that communicability of the mystic experience is hardly attainable is in part due to the imprecise nature, i.e. inadequacy of language. Here an incompleteness, a shortcoming of the created order is stated which is exacerbated in the Judeo-Christian perspective by original sin. Language is unable to grasp adequately what is prior to the occurrence of difference. It merely can demarcate and grasp negatively this state of affairs. Only if one can suppose a similar experience, may one hope communication could succeed. "Who has seen it, knows what I speak of."[109] Nevertheless, Plotinus addresses also those who have not (yet) "seen" it, because the gravitational center of his philosophy is the notion of unification. Every person's fulfillment hinges on this. Whatever one rationally explicates in a manner demarcating, albeit negatively the cause and the aim of unification, it is - apart from experience - a sufficient hint of the intensive, all-thinking and action-determining reality of the One and unification.

Some may regard Plotinus' protreptics for a mystic ascent and unification with the One - the "flight of the lone to the Alone" to put it in the philosopher's own words[110] - as favoring individualism or even solipsism. However, Plotinus

---

[105] Enn., VI 9,55ff.

[106] Enn., VI 7,36,17ff.

[107] Enn., VI 9,11,6ff; cf. also 10,14f. Here and afore: own translation.

[108] In the negation of the immateriality of the pure insight into knowledge of essence Anselm perceives the danger of Roscelin's nominalism. While Anselm insists on "universal substances," Roscelin prefers to leave "substantia" unqualified. In this case Anselm pleads for the supra-individuality of essence; it is a higher and solely spiritually apprehendable cause of being. Cf. I,9.21f. This reminds one of the central Anselmian concept of "sola ratione" (M 1:13,11; Cu I 20:88,5; Cv 11:111,28): there exists an inner necessity for the essence to be revealed in a spiritual beholding or vision. Cf. P 2-4.

[109] Enn., VI 9,47f.

[110] "phyge monou pros monon," Enn., VI 9,11,51.

did not allow his fundamental insight or his praxis to ossify into an esoteric attitude extricating him from social relations or political responsibility. This is suggested by Porphyry´s description of Plotinus' interactions with his disciples, politicians and orphans. He depicts him as affable, sociable, patient and mild. These features are characteristics of the "Agathon."[111] The mystic movement out and beyond the palpable world and its attendant societal interests does not necessarily exclude these two elements in Plotinus' mind. Porphyry judges his mild, tender and kind nature as manifesting itself as such in his social interactions and at the same time as expressing his yearning for the divine.[112] The individuated particular objects remain indebted to their common origin, Being, without negating their being created.

In the last recorded words of Plotinus the ever-current and, therefore, ever-recurring aim, namely to know the Divine through the Divine, is summarized: Attempt to lead yoursself up to God ("anagein pros en to panti Theou").[113] Within the Anselmic horizon of "aliquid quo maius cogitari nequit," in a manner that through the disciplined treatment of the argument one recognizes the absolute Thou, one may dispose of oneself and know oneself resting in the "Gelassenheit" (composure) of the absolute Thou.

2.3 The Centrality of Henology for Occidental Thought

We must not disregard the differences between Plotinus and Christian thought in some areas. While not a pantheist, a difference between creation and creature is not sufficiently clear at times in Plotinus´ writings. The Absolute is set outside the categories of being and rationality. The relation between nature and supernature is not seen as mediated by the element of grace.[114] It goes without saying, Plotinus lacked the central Christian notions of grace and personality.

2.3.1 in Greek Philosophy

Salient features of Plotinus' philosophy have become central - through a direct and indirect "Wirkungsgeschichte" (history of effectiveness) reaching to Goethe and German Idealism - for subsequent mystical philosophy or theology. Some aspects have been developed more intensely and have received new impulses from Christian revelation/philosophy which have strengthened the salvific relevance of mysticism.

In the quest for the crucial nexus between Antiquity and Christianity Plotinus' notion of the absolute One is foundational - though not always the focal point of attention - as a philosophical and theological principle. It finds its

---

[111] Enn., V 5,12,33; cf. Porphyry, Vita Plotini, 9,18; 13,8.
[112] Vita 23,1ff.
[113] Vita 2,26f.
[114] Knowles, The Evolution 29f.

congruent counterpart in the Christian concept of trinitarian unity. In retrospect a general line of Occidental thought can be discerned, which, in spite of numerous detours, estuaries, etc., is surprisingly consistent well into modernity.

Already in the recorded writings of Parmenides and Heraclitus the One (= "Hen") is thought as the relationless and synthesized one. To Parmenides neither is it generated nor completed. It is immutable, eternally complete and self-sustaining. Possessing already from the beginningless beginning the fullness of being, "it is indivisible."[115] It is per se. This fullness excludes both not-being and mere possibly being. In spite of its inner cohesion and in spite of the thought expressed within it, it is radically the unchangeable and difference-less One.[116] Such a constancy is identical with its truth.[117] By virtue of its self-identity (Being = Verity), the intimation is that it is both verity and veracity per definitionem.

In contrast, Heraclitus perceives the One as a joining of contraries: complete and incomplete, concordant and dissonant things are being combined.[118] This joining process is possible because the diverse originates from one common ground or reason. This unifying ground for the universal unity and completeness of the cosmos is the Logos. The Logos is "the invisible harmony" immanent to all things: such as bow and lyre.[119] It is wise and in accordance with the Logos to state the One to be all.[120]

While the One-Being of Parmenides and the One Logos of Heraclitus implicitly may possess a divine character, to Xenophanes the principle common to all things is explicitly primarily theological in nature. As He is immutable, God effortlessly governs and guides all things.[121]

It is difficult to reconstruct the authentic teaching of the Pythagoreans subsequent to the blow Aristotle's critique had dealt them. However, it appears that also to them the diverse emanations find a cosmic harmony by virtue of the One.[122]

The question concerning the relationship between the One and the many and in turn of the many to the One is central to Platonic philosophy. When Socrates asks for the "what" or "the essence" of a matter, then he aims already at the One in the many. Plato gives it a particular twist by introducing the "idea" of a matter. What is this Being per se which is proper to everything: which is true or actual being?[123] This One is perceived as being in itself, immutable, free of

---

[115] "oude diaireton estin:" Hermann Diels, Die Vorsokratiker (= VS). (Berlin: Weidemann, 1954) 28 B 8, 22.

[116] VS, 8,6.25.34.

[117] VS, 1,29.

[118] VS 22 B 10.

[119] VS, B 51.

[120] Fragment 22 B 50.

[121] VS 21 B 23 and 24.

[122] VS 1, 5, 986a 3; 14, 3, 1091a 15/22.

[123] "Haplous ontos on which is itself auto o esti," in: Phaedo 75d 2.

temporal or spatial categories, endowed with one form and by virtue of its presence the reason for the limited thus-being and recognizability of the many different, contingent things.[124] This causative and identity-giving of the individual thing through the presence of the idea corresponds to the participation of the "ideal-ized" (i.e. endowed with an idea) object with the idea.[125] The central task of philosophy is to verbalize the in-itself-being-idea as the unitary reason for the manifold insofar as its phenomena are recognizable.

Plato calls this method of articulation "dialectics." The aim of such an art is to define the idea of the Good as the reason of all ideas. The identification of the idea as a principle that is good and one at the same time[126] had been adopted and further developed by Plotinus and Proclus.[127] The thus thought identity was one reason for Neo-Platonism's perceiving of the One as a first principle unambiguously prior to a duality as transcendent. Unity is absolutely different from all forms of multitude. As "an intelligible material" duality it self-defines itself vis-à-vis the One. In this way Plato's teaching of principles - i.e. of the "Hen" and "aoristos duas" - supplies the essential outline for Neo-Platonic philosophy and, therefore, provides also a modifiable conceptual foundation for Christian theology.[128]

The term of the One is more significant in Plato's writings than a cursory survey might intimate. His oral observations in the Academy reveal more of Plato's philosophy than he was willing to convey in the *Dialogues*. They simultaneously confirm what internal conjectures the written texts permit and what external remarks other philosophers of Greek antiquity suggest.[129] Contrary to Plato's Dialogues, Aristotle holds that in the first book of the *Metaphysics* Plato taught three levels of being: that of the objects, of the ideas and of the One.[130] Keller speculates that whenever Plato mentions the good in the *Dialogues*, he actually meant the One.[131]

For Plato the final and ultimate knowledge ("Letzterkenntnis") always meant vision; intuitive insight. Citing the priestess Diotima from Mantineia, Socrates speaks in a way very akin to the three levels of philosophical-mystical insight of Plotinus: "katharsis" ("purificatio"), "photismos" ("illuminatio") and "henosis" ("unio"). While it is not clear whether Plato indeed intended to write

---

[124] Phaedo 78d 5/7 and 100d 5; conv. 210e 2/1b 5.
[125] Phaedo 100c 5f.
[126] Parm. 137c 4/42a 8; 142b 1/55c 3; cf. Eric Robertson Dodds, "The Parmenides of Plato and the origin of the Neo-Platonic 'One;' " Classical Quarterly 22 (1928): 129-142.
[127] Gaiser, Platons ungeschriebene Lehre, 2nd ed (1968) 452.
[128] Eric Osborn, The Beginning of Christian Philosophy (Cambridge: Cambridge UP, 1981) 54-56.145-148.
[129] Giovanni Reale, Zu einer neuen Interpretation Platons (Paderborn, München: Schöningh, 1993).
[130] 988a 10f.; cf. 988 b 4-5.
[131] Keller, Einführung 105.

on mysticism he undoubtedly prepared the ground work for such subsequent development in Neo-Platonism.

Aristotle's contributions to the notion of the One were less influential on subsequent philosophies. The One and Being are the most common and generalized ways of speaking.[132] Therefore, the two form an indissoluble unity.[133] In contrast to Plato, the One does not constitute here an ontological principle. It is an attendant definition to that of being.[134] Aristotle's *Metaphysics* ends by stressing unity as the ultimate, underlying principle. The "nous" is the unity of all definitions.[135] Nevertheless, his indexing of unity and multitude - the essentials of the One - as a continuum, an indivisible whole, have been assimilated by the following periods.

Plotinus builds upon this intellectual inheritance. It gives him the liberty not to have to reflect anew on the notion of the One solely as a unity but to go beyond: the question of the relationship between the One and the many now comes to the fore as the primary topic. As suggested above, it is Plotinus' epochal achievement to have developed on the whole a consistent theory of this relationship.[136] Plato's *Parmenides* is his point of departure. He appropriates the first three "hypostaseis" (= person or substance).

The first "hypostasis" stipulates the One ("Hen") to exclude all multitude within itself.[137] Only by way of a radical negation is it accessible. Beyond all categoriality it evidences itself as the pure, absolute, in itself resting unity. The second "hypostasis" ascribes being to the One. This establishes the first link between the One and the many. This is the reason to assume that the time-free nous brings forth thinking self-actuation. The third "hypostasis" is for Plotinus the soul ("psyche") which enables - in marked contrast to "nous" (reason) an immediate unity - a contact between the One and the manifold in time, space and matter.[138] As a consequence, he perceives reality as having three different degrees of intensity: the One, Reason and Psyche ("hen," "nous", "psyche"). The soul is the immediate causative principle of the world of phenomena.

Indebted to this Plotinian relational unity the Christian term of trinity receives in part its philosophical justification. Beierwaltes rightly observes:

> Relationalität zwischen den drei "Personen" des Einen göttlichen Seins stellt einen zeitfreien Prozeß des gegenseitigen - denkenden und liebenden - Inne-Seins dar. Das Eine substantiale Sein schließt sich zur Dreiheit auf - mira quaedam tam ineffabilis quam

---

[132] Metaphysics 10, 2, 1053b 20.

[133] Metaphysics 1054a 9/15.

[134] Cf. Hans Joachim Krämer, "Grundfragen der aristotelischen Theologie," Theologie und Philosophie 44 (1969): 363-382; Philip Merlan, From Platonism to Neoplatonism, 2nd ed. (The Hague: Nijhoff, 1960).

[135] Aristotle, De an. III, 5, 430a 14f.

[136] He considers himself as successor to Plato (Enn. V,1,8, 12/4).

[137] Enn. V, 5, 6, 26/8.

[138] Enn. V, 1, 8, 12/27.

inevitabilis in summa unitate ... pluralitas[139] und konstituiert sich gerade dadurch als Einheit: Drei-Einheit als absolute, sich selbst gegenwärtige Einheit *vor* jeder Vielheit oder Differenz im eigentlichen Sinne, die das Einzelne in ihr nicht nur unter- sondern primär ab-scheidet und trennt. Das Verhältnis von Einheit und Dreiheit, die nicht als Zahlbegriffe zu denken sind, ist das philosophische Fundament des theologischen Gedankens.[140]

Henology can be termed a consistent and sustained philosophic effort, that involved in a personal - at times perhaps even in a mystic manner - the thinking subject.[141] Along with Plato, the One is identified with the Good.[142]

These considerations lead to a systematic unfolding of the nature of the One. It is identified with the Good.[143] A thus constituted One gives itself by virtue of its plenitude of being "without resentment" and thereby sets into being other entities, which are related back to the One in such a way that they remain inalienably participatory in their origin.[144]

This emanating process of the One into the corporeal multifariousness is defined as "prohodos," procession from within the One. It seems that Plotinus draws at this point on the unrecorded teachings of Plato.[145] The return, called "epistrophe," is the third phase of this development. The aloneness ("mone") of the One gives cause for the emanation ("prohodos") from the One and the return ("epistrophe") of the many to the One. This event occurs in philosophical insight. Because the One is pure and full of integrity it attracts all and is thereby cause for reality's dynamism.[146] The "epistrophe" to the "Hen" is the final and ultimate goal of Plotinian philosophy.[147]

He uses the image of the roundelay dance to convey his thought. Though the dancers do not always look to the center, they constantly dance around it. Yet when looking at the center, which he identifies as the leader and personal One, we arrive at an aim and at a resting-point.[148] Quite remarkable is the fact that he uses terms similar to those Plato used in his cave-parable: aim ("telos") and rest ("anapaula"). This metaphor teaches a twofold meaning concerning the relationship of intelligent beings to the one. Either their relationship is merely an ontic one or they have the chance to direct their eyes to the dancers' leader.

---

[139] Here the author quotes quite tellingly in Latin Anselm: Monologion 43 (I 59, 15f. Schmidt); "..." in the text of Beierwaltes.

[140] Beierwaltes, Denken des Einen 10.

[141] For a discussion of the pervasive presence of henology in Western thought cf. Plotino e il Neoplatonismo in Oriente e in Occidente no ed. noted. (Accademia Nazionale dei Lincei Anno CCCLXXI - 1974 (Roma).

[142] Enn., VI 9: "Peri t'agathon e ton henos:" (= Concerning the Good or the One).

[143] Enn., II, 9, 1, 5; V, 5, 9, 35f.

[144] Enn. IV, 8, 6, 8.18; V, 4, 1, 35.

[145] Keller, Einführung in die philosophische Mystik 108.

[146] Enn., V 4, 27.

[147] Hans von Schubert, Plotin, Einführung in sein Philosophieren (München, Freiburg i. Br.: Alber, 1973) 64.

[148] Enn., VI 9,8.

Unlike the dance, this concsious relationship requires a mystical asceticism. It is then granted a vision which afterwards should be communicated to others.[149] Such a vision has both epistemological and ethical ramifications. It occasions a new life and an intensification of existence. To remain distant from this experience implies a weaker form of being.[150] One should be on guard lest the consciousness of the passing union of subject and object, which constitutes the insight into ultimate essence, is lost in mundane, daily life. In eternal life, however, such a union between subject and object, later termed "unio mystica," will be a constant feature. While contingent being calls for reason in order to attain this state, it will then be achieved without the aid of reason.[151] Such a state is constantly granted; no longer is an intellectual or ethical effort required.

Plotinus attempted to grasp the nature of the being-constituting and being-determining character of the One with the Platonic metaphor "King of all Matter"[152] and with the term "measure."[153] He also used the term "strength of all objects."[154] The latter defines the active omnipotence of the One over all in the ontological sense of being preceding all in the manner of absolute unity. The way this dynamic expresses itself to the "outside" (a term one may use only with the utmost caution) world, i.e. its creative manifestations, is goodness. To express this situation of the procession from the One, and yet remaining within it, Plotinus employs metaphors: root, seed, source, light, sun and circle.[155]

The universal effects of the One or the Good are grounded as beginning and aim - "arche kai telos" - in the human being, who possesses the possibility of a simultaneous turn to oneself and to the One. The one that is "similar" in us allows the soul's ascent to the ground for this similarity. This unifying process eclipses cognitional reflection. It is Plotinus´ consistent conviction that the One is Theos in its most intensive and highest meaning.[156] Hence all comprehending approximations and demarcations are at the same time applicable to the One and God; for they are synonyms.[157]

On this point Plotinus appropriates Aristotle's critique of the Platonic concept. Both the thinker from Stagira and Plotinus agree that the one (oneness = being an entity) and being must be one and the same. Thought further, it entails that being and one are identical with its (their) substance. Such a substance, however, is composed of a multitude, and therefore, is in turn still

---

[149] Enn., VI 9,7.
[150] Enn., VI 9,9. Meister Eckhart will call the thereby acquired "habitus" "Gelassenheit" or "Abgeschiedenheit."
[151] Enn., VI 9,10.
[152] Plat. ep. 2, 312e.
[153] Enn. 5, 5, 4, 13f.
[154] "dynamis panton:" Enn., III, 8, 10, 1.
[155] Cf. Enn., III, 8, 10, 5/28; V, 1, 6, 28; V, 1, 6, 28; IV, 3, 17, 13f.; VI, 8, 18, 7/32.
[156] Enn., 6, 9, 11, 28.
[157] Cf. John Rist, "Theos and the One in some texts of Plotinus," Medieval Studies 24 (1962): 169-180.

insufficiently defined as the highest.[158] For the being of multitude requires again an absolute one. Even the first essence is still a multitude as it lives and thinks. Pure thinking remains a multitude because it connotes a subject that thinks itself as an object. To Plotinus even ideas remain multitudinous as they are numbers.[159] As a consequence, to Plotinus the One is an absolutely simple principle, combining all multitude, an absolutely indivisible, whose absolute immediacy is not that of infinite smallness, but rather on the contrary that of infinite ability.[160] It is a limiting infinite, that becomes the measure precisely due to its infinitude.[161] By thinking further within the parameters set by Plato and Aristotle centuries earlier, he comes to affirm the absolute transcendence of the One. Here the tracing of the hermeneutical process is not one of curiosity, nor of an arbitrary appropriation. In the event something - such as otherness or passive infinitude - can be derived from it, it is then only as a mere abundance of the One which leaves the One undefined, untouched and unmoved by it.[162]

Porphyry thinks the One as a differentiated Unity of prior-to-being One along with the Being self as pure effect and self-thinking. Since Porphyry combined the highest thought of Aristotle[163] with the concept of the transcendent One,[164] he created one decisive material prerequisite for Christian theology as an intellectually accountable science. The latter - mandated by scripture - was compelled to reflect upon divine being, His wisdom and His Logos as a unit.[165]

2.3.2 in Scripture

The Old Testament defined God as one and unique. This made the Jewish God singular among religions and rendered Israel an exception in a world in which a polytheistic world-view prevailed. These features implied his actions as creator and his covenant with the Israelites. This uniqueness as the sovereignty of Jahweh has as consequence a relationship sui generis between God and Israel: "You shall have no other gods to rival me" (Ex 20:3). Moses' and Israel's historical experiences and insights are a form of early monotheism or at least of henotheism (Dt 4:39 and 6:4 - the latter is quoted in Mk 12:29 by Jesus). His deeds demonstrate His greatness: He is without competition and His status is

---

[158] Enn., VI, 9, 2, 1-10.19.

[159] Enn., VI, 9, 2, 24.27.

[160] Enn., VI 9, 6 1-12.

[161] Enn., VI, 7, 17, 15-20.

[162] Enn., V, 2, 1, 8.

[163] God is pure reality and absolute self-possession by thinking Himself.

[164] Not-being and being One (= 1. and 2. hypothesis of Parmenides) constitute in the thinking act the pure being of the One.

[165] Cf. Pierre Hadot, Porphyre et Victorinus 1/2, (Paris: Etudes Augustiniennes, 1968); Gerhard Delling, "Monos Theos," Theologische Literaturzeitung 77 (1952): 46-76.

incontestable (cf. Is 37:16,20). The greatness of this God ("For you are great and do marvellous deeds, you, God, and none other," (Ps 86:10)) is the attendant corollary to His uniqueness and unity. Only one God can be the greatest and His singularity is based on His unsurpassable greatness.

Upon this background - a combination of Platonism and the Septuagint - Philo of Alexandria develops a Jewish-Hellenistic theology, which is to exert major influence upon early Christian theology. The various descriptions of God (the unique one, "monos", a one (= unit) "eis," the one ("hen"), a unit or the uniqueness ("monas")[166] serve as semantic circum-definitions of the unitary nature of God. The unique being of God excludes all real multitude. Therefore God is identical with simplicity ("physis aple," "no mixture," without inner difference).[167]

As the naming of God as "monas" may suggest God´s being as one - just as the number one implies the first in a chain of multitudinous things - Philo localizes the absolute unity of God beyond monas. God is unity and at the same time above it. In the most intensive sense of Oneness, God is "older than the monas and purer than (the number) one."[168] Such simultaneous affirmation and negation is an adequate predication of God only insofar as it is understood as an "icon" of God.[169] On the one hand the absolute one-ness of God is "unmixed" and "pure." On the other hand God is through the mediation of the Logos as "God's Son" in the world created by Him - as both effecting and ordering entity - immanently present. Here one also finds present along with biblical aspects of creation and grace God as the term for a transcendent and universal reason, likewise the Platonic notion of God present in and effecting the cosmos. Both the biblical and the Platonic terminologies are expressions of modes of the Divine granting participation in Himself. Also the Stoa[170] and the Pseudo-Aristotelian writing *De mundo 6* [171] had already prior to Philo developed a concept of a One-God universally penetrating (from the exterior) and permeating (from the interior) the world.

The New Testament continues these already established strains of the Old Testament (cf. Dt 6:4 and Mk 12:29). The profession of the One God serves as a particular form of delimitation of the new creed from its surrounding Hellenistic-ecclectic religiosity. In the speech on the Areopagus (Acts 17:22-31) Paul proclaims the one God. While establishing a link between the Christian God and the as yet "unknown God" of the Greek tradition, he equally stresses the difference of the uniquely true God who creates and bestows grace unto the world. Thereby a clear distinction is drawn from pagan - often demons-adoring

---

[166] Cf. leg. all. 2,2f; 3,82; quis rer. div. her. 183; gig. 64; migr. Abr. 134f.
[167] leg. all. 2, 2,; mut. nom. 184.
[168] praem. et poen. 40; cf. also vit. cont. 2.
[169] quis rer. div. her. 187; spec. leg. 2, 176.
[170] Kleanthes' Hymn of Zeus: SVF no. 537.
[171] 397b 33; 398b 8.22; 399a 13.

- faith and its cultic praxis (1Cor 8:4f.). By His incommensurable uniqueness, the Christian God is elevated: exclusively He deserves to be predicated "the eternal King, the undying, invisible and only God," and "the only wise God" (1 Tim 1:17; Rom 16:27). Scripture also conveys a notion of unity in relationality when speaking of the reciprocal interior being of God the Father and God the Son in the one Godhead: "The Father and I are one" (Jn 10:30). This implies a pure identity of essence. Whoever hears Jesus, hears the Father; whoever sees the Son beholds the Father; the Father bears witness for the Son: these statements reveal a unity in volition, action and charity which refers back to the unity of the two in the one being (Jn 5). As this unity is a living one, the divine unity of the One becomes the obliging paradigm for the Christian community:

> May they all be one, just as, Father, you are in me and I am in you, so that they also may be in us, so that the world may believe it was you who sent me... With me in them and you in me, may they be so perfected in unity. (Jn 17:21.23)

This unity does not come about at random or by chance. Rather, it is facilitated and communicated in a manner both foundational and original in baptism: "But at work in all these is one and the same Spirit" (1 Cor 12:11). It is Christ Himself who unites all to one organism, incorporating the community's multitude into the existing unity between the Father and the Son:

> baptised into one body in a single Spirit. Jews as well as Greeks, slaves as well as free men, and we were all given the same spirit to drink. (1 Cor 12:13)

This implies:

> you are all one in Jesus Christ. (Gal 3:28)

2.3.3 in the Patristic Era

In intensive borrowing of Middle-Platonic and Neo-Pythagorean theorems, Athenagoras, Hippolytus and Clement of Alexandria gave prominence to divine uniqueness - in the sense of God's incomparable oneness.[172] This leads to reflection on God´s inner unity. Thereby both the one essence and the trinitarian differentiation in the one Godhead can be articulated. At the same time the radical difference of God and His unknowability as well as His beyond "sayability" are documented.[173] His essence is neither separable nor divisible. Insofar as language is always prone to divide, form categories, distinguish, etc., there exists no adequate manner of speaking of the Divine.

---

[172] leg. 6,1; strom. 5, 78, 4; 81, 5/82, 2 respectively.
[173] strom. 81/5f.

This leads Clement to conclude that "God is beyond one and above unity."[174] What must be later observed as paradigmatic for Marius Victorinus, Augustine and Western trinitarian thought in general, is valid already early on for the Greek Fathers: the effort to harmonize divine uniqueness, simplicity, uncomposedness and indivisibility with the trinitarian notion of variedness in the one Godhead.[175] To fend off anthropomorphizing tendencies, Irenaeus emphasizes God's simplicity:

> simplex, et non compositus ... et totus ipse sibimetipsi similis, et aequalis est, totus cum sit sensus et totus spiritus ...[176]

Arian disputes also caused a stress on the unity of the Logos with the Father.[177] This promoted a further integration of monotheistic and trinitarian dimensions. First the fathers developed the topic of unity and uniqueness, in order to thematize subsequently the variedness (i.e. properties) in God. A motion, a "movedness," an inner relationality, is being unfolded as a reflexive corollary moment revealed when contemplating divine oneness within the one Godhead. Upon this background even the more intensive relationship of God to the multitude entailed in the Logos´ incarnation can no longer provoke an essential transformation of the divine One into the many - both in the economic and in the immanent sense.[178] Both in the inner and outward procession God manifests His Oneness in and through the Trinity.

In such an intellectual milieu Gregory of Nyssa predicates prominently the One as the infinitely-being ("apeiron"). Thereby he identifies the essence of God as - in spite of His relationship to the world - a negation of all finite, temporal and extended matter.[179] Along with Plotinus he apprehends the One as without-form, prior to any determined-ness, not-something, without-confines and not-finite.[180] Like Plotinus Gregory uses the terms "Hen" and "apeiron" to express the One as the origin par excellence. Both predications remain beyond the reach of human verbalization. The term "katholou apeiron"[181] suggests a quality equally mutually embracing the monotheisitic and trinitarian moments in the One.

This must be seen in the light of the then virulent tritheistic and Arian (particularly of Eunomian provenance) debates. Both tritheism and Arianism threatened to dissolve the unity and the identity of the One's essence ("toutotes

---

[174] pead. 1, 71, 1.
[175] Orig. c. Cels. 4, 14.
[176] adv. haer. 2, 13, 3.8.
[177] Cf. Basil, c. Eunom. 1, 25.
[178] Origen, in Joh. comm. 1, 20, 119.
[179] Basil, c. Eunom. 1, 169/71. 236f. 683. 690.
[180] Enn., VI, 9, 6, 10f; V, 5, 10, 19/11, 3.
[181] tres dii: 3, 1, 52, 19 Jäger/Mueller.

ousias"): "eis gar theos kai ho autos."[182] This because God is the one and same essence: each Person is predicated equally "substantial" and "God." The thus described infinite unity of the divine essence ("ousia") makes the three divine persons one with themselves as well as renders dissolved and overcome all other predications within itself.[183] The trinitarian unity of the One divine essence confirms also its boundlessness and vice-versa. Boundlessness brings forth the thought of Unity in Threesomeness. The One Boundlessness is thinkable but once. Here the convergence of Greek Philosophy (Plotinus) and Christianity is complete.[184]

The Pseudo-Dionysian writings further attest to a synthesis between Plotinian thought and Christian theology. The divine predication as the "Hen" figures prominently. Through the translations of Pseudo-Dionysian teaching by John Scotus Erigena, the Plotinian thought on the One-God influenced Europe in the Middle Ages and well into the Renaissance.

Marius Victorinus additionally transforms the Plotinian notion of the One into a Three-Unity. In the anti-Arian polemics he states that the trinitarian unity constitutes itself by the progression of the "not-" or "before-"being One ("unum solum," "unum simplex," "unum ante ipsum on")[185] into the "being One" ("existentialiter unum")[186] or "unum unum" - not as duplication - but rather as unfolding of the "potentia" of the first One. This illustrates to Marius Victorinus the unity of being, life and thinking as the, in relationship to the Father, consubstantial Son. The Son is "Logos," "vita" and "forma Patris."[187] In the final stage of this unfolding of the trinitarian self-constitution stands the reflexive, thinking recourse of life to its proper origin and constituting beginning: in the Spiritus Sanctus.[188] It is the reflexive bond ("copula," "conexio")[189] which renders the self-revelation of the before-being into the being One to a "triplex unitas" or "unalis trinitas"[190] in the difference of the two

---

[182] comm. 20, 27/21, 1. 26, 1/5.
[183] tres dii: 3, 1, 55, 13/20; cf. to the whole question c. Eunom. 3, 10, 9, 47/9.
[184] Cf. Ekkehard Mühlenberg, Die Unendlichkeit Gottes bei Gregor v. Nyssa. Gregors Kritik am Gottesbegriff der klassischen Metaphysik (Göttingen: Vandenhoeck & Ruprecht, 1966).
"Seine (Plotinus´) Schau des Einen bietet eine direkte Parallele zu der "Mystik" Gregors, weil auch hier die Gottesschau das Ziel ist" (at 174).
While at pages 174-178 the positive elements of Plotinus´ influence on the thinking of Gregory are discussed, pages 82-88 point to the not insignificant differences between Plotinus and Christianity: the infinite boundless is predicated as evil by Plotinus. While Gregory defines divine infinity on the background of divine simplicity, Plotinus sees - much like Plato - in the multifarious a breaking away from the One (Enn., VI, 6, 1, 1-3) precisely because it is an infinite multitude.
[185] adv. Ar. 1, 49.
[186] adv. Ar. 1,50.
[187] adv. Ar. 1,51.
[188] adv. Ar. 1,51.
[189] hymn. 1, 5; 3, 205.
[190] gen. div. verb. 31.

(Father and Son) in the identity[191] eliminated or sublated. Indeed by virtue of this circular trinitarian procession to its base, the Trinity is a moved relationality or reflexivity of the most intensive One-ness.

Here a model is developed from a primarily philosophical point of view which corresponds precisely to a theological intention. Plotinian philosophy permits thinking of God as trinitarian difference, as thinking self-relationality and equally as absolute unity. This congeniality of philosophy and theology is noteworthy as paradigmatic for subsequent centuries. Revelation can be opened, indeed "revealed," in philosophy.

In this philosophical vein Augustine perceives the God of revelation to be the universal One "forma" from which all being comes into being.[192] Unity is considered the criterion of true being.[193] True thinking and particularly philosophy thematize the "unum." The reader is being introduced to the two central Augustinian questions: God and the soul, by demonstrating them as parts of the overarching quest for the One.[194] This he justifies by suggesting that the Latin word "universum" has its etymological roots in "unum."[195]

The creative effect of the "summum unum" is the basis for the correspondence of being and being-one in the created order. Or to express the same in a different manner: that something can be only insofar as it is one:

nihil est autem est quam unum esse. Itaque unum quantum quidque unitatem adipiscitur, in tantum est.[196]

The concrete being-one of being is the most common aspect of the fact that all created matter is structured according to numbers. This quality of being numbered is the ontological pre-condition for the inner cohesion or unity of being things perduring in time;[197] i.e. for its being ordered, being in accordance with oneself and with its origin and for its own identity vis-à-vis its self-destruction through the "aversio ab uno."[198] In the created temporal situation of the human condition, marked by "dispersio," "discissio," "distentio," "dissimilitudo," etc., human beings are called to a self-collection towards the

---

[191] adv. Ar. 1, 54.

[192] vera. relig. 30, 55; 35, 65; 43, 81; 55, 112f; Gen. ad. litt. imperf. 10, 32.

[193] Augustine, De vera rel. cc. 30-32; c. 36, n. 66; Conf. II, 1, n. 1; Sermo 104, c.2, n. 3; Sermo 255, c. 6, n. 6.

[194] Augustine, De ord. II, 17, nn. 42-48.

[195] Augustine, De ord. I, 2, n. 3; cf. Josef Koch, "Augustinischer und dionysischer Neuplatonismus und das Mittelalter," Kantstudien 48 (1956/57): 117-133.

[196] mor. Manich. 2, 6, 8 (PL 32, 1348).

[197] "formas habent, quia numeros habent: adime illis haec, nihil erunt:" lib. arb. 2, 16, 42; mus. 6, 13, 38 (PL 32, 1184).

[198] In the original the predications for such a unity of the created order are: "ordo," "convenientia," "concordia," "similitudo" and "salus" (cf. mor. Manich. 2, 6, 8; vera relig. 31, 58; 36, 66f; mus. 6, 17, 56 (PL 32, 1191).

One, a being around the One ("circa unum"), a re-course (retracing) towards and a "reformatio" of the self. This process Augustine understands as a return from a "deformatio" to the "forma omnium."[199]

Already for Augustine[200] the intellectual return into one´s own, personal interiority, which means cognitional self-ascertainment, is a necessary prerequisite for experiential evidence of numenous, divine being.[201] By also transcending the "mens," evidential experience of truth achieves this. It acknowledges God to be both more interior and higher than the self. By striding through the dialectic path - mustering the interior eye and interior listening as devices - the self tears itself apart from the realm of dissimilarity ("regio dissimilitudinis")[202] and beholds the unchanging light ("lux incommutabilis"), which now not only is, but also speaks: "I am who I am." In this process Being is apprehended as being pure, perfect, unchanging goodness, truth and justice. This includes the fullness and time-free perfect completion of Being as essentially different ("valde aliud") from time-constrained, creaturely, finite being, yet related to it. To achieve this perfection of the self, Augustine calls repeatedly for "the songs of steps" ("canticum graduum"). To this end (transcending) conscious interiority is required. In a manner proper to the human being this grace effects - analogous to and at the same time different from the Plotinian "eros" - the moving element and bequeaths freedom to the human being:

inflamed and lifted upwards through your gift we burn and go thus. We climb the ascents in the heart and sing the chant of steps.[203]

Like Plotinus Augustine does not subscribe to the belief that such a state could be achieved effortlessly. The Platonic conditions for the "visio beatifica" are adopted: The soul can grasp the ideas only with her interior eye. It must be holy and pure. The eye must become similar to what it desires to behold:

Et ea quidem ipsa rationalis anima non omnis et quaelibet, sed quae sancta et pura fuerit, haec asseritur illi visioni esse idonea: id est, quae illum ipsum oculum quo videntur ista, sanum et sincerum et serenum, et similem his rebus quas videre intendit, habuerit.[204]

---

[199] vera relig. 52, 101; 55, 113; mus. 6, 17, 56; conf. 2, 1, 1,; 10, 29, 40; 11, 29, 39; serm. 96, 6; 104, 2, 3; 255, 6, 6.
[200] It cannot be ascertained with certitude whether he had been familiarized with Plotinian thought via Marius Victorinus' translation. Cf. in general for this passage Joseph Geyser, "Die Theorie Augustins der Selbsterkenntnis der Seele," Aus der Geisteswelt des Mittelalters, Beiträge zur Geschichte und Theologie des Mittelalters - Supplementband III/ 1. Halbband, A. Lang, J. Lechner, M. Schmaus (eds.), (Münster: Aschendorff, 1935): 169-187.
[201] "Noli foras ire, in te ipsum redi. In interiore homine habitat veritas" (de ver. rel. 39,72).
[202] Cf. Plotinus, Enn., I, 8,13,17.
[203] "dono tuo accendimur et sursum ferimur; inardescimus et imus. Ascendimus ascensiones in corde et cantamus canticum graduum." Conf. XIII 9,10; cf. also Conf. VII 10,16 and En. in Psalm. 119,1 (my translation).

A collaboration difficult to define between God and man, between grace and conversion is a prerequisite for a beatific vision.[205] Purity of heart is indispensable.[206] Antiquity knew a sequence of steps leading to knowledge. Because of the nature of the beheld and of the acquired beatitude, however, one can no longer speak in Augustine's judgment of a purely theoretically oriented pursuit of life. Here, grace becomes the decisive ingredient. In this context one can no longer observe solely a "videre per speciem" but also a "videre per fidem" -echoing 2 Cor 5:7.[207]

As the above documents - and contrary to Keller's position[208] -, Augustine does not surrender the notion of the One, as articulated in Platonic and Plotinian metaphysics, in spite of a preponderance of "veritas" and "vere esse" as equivocal terms for God. The Christian teaching of a trinitarian God is not perceived in direct contradiction to Neo-Platonic metaphysics, but as its logical fulfillment.[209] Both God in the categoriality of the One and in trinitarian categoriality are developed from a unitarian ontology. Unity is the basis for being and the criterion for any statement concerning it: "in quantum quidque unitatem adipiscitur, in tantum est"[210]

Augustine, as later likewise Boethius, also approaches the decisive term "forma" from the notion of unity and the concept of ontological unity:

vis ipsa formae commendentur nomine unitatis. Hoc est enim veri formari, in unum aliquid redigi: quoniam summe unum est omnis formae principium.[211]

or:

Omnis enim forma ad unitatis regulam cogitur.[212]

Plotinus' teaching that only through the principle within us do we reach the primordial principle - mediated and prepared by thinking, ultimately attained only through non-thinking[213] - had been intensified and adumbrated by Proclus. He also adopted the teaching of the traces of the One or divine in us as

---

[204] De diversis quaestionibus qu. 46, Oeuvres de Saint Augustin, Vol. 10: Mélanges doctrinaux, Paris 1952, p. 124. For Plato's observations concerning the inadequacy of demonstrating the situation, cf. Timaeus 29A-D.

[205] Augustine, Ep. (ad Paulinam) 147, 6, 18.

[206] In Ps. 5. 63. 130. cf. Anselm, E 185, 27f; 446, 15-17.

[207] Augustine, in Ps. 119.149.

[208] Keller, Einführung 113.

[209] Augustine, De musica VI, c. 17, n. 56

[210] Augustine, De mor. Manich. II. 6, n. 8; cf. Ep. 18, n. 2.

[211] De Gen. ad lit. c. 10, n. 32.

[212] De Gen. c. Man. c. 12 n. 18.

[213] "os arche archein ora," Enn., VI 9,11,31f.

the ontological prerequisite of unification. The One in us - as the "concept of the One" (= "intelligentia unius") - denotes the preliminary nature of the One in our thinking. It signifies the timeless beginning of a thinking process collecting itself in time towards the One. Exclusively through "the One in us" does the nonconceptual and nontemporal accessible One communicate itself. It is the analogous conceptuality and expressivity (= speakable) of the One that is therein implied. The illumination of the soul ("illustratio," "claritas," "auge") enables unification with the transcendent One. The soul's illumination is a luminosity of thinking originating within the One itself.[214] The light immanent to the soul permits the transcendental light to be beheld and to be united with it. We must therefore - analogously to Plotinus' enlightenment of the intelligible cause - render the One in us conscious - "awakened" - in order to be capable of recognizing - precisely through One's analogous, trace-like presence within us - the One itself: "to eni to hen."

This insight echoes in the following observation:

Aware of this, what excels all being objects, a divinizing (upward) swing is required, so that we might not secretively be pushed by an uncertain concept into nothingness and its abyss, but rather, when having awakened the One in us to a glow, unite thereby the soul with the One, and as if cast anchor there, by standing aloof of all things thinkable and taking every other (conceivable) form of effectiveness from us, in order to come to communion with it and to dance around it.[215]

Last but not least thanks to the apostle-like authority of Dionysius the Pseudo-Areopagite during the Middle Ages - who had integrated into his theology central Proclusian philosophems - Neo-Platonic concepts, such as "flos intellectus," "acies mentis,"[216] "in nobis unum," "unum animae" and "the soul's ground" have become considered materially authoritative. Dionysius adopts the Plotinian notion of the terrestrial-human and divine circles. Unification is now caused by the causing principle itself, by the divine love. It impels the human circle to join the eternal One, forming two "eternal circles."[217] Divine, luminous ekstasis enkindles the "ekstasis" of human longing towards God. In Dionysius' writings also Plotinus is found in agreement with Scripture:

---

[214] Within Christian revelation (Mt 23:8-10) this moment of illumination experiences further maturation. Christ is "doctor interius:" the inner teacher for He is Truth itself. This spans from Augustine (De magistro XI 38: Christ as "intus ipsi menti praesidens veritas," XII 40: "Deo intus pandente (res); intus magister," XIV 46: "ut ad eum, scil. unum omnium magistrum, intro conversi erudiamur") to Bonaventure (Hex. I 11 (331a): "ipse (Christ) est medium omnium scientiarum," XII 5 (385a): "doctor interius" and It. III 3 (304b): "aeterna veritas ... docens." cf. to this complex Historisches Wörterbuch der Philosophie, Vols. 2 (1972), 5 (1980): articles "Einsprechung," "Erleuchtung," "Licht" and "lumen naturale."

[215] Plato, in Parm. (Cousin) 1072,3-13 (author's translation).

[216] Cf. Anselm: P P: 93,12: "aliquando mentis aciem omnino fugeret..."; O 7:21,88: "animae meae, quo aufugis aciem mentis meae?," also: M 33:52,21 and 64:74,31.

[217] Dionysius, div. nom. IV 14; 712 D.

"it is no longer I who live, but Christ who lives in me..." (Gal 2:20b).[218] Christian philosophy is not merely a strained and artificially retouched version of "pagan" philosophy. One must more correctly conclude to an inner congeniality between the two grounded in the universal human condition.[219]

Reflecting in connection with Ex 3:14 on the divine name, Dionysius strongly identifies God with the One.[220] This God cannot be spoken of as unity. Like Plotinus he knows of three hierarchies - purification, illumination and perfection - in order to attain similitude and unity with the Divine.[221] This deification of its members is the aim of the ecclesiastic hierarchy.[222]

As a theologian, Dionysius himself is indebted to and lives from a philosophical reflection and this in turn is productive for the demonstration of his own faith. Dionysius - one of the authorities for the Medieval mind - is a further example of how relevant Plotinian thought had been for Christianity.[223] The concept of the One plays a yet more significant role in his thinking than in that of Augustine.[224] Koch refers to Augustine's philosophy as "Seinsmetaphysik" and contrasts it to the "Einheitsmetaphysik" of Dionysius, thereby accentuating the different valences of the two.

Of equal relevance to the Middle Ages is Boethius. Roughly from the 9th to the 15th centuries De Hebdomadibus was used as a primer for the study of philosophy. He also transmits in varied ways Plotinian concepts.[225] When a worldly objector claimed that there is nothing good in mere existence, Plotinus rejoined that life is rendered good by the pleasures it offers, including that of philosophical contemplation.[226] This becomes the tenor of Boethius' opus magnum.

Boethius, "last of the Romans, first of the scholastics," to quote the humanist Lorenzo Valla of the fifteenth century,[227] refers to Plato, Aristotle and Plotinus as possessed with "auctoritas."[228] The central notion of the will, as an impelling volition towards oneself - figuring prominently in the Enneads [229] -

---

[218] div. nom. IV 13; 712 A.

[219] In this context the role of providence and grace in history merits further consideration: the terminological congeniality of the canonized Greek Septuagint and Greek philosophy etc.

[220] DN XIII 2.

[221] CH III 2.

[222] EC I 3.

[223] Barbara Faes de Mottoni, Il "Corpus Dionysiacum" nel Medioevo (Milano: Jaca, 1977).

[224] Josef Koch, "Augustinischer und Dionysischer Neuplatonismus und das Mittelalter," Kantstudien 48 (1956/57): 117-133; Kurt Ruh, Geschichte der christlichen Mystik, Bd. I. (München: C.H. Beck, 1990) 31-82.

[225] In Divis 875D he refers to Plotinus as possessed of "auctoritas."

[226] Chadwick, Boethius 205f.

[227] Chadwick, Boethius XI.

[228] Divis 875D.

[229] Enn., VI, 8,13.21.

resurfaces in Boethius' *De Hebdomadibus* [230] Boethius also inherited from Plotinus the notion of the One being singularly identical with itself not composed of different and alien components. Similarly to Plotinus all being must - insofar as it is -necessarily emanate from the infinite, inexhaustible source which he calls "ipsum esse," as absolute and simple Being, and which is materially identical with the Plotinian One.[231] By stressing the volitional moment, Boethius adds further personal features to Plotinus' One, thus bringing the One in greater proximity to the dynamic Christian and Semitic concept of the divine. This small treatise plays a significant role in subsequent Christian philosophy. The confrontation of a yet primarily static, unchanging One of Plotinian provenience with the alive and dynamic God of Israel results in the tense, vibrant trinitarian God of Christian revelation on a philosophical plane. It is important to note in this context that Plotinus' thought points in a direction which only Christianity could have fully developed.[232]

In his hymn "O qui perpetua mundum ratione gubernas" Boethius holds like Plotinus that philosophical inquiry enables the soul to attain to a vision of the divine. Thereby human beings are capable of obtaining consolation. To illustrate this cardinal moment he recurs to Plotinus' notion of the two circles:

> quae cum secta duos motum glomerauit in orbes,
> in semet reditura meat mentemque profundam
> circuit et simili conuertit imagine caelum.[233]

In a way this hymn is the pivotal hingepoint of the *Consolatio*. Only by attaining the Divine is this bliss guaranteed: 'divinitatis adeptio facit beatos.'"[234] The insight resulting from this beholding transforms existence: "in te conspicuos animi defigere visus."[235] From such a defined beatitude no ephemeral consolation can be deduced. The evidence of the divine foundation of being (which includes the world of senses) gives a convincing response to the question as to the reliable purpose of this world's joys, trials, vicissitudes and perils. The insight into the cause of all being changes perspectives. A passionate "aeternitas caritate flagrare"[236] as one's disposition to life calls for a consistent determination to this aim: philosophizing with God as its root and center. In a concise manner this hymn conveys notions with major future

---

[230] De Hebdomadibus, Lines 117-121. 155-162.

[231] De Hebdomadibus, 32-35.61-66.

[232] Philo of Alexandria is already a prefiguration. Cf. Emile Bréhier, Les idées philosophiques et religieuses chez Philon d'Alexandre (Paris: Vrin,1950).

[233] "though by their own split, molding by (divine) movement to two circles, they return again to themselves," (author's translation; cf. Cons. Phil m.9, lines 15f. - CCSL XCIV, Anicii Manlii Severini Boethii Philosophiae Consolatio (Turnhout: ed. L. Bieler, 1957).

[234] Cons. Phil. III 10, 24. Cf. Beierwaltes, Denken des Einen 323f.

[235] Cons. Phil. III 10, 24.

[236] Augustine, ver. rel. 46,89.

implications. Implicitly, it also contains the view that Genesis and Plato's *Timaeus* form a unit. This perception allowed the latter to become a primary object of reception for Medieval commentators.[237]

As creation, so also the mystic movement is perceived in volitional terms. This is found in Plotinus as the will of the One to itself - which causes and is paralleled by human emulation.[238] The Plotinian notion of the self-relationality of the One is contained in Boethius' concept of the "ipse esse." The "esse" of the "ipsum primum bonum" is cause and ultimate aim of "emanatio." The single thing partakes in the One's "esse." Upon this profoundly Plotinian ontological horizon the insight "omne ens est bonum" is then deduced.[239]

2.3.4 in the Middle Ages

Transmitted particularly by Augustine and Boethius, the Platonic and Plotinian formal circumscription of philosophizing in the categories of "unum," "unio" and "separatio" has retained its familiarity also to the Medieval mind. Historically this terminology could be conveniently invoked to reject Manichean and Katharist heresies postulating dualism as the underlying principle.

Plotinian and generally Neo-Platonic thought, as transmitted by Dionysius the Pseudo-Areopagite, figures prominently also in Eriugena's writings. In a lengthy discusion he evidences the Aristotelian predications as not being irreducible, final and most common. They yet can be reduced to status, motus and relatio.[240] A separation of theology and philosophy is unthinkable. Like others, not a diffuse amalgamation of Christian revelation and ancient philosophical themes occurs, but rather a critical, transforming synthesis very much in the Ricoeurian meaning of an original "refiguration"[241] of things analogous and different to one single thought. What Beierwaltes observes of Eriugena concerning the Plotinian notion of the One can be observed in general for all of Christian philosophy:

---

[237] Pierre Courcelle, "Etude critique sur les commentaires de la Consolation de Boèce (IXe-XVe siècles)," Archives d'histoire doctrinale et littéraire du Moyen Age 12 (1939): 5-140; Joachim Gruber, Kommentar zu Boethius, De Consolatione Philosophiae (Berlin: de Gruyter, 1978) 278ff. In her dissertation, Die Gedichte in der Consolatione Philosophiae des Boethius (Heidelberg: C. Winter, 1972), Helga Scheible supplies ample evidence of a Plotinus-Boethius link. These henologic moments have been further corroborated by Chadwick, Boethius 234f.

[238] Enn., VI, 8, 13. 21.

[239] DH 92f. Scholasticism concurs by stating "ens et bonum convertuntur." Boethius and Scholasticism will not use the term „emanatio."

[240] De div. nat. I, 22.

[241] Cf. Ricoeur, Du texte à l'action.

Trotz der plotinischen Differenz von nicht-denkendem Einen und sich denkendem absoluten Geist bleibt in der christlichen Konzeption des einen, sich trinitarisch reflektierenden Gottes als sachliche Analogie zum Neuplatonismus der Begriff der sich selbst - in ihren immanenten Differenzen - denkenden Einheit.[242]

In Christian thought Trinity reflects itself with indescribable intensity. Such a notion requires a parallel further development of the term "prosopon," "persona." Here Plotinian (Greek) static divine self-reflection gives way to the dynamic God of revelation.

The incommensurability of God insisted on as the "superessentialis-esse" vis-à-vis the being things reminds one of Plotinus.[243] Taking Plato's *Parmenides* - via Proclus' *Parmenides* commentary - as point of departure, the One is named as without form[244] and at the same time as infinite "dynamis." He therefore likewise - in the tradition of Plotinus - favors negative dialectics to explicate the paradoxicality of the One. In unification with the One ("Henosis") a leap beyond all categoriality occurs; the negation evidences itself as the negation of the negation: "per negari ... (omnes) abnegationes removere."[245] At another place unity is defined as "id cui nihil oppositum."[246] In this sense, unity is a priori to "esse," because esse still possesses not-being as an opposite. As the coincidence of opposites of unity and multitudinous plurality, it is the Plotinian "hen," which had integrated the "nous." As the incommensurable "unum," the One encompasses the multitude: "Deus est unum multiplex in seipso."[247] The salient feature of divine unity is not opposition between the unity lacking a multitude and the multitudinous unity of human thoughts and sentences. Thus the Augustinian and Dionysian traditions of negative theology and "docta ignorantia" reach a new plateau. By virtue of this development, Eriugena became a stimulus for the thought of Nicholas of Cusa, Giordano Bruno, the early Schelling and Hegel.

This occurs particularly in the Dionysian understanding of theophany. When thinking infinite unity, one defines the undefinable infinite. Thereby the formless infinite obtains form in the thinking subject. The infinite begins to appear in angels and humans; preferably in humans who are the most complete

---

[242] Beierwaltes, Denken des Einen 339.

[243] "nullam categoriam in Deum cadere." Eriugena, Periphyseon I 208, 29f.

[244] Periphyseon II 4,23; I 166, 18ff: the One is "in forma principium" and simultaneously "formarum omnium causa." Cf. Plot., Enn., V 5,6,4; VI 7,17,40.32,15; V 3, 12,50ff.; also: Procl., in Parm. 1118,19.1124,14. Eriugena's radical negation of the One's categoriality is occasioned probably via Dionysius' mediation: de div. nom II 10; 648 C. IV 3; 697 A.IX 3; 980 C.

[245] Procl. in Parm. VII 76,6; cf. Plato Parm. 141 e 9 and 12; also: Plot. Enn., VI 7, 38, 1; further: Procl. in Parm. 1240,29f and 1241,26: "if the One `is', it is not the One."

[246] De div. nat. I, 14.

[247] De div. nat. III, 17.

representation of the whole and who partake in the property that contradictory sentences can be true at the same time and under the same conditions.[248]

The unity of all being - while retaining their particular characteristics - is to appear in and through human beings eschatologically as the truth it is already from all eternity: "omnium ... unum ... erunt."[249] Eriugena interprets Christian history as salvation. Salvation occurs as a realized metaphor of the restoration of the unity after overcoming evil. This illustrates his metaphysics of unity which corrects Plotinian thought by way of the concept of coincidence. This metaphor is the main connecting thread for the interpretation of Christian tradition. In the process henology is expanded by the dimension of unity's relationality to the human being, to his cogitations and his history.

In Plotinus' vein the One is pure identity and the More par excellence ("plus quam").[250] Thereby it becomes Plotinus' relationless Above-All. The eternal ideas think themselves and explain their being-causing-essence from the One. Thinking and Being are identical.

Confronted with the credal content of the Trinity, Eriugena thinks the One as absolute relationality and reflectivity.[251] Thereby Plotinus' Nous-concept is enriched and transcended. The One becomes the thought of dialectics within itself. In this way the One as Divine Above-All exceeds all categories of formulation.[252]

Platonism is certainly not very openly visible in Anselmian writings. It must be distilled as an implication of his thought. The stringency of the ontological proof rests on the not expressly stated prerequisite of the pre-existence of our rational ideas.

Anselm also perceives reason as a tool in meditating and in approaching the Divine. A difference or even an irreconcilable contradiction between prayer and reason cannot be sensed in his writings. Quite the contrary, reason and prayer are conjoined in an ancillary and almost unreflected manner. It is by way of an introductory prayer that Anselm strives to prove divine existence in the *Proslogion* and yet claims to using as reason alone for his *Excitatio ad contemplandem deum*. The first chapter of the *Proslogion* corresponds to the Plotinian "katharsis" (purification) through which one is free for God and comes to rest in God. The second chapter contains both the "photismos" (illumination) and the "teleiosis" (perfection) as levels of insight into and as one's movement towards participation in divinity. Exclusively mustering the

---

[248] De div. nat. IV.

[249] De div. nat. I, 30.

[250] Periphyseon III 19, 170,8f: "Et neque erat, neque erit neque factus est neque fit nec fiet, magis autem neque est ..."

[251] See Anselm: The (One) substantial Being "evolves" towards a Triune: "mira quaedam tam ineffabilis quam inevitabilis in summa unitate ... pluralitas" - and constitutes therein itself as Unity. cf. M 43: 59,15f.

[252] Periphyseon IV 4; 749 A.

mind he arrives at God: "et quidem credimus te esse aliquid, quo nihil maius cogitari possit." Thus that beyond which one cannot think is recognized as God. This final step is Plotinus' "teleiosis." Anselm's steps are congruent with Plotinus' levels of insight. This should not suggest a separating "chorismos" between faith and reason, between daily life and mystical vision, which would be untenable as a description of Anselm's thinking. The "sola ratione" principle does not justify an accusation of rationalism. Equally Anselm's utilization of prayer does not supply an argument in favor of fideism.[253] Anselm departs from any verbalization onto the plane of pure being outside which there is no being. Like Plotinus he is not interested in multifarious being but exclusively in what cannot be considered greater than itself. This concentration on that beyond which no thing is, merits to be called mystical.

To Anselm, thinking and recognizing are impossible without an inner vision and experience. Thinking means rendering something spiritual intellectually apprehendable - be it only that it is incomprehensible. Moreover, the beholding process is not beyond intelligibilty. Particularly in the Anselmian context Balthasar speaks of: "Videre ist das Grundwort für Verstehen."[254] There is also something intellectually irrefutable in the luminosity of the beheld form. The whole of the "intellectus fidei" becomes apparent as a complex interaction of cognitive beholding, dialectic-conceptual effort and personal experience. Mysticism is an important element of this multiplication. Were the beheld zero, the complete undertaking would be destined to failure. This mystic dimension has equally not been unambiguously appreciated by Karl Barth in his radicalized theological appreciation of Anselm, nor by Malcolm and Hartshorne who considered only linguistic and logical points. The latter two no longer considered the subject of the argument, namely God, but only the predication of the existentially necessary.

There is admittedly a paucity of "unum" as the predication of the Divine in Anselmic reflections. He prefers to use such terms as "substantia", "natura" and "essentia". Nevertheless he is familiar with the term from Scripture (Lk 10:42) and from Augustine: "unum est necessarium."[255] However, even a cursory, systematic analysis of Anselm's writings reveals that he builds his philosophical teachings of God upon the necessity that we must presume both in

---

[253] The critical editor of Anselm's writings, Franciscus Silesius Schmitt OSB, rejected roundly any mystical interpretation of Anselm's approach. Barth and Söhngen favored a theological view and Gilson even considered it akin to Gnosis. It is quite true that Stolz' argument for a mystical interpretation is difficult to defend. Yet are there to Anselm differences between philosophy, a qualified form of gnosis, theology and mysticism? Anselm knew of no differences and supposed each of these factors to condition and enable the other three. Only upon the backgound of Plotinian philosophy is the riddle "Anselm" resolved.

[254] Hans Urs von Balthasar, Herrlichkeit Eine theologische Ästhetik. Bd. II. Fächer der Stile. Teil 1: Klerikale Stile (Einsiedeln: Johannes, 1962) 226.

[255] P 23: 117, 20. Meister Eckhart recurs to this Neo-Platonian connotation: In Joh. n. 113, lat. Werke 3,97.

being, in cognition and in speaking an "unum aliquid" preceding all multifariousness.[256] To him the "unum" is the "summa essentia." Yet the identity of both is conceived from the necessity of an "unum." Without any direct knowledge of Plato, he reestablishes the dialectics encountered in *Parmenides* insofar as he declares that one need assume divine unity to be "an equally inevitable and incomprehensible multifariousness (mira quaedam pluralitas),"[257] if one maintains that this principle is relational. From this angle he develops his reflections on the Trinity. He explicitly claims to be strictly philosophical. Without raising the issue, he thereby touches the question concerning the validity of the Aristotelian principles of insight and the categories of the metaphysics of the One. This aspect remains for later Scholastic philosophy to resolve. By all accounts, already in Anselm's writings the One, which contains all multitude, loses its principal disproportionality to human thought and speech - while retaining its numinous sovereignty. This notion previously began to dawn already with Eriugena. Anselm holds - he has a historically conditioned inclination towards formal-logical constructions -: the ability to enter into a disciplined system of necessary sentences is the unmistakable sign of their divine and therefore not accidental contents.

Nominalism as the negation of the universals as constitutive elements of being is a rejection of a central Platonic philosophical tenet. To Nominalists universals are a merely human "flatus vocis." As in a reaction, Anselm of Canterbury thus perceives Nominalism as the perdition of theology and of humanity in general. Accordingly, he vocally rails against Roscelin's Nominalism. These "dialectic heretics" recognize the concrete being of the separate objects but admit no statement concerning the property or nature apart from the individual, concrete bearer. Faithful to Platonism and Augustine, Anselm defends the concreteness of the non-concrete. Nominalists stay captives to the opacity (= lack of light) of corporeal imagery and are thereby unable to rise to pure insight into the essence of being. He argues:

... illi utique nostri temporis dialectici, immo dialectici haeretici, qui non nisi flatum vocis putant universales esse substantias (!), et qui colorem non aliud queunt intelligere quam corpus, nec sapientiam hominis aliud quam animam, prorsus a spiritualium quaestionum disputatione sunt exsufflandi. In eorum quippe animabus ratio, quae et princeps et iudex debet omnium esse quae sunt in homine, sic est in imaginationibus corporalibus obvoluta, ut ex eis se non possit evolvere, nec ab ipsis ea quae ipsa sola et pura contemplari debet, valeat discernere. Qui enim nondum intelligit quomodo plures homines in specie sint unus homo ... Et cuius mens obscura est ad diiudicandum inter equum suum et colorem eius ...[258]

One easily detects a moral undertone, insofar as a prerequisite for pure and spiritual knowledge is to keep oneself free from sensual-corporeal

---

[256] Cf. particularly the first four chapters of the *Monologion.*
[257] M 43: 59,15f.
[258] I 1: 9,21-10,7.

imaginations, which only daze the intellect. The implication is that Nominalism is an a-spiritual attitude or disposition. The conviction only of those who are free of sensual arrest and of subjective constraints is capable of essential insight in keeping with Platonism and was then a common-place.

The term "substantia" illustrates well the systematic point of contention between Anselm and Roscelin. Roscelin recognizes only the existence of individual substances. The being of qualities and yet more decidedly the being of the essence of a kind, such as the essence of "human being," is merely the being of the bearer of the specific quality, or to be more precise of the species "human being." In contrast Anselm subscribes to the concept of the supra-individual essence: it is the higher and only spiritually recognizable ground of essence.

The theologian's ire has its particular reason in Christology. The mystery of Christ's incarnation, of God's son, i.e. the communicability between the absolute and contingent orders of being, can be identified theologically if one can distinguish philosophically between "essence," "nature" and "person." Christ possesses two natures (divine and human) in one person. Precisely this the opponent denies:

     ... qui non potest intelligere aliquid esse hominem nisi individuum, nullatenus intelliget hominem nisi humanam personam ...[259]

Anselm defends universals' realism not only for specifically theological grounds, but equally to preserve the rationality of philosophy. The (Plotinian) ascent of - the origin-seeking nota bene - thinking towards God is secured and facilitated "sola ratione." This means the ascent occurs within the inner necessity, i.e. the immanent structures, of cognition. This does not involve solely formal logical consequences, but equally an ontic necessity, which reveals itself in the spiritual beholding, gaze or vision of the essences. Christian faith is not a material part of the demonstration nor the "conditio sine qua non" for such insight. On the other hand, the confirmation, perseverance and validation of the philosophically gained insight, a first intimation of religious truths in daily religious life and of the fundamentals of faith through rational insight is an aid for the human being, whose faith is constantly contested.[260]

The exclusively philosophical character of the line of argumentation is evidenced by the *Monologion's* first chapters. Its point of departure is not the supposition of ideas being original and true images/pictures of various kinds of being. The reflection sets out on a higher level: the most common observation about things; namely insofar as they are good and being. These things do not

---

[259] I 1: 10,9f.

[260] This is the "ductus" of the *Proslogion*. The proof of divine existence can well be followed if read in its full context; and not only chapters 2-4.

confer upon themselves the properties of goodness and being. Rather they receive that which essence is completely from: that which is exhaustively good and fully being. Here a trite hypostatization of the principle of the good and of being as the highest universals does not occur. Rather, that things are and are in a specific manner is postulated as their nature. This situation antecedes the things and does not necessarily reside in them. One may use the terms archetype-image (= "Urbild-Abbild") to express the relationship.[261] But Anselm´s elaboration is less defined. He simply distinguishes between being thanks to something else ("per aliud") and being through itself ("per se"). Diverse objects depend on that which is completely through and out of itself:

> Restat igitur unam et solam aliquam naturam esse, quae sic est aliis superior ut nullo sit inferior. Sed quod tale est, maximum et optimum est omnium quae sunt. Hoc autem esse non potest, nisi ipsa sit per se quod est et cuncta quae sunt sint per ipsam id quod sunt.[262]

In this context it is important to bear in mind how after an ascending line comes the highest insight, but as truly highest at the same time it radically differs from the members of this line. It is caused through itself, while the members of the chain are caused by it; i.e., their essence is determined by the highest - which is therefore infinitely more than the merely highest. The ascent is stepwise, according to the ontological difference in rank between the natures of the various kinds. Anselm holds it to be absurd not to countenance differences in values, being and quality. His comparison between wood, horse and human being serves to illustrate this gradation.[263]

As there cannot be a "regressus ad infinitum" for things and degrees of being, there must necessarily ("ex necessitate") be something which is the highest that may not again be subordinate to something else yet higher.[264] Considering this thought by itself and superficially, one might misjudge its purpose and valence. The highest is not the last member in a finite row of ascending ranks for it distinguishes itself from all other objects by its being: it is through and of itself. While it is true that there is an order of being in the cosmos, God stands above and beyond all created order.

For this reason Anselm introduces chapter sixteen of the *Proslogion* with 1 Tim 6:16: "Truly, O Lord, this is the inaccessible light in which You dwell" to justify the statement, "He is greater than can be thought." His greatness is such that it is inaccessible to human insight: "non potest intellectus meus ad illam."[265] Centuries later, a Plotinus-influenced Nicolas of Cusa summons

---

[261] Anselm does not employ such terminology. Nor does he call this relationship in Platonism's wake "participation." Cf. Franciscus S. Schmitt, "Anselm und der (Neu-)Platonismus" 39f.

[262] M 4: 17, 24-29

[263] M 4: 17,1f.

[264] M 4: 17, 5-10.

[265] P 16: 112, 24.

Anselm to buttress his understanding of any knowledge into divine matters as "docta ignorantia."[266]

Owing to Plotinus' interrelationality of matters divine and terrestrial, Anselm skillfully develops an organic connection, yes even something of a reciprocal[267] permeation which is by no means exterior or eclectic. "Ratio" and sentiment, "individuum" and "Deus" find in the overarching context of his response to the Nominalist rejection of universals a synthesis upon which Bonaventure could subsequently build: the inner harmony and consonance of the natural and supernatural realms. Neither component is negated by Anselm. Through recourse to the Plotinian "visio," the palpable and tangible order loses nothing. The reverse occurs: reality becomes graced, the signature of the noble, by being seen from the source of its being: Being. This insight Anselm sums up in the words, "credo ut intelligam." It resonates - sometimes mutedly, on occasion forcefully - in all of his writings and is "the" expression of the inner structure of his theology.

As many before him, Bonaventure combines henology and Christology[268] when preaching "Christus unus omnium magister."[269] He even holds, like Plotinus - in reference to the One instead of to Christ - and Augustine, that Christ is the "doctor interius" of all illumination.[270] Christ as the innermost teacher is the legitimation and guarantor of illuminating evidence through the truth identical with Him and through the ideas immanent to Him. Already to Anselm this situation is materially very much present: "mihi non expedit IESU, magister eius, aspice nos Dominus."[271]

Similar things can be observed yet later of Ficino. He distinguishes between the "true, pure and simple" One and the absolute self-reflecting Nous. As a result he concludes, thinking as well as being entails relationality.[272] Appropriating Plotinian thought, he speaks of God as the unity of the One. This signifies that God is and effects as the One: he is "rerum centrum simplicissimum,"[273] pure transcendence and not joined with some being.[274]

Meister Eckhart lived prior to Ficino. His early phase very much reflects Neo-Platonic thought. The One occupies center stage in his writings. Nothing

---

[266] Nicolas of Cusa, De veneratione sapientiae, cap. 26 Paragraph 77.

[267] "reciprocal" with provisos.

[268] Cf. as locus classicus: Mt 23:8-11: "You, however, must not allow yourselves to be called Rabbi, since you have only one Master ... you have only one Father ... you have only one Teacher, the Christ ..."

[269] Bonaventura, Collegii S. Bonaventurae, Quracchi 1882-1902, Vol. V, 567-574.

[270] Bonaventura, Vol. XII 5 (385a). Cf. I Sent. 2, 1, 1.

[271] O 12:49,113; cf. O 15:63,51; 16,66,57.

[272] A VI 15; 231f. VII, 13; 257.

[273] PT II 8; I 98. A II 3; 148. For the circle metaphor cf. Plot., Enn., I 7,1,24. IV 3,17,12. VI 8,18. VI 9,10,17.

[274] PT II 7; I 93: „Rebus aliis non immixtam (summa essendi necessitas = Deus), ne minuatur per mixtionem." Cf. Plot. Enn. V 5,13,35: the Good or One causes all but is above all.

multifarious is capable of diluting God. Man is protected from any form of dissipation by being in union with the One.[275] During his years in Paris he explicated Gal 3:16: "Deus unus est." This is thought to contain two messages. God is one and God is by virtue of His oneness God. Only unity can be credible, because only then is it pure being[276] Eckhart comprehends and experiences God from this definition as the One. The human intellect comes to its own by resting in this one God. The "unio mystica" is a rational approach; just as with Plotinus and as implied by Anselm.[277] At this phase of his teachings Eckhart uses solely the word "oneness" to predicate the numinous. Being is associated with accidental things. God is one and therefore only intelligence. By utilizing the intellect human beings therefore form a bond to God. Therefore, intellectual insight conveys as implication piety and an enablement of becoming God-like.[278] Cusa's thought reflects Plotinian influence too. This is particularly the case in his concept of the "coincidentia oppositorum" and the "docta ignorantia." Because all is contained in God, God is one. This "non-aliud" is then brought into relationship with the trinitarian notion of God.[279]

2.3.5 Modernity

Giordano Bruno echoes Plotinus when contemplating the all-in-all being principle as not a negation of the all-above-all principle:

(Deus) intra omnia non inclusus, extra omnia non exclusus ... in quo sunt omnia, et qui in nullo ... sed est ipse.[280]

The history of reception[281] evidences the present topic's relevance - always allowing for different, modifying and differentiating historical pre-conditions. Though one certainly cannot assume an unchanging problem-awareness within the course of the history of thought, there does seem to be a certain invariance as regards thoughts, their elements, aspects and questions. They illustrate a historical continuity, in spite of all the fractures and deviations/detours the history of philosophy might suffer. Thus, even with little

---

[275] DW V 202.
[276] LW IV 267.
[277] LW IV 269f.
[278] LW V 608f.
[279] Keller, Einführung 116f.
[280] De triplici minimo et mensura, Opera Latina, ed. Fiorentino, Tocca i.a., Naples/Florence, Vol. I 3, 147,5.
[281] Cf. also: Thierry of Chartres (Marie-Dominique Chenu, La théologie au XIIième siècle (Paris: Vrin, 1957)); Nicolas of Cusa (Stephan Gersh, "Platonism - Neoplatonism-Aristotelianism. A Twelfth-Century Metaphysical and its Sources," Renaissance and Renewal in the Twelfth Century, ed. by R.L. Benson and G. Constable (Cambridge, Mass.: Harvard U P, 1982): 512-534).

84

critical actualization one can join in Zelter's 19th century quote of Goethe regarding Plotinus' relevance: "Under all account the `old mystic´ belongs to us."[282]

While it is debatable whether early 19th century thinkers appropriated the categories of "one," "unity," "unification" and "separation" via the Middle Ages or directly from the writings of Plato and Plotinus, they certainly did identify the very nature of philosophy as gyrating around them.[283] Hegel perceives philosophy as the science of unity per se: "die ganze Philosophie (ist) nichts anderes als das Studium der Bestimmungen der Einheit."[284]

Conscious experience of unity is a pure experience. It is undiluted and apart from the multifarious experience of daily toil. While rare, this experience is the proper center of our awareness in Albert Camus' view. It is the soul's home-country. Camus had written his thesis on "Christian metaphysics and Neo-Platonism." It was Plotinus who had understood the insight of unity as the soul's home-country. To Camus this insight as an intimation of the underlying ontic unity is not one which awaits one in heaven, but is already now proclaimed by the sun and the oceans.[285] All human yearning comes to a final rest in this unity of being.

2.3.6 Concluding Summary

The above discussion demonstrates the inalienable relevance of the philosophical insights of Occidental antiquity for the intellectual ambience of the Middle Ages and well beyond. Yet what benefit does this excursion have for the beginning of the third millenium? Is it of mere statistical interest, a desultory, seemingly unchallenged and uncritical reproduction of things bygone with no current value? Such unreflected positivism, such a naively critical disposition fails to recognize that intensive knowledge of the history of reception of a thought is highly revealing for the sake of that thought but also for (possible) future beneficial potentials lying possibly therein. Rejecting the relevance of the history of ideas as relevant to mastering the present, one becomes too blind to countenance the ephemeral nature of current fashions and to the rapid change of questions posed. Positions ardently held now may prove

---

[282] "Er - der 'alte Mystiker' - gehört in jedem Falle zu den Unsern." Cf. Beierwaltes, Platonismus und Idealismus (Frankfurt am Main: Klostermann, 1967) 100.
[283] For the late J. G. Fichte see Anweisung zum seligen Leben (1804); F.W.J. Schelling, Bruno (1802).
[284] Hegel, Philosophie der Religionen. 15, 113. or: WW 17,390.
[285] Evidently Camus misunderstood Plotinus to mean that such an experience of unity can be had only in paradise: "Cette union que souhaitait Plotin, quoi d'étrange à le retrouver sur la terre?" Camus, Hochzeit des Lichts (Zürich: Arche, 1954) 45f.

déjà vu tomorrow. As both Scripture and Hegel remind us: "daß die Füße derer, die (auch sie) hinaustragen werden, schon vor der Tür stehen."[286]

Vice-versa, the same holds true. The thinking through of recent and modern problematics illuminates historically preceding concepts. It makes one acutely aware of the differences vis-à-vis the latter and, therefore, appreciative of the value of the earlier. Precisely the awareness of the difference may allow one to highlight the affinities all the more clearly. Modern consciousness of awareness of the present need not necessarily lead to either a curt opposition to or to a terminological transformation - and thereby to the destruction - of an earlier thought. Rather it renders one receptive to the hermeneutical difference of the respective areas - insofar as this awareness remains determinative for the understanding process. Only thus can one arrive at a genuinely "origin-al" "Horizontverschmelzung."[287] The understanding subject acquires the "otherness" or "alienness" - transforming it yet without depriving it of its very value and nature. Such actualizing comprehension produces something new, and experiences nevertheless an indebtedness to past generations. A human continuum is experienced in the process that may transcend the merely human: it permits the a posteriori participation in previously made experiences of the otherness of existence.

Whenever confronted with the seriousness and solemnity (for reality's sacredness in a philosophical-religious sense) of reality, society plays collectively possum. Kant still musters all cognitional energies to reflect upon the unifying structures of the palpable. Since the days of Auguste Comte, metaphysics is considered a futile endeavor. Adorno's "critical theory" establishes this discipline even in the vicinity of totalitarian efforts. The attempt to apprehend a unity in existence is being sacrificed for the sake of finding one's own self-identity, as the systematization of reality under a unifying one led (thus the claim) to non-identity. Socio-theoretical arguments take precedence over systematic-philosophical ones (cf. also Carnap).

From a different angle Heidegger developed his very own project to recover being in view of a generally perceived "Seinsvergessenheit." He equally criticized metaphysical language for its supposedly deleterious effects on ontology.[288] By declaring conventional metaphysical thinking an example of "Seinsvergessenheit," Heidegger strove to distinguish between his rigorous pursuit of "Sein" - in constant dialogue with philosophy - and the "verrechnendes Etwas" or "Seiendes." He perceives technical aggressivity, "Gemächte," "Gestell," as signifying a progress-mad inclination of humankind in the technical era. This "Machen des Machbaren" is the deleterious result of incorrect metaphysical thinking.

---

[286] Hegel, Vorrede zur Phänomenologie des Geistes (Hoffmeister) 58; quoting Acts 5,9b: "At the door are the footsteps of those who ... will carry you out ..."

[287] Gadamer, Wahrheit und Methode 289f. 356f.

[288] Martin Heidegger, Was ist Metaphysik? 14th ed. (Frankfurt am Main: Klostermann, 1992).

Neopositivism and linguistic analytical philosophy claim that metaphysics juggles with illusory problems. C.S. Peirce, J.P. Sartre and A.N. Whitehead have expressed similar views.[289]

Neopositivistic and language-analytical approaches, such as that of Wittgenstein, decry metaphysics as sounding brass and a tinkling toy. Its problems are feigned. Therefore it is their intent to return "die Wörter von ihrer metaphysischen wieder auf ihre alltägliche Verwendung."[290] Only what is empirically verifiable - "was der Fall ist" - may remain in the realm of intelligent discourse. All other, non-empirical statements, aiming towards a system, are categorized in the pejorative sense of the word as "mystical."[291]

The remarkable unanimity of such diverging positions is a characteristic of the present intellectual state. It leads directly and invariably to the postmodern state of affairs: "everything goes." However, such an eclectic temper requires the existence of (already twenty to fifty, even 200 years earlier claimed to be intellectually and/or morally unsustainable) positions with clear, immanent merits to choose from. Yet if postmodernity proves unable to allocate lasting value or convincing arguments to at least two or more different positions, it necessarily heralds the dissolution of the same (= postmodernity; i.e. to take clear - also judgmental - positions). By so doing it also inaugurates - though with some delay - its own demise: if there is nothing to choose from, postmodernity reveals its own vacuity. Precisely the very characteristic feature of postmodernity prepares the foundation for its own overcoming and sublation.

In marked contrast to this are the philosophical endeavors well into the 19th century. In spite of varied fractures Greek philosophy, Neo-Platonism and Christian philosophy are characterized by a remarkably synthetic intention and by historical and material continuity. The anamnesis of the same should be the task of current thought. It should sensitize us for the loss of questions and offer corrections of the current world view. The accusation of an inexpensive repristination of bygone times does not hold if there does exist something perduring in history which requires ever anew an "original" appropriation.[292]

---

[289] Charles S. Peirce, The Collected Papers of Charles S. Peirce Charles Hartshorne and Paul Weiss (vols. 1-6) and Arthur W. Burks (vols. 7-8) eds. (Bristol: Thoemmes, 1997); Jean-Paul Sartre, L'être et le néant essai d´ontologie phénoménologique (Paris: Gallimard, 1943); Alfred North Whitehead, Process and Reality. An essay in cosmology (New York: Humanities Press, 1955).

[290] Ludwig Wittgenstein, Philosophische Untersuchungen (Frankfurt am Main: Suhrkamp, 1967) 67.

[291] At this point it would be worthwhile to investigate whether the global, sweeeping accusations levied against metaphysics really stand. Does not the description of the historical phenomenon of Ausschwitz as "cruel and inhumane" actually not negate the possibility of metaphysics but rather, on the contrary, require it to arrive at such a valuation?

[292] "Original" both in the etymological sense "from the origins," "origin seeking" and "creative."

Active remembrance of past reflections does not prevent one from attending to the cognitional tasks requiring attention now. Quite the contrary, such labor will serve the internalisation of one's own pre-history and render one yet more acutely conscious of one's own and present awareness in general. Neither the apotheosis of the present nor the suppression[293] of the past serves being oneself - i.e. being original, authentic and faithful to oneself - or does justice to the exegencies of an era. Only critical mediation of past and present appears as a viable, intellectually honest and credible avenue.

This section wishes to have established:

1. the hermeneutic optimism as regards the tradition of reception history as a living part of today's (global) consciousness in general.

2. the significance of the concept of the One and unification with the same for a proper appreciation of Anselm's writings.

3. the philosophic recourse to creation's oneness and unity as a significant building-stone for a future global community.

---

[293] To do the process justice one should rather use the term sublimation.

CHAPTER THREE
3.0 Monastic Theology

Monks dominated the spiritual, intellectual and artistic life of the Western Church between the 6th and 12th centuries.[1] Boniface, Ansgar and Willibrod founded dioceses and missionized throughout Europe. Alcuin and Rabanus Maurus transmitted antiquity's erudition and Patristic theology. Notker Balbulus, Guido of Arezzo and Tuotilo excelled as musicians, artists and poets. The Venerable Bede and Otto von Freising recorded history. Peter Damian and Gregory VII renewed and reformed the Church. Hildegard of Bingen and Bernard of Clairvaux left their imprint on their age as ardent and dedicated preachers and community heads.[2] It is within a monastic context that the Benedictine monk Anselm wrote his treatises, gained insights and argued. Therefore, it is useful to establish whether indeed one may legitimately speak of a "Monastic Theology" and what its nature was.

It would be hazardous and an injustice to ascribe a specific year to an intellectual current with such longevity and as broadly based as monasticism. In this case it would, however, be of a symbolic value. Hegel in his *Vorlesungen zur Geschichte der Philosophie* [3] identifies the year 529 A.D. as the "Untergang der äußeren Etablissements der heidnischen Philosophie." Because of an edict of Emperor Justinian the Platonic academy in Athens had to close after an uninterrupted 900-year existence. Yet, unnoticed by Hegel, something else occurred in the same year. Benedict of Nursia founded the monastery of Monte Cassino. This year marks the finale of an exhausted and worn-out age and inaugurates a new age.

In spite of a noticeable difference in style and pursuit, an inner congruence also exists between the academy and the monastery. Both attend to intellectual life and both are pre-occupied with the quest for truth. They inquire into the essence of matter, the nature of reality in its totality and what its purpose might be. Both enjoy in their respective environments a degree of commonly accepted immunity. Both had a central, religious character. In the grove of the Academy the philosophers convened on a regular basis for religious sacrifices. They understood their community not merely as a gentlemen's club in the measured search of the underlying "what" of life, but

---

[1] Karl Suso Frank, Geschichte des christlichen Mönchtums: Grundzüge (Darmstadt: Wissenschaft-liche Buchgesellschaft, 1988) 35ff.

[2] Cf. i.a. the seminal reflections on this topic by Hans v. Schubert, Geschichte der christlichen Kirche im Frühmittelalter 600-631 (Tübingen: Mohr, 1921); Christopher Brooke, The Monastic World 1000-1300 (London: Elek, 1974); Ludo J. R. Milis, Angelic Monks and Earthly Men, Monasticism and its Meaning to Medieval Society (Woodridge: Boydell, 1992).

[3] In this citation one discerns the generally held hiatus - one is reminded of Tertullian's remark: "What has Jerusalem to do with Athens?" - between pagan philosophy and Christian faith. Little attention is given to the inner kinship of the two. The unreflected presumption of an equal hiatus between the created order and grace in much Protestant thought plays no small role in this case.

also and at the same time intrinsically linked to it as a cultic community. Leclercq does not tire of demonstrating for this theology the inner unity of "monasticism of worship" ("Kultmönchtum") and "monasticism of culture" ("Kulturmönchtum").[4] This was already the case with ancient philosophy. In this sense the overarching term uniting both spirituality and erudition is "spiritedness" ("Geistigkeit").[5] In contrast to the subsequent era, monastic theology is less method than person oriented. It resulted from a well cultivated life-context and the insights gained therein were intended again to make this environment flourish. To facilate the proper understanding of this theology, Leclercq also introduces the term "théologie admirative."[6] It longs to ascend to God. To the French scholar there exist principally three different modes, yet equally legitimate in pursuing the theological enterprise: Patristic, Monastic and Scholastic theology. All three have their rightful place within the Church. All should be allowed to contribute to Church life.

3.1 The Benedictine Understanding of the Monastic Community as "Domus Dei"

God's plan and order become apparent in every spiritual or material edifice. The notion of the Church as an image and terrestial realization of the Divine City is common in the Middle Ages. The abbot of St. Denis, Suger, describes the church:

> In the centre were twelve columns lifting the edifice upward according to the number of apostles, and an equal number of naves, signifying the number of prophets, faithful to the apostolic words: "So you are no longer aliens or foreign visitors; you are fellow-citizens with the holy people of God and part of God's household. You are built upon the foundations of the apostles and prophets, and Christ Jesus himself is the cornerstone. Every structure knit together in him grows into a holy temple in the Lord; and you too, in him, are being built up into a dwelling-place of God in the Spirit (Eph 2:19-22)."[7]

Shortly after Anselm's death this church had been consecrated in 1144. To this degree it is reflective of the then common understanding of the Church as a building and community of the faithful. One can discern some guiding principles from Suger's observations. The apostles' words built the edifice spiritually and materially. Apostles and prophets form the foundations, while the incarnate Word is the cornerstone. Churches constitute a part of the "ordo" of the salvific plan. Symbolizing the apostles and prophets, the columns take on

---

[4] Leclercq, The Love of Learning 180.

[5] In this vein of argument cf. Louis Bouyer, Le Sens de la Vie Monastique (Turnhout: Brepols, 1950) particularly 113-132.

[6] Jean Leclercq, L'amour des lettres et le désir de Dieu. Initiation aux auteurs monastiques du moyen âge (Paris: Cerf, 1957) 216.

[7] Ernst Gall, Die gotische Baukunst in Deutschland und Frankreich, Vol. I (Leipzig: Klinkardt und Biermann, 1925) 99.

anthropomorphic significance. Christ keeps all the stones in place. The faithful are citizens, not slaves, in the Church. That means they possess rights and responsibilites. The heavenly Jerusalem is in this context not a final state but the most sublime meaning of the present state. The faithful emerge into the sanctuary as if entering heaven. The church is not only image, it is the reality of the heavenly Jerusalem. Every member expresses in the sacraments and reliquaries its fidelity to the cornerstone and the columns.

In the sixty fourth chapter of the *Regula*,[8] Benedict takes for granted that the monastery in its entirety is the House of God. This comes as quite a surprise as one is not accustomed to perceive the whole of the monastery, including the fields, vineyards, dormitory, refectory, church inventory and members, as sacred and as bearers of a liturgical significance. This comprehensive view of the monastic community is found in different places, for example, where reference is made to the cellarer and reception of guests in the monastery (RB 31, 19; 53, 22). Benedict is keen at seeing a worthy abbot installed as head of the community: "sed domui Dei dignum constituant dispensatorem" (RB 64,5).[9] The abbot is the visible representative of Christ. Since Christ is God's vicar, the representative of Christ is at the same time the representation of God. Consequently, the abbot is the representative of the cosmic Father; "abba pater" (RM 8). Hence the monks are the sons of the invisible Father and as a consequence brothers to one another. The centralizing peak of this community lies in the invisible, celestial realm. The abbot is the divine "pater familias" of Roman antiquity both in the concept's spiritual and economic meaning (RB 2,7). The divine "dignitas" of the monastic community is the ontological reason for the "dignitas" required by every abbot. In the concept of the monastery as "Domus Dei," one apprehends the essence of Benedict's intuition: the inner form of the monastic community is the cognitionally reflected and existentially explicated becoming form of "ut in omnibus (= the entirety of the monastic community) glorificetur Deus." No nook is left for profanity to seek refuge from God; all is perceived as resting in God. To the monk all of monastic reality is permeated by prayer and liturgy. From here it is but one logical step to apprehend all of the world as ordered towards the prototypical "Domus Dei" in heaven.

The monastic community is seen as a central place of awareness of a cosmic movement also encompassing the present situation. All of life makes sense when beheld as God's creation. The monastery is where creation is aware of this and consciously participates in creation. This synthesis of the divine and terrestial order as the result of the human world's reflection and imitation of the

---

[8] Adalbert de Vogüé, The Rule of Saint Benedict, a Doctrinal and Spiritual Commentary (Kalamazoo MI: Cistercian Publications, 1983); Clifford Hugh Lawrence, Medieval Monasticism (New York: Longman, 1984) 17-35; Frank, Geschichte des Mönchtums 51-65.

[9] Cf. Constable Giles, Monks, Hermits and Crusaders in Medieval Europe (London: Viviarum, 1988) 189-210.

divine world is well enunciated in Augustine's *De Civitate Dei*. Emulation of the divine world is also the acknowledged raison d'être of the Carolingian and Ottonian empires. In this theological vision of history it was considered imperative to renew the Roman Empire ("renovatio imperii"), lest Christians would fail to fulfill their responsibility in history, i.e., they could no longer imitate the celestial order.[10] If the world does not recognize Jesus Christ as the Son of the Living God (Jn 1:10f.) then the end of the world must be at hand. This explains the rendering of God as the supreme judge, separating good from evil on the last day of judgment in the tympanae of romanesque churches.[11]

In Benedict's worldview, the monastery is the place where Church - in the fullness of the word's meaning as the life-community of the faithful - is realized.[12] Herein lies the unique significance of the monastery for the world and to that degree the import and proper nature of monastic theology. In the last supper Christ gave His disciples and the Church in the institution of the eucharist table-community with Him. In the ancient world - and to this day this still applies in the Middle East - this gesture entailed life-community. The room with the table, called the "tablinum" or "exedra," is the fulcrum of the Roman house. To express their life community with the risen Lord, Christians applied this notion of the "tablinum" to the "basilica" (= (the house) belonging to the Lord). The table or altar becomes the center of the church. Refectories in both Western (Catholic) and Eastern Christendom not infrequently attest to this community with Christ:[13]

So you are no longer aliens or foreign visitors; you are fellow-citizens with the holy people of God and part of God's household. You are built upon the foundations of the apostles and prophets, and Christ Jesus himself is the cornerstone. Every structure knit together in him grows into a holy temple in the Lord; and you too, in him, are being built up into a dwelling-place of God in the Spirit.[14]

Upon this background it becomes evident that the monastic community is the realization of the ideal Church of Christ. No friend of lofty, abstract theology, Benedict was a practitioner with rather a profound theological orientation. Naturally his definition of the Church is also practical, albeit particularly a Benedictine ecclesiology still awaits development.[15] Yet already the material evidence is sufficient to establish the link between the monastery

---

[10] Karl H. Krüger, Die Universalchroniken Vol. 1 (Turnhout: Brepols, 1976) 23-30.

[11] Milis, Angelic Monks and Earthly Men, Monasticism and its Meaning to Medieval Society 10f.

[12] Waldemar Kurtz, "Domus Dei, der Kirchenbegriff des Hl. Benedikt," Regulae Benedicti Studia, Annuarium Internationale 5 (Hildesheim: Gerstenberg, 1977): 119-130, at 121.

[13] Particular care in many Eastern monasteries is given to the refectory's being on the same axis with the church. After the eucharist monks eat at the table(s) directly opposite to the altar.

[14] Eph 2:19-22.

[15] Basilius Steidle, Die Regel St. Benedikts (Beuron: Beuroner Kunstverlag, 1952) 41.50.

and the church. The local bishop should act in case of irregularities (RB 62; 64). Benedictines live the interior part of the catholic ecclesial life, particularly via liturgy but also hierarchically. As the diocese's bishop is assisted by priests, deacons and clerics, so likewise the abbot is assisted by priest-monks and provosts. Both hierarchies feel addressed by Christ's call to the apostles and their successors: "Feed my sheep ... Behold I am with you until the end of the world ... He who hears you, hears me."[16] Therefore, the abbot fulfils a twofold task in one person. He is, as successor to the apostles, teacher (doctor) and, as representative of Christ, pater familias (abbas). This is the message of the two first chapters of the *Regula Benedicti*. Christ is the scola's doctor. In this way the two terms possess different foundations but bear the same import. Together they indicate the abbot's authority emanating from Christ: "because he appears as the representative of Christ" and "for the honor and love of Christ"(RB 63).

More clearly than the *Regula Magistri*, Benedict shows the abbot to be entirely in charge of the monastic council (RB 3). Considering divine judgment, the Rule invites the abbot to "dispose all things with foresight and justice" and to "do all things in the fear of God and respect for the rule." Though displaying a sensibility for the abbot's fallibility, Benedict does not limit his authority. Rather, the rule should prevail throughout the vicissitudes of life as the guiding norm of monastic life. From this it follows that the worthiness of the elected does not arise from the votes cast but from the law of God. As Benedict states: "secundum timorem Dei" (RB 64). Personal and communal sanctification occur in fidelity with Christ through obedience to Scripture, the Rule and the monastic community. Vogüé concludes in this context:

> No majority, no unanimity can prevail against the imprescriptable rights of the Rule. ... Our two legislators (= Magister and Benedict, author´s note) say not a word about knowledge of the world and of men, of intellectual and practical talents, of charm, of suppleness and sensibility to the taste of the day, for their look is fixed upon a point transcending every human horizon: holiness according to the Gospel.[17]

Since the abbot is a grace-bestowing gesture of the Church, the mystical body of Christ,[18] there exists no other yardstick to measure the worthiness of men, the quality of theology, of manual labor, of prayer, etc. but Scripture - and the Rule - as parameters of the Spirit.

---

[16] RM 1 with Jn 21:17; Mt 28:20; Lk 10:16. Cf. Basil and Jerome invoking similarly: Basil, Reg. 70; Jerome, De oboedientia; CC 78: 552,12. Likewise, Horsiesius sees the words of Christ addressed to Peter "feed my sheep" applying to all the heads of the households: Liber 19 (Heb 13:17).

[17] de Vogüé, The Rule 74.

[18] For the central role the category "corpus mysticum" plays in the Middle Ages cf. Henri de Lubac, Corpus Mysticum, L'Eucharistie et l'Eglise au Moyen Age, Deuxieme édition revue et augmentée (Paris: Aubier,1949).

This gives cause to reflect on obedience in its particular form as a Benedictine virtue. The Master[19] quotes Jn 6:38[20] to show that Christ is the prototype for obedience. The obedience of the disciple in the scola is connected with the God he seeks through the authority of the abbot (RM 2 and 7). The obedience to God and the superior are not understood as divorced from one another, but two faces of the same coin. Obedience is the art of renouncing oneself in order to seek God.

If nothing obliges us to identify Christ's obedience to his Father with the monk's obedience to his abbot, we should at least recognize that the latter is analogous to the former, and find(s) in this analogy the most powerful of motives.[21]

Benedict considers the monastic community legally bound to the Church and holds that it has a responsibility for the Church's edification. He thereby continues in the already established path of Basil. The monastery is the ideal church of Jerusalem.[22] The monastery as the coenobium is the realization of the ideal community, as it exists sacramentally between Christ as abba and the Church.[23] Consonant with this view, he calls the church as well as the monastic community "corpus" and the monks "membra" (RB 61) for "omnes in Christo unum sumus" (RB 2). The praise of God in the hours is sacred and takes precedence over all other matters (RB 43). Conversely, the exclusion from choir and table is the severest form of punishment a monk can possibly envision (RB 23-27).[24] In the regula-scholar Steidle's opinion this demonstrates to what a profound degree Benedict knew the monastic community to be ecclesial in nature. The Rule mentions excommunication as an important element of monastic discipline.[25] In the monastic community, the individual monk thus experiences the mystery of the whole church.

Benedictine - as well as any ecclesial - authority is a form of deputized Christian charity and fatherly responsibility. As the abbot is to love his monks (RB 64), likewise the monks should vice-versa extend devout and humble love to the abbot (RB 72). The primordial image for this relationship between abbot and monk is the Trinity (RB 2). Mirroring the heavenly Father, the abbot is "auctor vitae."[26] Obedience is thus not an accidental feature, installed for

---

[19] As the RB is sometimes too brief, one sometimes is forced inspite of noticeable differences between the two to refer to the RM.

[20] "I have not come to do my own will, but the will of him who sent me."

[21] de Vogüé, The Rule 107.

[22] Benedict refers to Basil as "our Father Basil" (RB 73).

[23] Steidle, Die Regel 17.

[24] Cf. Lawrence, Medieval Monasticism 28ff.

[25] Steidle, Die Regel 211.

[26] Emmanuel M. Heufelder, "St. Benedikt von Nursia und die Kirche," FS Hugo Rahner, Sentire Ecclesiam, Jean Danielou, Hubert Vorgrimler (eds.) (Freiburg i. Br.: Herder, 1961): 176-184, at 181.

convenience sake. It is the willingness always and everywhere to seek the will and call of God.

In his stages of humility Benedict attempts to free human beings from ego-centeredness, until he is fashioned according to the Lord's example (Phil 2:5ff.) to complete divestment of the self, "kenosis," reaching the apex of humility, perfect love, which knows no fear.[27] Here the Lord bestows abundant graces upon his servant through the Holy Spirit so that he is free of sin and faults. One senses at this point how much Benedict himself struggled to obtain these graces from the Holy Spirit on this charismatic journey. To this end he sought to secure that the sources for the Holy Spirit remain open and readily available in the monastic church's daily schedule. Liturgy is the formative element placing the monk ever anew in the immediate presence of the Lord so that heart and word may be in unison (RB 19). In addition, the monk is urged vividly to participate in the "oratio" (personal prayer), which is to be brief, unadorned, genuine and pure if not extended by the "affectus inspirationis divinae gratiae" (RB 20). The decisive disposition of harkening to God's call is an openness to the Spirit's initiative (Rom 8:14,26), the willingness for grace, for "the prize for which Christ Jesus took hold of (for) me" (Phil 3:12). These observations emphasize both the absolute liberty of divine grace and the human being's inner freedom vis-à-vis this grace. Grace flourishes in every single human being in a most personal, charismatic manner. Benedict urgently entrusts to the abbot's care precisely the reverent recognition and preservation of particular and special features and talents in every monk (RB 2).

The age-old yearning to encounter the numinous is articulated in an earnest and sober manner in the *Regula Benedicti*. One senses a profound underlying affinity between Greek philosophy (as also summarized by Plotinus), Roman "gravitas," Christian revelation of the personal God and the sober maturity of someone who had wrestled with himself/herself to attain this goal. The "domus" is the Lord's because He is present in the monastery. For this reason, Christian monasticism knows of no hiatus between idea and reality, between idea and image. Benedict's notion of the church - as likewise of faith - is remarkable for its sense of the concrete and tangible. This theological-monastic concept manifests itself in word, architecture, painting, world-view, etc. It finds its intellectual and existential legitimization in the incarnation of the eternal Logos, in Jesus the Christ.

Benedict himself displays a terse retenence in defining terms and in introducing abstract concepts. To understand his presumptions when applying the term "scola" to the monastery one is once again forced to refer to the *Regula*

---

[27] It is perhaps by virtue of this consideration that both RM and RB permit nothing to take precedence over the abbot. They remind the reader of Horsiesius in his Liber (7-18 on superiors, 19 on obedience). Both Basil and the Augustinian Rule first mention the union of hearts and the community of goods and refer to the abbot only later (cf. Augustine, Praec. 7,3; Basil, Reg. 15 (superior) and 3 (community)).

Magistri.[28] There the monastery is presented as "the school of the Lord's service." This results from the discipleship of Christ: "Put yourself in my school" ("Discite a me").[29] The equation of "monasterium" and "scola" permits the monastery to appear as the primary place where not merely are things taught about Christ, but rather Christ Himself teaches (RM 8). Monastic existence is intimately tied to the renewal occurring in baptism and resurrection.[30] A conformation of the monastic sons to their Father, God, is intended.[31] The French scholar Vogüé observes:

> The scola of the monastery therefore plays in the Master's thought a mediating role between the baptismal spring and the fulfillment of the kingdom. It allows passage from one to the other. After having been "recreated" by the sacrament, one must "place oneself in the school" of Christ in order to arrive at the ultimate "repose" which he has promised.[32]

The monastery is the training ground conducted by the Lord where the monks serve Him. Here Christ dispenses divine doctrine. The church in turn is seen as mother of all graces: in the sacraments. Within the greater context of the "ecclesia," the "scola" brings the life-giving work to its completion. There is a close correlation of the two terms. "Scola" is an extension of the "ecclesia" because it resides in the "domus Dei." In a certain sense, the church is brought to its perfection within the monastic context.

Yet it would be an oversimplification of the term "scola" to assume it contains exclusively the meaning of "school." In Latin antiquity it refers equally to a place set apart for a professional fellowship and the activities it wishes to promote. It also may mean a body of soldiers or civil functionaries. The *Master* must have had this broad meaning in mind when refering to the scola as a "dominici scola servitii" for the Lord's service. Whoever wishes to serve the Lord must be willing to bear all kinds of things.[33] Well before reaching the heavenly kingdom, this "schola" of the monastery brings about a certain happiness, which Benedict qualifies as "ineffabile" (RB 61).

In summary the Benedictine idea of "scola" designates central features of monastic life. The "scola" encompasses all of life. It is the place of grace, of ascetic and moral effort. Christ is the actual superior and teacher. He is both the teaching master and the ruling Lord in the monastic "scola." It enables and calls

---

[28] de Vogüé, The Rule 33.
[29] RM, Thema 14; cf. Mt 11:29.
[30] Cf. Thema 12 "resurrectionem"; Thema 13: "recreaverat"; Thema 17: "recreationem".
[31] Thp 12-14.16: conformation of sons to the Father; Th 25: rebirth - "renativitate"; Thp 5: "denuo renati per baptismum".
[32] de Vogüé, The Rule 18f.
[33] "Omnia debet pro Domino sustinere, qui eius cupit militare scholae," cf. RM 90. 12. 46. The "schola" = "ecclesia" equation is missing with the RB. This should not, however, imply that the notion is altogether foreign to it.

for a certain distance to the marketplace of the world so that the monk may be a good "militans Deo" (RB 4).

The notion of stability as an outgrowth of obedience to the abbot "meant the preservation of a common memory."[34] It enabled the monastic community to participate more fully in the divine communication: receiving it better and transmitting it to medieval society and recording it for posterity. At the courts of Charlemagne and the Ottos monks played a significant role.[35] The intellectual contribution of monks manifested itself best in the "scriptorium" and its products; however, it was not limited to that. The scribe or copyist should not expose his personality and should refrain from revealing his personal handwriting. This was also the general attitude arising from obedience and stability: the Lord's will should be the center of attention and should dominate. The individual monk is merely a transmitter. In this sense Church and monastery were seen as a large "scriptorium" of the divine will and presence: expressed and conveyed through liturgy and scripture. When the RB mentions objects, which may never be possessed personally, it enumerates as a telling example for the time writing material (RB 33). By oral memorization the acquired insights were regularly verified. Novices learned to recite the psalter by heart. Knowledge was perceived as static and divinely revealed. In such a context obedience and authority were understood as indispensable aids to enforce insight.[36] The striking lack of major Benedictine contributions in Scholastic and later medieval thinking - quite in contrast to their omnipresence in the field of learning in earlier centuries - can be explained by the Rule's inflexibility on this point.[37]

Milis describes the paradigm shift to which the monks were not party as follows:

There is no doubt that the purpose of education in general, and of writing in particular, became increasingly pragmatic. The sort of education intended to better the performance of the laus perennis, the continuous praise of God, or to enhance His glory by what monks called science, faded into the background.

Henceforward a career became of interest. The study of law and of theology, although initially directed towards the accumulation of pure knowledge became, certainly in the thirteenth century and perhaps already earlier, mainly a professional choice. Law and theology engaged less in scientific thought and speculation than in finding a patron, ecclesiastical or lay, to serve faithfully as good civil servants do. Clerics became clerks that way. The "closed schools" and the life-style of the monks did not fit into this mentality of pragmatism.[38]

---

[34] Milis, Angelic Monks 12.
[35] Milis, Angelic Monks 98.
[36] Jan Vansina, Oral Tradition. A Study in Oral Methodology (London: Routledge, 1973) 33f.
[37] Milis, Angelic Monks 108ff. This inflexibility prevented monastic theology from losing its proper profile.
[38] Milis, Angelic Monks 111.

Soon Augustinian, Cistercian, Franciscan and Norbertines had their respective schools in the medieval cities and energetically participated in academic life. Benedictines followed their example in small numbers and only belatedly.

The term "Monastic Theology" was in all probability first given modern notoriety by Jean Leclercq (1957).[39] Previously one spoke only of a preliminary or early stage of Scholastic theology when characterizing theology prior to the 12th century. In this vein Anselm is noted not as a monk but as the "Father of Scholasticism."[40] However, the life-context in which he conducted theology was radically different from that of the later Scholastics. His was the world of monastic retreat in the countryside, of prayer and reflection - a context most condu-cive to meditating on the divine in the community of the like minded. The primary purpose was searching for God. All social activities were secondary and subservient to this overarching goal. The search was for spiritual wisdom ("sapientia"). The Scholastics[41] on the other hand lived in the ambience of the newly established universities, increasingly dominated by a new, altogether different style of architecture: Gothic cathedrals and spires surround them. Geometric designs abound. The world and even heaven seem expressed in mathematical rules. In the burgeoning cities these academics developed their thoughts and engaged in disputations from an altogether different heuristic principle than their monastic counterparts. Questions and disputations gave rise to insight, while the monks were completely oriented toward the all-encompassing and all-permeating liturgical "opus Dei." The monks perceived

---

[39] Leclercq, L'Amour des lettres et le dèsir de Dieu. For further discussion on the term cf. Jean Leclercq, "A propos de `La renaissance du XIIe siécle.´ Nouveaux témoignages sur la `théologie monastique´," Collectanea Cisterciensia 40 (1978): 65-72.

Unfortunately Anselm is assigned in many respects to Scholasticism, although the author concedes that his writings also contain "a truly monastic doctrine" in L'Amour des lettres 204. Here Leclercq is guilty of some kind of inconsequence. Quoting Bernard's, De consideratione - whose writings are particularly familiar to Leclercq - he demonstrates that for monastic theology it is worthier and easier to seek God in prayer than in logical dispute. Nowhere could he have found this better illustrated than in the "corpus Anselmi," a devout disciple of Benedict. Unless considered apart from Thomas, Abelard and Gilbert, one cannot fathom the valence of the Anselmian meaning of "fides quaerens intellectum". cf. pages 265ff. in the English-language edition of L'Amour des lettres. For a comparison, cf. Wolfram von den Steinen´s felicitous solution of the problem of Anselmian categorization: Wolfram von den Steinen, Der Kosmos des Mittelalters. Von Karl dem Grossen zu Bernhard von Clairvaux. (Bern, München: Francke, 1967) 253-279.

[40] Grabmann, Die Geschichte der scholastischen Methode, vol. I, 258.

[41] Joachim Ehlers, "Monastische Theologie, historischer Sinn und Dialektik, Tradition und Neuerung in der Wissenschaft des 12. Jahrhunderts," in: Albert Zimmermann (ed.), Miscellania Mediaevalia, 9, Antiqui und Moderni (Berlin: de Gruyter, 1974): 58-79, provides a summary comparison of Monastic and Scholastic theologies in the 12th century. To delineate the dissimilarities he presents the positions of Bernard, Hugh St. Victor, and Abelard.

the Christian "ratio" as sanctified and sanctifying in a liturgical context which enveloped the totality of life. Reason is thought of - much in continuation of Plotinus - as the divine in the human being, enabling the monk to envision - after due asceticism - already in his terrestrial existence the heavenly Jerusalem. Monks knew the dangers rationalization holds for those who struggle in fidelity to Christ. The stability of one's commitment assisted in attaining the "ratio fidei" so much mentioned by Bernard,[42] who in this regard was also much indebted to Anselm.[43] The Scholastics strove for terminological clarity and philosophical precision in the bustle of the cities in the intellectual intensity of university life. While the monks struggled to gain spiritual experience ("experientia"), the Scholastics' aim was purely to arrive at intellectual knowledge ("scientia").[44] The monks saw the purpose of "lectio" in coming to "meditatio" and "oratio" in front of the divine presence.

Yet common to both the monastic and scholastic minds was a sense of historic continuity. There existed no absolute, unbridgeable distance to history. Even antiquity felt more of the difference between past and present. It knew both progress and yearning for a better bygone time, which one strove to renew or rekindle. One was aware that everything is subject to "educatio," the process of gradually bringing something forth. Nevertheless, neither antiquity nor the Middle Ages were familiar with the sense of breaking off all bridges to the past. The disposition was not one of revolution - of abrupt or sudden overthrow. This becomes a dominant attitude only in modernity.[45]

The actual achievement of a piece of art, a theological treatise, etc., does not lie in individuality and originality but in its praise of the divine plan of

---

[42] In his Sermo 36 he argues:

„Non ignoro quantum Ecclesiae profuerint litterati sui et prosint, sive ad refellendes eos qui ex adverso sunt, sive ad simplices instruendos."

Bernard of Clairvaux: Sermones super Cantica Canticorum, J. Leclercq, C.H. Talbot, H.M. Rochais, eds. Roma, 1959 (= S.Bernardi Opera 2) at 4. The result ("fructus") and usefulness ("utilitas") of scientific labor for the Church's life must be secured. He sees in Scholastic theology a peril for the "holy relevance" theology need always preserve.

[43] Anselm does not mention this term, but materially anticipates it - for example "ratio veritatis" in Cu II 19:130,29.

[44] This comparison should not suggest opposites or contradictions but different emphases: cf. Leclercq, The Love of Learning and the Desire for God at 2-9.

Also Scholasticism brought forth great mystics in Thomas and Bonaventure. Both monks and scholars strove to partake in the "visio beatifica." Cf. Thomas Aquinas, Compendium theologiae, pars 1, cap. 1.

Yet, monks viewed pure intellectual "curiositas" with reservation: intellectual research in Scripture serves to make man gain more insight into God so that the interior man may come to life. Those who conduct such inquiry in order to obtain honor and glory in front of fellow human beings have difficulties loving God - as Abbot Gottfried of Admont (Austria) in the 12th century argued. Gottfried of Admont, Hom.Dom., 51, in PL 174, 339B-C.

[45] Günter Bandmann, Mittelalterliche Architektur als Bedeutungsträger 9th ed. (Darmstadt: Wissen-schaftliche Gesellschaft, 1990) 50.

creation. Even the 15th century notion of "rinascità" still endeavors to rekindle an old flame. The concept of universalism is much alive. The sciences, theology and art are necessarily viewed in relationship to revealed truth, to credal sentences no longer subject to alteration. For this reason authority and the citation of the Fathers enjoyed such popularity.

One of the principles was that the Roman Empire is the last "aeon." After this reign final judgment would arrive. Jerome, Orosius and Origen applied Hellenistic periodizations of history dating back to Claudius, Ptolemy and into the Assyrian-Babylonian, Median-Persian, Greek-Macedonian and Roman empires to the Christian world-view.[46] Bede stated categorically "Quando cadet Roma, cadet et mundus."[47] In a way this sense of continuity with antiquity was to perdure into the Enlightenment.[48]

As Paul admits to an "epithymia," a desire for the end of temporal time, not so much to be in the thereafter but rather to be "with Christ" now, many monks echo this yearning.[49] Therefore, Benedict advises his confrères not to have a longing for God, but to struggle for Our Lord, the true king in the here and now. In a way difficult to follow for the current temper, the monks felt definitely formed and determined by Christ in this world: God Himself had become man; i. e. divinity had appeared to humanity. The divine inclination and affection shown to humanity in incarnation takes on a dramatic and historical form. The cosmos constantly reverberates from this singular event. It beckons with a sense of irresistable urgency for a corresponding form of response.[50] The "Deus-homo," incarnation and the corporealization of eternity stood in the gravitational center of all actions and reflections. The "Deus-homo" was considered the most complete human being since the fall of Adam. Everything yearned to partake in this perfection. Christ is the measure of all human concepts: beauty, earnestness, courage, lineage, royalty, etc.[51]

---

[46] Johannes Spoerl, Grundformen der hochmittelalterlichen Geschichtsbetrachtung. Studien zum ethos der Geschichtsschreiber des 12. Jahrhunderts (München: Hueber, 1935) 29.

[47] Beda, Collectan. et Flores. III, 483, PL 94, 543.

[48] Otto Lauffer, Die Begriffe „Mittelalter" und „Neuzeit" im Verhältnis zur deutschen Altertumskunde (Berlin: Deutscher Verein für Kunstwissenschaft, 1936) at 6ff. There also instances of disregard for the „translatio imperii" concept: Orderius Vitalis, William of Malmesbury and Ronald of Salerno.

[49] Phil 1:23. "I am caught in this dilemma: I want to be gone and to be with Christ, and this is by far the stronger desire - and yet for your sake to stay alive in this body is a more urgent need."

[50] von den Steinen, Der Kosmos im Mittelalter, 1. part, "Das Dasein und seine Deutung:" at 90-113. The author possesses the precious gift of rendering an erudite exposition in most literary prose.

[51] From this perspective one must challenge Jakob Burckhardt's view that humanism is of exclusively early Italian Renaissance origin. Richard W. Southern in: Medieval Humanism and Other Studies (Oxford: Basil Blackwell, 1970) as well as Deborah Vess in: Humanism in the Middle Ages: Peter Abailard and the Breakdown of Medieval Philosophy (Denton: U

While differences in the monastic context were theoretical (in its etymological meaning), and visible primarily in written exchanges, the Scholastic method found its forum in the personal disputation.[52] This calls for a consideration of the hermeneutical locus of the monastic mind, which due to the monks' specific form of life and occupation ("ora et labora") possessed differing accents and functions. Leclercq defines a bit one-sidedly the medieval mind, however, thereby better bringing the accents to the fore. Scholasticism seeks

> (an) impersonal and universal knowledge of God ... whose purpose is to organize Christian erudition by means of removing any subjective material by making it purely scientific.[53]

Already the lack of interest for the specificity of monastic thought is quite revealing. The relationship of dogma to theology is a radically different one for Scholastic and modern systematic theology.[54] Their intention is to present a historic-genetic development of an aspect of theology, but not the full length and breadth of a religious notion. The theological effort is increasingly divorced from the subject's movement in and to the One - as Plotinus and Christian theology had understood the enterprise. Having a preconceived understanding of theology as scientific and speculative in nature, as opposed to spiritual, edifying, ordered towards a homily and the personal ascent of the subject typical for monks, Scholasticism aimed at removing intellectual barriers to believe in God. However, daily interpretation of credal contents, of dogma and bible exegesis also deserve to be called theology. A departmentalization of theology is not necessary in order for a thought to merit the term "theology."[55] Quite the contrary, one must hold the three moments of theology - Patristic, Monastic and Scholastic - in distinct but related mental balance when reflecting on Christian faith as a self-execution of that very same faith.

North Texas, 1991) argue for an earlier dating of humanism. Humanism's inner justification can ultimately be found in the incarnation.

[52] Manuals on theology and the history of dogmas generally fail to appreciate the specific nature of monastic theology: Gustaf Aulén, Dogmhistoria; den kristna lärobildningsgens utvecklingsgang från den efterapostoliska tiden till våra dagar (Stockholm: Norstedt, 1917); Grabmann, Geschichte der katholischen Theologie seit dem Ausgang der Väterzeit.

[53] Leclercq, The Love of Learning 233.

[54] Alf Härdlin, "Monastische Theologie - eine `praktische´ Theologie vor der Scholastik," Münchener Theologische Zeitschrift, 39/2 (1988): 108-120, here 109.

[55] Wolfgang Beinert, "Theologie und christliche Existenz," Catholica 30 (1976): 101-109, at 101; François Vandenbroucke, "La divorce entre théologie et mystique, ses origines," Nouvelle Revue Théologique, 72 (1950): 289-372.

3.2 The inner Structure of Monastic Theology

One can follow Härdlin and call monastic theology "practical."[56] It arises from praxis - liturgy, "vita contemplativa," etc. - and again serves this very praxis:

> ... sie nährt sich daraus, aber findet auch ihren Zweck und ihr Ziel in eben diesem Leben. Aus diesen beiden Beziehungen zur Praxis erhält sie ihren Charakter. Diese Praxis bestimmt die Gattungen und Formen dieser Theologie, gibt ihr die spezifischen inhaltlichen Strukturen und prägt ihre sprachliche Form.[57]

This praxis determines the styles and form of this theology, endowing it with particular structures and developing a specific language.

Up to now little is known of the specific inner structure and inherent systematics of monastic theology. Frequently scholars approach monastic writings with inadequate methods and with questions wrongly posed. These reflect a theology of later times, oblivious to the foundational difference the varieties of hermeneutical approaches occasion.

Such misperceptions seldom come truly to the fore. Examples are the attempt to discern an ecclesiology in the works of 12th century Benedictine monks Rupert of Deutz or Bruno of Segni. After some scrutiny one arrives at the conclusion that neither possesses a thoroughly developed ecclesiological tractate. These monastic theologians provide no comprehensive, systematic presentation of the nature of the church or of the sacraments. Similarly they know of no teaching of the "sacraments" or of a concise definition of what sacrament to their minds may be. However, one does discover interspersed at diverse and seemingly at randomly chosen places ecclesiologically or sacramentally relevant observations. Modern scholars separate these from their respective contexts and order these fragments in a systematic manner. Thereupon the statements are compared with diverse contemporary Scholastic schools. Such studies show well that the monastic author is cognizant of the current debates but usually conclude that the author studied provides no new insights.[58]

The main sources of monastic education were Scripture, Patristic writings and classical literature. The monk moved from "lectio via meditatio" to "oratio". The academic reader in contrast approached the texts with questions and probed the viability of his presumptions in disputations, i.e., through the discursive method. "Meditatio" and "oratio" were no longer constitutive

---

[56] Härdlin, "Monastische Theologie" 111.

[57] Härdlin, "Monastische Theologie" 111.

[58] Wolfgang Beinert, "Die Kirche - Gottes Heil in der Welt. Die Lehre von der Kirche nach den Schriften des Rupert von Deutz, Honorius Augustodinensis und Gernoch von Reichersberg," in: Beiträge zur Geschichte der Philosophie und Theologie des Mittelalters, N.F. 13 (Münster: Aschendorff, 1973); Réginald Grégoire, Brune de Segni. Exégète médiéval et théologien monastique (Spoleto: Centro italiano di studi sull'alto medioevo, 1965).

moments of the one credal-theological movement. Drawing on the "septem artes liberales" he favored dialectics over grammatical considerations as a method.[59]

Monks perceived a correspondence between Old and New Testaments as both convey knowledge of salvation. The Old Testament is seen in constant reference to and anticipation of the deeds of Christ and the apostles. This salvation-historical aspect was a principle for monastic exegesis. It defined monastic existence, study and scholarly production. Ever new nuances were devised to apply typological interpretation for the purpose of discovering secret meanings in Scripture. Typological interpretation is capable of relating distant and causally hard to connect events, by separating them from their actual context and connecting them in order to obtain a new meaning. Daniel's rescue from the lions' den is interpreted by Otto of Freising as a sign of Christ's resurrection. Babylon is a symbol of the Roman Empire.[60] The prerequisite for this approach was the representation of a later spiritual reality in an exemplary manner by the prefiguring situation. This prefiguration in turn also supplied a part of the evidence of the spiritual reality.[61] In Israel's history the monks beheld the way of the Church prefigured. Exegetes considered it their task to find direct references for occurrences in church history, official ecclesial pronouncements and institutions in Scripture.

A point in case is a modern study undertaken by A. Hallier concerning the Cistercian monk Ailred, whose writings show similarity of attitude and interest primarily with fellow monks Bernard of Clairvaux and William of St. Thierry. He concludes with a representative observation:

An examination of his works reveals a doctrinal unity. But to guard against misconceptions, we should point out that a synthesis is not elaborated in the way we understand a synthesis today. Nowhere in his works will we find a complete and methodic presentation of this. Therefore we have to reconstruct and arrange such a synthesis, something which seems to be required by his whole work.[62]

Such an orientation in research appears unlikely to yield insights into the specific nature of monastic theology. The methodological presumptions with which theologians for perhaps the last two centuries had approached such texts are little suited to reveal the inherent structure and world-view of monastic authors. The assumption is that these texts might contain material for a theology yet to be formulated by systematization. Pre-Scholastic theological literature serves merely as a quarry for actual theology. Theological value must be given to these writings a posteriori by dissecting and altering their format. As the texts are read they convey to the modern reader a pre-scientific naiveté. The question

---

[59] Leclercq, The Love of Learning 111-184..
[60] Ehlers, "Monastische Theologie" 66f.
[61] This illustrates well Ricoeur's notion of prefiguration. cf. above.
[62] Amadée Hallier, The Monastic Theology of Aelred of Rievaulx. An Experimental Theology (Shannon: Irish UP, 1969) 162.

that must be addressed is whether the texts in precisely the form their authors have given them contain a message arising from their chosen context and method. Perhaps it is modern scholars who are tempted to approach the texts in a naive and uncritical way?

The abundant use of biblical citations, allusions and imagery is obvious even when reading few examples. The same applies to the texts' homogeneity and their concrete language. As Härdlin rightly points out, monks did use Scripture to write sermons or as supporting pillars for elaborately composed arguments as the Scholastics would be accustomed to do yet more intensively.[63] In monasticism papers, conjectures and thoughts arose from an existence within a scriptorial context. Pericopes within the Bible become the pattern for the evolution of thought. The intensive preoccupation with the biblical text makes of the written text something of a non-canonical continuation of Scripture. Words are primarily considered not as containing a rational meaning but rather as the bearers of a secret revealed gratuitously in meditation. This meditative language cannot be translated into a univocal, conceptual terminology. These manuscripts demonstrate the particular strength of monastic speech in their aequivocal language, which was far from ambivalent, emulating in its vividness and concreteness (oftentime un-) consciously Scripture and are, therefore, seemingly equally unfathomably profound and multilayered. This is well demonstrated, for example, in the commentary on the Revelation of John by the abbot of Volpiano, Ambrosius Autpertus, in the middle of the 8th century.[64]

In order to comprehend the underlying presuppositions of the monastic authors, it is important to consider the significance the *Regula* of St. Benedict played in the monastic setting. Daily monastic life is divided into three equal parts: the "opus Dei," "lectio divina" and "labor." The "opus Dei" is the common liturgy in the choir, which takes precedence over all other activities. "Lectio divina" refers to the spiritual readings, and "labor" to manual labor. Liturgy meant for the monks of that time the "officium," i.e., the liturgy of the hours prayed in common during day and night in the choir. Liturgy comprises also the eucharist. But it was then reserved for Sundays and feast days only. The sung psalms constituted the larger part of the office. They were considered as both praise of God and as His word to the congregation. If one wants to praise God "with insight" as the Psalmists call it, one must receive the words with an attentive spirit and heart and utilize it during meditation as interior nourishment.[65]

It is but one logical step from liturgy to "lectio divina." In reading and meditating Scripture the monks pray and seek the face of God. Later this evolved into a study of spiritual and theological books in general. However, in

---

[63] Härdlin, "Monastische Theologie" 117f.

[64] André Winandy, <u>Ambroise Autpert, moine et théologien</u> (Paris: Vrin, 1953).

[65] Adalbert de Vogüé, "Prayer in the Rule of Saint Benedict," <u>Monastic Studies</u> 7 (1969): 113-140.

the older tradition the "lectio divina" retained its character as a meditative reading of Scripture and of the Fathers' commentaries. There is no gainsaying that the monks also read in order to comprehend. For one cannot love something one has no idea of. Yet primarily the "lectio divina" served the purpose of finding God: to be invigorated in His presence.[66]

The third element of monastic existence is also significant for an appreciation of monastic theology. To Benedict labor was always manual. Such labor not only served to secure supplies and create the visible monastic conditions. It was service in front of God and a spiritual exercise, promoting asceticism. Humility and simplicity were thereby learned. Manual labor reminds one of humanity's banishment from paradise. Without seeing God, one performs these labors in His view and for the wellbeing of the community.[67]

3.3 Genres of Monastic Theology

As the above has demonstrated, the "Sitz im Leben" of monastic theology is not the "disputatio scholastica" but the contemplative search for and in God. This already delineates the forms and genres in which it manifests itself.[68] A poetic and literary language is also capable of expressing ideas clearly. In addition, one detects early on in the texts an order of thought, clarity of vision and logical consistency.

Monasteries produced rich liturgical poetry in the form of hymns, sequences and tropes. Further, they brought forth biblical poetry in Latin and the vernacular. This literature easily betrays its liturgical and bible-meditative origins. Nevertheless, a subjectivistic attitude rarely arises. The enthusiasm and urgency marking this poetry originates entirely from within the celebration and contemplation of the divine mysteries. One wishes to laud this and not one's own joy. Von den Steinen illustrates well that these texts oftentimes contain subtle and well developed theological insights. Chronicles and "vitae" show how human life, fidelities and infidelities, obedience and disobedience, honesty and falsehood, perfection and failure are inserted into the history of God. Thereby an understanding of history is unfolded in which every human being and every episode plays a role. In the process a unique theological view and a Christian reading of life is given expression to.[69]

---

[66] See Jacques Rousse, "Lectio divina et lecture spirituelle," Dictionnaire de spiritualité ascétique et mystique, Vol. 9 (Paris: Beauchesne, 1975) rub. 470-487.

[67] von den Steinen, Der Kosmos des Mittelalters, Von Karl dem Großen zu Bernhard von Clairvaux 138-146.

[68] It must be admitted here that the present-day understanding of theology is so much indebted to the Scholastic definition that monastic theology may have difficulties passing as theology. However, one must part from such a definition if one intends to discover monastic - as well as Patristic - theology.

[69] Ian Dunn, "The Saint's Legend as History and as Poetry," American Benedictine Review 27 (1976): 357-378; von den Steinen, Der Kosmos 138-146.

Sermons, collections of sermons and biblical commentaries are very common. As regards language, contents and manner of formation, they are similar. Sermon and biblical commentary originate in the divine word, which is being proclaimed and celebrated during service and meditated in the "lectio divina." The biblical commentaries do not constitute deliberations about Scripture as if it were a document of the history of religions. Very much like the sermons, the commentaries also want to serve as theological explanations and guiding instructions.[70] Frequently commentaries retain indications that they originated in a proclaiming context. As a result series of sermons on complete books of Scripture in the manner of the "lectio continua" were not uncommon. Being incentives to and instructive for a deepened search for God, they were often recorded, revised, copied and distributed.[71]

These forms and genres are representative and distinguish the monastic approach from that of Scholasticism. Systematic theology with its division into thematic tractates is essentially a creation of Scholasticism. Monastic theology is not motivated by a desire to analyze and, therefore, to divide, but rather to behold and participate in the essential and eternal One. Consequently it is oriented towards the whole of theology as the expression of the One, of God. It would never have occurred to a monk to labor on a text in order to be of service for the theological discipline alone. He perceived himself always living in an impelling movement towards the One. Nevertheless the monk did sometimes write tractates. Peter Damian wrote not less than fifty of them - only to argue against nascent dialectics. Generally speaking, these tractates were biblical in scope and made use of biblical language. Abstract, philosophical terms, distinctions and analytic investigations are rarely used. Consonant with their aim, these works are synthetic and integrative. Monastic theology is in one work simultaneously exegesis, dogmatics, liturgics, moral theology, sacramentology and christology.

While comparatively "unsophisticated," monastic theology does contain firm cognitional structures and, although not always apparent, a systematic element. The artistic decor of Bernard's writings is an expression of a synthetic mind.[72]

3.4 The Presence of Salvation

As already indicated, monastic thought does possess a structure, albeit a difficult one to detect.[73] As the sequence "Mundi aetate octava" from about 900

---

[70] Leclercq, The Love of Learning 187-232.
[71] Cf. for example the sermons on the Song of Songs by Bernard of Clairvaux. See Friedrich Ohly, "Geist und Form der Hoheliedauslegung im 12. Jahrhundert," Zeitschrift für deutsches Altertum und deutsche Literatur 84 (1954/55): 181-197.
[72] Leclercq, "Essais sur l'esthétique de S. Bernard," Studi Medievali Ser. III:9 (1968): 688-728.
[73] Hallier, The Monastic Theology 64f. and 102f.

illustrates, the movement of that era is one from creation to beholding, from paradise to heaven as the - in the event of resurrection - re-opened paradise. God's salvific plan rules history: the world under the governance of His economy ("oikonomia"). For this reason the Son is always present in history. He unites in the perfection of all time all things in His person. He becomes the key to understanding the course of history, created and written, etc., for in Him everything possesses meaning, purpose and context. The old covenant is the example of the realization of His life, person, death and resurrection. To the day of the "parousia" salvation history continues in the Church. In the Church, His body, He is through the mysteries of faith and the sacraments constantly and actively present. In the faithful He acquires form ever anew.[74]

While the modern mind thinks history as an irregular chain of points, the monks understand history as a unity of one action. All of time is composed in Christ, forms a unit and is made conscious in liturgy. Allegorical exegesis did not display the monks' low esteem for history. Through allegory they were able to give history in Christ its context, meaning and aim.[75]

Attentive philological analysis reveals the salvation historical structure as characteristic of monastic theology. The commentaries and homilies follow a verse-by-verse approach. A lack of original disposition is not the cause for this situation. By remaining faithful to the exterior structure of the original text, it is the authors' then commonly assumed task to bring to life something of the salvation which Scripture attests. The cultivation of a terminology serves this purpose. Diverse terms are used to show concepts and the reciprocal relationships and dependencies between grammatical tenses, namely between past, present and future tenses. The ecclesial mystery in which the Christian partakes now is kept in present tense, but is rooted in the indelible antecedence of divine action and meets its full realization when the mystery is beheld in the future. Their presupposition was that salvation occurred once and for all (= "semel") so that it is always present in the age of the Church. Every day it receives new form in the sacraments, discipleship and sanctification. Such daily exercise (= "quotidie") is a daily sacramental representation and daily existential self-execution, all viewed as preparatory for eternity when creation will not only be redeemed but definitively glorified. This illustrates how monastic theology is a theology in progression, on the way: something of a realized exodus. Time and history are ways toward the day of last judgment.[76]

---

[74] Cf. Wolfram von den Steinen, Notker der Dichter und seine geistige Welt, Darstellungsband. (Bern: Francke, 1948) at 81f.

[75] Härdlin, "Monastische Theologie" at 119.

[76] Aelred of Rievaulx, Sermones inediti, ed. C.H. Talbot. (Roma: Gregoriana, 1952) at 94-100.

The outstanding feature of monastic theology is its structure: history as the salvific way. [77] The center of this history, however, was not an abstract, rational meditation upon the One principle, as is the case with Plotinus, but the present and ever new obtaining of the form of Christ's last supper. The thus-constituted Church is spotless in spite of her members' failings: the temple of Jerusalem in which He resides. Resulting from this perspective, a distance between the believer and the believed - common to Scholastic and later theologies - is impossible. One can no longer separate subject and object, mystery and personal existence, divine address and human response. The purpose of insight in monastic theology is not to excel in the sciences but to impel the reader or listener to follow Christ and to adore God in word and deed. This had been antiquity's claim, too. Like the monks it aimed at the "homoiosis theou," the increasing similarity with God in the here and now.[78] Leclercq, we recall, had described this theology as "une théologie admirative." It is meant to fill the heart with wonder and not simply the mind with knowledge.[79]

Such a theology fosters a less formal and more literary and poetic language. Steeped in Augustine, these monks (and nuns) heeded the trivium of "docere," "delectare" and "flectare." As Härdlin in his seminal article well summarizes it:

(e)s kommt darauf an, die wahre Kenntnis zu lehren und durch sie zu bezaubern, damit die Wahrheit in ihrem vollen Glanz anziehend und begehrenswert wird, schließlich den Willen zu beeinflussen, damit die Erkenntnis in Güte verwandelt wird. Erst dann wird die Theologie nach der Auffassung der Mönche eine praktische Theologie. Erst dann wird sie, mit den Worten Ciceros ausgedrückt, eine "magistra vitae," eine Lehrmeisterin für das Leben, für das Leben in Gottes Geschichte und aus dieser Geschichte, vom ersten Paradies zum Paradies der Vollendung.[80]

Through Jesus Christ true knowledge is imparted to the Church. The monks desire to give this truth palpable and existential form, thus rendering it desirable. Finally, insight is to be transformed into goodness: "benignitas." In light of this monastic theology remains preeminently practical in nature.

---

[77] Härdlin showed convincingly the independent and careful catenation of thoughts. Härdlin, "Monastische Theologie" at 119.

[78] Plato, Republic, 613a4-b1; ibid, Phaido 83a; Aristotle, Metaphysics, Book Lambda; Plotinus, Enn., V 8,11,5; VI 9,10,13ff.

[79] Jean Leclercq, in his introduction to Baudouin de Ford, Le sacrement de l'autel, (Sources Chrétiennes 93), at 47-51.

[80] Härdlin, "Monastische Theologie" at 120.

CHAPTER FOUR
4.0 Saint Anselm's Concept of the "One" - Cognitional Unity as Real Unity

The observation "bonitas sibi sufficiens"[1] as the description of the One is decisive. The One is goodness and at the same time "selfstanding." Cogitation remains in its endeavors and interest oriented toward the thus perceived One. To Anselm's mind this orientation towards the One - in contrast to Plotinus - does not allow cogitation to reach its intended goal by itself, taking recourse only to its own resources. Only if the good One relates itself to cogitation before this relationship has already constituted - "bonitas sua dans et faciens" - can this be achieved.[2] Thereby the one "bonitas" appears to thought as the "bonum per se." At the same time thought comes to its own by entering into this relationship and adopting this relationship as its own. In the process it acknowledges itself as interesting and affirms itself. Cogitation becomes self-knowing. It perceives all things endowed with "bonitas" including thought as good: "hoc ipsum quod aliquid sunt aut aliquomodo bene sunt."[3]

Anselm situates at the beginning of the cognitional process the multitude of good things: "tam innumerabilia bona" which occasion a "discernere" of the innumerable good: "Cum tam innumerabilia bona sint, quorum tam multam diversitatem et sensibus corporeis ... ratione mentis discernimus."[4] The discernment leads to the recognition of a gradation in the quality of the good. This leads to a "iudicare:" a determination of the goodness of the cognitional act and what else may in fact be good.[5]

Thought asks itself how it arrives at this "iudicare." How is this thought structured that it may arrive at the Good? The Good must give itself in its oneness as what it is. Anselm concludes that the Good appears with inner necessity as itself. The multifarious good things can only be reflected upon if there is some One which corresponds to the "one" thought, so that cogitation can arrive at a judgment. The (intellectually) meditating monk must grasp the good in such a foundationally radical manner as the one "unum aliquid ... bonum" that otherwise he cannot think himself. To think the "unum" as the "bonum" and as "aliquid" is the common (basic) cognitional form. It is this that is being thought as something (= "aliquid"). Then the possible unity of the quality of the good things corresponds to the one thinking process. Only by bringing to unity the multitude, is it possible to think that which is to be thought.

As Anselm does not tire of illustrating with the concept of the Good, thought always presupposes the One. Otherwise the manifestation of the good

---

[1] M 1: 13,5f.
[2] M 1: 13,8.
[3] M 1: 13,6f.
[4] M 1: 14,5-7.
[5] M 1: 13,15.

as the good would not occur. This permits for a graduated appreciation of the various intensities of the good. This quality is found "idem in diversis"[6] wherein only "per aliud" is goodness encountered. In connection with this, Anselm makes reference to the horse. The good may be predicated by virtue of its strength or by virtue of its speed. When one speaks of a good human being, however, something else is meant. A horse may be found good for utilitarian purposes, "propter aliquam utilitatem," whilst a human being can be predicated as good exclusively in a moral sense: "propter honestatem."[7] This cognitional progression only comes to rest when finding a final, unexcellable good. This final good is no longer a "per aliud" good but one per se and is the causation of the various diverse manifestations of good: "Ergo consequitur, ut omnia alia bona sint per aliud quam quod ipsa sunt et ipsum solum per seipsum."[8]

In a Platonic vein one recognizes the quality of the good by partaking in the One that is good: "dicuntur (unum) aliquid ita, ut ad invicem magis vel minus aut aequaliter dicantur."[9] The cause - now thought of in descending ontological order - is "unde sunt bona."[10] In this context Kienzler poignantly observes:

> Die Frage nach der Einheit des Guten stellt sich dem Denken mit Notwendigkeit. Es ist zugleich die Forderung des Denkens an das Gute, soll dies je zu denken sein.[11]

As a consequence cogitation recognizes unity as unity. This One presents itself either as "unum per se" or as "unum per aliud."[12] Thought arrives at the common cause of all "per aliud." The unity of the good allows one to think the One and as a consequence to apprehend the unity of human thought. The many facets of the good yield not only the generic term "good" but the necessary prerequisite for all, namely the One ("unum").

---

[6] M 1: 14,12.
[7] M 1: 14,23-15,18.
[8] M 1: 15,6f.
[9] M 1: 14,10f.
[10] M 1: 13, 14.
[11] Klaus Kienzler, Glaube und Denken bei Anselm von Canterbury (Freiburg i. Br.: Herder, 1981) 90.
[12] M 1: 14,7.11.

4.1 The "Unum" as the guiding Principle of the "Ratio"[13]

Subsequent to considerations on the nature of "bonum," chapter two of the *Monologion* treats the "unum." The reader detects a necessary train of thought. Only the One as the unity of the many goods in the one good enables cognition - which is a thinking from within the one - to reflect upon the good at all. As the first chapter via the "bona" and "unum aliquid" arrived at the highest good- "summum bonum" - the second chapter derives from the "magnum" a highest magnitude -"summum magnum." The third chapter deduces from the being things -"quidquid est" - the highest being: "summum omnium quae sunt."[14] The "unum" is the guiding principle for epistemological progress.[15] The derivation of the "summum bonum" from the merely "bonum" already illustrates the central, axiological and teleological role the "unum" plays.[16] The discussion of the "bonum" reveals a twofold relationship. The Good itself implies unity and at the same time cognition requires this unity. After *Monologion's* first chapter the "bonum" has served its purpose and no longer occupies central stage. Yet, the insight remains that there is a fundamental convenience, or perhaps better even inner correspondence between goodness and unity which both preceeds and constitutes this relationship. This convergence already establishes a first unity. It also yields an additional insight. There is but one thinking and it is only such inasmuch as it comes into concurrence with itself.

---

[13] Cf. Werner Beierwaltes, Proclo: I fondamenti della sua metafisica (Milano: Vita e Pensiero, 1988); Kurt Flasch, "Der philosophische Ansatz des Anselm von Canterbury im Monologion und sein Verhältnis zum augustinischen Neuplatonismus," Analecta Anselmiana. Untersuchungen zu Person und Werk Anselms von Canterbury. II. Vol. Franciscus Salesius Schmitt ed. (Frankfurt am Main: Minerva, 1970): 1-43, at 9ff. 35ff.; Kurt Flasch, "Zum Begriff der Wahrheit bei Anselm von Canterbury," Philosophisches Jahrbuch 72 (1965): 322-352, at 339ff.; Helmut Kohlenberger, Similitudo und Ratio. Überlegungen zur Methode bei Anselm von Canterbury (Bonn: Bouvier, 1972) at 173ff.; Franciscus Schmitt, "Die wissenschaftliche Methode in Anselms `Cur deus homo.'" Spicilegium Beccense I (Paris: Vrin, 1959): 349-370, at 358ff.; as well as Karl Barth, Fides Quaerens Intellectum. Anselms Beweis der Existenz Gottes im Zusammenhang seines theologischen Programms. 2nd rev. ed. (Zollikon: Evangelischer Verlag, 1958) at 42ff.

[14] M 3: 15,26.

[15] M 1: 14,7; 2: 15,16; 3: 16,2.

[16] Sofia Vanni-Rovighi, "L'etica di S. Anselmo d'Aosta," Analecta Anselmiana Bd. 1. (Frankfurt am Main: Minerva, 1969): 73-99, at 73ff. Flasch observes as regards the term "truth":
"Die Wahrheit ist für Anselm zugleich Sein und Gutheit. Das ergibt sich aus ihrer teleologischen Ableitung; wenn ein Wesen oder eine Tätigkeit die spezifische Aufgabe erfüllt, die ihnen gestellt ist, dann erreichen sie ihr wahres Sein und ihre Gutheit." Flasch, "Zum Begriff der Wahrheit" 336. Bonaventure explicitly borrows this approach from Anselm: Itinerarium V, 2 and VI,2.
This correlation of truth, goodness and unity/oneness establishes an ontic bond between empirical and moral statements.

Later this relation will be defined in the words: "bonum et unum convertuntur."[17]

Thus the Anselmian path leads to results with an inner necessity. This is a consequence of the reflection on the "unum": thinking is henceforth restricted to that which follows "ex necessitate" or what "necesse est."[18] Hence Anselm's assumption has thought think only and exclusively that which "cogitari potest."[19] From the above considerations on the "unum" of mental reality Anselm follows the restriction of the cognitional process to that which evolves from thought. Whatever is multifarious, diverse and disparate is reduced to the one ground in chapters two and three of the *Monologion*. The ground reveals the unity as constitutive for both the ontic reality and for thought. In the tension between the terms "aliud," "aliquid" and "unum" a comprehensive connection between the multitudinous and the One becomes apparent to thought. To deduce from this an Aristotelian appreciation of causality is perhaps too rash. Nothing indicates Anselm's familiarity with Aristotle.[20]

The necessity of thinking alters thinking's very character with necessity into that which necessarily needs to be thought. Under the conditions established by the categories of "unum," "necessitas" and the explaining of their connection, the to-be-thought comes to be thought necessarily. The necessity of thought becomes the necessity of that which is to be thought - yet only the latter finally makes thought possible. As with the terms "bonum" and "unum," there is now a necessary concurrence between the terms "unum" and "ens." Thought and being condition each other reciprocally.

The notion of the "unum" vouches for the openness of being and thought for one another. The "unum" reveals the multifarious things in their one ground and compels the thinking process to recognize the necessary connection with this ground. Very much like Plotinus Anselm does not so much argue and establish at the beginning the reasons for the inner connection between

---

[17] These are also present in De Veritate. They lay the groundwork for a transcendentally formulated question. Cf. Adolf Schurr, Die Begründung der Philosophie durch Anselm von Canterbury. Eine Erörterung des ontologischen Gottesbeweises (Stuttgart: Kohlhammer, 1996) at 37f.73ff. After a "phenomenology of natural consciousness" has been established, Anselm turns his attention to conditions for consciousness per se. Cf. Flasch, "Zum Begriff der Wahrheit" 326: while Kant first establishes this case explicitly, this by no means implies that this circumstance was heretofore unknown.

"Daß Anselm Phänomenologie des natürlichen Bewußtseins und transzendentale Fragestellung nicht terminologisch trennen konnte, ist bei seiner philosophiegeschichtlichen Stellung selbstverständlich, das schließt aber nicht aus, daß er beides betrieben hat und daß seinem Interpreten die Pflicht erwächst zu unterscheiden, wo er das eine, wo er das andere im Sinn hat."

[18] M 2: 15,17; 3: 16,16.

[19] M 3: 15,30.

[20] Kienzler, Glaube und Denken 98 against, Flasch, "Der philosophische Ansatz" 29ff and Schmitt, "Anselm und der (Neu-) Platonismus" 41ff. Cf. Anselm's treatment of causation in M 6: 18,27-19,5.

"cogitare" and "ens," but rather trusts in the existence of this connection.[21] Thought finds its own necessity, "origin-ality" (= ground/reason) and unity by recurring to the necessity, "origin-ality" and unity of Being.

Building upon the ascending line of thought of the first chapter, the second chapter establishes that the many Great ("quaecumque magna sunt") is great "per unum aliquid magnum" which must be in itself great: "magnum per seipsum."[22] The pattern established in the previous chapter is thus confirmed. Chapter three provides a further concentration. The premises of thought stand the test in view of the highest object of thought: Being. "Quod sit quaedam natura, per quam est, quidquid est, et quae per se est, et est summum omnium quae sunt."[23] Everything that is, "quidquid est," must be "per unum aliquid." Such an "unum aliquid" must finally be recognized as an "unum per seipsum" and a "summum omnium quae sunt." Since here the "unum" plays the crucial role, Anselm problematizes the notion of "unum" to its very extreme to demonstrate its viability and significance for every preceding and subsequent reflection.[24] Up to this point the "unum aliquid" yielded both the "bonum per seipsum" and the "magnum per seipsum." Anselm wants to know whether it is able to yield also the "Unum per seipsum" as the ultimate all-explaining cause. On this rests the unity of thought. Thinking and the (im-)possibility of thinking decide at this point the question. He concludes that there cannot be something that cannot be thought and vice-versa that there must exist something that is necessary to the thinking process.[25]

The Anselmian progression from the notions of unity and necessity of a final cause to the necessity of an actual final, really existing cause occasioned much discussion. While a thorough discussion must be reserved for the analysis of the *Proslogion*, it should be pointed out already here that Anselm does not make recourse to a mathematical-quantitative approach.[26] The solution to this crucial aspect of Anselm's writings becomes apparent when considering the whole of the Anselmian train of thought.

First Anselm removes what is impossible to think: "omne namque quod est, aut est per aliquid aut per nihil."[27] The possibility of the existence of a reason for the concrete being thing determines the thinkability of a being thing. Otherwise the thinkability of the being thing would be impossible. This extreme impossibility of no causation would be nothing. Such a hypothesis negates itself

---

[21] Multifarious impressions lead to the idea of the One: Plato, Phaidrus 249b.

[22] M 2: 15,19.

[23] M 3: 15,25f.

[24] M 3: 16,18ff.

[25] M 3: 15,30.

[26] Against Helmut Kimmerle, Die Gottesbeweise Anselms von Canterbury. Ihre Voraussetzungen und ihre Bedeutung für die philosophische Theologie (Berlin: Freie Universität P, 1958) 16ff. along with Kienzler, Glaube und Denken 99ff. 220ff; and Jules Vuillemin, Le Dieu d'Anselme et les apparences de la raison (Paris: Aubier, 1971) at 34ff.

[27] M 3: 15,29.

as impossible to think: "sed nihil est per nihil. Non enim vel cogitari potest, ut sit aliquid non per aliquid."[28] The hypothetical nothing evidences thinking, however, and it is equipped to negate something that is not equally "non potest cogitari." Thinking shows itself capable of prevailing.

The next step is divided into three phases. First the being object is "per aliquid" in its constitution. Subsequently Anselm asks whether there is one cause or several causes.[29] Were there to be several causes at the beginning of the being object, then three possibilties would logically occur to the mind:

1. the many causes have a common ground; this ground would then be an "unum aliquid."[30]

2. The causes are per se what they are independently. In that case they would possess a proper power, "una aliqua vis vel natura existendi per se." Yet were this the case, then this "una natura existendi per se" would in turn be their common ground: "per id ipsum unum sint, per quod habent, ut sint per se."[31]

3. Finally, they could possess causes independently from one another: "plura per se invicem sint."[32] This, however, Anselm precludes, for these relationships presume but do not constitute a relation. As a consequence he concludes: "(c)um itaque veritas omnimodo excludat plura esse per quae cuncta sint, necesse est unum illud esse, per quod sunt cuncta quae sunt."[33] The final cause, an "unum per se," is found and thereby the unity of thinking and Being is established.

4.2 The Categoriality of Thought

The previous train of thought permits one to establish the concept of the One as the principle of the thinking process. The thinking process evidenced itself as a self-unfolding execution. In this respect Anselm's notion of thinking as a meditation on the One is strikingly similar to that of Plotinus. Going beyond Plotinus' use of "being," he uses the most common terms "bonum," "magnum" and "cause" to distill the final "unum." Yet all terms must imply evidently far more than the notion of "unum" can capture. Anselm is quite mindful of the danger of a simplification to exclusively one principle. The terms "summum magnum" and "summum bonum" are also employed to illustrate that the One is infinitely more than merely a unit.[34]

Chapter one sums up the result of these reflections:

---

[28] M 3: 15,30-16,1.
[29] This is in keeping with the Platonic tradition. Cf. Flasch, "Der philosophische Ansatz" 20f.
[30] M 3: 16,2-6.
[31] M 3: 16,8f.
[32] M 3: 16,10.
[33] M 3: 16,12-17.
[34] M 3: 16,18-28.

(n)am quaecumque iusta dicuntur ad invicem sive pariter sive magis vel minus, non possunt intelligi iusta nisi per iustitiam, quae non est aliud et aliud in diversis.[35]

Such "non possunt intelligi" as a cognitional necessity permits him to assume terms - as for instance "bonitas" or "iustitia" - to signify something transcending cognition. He similarly proceeds in the second chapter. The discussion does not result in a quantitative greatest, but in a qualitative greatest, namely "sapientia."[36] The same applies to "magnitudo." As Rousseau and Vuillemin convincingly demonstrate, these exhibit parallels to both Plato and Augustine.[37]

For Anselm such a cause cannot solely originate in the mind, because the cause of a quantitative entity necessary to the mind would be a mere quantitative maximum but not a qualitative and transcendental entity such as "sapientia."

Towards the end of chapter four of the *Monologion*, Anselm approaches unity from a different angle: the possibility of a "regressus in infinitum."[38] The order of "disparitas graduum" as the background of the "res," causes the ontic differences to take center stage. The cause for this difference is addressed. Previously a real danger existed that the differences could be merged into an identity. This new order of inequality calls for a new cognitional approach. This qualitative "imparitas graduum" possesses its very own value.[39] Both orders, that of sameness and of difference, must in Anselm's view be thought together. This requirement entails amplifying and correcting the order of sameness along lines of gradations and explaining and grounding in thinking must occur in another way. To this point the "summum" remains undefined. It is not merely an elongation of the thinking process, if one is to do justice to its necessity. Hence the many righteous are caused by the transcending category of the one justice. Similarly the term of the many big things does not exhaust itself with the construction of the "maximum" but in the term "sapientia."[40] Must not the final

---

[35] M1: 14,13-15.

[36] Cf. Augustine: "Non enim mole magnus est, sed virtute; et eadem bonitas quae sapientia et magnitudo ... in iis quae non mole magna sunt, hoc est maius esse quod est melius esse" (De trinit. I.6,c.7,8,9 - PL 42, 929); Flasch, "Der philosophische Ansatz" 42.

[37] Cf. Plato, Symposion, 210c-211c and Augustine, De civitate Dei I.8,c.6; Rousseau, Introduction 30; Vuillemin, Le Dieu d'Anselme 78ff. Henry compares these terms (i.e., "iustitia," "fortitudo," and "participatio") to Aristotle: Desmond P. Henry The Logic of Saint Anselm (Oxford: Clarendon P, 1967) at 62ff. Particularly the last term is for Henry cause to detect a clearly visible (neo-) Platonic vein in Anselm's thinking. This Flasch buttresses. To him Anselm connects causality and participation into one single moment; thus "es versteht sich von selbst, daß das, woran partizipiert wird, auch die eigentliche causa ist." Cf. Flasch, "Zum Begriff der Wahrheit" 329ff.

[38] For the time being the question of whether in this chapter a proof of God's existence is being provided may be disregarded.

[39] M 4: 16,32 and 17,1.

[40] M 2: 15,22 and 19ff.

cause of all being be equally a being-transcending cogitation? Here causation does not suffice. A new perspective is called for.

Such thinking would recognize the proper rank and value of the things. There exists a more or less.[41] Quite clearly there is for Anselm a qualitative, ontic difference within the created order. In the new ascent within the order of "more" and "less" cognition reaches anew a "summum." But in the process of this ascent cognition now experiences a mutation. There are no longer grades towards the "summum" but a giant leap. In this manner Anselm overcomes the "regressus in infinitum" which holds the danger of the existence of merely an infinite number of causes.[42] The prospect of qualitatively identical causes appears absurd to the Benedictine monk. The cognitional effort requires causes of varying valence, lest the cognitional process itself becomes absurd. This process realizes that it itself cannot provide the final cause. It must occur unto it from the outside. In this sense the "summum" assumes the quality of the necessary. Cognition must venture to let itself be involved in a leap beyond the finite number of causes towards the final and final-causing cause. This requires that cognition be willing to surrender its uniquely necessary character in order to become a self-transcending cognition. Only such cognition is able to do justice to reality. Either cognition tries to explain everything, or it dares to leap beyond its own confines. Anselm unequivocally opts for the latter: "id quod omnem humanum intellectum transcendere intelligo."[43]

By transcending itself, cognition does not abolish itself but rather considers the conditions and possibilities of self-transcendence in a way mindful of its origins.[44] Koyré summarizes this circumstance as follows:

St. Anselme remonte par une sorte d'induction du monde à Dieu, de la créature à son créateur, des perfections et des biens finis et complets de ce monde, à la perfection infinie qui en est le fondement et la source.[45]

In this sense a transcending cognition does not render thinking futile but enables it to acquire a new significance: it is a transcendental necessity. Thinking undergoes a transcendental reduction unto itself. In Evdokimov's words:

La réduction apophatique rend impossible toute identification de l'Absolu avec le transcendentale ou l'intelligible. Dieu est trans-transcendentale et trans-intelligible .. Dieu transcende le plan des causes et des effets. Il est trans-causal et trans-ordinal.[46]

---

[41] M 4: 16,31-17,10.
[42] Alexandre Koyré, L'Idée de Dieu dans la philosophie de Saint Anselme (Paris: E. Leroux, 1923) at 14.
[43] M 65: 76,26.
[44] Schurr, Die Begründung der Philosophie 37f.73ff.
[45] Koyré, L'Idée de Dieu 37.

In this manner the cognitional process includes a self-reflecting moment which renders it self-conscious: at the same time and under the same consideration it both gives a gift and receives a gift.[47]

For this reason Anselm considers it required to prove again the unity of the "summum" from another perspective. The criterion is no longer the necessary causation of many reasons/grounds by one reason/ground. Rather he investigates what being is "superior" or "maius." Are the many or is the one greater, beyond which one can no longer think? He concludes there exists one, no-longer-to-be-excelled-greatest which is also the highest.[48] Going beyond what has already been established in the previous chapters, it must now be shown to contain the fullness of "natura" and "essentia." Therefore, it would be the highest and fullest of all beings. No longer is this "unum" the unity of cognition but the fullness of Being which stands beyond and above all being things. It even contains the definition of unity as the "maximum et optimum" and the "summum omnium existentium."[49]

Anselm employs two distinct cognitional tracks. The one ascends from the many to the final and necessary "per se" and identifies it as the "summum." The other has arrived at the "summum" and perceives all grounded in the "summum" in retrospect. This "summum" is its own cause: "per se," and thus the final cause of all being objects (things): "per quod alia cuncta sunt."[50] In the subsequent chapters 5 - 8 a discussion of the "per se" and "per aliquid" ensues.

Chapter five establishes that the being things possess being "ex alio" while the "unum" is "ex se ipso."[51] The change in the text from "per" to "ex" has been characterized by Balthasar as a turning point within the *Monologion* from a "philosophischen (oder antik-theologischen) zur (christlich-) theologischen Vernunftschau."[52] Chapters 6 to 8 contrast the manner of causation between the one and final cause and its created things with the manners of causation within the created order. Anselm relates three forms of finite causation: "Quod enim dicitur esse per aliquid, videtur esse aut per efficiens aut per materiam aut per aliquod aliud adiumentum, velut per instrumentum."[53] It is the monk's intention to demonstrate the qualitative difference of causations between the "unum" and the created order. The highest being relates to the created order as "lux" does to

---

[46] Paul Evdokimov, "L'aspect apophatique de l'argument de Saint Anselme," Spicilegium Beccense (Paris: Vrin, 1959): 233-258, at 237, cf. also 246f.

[47] Ferdinand Ulrich, "Cur non video praesentem? Zur Implikation der `griechischen´ und `lateinischen´ Denkform bei Anselm und Scotus Erigena, Freiburger Zeitschrift für Philosophie und Theologie 22 (1975): 70-170, at 92ff.

[48] "Restat igitur unam et solam aliquam naturam esse, quae sic est aliis superior, ut nullo sit inferior." M 4: 17,24f.

[49] M 4: 17,26 and 30.

[50] M 4: 17,29f.

[51] M 6: 20,6.

[52] Balthasar, Herrlichkeit II 233.

[53] M 6: 19,1-3.

118

"lucere" and "lucens."[54] Kienzler describes this relationship as the being-ground of the final cause as transcendent difference which simultaneously is immanently present.[55]

Repeatedly investigating in his writings "nothing," Anselm states in chapter 8 that the highest Being creates "ex (de) nihilo" all that is created.[56] The reflections on the foundational matrix of the highest Being as the ground of being receive in chapters thirteen and fourteen their climax. The ground of being does not simply precede ontologically all creation but is as such present in the created order every single moment, in a way manifesting an intimate relationship between the finite with its final and infinite cause: "Ubique igitur est per omnia et in omnibus .... eadem est, quae in omnibus, et ex qua per quam et in qua omnia."[57] Thereby Anselm defines the connection between absolute Being and created being in an altogether new fashion. The necessary foundation of cognition is no longer reduced to evidence provided by finite causes. Causation "per aliud" moves suddenly to a cause transcending all causes. The cause-explaining thinking mutates into a self-transcending thinking in order to explain and constitute itself. This means that for Anselm to comprehend oneself from the final cause and thereby to perceive oneself in an explaining and grounding of thinking, because all causations of thinking are ultimately grounded in the being-ground of the ultimate cause of all causes.

We come upon a very positive insight: finite cognition remains inadequate in its thinking before the One, yet it is fitting to perceive itself with this shortcoming: "non ostenditur quid sit, sed potius qualis vel quanta sit."[58] While it can state the greatness of the One, finite thinking is not able to predicate from its own perspective "quid sit." Certainly this One is also "iustitia" and thereby "iustus." Yet it is more than quantity or quality because it is Being. It is not "iustus" as finite, created things are "iusti," but because being just is its very own property. In this manner the cognitional process is held back by the qualifiers "qualis" and "quanta." On the other hand this cognitional labor is capable of being mindful of its inherent limitations and can think toward the unthinkable One, the "Summum" in its "quid sit" in an asymptotic way: "Quidquid igitur eorum de illa dicatur: non qualis vel quanta, sed magis quid sit

---

[54] M 6: 20,13-19. "Quemadmodum se habent ad invicem lux et lucere et lucens, sic sunt ad se invicem essentia et esse et ens, hoc est existens sive subsistens." M 6; 20,15f.

[55] "Anselm beschränkt sich also darauf, das Grundsein des letzten Grundes als transzendentes Anders-sein und gleichzeitig immanentes In-sein zu beschreiben. Wichtig ist ihm offensichtlich die Transzendentalität dieses Begründungsverhältnisses." Kienzler, Glauben und Denken 115.

[56] M 8: 24,5. "Nihilo" occurs 81 and "nihil" 776 times in Anselm's writings. Cf. Gillian Rosemary Evans, A Concordance of the Works of Saint Anselm (Millwood N.Y.: Kraus International, 1984) at 933 and 927-932 respectively.

[57] M 14: 27,20-26.

[58] M 16: 30,5f.

monstratur."[59] The unbridgeable difference in its unbridgeability becomes apparent. All predications to which cogitation advances must be understood in this sense as modi of the highest Being. These Anselm enumerates:

> Illa igitur est summa essentia, summa vita, summa ratio, summa salus, summa iustitia, summa sapientia, summa veritas, summa bonitas, summa magnitudo, summa pulchritudo, summa immortalitas, summa incorruptibilitas, summa immutabilitas, summa beatitudo, summa aeternitas, summa potestas,

and finally

> summa unitas, quod non est aliud quam summe ens.[60]

While already previously encountered in the *Monologion*, they now are firmly anchored in the One and highest Being as the "simplex" and "unum." Thus the One becomes the coincidence of all predicates.

The One's transcendence is further adumbrated in chapters 18 to 26. It has neither beginning nor end. It precedes and follows all temporality and spatiality. It is immanent in a manner that cannot be defined as in time and space, because it is equally nowhere. It asserts its transcendence in its immanence and remains nevertheless immutable. These qualities are summed up as "quod sit extra omnem substantiam et singulariter sit quidquid est."[61]

4.3 Summary

At the beginning of his reflections Anselm posits the "sola ratione" as the cognitional principle. It possesses no prior exterior assumptions. It is radically left on its own: almost forlorn and forsaken in a Heideggerian sense. It departs from a "tabula rasa." Using rational means exclusively Anselm threads a cognitional path which does not originate solely in thought and leads him well beyond cognitional confines.

From its very beginning cognition is posited as possessing a relationality with the "bonum." Becoming aware of its relationality it encounters unity. It experiences it in a self-constitutive self-reflective moment and thereby as its very own think-ability and its necessity. This cognitional path, however, leads the thinking process beyond itself. This surplus it perceives as a being wanting a cause, even when it merely defines itself by thought. In the process cognition feels itself bereft of a cause were it not grounded in a transcending cause. Such a transcending-thinking does not deprive thinking of its originality but rather reconstitutes it in its essential constitution as "necessarily-causing," as necessity and as unity. The cognitional process apprehends itself as necessarily defined

---

[59] M 16: 31,1f.
[60] M 16: 31,3-8.
[61] M 26: 44,3f.

from a transcendental cause. Only via a detour to its own transcendence does it define itself properly and does transcending thought experience its own originality.

CHAPTER FIVE

5.0 The Relationship of Faith and Thought as a Cognitive-Ontic Process - Fides quaerens intellectum

There is an intellectual and existential progress to be realized as a task in the tension between faith and thought which can be termed the monk's personal, yet objective movement toward the One, revealed in scripture and beheld in monastic life and yet remaining the God who is yearned for. Defying any simplification of his position as akin to that of rationalism[1] and fideism,[2] Anselm postulates an intertwinedness of faith and reason that seems to run counter to his heuristic principle of "sola ratione"[3] in "Epistola de incarnatione verbi:" "quoniam sentio plures in eadem laborare quaestione, etiam si fides in illis superet rationem quae illis fidei videtur repugnare, non mihi videtur superfluum esse repugnantiam istam dissolvere."[4] Therefore, while he readily admits a contest to exist amongst the two he presumes a yet more basic connection underlying and constituting their diverse modi of existence. This is for the time being his assumption. Nowhere in his writings is a justification for this premise supplied.[5] Nevertheless, it is this foundational assumption which gives him the courage to dare advance cognitionally to the innermost secrets of divine being. In the shadowy dawning of Medieval rationality he endeavors to develop anew for his contemporaries the whole of theology.[6]

---

[1] Cf. particularly Maxwell John Charlesworth, Introduction to the *Proslogion* in St. Anselm´s Proslogion with a reply on behalf of the fool by Gaunilo and the author´s reply to Gaunilo (Oxford: Oxford UP, 1979); Schmitt, "Die wissenschaftliche Methode" at 349ff. 366f; Cipriano Vagaggini, "La Hantise des 'rationes necessariae' de S. Anselme dans la théologie de processions trinitaires de S. Thomas." Spicilegium Beccense I Paris: Vrin, 1959): 103-139, at 103f.

[2] Represented perhaps in a very remote sense of the word "fideism" by Barth, Fides Quaerens Intellectum; Arrigo Levasti, S. Anselmo; vita e pensiero (Bari: G. Laterza, 1929); Anselm Stolz, " Zur Theologie Anselms im Proslogion." Catholica 2 (1933): 1-24, at 1ff; Anselm Stolz, "Das Proslogion, des Hl. Anselm." Revue Bénédictine 47 (1935): 331-347, at 331ff. This qualified fideistic position receives a rebuttal already in Etienne Gilson, "Sens et Nature de l'Argument de Saint Anselme," Archives d'Histoire Doctrinale et Littéraire du Moyen Age. 7 (1934): 5-51, at 31ff (intended particularly towards Stolz' mystical interpretation in Catholica 2 (1933)).

[3] Cf. Gilson, "Sens et Nature" 5ff.19ff.39ff; Grabmann, Geschichte der scholastischen Methode 258ff; Kienzler, Glauben und Denken 20ff; Koyré, L'Idée de Dieu; Paul Vignaux, "Structure et sens du 'Monologion.'" Revue des sciences philosophiques et théologiques 31 (1947): 192-212, at 192ff.

[4] I 1: 6,2f.

[5] Johann Adam Möhler had been one of the first to apprehend the whole of the Anselmian oeuvre as critical for a proper understanding of Anselm's thinking: "Anselm, Erzbischof von Canterbury. Ein Beitrag zur Kenntniß des religiös-sittlichen, öffentlich-kirchlichen und wissenschaftlichen Lebens im elften und zwölften Jahrhundert,"Gesammelte Schriften und Aufsätze. Bd. 1, ed. I. Döllinger (Regensburg: n.p.,1939) at 32ff.

[6] Thus Henri de Lubac, "'Seigneur, je cherche ton visage.' Sur chapitre XIVe du Proslogion de saint Anselme," Recherches dans la Foi. Trois études sur Origène, saint Anselme et la

5.1 Praeliminaria

The challenge Anselm is willing to face is how to permit each of the two entities, i.e., faith and reason/cognition, not to dissipate into the other but rather retain their autonomy. "Without confusion or change, and without division or separation." How can one relate reason to faith without reason becoming submerged under credal assertions (fideism)? On the other hand how can also faith prevail in its own right without becoming subservient to reason (rationalism)? For the moment Anselm claims more than a mere formal interrelatedness. Correlation can only be determined from an inner recognition of the constitution of both "fides" and "ratio." To uncover this a posteriori is difficult, as the author nowhere treats this in a systematic and coherent manner. Some preliminary considerations are found in the introductions to some of his writings: *Cur Deus Homo, Monologion, Proslogion* and *De Incarnatione Verbi.*[7]

When making the assertion "sola ratione"[8] his guiding star in the intellectual endeavor he undertakes, then this means the point of departure, for thinking starts with itself. It constitues itself within its own thinking process and is not satisfied without uncovering the "rationes necessariae" of what is to be thought from its own inner necessity. As a consequence Kohlenberger describes the "ratio" as the "letzte Instanz."[9] Yet the further determination of the "autonomy" and "heteronomy" of Anselm's reason is subtle.[10]

Calling to mind Plotinus' method, Anselm defines reason as "quae et princeps et iudex debet omnium esse quae sunt in homine."[11] This defines reason as something proper to the human condition in a most common manner. It is related to "all" that is within the human being. The Latin term evokes several meanings in English. Reason is a "princeps" as both "duchess" and guide of human "esse," for it is also its origin. In a way not further elucidated, the human being is not a derivative of other things but rather the place wherein all being is present. He need not search in the outer world to uncover the key to all that is. There is something like an "interior castle" in each human being.

---

philosophie Chrétienne. Henri de Lubac ed. (Paris: Beauchesne, 1979): 6-124, at 109ff. Karl-Friedrich Ubbelohde, Glaube und Vernunft bei Anselm von Canterbury. Eine Studie zur Genese systematischer Theologie und zum Verständnis von "Theologia" und "Philosophia" zwischen Patristik und Frühscholastik (Göttingen: Göttingen UP, 1969) at 1ff situates Anselm well in the theology of his day.

[7] As regards methodological questions cf. also Flasch, "Zum Begriff der Wahrheit" 322ff; Carmelo Ottaviano, "Quaestioni e testi medioevali. I.: Le `rationes necessariae´ in S. Anselmo," Sophia 1 (1933): 92-98 at 92ff; Schmitt, "Die wissenschaftliche Methode" 360f; Schurr, Die Begründung 14ff.31ff; Söhngen, Die Einheit der Theologie 24ff.

[8] Cu I 20: 88,4-8.

[9] Kohlenberger, Similitudo et Ratio 122, Fn. 89.

[10] Balthasar, Herrlichkeit, Vol. II, 226; Ulrich, "Cur non video" 70ff.

[11] I1: 10,1f.

Such a definition of the human being and reason leads Anselm to summon people to collection of thoughts, reflection and meditation. By beckoning the human being to meditate, he simultaneously invites to reflection upon reason using reason. His is in a way an apodictic insistence on reason's exclusive role as the self-execution of the divine (in the sense of "similitudo" because of humans' "imago Dei" quality) as a self-reflection of reason. As the following quotation illustrates, this justifies the title of the *Monologion*: "Quaecumque ibi dixi, sub persona secum sola cogitatione disputantis et investigantis ea quae prius non animadvertisset, prolatat sunt."[12] As in the Christian tradition this recourse unto the self is a genuine grasp towards the infinite contained in the finite, it does not wither into a truncated solipsistic exercise: "Deum et animam scire cupio," Augustine states in the *Soliloquy*.[13] In the cognitional process truth becomes apparent as a personal, ontic and divine moment. Knowledge is, therefore, insight into God and the self. These two are recognized not in two separate, successive and distinctive steps, but together. The outward thrust to the infinite One is the encounter of the innermost depths of being. God is indelibly and non-accidentally written into the cognitional process. As Kienzler summarizes: "Das Denken hat bei sich anzufangen, um sich in Gott zu finden."[14] The cognitional encounter of the thinking self is already a relational event in a way essentially intimate for thinking: between the recognizing and the recognized. Insofar as thinking is authentic it fundamentally opens towards the totality of being. Thinking contains all, isolates nothing and brings all into a foundational relationship. It is thus the "densest" of all possible acts. Anselm concludes: "Spiritualis iudicat omnia, et ipse a nemine iudicatur."[15]

Having established the principal role of reason, Anselm follows the necessities of thought. It is in cognition that the freedom and sovereignty of thinking becomes evident, along with the all-encompassing coherence of cognition. The yearning for God is implied and indeed contained already in the creative act and is expressed in the "rationes necessariae" of Anselmian thought. They are not random extrapolations but are components of the interior of the thinking act. From this perspective one may dare state that there is nothing prior to thinking; it is the a priori per se.[16] This means that the thinking human being is not everything, but in thinking everything is present. Human beings are inextricably involved in the relationality of all things. This is the Anselmian message in the sentence, "ratio est princeps omnium quae sunt in homine." The

---

[12] M Intro : 8,18-20; cf. P Prooem: 93,2-4.
[13] Augustine, Soliloquium 1.1,c.2,7 (PL 32,872).
[14] Kienzler, Glauben und Denken 29. For cognition as means to recognize both God and the self, cf. Flasch, "Zum Begriff der Wahrheit" 322ff; Kohlenberger, Similitudo et Ratio 114ff.
[15] I 1: 8,18f., evoking 1Cor 2:15.
[16] Schmitt, "Die wissenschaftliche Methode" 361ff; Barth, Fides quaerens intellectum 47ff introduces a distinction between "noetic" and "ontic" necessity and supposes the latter to precede.

origin of cognition contains a radicality which is also a vocation. Reason[17] fails to find a cause beyond itself.

Flasch apprehends in the last quotation also an additional dimension. If it implies relationality to all things, the "ratio" must address truth claims.[18] Indeed, to Anselm's mind the terms "iudicare" and "discernere" belong to the "ratio's" essence: "rationali naturae non est aliud rationale, quam posse discernere iustum a non iusto, verum a non vero, bonum a non bono, magis bonum a minus bono."[19] Reason acts in a manner both judging and discerning among the good or bad, less or more, and what is and what is not. In the *Proslogion* reason is even perceived as judge concerning "esse in solo intellectu" and "esse et in re." Thus it is the arbiter of "thought" and "being."[20] In this sense cognition does not merely judge what is the case in the outside realm but also within the thinking process in a comprehensive way. It even passes a verdict on whether something in the mind truly is and what its nature is. Thought problematizes this latter aspect by investigating its relationship to being. The relationship between thought and being does not mean that thought is simply "captive" to thought. It is a relationship put to the test ever anew.

It would, however, be incorrect to posit an original hiatus between thought and being. Were one indeed to do this, one would become either a realist or idealist. Such would hold to an unbridgeable difference between the two within finite cognition. Yet by being mindful of this difference the thinker is capable of overcoming this difference albeit in an incomplete way.[21] This is the task of the "iudicium." Analytic judging arrives at a synthetic verdict. This verdict may also be a spoken one. In the word "similitudo" the ontic relationality of thought and speech is contained. Speaking overcomes the difference also by demarcating the difference. In Kohlenberger's view this encapsulates a moral element: the "Sollens-Charakter" of thought and speech.[22] Already prior to speech, cognition bridges the difference by thinking. Thinking as thinking considers ontic reality and thereby overcomes the finite difference between thought and being. Being is ever present to thinking. On the one hand it is mindful of its origin in being, on the other it is equally aware of its analytic "iudicare"-function vis-à-vis being. It is aware of its relationality with being. Being "princeps," it is privileged to formulate also the synthesis between the two. This is not a secondary event; rather it is its central task to mediate between the two.

The question arises: How to think a relationship which is so foundational to thinking? Balthasar perceives the answer in the word "aperta." In the preface

---

[17] In English "reason" may mean both "ratio" and "principium."
[18] Flasch, "Zum Begriff der Wahrheit" 322ff.
[19] M 68: 78,21-79.
[20] P 2: 101,1-102,3.
[21] Gilson, "Sens et Nature" 7f.
[22] Kohlenberger, Similitudo et Ratio 80.

to the *Cur Deus Homo* Anselm writes, "aperta ratione et veritate."[23] The relationship prospers in its openness. Both thinking and being must be reciprocally open and feel impelled towards truth. On the one hand being is open for cognition, i.e. mindful of itself as a thinking being. On the other hand cognition is open for being to ponder the same. In this scope, thinking's openness implies an unconditionedness. Thinking exhibits a dynamic component transcending mere facticity. The relationality of both and their respective constitution in their proper contexts occur where truth comes about.

This can be elucidated by recurring to the phrase "claritas veritatis" which also occurs in the *Cur Deus Homo.*[24] Truth by its very nature is open and lucid. It is yet an ongoing task to bring being to the "claritas veritatis." This occurs in thought which mediates between the two. Truth expresses the concord of being and thought. When being and reason collaborate, truth occurs and light appears. For this reason Anselm speaks of the luminosity of being and of the luminosity of reason: light "micat omne verum quod rationali menti lucet."[25] In light truth is evident. For this reason Ulrich chose the light motif as the keyword with which to interpret Anselm´s writings.[26]

As thinking is a process, it is also temporal. Temporality is typical for finite cogitation and characterizes also its ontological difference from being. In temporal reflection "esse in intellectu" and "esse in re" are different. And yet finite cogitation thinks in a seemingly timeless manner. Upon this background Anselm defines reason as follows: "mens ipsa ex omnibus quae facta sunt, sui memor et intelligens at amans esse potest."[27] "Ratio" is thereby the concurrence of three elements: "memoria," "intelligentia" and "amor."[28] They are constituting modi of the "ratio." The three are posited in a temporal sequence.[29] Thought aims at uniting in love what it produces from memory[30] and insight. Thought is remembering what is and what precedes it. Equally, thought implies recognition of objects. Finally it contains the moment of loving the contents of the cognitional process. This illustrates the personal and ethical involvement of the thinking subject. Thinking entails an ethical effort which expresses itself in the identification of the subject of cognition with the truth arrived at. The temporality of the cognitional act does not free one from the compulsory nature of truth.

The dimensions of memory are well discussed in the *Monologion.* This pre-cognitional memory (i.e. an a priori to memory) is constantly cause for new

---

[23] Cu Praef : 42,14f; Balthasar, Herrlichkeit II 226ff.
[24] Cu Praef : 42,14f. Cf. Balthasar, Herrlichkeit II 228.
[25] P 14: 112,5f.
[26] Ulrich, "Cur non video" 101ff.
[27] M 67: 78,1-2.
[28] M 50: 65,3-10.
[29] M 68: 79,5-6.
[30] Kohlenberger, Similitudo et Ratio 35.

insights and questions. "(P)rimum itaque quaerendum esse puto"[31]; "verum videor mihi vider quiddam quam studiose possum inquirere quod non negligenter discernere cogit"[32]; "sed ecce videtur mihi suboriri nec facilis nec ullatenus sub ambiguitate relinquenda quaestio."[33] The remembering is not only a recall of what precedes but also and yet more significantly constitutes it. This is the "se intelligere."[34] By not distinguishing between cogitation and awareness, Anselm seems to identify thought with the beginning of what precedes it. Thought and being are from the very beginning and in this respect original categories. Memory is a modality of thought.

This interpretation seems to be confirmed when considering, for instance, the observation a little further in the same chapter: "mens rationalis seipsam cogitando intelligit."[35] A certain degree of identity without a difference and, therefore, a remaining element of tension occur. By permitting itself to be engaged by itself cogitation understands itself. Then at the very same time unity and discernment occur. "Si enim mens humana nullam eius aut suam habere memoriam aut intelligentiam posset, numquam se ab irrationabilibus creaturis et illam (i.e. highest wisdom) ab omni creatura, secum tacite disputando, sicut nunc mens mea facit, discerneret."[36] Thinking apprehends itself through the cognitional act as different from all other things. It thinks from a unity and perceives differences. The immediacy of memory renders thinking primordial. By acknowledging differences among the objects perceived - and thus always considering the difference between thinking and being - it already overcomes the notion of difference towards a synthetic unity. This categoriality of unity does not merely mirror a cognitional effort towards those objects outside cognition; rather, it arrives at its very own unity.

Interpreting Anselm yet further: thought apprehends the primordial immediacy of all in all at the beginning. At that point of primordial immediacy, however, both thought and being have not yet arrived at their respective selves (awareness of the self in its proper constitution, i.e., givenness). Only by executing its proper self (i.e. by thinking) does cognition come to its own; it is more than mere potentiality. This act allows thought to perceive its contours. In their discerning act being and thought are apprehended as relational and thereby in their proper independence.

An additional definition of thought is amor.

---

[31] M 7: 20,29.

[32] M 9: 24,10.

[33] M 31: 48,17f.

[34] Cf. "rationalis mens possit non solum suimet et ipsius summae sapientiae reminisci, sed et illam et se intelligere." M 32: 51,8-9.

[35] M 33: 52,13.

[36] M 32: 51,9-12.

Cum et mens rationalis se et illum (God) amare posse convincatur, ex eo quia sui et illius memor esse et se et illum intelliger potest. Otiosa namque et penitus inutilis est memoria et intelligentia cuius libet rei, nisi prout ratio exigit res ipsa ametur aut reprobetur.[37]

The apprehended object is loved by thinking. Love perfects and completes cognition's self-execution. In so doing it ultimately apprehends God as the culminating and beloved object. Monastic contemplation thereby becomes the culmination of human cogitation. But this moment is contained and implied in every thinking act. True thought must be accompanied by love/charity. Otherwise, memory and recognition would be rendered futile.

In a way similar to Plotinus, Anselm perceives along these lines love has an undivided interest in the recognized "res ipsa." Love means unity. Love knows the vis-à-vis - ist a counterpart - in its proper valence and as a consequence also itself. Such love is more than mere recognition and acknowledgement of the other's existence. It is also a positive, welcoming affirmation. It constitutes a conscious decision for the other as expressed in confidence and fidelity. Such love affirms each in its distinctiveness and independence. Philosophy does not hesitate from the consequences its own endeavor entails. In this way it is more than "only" philosophy, - at least in the modern sense. It is open towards theology in way necessary for its self-understanding. This openness is a constitutive element of its self-definition.

This fiduciary moment of thought demonstrates the decisiveness and daring nature of cognition. These qualities are found at the beginning of every thinking act. Fidelity accompanies the thinking process. It implies acceptance of a yet unknown, thought-preceding origin. Such cognition yearns for a unity of thought and being, of "ratio" and "res ipsa." This union as relationship is not mere facticity but a task to be fulfilled ever anew. No one side can force it; it requires both to realize it. The one must trust the other to contribute its share. As a result one must conclude that cognition is

es in seiner Sinnspitze Lieben ist; denn nur so findet es seine Einheit und seine Vollendung, realisiert es die Beziehung zum Sein, die es will.[38]

Hence the relationship requires much more than what cognition alone can provide. The result implied at the beginning of thinking precedes thinking. In a way thinking traces these a priori footprints in its self-execution. Such pensive reflection reveals a surplus proper to cognition. This surplus has thinking address an agenda remaining always unfinished. Undeniably it is Karl Barth's contribution to Anselmian research to have pointed out this "eschatological" character of Anselm's writings.[39] Schmitt has drawn attention to the "futurum"

---

[37] M 49: 64,19-23.

[38] Kienzler, Glauben und Denken 46.

[39] Barth, Fides quaerens intellectum 19f.

in which so many of Anselm's verbs are set.[40] This surplus is also a part of what cognition must ponder. It thereby realizes that the envisioned unity of cognition and being can be anticipated but remains ever incomplete.

5.2 Consequences for Faith

Cogitation must be seen in its mental tension and balance with faith in order to appreciate the Anselmian way. Faith is the other beginning.[41] Faith does not commence with cogitation but with faith. This is the message of "fides quaerens intellectum" in the introduction to the *Proslogion*.[42] Faith begins by asking as regards its own cause and self-understanding. By understanding itself it desires to give itself an account and make itself transparent. Such is Anselm's definition of "intelligere." Faith entrusts itself completely and without reservation to reason/cogitation. The causes of the "fides" are found by way of the "ratio." The "ratio fidei" illumines faith for faith. Yet more than contributing to its self-understanding, reason renders faith luminous and reasonable. In some sense faith grounds a "ratio" yet without subverting the "ratio" - this quite analogous to Plato, who grounds dialectics in the state of puzzled bewonderment and mystical experience.

Again one sees applied the principle of the "sola ratione." Although possessing a separate and distinct origin, faith's origin can only be properly apprehended by reason. For all the "ratio" is the sole and ultimate arbiter. Anselm rejects all criteria commonly accepted by the Church and the general public. Scripture,[43] tradition,[44] church fathers[45] and other authorities[46] are roundly rejected. Even the historical Christ is being bracketed: "remoto Christo."[47] "Sola ratione" is his point d'appui to converse on matters of faith.[48]

---

[40] Siegward Richthammer, Die Systematik des Proslogionbeweises. Transzendentalphiloso-phische Überlegungen zu Anselms Beweis der Existenz Gottes, Diss. (Regensburg: Regensburg UP, 1996) 104; Schmitt, "Die wissenschaftliche Methode" 364; cf. Gilson, Sens et Nature 29ff.

[41] Either Barth does not appreciate this dual view he is thinking in terms of the concrete historical economy of salvation. He sees both in one moment combined: "Als credere des Credo ist der Glaube selber schon gewißermaßen ein intelligere, von dem intelligere, nach dem er 'verlangt', nur durch den Grad, nicht durch die Art verschieden." Fides quaerens intellectum 23f.

[42] P Proem: 94,7.

[43] Cu II 22: 133,6-8.

[44] I 1: 3,7ff.

[45] Cu I 1: 48,5-10.

[46] Cu I 2: 50,3-13.

[47] Cu Praef : 42,11-25.

[48] Barth, Fides quaerens intellectum 40ff; Koyré, L'idée de Dieu 32f.; Robert Pouchet, La Rectitudo chez Saint Anselme. Un Itinéraire Augustinien de l 'âme à Dieu. (Paris: Etudes Augustiniennes, 1976) at 19ff; Schmitt, "Die wissenschaftliche Methode" at 359f; cf. already Grabmann, Die Geschichte der scholastischen Methode 266; Richthammer, Die Systematik des Proslogionbeweises 30-33.

In a way Anselm stresses the beginning of reason to such an extent that the other beginning, namely that of faith, receives an elevation. This means faith and reason are so near to one another. One mirrors the other.[49] Precisely because of this reason Anselm can disregard faith. The demarcation of reason from faith signifies also the originality of faith vis-à-vis reason. Both possess their respective originality. This situatedness of both in a different ground is cause for reason to reflect on the cause of faith: "intelligere quod credimus,"[50] "quaecumque ... credimus;"[51] "ut quod fide tenemus ... necessariis rationibus probari possit."[52] One almost senses here that the exterior force of nature would suffice without a conscious integration with faith . However, this would imply too great a hiatus between the two.

Whereas the *Monologion* is defined as a "soliloquium," Anselm defines the *Proslogion* as an "alloquium," as an address of someone.[53] Its dialogic structure serves as underpinning for the author in this tractate. He addresses, prays to and narrates God. Pouchet demonstrates well Anselm's indebtedness in this regard to Augustine.[54] Here one beholds a countervailing moment. While the guiding star had previously been "Christo remoto" and "sola ratione," it now is faith. God is divined not merely as the object but also as the preceding origin and therefore subject of faith. We have a "solo Deo." "Intra in cubiculum mentis tuae, exclude omnia praeter deum et `clauso ostio´ quaere eum."[55] Everything but God should recede. When thinking approaches faith only God is a worthy object. The "mentis tuae" refers to the place where the intellectual theophany occurs. Simultaneously the whole of the human person is challenged to confront divine presence: "Dic nunc, totum `cor meum,´ dic nunc deo: `Quaero vultum tuum.´"[56]

In spite of all pondering, the desire of God remains sober enough to admit the existence of a "lux inaccessibilis." Human beings are unable to find the origin unless the origin yields itself. Both reason and existence must hope the origin will unveil itself. In this sense all history of faith, and this includes the history of thinking about God, is an unpronounceable catenation of histories of God with human beings. This becomes acutely present in a monastic context:

---

[49] Kienzler, Glauben und Denken 48; Schmitt, "Die wissenschaftliche Methode" 359f.

[50] P Proem: 94,2.

[51] P Proem: 93,9.

[52] I 6: 20,18f.

[53] P Proem: 93,20-94,12.

[54] Pouchet, La Rectitudo chez Saint Anselme 70ff.

[55] P 1: 97,7-9.

[56] Cf. Kohlenberger, Similitudo und Ratio 31.151, footnotes 9 and 90 respectively for references to the Augustinian concept of "cor." Kohlenberger holds the "mens" to be the place where the relationship between being and thinking is communicated:at 31; where practical decisions are made: 120ff. For "Quaero vultum tuum" cf. Henri de Lubac, Seigneur, je cherche.

doce cor meum ubi et quomodo te quaerat, ubi et quomodo te inveniat. Domine, si hoc non es, ubi te quaeriam absentem? Si autem ubique es, cur non video praesentem? Sed certe habitas, `lucem inaccessibilem.' Et ubi est lux inaccessibilis? Aut quomodo accedam ad lucem inaccessibilem? Aut quis me ducet et inducet in illam, ut videam te in illa? Deinde quibus signis, qua facie te quaeram?[57]

Nevertheless, one reads a few lines down that all existence already contains an indelible sign of the divine: "Denique ad te videndum factus sum, et nondum feci propter quod factus sum."[58] This origin impels the thinking subject to its destination: the "visio beatifica," face to face. In as much as one ponders history one becomes more intensely aware of the incongruency between the present and the past, between origin and reality. Alienation from God and divine seclusion and sovereignty increase proportionately. "O misera sors hominis, cum hoc perdidit ad quod factus est. Quare sic nobis observavit lucem, et obduxit nos tenebris? Quando restitues te nobis?"[59]

The history of God deigns not to bypass, or to ignore that of humanity but provokes and inspires human beings to take up the task of their own history. In the event of beholding the origin, the whole human being is addressed; therefore the use of the word "cor." This originating event is to become present ever anew. Such is the abiding call and task of both reason and faith. The primordial history is made into current history. Nothing less than this is the import of the words: "Fateor, domine, et gratias ago, quia creasti in me hanc imaginem tuam, ut tui memor te cogitem, te amem."[60] Remembering one's own past and pre-history ("memor tui") human beings arrive at the "te cogitem" in the sense of an assuring oneself of divine presence. The central chore is to realize "cogitare et amare."

A thus constituted faith seeks intellectual verification: "fides quaerens intellectum."[61] This understanding of faith is pivotal,[62] for only thereby does faith become luminous and reasonable: "negligentia mihi videtur, si postquam confirmati sumus in fide, non studemus quod credimus intelligere."[63] The two terms "deus" and "mens" play a central role. In the interplay of these words faith turns into temporal reality.[64] It comes from an origin, struggles for presence and awaits fulfillment. This dynamic element requires divine initiative: "esuriens incepi."[65] Every step taken by Anselm is undertaken under divine guidance. Yet it requires his own effort of walking along. For this reason he prays: "Doce me

---

[57] P 1: 98,1-6.
[58] P 1: 98, 14f.
[59] P 1: 98,16 and 99,2.
[60] P 1: 100, 12f.
[61] P 1: 100,17.
[62] Kienzler, Glauben und Denken 55.
[63] Cu I 1: 48,17.
[64] "Intellectus est medium inter fidem et speciem." Cu Com: 40,9f.
[65] P 1: 99,23f.

quaerere te, et ostende te quaerenti, quia nec quaerere te possum nisi tu doceas, nec invenire nisi te ostendas. Quaeram te desiderando, desiderando quaerendo. Inveniam amando, amem inveniendo."[66] The investigation, even the formulation of the question, require divine assistance. But it belongs to the paradox of human existence that one needs to inquire to discover God. Equally one cannot find God if one does not love Him. Yet one cannot love God if one does not find Him. The opportunity of temporality is that faith as a gift can occur. "The time is fulfilled, and the kingdom of God is close at hand. Repent, and believe the gospel: (Mk 1:15). Time may be the kairos of faith, provided God and human beings collaborate. Time as reflected presence is a gift; it is a surplus. This is the import of the following lines referring to God's image:

Sed sic est abolita attritione vitiorum ... ut non possit facere ad quod facta est, nisi tu renoves et reformes eam. Non tento, domine penetrare altitudinem tuam, quia nullatenus comparo illi intellectum meum; sed desidero aliquatenus intelligere veritatem tuam, quam credit et amat cor meum. Neque enim quaero intelligere ut credam, sed credo ut intelligam.[67]

As a consequence, faith transcends itself and reaches farther than the subject ever could envision. This results from the fact that faith is indebted to someone else than exclusively the believer. This someone else sustains the subject. Yet as this is being apprehended by the subject (who experiences him/herself also as the object of the faith event), he/she also beholds his/her alienation from the goal. God reveals Himself in His divinity. In this sense the believer remains pilgrim towards a goal: "fides quae per dilectionem operatur."[68] As the previous citation attests (= "nen tento ... penetrare altitudinem tuam ... sed desidero aliquatenus intelligere"), this cogitating subject of faith is well cognizant of this difference. Nevertheless, faith is a project to be realized in everyday life. The primordial "fides" demands an actualization which finds its concretization in and to the infinite tomorrow. Precisely it is cognition's nature to maintain the tension between "intellectus" and "visio." In fact, precisely by maintaining this tension, faith becomes current and present. Mindful of these factors, thought turns into rapt, reverent and prayerful thought. By remembering the preceding nature of faith, i.e. its primordial, originating origin, thought changes to grateful faith: "credit et amat cor meum."[69] The believer delights in the giver of the present of faith.[70] Such a grateful attitude on the part of the believer occasions a surrender to the giver, as a self-alignment towards the numinous, as a "tendere in deum."

---

[66] P 1: 100,8-11.
[67] P 1: 100,13-18.
[68] M 78: 85,6.
[69] P 1: 100,17.
[70] Both Balthasar, Herrlichkeit II 238ff and Barth, Fides quaerens intellectum 14f appreciate the notion of "delectatio."

132

The established formula of "fides quaerens intellectum" is also an indirect
predication of God. God is friendly towards human beings, for He had
established the cognitional, linguistic, historical and ontic conditions for a
rapport between Himself and humanity. Here Anselm draws heavily inter alia
on Augustinian thought. Augustine had observed, "Fides quaerit, intellectus
invenit" in his treatise *De Trinitate*.[71] In *De Libero Arbitrio* Augustine
observes

> Quamquam haec inconcussa fidei teneam, tamen quia cognitione nondum teneo, ita
> quaeramus quasi omnia incerta sint. ... Iam credentibus dicit (i.e. Jesus Christ): Quaerite ut
> invenietis: nam neque inventum dici potest quod incognitum creditur; neque quisquam
> inveniendo deo fit idoneus, nisi ante crediderit quod est postea cogniturus.[72]

The "quaerere" connotes the dynamic element in Christian existence. Ever anew
the quest must be undertaken to find a congruence between today and eternity.

Faith's point of departure in human existence is the "intellectus" already
to Augustine. "Aderit enim deus, et nos intelligere quod credimus faciet.
Praescriptum enim per prophetam gradum, qui ait: Nisi credideritis, non
intelligetis."[73] Out of its own freedom and its own origin can humanity
commences to begin. This occurs preeminently by way of initiating the
strenuous process of thought. The fact that the numinous is at the beginning of
this path requires more than what humanity by itself is able to muster. Faith
entails an "intelligere" as a symphonic accord between God and humanity;
between faith and reason.[74] For this reason no cheap excuse exists extricating
humanity from thinking credal contents. What faith states is also meant to be
reflected upon. This obligation is a part of what is meant by the term "imago
Dei." It is the "insipiens" who is unwilling to realize this and whom Anselm
feels called to criticize: "certe ipse idem insipiens cum audit hoc ipsum quod ...
intelligit est potest ipsi sibi saltem sola ratione persuadere."[75] This
understanding of faith is of such a general, common and universal nature that

---

[71] De trinit. I.14, c.2 (PL 42, 1058). In this context one might mention the Augustinian
correlation of "credere" and "intelligere" in: De liberum arbitrium I.1,c.2,4 (PL 32, 1224f);
I.1.,c.3,6 (PL 32, 1224f). For a more extensive discussion of Anselm's indebtedness to
Augustinian terms cf. de Lubac, Seigneur, je cherche 213ff. and especially Pouchet, Rectitudo
70ff.
[72] De lib. arb. 1.2,c.2,5f (PL 32,1243f).
[73] De lib. arb. I.1,c.3,6 (PL 32, 1225).
[74] M 1: 13,5-11; Cu 1: 48,2.22; P 4: 104,6f.
[75] P 2: 101,5-9. cf. already Augustine's reference to the "insipiens" in De libero arbitrio.
   "Si quis ergo illorum insipientium, de quibus scriptum est: Dixit insipiens in corde
suo. Non est Deus (Psal. LII,1), hoc tibi diceret, nec vellet tecum credere quod credis, sed
cognoscere utrum vera credideris; relinqueresne hominem, an aliquo modo, quod
inconcussum tenes, persuadendum esse arbitrareris; praesertim si ille non obluctari
pervivaciter, sed studiose vellet agnoscere?"
De lib. arb. I.2,c.2,5 (PL 32, 1242).

everyone is called to entrust him/herself completely to cognition. By believing and hearing the credal contents, the believer is empowered to think faith: "aut non audiendo aut non credendo ignorat intelligit."[76] Thought must engage the credal contents. This is the most radical of forms. However, the yield is equally radical, for it demonstrates the congruence of the two goals (of faith and thought) to be one and the same. Thought and faith are one in the cognitional investigation. In the *Cur Deus Homo* Anselm observes of the infidel: "Quamvis enim ideo rationem quaerunt, quia non credunt, nos vero, quia credimus: unum idemque tamen est quod quaerimus."[77]

Upon this background Anselm observes, quoting from Scripture in the *Proslogion* "Nam et hoc credo: quia, `nisi credidero, non intelligam.'"[78] The Anselmian notion of "credere" encompasses both thinking and faith. The one occasions the other. While not mentioning it, of course, Anselm as a pre-Scholastic monk, assumes a unity of philosophy and theology which is existentially important for both disciplines to be cognizant of. Only by bearing this in mind can each discipline live up to its specific mission. Both must be interdisciplinary and make cross references in order to acquire their proper profiles. As theology is the fulfillment of philosophy, faith is the fulfillment of thought: "ut eorum quae credunt intellectu et contemplatione delectentur."[79]

Faith stimulates thought in two ways. It keeps the destiny of thought present and prevents thought from subjugating and perverting the contents of thought. Faith safeguards the orientation, purity and veracity of thought.[80] Thus perceived thought can never degenerate into a sophistic exercise. Faith never permits thought to come to rest, unless it is transfigured into faith.[81]

Precisely for this reason there is a unity of purpose and yet a difference between faith and reason. This difference is again a relational one. This means it arises from their relationship and serves this relationship. While the believer may begin from faith, the non-believer may start from reason. The outcome of both diametrically opposed endeavors is the same: "Quamvis enim (= non-believers) ideo rationem quaerunt, quia non credunt, nos vero, quia credimus: unum idemque tamen est quod quaerimus."[82] As this evidences, cogitation is in constant rotation from and around itself by virtue of rotating constantly from and around its origin. Genuine thinking thereby demonstrates the actualization of the origin. Again one apprehends the unity of thought/meditation and ontic

---

[76] M 1: 13,9.

[77] Cu I 3: 50,18ff.

[78] P 1: 100.19; again cf. Augustine, <u>De lib. arb.</u> I.1,c.2,4 (PL 32, 1224).

[79] Cu I 1: 47,9.

[80] This is what Söhngen wishes to convey: "Anselm faßt augustinisch den Glauben heilspädagogisch als `fides purgans' (cor, intellectum) auf (mit Berufung auf Apg 15,9)." Söhngen, <u>Die Einheit der Theologie</u> 90.

[81] Cu Com: 40,9f; cf. Lubac, <u>Seigneur, je cherche</u> 216f.

[82] Cu I 3: 50,18ff.

reality. And yet do God and faith remain on the outermost fringes of cogitation. Also this attests Anselm's affinity to Plotinus.

In this temporality of the two parameters of human existence, faith and reason, not nothing but something is being revealed, albeit as ineffable. The difference of faith and reason is qualitatively different from the difference between the donor of the gift of faith and the recipient. While the first difference is caused by temporality alone, the second difference is caused by the ontic difference of finite and infinite being.

In summary one can agree with Kienzler's remark:

> Anselms Denken ist ein Ganzes, das nach seiner Einheit sucht, wenn diese Einheit auch nur approximativ angedeutet werden kann, da sie selbst nicht im Denken, sondern in der Übergabe des Denkens an den Glauben, letztlich in Gott, stattfindet.[83]

Anselm's vision is a complete, coherent and exhaustive one. Yet, it refrains, precisely for that reason, from becoming a complete, self-contained system. Anselm's writings contain careful, faint hints. They require further adumbrations which this reflection attempts to accomplish in part. Anselm's innovation is the - at first glance almost heretical - emphasis on the role of the "ratio."

Does this, the first reflection on the relationship of faith and reason, already permit a new appreciation of Anselm's writings? For this reason it is of particular importance to see what role it plays in his subsequent writings. Does it assume a formative role not only in a part but in the whole of his theological program? Only after establishing this overarching tension of philosophy and theology in the treatises *Monologion* and *De Veritate,* can one then address the ontological argument in the *Proslogion* and subsequently and finally the central issue of incarnation and atonement in *Cur Deus Homo.*

5.3 The "Ratio" as the *Monologion's* Leitmotiv

This treatise represents Anselm's first attempt to reflect in a thorough and radical manner on the import of the notion of "ratio." As this thinking thinks matters divine, one asks the possibilities of thinking truth. How do true statements come about? For this purpose it is helpful to consult subsequently *De Veritate.*

It is noteworthy that Anselm himself professes the intention of speaking not of the "ratio" but rather of God and the divine properties. Yet he wishes to do this solely by using "ratio." "Ratio" may be used in the undifferentiated sense of "thinking." This is a felicitous translation, for Anselm introduced no subtle distinctions and because it expresses best the unity, originality (in the meaning of "going back to the origins") and wholeness of the Anselmian understanding

---

[83] Kienzler, Glauben und Denken 69.

of the "ratio." Never again would a period provide a similar context in which to reflect upon the term in such a singularly merciless and radical form.

Unfortunately Anselm is not very helpful in providing a logical presentation of the material. Only in chapters 64 to 68 does he treat the notion "ratio." Prior to these chapters he addressed issues of divinity and trinity. After chapter 68 he turned to the "visio beatifica." The recourse to the conditions for knowing God renders a pondering of the possibilities and limits of thought necessary in order to determine its range. After preparatory considerations in chapters sixty six and sixty seven, chapter sixty eight provides an abbreviated definition of "ratio."

In chapter sixty six Anselm defines two steps for thought

Cum igitur quia nihil de hac natura possit percipi per suam proprietatem sed per aliud, certum est quia per illud magis ad eius cognitionem acceditur, quod illi magis per similitudinem propinquat.[84]

Thought does not arrive at the interior of divine existence: the "esse per se." Thought remains a foreigner. "Per aliud" is as a consequence the way for thought to proceed. Yet by premonitions of divine essence, "ratio" experiences its very own agony. Its only possibility is to contemplate via "similitudo." No longer then does thought consider its limits, but it apprehends itself as posited in a creaturely relationship to God. The reflecting human being knows himself "qua homine creato." Then God is no longer a distant entity and the most extreme towards which the human mind can wander, but simultaneously the innermost that is given to thought. This "similitudo" then is so central for the constitution of the human mind that without it it no longer is capable of functioning.

The second step follows from this:

Quid igitur apertius quam quia mens rationalis quanto studiosius ad se discendum intendit, tanto efficacius ad illius cognitionem ascendit; et quanto seipsam intueri negligit, tanto ab eius speculatione descendit.[85]

In an almost apodictic manner Anselm asserts that the approach towards God can succeed only via thought. This means a fundamental disposition of thought is to place itself into the question of God and to comprehend itself from within the relationship to God. By recognizing and understanding itself, i.e. by becoming self-conscious, it becomes aware of its "similitudo" with the Divine.

As a consequence, from its very inception (contingent) thought is relational thinking: as it is self-recognition (as being contingent) it acquires therein (i.e. in the act of self-recognition) a pre-disposition for the recognition of God (as "actus purus"). This relationality to an absolute as the unconditioned

---

[84] M 66: 77,7-9.
[85] M 66: 77,21-24.

136

- the numinous - is incontrovertibly and irrevocably engrained in every human consciousness. Later the "similitudo" between created thinking and highest thinking will become Anselm's main concern. This idea is already further elaborated in the subsequent chapter where Anselm introduces the concept of "imago Dei." Thought experiences itself by apprehending itself as "imago Dei." It not merely acknowledges but affirms in a loving way this facticity. "Quod mens ipsa speculum eius et imago eius sit ... sui memor et intellligens et amans esse potest."[86] In the cognitional process thought becomes "speculum Dei" and is aware of it. By recognizing itself it intimates some of the modi of being within God: "Nam si mens ipsa sola ex omnibus quae facta sunt, sui memor et intelligens et amans esse potest: non video cur negatur esse in illa vera imago illius essentiae, quae per sui memoriam et intelligentiam et amorem in trinitate ineffabili consistit."[87] The reciprocal mirroring of the Divine and of thought becomes perfect when considering that he had distilled in previous chapters the concept of a trinitarian God from the terms "memoria," "intelligentia" and "amor." This mirror is the only approach to knowing God. For this reason knowing God is knowing oneself.

After establishing the context within which thought can be thought, the necessary connection of God and thought and the wholeness of thought, Anselm investigates the purpose and meaning of creating thought: "propter quid rationalis creatura facta sit?" and follows "(c)onsequi itaque videtur quia rationalis creatura nihil tantum debet studere, quam hanc imaginem sibi per naturalem potentiam impressam per voluntarium effectum exprimere."[88]

It is telling that Anselm sees thought confronted with an ethical task. In all of the "corpus Anselmi" a "debere" is always contained as a prevenient moment to thinking. Thought must correspond to "debere," a "should," which it is not at thinking's disposition to accept or reject. Thinking must correspond in its self-execution of this obligation. Thinking is called to this ethical effort, to this travail. This "studere debet" calls thought to confront reality and yet it does not arise from palpable reality alone. Rather it is a consequence of humanity's constitution as "imago Dei." This is connatural to the human state: "per naturalem potentiam impressam." So it comes that thought is by its nature mirror or image of its origin. This seems a chance, a possibility, at first glance. The call to actualize this potential is the constitution of thought's freedom and consequently of human freedom per se. By following this "debere", thinking actuates its "imago Dei." Thought liberates itself towards its being-image and, therefore, to its origin. By actuating this freedom, thought is brought in relation to and from God. From the createdness and from the awareness of the same it follows that thought thinks itself under an obligation. This call again implies that thinking knows itself to be created ("creanti se debet"). This is the meaning

---

[86] M 67: 77,26 and 78,1-2.
[87] M 67: 78,1-4.
[88] M 68: 78,14-16.

of: "Et enim praeter hoc quia creanti se debet hoc ipsum quod est: hinc quoque
quia nil tam praecipuum posse quam reminisci et intelligere et amare summum
bonum cognoscitur, nimirum nihil tam praecipue debere velle convincitur."[89]
Therefore, the "debere" is not merely co-implied with thinking but equally with
the concept of God. God also provides the thinking subject with the necessary
"posse." A fundamental volition which is not all accidental underlies all
thought. It is significant that this volition is acknowledged and wanted by
thought. This means a "posse." Yet this ability would not be helpful were it to
lead to a judging.[90] There is no at-randomness in the thinking of Anselm. This
means that, thinking bethinks its ethical imperative according to its fittingness,
which is revealed when contemplating its origin.

In this way thinking matures into knowledge of its "imago Dei"quality.
Reality is a surplus going beyond mere "potestas." Thinking is the freedom to
become that towards which it had been created. As thinking is more than mere
thinking, likewise "posse" is more than plain potentiality. Freedom is more than
a grand scheme.

Thinking becomes the volitional execution of its own originality. In this
manner it actuates itself. Such is the import of "(q)uis enim neget quaecumque
meliora sunt in potestate, ea magis debere in voluntate?"[91] There is a tension-
filled space through which the monk guides the reader. Between potentiality
and volition, should and doing, givenness and execution, possibility and reality,
destiny and freedom, thinking becomes apparent as a dynamic entity. Is,
therefore, the "ratio" merely the intersection of various vectors which the
thinking subject is forced to approve of?

The text continues:

(d)enique rationali naturae non est aliud esse rationalem, quam posse discernere
iustum a non iusto, verum a non vero, bonum a non bono, magis bonum a minus bono. Hoc
autem posse omnino inutile illi est et supervacuum, nisi quod discernit amet aut reprobet
secundum verae discretionis iudicium. Hinc itaque satis patentur videtur omne rationale ad
hoc existere, ut sicut ratione discretionis aliquid magis vel minus   bonum sive non bonum
iudicat, ita magis vel minus id amet aut respuat. Nihil igitur quam rationalem
creaturam ad hoc esse factam, ut summam essentiam amet super omnia bona, sicut ipsa est
summum bonum; immo ut nihil amet nisi illam aut propter illam, quia illa est bona per se, et
nihil aliud est bonum nisi per illam. Amare autem eam nequit, nisi eius reminisci et eam
studuerit intelligere.[92]

The corollary function to the "ratio" is "discernere." That term frequently
recurs in Anselm's writings. It connotes the discriminatory function of "ratio."
By discerning between good and incorrect statements, good and bad, more good

---

[89] M 68: 78,16-19.
[90] M 68: 78,21-79,6.
[91] M 68: 78,19f.
[92] M 68: 78,21-79,6.

or less good the fundamental feature of thinking as image of God is conveyed. It is the "posse" which enables the "discernere." While this action of distinguishing is necessary to thinking, it does not occur automatically. The "posse" implies also a difference between what is and what should be. A thinking that is content in being mere potentiality is completely useless: "inutile et supervacuum." Using "discernere", it must struggle to reach a "iudicium."

Thinking must confront the decisions it ought (= "debere") to make. To this extent a qualifying, i.e. evaluating, confrontation with reality is its innermost obligation. However, in the deciding process it also defines what reality is. A thinking corresponding to the call of "iudicare" either loves or rejects something: "amet aut reprobet." In this way Anselm prepares the reader for the final chapter in the *Monologion*. This is the purpose particularly of the summarizing sentence of chapter sixty eight: "Clarum ergo est rationalem creaturam totum suum posse et velle ad memorandum et intelligendum et amandum summum bonum impendere debere, ad quod ipsum esse se cognoscit habere."[93] This may serve as a definition of Anselm's understanding of "ratio." It is creaturely in its constitution and therefore (as self-awareness) contains an "imago Dei" quality. The totality of such a constituted "ratio" is "posse et vele." This potentiality and volition receive their proper drive from the "debere." Thereby it realizes freedom. By wanting what it should, it realizes its "imago Dei" quality. By remembering, recognizing and loving cognition comprehends its proper self.

Thinking is for the monk the correspondence, or "similitudo," to the thought object in the preceding manner. Thinking is called to relate to its very own originality. This is the abiding concern. To become "imago Dei" is the great enterprise of cognition. In the categoriality of thinking, it retraces its prehistory by virtue of its "potentia impressa." Nevertheless, thinking reaches its destiny "per voluntarium effectum."

The preceding reflections convey Anselm's emphasis on the relationality of thought both as an intellectual facticity and as a task yet to be realized by thinking. It possesses apart from any other (natural) human component the quality of "imago Dei." The circumstance of being image evokes as task the endeavor to have this image take on figure, gain profile and take on form. This is the central meaning and consequence of the concept of "debere." It is the burden and joy of freedom to address this task head on "per voluntarium effectum." This "velle" represents the lasting reflectivity of thinking.

Upon this background the previously supplied outline of Anselm's understanding of "ratio" as akin to that of Plotinus gains credibility. It is the direct result of the afore-presented considerations.

The introductory lines of the *Monologion* lose their quality of over-confidence. The words are corroborated by the subsequent argumentation: "Si

---

[93] M 68: 79,5-11.

quis unam ... aliaque per plura, quae de deo sive de eius creatura necessarie credimus, aut non audiendo aut non credendo ignorat: puto quia ea ipsa ex magna parte, si vel mediocris ingenii est, potest ipse sibi saltem sola ratione persuadere."[94] The "ignorans," i.e. the one who rejects faith - "aut non audiendo aut non credendo ignorat,"[95] - can discover the afore-described exclusively by thinking. Absolutely no precondition is admitted to this discussion. [96] This "sola ratione" principle is a self-securing step for Anselm.[97] Such confidence or faith thrusts forward toward thinking. The beginning credal statement can be transformed into thought: the "bonitas" of religious thought can be translated into the "bonum" of philosophy. The self-assurance gained from the credal statement thereupon is put aside. Exclusively via thought, thought is to come to its own: to its origin and destination - God. The "bonitas Dei" enjoys a central position in Anselm's theological reflections. For this reason the aim of thought is not merely a nebulous, undefined or unencountered God but the God already experienced as "bonus." Hence he intends to arrive "sola ratione" at the property of God and at the same time at the "bonitas Dei." The "bonitas Dei" is both his point of departure and the port of destination for all cognitional travail.

This determination is of no small importance for determining Anselm's philosophical lineage. Schmitt claims the "bonum" is avoided in Anselm's writings.[98] Flasch particularly argued against this position. The question is important insofar as it can define Anselm as either a Neo-Platonist (Flasch) or more as an Aristotelian (Schmitt). While there is no gainsaying that one does not encounter in Anselmian literature the term good that often, it does enjoy a prominent and indeed pivotal role in the "Corpus Anselmi."[99] Proponents of an Aristotelian reading of Anselm fail to consider the numerous places he mentions "beatitudo" as the eschatological arrival of the human being at the Divine "bonum" and the history of reception Anselm is placed into.[100] Whoever affirms the central role "bonum" plays in Anselm's thinking will agree with an

---

[94] M 1: 13,5,11.

[95] M 1: 13,9f.

[96] Koyré, L'Idée de Dieu 35ff; Schmitt, "Anselm und der (Neu-)Platonismus" 39ff; Schurr, Die Begründung der Philosophie 31ff.; Paul Vignaux, "La Méthode de Saint Anselme dans le Monologion et le Proslogion." Aquinas, Ephemerides Thomisticae VII (1965): 110-129, at 110ff; Vignaux, "Structure et sens" 132ff.

[97] Barth, Fides quaerens intellectum 40ff.

[98] Schmitt, "Anselm und der (Neu-)Platonismus" 39ff, "Anselm weicht ... dem Wort bonum aus" 53.

[99] M 1: 13, 4-15,2; 4: 16,31-18,3; 6: 20,1f; 7: 21,20-28; 16: 30,9-11; 19: 34,11-14; 53: 66,11f; 68: 79,16-19; 69: 79,21; 70: 80,21f; 74: 83,5; 80: 86,22. 87,1-7; 71: 81,9; P Proem : 93,7ff; 5: 104,14ff, 12: 110,6-8; 22: 117,18; 23: 117,6.20.22; 25:I 118,25f; Ca 1: 234,29-235,7; I 8: 22,22ff; 23,3-5.

[100] This is particularly the case with Cur Deus Homo; cf. Flasch, "Der philosophische Ansatz" 5; Vanni-Rovighi, "L'Etica di S. Anselmo" 86ff. Yet see also M 1: 13,5-14,3; 69: 79,28-80,2; P 25: 118, 11-120,20; 26: 120, 21-122,2; Ca 4: 241,13f; Cu I 11: 281,5-12; I 13: 285,19ff.

140

axiological and teleological character to his thinking.[101] Flasch argues for a close relationship between "ens" and "bonum" - as will later become yet more present in the Scholastic axiom: "ens et verum convertuntur."[102]

Very much in the tradition of Plato, Plotinus and Augustine the "bonitas Dei" is the "bonum per se." Nevertheless, Anselm is much intent on stressing that there is a multitude of possibilities which start thinking. Yet the "bonum" seems most suitable: "Si quis unam naturam, summum omnium quae sunt, ... sunt aut quod aliquomodo bene sunt, per omnipotentem bonitatem suam dantem et facientem, ..."[103] As Schmitt readily admits, Anselm chose the "bonum" as his point of departure because this had been familiar to him from reading Augustine.[104] By making such a decision, however, no credal assent is required, for universally every human being strives for the good: "Et enim cum omnes frui solis iis appetant quae bona putant."[105]

By positing the "bonum" at the beginning of his deliberations as a commonly self-evident value, Anselm has made a significant preliminary decision.[106] Well prior to any cognition, human beings are placed in the position of choosing and deciding between things according to a subjectively assumed criterion of good. This sheds light both on Anselm and on thinking as such.

While not thematizing the "bonum" in a manner commensurate to the role it plays in his thought, it is nevertheless the formative element in Anselm's philosophy.[107] The facticity of the human state as one poised between the good and the bad is to him so blatantly obvious that further discussion would likely have seemed redundant to him. Choosing the life of a monk along with a multitude of others in a monastery and the fact that in early Medieval society monastic life was frequently considered the pinnacle of what a human purpose could desire, may explain why the Abbot of Bec saw no need to elaborate in extenso on this central aspect of his writings.

A further reason for the choice of the "bonum" as the formative principle of his reflections may have been that cognition does not depart from a tabula rasa. It does not produce "ex nihilo" the "bonum." Rather "bonum" is pre-

---

[101] Flasch, "Der philosophische Ansatz" 2ff; similarly Kohlenberger, Similitudo und Ratio 173ff.
[102] In this vein Flasch argues: "Die Wahrheit ist für Anselm zugleich Sein und Gutheit. Das ergibt sich aus ihrer teleologischen Ableitung; wenn ein Wesen oder eine Tätigkeit die spezifische Aufgabe erfüllt, die ihnen gestellt ist, dann erreichen sie ihr wahres Sein und ihre Gutheit." Flasch, "Zum Begriff der Wahrheit" 336.
[103] M 1: 13,4-8.
[104] Schmitt, "Anselm und der (Neu-)Platonismus" 47ff.; cf. De trinit. I.8, c.3.4 (PL 42, 949ff).
[105] M 1: 13,12f.
[106] Flasch well illustrates the ramifications of this choice, cf. Flasch, "Der philosophische Ansatz" 4ff.
[107] Cf. Henri Rondet, "Grâce et péché, l'augustinisme de Saint Anselme." Spicilegium Beccense I (Paris: Vrin, 1959): 155-169, at 158ff; Sofia Vanni-Rovighi, Sant' Anselmo e la filosofia del secolo XI (Milano: Vita e Pensiero, 1949) at 64.

141

cognitional and therefore what cognition is given as a task to contemplate on. By considering the self-evident as self-evident, cognition experiences its very own self. As a consequence its self-consciousness is heightened.

It is of interest to examine more closely how Anselm perceives the dimensions of reflection in cognition. As he observes already at the beginning, his thinking wants to persuade: "persuadere."[108] It is his intention to remain attentive to what all people do: "aestimo esse promptissimum ... mentis oculum convertere."[109] Only in this openness of cognition for all assumed things can thinking commence working:

> in promptu est, ut aliquando mentis oculum vertat ad investigandum illud, unde sunt bona ea ipsa, quae non appetit nisi quia iudicat esse bona, ut deinde ratione ducente et illo prosequente ad ea quae irrationabiliter ignorat, rationabiliter proficiat.[110]

Obviously in this passage a distinction is introduced between "mens" and "ratio." "Mens" is the place of experience and perception of something pre-cognitional. In contrast, "ratio" is the self-execution of cognition.[111] Anselm takes "Quasi necessarium" as a beginning as long as no other convincing authority comes in sight ("maior auctoritas").[112] It is the human being him/herself who gives testimony to this facticity, however "tacitus" this may occur. In a way his approach is quite modern and very anthropocentric. As a result every well-intentioned person ought to be capable of following his or her deliberations and sharing with one another the truth of the results one arrives at, lest one be an "insipiens." For what is obvious to human action is necessarily also obvious to human thinking. In his judgment there can be no intelligent argument raised against his conclusions. From such an approach, that departs in this way from within itself, indubitable and indispensable conclusions result: "Ergo consequitur."[113]

Unfortunately, Anselm does not intimate the ramifications of the choice which "bonum" has for thought, yet the consequences of such an approach would render these more lucid. Perhaps Anselm chose something as commonplace and as tangible as the good to offer an easier access to the highly unnatural and uncommon way of thinking about thinking itself. Moreover, the thinking subject and thinking itself possess a vested interest in the good. The

---

[108] M 1: 13,11.
[109] M 1: 13,12.14.
[110] M 1: 13,13-14,1.
[111] Kohlenberger, Similitudo und Ratio 113f; Schmitt, "Die wissenschaftliche Methode" 358ff.
[112] M 1: 14,1ff.
[113] M 1: 15,6. Flasch calls this modus operandi a "Phänomenologie des natürlichen Bewusstseins" and compares it with Kant's transcendental procedure. Flasch, "Zum Begriff der Wahrheit" 326.

142

interest in the "bonum" is always expressive of a curiosity in the self. This in turn entices thinking to think the beginning and origin of its thinking.

In a certain sense the good awakens thinking to its very own origin by drawing it (= reason) outside itself. The consequences for cognition are not paltry. The "bonum" structures thinking and its execution. It arouses interest in something beyond the subject's immediate horizon and this object refers back to the self of the subject. Thus two interesting movements in opposite directions are occasioned by the "bonum." These movements render thinking conscious thinking. The something that thinking apprehends is again open for something else and opens in turn thinking for yet more and this may continue an infinite number of times. Thinking is never satisfied, never exhausted with something singular, a concrete good, but remains open to an all-encompassing whither and whence.

Thinking broadens in the process in such a way that anything approaching it as thinkable arouses thinking's interest. Kienzler defines this principal self-transcending constitution of thinking as:

So findet sich das Denken in einem unendlichen Zug des Strebens und Erfülltwerdens vor, wenn es sich mit dem "bonum" befasst, das das menschliche Denken überhaupt prägt.[114]

The Augustinian tension of "appetere" (= "strive" for something) and "frui" (= "fulfillment") is very much present also in Anselmian thinking. Together these terms point to a salient feature of finite thinking. It contains something outstanding - the not-yet of creation. It contains already in the now of contingent existence an eschatological anticipation.

Original (= "origin-making") interest relates to a "bonum" which is not a simple given and at one´s arbitrary disposition, but which is withdrawn and even withheld. Since it has an immanent interest to be itself in the other, thinking is fundamentally relational. Not merely is it passively posited into a relationship, it also discovers interest in itself and as a consequence defines itself from within this relationship. Once the "bonum" is recognized by thinking, thinking wants to maintain this relationship with the "bonum" and uphold it as its goal.

Vice versa, the "bonum" is also a dynamic entity that not merely is but at the same is for something else. It is true to itself when it also reaches beyond the self. Consequently it also contains moments of unity and alienness, of self-identity and its intrinsic transcendent orientation, of identity and difference. First and foremost the "bonum" is a whole which supplies the justification for any yearning for goodness and unity. Anselm calls this union of unity and goodness: "unum bonum."[115] It belongs to the intrinsic feature of the "bonum" to be yearned for. Therefore, it is equally relational as thinking in Anselm's

---

[114] Kienzler, Glauben und Denken 86.
[115] M 17: 31,14.

understanding. It communicates itself in the "iudicare" so that other things might be found good. Only insofar as the subject perceives something as good can the confronted object also gain the profile of being known as good. The dialogical structure of thought is mirrored in the dialogical structure of the "bonum."

Such a defined relationship is, however, more than only the total sum of two entities. It expresses a surplus which can be translated into a moral "more" or "less:" "magis et minus bonum."[116] The relationship requires a concrete vis-à-vis. Only by being good through the one or other good - "aliud per aliud"[117] - does it arrive at the primarily intended good: "bonum per seipsum."[118]

The expression "per aliud et aliud" of the individual things being good also implies that the "bonum" occurs in temporality and in sequence. The (contingent) subject is inextricably placed into a network of relations: withholding and fulfilling; by striving for good it labors to have past and future become present; the relationship is not itself, but always precedes and antecedes the subject. It must relate to individual "bona" in order to relate to the "bonum."

In this manner both thinking itself and the beginning of thinking can be retraced and read from the "bonum." The "bonum" embraces not merely the individual "bona" but equally the whole of thinking. The "bonum" is in such a radical manner relational that it unfolds itself in the striving of thinking. Again the thinking has the "bonum" unfold itself by perceiving it in its very own self-execution as desirable. Thereby the relationship between the good and thinking can in turn be predicated as good.

5.4 Thought and Similitude

The question arising now is how to preserve the unity of thinking in spite of its own transcendentality. This, however, can be achieved by utilizing the term "similitudo." It permits correlations which bring forth the relationship of the whole to the part, cause to effect, image to original.[119]

This central connection between transcendence and "similitudo" has also been addressed by Vuillemin. He considers it a hinge point for a proper appreciation of the ontological argument.[120] According to him transcendence and similarity are two indispensable terms for any philosophical treatment of the question of God. In his judgment any thought of God requires three prerequisites:

1. the created world - insofar as one is able to perceive it through senses and cognition,

2. a positive or negative relationship to God and

---

[116] M 1: 14,10f.

[117] M 1: 14,18.

[118] M 1: 15,5.

[119] Kohlenberger, Similitudo und Ratio 61.

[120] This argument will be treated further down.

3. an understanding of the transcendence which protects God vis-à-vis the created order.

These three conditions can be described as those of the concrete given, the condition of a chain of similarity and the condition of transcendence. Reason's challenge is to arrive from the plateau of the created and similar to something transcendent.[121] This suffices to illustrate how important for Anselm it must be to discuss creation in chapters 1 through 4, transcendence in chapter four of the *Monologion*, and subsequently at disparate locations "similitudo" before arriving at the ontological argument in the *Proslogion*.

Without this consideration, the previous path in the *Monologion* apppears altogether strange and wanting bearings. Anselm intended to speak of matters divine, and instead he spoke of the "ratio" without any prerequisites: "sola ratione." On such secure foundations he wanted to approach the divine. Within the course of these reflections he discovers this only to be possible if thinking radically changes itself. The path to God changes into the path to thinking. By contemplating the highest possible object, thinking discovers itself. In search of knowledge of God, it found self-knowledge. By discovering its heteronomy it recovered its autonomy.

At first sight two different cognitional paths seem to exist. The first, causal approach intends to uncover in thinking its very principles and constitution. Thinking strives to illumine, and thus ground itself. No matter how hard this grounding of thinking pushed, it could only discover an unending number of finite causes. The searched for a "summum" became proportionately nebulous. As the searched for the object became invisible, thinking also experienced itself as groundless and began to founder.

The second way, best termed transcending thinking, leads beyond the confines of thought. It resembles a daring leap into the unknown, seeking a ground beyond the self. By so doing, thinking experienced itself as open for transcendence. To the same degree that it was reaching out into a transcendent realm, it found a greater self-awareness. Dialectical movements result in unity. Thinking's heteronomy acquires the quality of its own autonomy. Thinking becomes more what it is by becoming cognizant of its transcendence.

There is no gainsaying as it stands, the position arrived at must pose a riddle to the reader, for what is presumed to be the cause of a transcending thinking - which is an original and originating thinking - has not yet been disclosed. Equally it is an enigma how heteronomous thinking actually is autonomous thinking. How should self-identical thinking remain true to itself by beholding in something else its beginning and cause? How can a heteronomous God be the cause of an autonomous "ratio?"

[121] Jules Vuillemin,"Id quo maius cogitari potest. Über die innere Möglichkeit eines rationalen Gottesbegriffs." Archiv für Geschichte und Philosophie 53 (1971): 279-299, at 281.

There must be a correspondence[122] between thinking and its transcendent cause. Otherwise the two movements - namely reaching out to the infinitely other and grasping the intimately known - cannot form a unit which constitutes an epistemological and ontic process for thinking. From itself thinking needs to be open for and toward self-transcendence. Anselm had expressed this foundational correspondence between thinking and its transcendence as "similitudo."[123]

A transcending thinking implies a cognitional faculty as its cause and ground. This faculty is at the same time and under the same consideration both within itself and outside itself. In order for this cause to be truly the cause for all further causations and thinking it must be transparent and luminous. Only thereby can it become the foundational cause of all. In the process of thinking, it turns into an image or a mirror of transcendence, namely into a "similitudo."[124] Thinking is both this "similitudo" and an actuation of this "similitudo." As all thinking is thought from this transcendent source/cause, all must become transparent and luminous upon this transcendent background. On the other hand, all must be apprehended and defined as caused from this final cause. Thinking as thinking uncovers this cause. Indeed, it belongs to the essence of thinking not only to stand in relationship with this first thought but to realize constantly anew this "similitudo."[125]

When speaking of "similitudo" in the greater context of the *Monologion,* Anselm is not concerned in delineating the nature and structure of the term itself. By necessity the term is arrived at as a result of pondering the natures of divinity and thought. As a result the present definition of Anselm's understanding of "similitudo" is but a preliminary one. Nonetheless, this definition of "similitudo" is imperative. Without it, the correspondence of first thinking and transcendental cause to thinking cannot be established. Thinking does not find first thinking and its transcendental cause available and present. The *point d'appui* of thinking is solely "similitudo." The next question is from what does thinking know "similitudo" to be its ancillary entity? Moreover, from where does contingent thinking possess the certitude that in company with "similitudo" it has the ability to apprehend thinking per se? It is only within the thinking act that this circumstance becomes apparent. How, or yet better (thought from cognition's result in hindsight) who can it be that thinking becomes cognizant of in its own measure and mindful of its own origin? This measure must be gained by thinking from within itself. To this extent it is correct to speak of a circular movement.[126]

---

[122] Cf. for the Platonic-Augustinian background, Flasch, "Der philosophische Ansatz" 34ff.
[123] M 31: 49,9-11.21-23; 66: 77,7-19; cf. P 1: 100,12f. for "imago."
[124] Kohlenberger, Similitudo und Ratio 37ff.
[125] Gillian R. Evans, "St. Anselm's Analogies," Vivarium XIV (1976): 81-93, at 81ff; Flasch, "Zum Begriff der Wahrheit" 349ff; Schmitt, "Anselm und der (Neu-)Platonismus" 60ff.
[126] Vuillemin, Le Dieu d'Anselme 32ff.

To sustain the assertion that thinking is the only way to reflect upon one's own thinking of and towards the highest Being, we must consider a tension in contingent thinking. It is both a creative art and an interior speaking. The correspondence of such thinking with first thinking does not hinder Anselm from pointing out the "dissimilitudo" that becomes apparent in the process.[127]

The causality operative in the Christian notion of creation had already been described in the *Monologion,* chapter five in the term "artifex" (= artist).[128] The artist must use more than merely material to produce art. In the subsequent chapter the metaphor of the artist is used to distinguish the causality of the highest being's creative act from all finite causes. The artist depends on categorial causes, whereas the creator's causality is transcendental in kind.[129]

The idea of unity plays a significant role as well. The product is a unit. But there is also a unity between the artist and the art he or she produces. The artistic process represents, then, a further unit. In addition, the created object forms a unit. This metaphor thus enables Anselm to demonstrate how a multitude of different moments can contribute to ever greater forms of unison. As Kienzler observes:

> Dies war für uns und für Anselm die Grundform des Denkens, aus der Differenz unterschiedener Momente zur eigenen Identität und Einheit finden.[130]

Thinking is the means to overcome difference, ontic isolation and disparate forms of existence and to discover one's own identity and untity and simultaneously the unity of causes and of all being.

Artistic creativity is made possible only by the principle of "similitudo"and this principle of "similitudo" equally applies to thinking. A "similitudo" between the artist's original idea and the finished piece must exist.

> Nullo namque pacto fieri potest aliquid rationabiliter ab aliquo, nisi in facientis ratione praecedat aliquod rei faciendae quasi exemplum, sive aptius dicitur forma, vel similitudo, aut regula.[131]

Thinking is evidenced neither as a static process nor as a reflective reproduction of the ontically tangible, but rather as creative reason: "ratio faciens." "Similitudo" regulates the correct relationship between idea and form. First there is but the "exemplum" in the artist's mind. The metaphor of the artist can be amplified by the model of the interior speaking. Both artistic creativity and thinking can be perceived as an interior speaking. Thinking attains a personal,

---

[127] Kohlenberger, "Similitudo und Ratio" 98ff.

[128] M 5: 18,11-14. The concept "creation" is inconceivable in Plotinian philosophy. In this regard Anselm and Plotinus do not occupy the same thought-world.

[129] M 6: 18,18ff.

[130] Kienzler, Glauben und Denken 125.

[131] M 9: 24,12-14.

indeed an interlocutory quality.[132] The artist allows the created to speak within himself: "sicut faber primum apud se dicit, quid facturus est."[133] The idea, or form preceding the piece of art, has its cause in the artist's soliloquy and freedom.[134] In an analogous manner Anselm defines thinking as a monologue of thinking with itself: "locutio in ipsa ratione."[135] Thus, thinking is more than a solipsistic exercise: the objects produced may not remain outside thinking, but must simultaneously be present to thinking. This is explained by the Augustinian concept of "similitudo." Different levels and qualities of thinking exist:

> Frequenti namque usu cognoscitur, quia rem unam tripliciter loqui possumus. Aut enim res loquimur signis sensibilibus ...; aut eadem signa, quae foris sensibilia sunt, intra nos insensibiliter cogitando; aut nec sensibiliter nec insensibiliter his signis utendo, sed res ipsas vel corporum imaginatione vel rationis intellectu pro rerum ipsarum diversitate intus in nostra mente dicendo.[136]

While there is always "similitudo" present in the relationship - i.e. of the things and their being thought, of the sense perception and the perceived, of thinking and thought -, thinking reaches its culmination of "similitudo" when it no longer thinks sense impressions or intelligible content, but where it directly addresses the "res ipsae" in its "quidditas." Thinking preserves the object of thought as "verbum" by virtue of the inherent "similitudo" as quality. Thereby objects are present to the mind in their proper form of being. Yet the difference between the concrete object and object of thought remains unbridgeable.[137]

Thinking attains the highest degree of similarity with the object of thought:

> exceptis inquam his nullum aliud verbum sic videtur rei simile cuius est verbum, aut sic eam exprimit, quomodo illa similitudo, quae in acie mentis rem ipsam cogitantis exprimitur.[138]

This insight is granted by the object of thought. While the object/things are not in cognition, cognition remains only in similarity to things. The mentally actuated words are capable of achieving such a degree of similarity that by their

---

[132] Kohlenberger presents this relational dimension as his main thesis.

[133] M 10: 24,22f.

[134] Nota bene: freedom contains in a constitutive manner the dimension of relationality. Therefore one must not confuse freedom with mere autonomy.

[135] M 10: 24,25.

[136] M 10: 24,29-25,4.

[137] Cf. M 10: 25,15ff. For "verbum" see Kohlenberger, Similitudo und Ratio 94ff; Victor Warnach, "Wort und Wirklichkeit bei Anselm von Canterbury," Salzburger Jahrbuch für Philosophie 5/6 (1961/62): 157-176, at 157ff.

[138] M 10: 25,19-21.

own accord they are present as "res ipsae." For this reason Anselm describes their presence as

> locutionis verba ... naturalia sunt et apud omnes gentes sunt eadem. Et quoniam alia omnia verba propter haec sunt inventa: ubi ista sunt, nullum aliud verbum est necessarium ad rem cognoscendam; et ubi ista esse non possunt, nullum aliud est utile ad rem ostendendam.[139]

There are words existing exclusively in cognition. And yet, the other words become necessary only because of the first, non-concrete words: "Illud igitur iure dicendum est maxime proprium et principale rei verbum."[140] When this "acie mentis"[141] is achieved one has the highest form of thinking. Then thinking is most intimately aligned with the things and the things are present to thinking. Conversely, in the occurrence of their most intense culmination in thinking, thinking attains the highest level of "similitudo" with the things and is simultaneously present to itself. It is a congruence of the intense presence of the "res ipsae" and the "mens." Nonetheless, cognition remains thinking and the objects remain things.

At this moment the highest degree of unity of thinking and the object of thought occurs. All predications of the object are found present in the "similitudo." There are - according to Kohlenberger - three acts or levels of "similitudo:" 1. sense perception, 2. rational thinking and 3. comprehensive thinking.[142] In thinking, thinking experiences both its own unity and its union with things. Both are reciprocally conditioned.

Here the "similitudo" as an interior process of thinking is demonstrated but not explained. Is thinking the cause for "similitudo?" This would render "similitudo" merely a self-explication of cognition. Anselm roundly rejects this. Never could a "similitudo" so constituted reach out to the "res," or essence, of the objects of thought. For Anselm only God can satisfy the criteria for a cause of the "similitudo." As creator, God is "similitudo" to both his creatures and to thinking. One can think of God as in "similitudo," in similarity, with thinking. From this it follows for Anselm that thinking in its totality is a "similitudo" to the highest being. But this is not granted lightheartedly to the faint hearted. An ethical effort is in order: "non immerito videri potest."[143]

As demonstrated with creation, "similitudo" also exists apart from tangible things. For this reason a "creatio ex nihilo" is viable: "Patet itaque, quoniam priusquam fierent universa, erat in ratione summae naturae, quid aut

---

[139] M 10: 25,11-15.
[140] M 10: 25,21f.
[141] M 10: 25,21.
[142] Kohlenberger, Similitudo und Ratio 30ff; Warnach, "Wort und Wirklichkeit" 158ff.
[143] M 10: 25, 25.

qualia aut quomodo futura essent."[144] This makes "ratio faciens" possible in first place.[145]

As the model of an interior speaking intimates, it is both something within and outside God. In the "locutio rerum" something of a divine quality is communicated as an "intima locutio" to the created order. The notion of the "locutio rerum" is extrapolated from contingent matter in finite thought unto the highest Being. "(N)on immerito videri potest apud summam substantiam, talem rerum locutionem et fuisse antequam essent ut per eam fierent, et esse cum facta sunt ut per eam sciantur."[146] As the created piece of art is first contained in the artitst's imagination, so creation is first contained in nuce in the highest Being. The highest Being brings these into being through "locutionem rerum."

In its highest potency (= third level), human thinking perceives in an asymptotic manner - "per similitudinem" - how things actually are in the Divine Spirit. Therein occurs the highest similarity between thinking and Being. "Per similitudinem" all of creation is contained in a non-pantheistic way in the highest Being. Departing from a logos-theology, the highest Being is speaking, progression and pronouncement of the created things: namely "locutio rerum." A demarcation between thinking and consciousness is not drawn. Even at this point "similitudo" is not proven. Rather the reciprocal and explanatory congruency of thinking and the highest Being is evidenced through the concept of "similitudo." Anselm does supply a fully satisfactory explanation. However, one can agree with Kohlenberger when he concludes that the Anselmian "similitudo" constitutes by itself a "similitudo" to the highest Being.[147] Thinking does not cause but finds "similitudo" already ever present in itself. Nevertheless, the explanation for the facticity of "similitudo" in cogitation must be sought outside contingent thinking. All of thinking must be a "similitudo" in order to have the capacity to actuate itself: i.e. in order to apprehend the object in a way objectivizing the perceived:

Etenim omnia huiusmodi verba quibus res quaslibet mente dicimus, id est cogitamus, similitudines et imagines sunt rerum quarum verba sunt; et omnis similitudo vel imago tanto magis vel minus est vera, quanto magis vel minus imitatur rem cuius est similitudo.[148]

The measure of this "similitudo" is not defined by thinking itself. This measure as measure is a pre-given for thinking and not at its disposition. This "similitudo" seems anchored firmly in the truth that is the highest Being. As it is a property of thinking, finite "similitudo's" highest realization occurs when thinking ascends to the third level.

---

[144] M 9: 14,14f.
[145] M 9: 24,19f.
[146] M 10: 25,25f.
[147] Kohlenberger, Similitudo und Ratio 102.
[148] M 31: 48,18-21.

Precisely for this reason Kohlenberger divines that contingent thinking is an "imitatio" of the Numinous´ creative thinking. Equally, contingent being is a "similitudo" of the highest Being. The degree of "similitudo" finite thinking achieves corresponds best to the "similitudo" prevailing betweeen creature and creator.

Cum igitur pateat quia nihil de hac natura possit percipi per suam proprietatem sed per aliud, certum est quia per illud magis ad eius cognitionem acceditur, quod illi magis per similitudinem propinquat ... Quapropter id et per maiorem similitudinem plus iuvat mentem indagantem summae veritati propinquare, et per excellentiorem creatam essentiam plus docet, quid de creante mens ipsa debet aestimare.[149]

Thinking must contain and actuate this higher "similarity." This "similitudo" as an instrument towards the "summa ratio" is something recognized by thinking in its self-actuation.[150] Such is the case because contingent thinking in its totality is similar to the highest Being. In a way constitutive for the cognitive act, "similitudo" contains a dynamic, self-impelling component.

Yet, this understanding of "similitudo" in no way endangers the sovereign and numinous nature of the "summa ratio." "Quod tamen multa sit in hac similitudo dissimilitudo."[151] Again Anselm uses the example of the artist to demonstrate what he means. Divine creativity remains infinitely dissimilar to contingent creativity. Whatever the creator uses is already contained within the Godhead. God actuates His own "similitudo," concepts, ideas, notions, etc. While contingent thinking knows of different levels, realizing different qualitative degrees of "similitudo," divine "similitudo" is already fully realized. Divine thinking is a fully realized unity.[152]

quidquid summa substantia fecit, non fecit per aliud quam per semetipsam, et quidquid fecit, per suam intimam locutionem fecit, sive singula singulis verbis, sive potius uno verbo simul omnia dicendo: quid magis necessarium videri potest, quam hanc summam essentiae locutionem non esse aliud quam summam essentiam?[153]

The "res ipsae" are not mere allusions or shades but already permanently - without beginning and without end - realized ideas fully in God, namely as a unity in plurality. Anselm further unfolds this plurality in his theology of the Trinity in the inner-trinitarian components of "verbum" and "amor." For this eternal commerce between the two, one can never simplify contingent thinking into simply an image-quality of divine thinking.

---

[149] M 66: 77,7-13; cf. Kohlenberger, Similitudo und Ratio 99f..
[150] M 34: 53,18.
[151] M 11: 26,1 - used by Anselm as a heading. Cf. Kohlenberger, Similitudo und Ratio 102f.
[152] M 11: 26,16-20.
[153] M 12: 26,26-31.

Though the "summa ratio" is also described as "vivit et sentit et rationalis,"[154] finite thinking contains an infinite "dissimilitudo" vis-à-vis the "summa ratio." In spite of its intellectual acuteness, the human intellect remains a weak imitation of the divine "ratio." Its greatest achievement is perhaps to apprehend in the "similitudo" a double-function. The latter is both a bridge and the demarcation of a boundary between an absolute and finite thinking.

Satis itaque manifestum est in verbo, per quod facta sunt omnia, non esse ipsorum similitudinem, sed veram simplicemque essentiam; in factis vero non esse simplicem absolutamque essentiam, sed verae illius essentiae vix aliquam imitationem.[155]

5.5 "Verum" as an ethical Imperative - *De Veritate*[156]

The heteronomy and autonomy of human reflection is expressed in a dense manner by the term "similitudo." The transcendental causes of thinking become apparent. The "similitudo" is not caused or sustained by contingent thinking. Contingent thinking is merely capable of recognizing a convergence between human and divine "similitudo." How does truth, i.e. the congruency between a statement and reality, occur? This is the concern of the *De Veritate*.[157] In the *Monologion* the conditions for truth are delineated: namely transcendentality, necessity and unity.[158] Subsequently *De Veritate* is able to thrust forward to Anselm's core issue: "le fondement épistemologique de toute sa doctrine."[159]

In order to explore the nature of truth, Anselm looks to the various manifestations of truth in the common use ("usus communis").[160] This term serves him as a heuristic principle for the discovery of truth. His point of departure is natural consciousness. For this reason both the *Monologion* and *De Veritate* start with a phenomenology. The latter begins with the disciple's

---

[154] M 31: 49,15f.

[155] M 31: 50,7-10.

[156] For this treatise cf. Barth, Fides quaerens intellectum 44ff; Donald F. Duclow, "Structure and Meaning in Anselm's De Veritate," American Benedictine Review 26 (1975): 406-417, at 406ff; Flasch, "Zum Begriff der Wahrheit" 322ff; Gilson, "Sens et Nature" 9ff; Kienzler, Glauben und Denken 135ff; Pouchet, La Rectitudo 55ff; Schurr, Die Begründung der Philosophie 39ff;Vanni-Rovighi, "L'etica" 73ff.

[157] Cf. Heinz Külling, Wahrheit als Richtigkeit: eine Untersuchung zur Schrift `De veritate' von Anselm von Canterbury (Bern: Lang, 1984). Also: Markus Enders, Wahrheit und Notwendigkeit: die Theorie der Wahrheit bei Anselm von Canterbury im Gesamtzusammenhang seines Denkens unter besonderer Berücksichtigung seiner antiken Quellen. Habilitationsschrift (Leiden: Brill, 1999). Enders' "Habilitationsschrift" is the most thorough discussion yet on this treatise. He discusses the contributions of Aristotle, Cicero, Augustine and Boethius to Anselm's writings.

[158] For a discussion of the interrelationship between the two treatises cf. Flasch, "Zum Begriff der Wahrheit" 227; Pouchet, La Rectitudo 55f.

[159] Gilson, "Sens et Nature" 9.

[160] V 2: 179,27.

observation that faith knows God to be the highest truth: "Quoniam deum veritatem esse credimus, et veritatem in multis aliis dicimus esse,vellem scire, an ubicumque veritas dicitur deum eam esse fateri debeamus."[161] Here the insights gained concerning the highest being in the *Monologion* are presupposed. The transcendental quality of truth renders evident a surplus of truth when confronted with contingent thinking. To underline this central insight of the *Monologion*, Anselm explains: the highest truth "non habere principium vel finem."[162] Therefore it is eternal and immutable. Truth is not a corollary of thinking.[163] Truth need not "predate" thinking for it is valid always and everywhere.[164] All veracity has this as its measure. Faithful to (Neo-) Platonism, every truth statement partakes in (highest) truth.

> Una igitur est in illis omnibus veritas ... ita summa veritas per se subsistens nullius rei est; sed cum aliquid secundum illam est, tunc eius dicitur veritas vel rectitudo.[165]

Again Anselm applies the concept of "similitudo." For this reason he writes: "cum aliquid secundum illam est." According to Torrance[166] he goes further than any known philosopher. Thinking suggests the frame for truth but no adequate description is found of when and how truth becomes an event.

Anselm's guiding star is the Johannine "veritatem facere" (Jn 3:20f). Depending on how one relates to truth, one derives the appropriate consequences. Little wonder then that the insight, "Qui male agit, odit lucem," is a recurring motif in Anselm's writings.[167] Equally, the use of the term "lux" and its derivatives "lucere" and "lucens" is very common in the *Corpus Anselmi* and not restricted to the *De Veritate*.[168] His is an incarnational understanding of truth. Yet the incarnation does not do violence to the world it enters. It is a truth most akin to the reality it enters. Indeed, the tension between reality and the "other world" is mirrored by the tension between theory and praxis in reality. Doing truth entails having its light appear as luminous and resplendent in both action and theory. Thereby this light emerges in a twofold modi: as reality and as the luminous cause for concrete action.

By doing truth - "stare in veritatem" - , one approaches light: "venit ad lucem." All action is inextricably a relationship to truth, often becoming a part of truth. Thus action is also a testimony to the truth. It is also a participation in

---

[161] V 1: 176,4-6.
[162] V 1: 176,18.
[163] Kohlenberger, Similitudo und Ratio 95.
[164] V 1: 176, 6-20.
[165] V 13: 199,11.27-19.
[166] Thomas F. Torrance, "The Ethical Implications of Anselm's `De Veritate" Theologische Zeitschrift 24 (1968): 309-319, at 313.
[167] Kohlenberger, Similitudo and Ratio 56, fn. 14; Pouchet, La Rectitudo 29ff.
[168] Külling, Wahrheit 125ff; Schmitt, "Anselm und der (Neu-)Platonismus" 62ff; Warnach, "Wort und Wirklichkeit" 167ff.

truth. This is expressed in the words: "qui facit veritatem, venit ad lucem; idem est veritatem facere quod est bene facere."[169] The struggle for the felicitous congruency of action with the first truth is the permanent aim of human existence: "facere veritatem, " "stare in veritate" and "bene facere." The salient feature of human action is that it is ever anew the self-execution of humanity. Being human calls for a responsiveness which transcends the merely palpable relationship. Every human action, then, acquires "qua actione humana" an ethical quality.

With Flasch and Kienzler one might state that while the *Monologion* is an elaboration on the nature of theoretical reason, *De Veritate* contains the program for practical reason. "Schon beim ersten Lesen des Dialogs fällt auf: die ethische Fragestellung und Terminologie durchdringt das kleine Werk. Theoretische und praktische Vernunft sind hier noch nicht (wieder) zu einer relativen Scheidung auseinandergetreten wie bei Aristoteles und in der aristotelischen Scholastik. Wahrheit ist für Anselm gerade das, was sie wesentlich gemeinsam haben."[170]

The qualification and clarification of all action occurs in the first truth. *De Veritate* investigates the conditions of practical reason. Anselm assumes practical reason to receive truth's demand that every action must be predicable with the adjective "true." "Facere" alone does not suffice to describe the imperative of the human condition. It must result in "bene facere."[171] The imperative encountered in life is always endowed with an ethical quality. By doing the "bonum," the action becomes "bene." This ethical intentionality of action is touched upon already in the *Monologion*: "Etenim cum omnes frui solis iis appetant quae bona putant."[172] Reason is under this call. The "bonum" belongs to human fulfillment. The call to do good is subject to failure. However, if failure to fulfill this relationality between reason and the good occurs, then something central to the description of human existence suffers shipwreck. Therefore, there is a "debere" resonating powerfully in all human action.[173] Practical reason is completely ordered toward hearing the "debere." "Debere" belongs to the destiny of human existence. Consequently "debere" connotes a comprehensive imperative encapsulated in the "facere quod debet."[174] This is the formula which expresses when the discernment of truth occurs. The "verum" is a should/ought/must to be realized. Finite truth is

---

[169] V 5: 181,20ff; cf. Philippe Delhaye, "Quelques Aspects de la morale de Saint Anselme," Spicilegium Beccense I (Paris: Vrin, 1959): 401-422, at 403.
[170] Flasch, "Zum Begriff der Wahrheit" 327; cf. Balthasar, Anselm (this refers to Herrlichkeit, vol. II, where a section is dedicated to Anselm) 222; Külling, Wahrheit 9-36; Hans-Joachim Werner, "Anselm von Canterburys Dialog `De Veritate´ und das Problem der Begründung praktischer Sätze," Salzburger Jahrbuch für Philosophie XX (1975): 119-130, at 119.
[171] V 5: 181 19-28. See Kohlenberger, Similtudo und Ratio 124f.
[172] M 1: 13,13.
[173] Flasch, "Zum Begriff der Wahrheit" 335ff; Kohlenberger, Similitudo und Ratio 55.
[174] V 5: 181,30; 182,4.5.

subject to an ethical claim to actuate itself in dialogue with "transcendental truth."[175]

Truth, so constituted, is beyond the palpable realm and therefore is neither simply found in thinking nor in the "res." Rather finite truth is the agreement of both in the transcendental truth sustaining them. Flasch sums up Anselm's view of truth as an "eidetisch-teleologisch-ethisch gefaßte rectitudo."[176] The "bonum" is the well from which springs forth the concrete call to fulfill the "debere."[177] This transcendent cause is also the transcendent measure for the concrete "debere." A further, non insignificant measure for the "debere" arises from the actual act. This is the immanent yardstick for the "debere." How is one to perceive this "ought"?

"La rectitudo nous parait être chez Anselm le centre vital où se nouent la pensée et l'action, ... unification de la science et de la vie ... de la connaisssance et de l'action."[178] One must agree on this point with Pouchet, for all of Scripture, and Greek and Christian antiquity can be subsumed under the term "orthes." The whole of the cosmos possesses an inner harmony and lack of contradictions, i.e., positively formulated, a consistency to which the human being is called to relate.[179] "Rectitudo" is the pivotal circumscription of the "debere" as the constituent of practical reason. Besides "debere" "facere," "veritatem facere" and "bene facere" are also defined by the rectitude of the ontic order. Every human act possesses and acquires in its self-execution its very own measure with itself. By being good and judicious every act actuates truth: "Recte facere" or "veritatem facere." The act thereby corresponds to and is congruent to its a priori intentionality. Verity, hence, arises from the rectitude proper to every isolated act and yet it is free of contradiction with the ontic order.

In *De Veritate* truth takes on a multitude of forms. Truth is pluralistic. By fulfilling its "rectitudo," the isolated act constitutes truth: "recte facit, veritatem facit, bene facit."[180] The isolated act bears testimony to verity because it is

---

[175] Kohlenberger, Similitudo und Ratio 90ff; Külling, Wahrheit 157-174.
[176] Flasch, "Zum Begriff der Wahrheit" 328.
[177] V 4: 181,1.4.6.8.
[178] Pouchet, La Rectitudo 6.15.
[179] For the philosophical background of "rectitudo" cf. Franz Wiedmann, "Wahrheit als Rechtheit," Epimelia. Die Sorge um den Menschen. FS H. Kuhn (München: Hueber, 1964): 174-182, at 174; biblical background of the term cf. Pouchet, La Rectitudo 29ff; for the Augustinian background cf. Pouchet, La Rectitudo 35ff; Flasch, "Zum Begriff der Wahrheit" 331 fn. 24; Pouchet, La Rectitudo 40ff elaborates on the Patristic (esp. Gregory the Great's) use of this word.
[180] V 5: 182,22f. For a discussion of the interrelatedness of ontic order and "rectitudo" cf. also Balthasar, Anselm 217ff. 243; Delhaye, "Quelques Aspects" 402ff; Flasch, "Zum Begriff der Wahrheit" 327ff; Külling, Wahrheit 175-186; Gottlieb Söhngen, "Rectitudo bei Anselm von Canterbury als Oberbegriff von Wahrheit und Gerechtigkeit," Sola Ratione. FS F.S.

veracious. The purpose of such a givenness of reality is not utilitarian; it actuates and enunciates its very own "rectitudo." "Ergo non est illi aliud veritas quam rectitudo."[181] The judgment arising from this matrix is immutable, always valid and natural.[182] Only if the judgment is incorrect do these adjectives not apply. "Rectitudo" is the sovereign arbiter of whether the judgment is correct or incorrect. The "rectitudo" is not again subject to an opinion: "nobis datum est,"[183] for its yardstick is truth, which is without beginning and without end.[184]

Chapters nine and eleven of *De Veritate* demonstrate that transcendental truth possesses an equally significant immanent component. It is through praxis that truth realizes itself. "Quoniam namque non est ab aliquo faciendum nisi quod quis debet facere, eo ipso quod aliquis aliquid facit, dicit et significat hoc se debere facere."[185] Concrete action and thought are "facere." In this comprehensive view of "facere" an interior imperative becomes transparent: "Similiter cum cogitat aliquis aut vult aliquid, si nescires an deberet id velle sive cogitare: si voluntatem eius et cogitationem videres, significaret tibi ipso opere quia hoc deberet cogitare et velle."[186] The truth of thinking and intention must be done so that truth comes about. In thinking "rectitudo" and truth are beheld. "Possumus igitur, nisi fallor, definire quia veritas est rectitudo mente sola perceptibilis."[187] "Veritas" is experienced exclusively rationally - here again Anselm echoes a Plotinian philosopheme: "sola mente." Yet one must be mindful that the mind does not cause or form "rectitudo." "Veritas" is the yardstick for uprighteousness ("rectitudo") and because all action stands under a truth claim - an imperative "debere" to align oneself with the idea of truth - "rectitudo" is also the yardstick of all actions. The transcendental idea of truth is realized in different degrees in finite and concrete truth. There is a closed and circular train of thought: Reason is for the "homo rationalis" a burden because it exists under an ethical claim - and yet, it is the only way, better yet: chance, to be human. Vanni-Rovighi, interpreting this circumstance in a positive manner, sees the ethical call as the enablement of freedom: every action has its very own inner measure.[188] "Rectitudo" occurs in the congruence of the heard "rectitudo" with the "rectitudo" per se and at the same time as the correspondence of every action. This congruence and its attendant correspondence "sola mente" can be perceived. Consequently transcendence is recognized only by thinking.

Schmitt (Stuttgart - Bad Cannstatt: Friederich Frommann, 1970): 71-86, at 71ff; Speck, Grundprobleme 48ff; Vanni-Rovighi, "L´etica" 73ff.
[181] V 2: 178,25; Gottlieb Söhngen, Grundfragen einer Rechtstheologie (München: Pustet, 1962).
[182] V 2: 179,13f.
[183] V 3: 180,12.
[184] V 5: 182,13.
[185] V 9: 189,4f.
[186] V 9: 189,20ff.
[187] V 11: 191,19f.
[188] Külling, Wahrheit 149-157; Vanni-Rovighi, Anselmo 126ff.

5.6 The Tension between the Objectivity and Subjectivity of "Rectitudo"

There is a two-fold dimensionality to "rectitudo." On the one hand it is the exterior criterion for every morally good action. But on the other hand, the action is measured twice: from the outside and from the inner sense. Henry sees these dialectics of the "rectitudo" implied particularly in the term of "dari" and its derivatives.[189]

The "dari"[190] of the "rectitudo" to each and every action is cocreated with human consciousness: "ad hoc facta est." [191] Creatures received this gift along with their being from the Creator. Therefore, "naturaliter" matter has, as its "essentiae rerum,"[192] "rectitudo."[193] Consequently there is an orientation toward "rectitudo" "ex necessitate." This givenness is no longer at their disposition: "non habere non potest."[194] In contrast to all other creatures, rational beings possess "rectitudo" for a purpose: "propter quod."[195] As such "rectitudo" entails a responsibility which is apprehended as an obligation toward an alignment.

These features of human existence become acutely apparent in Anselm's notion of receiving. "Rectitudo," intentionality, truth, etc. have been received for a purpose. These terms denote an ontic entelechy. "Quod significare accepit."[196] Upon this background of givenness the transcendentality of "rectitudo" is demonstrated. Yet more than being transcendental, it beckons the receiver to be in relation to something: "recipiet prout gessit."[197] These dynamics of granter and grantee impel the receiver forward towards the "facere quod debet." As such there are two origins for action: truth per se and the origin itself. The tension of the two brings forth freedom ever anew. The "mens" correlates with and enables the relationship between the concrete and actual truth and the highest truth. In finite form this relation is called to succeed. Anselm encapsulates the whole of this complex, dynamic process in a concise and succinct form as a hypothetical objection in the twelfth chapter of *De Veritate* beginning:

... forte dicet aliquis:
Si rectitudo voluntatis non nisi cum servatur dicenda est iustitia: non mox ut habetur iustitia, nec accipimus iustitiam cum illam accipimus, sed nos servando facimus eam esse iustitiam.[198]

---

[189] Henry, Logic 185ff; Külling, Wahrheit 175ff.
[190] V 2: 180,13.
[191] V 2: 179,4.
[192] V 7: 185,7.
[193] V 7: 186,1.
[194] V 2: 179,28.
[195] V 2: 179,7.
[196] V 2: 179,7.
[197] V 5: 182,16.
[198] V 12: 195,1-4.

We are called to preserve (= "servare") the given "rectitudo" so that "iustitia" is being done. It is not simply "datum." Rather therein (in the "datum") the call for us is contained: "facimus." Not simply is something "habitur" but we must actively accept it (= "accipimus"): "nam prius illam accipimus et habemus, quam servemus."[199] The relationality of givenness and receivedness opens towards a - always personal in nature - responsibility which strives to preserve the "rectitudo." "Sed ad haec nos respondere possumus, quia simul accipimus illam et velle et habere. Non enim illam habemus nisi volendo; et si eam volumus, hoc ipso illam habemus."[200]

These elaborations on the dimensions of the "rectitudo" permit Anselm to define justice.[201] Justice is in Anselm's mind intertwined with the notion of truth: "invicem esse definiunt veritas et rectitudo et iustitia."[202] For justice is the yardstick of "rectitudo." Justice becomes nothing less than the fulfillment of its own "rectitudo." It is characteristic in a way central to the "animal rationale" to yearn for a correspondence of the just action with the measure of its "rectitudo." It is again characteristic for the specifically human "rectitudo" to possess knowledge and intentionality towards justice so defined: "Constat quia illa iustitia non est in ulla natura, quae rectitudinem non cognoscit."[203] This justice is a constrained one: "mente sola perceptibilis."[204] Truth becomes defined as correct and just action. Truth is the rational congruence between what is correct and at the same time the active execution of what "debere" calls to be done. All these components appear equally important in Anselm's system. This "debere" implies no exterior compulsion which would render the concrete and single act incongruous with its subject's cast of mind or nature. Rather it calls for its realization "sponte," which seems to mean in freedom.[205] Only if intention and "debere" are one in praise (= "cui laus debetur")[206] does the act do what it ought: "facit volens quod debet."[207] There is no higher criterion than "rectitudo." "Iustitia igitur est rectitudo voluntatis propter se servata. .... Voluntas ergo illa iusta est, quae sui rectitudinem servat propter ipsam rectitudinem."[208] Justice and "rectitudo" mirror each other and are therefore reciprocally dependent entities. "Rectitudo" brings the immanent and transcendental dimensions of moral humanity and truth to bear.[209] "Die `iustitia´

---

[199] V 12: 195,4f.
[200] V 12: 195,7-9.
[201] Külling, Wahrheit 113ff; Pouchet, La Rectitudo 88ff; Schurr, Die Begründung der Philosophie 51ff.
[202] V 12: 192,8.
[203] V 12: 182,30f.
[204] V 12: 192,7.
[205] V 12: 192,19.
[206] V 12: 192,27.
[207] V 12: 192,24.
[208] V 12: 194,26.23f.
[209] Kohlenberger, Similitudo und Ratio 90.101.

kommt in der inneren Entsprechung der ihr gegebenen und aufgegebenen eigenen transzendenten Bestimmung zu sich; sie findet aber ihre eigene Transzendentalität nur in sich selbst."[210] Justice comes to its own, its actual correspondence of its transmitted and own transcendental destiny given as task. Yet it finds its own transcendentality only by recourse to itself, which means inevitably by recourse to the "totaliter aliter."

5.7 Summary

The path threaded in the *Monologion, Proslogion* and *De Veritate* evidences thinking as both grounded in itself and in the highest object, namely in the "summa ratio." The previously autonomous principle of the "sola ratione" has not thereby been surrendered. Quite the contrary: by recourse to the divine thinking it is properly caused and instituted. Relationality and independence of thinking are not contraries.

Up to this point Anselmian philosophy has unfolded in three phases. The first one enunciates the constitution of cognition as transcendental. The second phase defines this cognition as based on its "similitudo." Thirdly, in becoming practical it evidences itself as true.

The first level deals with theoretical reason. It transcends itself. In doing so it not only finds its very own nature in a self-constituting manner, but it also re-constitutes cogitation as a necessary self-transcending reflection. In the process this theoretical reason illumines its own causal context. All these factors permit reason to be transparent for its cause, namely for its transcendental cause, which is ultimately God. This occurs not only from within a stringent system as a stringent result. Its existential ground and cause is the divine one.

This causation is expressed in the Anselmian systematization by the term "similitudo." The implication Anselm suggests to the reader is that theoretical cognition is not capable of supplying its own basis. An ontic explanation is called for. This is the task of "similitudo." This term expresses the critical nexus between seemingly incomparable entities: God and thinking, divine existence and the existence of contingent thinking. These relationships are, by way of the "similitudo" concept, seen not to be blasphemous. This notion permits thinking to perceive itself as a divine image. God is the original of this image. Contingent thinking experiences two wellsprings for its own being: 1. the one transcendental cause who is God and 2. its own being by virtue of being image.

Finally, practical reason carries out this causative thinking within the parameters noted in the term truth. Truth thematizes the insight into God and the self as the consummation of truth per se. Truth in this perspective is seen as having several origins. As transcendent truth it is called to be done in praxis. As the immanent truth of thinking it is called to orient itself according to the first

---

[210] Kienzler, Glauben und Denken 155; Külling, Wahrheit 219-261.

truth and to execute the same. Thereby it executes itself by finding in God its origin and by actuating itself in praxis. While executing itself in thinking, the truth of cogitation remains infinitely greater than its executing agency: cogitation.

CHAPTER SIX
6.0 Reason's Itinerary - Perceiving God - Understanding the "I"

The prominent discussion of reason in Anselmian writings has had some authors suppose a strong philosophical proclivity in the Archbishop's treatises. Barth is notable for insisting on a preeminence of the theological moment.[1] Balthasar had already inaugurated a correction of this approach by distinguishing Anselm's "form" and "method" as philosophical, but his "contents" and "object" as theological.[2] Although Balthasar perceives in Anselm's writings an aesthetic balance between the two disciplines - namely philosophy and theology - he perhaps fails to appreciate the a priori unity of the two. Pouchet is probably the first scholar to analyze Anselm from a pre-Scholastic angle. Particularly in *De Veritate* he sees a fruitful synthesis of the two at work:

> Le `De veritate' apparait ... comme l'oeuvre charnière par excellence, le noeud vital qui relie théologie, christologie et anthropologie anselmienne; c'est le phare qui projette sa lumière sur l'ensemble de la doctrine et permet d'en esquisser la synthèse.[3]

6.1 Thinking as Salvation

In Pouchet's judgment the unifying, synthetic principle is made most evident by Anselm's employing the term "rectitudo." It is the present author's opinion that "ratio" is yet more suitable to express Anselm's all-encompassing vision. This approach seems viable as the above exegesis of *De veritate* has demonstrated. The "sola ratione" is the guiding star and formative principle underlying the whole of Anselm's corpus. By attending to "ratio" as the key term one simultaneously claims positively a rational moment, indeed rationa(bi)lity. What theological and more precisely soteriological consequences are to be drawn from such a view?

First one ought to bear in mind that a "sola ratione" by no means implies an autonomous notion of human reason. Anselm's assumed program is the connection of knowledge of God and self-knowledge. As with Plotinus, recognizing the self implies the mind's disposition to recognizing God - the origin and aim of all thinking. Anselm asserts unequivocally that God Himself designed cognition to fathom divinity. Lest there be a fracture in Anselm's

---

[1] Barth, Fides quaerens intellectum 54, fn. 59. He divines a rupture in Anselm's thought. The original philosophical element receives a purifying and mature theological treatment through theology. Cf. Ubbelohde, Glaube und Vernunft 26ff.
[2] Balthasar, Anselm 218f.
[3] Robert Pouchet, "Existe-t-il une `synthèse anselmienne,' Un itinéraire augustinien de l'âme à Dieu," Analecta Anselmiana I. (Frankfurt am Main: Minerva, 1969): 3-10, at 5f.

thought, these presuppositions also need to hold true in soteriological considerations. The "sola ratione" approach conveys "ratio's" three dimensions. The condition for the possibility of cogitation is thinking and its attendant conditions. This "ratio" is further grounded in the "similitudo." Finally, and perhaps from a practical point of view most importantly, it necessarily relates in a self-constitutive way to truth. Rationa(bi)lity means therefore that thinking brings forth its very own conditions but at the same time is based on these: "similitudo" and "veritas." As a result every Anselmian observation not only originates in truth and similarity but reveals an aspect of thinking. Expressed more concretely this means that thinking not only is indebted to salvation but participates in an active manner in the ongoing story of salvation history.

6.2 Perceiving God

Anselm's teachings on God are delineated in the *Monologion*, in the *Proslogion* and in the *De processione spiritus sancti*. It is always the unthinkability of matters divine that stands in the foreground. In this regard he is faithful to Augustine.[4] For Anselm the view is that thinking by itself can apprehend the unthinkability of God:

> Nam si superior consideratio rationabiliter comprehendit incomprehensibile esse, quomodo eadem summa sapientia sciat ea quae fecit, de quibus tam multa nos scire necesse est ...[5]

The unthinkability of God is arrived at by making use of reason: "rationabiliter." Many things that touch the relationship between the created and creator must be thought necessarily. For this reason Anselm was able to assert already a few lines further up: "necessariis sunt rationibus asserta." Not only does one behold the necessity of some aspects of existence, one also penetrates reality through this insight in a way one can define as necessary. This reveals a second dimension: there is a principle of non-contradiction permeating reality. This second insight strengthens credal certitude. The unthinkability of matters divine thereby evidences itself neither as a paradox nor as an absurdity and certainly not as an aporia. It is neither unreasonable nor in contradiction to cogitation: rather it is something necessarily transcending thinking. The unthinkability of the infinite is a significant element of contingent, finite thinking. Such is the import of the following:

---

[4]   Augustine, De trinit.; cf. Pouchet, "Existe-t-il" 36 and Michael Schmaus, "Die metaphysisch-psychologische Lehre über den Heiligen Geist im Monologion Anselms von Canterbury," Sola Ratione. FS F.S. Schmitt (Stuttgart-Bad Cannstatt: Friedrich Frommann, 1970): 189-219, at 199ff. Anselm expressedly referred to Augustine in Cu I 2: 50,1-12; I 16: 117,23f; Co 21: 161,4-6; Pr 2: 177,10-15.
[5]   M 64: 75,11-13.

Sufficere namque debere existimo rem incomprehensibilem indaganti, si ad hoc ratiocinando pervenerit ut eam certissime esse cognoscat, etiamsi penetrare nequeat intellectu quomodo ita sit; nec idcirco minus iis adhibendam fidei certitudinem, quae probationibus necessariis nulla alia repugnante ratione asseruntur, si suae naturalis altitudinis incomprehensibilitate explicari non patiantur.[6]

When contemplating matters divine one invariably reflects upon the vehicle which is to transport one in this direction: namely contemporaneous cogitation. One invariably must confess the object - God - to be at the same time and under the same consideration the basis and sole enabling agent for thinking. This intimates a close proximity of object and subject - which is not too unfamiliar to Plotinus even if it is more sublime and personal.[7]

The second principle of Anselm's thought on God is that of "similitudo." The trinity-psychology of Augustine finds an application here. God is one but has three modes of execution: "memoria," "intelligentia" and "amor." But in contrast to Augustine, Anselm is not content to see these three psychologically; rather they are modes for understanding something of the real "similitudo" of finite thought. Since these three elements of "memoria," "intelligentia " and "amor" are components of finite thought critical reflection upon the nature of cogitation cannot but be a contemplation of God, and vice- versa, the investigation of divine existence cannot help but reveal the nature of human thinking. In this sense the execution of the "ratio" becomes more than a mere intellectual act. It becomes a spiritual one - an "intima locutio." In spite of these statements, Anselm is careful to note a yet greater "dissimilitudo" surpassing qualitatively any stated "similitudo." [8] The considerations on the "dissimilitudo" introduce an element of incertitude and - particularly important for postmodernity - a distance to anything akin to a modern ideology or an other form of closed system.

The properties of the highest Being are characterized as spiritedness: "utique eadem asserenda esse spiritus."[9] The "intima locutio" is an expression of the highest Being's spiritedness. While this does describe the highest Being as "unus spiritus" the concrete "intima locutio" is constituted by a multitude of different acts. Thereby a dialectics of unity and multitude/diversity becomes apparent. Spirited activity is the highest self-execution of the "intelligentia." In

---

[6] M 64: 75,1-6.
[7] For the influence of this approach on subsequent theologies cf. Kohlenberger, Similitudo and Ratio, pp. 84ff; Michael Schmaus, "Die theologiegeschichtliche Tragweite der Trinitätslehre des Anselm von Canterbury," Analecta Anselmiana. Vol. 4/1 (Frankfurt am Main: Minerva, 1975): 29-45, at 29ff; Vagaggini, La Hantise 103ff.
[8] Helmut Kohlenberger, "Konsequenzen und Inkonsequenzen der Trinitätslehre in Anselms Monologion." Analecta Anselmiana V (Frankfurt am Main: Minerva, 1976): 149-178, at 159.176ff; Vignaux, "Structure et sens" 198ff.
[9] M 27: 45,17.

the divine context Anselm readily admits the existence of a problem already in the introductory title. "Quod eius locutio idipsum sit quod ipse, nec tamen sint duo, sed unus spiritus."[10] While there is in the finite realm a difference between "locutio" and "intelligentia," in infinite cogitation there must be a unity of both, by virtue of the "dissimilitudo:" "Quid enim est aliud illi rem loqui aliquam hoc loquendi modo quam intelligere?"[11] In the divine world "locutio" and "intelligentia" are diverse modi of the one spiritedness. In every single act the whole Spirit present for every act at the same time is a moment of self-execution of the Spirit because of its fundamental unity: "necesse est ut sic illi haec sua locutio sit consubstantialis, ut non sint duo, sed unus spiritus."[12]

The "verbum" is for Anselm the equivalent to the self-execution of the Spirit in the finite world. In this finite realm the problem might repeat itself. Need not as many "words" exist as there are human utterances? This is not the case because of the dissimilarity between the divine word and human words. The highest Being's word is at the same time the most all-encompassing statement possible; it is the most basic and common observation. God's word is the self-expression of His being. Highest Being can be thought without seeing an obligation or necessity to create. The highest Being's spiritedness implies both independence and primordial unity. Nothing in the ontic existence of the highest Being is altered by creation. By being "verbum" the creative utterance is nevertheless the highest Being's interior word.[13]

The infinite distance and yet intimate relationship between the eternal word and the finite word is best preserved by the term "similitudo." It already implies a "dissimilitudo." This safeguards the inner unity of the highest Being's word. Strictly speaking the term "similitudo" applies only to the created word but not to the eternal word. Every effort of emulation, of "imitatio," never rises to a definition of the divine word.[14] "Similitudo" is a one-way analogy of two generically but not materially similar entities. The finite spirit is endowed with an affinity for matters divine, yet the divine word is not similar to the first.

Ergo summus ille spiritus sicut est aeternus, ita aeterne sui memor est et intelligit se ad similitudinem mentis rationis; immo non ad ullius similitudinem, sed ille principaliter et mens rationalis ad eius similitudinem.[15]

This similarity of spiritual activities of both the finite and infinite spirits must be seen particularly under the considerations of the self-execution of

---

[10] M 29: 47,2f.
[11] M 29: 47,21f.
[12] M 29: 48,3-5.
[13] M 31: 48,14-50,13.
[14] M 31: 50,10.
[15] M 32: 51,12-15.

"memoria" and "intelligentia."[16] This safeguards under all circumstances the unity of the highest Being's word. Unity is being claimed with necessity. God's creative action is one of unity: "nec tamen sunt duo, sed unus creator et unum principium."[17] Spirit and word form a part of one subject. Yet this unitarian duality remains in his judgment an unexplainable mystery. Nevertheless Anselm ventures to attest the respective proprium of both "verbum" and "spiritus."

> Sed cum haec ita sint, miro tamen modo apertissimum est, quia nec ille cuius est verbum potest esse verbum suum, nec verbum potest esse ille cuius est verbum. Ut in eo quod significant vel quid sint substantialiter, vel quid sint ad creaturam, semper individuam tenent unitatem; in eo vero quod ille non est ex isto, hoc autem est ex illo, ineffabilem admittant pluralitatem.[18]

While the multitudinous nature of creation does not imperil the highest Being's unity, it does grant intimations of the multitude of acts possible within the highest Being. This leads to the question of how one can still preserve the unity of the infinitely dynamic entity.

The duality within the Godhead must be different from the duality of finite substances or persons. Indebted to Boethius' definition of "persona,"[19] Anselm observes:

> Constat igitur quia exprimi non potest, quid duo sint summus spiritus et verbum eius, quamvis quibusdam singulorum proprietatibus cogantur esse duo.[20]

He is compelled by the inherently underlying drive of his own thought to make observations concerning the highest Being which this cognition can no longer verify. Scheeben already acknowledged that on this point Anselm proves

> mit keiner Silbe, daß man die göttliche Weisheit und Erkenntnis nicht denken könne ohne ein aus ihr hervorgehendes Wort, welches dem ursprünglichen Inhaber derselben als Produkt des Erkenntniswortes hinzunimmt.[21]

---

[16] On the critical side one must note Anselm's failure to discuss the relationship of the creating word and the inner divine word. How can the self-execution of the divine Word have no immediate mediation to the outside? Kohlenberger draws the radical conclusion: "Damit ist faktisch die Schöpfungslehre aufgegeben." Kohlenberger, "Konsequenzen und Inkonsequenzen" 157. The creative word as an inner possibility is predicated by Anselm with a "fortisan" (M 34: 53,17). As enigmatic as this may sound he is unequivocally clear about defending its unity.

[17] M 37: 55,24.

[18] M 38: 56,11-16.

[19] Palémon Glorieux, "Quelques aspects de la christologie de Saint Anselme," Spicilegium Beccense I. (Paris: Cerf, 1959): 337-347, 339f; Maurice Nédoncelle, "La Notion de personne dans l'oeuvre de Anselme," Spicilegium Beccense I (Paris: Cerf, 1959): 31-43, at 31ff.

[20] M 38: 56,28-30.

[21] Scheeben, Mysterien 29.

He presupposes an idea of an actual production of insight arising from pure faith. One could not immediately adduce from the unity the multifariousness of the highest Being, if this highest Being had not revealed a priori its multifariousness as its "proprietas." The subsequent considerations on the divine properties are deduced from the trinitarian teachings.[22]

Within Anselmian systematics the connection of multifariousness and unity is also brought out by utilization of the term "processiones." This safeguards the assumed priority of the concept unity. Every single procession demands an underlying unity. To express the "verbum's" procession Anselm draws on the word "nascere." This "nascere" is a spiritual act. Of course, only the careful use of the term "similitudo" permits humans to speak in this context of a birth.

Nam nulla ratione negari potest, cum mens rationalis seipsum cogitando intelligit, imaginem ipsius nasci in sua cogitatione; immo ipsam cogitationem sui esse suam imaginem ad eius similitudinem tamquam ex eius impressione formata.[23]

In this sense the Father "gignat" and the Son "gignatur," the Father is "parens" and the Son is accordingly "proles."[24]

On the basis of this primary distinction Anselm is then well equipped to stipulate a principle for all further considerations on the Trinity:

Sic sunt oppositi relationibus, ut alter numquam suscipiat proprium alterius; sic sunt concordes naturae, ut alter semper teneat essentiam alterius.[25]

Both unity and multifariousness originate within the one Godhead. The first comes from the spiritedness, the latter, from the relationality of the Trinity. The divine attributes are deduced from the "oppositio relationis." The divine persons' common basis within the one Godhead is their divine essence.[26] And yet Anselm attributes the quality of "intelligentia" more to the Son, that of "memoria," more to the Father. Nevertheless, when considering their distinct ontic forms, one should ascribe "memoria" primarily to the Son and "intelligentia" primarily to the Father. He specifies this insofar as the Son is the

---

[22] In order to introduce some precision into Anselm's terminology, Kohlenberger suggests the distinction between "constitutive" and "functional" aspects of Anselm's understanding of the trinity. This, he believes, functions to express well the trinity's multitudinous nature, while the constutive element accentuates best the Godhead's unity. Cf. Kohlenberger, "Konsequenzen und Inkonsequenzen" 157f and 173ff.

[23] M 33: 52,12-15.

[24] M 42: 58,15 and M 39: 57,3ff respectively.

[25] M 43: 60,5-7.

[26] M 44-46: 60,13-62,26.

"intelligentia intelligentiae" and the "memoria memoriae patris."[27] This allows him to remark already previously:

> Inventis tot et tantis singulorum proprietatibus, quibus mira quaedam tam ineffabilis quam inevitabilis in summa unitate probatur esse pluralitas.[28]

By thinking the Augustinian psychological model of the Trinity to its very end, Anselm moves from the notion of trinitarian unity to its triune nature. This results by pondering the spiritual dimension of the already ascertained duality.

> Quam enim absurde negetur summus spiritus se amare, sicut sui memor est et se intelligit, cum mens rationalis se et illum amare posse convincatur, ex eo quia, sui et illius memor esse et se et illum intelligere potest? Otiosa namque et penitus inutilis est memoria et intelligentia cuiuslibet rei, nisi prout ratio exigit res ipsa ametur aut reprobetur.[29]

Spiritual action finds its proper completion and culmination in the "amor." To adequately value this one must note the proper order within which it executes itself. The "amor" embraces both "intelligentia" and "memoria" in a manner which allows all to be and to fulfill their proper selves in a way commensurate to their inner trinitarian ontic valences. It is an expression of a reciprocal being-in-one. "Quod uterque pari amore diligat se et alterum." [30] Love is the outflow of divine essence. This "amor" expresses, perfects and represents trinitarian unity. It originates from the Father and the Son and yet this love is not created. The "amor" thus perceived is the Spirit of both other divine persons: "patri filioque commune."[31]

6.3 Pneumatology

The "filioque" is a particularly central concept in which, to Anselm´s mind, the Christian understanding of the trinitarian God is put to the test. As a consequence he dedicated one full treatise - namely *De processione spiritus sancti* - to resolving the trinitarian disputes of his day. Again he places the notion of unity on center stage. Ignoring the Augustinian trinitarian psychology, he focuses exclusively on the dialectical relationship of multitude and unity. It is from within the center of divine unity that the Spirit proceeds from eternity from Father and Son. This assumption of a trinitarian unity is not only his theological-philosophical point of departure, it also serves quite conveniently as

---

[27] M 46-47: 63,2-11.
[28] M 43: 59,15f.
[29] M 49: 64,18-23. Anselm´s understanding of "relatio" arises from Boethius´ interchangeable use of the terms "relatio," "persona" and "ad aliquid." Cf. Nédoncelle, La Notion de Personne 33. The "amor" actually produces spiritually just as the "verbum" does.
[30] M 51: 65,12.
[31] M 57: 69,8.

a common ground with the Greek theologians. [32] All the more so, as it is also a credal confession. The procession and giving birth of God from God plurality is founded in unity. Only in the mode of procession may a difference be noted:

> Haec itaque sola causa pluralitatis est in deo, ut pater, et filius et spiritus sanctus dici possint de invicem, sed alii sint ab invicem, quia praedictis modis est deus de deo.[33]

The "quomodo" of this generation results in the dissonances between Greeks and Latins. Anselm resolves the tension between the "invisibilis unitas" and "insociabilis pluralitas" within the Godhead by applying the "oppositio relationis" as the relevant principle:

> Quatenus nec unitas amittat aliquando suum consequens, ubi non obviat aliqua relationis oppositio, nec relatio perdat quod suum est, nisi ubi obsistit unitas inseparabilis.[34]

This rule regulates the procession of plurality from unity. The totality of divinity comes forth. The full divine essence is being transferred. But it remains undeniable that one can never remark of God the Father: "deus de deo." As, however, the Spirit is from the divine essence, it is equally from the Father and from the Son. The contrary is not possible. The Son is born from the Father and therefore only from the Father, whereas the property of "procedere" implies that the Spirit comes forth from both persons.[35] The generation of the Spirit is explainable by way of divine unity and not through the diverse divine attributes of Father and Son. As a result Anselm defends the "filioque" as an expression of this divine unity:

> Constat inexpugnabili ratione spiritum sanctum esse de filo, sicut est de patre, nec tamen esse quasi de duobus diversis, sed quasi de uno. Ex eo enim quod pater et filius unum sint, id est ex deo, est spiritus sanctus, non ex eo unde alii sunt ab invicem.[36]

Similarly to chapter fourteen of the *De processione spiritus sancti* also the *Monologion's* chapters fifty eight and following defend the teaching of the third divine person. The properties arise from within the foundational "communio" of the Spirit with the Father and the Son.

The insistence on the unity of the Godhead is quite important, for only upon this background can the postulate of rationality's necessity be sustained. Thereby Anselm reaches the outermost of reason's and language's fringes. From here on one must speak of a "mirum" and a "dissimilitudo." Schmaus notes in this context that Anselm had not yet sufficiently developed the terms

---

[32] Pr 1: 177,18ff.
[33] Pr 1: 179,12-14.
[34] Pr 1: 181,2-4.
[35] Pr 1: 185,19-28.
[36] Pr 14: 212,10-14.

"relation," "property" and "notion." While having developed the brilliant principle that everything which does not consist of a relational opposition must be one in God, he failed to make adequate use of the Augustinian "metaphysisch-psychologischen Trinitätserklärung."[37] In spite of this defect, Anselm's thesis of divine transcendence has been succesfully put to the test by cognition.

6.4 Understanding the thinking "I"

Since the writings of Anselm the "mens rationalis" and therefore the "zoon noetikon" appear in an altogether new way in philosophical discourse. This "mens rationalis" is not only in Balthasar's opinion the center of Anselm's thought.[38] The rational structure of the human being is not only the hinge point for understanding God but also for God's history with humanity. "Saint Anselme a esquissé .. une doctrine de la personne qui lui est propre et qui est fondé sur les idées de liberté, de rectitude et dignité spirituelle."[39] An anthropology so defined is the hub and heart of Anselm's philosophy. The teleological orientation of this rational constitution as delineated in *De Veritate* also belongs to the definition of the human being; likewise the general rational human nature as brought out in the *Monologion*. This teleogical orientation actualizes itself in the praxis of, for and in truth. The "ratio" is the critical link between Anselm's theoretical and practical philosophy. Upon this canvas the central term freedom receives its particular flavor in practical philosophy.

Pouchet was particularly successful in illustrating Anselm's indebtedness to Augustine. In the latter's treatise *De libertate arbitrii* one already encounters terms such as "recte," "iuste," "rectitudo," "bona voluntas," "recta et honesta vita," "recta ratione," "sponte" and finally "debere."[40]

In the preface to *De Veritate* Anselm himself identifies a broad connection and essential interrelation between the treatises *De Veritate, De libertate arbitrii* and *De casu diaboli*.[41] The common ground of these three is

---

[37] Schmaus, "Die theologiegeschichtliche Tragweite" 40 and 221ff.

[38] Balthasar, Anselm 217. 241ff; Richard Heinzmann, "Veritas humanae naturae. Ein Beitrag zur Anthropologie Anselm's von Canterbury," Wahrheit und Verkündigung. FS für Michael Schmaus. Vol. 1 (München: Schöningh, 1967): 779-798, at 779-783; Gisbert Greshake, "Erlösung und Freiheit. Eine Neuinterpretation der Erlösungslehre Anselms von Canterbury," Theologische Quartalschrift 153 (1973): 323-345, at 340ff; Kohlenberger, Similitudo und Ratio 113f; Nédoncelle, "La Notion de personne" 31ff; Pouchet, La Rectitudo 85ff; Rondet, "Grâce et péché" 155ff; Ubbelohde, Glaube und Vernunft 273ff; Vanni-Rovighi, "L'Etica" 73ff; Paul Vignaux, "Necessité des raisons dans le Monologion," Revue des sciences philosophiques et théologiques 64 (1980): 3-25, at 14ff.

[39] Nédoncelle, "La Notion de Personne" 31.

[40] Pouchet, La Rectitudo 35ff.

[41] V Praef: 173,2ff.

the concept of "libertas." This term receives its proper context by being correlated with that of "ratio." By implication "ratio" has necessarily a practical consequence for Anselm. The whole of human existence stands under reason's claim. The theoretical basis for Anselmian anthropology is the "ratio;" its practical manifestation is freedom's history. Thereby reason acquires inevitably a historical perspective and must be considered under soterio-historical considerations. There is a processional component in this understanding: either the history of reason entails a coming-to-one's-senses (in the sense of becoming self-conscious) or failure to achieve this state. In an examplary way Anselm defines this situation of reason in the *De casu diaboli*:

> Quamdiu enim voluntas primum data rationali naturae et simul in ipsa datione ab ipso datore conversa, immo non conversa sed facta recta ad hoc quod velle debuit, stetit in ipsa rectitudine quam dicimus veritatem sive iustitiam in qua facta est: iusta fuit. Cum vero avertit se ab eo quod debuit et convertit ad id quod non debuit: non stetit in originali ut ita dicam rectitudine in qua facta est.[42]

Anselm expresses his central concern in the words "stare in veritate" and "stare in rectitudine sive iustitia."[43] These two concepts express the ontic intentionality of the "homo rationalis." There is a purpose in being created "homo rationalis." This giftedness with a "natura rationalis" entails an "ab ipso datore." The "ratio" so intended is equipped with a transcendentality, a destination towards the (ultimately to be thought as personal entity) "bonum" and finally ordered towards its own "beatitudo." The "beatum esse" requires, however, a "recte et iuste facere" as a prerequisite. Reason's self-execution occurs within the doing of truth. This in turn calls for a volitional (i.e. "voluntas iusta") decision on the part of reason. The creator has endowed the human race with all the means necessary to attain the state for which it had been destined. The human condition was equipped with an "originalis rectitudo" which permitted humans to correspond to an inner transcendalism. Therefore, in a primordial state there was the intention to will what is good, " facta recta ad hoc quod velle debuit." The will must will that for which it had been created - "quod velle debuit" - in order to stand in truth and justice. Such is the call humanity hears to its own history - a chance, yet also a necessity. Creation calls for fulfillment. In the original state humanity had turned away from that towards which it had been made: "avertit se ab eo quod debuit" and turned to that for which it had not been created: " et convertit ad id quod non debuit." As a result humanity fell from a particular form of grace: "rectitudo originalis." Human history is a constant descent from rational nature. This in turn is a challenge for redemption. To Anselm's mind salvation history is also a process of reason's restitution. In this sense freedom is by no means an abstract category in

---

[42] Ca 9: 246, 26-247,1.
[43] Cf. Delhaye,"Quelques Aspects" 403; Pouchet, La Rectitudo 29ff.

Anselmian literature. It is a part of salvation history and profoundly related to reason. Both are imbedded in concrete salvation history. Freedom is the topic of human existence.

6.5 Freedom and Truth

The gravitational center of Anselm's anthropology - as delineated in *De libertate arbitrii* - is the notion of freedom as the tenor of human history. The corollary term to freedom is reason. In the field of tension between these two terms life appears as a call to an ethical effort. The "homo rationalis" ought to want what he or she should and ought not to want what he or she should not: "velle debere." Historicity is the direct result of such facticity. Sin becomes the antagonist of freedom. [44] One asks to what degree sin could be the direct consequence of freedom. Is freedom as a result itself infected in some way? Has freedom thereby failed her destiny by wanting exactly what is diametrically the opposite to her purpose? In what way did original sin affect the nature of freedom? What imprint did this sin leave on the essence of the human race? More specifically, how does it impinge upon humanity's rational nature? Is humanity corrupted altogether beyond repair with no glimmer of hope? A pupil formulates this central question and the resulting dilemma:

Quoniam liberum arbitrium videtur repugnare gratiae et praedestinationi et praescientiae dei: ipsa libertas arbitrii quid sit nosse desidero, et utrum semper illam habemus. Si enim libertas arbitrii est `posse peccare et non peccare,´ sicut a quibusdam solet dici, et hoc semper habemus: quomodo aliquando gratia indigemus? Si autem hoc non semper habemus: cur nobis imputatur peccatum, quando sine libero arbitrio peccamus?[45]

If human freedom has in no way been altered by the event of sin, the pupil asks, and therefore the human being remains equally capable of doing good or committing sin, why should human freedom be in need of grace? However, if freedom has been totally corrupted by sin, how could one count something as a failure; how could a human being ever be culpable?[46]

Anselm does not hesitate to respond directly: freedom does not exhaust itself in a negative definition. It is positively more than the ability to commit a sin: "libertatem arbitrii non puto esse potentiam peccandi et non peccandi."[47] Freedom could exist outside the possibility of sin. Anselm asks the reader to consider that God and the angels are free and yet have not sinned. Nevertheless, this does not suffice to illumine the true nature of freedom. Freedom is defined by its rationality and intelligibilty. It is against the background of "ratio" that freedom can obtain the quality of "rectitudo voluntatis." Human volition

---

[44] L 1: 207,3-209,6.
[45] L 1: 207,4-10.
[46] Cf. Delhaye, "Quelques Aspects" 413ff.
[47] L 1: 207,11f.

becomes free by doing the good: "quod decet et quod expediet."[48] Rectitude is the intentionality, the justification and purpose of freedom.

> Ergo ad rectitudinem voluntatis habuerunt libertatem arbitrii. Quamdiu namque voluerunt quod debuerunt, rectitudinem habuerunt voluntatis.[49]

The intentionality so defined is not accidental to human nature but a constitutive element of human essence. No matter how one sinned, one remains imbedded in this rational structure.The free will is circumscribed by the definition of justice already explained in *De Veritate*. "Quapropter restat libertatem arbitrii datam esse rationali naturae ad servandam acceptam rectitudinem voluntatis ..."[50]

Since nobody can sin out of pure necessity - this would defy the definition of freedom - human beings sin out of free will.This free will obtains and retains the adjective "free" only insofar as it is bound to a "iudicium" or "arbitrium." This, however, can only be the case if these are subject to a rational verdict and therefore to reason itself.[51] This "libertas arbitrii naturalis" can never and at the hands of nothing, suffer destruction. It belongs to the most natural of human faculties. Also "post lapsum" the human being is capable of using reason.[52] The same holds for human freedom. She remains incorruptible and able to fulfill its very essence:

> Ergo quoniam omnis libertas est potestas, illa libertas arbitrii est potestas servandi rectitudinem voluntatis propter ipsam rectitudinem.[53]

Original sin can never be so deleterious that freedom cannot preserve its own rationality and hence also "rectitudo." This applies to the same degree also to free will.[54] This will is ordered towards the "rectitudo voluntatis." Even when failing its goal, volition´s intentionality and purpose remain intact, be it only in potentiality. While free will did lose its rectitude in original sin, it is not altogether deprived of its instrument. It is by means of rationality that the original state of freedom remains somehow present also "post lapsum."[55]

Anselm´s disciple insists on knowing what this freedom precisely to sin conveys. The response is that this "potestas peccandi" is grounded in finite volition. This volition retains its ability to fulfill rectitude: "velle ipsam

---

[48] L 1: 208, 14-17.
[49] L 3: 211,9-11.
[50] V 3: 143, 7-17; cf. L 3: 212,8f.18.
[51] C 6: 257,13.
[52] L 3: 210,28f.
[53] L 3: 212,19f.
[54] L 3: 212,22f.
[55] L 4: 214,4ff.

rectitudinem perserverantur."[56] Even if the situation is such that it cannot fully fulfill its own rectitude, it retains this ability. This "rectitudo voluntatis" is indefatigable. Not even God can abolish this givenness. Not only is this "libertas" part of the human volition, it is also part of the divine will. "Sed iam positum est servare hoc modo rectitudinem voluntatis esse omni servanti velle, quod deus vult illum velle."[57] Freedom of will is grounded in a transcendent cause. Its own necessity is explained by its correspondence with the divine will. The agencies for the appropriate existential correspondence are "ratio" and "voluntas;" which are in turn also transcendentally grounded. Both arrive at their proper rectitude by virtue of their own transcendality. This necessity is inalienable and can never be neutralized: "Igitur nihil magis impossibile, quam deum rectitudinem voluntatis auferre."[58] The very concrete history of freedom and rectitude well illustrate in Anselm´s judgment the necessity for salvation. Only redemption can fully restore rectitude.

Quippe sicut nulla voluntas, antequam haberet rectitudinem, potuit eam deo non dante capere; ita cum deserit acceptam, non potest eam nisi deo reddente recipere.[59]

In conclusion Anselm presents a definition and differentiation of the various manifestations of freedom. Light is shed on the salient features of freedom. Freedom is the key term to describe the drama of failings and of salvation in the history of humankind.

Restat nunc ut dividas eandem libertatem. Quamvis enim secundum hanc definitionem communis sit omni rationali naturae, multum tamen differt illa quae dei est ab illis quae rationalis creaturae sunt, et illae ab invicem.
Libertas arbitrii alia est a se; quae non facta esat nec ab alio accepta, quae est solius dei; alia a deo facta et accepta, quae est angelorum et hominum. Facta autem sive accepta alia est habens rectitudinem quam servet, alia carens. Habens alia tenet separabiliter, alia inseparabiliter. Illa quidem quae separabiliter tenet, fuit angelorum omnium antequam boni confirmarentur et mali caderent; et est omnium hominum ante mortem, qui habent eandem rectitudinem. Quae vero tenet inseparabiliter, est electorum angelorum et hominum. Sed angelorum post ruinam reproborum, et hominum post mortem suam. Illa autem quae caret rectitudine, alia caret recuperabiliter, alia irrecuperabiliter. Quae recuperabiliter caret, est tantum in hac vita omnium hominum illa carentium, quamvis illam multi non recuperent. Quae autem irrecuperabiliter caret, est reproborum angelorum et hominum; sed angelorum post ruinam, et hominum post hanc vitam.[60]

[56] L 5: 216,17.
[57] L 8: 221,2f.
[58] L 8: 221,8f.
[59] L 10: 222,10-13.
[60] L 14: 226,3-18.; Delhaye, "Quelques Aspects" 409 and Nédoncelle, "La Notion de Personne" 31 discuss the differences between Augustine´s and the Stoa´s understanding of freedom respectively. In general cf. Vanni-Rovighi, Sant´ Anselmo 123ff.

6.6 Angels and Truth

In the introduction to *De casu diaboli* Anselm informs the reader of his intention to speak of the angels' fall. In reality he discusses the conditions for the fall. He rejects on grounds of the nature of freedom the possibility of the fallen angels' freedom. He never loses sight of the actual topic of his writings - human freedom - and it is precisely for this reason that he dwells on the nature of angelic freedom. In Anselm's understanding the predication "free" may not be restricted in Anselm's understanding to the human condition as it is closely linked with reason. The Godhead, angels and human beings share in this predication, as the final chapter of *De libertate arbitrii* has shown.

Angelic freedom has as its pendent the "rectitudo." A bad angel "in veritate non stetit."[61] Further down the text this situation is transposed into the words "in rectitudine non steti."[62] Some angels have lost their "fortitudo naturalis." Both angels and human beings have a received freedom and their volition towards their own rectitude is likewise received from the creator. Therefore, Anselm asks whether, not the angels, but God Himself is to be held responsible for the sins angels have committed. Here one senses the tension between the terms "accipere" and "habere;" as well as between "rectitudo voluntatis" and "iustitia." Anselm intends to illumine the mysterious nature of freedom, since it is the common predication of all rational beings. Yet what is the angel's share in this "facere" if so much is received?

To have received freedom is in Anselm's mind a "bonum." The angels's failure, however, is to have failed to preserve the received gift: "servare."[63] Though the perseverance in the good is God's gift, this must also be preserved by the angels. The good angels were successful in preserving this "perseverantia" which they had received and which they had possessed because God had given it. The bad angels had not been given this "perseverantia" because they had refused to receive it and they had not been in possession of it because they had not preserved it. To stand the test of one's own freedom means to play the dialectics of "to give" and "to preserve." In the words of the "discipulus" the difference between those who accede to being "personae dramatis" to God and those who refuse is evident.[64]

Receiving depends in Anselm's dialectics on giving: "datio est causa acceptionis."[65] The fallen angels have not received because they have not been given: "non accipimus quia non datur"[66] the "discipulus" interjects. How could God then be in any way responsible for the angels' non-preserving? To ascribe any guilt to God would mean seeing only one side of a dialectical relationship

---

[61] Ca 2: 235,20.23.
[62] Ca 9: 246,29.
[63] Ca 2: 235,18-31.
[64] Ca 2: 235,20ff.
[65] Ca 2: 236,1.
[66] Ca 2: 236,5.

in which God is also a dependent partner. God depends on the angels′ acceptance? "Quod ideo deus non dedit, quia ille non accepit."[67] Giving depends on the mode of being received. It does not, however, follow that the refusal to accept something depends on its not having been given in the first place. "Potest enim non dare non esse causa non accipiendi, etiamsi dare semper causa esset accipiendi."[68] Receiving and accepting have their cause in the being-given of something. The refusal to accept something does not, however, have its cause necessarily in the donor. Even the one who ultimately rejects acceptance could have been divinely equipped to accept and receive: "deus dedit illi voluntatem et potestatem accipiendi perseverantiam."[69] Acceptance is the responsibility of the one who receives. As "pervelle" indicates, the fallen angel refused to accept the "perseverantia." He qualifies this reaction (= refusal) on the part of some angels as "sponte." This means it occurs out of a free will. In this avenue Anselm is able to safeguard the "bonitas Dei" and the sovereignty of both God and the fallen angels. The gift of being capable of doing the good deed God had not withheld, but the fallen angels have rejected acceptance.

The insights thereby gained permit Anselm to draw some conclusions for creaturely freedom in general. In *De libertate arbitrii* sin becomes the antagonist of freedom. In this regard the angle under which "peccatum" is considered undergoes an interesting change. "Peccatum" evolves into something more than mere disobedience. Both the fallen angels and the post-lapsarian human race have violated the "similitudo."[70] "Quomodo ille peccavit et voluit esse similis deo."[71] Angels are called to "will" what they had received, but never what had not been given to them. The fallen angels′ hybris lies in their presumptuous assumption that they can dispose of the creaturely dialectics of being endowed and receiving. This entails a disregard for "iustitia." "Nihil autem velle poterat nisi iustitiam aut commodum."[72] The angels′ will went beyond that which had been destined for them "quia plus aliquid quam accepit inordinate volendo voluntatem suam extra iustitiam extendit."[73] The inordinate craving went so far that it wished to supplant "similitudo" with "identitas." Sin is defined in this context as presumptuousness. The fallen angels have laid claim on something they do not hold title to. This situation can experience an

---

[67] Ca 3: 236,11.

[68] Ca 3: 236,12.

[69] Ca 3: 237,27f.

[70] Ca 4-6: 240,15ff.

[71] Ca 4: 240,15; this line is again conventional. By opting to change the divinely ordained role in the dialectics of "similitudo" the one partner of this relationship threatens the relationship which is built on "similitudo." This is no longer an unjustly usurped "similitudo" but a rightfully laid claim on identity (against Kienzler, Glauben und Denken 188).

[72] Ca 4: 241, 13.

[73] Ca 4: 241,22f.

amelioration only if a recourse to the rational structure is found. This appreciation and re-alignment of human beings with "ratio" always means a reconstitution of the "similitudo." The uniqueness of divine nature must be recognized. The respect for God's sublime sovereignty must always be taken into account. Disrespect for divine authority and uniqueness as well as an abuse of the constitutive definition of human existence as rationally structured define sin.

> Si deus non potest cogitari nisi ita solus, ut nihil aliud deo simile cogitari potest: quomodo potuit diabolus velle quod non potuit cogitare? Non enim ita obtusae mentis erat, ut nihil illi simile cogitari posse nesciret.[74]

The *Proslogion's* understanding of the Godhead resonates here; equally its definition of sin's nature. Sin constitutes a violation of divine uniqueness. Simultaneously sin abuses rationality and similitude: "deus non potest cogitari nisi ita solus." The failure to remain within the divinely ordained matrix - perceived as both ontic and ethic - entails a diminution of existence, for the Godhead is nothing less than ontic fullness and therefore consequently ethical plenitude.

This established, Anselm proceeds to contemplate in greater depth the nature of evil.[75] He investigates the problem the existence of "malum" poses when bearing in mind divine omnipotence and the assumption of an all-good God.[76] The bad deed is grounded in the bad intention (= "voluntas"); insisting nevertheless that this volitional capacity was created so that human beings may do good and thereby participate in divine goodness. Thus, human "voluntas" is able to pervert its actual destiny into its opposite.[77] Anselm arrives at the conclusion that the "malum" is not in and of itself an "aliquid" but merely the "privatio" of the good and hence "nihil."[78] He observes on this aspect:

> Iustitiam credere debemus esse ipsum bonum quo sunt boni ... et quo ipsa voluntas bona sive iusta dicitur; iniustitiam vero ipsum malum esse, quod nihil aliud dicimus quam boni privationem, quod malos et malam voluntatem facit, et ideo eandem iniustitiam non aliud esse asserimus quam privationem iustitiae.[79]

The good is identified with the ethical good per se, namely justice. It originates in the "bona sive iusta voluntas." The "malum," however, is the

---

[74] Ca 4: 241, 31-242,2.

[75] Ca 2-12: 244,8-255,18.

[76] Cf. Ca 7: 244,22ff. This is very much in the Augustinian line of argument. God is good, human beings are able to correspond to this predication and the bad is merely an ontic reversal, i.e. a perversion of the good (cf. Augustine, De lib. arb. 1.1, c. 1; c. 11,21. 1.2, c. 19f and c. 9,24. c. 12,35 respectively. See also Pouchet, La Rectitudo 39. 122f; Vanni-Rovighi, "L'etica" 91ff.

[77] Cf. Ca 7: 245,13ff.

[78] Ca 9: 246,19 and 10: 247,5.

[79] Ca 9: 246,22-26.

outgrowth of "iniustitia." The "malum" is defined as a "privatio boni scilicet iustitiae." From this statement it follows that it is a nothing in the - nota bene divinely ordained - ontic order. "Quod malum et nihil non possint probari per nomen suum esse aliquid, sed quasi aliquid."[80]

Chapters twelve through fifteen develop a theory of volition. Anselm distinguishes a first will. Both angels and human beings cannot dispose freely of this will. Rather it is divinely pre-given. Therefore any kind of will remains permanently oriented towards God. Already in *De veritate* Anselm had claimed that volition is fundamentally transcendental in character. This occurred already with the term "ratio" in the *Monologion*. Both terms are at their point of reference transcendental and both point towards the same goal: beatitude; or: "Omnes quippe volunt bene sibi esse."[81]

Resulting from his distinction between the first volition (= "prima voluntas") and a factual intention arising from one's own actualized freedom Anselm also refers to two "potestates." This bipolar perception is continued by the terminological pairs of double goods, double evils, "commodum" - which every intention intends to realize - and "iustitia," which is a posed task, and finally the "voluntas beatitudinis" and the "voluntas rectitudinis." These pairs in their sum-total also describe the phenomenon "homo rationalis." These words predicated of the human condition refer to a task given ever anew. Such a predicating endeavor succeeds if it results from within the predicating subject as a free act.[82] The act must arise from, be sustained in and executed by a single, undivided and free will:

nec potest nec debet esse beatus nisi velit et nisi iuste velit: necesse est ut sic faciat deus utramque voluntatem in illo convenire, ut et beatus esse velit iuste velit. Quatenus addita iustitia sic temperet voluntatem beatitudinis, ut et resecet voluntatis excessum et excedendi non amputet potestatem.[83]

In this perspective justice becomes the highest and ultimate goal of every intention. Rectitude and beatitude find their fulfilling culmination. "Iustitia" is the sublimest expression of rationality. For it is the manifestation of all that "ratio" recognizes as essentially substantive and therefore existentially authoritative. "Iustitia's" rationality occupies center stage in the Anselmian anthropology.[84]

In Anselm's anthropology, freedom and (practical) reason dominate. This is an altogether uncommon view of human existence at that time. Reason and freedom become reciprocally conditioning and enabling corollaries of

---

[80] Ca 11: 248,2f.
[81] Ca 12: 255,4.
[82] Ca 13: 255,20; 256,2f; along with Ca 12: 252,30ff.
[83] Ca 14: 258,6.20-24.
[84] Ca 15: 259,6ff.

humanity. By taking the "libertas" of humankind seriously, Anselm shows that the philosophical train of thought is compelled to postulate the "homo rationalis." "Libertas" articulates itself in "rectitude" in its most (and only) fitting expression.

Confronted with the then virulent formulation of soteriological questions, Anselm is challenged to greater precision as regards the nature of "rectitudo." The impulse of human nature towards "rectitudo" renders freedom, both under the consideration of "libertas arbitrii"and as "liberum arbitrium," as non-deprivable. It is constitutively relevant both in the transcendental self-execution of the human being - as "instrumentum" - and in practical self-executions - as "usus." It remains simultaneously responsible to reason. This ultimately transcendental cause of both volition and freedom does not serve to alienate the same but rather to render them - along with "ratio" in the *Monologion* - transparent towards their one and single cause.[85]

---

[85] Cf. Gerhard Gäde, <u>Eine andere Barmherzigkeit: zum Verständnis der Erlösungslehre Anselms von Canterbury</u> (Würzburg: Echter, 1989) at 23ff; Kienzler, <u>Glauben und Denken</u> 190f.

CHAPTER SEVEN
7.0 Soteriology

7.1 Introduction
This area is considered under the terminological pairs "lost justice" and the "personal justice" as well as "nature" and "person" necessary to restore the original state.[1] The tensions created in the human mind as the result of terms such as "peccatum," "satisfactio" and restauratio" are not belittled but come into reciprocal relationship by employing consistently the overarching term "iustitia."

7.2 *Cur Deus Homo*
Anselm's work *Cur Deus Homo*[2] articulates his grand soteriological design which enunciates the necessity of both humanity's redemption and its redemption by the God-Man: "Necessariis rationibus." These necessities are requirements of a rational kind. They are implications of comprehension, epistemology and cognition. By retracing these areas Anselm expressly wishes to do justice to their respective rationalities, subsumed under the one "ratio" permeating all ontic orders. Reason is the formative and epistemological principle of all things insofar as they are. Consequently, reason is the measure with which to recognize and comprehend all ontic concentrations. These ontic concentrations are nothing less than what faith reveals as Christian truths.

Yet it would be too simple, were one to reduce Anselm's understanding of ratio to this. "Ratio" is not merely an instrument, a cognitive tool for apprehending the created order, but rather inalienably the hingepoint and center of the Anselmian soteriology; i.e. it is the ideal means for apprehending the divine movement in history. Little wonder then that he confronts the reader with these central notions of his *Cur Deus Homo* already in the preface. The "ratio" is presented as the "creatura rationalis" in the sense that it itself is an artistic and dramatic moment of life.[3]

Omnis voluntas rationalis creaturae subiecta debet esse voluntati dei ... Hoc est debitum quod debet angelus et homo deo, quod solvendo nullus peccat, et quod omnis qui non solvit peccat. Haec est iustitia sive rectitudo voluntatis, quae iustus facit sive rectus corde, id

[1] Rudolf Haubst, "Anselms Satisfaktionslehre einst und heute," Analecta Anselmiana 4/2 (Frankfurt am Main: Minerva, 1975): 141-157, at 141ff; Kienzler, Glauben und Denken 192ff; Jean Plangieux, "Le Binome 'iustitia - potentia' dans la sotériologie augustinienne et anselmienne," Spicilegium Beccense I (Paris: Vrin, 1959): 141-154, at 141ff; Rondet, "Grâce et péché" 155ff; Ubbelohde, Glaube und Vernunft 266ff.
[2] For general introductions cf. Théodore A. Audet, "Problématique et structure de Cur Deus Homo," Etudes d'histoire littéraire et doctrinale 13 (1968): 7-115, at 7ff; Gäde, Eine andere Barmherzigkeit 13-22; Greshake, "Erlösung und Freiheit" 323ff; Haubst, "Cur Deus Homo" 302ff; Pouchet, La Rectitudo 145ff; Schmitt, "Die wissenschaftliche Methode" 349ff.
[3] Cf. Cu I 11: 68,12.14ff.

180

est voluntate. Hic est solus et totus honor, quem debemus deo et a nobis exigit deus ... Sic ergo debet omnis qui peccat, honorem deo quem rapuit solvere; et haec est satisfactio, quam omnis peccator deo debet facere.[4]

One encounters here again Anselm's coherent structure of reality as a correlation of truth, uprightness ("rectitudo"), honor and reason. Ideally, spirit and matter are in unison. This paragraph contains in nuce the whole of Anselm's agenda. The topos is the created "voluntas rationalis." This rational will is ordered towards and neccessarily is subject to the "voluntas dei." Every created (rational) creature, be it angel or human being, owes God obedience: "debet deo." This facticity of "debere" has two causes:
1. the createdness of the creature and
2. its being equipped with reason.
From this it then follows: the "creatura rationalis" is exclusively capable of this primordial fulfillment of justice and rectitude, as he alone amongst created beings is capable of reflecting upon the categoriality of facticity. Intriguingly for Anselm this creature not merely applies reason in order to fathom reality, but is able to reflect upon this rational constitution of its being. In this sense "ratio" is not merely a first, superficial reflection in the sense of a pragmatic analysis of reality; it is capable of a "meta-reflection" in the sense that it is able to ask not only in general terms about the meaning of existence but more specifically to reflect upon the rational categoriality of reality and more particularly of its, i.e. rationality's meaning. This is the import of the predication "rationalis." The transgression of this rectitude is sin. The honor of God is preserved by the justice humans practice. His uniquness and perfection are consequently respected. A created will is subject to the "debemus deo" and thereby becomes a just will. Since sin is not able to render God the honor due to Him, this transgression requires satisfaction. Every sinner must perform this satisfaction. The aim of such satisfaction is called "restauratio ordinis recti."[5] It would be a gross oversimplification were one to perceive the need for such a restoration as arising exclusively for juridic considerations. The "ordo rectus" is the form of the world which is linked to the "iustitia dei." Both nouns, "ordo" and "iustitia," are equally considered ontic realities. Through Jesus Christ's death this "ordo rectus" is restored. By the "reconstitutio" the original created order and - in a quite different manner - also the divine order are returned to their original state.[6]

---

[4] Cu I 11: 68,12-69,1.
[5] Cu I 3 and 15.
[6] Cu I 3: 50,29-51,12; cf. Pouchet, La Rectitudo 147ff: Pouchet illumines well the Augustinian background for the terms employed. Though borrowing heavily from Augustine, Anselm is seen as appropriating in an independent manner the motifs of "ordo," "iustitia" and "peccator." Cf. Gäde, Eine andere Barmherzigkeit 107ff; Plagnieux, "Le Binome 'iustitia-potentia'" 144ff.

The terms "divine order," "justice" or "rectitude of will," "satisfaction" and "the restoration of the correct order" are code words which Anselm uses to signify the drama of sin and the necessary salvation effected through Christ's redemptive acts. In this context the term "justice" serves as a kind of dominating brackets for *Cur Deus Homo*: "La définition de la justice commande tout le Cur deus homo."[7]

The topic of the *Cur Deus Homo* is defined as a theological one: "cuiusdam de fide nostra quaestionis."[8] This topicality remains ever current. This remark, however, does not serve to lure the reader into abandoning rationality as the hermeneutical principle of the discourse. Rather, this enables Anselm to illustrate the necessity of Christ's redemptive deeds and the inner rationality of the salvific event: "qua scilicet ratione vel necessitate deus homo factus sit, et morte sua, sicut credimus et confitemur, mundo vitam reddiderit."[9] The principle of rationality permits him to speak to anyone willing to lend him an ear, be he or she Christian or non-believer. He can address the infidels and instruct believers with arguments that must convince both parties.

In spite of the aforesaid, at first sight it is difficult to discern a structure in this treatise. According to the preface, the writing is divided into two books.[10] The first book is divided again into two large units. The first unit, concerning objections (I, 1-10), is intended as a general introduction to the overall problematics of incarnation, the human life of Jesus Christ and redemption.[11] The second part of this first book is concerned with systematics. It argues "remoto Christo," in order to illustrate rationally the necessity of thinking humanity's redemption to be utterly impossible without Christ (I, 11-25). The second book is altogether different. Here too the author is faithful to the voluntarily chosen methodological limitation: to disregard for the time being the historical Christ's revelation. The point of departure for his argumentation is humanity's divinely ordained destiny, namely "beatitudo" (II, 1-5). This is followed by the final large unit. It serves to illustrate that the aim of human existence, which is "beatitudo," can only be reached through and with the God-man. The Christian creed is necessary if we are to journey with some prospect of success on the earthly trail towards the heavenly kingdom: "omnia quae de Christo credimus fieri oportere."[12] So to say in passing, Anselm delineates once again the pivotal importance and yet also the limitations of contingent rationality. While reason is fully capable of recognizing and articulating the teleological categoriality of human existence, it alone does not suffice to attain this "telos." It can lead to faith and finds within faith its proper mode of

---

[7] Rondet, "Grâce et péché" 159.

[8] Cu I 1: 47,6.

[9] Cu I 1: 48,2f.

[10] Schmitt, "Die wissenschaftliche Methode" 351ff.

[11] Audet, "Problématique et structure" 34ff.

[12] Cu P: 43,2.

operation, because reason, while not fully imparted to post-lapsarian humanity, is of divine predication and in this constitutedness planned for humankind by God.[13]

The first part of the first book offers some clarification on the subject chosen (I, 3-10). The main objection raised by the "infideles" is their inability to reconcile the God of their imagination with Christian faith in the objective redemption of all of humanity effected by Jesus Christ: "multa...quae de deo non videntur convenire."[14] Anselm wishes to reconcile inconsistencies *within* human comprehension with divine reason, which embraces and gives sustenance to all of reality.[15] Anselm's partner, Boso, formulates this weighty objection in the following words: "qua necessitate scilicet et ratione deus, cum sit omnipotens, humilitatem et infirmitatem humanae nature pro eius restauratione assumpserit."[16] Boso represents the infidel. For the infidel it is utterly inconceivable that an almighty God might become incarnate and share in humanity's depravity in order to effect its redemption.[17]

The attack originates in the contestation of the claim that it is fitting for divine essence

1. to become human, i.e. to suffer the ignominy of the human condition, and

2. to liberate humanity from the same: "Obiciunt nobis deridentes ... infideles quia deo facimus iniuriam et contumeliam, cum eum asserimus ... descendisse ... crucem mortemque sustinuisse."[18] Anselm negates an inconsistency in this statement: rather than an inconvenience between the human condition and the divine omnipotence, what we have is the weakness of the human mind to bring human imagination into (albeit asymptotic) symmetry with divine will. Through His incarnation Christ has become the author of our justice and salvation. He restored humanity's primordial justice. More specifically, humanity's disobedience and its deleterious effects have been undone. Boso is not content with this response and probes further. He is only able to behold in Anselm's argument some exterior form of a "beautiful convenience," but not a fully convincing argument addressing the inner movement of salvation. The implication is that Boso does not hold the "verum"

---

[13] The outline presented by Audet, "Problématique et structure" 47ff appears more convincing than that of Schmitt, "Die wissenschaftliche Methode" 353.

[14] Cu I 3: 50, 27.

[15] The implication left unmentioned is that by achieving some consonance with divine reason, reality as a whole for the (contingent) thinking subject - and therefore also palpable reality - acquires greater cogency. Cf. Gäde, Eine andere Barmherzigkeit 107-112.

[16] Cu I 1: 48, 22-24.

[17] Henry recognizes (in The Logic of Saint Anselm 134ff) in God's predication as almighty ("omnipotentia dei") the crucial issue in the *Cur Deus Homo*. Anselm probes the viability of modal statements in the context of "potesse:" "posse," "non posse," "potesteas" and "potentia."

[18] Cu I 3: 50, 24-28.

to result from the "pulchrum." On the contrary, it is only after apprehending the "verum" that one is able to appreciate its aesthetic categoriality, namely "verum" as the "pulchrum"; "veritatis soliditas rationabilis, id est necessitas."[19]

A further objection raised by Boso concerns the concrete mode in which redemption occurred. Must it have come about in "hoc modo"? Does not this manner of redemption do violence to the divine properties? As God is "omnipotentia," God in his sovereignty could have redeemed humanity by choosing other means than having his only begotten son become man. Does one not in this case constrain the "sapientia Dei"? "Aut si fatemini quia potuit, sed non voluit nisi hoc modo: quomodo sapientem illum potestis ostendere, quem sine ulla ratione tam indecentia velle pati asseritis?"[20]

Boso queries whether Anselm when using the term "liberatio" does not presuppose an incorrect understanding of the "iustitia dei." To his mind divine justice serves to snatch away humanity from the devil's grasp. Anselm seems to argue that divine will is such that it cannot be reduced simply to the service of counteracting a fallen angel's intention.[21] This reference to divine will provokes yet another objection on Boso's part. It would not be fitting for divine nature to be compelled to die. Anselm responds to this by distinguishing between an obedience coerced by exterior factors and an obedience originating from within the very nature, the very essence, of an obedient act. While human beings are called to act "oboedientiam servare" or "non exigente oboedientia," true obedience occurs in the Godhead in a manner "sponte."[22] This obedience is freely performed by the divine son, illustrating the attitude in which every creature should be able to execute obedience. "Hanc igitur oboedientiam debebat homo ille deo patri, et humanitas divinitati, et hanc ab illo exigebat pater."[23] In his obedience Christ becomes exemplary for what God expects in fact from all of humanity. This is the case because Jesus lived the primordially intended relationship between God and humanity: "(Q)uia veritatem et iustitiam vivendo et loquendo indeclinabiliter tenebat."[24] In so doing Christ fulfills the destiny pre-ordained for every human being, and nevertheless, this freedom can never be a coerced one, lest Jesus is not the Christ, i. e. the son of God. If Jesus Christ is the son of God, then He fulfills the divine will as part of His very own essence which He has in common with the Holy Trinity. Jesus Christ as the true and, therefore, full human being, represents the obedience every human being

---

[19] Cu I 4: 52,3f. In spite of Boso's argument, Anselm holds "pulchritudo" to be an important indication of a coherent rational argument. It is from this Anselmian understanding of beauty, that Balthasar develops his "theological aesthetics." Cf. Hans Urs von Balthasar, The Glory of the Lord, Vol. I. Seeing the Form (San Francisco: Ignatius, 1982) 217ff.

[20] Cu I 6: 54, 3-5.

[21] Cu I 8: 59, 10f.

[22] Cu I 8-9.

[23] Cu I 9: 61, 18f.

[24] Cu I 9: 61, 13f.

owes God. In this connection Anselm quotes Phil 2:8. For this reason the redemption effected by Jesus Christ is fitting for God: "decet." The Son's action is laudable and was performed for the honor of God and for the salvation of humanity.[25]   Now even Boso seems to be satisfied, because the Son's redemptive action is obviously brought into a form which renders it congenial to the objective and universal principle of rationality. The "oboedientia" is an expression of the subjugation of the free will under the measure of "iustitia."

In spite of this admission Boso does note a last incongruency. Why can one not suppose another mode of salvation and why would God have rejected it? In the second part of the first book Anselm discusses Boso's objection and intends to illustrate the neccessity of why God could not have saved humanity in another way.[26]

At the beginning of the second part of the first book Anselm reiterates that his line of argumentation is "remoto Christo." His premises are facts lying prior to redemption; "constet inter nos homines esse factum ad beatitudinem, quae in hac vita haberi non potest, nec ad illam posse pervenire quemquam nisi dimissis peccatis."[27]

The second part of the first book supplies definitions. Sin is a violation of justice, and satisfaction is the restitution of the same.[28]   Audet distinguishes three meanings for justice, sin and satisfaction. Sin is the failure to supply the "debitum" due to God. Sin is violence against communal justice. As Audet points out, this justice is moral in its quality. Therefore, human justice is grounded in divine justice. A justice thus perceived in turn is honor to which every creature must do hommage.[29]   Consequently, sin is a gross violation of divine honor: "Hunc honorem debitum qui deo non reddit, aufert deo quod suum est, et deum exhonorat; et hoc est peccare."[30]   Since human nature is contingent and postlapsarian, it can neither perform the ontologicallly required[31]

---

[25] Cu I 10: 66, 17.

[26] Cf. Cu I 10: 66,19-22. 67,1ff.

[27] Cu I 10: 67, 13-15.

[28] Cu I 11: 68, 15.

[29] Audet, "Problématique et structure" 49; Gäde, Eine andere Barmherzigkeit 199ff..

[30] Cu I 11: 68, 19-21. Cf. Audet, "Problématique et structure" 49; Greshake, "Erlösung und Freiheit" 326ff.

[31] In Anselm's worldview one can substitute "ordo" for ontic. Being is perceived in the tradition of Plato as hierarchized. This "ordo" must be freed of blemishes. Life at the court of God must be put in order again, so that the court retinue - squires, courtiers, major-domo, etc. - can again live according to the court etiquette, i.e. pay God the honor due him.

Medieval imagination knew the known world to be contained in spheres which in turn pass into the space that is heaven's: the Augustinian Civitas Dei. It was understood as the purpose of human existence to endow the few earthly hours with purpose and value. Knowledge meant then to give thinking responsibility, and life profundity and dignity. Human life should find means to join in the cosmic harmony - "palintonos harmonie" as Hercalitus had expressed it in antiquity. The spirated reason was perceived as the call to follow the divine word. It was the Middle Age's longing to find its proper and fitting place in the cosmic restitution of its own nature nor return to God the honor due to Him. The effort required is supreme, and beyond the means of every sinner. Since no sinner is able to restore the divine honor, only God himself can address this issue. Anselm offers a variety of possibilities. One possibility would be that God forgives sinners out of His own mercy. Anselm rejects outright a forgiveness out of mercy alone.[32] The reasoning behind this rejection is that God´s actions could never possibly provoke an incongruency between the divine essence and the divine action. God does nothing which is not fitting to His being. Everything that God does must necessarily be reasonable. The exclusion of a "sola misericordia" results, furthermore, from the inner necessity of divine justice. Should God not be guided by His own justice, His decisions would be whimsical, arrived at at random. This contains and involves actively a twofold implication. For one, rationality presupposes an articulate and clear decision which is arrived at after due consideration and/or arises from an inner logic. The inner logic of the person and of the subject and of the act are not only consistent within their respective selves and vis-à-vis each other. They are also consistent with the overarching cosmic "ratio." As a consequence, a true act is not one taken easily or arrived at in passing and therefore in a theoretically or actually possible contradiction to the ontic-ethical order. From this it follows that a "by jingo" attitude is the mark of sin. Between being and decision no contradiction could possibly occur in the divine order, of which the orders of the cosmos, of the person and of the mind are mere subdivisions. "Similiter erit apud deum peccanti et non peccanti ... liberior igitur est iniustitia, si sola misericordia dimittitur, quam iustitia."[33] The principle of non-contradiction is applied to the area within the Godhead in order to distill ethical precepts applicable also to humanity. As a result, neither "misericordia dei" nor the allied divine attributes "libertas," "voluntas" and benignitas" may contradict divine "dignitas" and "iustitia." "Quod autem dicitur quia quod vult iustum est, et quod non vult non est iustum, non ita intelligendum est ut, si deus velit quodlibet inconveniens, iustum sit, quia ipse vult." From this follows the insight that God can never possibly be "inordinate" or "iniuste."[34] The "ordo rerum" corresponds to the

---

order - so that this order may be a healthy one. Christians are called to contribute to this *Civitas Dei.*

Perhaps still during Anselm´s life-time an Augustinian manuscript in Canterbury was illustrated with a depiction of this *Civitas Dei.* Maybe Anselm had known the artist. It shows Christ in a mandorla blessing the universe. Angels and apostles surround him. In the lower regions the crowned *ecclesia* reigns. The heavenly retinue is present. This painting reflects well the Medieval worldview.
Cf. Florence, Biblioteca Laurenziana, plu. 12, cod. 17, fol 2v. 35 x 25 cm.
See Wolfram von den Steinen, Homo Caelestis, Vol. I (Bern/München: Francke, 1967) at 172ff.252.
[32] Cu I 12-15.
[33] Cu I 12: 69,19.
[34] Cu I 12: 69,13-70,28.

"honor dei." With other words, there exist congruence and correspondence between the created and the creating orders. This does not bar a yet greater "dissimilarity.". Were God to leave the world "inordinate," then justice would not have been restored. Human endeavor experiences its climax precisely when preserving divine order in the created sphere. "Si deo nihil maius aut melius, nihil iustius quam honorem illius servat in rerum dispositione summa iustitia, quae non est alius quam ipse deus."[35] While no sin can diminish God´s honor, this honor nevertheless must also be upheld in the "ordo rerum." No one serving at the cosmic court can insult or detract from the divine honor.

Nevertheless, the honor of that court does suffer. More than merely the individual is corrupt and yet infinitely less than the whole: and yet the Godhead remains unblemished. Since no human being can sustain the divine honor, only God himself is equal to this task. God nevertheless expects homage from every created being. But precisely the just (= fitting, commensurate) homage can no longer be rendered to God. This applies particularly to the "creatura rationalis." "(E)t hoc maxime rationalis natura, cui datum est intelligere quod debeat."[36] However, if this order is indeed interrupted, then only through commensurate satisfaction can it be restored. To allow a "violata ordinis pulchritudine deformitas"[37] would be the go-ahead for creation to suffer shipwreck. This constitutes for Anselm the argument against a "sola misericordia" position. One cannot have divine mercy prevail at the expense of divine justice. Divine justice actuates itself in the concrete world only insofar as this world is an "ordo rectus." The necessary consequences from these considerations is the requirement that a satisfaction be divinely effected by God for humanity.

Satisfaction guarantees the restoration of a just and correct order. In a side-remark Anselm also considers the possibility that the divine will could prevail solely through the application of severe "poena."[38] Yet this excursus also comes to the conclusion that only through satisfaction could the restoration of humanity be effected. It would be inadequate were one simply to claim the principle of "aut poena aut satisfactio" to originate in a superficial appropriation of Germanic criminal-code-thinking still lurking in the background of the Middle Ages. As has been delineated above, Anselm´s understanding of justice is strictly based on philosophical-theological reasoning. This is also confirmed by his observation, "constat deum proposuisse, ut de hominibus angelos qui ceciderunt restauraret." How is such "restaurare" to be thought?[39] Anselm

---

[35] Cu I 13: 71,7f. cf. Felix Hammer, Genugtuung und Heil. Absicht, Sinn und Grenzen der Erlösungslehre Anselms von Canterbury (Wien: Herder, 1967) at 115; Pouchet, La Rectitudo 148f.

[36] Cu I 15: 73,2f.

[37] Cu I 15: 73, 19-25.

[38] Cf. Cu II 19-24.

[39] Cu I 19: 84,6f. Heinrich Ott, "Anselms Versöhnungslehre," Theologische Zeitschrift 13 (1957): 183-199, at 187ff argues in favor of a juridic reading of the "aut poena aut satisfactio"

repeats that God's purpose in creating humanity was for it to attain the state of "beatitudo." God leads humanity to this goal - which had already been established before humanity had sinned. Faithful to this position, satisfaction means the reconstitution of the "bonum." "Poena" alone does not suffice to achieve the goal of "beatitudo." Precisely on the grounds that "poena" is legalistic, it results merely in the "privatio beatitudinis" but does not occasion already the return to "beatitudo." Insisting on "poena" as the exclusive soteriological vehicle would have made Anselm indeed susceptible to the accusation of subscribing to juridic thinking.[40]

By excluding the "poena," one is invariably compelled to apprehend in the concept of "satisfactio" the ideal means for redemption. This necessity comes all the more acutely to the fore if one aligns it with the concept of justice. Anselm sums up his many-faceted argument in favor of the satisfaction theory in the words:

> Tene igitur certissime quia sine satisfactione, id est sine debiti solutione spontanea, nec deus potest peccatum impunitum dimittere, nec peccator ad beatitudinem, vel talem ualem habebat, antequam peccaret, pervenire. Non enim hoc modo repararetur homo, vel talis qualis fuerat ante peccatum.[41]

Having established the need for satisfaction, Anselm now turns his attention to the appropriate measure of such satisfaction. Since satisfaction fulfills the call for justice, justice itself becomes the final yardstick for satisfaction. In a twofold sense humanity opposes this justice by positing injustice. The first injustice results from of committing a transgression. The second form of injustice is the result of the first one. It is humanity's inability to render God the justice due to him. What is due to God, humanity has lost and, therefore, can no longer supply. Through its own fault humanity has been reduced to such a state that what it is called - in an obligatory form - to render God is larger than what it possesses. "Non ergo satisfacis, si non reddis aliqid maius, quam sit id pro quo peccatum facere non debueras."[42] God has a right to demand from humanity this "maius." But in the very same way humanity is unable to present this "maius." Humanity is guilty of this "impotentia." Through its own free will humankind has acquired the quality of a twofold injustice. The first injustice has befallen humanity through freely chosen sin.

---

formula. Hammer, Genugtuung und Heil 118ff; Kienzler, Glauben und Denken 207f; John McIntyre, Anselm and his critics. A re-interpretation of the "Cur Deus Homo" (Edinburgh, London: Oliver and Boyd, 1954) at 67f; Nèdoncelle, "Notion de personne" 35; oppose this interpretation or regard it as too narrow.

[40] Cu I 14: 72,14-18.

[41] Cu I 19: 85,28-32. As Delhaye, "Quelques aspects" 406ff and Kienzler, Glauben und Denken 208f rightly argue, Anselm's point of departure for his arguments is the notion of "beatitudo" and not "iustitia."

[42] Cu I 21: 87,27f.

188

Through this first injustice no contribution can be rendered to his own justice. Both the transgression and the resulting ignomiy must be undone.[43]

Applying this understanding of justice, no recourse to divine mercy alone can remedy the malcondition of injustice. The insult made is one that not only has had ramifications for the human condition but also for cosmic court-life. Injustice is not a positive quality and can, therefore, not contribute to justification. In the same vein the sinner cannot contribute to his own justification. The justice required can only originate from outside humanity. Also Boso must acknowledge the stringency of the argumentation: that the sinner is ill-equipped to contribute to his own redemption. "Sed hoc facere nullatenus potest peccator homo, quia peccator peccatorem iustificari nequit."[44] Chapter I, 25, presents a summary of the previous considerations. When Boso asks how humanity is then to be extricated from this dilemma, Anselm responds, "ex necessitate per Christum salvatur homo." After the exclusion of all other variants, this is the only viable avenue left. Anselm summarizes the reasons for the necessity of salvation effected through Jesus Christ, as follows:

An non intelligis ex iis quae supra diximus, quia necesse est aliquos homines ad beatitudinem pervenire? Nam si deo inconveniens est hominem cum aliqua macula perducere ad hoc, ad quod illum sine omni macula fecit, ne aut boni incepti paenitere aut propositum implere non posse videatur: multo magis propter eandem inconvenientiam impossibile est nullum hominem ad hoc provehi ad quod factus est ... Quod enim necessaria ratione veraciter esse colligitur, id in nullam deduci debet dubitationem, etiam si ratio quomodo sit non percipitur.[45]

By denoting the intrinsic impossibilities and inconveniences (= incongruencies and contradictions) Anselm infers a necessity. Boso is not content with this negative process of exclusion and asks whether one cannot demonstrate positively the inner necessity for Jesus Christ's redemptive deeds. The negative evidence may suffice to confound the "dubitationes fidei," but does not satisfy the "ratio certitudines." Here a remarkable distinction is introduced into the discussion. Alas, it is not further pursued.[46] One must prove positively the rational necessity of the actual occurrence of redemption. He formulates rather apodictically that redemption occured either through Christ or not at all. First Anselm responds that the inability to recognize salvation to have occurred in Christ does not supply an adequate argument for the impossibility of redemption. Otherwise put, the inability to recognize the mode

---

[43] Ludwig Heinrichs, Die Genugtuungstheorie des hl. Anselmus von Canterbury, neu dargestellt und dogmatisch geprüft (Paderborn: Schöningh, 1909) at 70; cf. Gäde, Eine andere Barmherzigkeit 234-247.

[44] Cu I 24: 91,24-26. Cf. 93.

[45] Cu I 25: 95,24-96,3.

[46] Cu I 25: 95,15ff. Cf. Henry, The Logic of Saint Anselm 134ff; Kohlenberger, Similitudo und Ratio 68ff. 213ff.

189

("quomodo") cannot supply enough evidence to weaken the argument in favor of Christ´s redemption of humanity.[47]

Boso´s argument is taken as the topic for the second book of *Cur Deus Homo*. Again Anselm insists on supplying an argument that is philosophical and not theological in nature.[48] Only the "homo deus" is able to effect redemption. The "esse oportere" of the Catholic profession of faith is evidenced. Upon this background Christ´s life and death are shown as necessary for salvation. Christology is soteriology.[49]

At this point Anselm presents - in condensed form - his program of rationality once again. His principal philosophical decisions form the basis for his christology and soteriology.[50] The divinely created, intended and hence ordained rationality of the human species is the necessary nexus for the redemption in Christ. Rationality allows human beings to discern between just and unjust, between good and bad, between a higher and a lesser good; to disapprove of evil and to choose the good. Rationality´s ethical implications have not been designed by God "frustra." Divine reason did not create by chance the rationality of created matter. The "ordo rerum" is reasonable and, therefore, intelligible. Only if reason exists can the existence of the will be justified. Without rationality human will would be "absurdum." These considerations are the "firmum fundamentum" for the *Cur Deus Homo*. A "homo rationalis" so defined is posited within the context of redemption: "Necesse est ergo, ut de humana natura quod (deus) incepit perficiat. Hoc autem fieri, sicut diximus, nequit, nisi per integram peccati satisfactionem, quam nullus peccator facere potest." Here Anselm needs the ready concurrence of Boso. "Intelligo iam necesse esse, ut deus faciat quod incepit, ne aliter quem deceat videatur a suo incepto deficere."[51] Only God can render the satisfaction which is due to God: "quod praeter deum est." But this salvific act cannot occur for humanity by disregarding humanity at the same time. For this reason it is imperative that God become human. It is important for the only true God to become fully human in order to render God satisfaction. For this reason God must also become of Adam´s lineage. Here one is witness to the congruency between Anselm´s teachings on God - as expressed in the *Monologion*, *Proslogion*, and in the *Epistola de incarnatione verbi* - and his soteriology.

Without sin Jesus Christ´s life is the fullness of human existence as intended by God. To emphasize that Jesus Christ was good and that human nature in its uncorrupted form is good, Anselm emphasizes that Jesus Christ did

---

[47] Cu I 25: 95,18-96,3.
[48] Cu I 25: 96,10ff.
[49] René Roques, Anselme de Cantorbéry. Pourquoi Dieu s´est fait homme (Paris: Cerf, 1963) at 140ff.
[50] Cu II 1: 97,4-98,5. Roques, Pourquoi Dieu s´est fait homme 137ff; cf. Gäde, Eine andere Barmherzigkeit 261ff.
[51] Cu II 4: 99,9-12.

not serve justice out of necessity but out of a freedom of an sovereignly free will. As with every rational creature Christ's life also has the properties of "iustitia" and of "libertas arbitrii".[52]

> Solemus namque dicere deum idcirco fecisse angelum et hominem tales qui peccare possent, quatenus, cum possent deserere iustitiam et ex libertate servarent arbitrii, gratiam et laudem mererentur, quae illis, si ex necessitate iusti essent, non deberentur.[53]

From his very terrestrial beginning, the God-man calls "iustitia" and "libertas arbitrii" his own by virtue of his earthly form of existence, which is grounded on his eternity, perduring ontic but also ethical union with God, whence all justice originates. In the God-man necessity and freedom coincide: "Hoc igitur modo habet a se iustitiam, quia creatura eam aliter a se habere nequit; et idcirco laudandus est de sua iustitia, nec necessitate sed libertate iustus est."[54]

Whatever Christ did, he achieved out of pure freedom. This applies particularly to his death. In no other way could he have completed redemption. The manner in which redemption occurred is to Anselm's mind indicative of the quality of justification: "Quod moriatur ex sua potestate."[55] The term "debere" as it is commonly applied to the human race in general cannot be applied to Christ, because there is no "debitum" which the God-man has to render to God. Christ has voluntarily taken unto himself the ordeal of death to express supreme dedication to God as well as self-abandonment. In Jesus Christ's death the required "maius" is "payed" and redeemed. "Ratio quoque nos docuit quia oportet eum magis aliquid habere, quam quidquid sub deo est, quod sponte det et non ex debito deo."[56] This "maius" is not rendered merely in obedience to God, because obedience is an attitude every creature qua creature is required to give God. In contrast, Jesus Christ's death actually effects satisfaction for the violated justice and simultaneously gives God the highest measure of honor due to him.[57]

In this manner Christ becomes the paradigm of human existence. In Christ creaturely rationality arrives at its divinely willed destiny: "beatitudo." Because sin is always personal in character inasmuch as it touches the relationship between finite humanity and the Absolute, it, sin, acquires an infinite quality. In this horizon Jesus Christ's death is "bonum incomparabiliter."[58] Furthermore, the "satisfactio" effected by Jesus Christ's death has universal ramifications. It reaches the first cause of sin, the first

---

[52] Cu II 10: 107,12.15f; 108,4.
[53] Cu II 10: 107,13-17.
[54] Cu II 10: 108,3-5.
[55] Cu II 11: 109,2.
[56] Cu II 11: 109f.
[57] Cu II 11: 110,25-111,17.
[58] Cu II 14: 114,23.

human being. With Christ the divine plan to lead all human beings to their destiny ultimately prevails.[59]

In a rather strange turn, Anselm now tries to consider redemption from the perspective of the "misericordia dei." In the first book divine mercy had been excluded from further consideration. Evidently the author at this point of the discussion wishes to point out the dialectical relationship between justice and mercy. In the first book mercy as a motive for salvation had been excluded because it contradicted divine justice.[60]

Boso asks whether anything else contributes to the divine honor if everything is subsumed under the term "justice." Evidently there must be something greater than mere justice. It must fulfill the requirements of justice and yet also serve to glorify God's honor. In fact, Christ's death constitutes a synthesis of "iustitia dei" and "honor dei": "video quia nulla ratione se ipsum morti ex debito ... dedit ad honorem dei, et tamen facere debuit quod fecit."[61]

The "melius" of justice which occurs in Christ is transferred to sinners. The satisfaction and retribution effected by Christ is a surplus of unowed grace. It constitutes more than mere divine justice. It is divine mercy for all of humanity. In this sense Anselm characterizes divine justice as divine mercy. The predication "almighty" allows no limitations to the divine nature. This includes no limitations in the sense of a protection against a partitioning of divine qualities. Not only justice but mercy too reveals the divine nature. Divine affection for sinful humanity is a communication from the essence of the divine being: "ut nec maior nec iustior cogitari possit."[62] Little wonder then that the end of the *Cur Deus Homo* flows over into a praise of the "misericordia dei." "Misericordiam vero dei quae tibi perire videbatur, cum iustitiam dei et peccatum hominis considerabamus, tam magnam tamque concordem iustitiae invenimus, ut nec maior nec iustior cogitari possit."[63]

The proper understanding of Anselm's soteriology depends on whether one understands his central notion of "iustitia". Only from this term does one appreciate the other soteriological terms: "peccatum," "satisfactio" and "restauratio." By developing these terms, Anselm thematizes in his soteriology the rational structure of both human nature and of history. Yet more radically, Anselm ventures to categorize and formulate divine properties, such as "iustitia dei," "honor" and "misericordia" out of an intrinsic rationality permeating all things insofar as they are, including the Trinity. So to speak even divine omnipotence is bound by rationality. The constitutive rationality of justice is invariable and indelible. This applies to both human (created) and divine

---

[59] Cu II 16: 119, 23f; the subsequent lines 16f are later interpolations. Cf. Kienzler, Glauben und Denken at 216.
[60] Cu I 25: 96,12.
[61] Cu II 18: 129, 14-16.
[62] Cu II 20: 131,29. Cf. Richthammer, Die Systematik des Proslogionbeweises 5.
[63] Cu II 20: 131,27-29.

(absolute) rationality. Here again one cannot fail to notice and appreciate the congeniality between Plotinus´ understanding of "νοῦς" and Anselm´s understanding of "ratio."[64]

In this sense, the *Cur Deus Homo* can be considered the culmination and apex of Anselm´s theology. On the one hand it confirms the previously held assumptions delineated in *Proslogion* and *Monologion*. The problematics of theological redemption find their climax in the *Cur Deus Homo*. On the other hand, the rational structure not only of God and of human nature, but more specifically the rational structure of philosophical discourse and theological reflection in general come to the fore. Both human justice and divine justice are unlocked by utilizing the principle of rationality. The topic of soteriology enables Anselm to illustrate the distinguishing traits of human and divine justice. At the same time, this topic serves him as a welcome opportunity to mediate between the two. It is hardly possible to address with a more acute mind the connection between autonomous human justice and heteronomous divine justice. The narrative of humanity´s redemption illustrates the restitution of both humanity´s justice and of the "homo rationalis." At the same time God is apprehended as the ever greater entity that the human mind cannot fathom. The divine mystery is not annulled, but receives an additional accentuation: it is yet more just and more merciful than the human mind can perceive: "ut nec maior nec iustior cogitari possit."[65]

7.3 *De Conceptu Virginali et de Originali Peccato*

Anselm first undertakes to define the lexical meaning of "originalis." He discerns two possible meanings for this word: "videtur dici aut ab origine humanae naturae ... aut ab origine, hoc est ab initio uniuscuiusque personae ... humanae."[66] In his judgment the first option is not convincing. One cannot claim original sin to have occurred at the beginning of the existence of the human race. Were this the case, the assertion that human nature and its origin were good ("origo illius iusta fuit"[67]) could not be sustained. Though a common feature of all humans, original sin contains a personal quality. He considers the adjective "naturale" in this context as problematic. Only in a very

---

[64] As there is no proof for a direct Plotinian influence on Anselm, one can only state a loose congeniality between the two, effected by the Neoplatonism present in the early Middle Ages. Anselm had no knowledge of the different view Plotinus held on the nature of the ˝nous˝ (i.e. the ˝nous˝ is to Plotinus beyond all rationality). Anselm´s style was to unite the various lines of tradition into one systematic whole.

[65] Cf. Rudolf Allers, Anselm von Canterbury - Leben, Lehre, Werke (Wien: Hegner, 1936) 98f; Kienzler, Glauben und Denken 216ff; Joseph Ratzinger, Einführung in das Christentum. Vorlesungen über das Apostolische Glaubensbekenntnis (München: Kösel, 1968) 187ff; Richthammer, Die Systematik des Proslogionbeweises 119; Roques, Pourquoi Dieu s´est fait homme 182ff.

[66] Co 1: 140,9-11.14.

[67] Co 1: 140,13.

qualified way has nature been affected by original sin. Sin is in its very essence violent; it does violence unto "iustitia." Subsequently in this system all forms of sin are a harm to justice. Negatively defined, sin is nothing less than "iniustitia." Much like "iustitia" it is thereby related to rationality and volitional freedom. In obvious contrast to perhaps some tendencies in the early Augustine he connects sin to volitional freedom and not so much to human nature[68] Original sin is to him "peccatum iniustitiae"[69] Both the good deed and sin have their origin in volition:

> Nihil enim, sive substantia sive actio sive aliquid, per se consideratum est iustum nisi iustitia, aut iniustum vel peccatum nisi iniustitia, nec ipsa voluntas in qua est iustitia sive iniustitia.[70]

As justice arises from the "bona voluntas," injustice arises from the bad will. This is in keeping with Augustine.[71] Yet quite adamantly Anselm insists that volition is not created with a procilivity toward sin. In order to distinguish between the good and bad wills he introduces again his previous distinction between "instrumentum volendi" and "usus voluntatis."[72] By thus distinguishing, Anselm is able to state in no uncertain terms that neither human talents, predispositions and assets nor the human volitional faculty are sinful. Only the concrete individual intention to will "iniustitia" instead of "iustitia" can be described as sinful. This is the import of his observation: "iustitia, quam habendo `iusta´ voluntas et qua carendo `iusta´ vocatur."[73] From this situation Anselm draws a significant conclusion which differs considerably from Augustine´s position. If sin occurs within the will, then punishment is in order for the will, but not for all of human nature in the judgment of „aliquis": "Non enim punitur nisi voluntas."[74] But merely stating this does not satisfy his inquisitive mind. What ramifications does original sin have for human nature in general? [75] The first human beings possessed the original justice which they were called to preserve and actualize in their lives. Original sin incurred the loss of this "iustitia originalis." Humanity can not attain this original justice by its own efforts. This is expressed in the word "impotentia." This weakness is so fundamental to human existence that it is transmitted through the generations. It indicates already the need for salvation through something else and through more than a mere human being. As *Cur Deus Homo* already developed, this agency must possess a personal and divine quality. These qualities are

---

[68] Cf. Rondet, "Grâce et péché" 161ff.
[69] Co 3: 142,21.
[70] Co 4: 143,25-27.
[71] Plagnieux, "Le binome `iustitia - potentia´" 144.
[72] Co 4: 143,25 - 144,3.
[73] Co 4: 144,1f.
[74] Co 4: 145,20f.
[75] Co 2: 141,7.

inherently necessary because original sin did not merely effect a loss of original justice which had devalued the quality of human existence in a lasting manner ("debitum iustitiae integrae"), but also resulted in a "debitum satisfaciendo" which addresses a third party. Only by rendering this "satisfactio" can justice be restituted:

> debitum iustitiae integrae sine omni iniustitia quam accepit, et debitum satisfaciendi ... per se nec satisfacere pro peccato nec iustitiam derelictam recuperare valet.[76]

The question of whether infants can also be called guilty because of their own sin is much pondered. The point of departure is the notion of personal sin. While one can not yet speak in the case of children of culpability, Anselm nevertheless does think of something akin to sin. Children are also in the state of "impotentia" and, therefore, unable to regain their original justice through their own efforts alone. Consequently children are also under the spell of original sin - though he readily admits that children are unable to recognize the nature of justice. Furthermore, children are lacking the rational and volitional capacities for a true "peccatum personale."[77]

As regards animation, Anselm subscribes to Aristotle´s understanding. Children are not immediately but only gradually equipped with an "anima." However, the "anima" is necessary in order for a premonition of what personal guilt might be to come about. And yet, he admits that a certain "necessitas" to commit sin exists simultaneously with nascent freedom.[78] The correlation of culpability to personality in Anselm´s system calls for an elaboration.

Much like "iniustitia" and "peccatum," "malum" is "nihil." It is merely the privation of good. Sin and evil merit punitive action, therefore, not "pro nihilo" but "propter aliquid."[79] Everything is a willful violation of the "ordo congruus universitatis rerum." This "ordo" is not the result of a chain of accidents; it is not the product of trial and error. It is the direct consequence of a personal and divine will. Sin is, therefore, not only a violation of an impersonal cosmic order but also a personal insult "ad personam Dei" affecting the cosmic order as "vestigium Dei." God demands "aliquid" as penance.[80]

Anselm is quite adamant when developing the "transmissio peccati originalis" that human nature in spite of the entry of the phenomenon of sin into the world remains just. Adam is not the bearer of a "debitum" as a human person "quia homo est nec quia persona est" but rather "non simpliciter quia est Adam, sed quia est peccator Adam."[81] Adam´s having-become-guilty is the

---

[76] Co 2: 141,21f.
[77] Co 2: 142,3f and 7: 148,1ff.
[78] Co 7: 149,9-13.
[79] Co 6: 147,13f.
[80] Co 6: 147,15f.
[81] Co 10: 151,16f.

primary cause for the propagation of the deleterious effects of original sin. Human nature per se is not the cause. Only insofar as Adam had become unfaithful towards his own rationality did he and his offspring lose original grace:

> Quoniam vero ADAM subditus noluit esse dei voluntati ... peccando sine omni necessitate deum exhonoravit, unde per se satisfacere non potuit, gratiam quam acceptam propagandi de se potuit semper servare perdidit, et peccatum secum comitante poena peccati, quantumcumque per datam propagandi naturam propagetur, trahit.[82]

Consequently Rondet concludes concerning the effects of original sin on human nature:

> Anselme ne cesse de dire dans son DCV: En Adam, la personne a corrumpue la nature; dans sa posteriorité, la nature corrompt la personne.[83]

This is of central importance to Anselm as he strives to demonstrate that the birth of the Son of God from the Virgin Mary is free from a "debitum primorum."[84] Original sin and the loss of original righteousness are the result of Adam's will. The God Son's decision to redeem humankind, however, is not the consequence of Adam's will but of that of divine providence. Jesus Christ is not subject to the "cursus naturalis" or to the "cursus voluntarius" of humanity.

> Quoniam ergo propagatio viri de sola virgine ita non est naturalis aut voluntaria sed mirabilis ... palam est quia nequaquam subiacet legibus et meritis illius propagationis, quam et voluntas et natura - quamvis discerete - operantur.[85]

As the Son of God is created exclusively from the divine will which also intended to have a perfect humanity, the Son bears witness to the original goodnessof creation. Jesus Christ is to Anselm's mind the prototypical human being living completely from the original "iustitia" and he must, therefore, be called "just." He is equipped for this task by His own liberty and is always able to preserve this received justice. Finally, He remained free of sin but accepted guilt ("debitum"). For this reason He is destined for beatitude.[86] This illustrates a larger masterplan than one generally could assume. *Cur Deus Homo* directly prepares the stage for *De Conceptu Virginali* and in this sense is a postlude to the centerpiece of soteriology.

---

[82] Co 10: 152,9-27.
[83] Rondet, "Grâce et péché" 137.
[84] Co 8: 149,28.
[85] Co 11: 154, 11-15.
[86] Cu I 1-5: 97,1-100,28.

CHAPTER EIGHT
8.0 Reason as a Divine Icon

Materially the *Proslogion* and the *Monologion* are the most related of Anselm's writings. In the former Anselm attempts to think matters divine in the wake of the latter. God is to be articulated in cogitation in a way commensurate to the divine being and essence. Anselm senses an inadequacy in the *Monologion* which he intends to overcome by introducing in the *Proslogion* the "unum argumentum." What he had previously attempted to argue, using many steps, he now attempts to develop through one succinct and comprehensive argument.

> considerans illud esse multorum concatenatione cotextum argumentorum, coepi mecum quaerere, si forte posset inveniri unum argumentum, quod nullo alio ad se probandum quam se solo indigeret, et solum ad astruendum quia deus vere est, et quia est summum bonum nullo alio indigens, et quo omnia indigent ut sint et ut bene sint, et quaecumque de divina credimus substantia, sufficeret.[1]

This argument[2] is one for the simple reason that Anselm presupposes God to be as "summum bonum" one as one unit. Nevertheless, this one and single argument presupposes nothing else ("nullo alio") but itself. It is interesting to investigate the requirements resulting from this novel "unum argumentum." The chain of arguments presented in the *Monologion* resembles cognition's ascent to God in various steps. While this mental itinerary applies the principle of "sola ratione," the reader beholds thinking's variety of dimensions. Unity is supplied to the text by the sustained object of deliberations: namely the unity of recognizing God and the self. Only after the unity of thinking's object (= God) prevailed in the text, did thinking itself arrive a posteriori at its own unity.

Mind's gradual ascent to the thought "God" propelled also the mind's recoil ever more into its own realm, until finally it reached its own ground. This cognitive movement was by no means an unreflected or nebulous one. True to its nature it was always accompanied by intellectual verifiability. Reason's accountability was the conditio sine qua non for ever increasing intellectual veracity. The increased objective encounter with divine truth occasioned

---

[1] P Prooem: 93, 4-10.

[2] Literature on this book is legion. Roger Payot, "L'Argument ontologique et le Fondament de la Métaphysique," Archives de Philosophie 39 (1976): 227-268.427-444.629-645 supplies a bibliography on 629ff; cf. among others Barth, Fides quaerens intellectum 69ff; de Lubac, "Seigneur, je cherche ton Visage" 295ff as well as 201ff. 407ff; Flasch, "Zum Begriff der Wahrheit" 322ff; Flasch, "Der philosophische Ansatz" 165ff; Gilson, "Sens et nature" 5ff; Henry, The Logic of Saint Anselm 142ff; Kohlenberger, Similitudo und Ratio 151ff; Adolf Kolping, Anselms Proslogion-Beweis der Existenz Gottes im Zusammenhang seines spekulativen Programms "Fides Quaerens Intellectum" (Bonn: Peter Honstein, 1939) at 145ff; Franz Sales Schmitt, "Der ontologische Gottesbeweis," Theologische Revue 32 (1933): 217-223, at 81ff; Schurr, Die Begründung der Philosophie 66ff; Söhngen, Die Einheit der Theologie 24ff; Warnach, "Wort und Wirklichkeit" 170ff.

simultaneously an ever greater intellectual interiority. The meeting of thought's personal vis-à-vis (i.e. the numinous, God) brought to light the transcendental conditions for thought's own constitution, which are grasped in the concepts of "necessity," "unity" and a coherence of causations. The greatest possible encounter with the absolute wrought the most intimate knowledge of mind's own facticity. The thought "God" has to correspond to the mind's conditions in order to be thought. From this perspective, thought has given cause for the numinous to arise from within itself as the one and necessary "summum." Through such predication, the absolute was apprehended as the base and apex of every explanation, of every "reasoning." Defined in such a way, God could not possibly be the immanent cause for a "finite-infinite" explanation, lest God were subject to thought's explanatory matrix. Rather, and quite on the contrary, God is the cause per se, i.e. par excellence. As the transcendent cause, God stands within and above every kind of immanent causal context. Hereby God preserves his true being-cause. At the same time he had to be the ground for all immanent explanations - and this precisely as the causal ground for thinking's transcendental conditions. Apprehending itself as transcendentally constituted a priori entails experiencing itself in the recognition of this circumstance as a thinking which transcends itself.

This nexus becomes evident in the term "similitudo." The transcendent cause must be of a kind that is both luminous and immanent to mind. This must be manifest in the mind's (as immanent cause) indebtedness to the transcendent cause. Both causes need to relate to each other "per similitudinem." Thinking occurs as a reflecting image of the divine image. This reflecting image corresponds to the primordial image in "similitudo" and in "dissimilitudo."

While the *Monologion* illustrates the gradual ascent to God, the *Proslogion* unfolds everything from the "unum argumentum."[3] The latter is summarized in the words "id quo nihil maius cogitari possit." Reason's highest term must be the term which is fitting and adequate for the highest being.[4] In a way it must contain all that can be said of thinking and of God. This argument needs no prerequisite. If this holds true, then everything, insofar as it is, must unfold with inherent necessity from this inner unity. Is one then not compelled to surrender the notion of pure transcendence and to speak rather of thinking as transcending itself? In the process the explanatory connection between God and thinking would become evident. Thinking would be seen as becoming God's "similitudo" and God as relating to thinking through "similitudo" and "dissimilitudo." Anselm thinks he has found in the "unum argumentum" indeed

---

[3] Cf. Gäde, Eine andere Barmherzigkeit 268f; Kienzler, Glauben und Denken 222; Vuillemin, Le Dieu d'Anselme 120ff.

[4] The description "fitting and adequate" defines the term only inasmuch as it describes a moment of God's self-revelation. Nothing is thereby stated positively as regards the divine immanence.

the one argument wherein God and thinking reciprocally relate to one another. Thinking mirrors God and becomes an icon in which divine thinking appears.

Noteworthy is the fact that Anselm begins with the highest term. In the *Proslogion* no further explanation or justification is supplied.[5] This beginning is exactly the focal point of contention between Gaunilo and Anselm. Needless to say, the whole of Anselm's thinking is put to the test here.

8.1 Terminology

The point of departure is the term "aliquid quo maius nihil cogitari nequit."[6] The person of faith believes with wholehearted conviction that there is no term greater than God.[7] This said, Anselm nevertheless insists that the term is primarily a philosophical one. As a consequence, the term can also be understood by the "infidels," that is to say by every human being qua human being. In this connection he introduces a significant distinction. While the "insipiens" may negate God's actual existence, he can not deny the philosophical term and what it conveys: "'... dixit insipiens in corde suo: non est deus.'? Sed certe ipse insipiens, cum audit hoc ipsum quod dico: 'aliquid quo maius nihil cogitari potest,' intelligit quod audit."[8]

The "intelligere" is reduced here to the pure "audire." Therefore one can claim the question to be primarily a philosophical one. Were this not at least cognitionally possible, all further discourse would be absurd. In spite of this universal claim, the term is drawn from religious praxis.[9] The comprehensibility of the term is presented by Anselm in a way of leaving no space for doubt. The hearing of the term occasions the necessity of its being understood.[10] No matter whether one accepts or rejects the proposition that God exists, one - insofar as

---

[5] As regards the ontological argument, cf. Dietrich Henrich, Der ontologische Gottesbeweis. Sein Problem und seine Geschichte in der Neuzeit (Tübingen: Mohr, 1960); Schmitt, "Der ontologische Gottesbeweis" 38ff.

[6] P 2: 101,8. God as the highest term is not Anselm's novel contribution to the history of philosophy. His is, nevertheless the most remarkable development and execution of this concept. Seneca, Tertullian, Augustine and John Damascene had already known this notion. Cf. Théodore A. Audet, "Une source augustinienne de l'argument de Saint Anselme," Recontres 30 (1949): 105-117, 105ff; Koyré, L'idée de Dieu 196ff; Vuillemin, Le Dieu d'Anselme 13.

[7] Cf. P 2 : 101,4f.

[8] P 2: 101,6-8. cf. Richthammer, Die Systematik des Proslogionbeweises 61.

[9] This position seems contested. The following contends the term to be exclusively a credal one: Barth, Fides quaerens intellectum 69ff; Jehangir N. Chubb, "Commitment and justification. A new Look at the Ontological Argument," International Philosophical Quarterly 13 (1973): 335-346, 335ff. Others come down clearly on the side of a philosophical assignment: Grabmann, Die Geschichte der scholastischen Methode 293ff; Koyré, L'idée de Dieu 201. While Gilson, "Sens et nature" 8f. 137f; Söhngen, "Die Einheit der Theologie" 53ff attempt to mediate.

[10] PR 9: 138,11-16.

one is gifted with reason - must understand the term first. This is the case even if one were to negate the term later. This the monk Gaunilo rejects outright.[11]

First Gaunilo contests the need to postulate the necessity of such a term in order to supply the proof.[12] Neither by defining the term as philosophical nor as exclusively theological is one able to prove divine existence. No matter whether one uses the term "God" or that of the "highest being," one can not prove that the predicate indeed exists: "Deinde vix umquam poterit esse credibile, cum dictum et auditum fuerit istud, non eo modo posse cogitari non esse, quo etiam potest non esse deus."[13] In the background is Gaunilo's assumption that the term "cogitare" enjoys a much too prominent role in Anselm's scheme. In principle, thinking is not the means for him to infer being. "Cogitare" is for him merely the opposite to "excogitare." The latter, however, connotes something merely thought, presumed.[14] Gaunilo cannot support an inference resulting exclusively from the imagined.[15] He is not satisfied with a term arrived at alone from "percipi intellectu." There must be more to sustain the argument. There need be certitude that the "re ipsa esse," that the notion exists in reality. Here Gaunilo demands the impossible. What is to be proven he presupposes: divine existence. Thinking is not able to think the absolute. He suggests that only insight can supply the certitude Anselm is seeking: " For this reason he proposes, Anselm should substitute for the term "cogitare" "intelligere." (Intuitive?) insight (= "intelligere") seems to Gaunilo the only locus from which to gain surety as regards the nature of being.[16]

To Anselm the question whether one is dealing with a philosophical or theological issue is by no means paltry.[17] From mere hearing knowledge can not be derived. The contrary is the case with a philosophical view. From a philosophical view, originating in thinking, one can gain knowledge. For Anselm "intelligere" means something akin to an original, primordial understanding. Anselm's "intelligere" does not claim to intimate a connection between a term and its existence. He, therefore, defends his distinction between "cogitare" and "intelligere." His argumentation results exclusively from the "cogitare." The "cogitare" should advance to the "esse." It is not by chance that Anselm had chosen "cogitare." It is from that term that with necessity God's

---

[11] For the debate between Gaunilo and Anselm cf. Barth, Fides quaerens intellectum 74ff; Jasper Hopkins, "Anselm's debate with Gaunilo," Analecta Anselmiana. Vol. 5 (Frankfurt am Main: Minerva, 1976): 25-37, at 24ff; Kohlenberger, Similitudo und Ratio 151ff; Koyrè, L'idée de Dieu 212ff; Schmitt, "Der ontologische Gottesbeweis" 81ff; Schurr, Die Begründung der Philosophie 75ff.

[12] Cf. for the subsequent Vuillemin, Le Dieu d'Anselme 5ff.72ff.

[13] PI 2: 126,4-6.

[14] PI 3: 126,24. cf. Richthammer, Die Systematik des Proslogionsbeweises 88.

[15] PI 2: 126,8ff.

[16] PI 2 :125,17-20.

[17] PI 4 - 5.

existence must be proven or the whole of the Catholic understanding of the nature-supernature matrix is undermined.

The dialogue betwen Gaunilo and Anselm sets the stage for future lines of argument in favor of or against the ontological argument: Thomas Aquinas, Bonaventure, Descartes, Leibniz, Kant, Hegel, Schelling and Blondel. The whole of the Anselmian enterprise rests on the term "cogitare." Every attempt to divorce "cogitare" and "esse" does not maintain Anselm's argumentative level.[18] It is only when simplifications of Anselm's position occur, that criticisms of the ontological argument generally arise: "Seule la forme négative et épistémologique est charactéristique de la preuve ontologique d'Anselme et la distingue essentiellement de toutes formes positives et dogmatiques soit des preuves ontologiques classiques, soit des formes auxquelles on a souvent réduit la preuve d'Anselm lui-même."[19]

8.2 The Viability of "cogitare" and "intelligere"

Gaunilo expresses doubt as regards the comprehensibility of the terms and as regards their inner cognitive potentialities. This actually and ultimately calls into question the term "God" itself.

> quia scilicet illud omnibus quae cogitari possint maius, quod nihil aliud posse esse dicitur quam ipse deus, tam ego secundum rem vel ex specie mihi vel ex genere notam, cogitare auditum vel in intellectu habere non possum, quam nec ipsum deum, quem utique ob hoc ipsum etiam non esse cogitare possum. Neque enim aut rem ipsam novi aut ex alia possum coincere simili, quandoquidem et tu talem asseris illam, ut esse non possit simile quicquam.[20]

Gaunilo argues that this term is not covered by reality (= "res"). It departs from all other definitions of possible terms. The coherence of the term within the whole of the rational realm is called into question. One cannot arrive at this term by applying "genus" and "species." Nor does analogy yield the basis for such a term's existence. One is confronted with an empty term with no correspondence with experience; there is no "res similis." Consequently "in intellectu habere non possum." One deals here with a hollow construct of the human mind based on sounds.[21]

---

[18] Barth in: Fides quaerens intellectum, first treats God as a term (at 69ff) and only later also as divine existence (at 85ff).

[19] Vuillemin, Le Dieu d'Anselme 19. cf. also Richthammer, Die Systematik des Proslogionbeweises 16ff.

[20] PI 4: 126,29-127,3. Materially Gaunilo poses the question of to what degree the presupposition of the "ars analogi rationis" of Greco-Roman antiquity, or as Scholasticism transposed it, more radically the question on the ontological level of whether "analogia entis" really supplies a coherent appreciation of reality.

[21] Cf. Kohlenberger, Similitudo und Ratio 157ff. PI 4: 127,1.

In response Anselm repeats the line of argumentation previously intimated.[22] Anselm concedes to Gaunilo that what is in the intellect need not necessarily be in matter. There is no doubt that Anselm does not subscribe to a necessary causal nexus or correlation between the mind, or to be more precise between the imagination, and ontological reality. Faithful to this insight the hypothesis of the verifiability of cognitive claims by ontic certitudes is upheld. Contrary to Gaunilo, Anselm sees no harm done to the "esse et in intellectu." Whatever is being heard can also be comprehended. If this initial comprehension is admitted, then one can no longer negate an initial viability of the term. The question of whether indeed this term corresponds to reality requires further investigation. To his mind what has already been established suffices to validate the "esse in intellectu" of the highest term.

Of course Anselm does not allow the argument to rest here. The aim is to prove that the highest term also possesses the quality of being "realiter." In order to do so, he distinguishes several steps.

1. The "intelligere" originates in the "audire."

2. This simple "intelligere" has its correspondence within the mind. Therefore, at least within the intellectual realm an "esse in intellectu" must be conceded. Moreover, the "esse in intellectu" comes about from external experience.

3. The mind is capable of distinguishing between an "esse in solo intellectu" and an "esse et in re."[23]

Whether the term is merely in the mind or indeed a tangible, concrete thing must be investigated. The means of investigation remains the mind: "intelligere." The mind is the pivotal agency in the quest for truth.

The aforesaid compels one to ponder in greater depth the valency of the term "intelligere." The labor still to be performed is not petty. After having delineated "intelligere" one must now probe the meaning of every term's "esse in intellectu." Upon this background one can then investigate the concept of "esse in re." Finally, this should yield knowledge of whether indeed the highest term is also contained in an "esse in re." In addition, this may supply in hindsight the plausibility of the assumed epistemological presuppositions or discredit it.

Vuillemin considers Anselm's line of argumentation to lead to a terminological fullness of the term "God". Within that term the notions of experience, of similarity ("ressemblance") and of transcendence must be contained in a mutually non-contradictory manner. It seems to be that the concept of transcendence eclipses the realms of experience and similarity. In spite of this recognition of divine omnipotence there must be a correspondence

---

[22] PR 2: 132,10ff.14ff.22ff.
[23] P 2: l01, 9.

and coherence contained within the term "God": "une vérité de la logique." The term must conform to strict logical criteria. [24]

8.2.1 The Mind's Grasp

The Anselm's "intelligere" contains several moments. First, it is pure and concentrated hearing: "audire." This effort allows the subject to be wholly engulfed by the object. In the subject's reflection an "intelligere" occurs between action and the heard. Yet this "intelligere" also occasions an understanding of the process. On a third plane it indicates that this understanding arises from within the mind and from within the appearing subject matter. The "intelligere" gives cause for the coming-to-the-fore or breaking-through of verity. Truth appears as the correlation of thinking and being. Gaunilo is also concerned with the quest for truth. Yet he rejects the primordial "intelligere" as establishing a relationship with the "res." "Intelligere" can always be prone to understanding something false. Moreover, "intelligere" is not univocal with understanding, rather it means only "appearing or approaching the mind." The "intelligere" of the highest term must be of an altogether different kind from the one containing the possibility of recognizing something false. [25]

Gaunilo defines "intelligere" as a comprehensive understanding. This understanding, as "scientia," desires to penetrate to the "res ipsa." Hearing something about an unknown person does not result in knowledge of that unknown person's existence. Nevertheless, one can categorize the person according to "genus" and "species." It is the "scientia" which supplies the "intelligere" with the suitable terminological tools. The definition "person" or "human being" is arrived at from experience. One can always verify the hypothetical object of inquiry by verifying it with the already experienced "secundum rem ipsam." [26] This experiential background cannot be presumed when speaking of the highest being. The "scientia" cannot supply the instruments for the "intelligere" of the "res ipsa." The "intelligere" cannot be supported by experience supplying a "notitia." Information merely from hearsay ("secundum vocem") is not sufficient: "secundum quam solam aut vix aut numquam potest ullum cogitari verum." [27] Life does not supply "scientia" but merely an inconclusive, nebulous "vox." As a result Gaunilo obviously subscribes to the propositions held by an empiricist (in a rather narrow sense). The "intelligere" is dependent on what the "res ipsa" grants.

---

[24] Vuillemin, Le Dieu d'Anselme 53f. The author claims that the Anselmian notion of God must conform to modern mathematical and logical principles. See at. 54.

[25] PI 2: 125,14ff. Cf. Hopkins, "Anselm's Debate" 30ff; Kienzler, Glauben und Denken 234; Kohlenberger, Similitudo und Ratio 157; Richthammer, Die Systematik des Proslogionbeweises 60ff.

[26] PI 4: 127,6.

[27] PI 4: 127,13f.

204

On the other hand Anselm insists that the "intelligere" is more than a rational reflection of what palpable reality offers. He states unequivocally "intelligit quod audit."[28] This observation does not help Anselm much. The same applies t o his remark that Gaunilo as a believer ought to advance better arguments. This merely gives the impression that Anselm would subscribe to fideism. The "intelligere" would then only originate from within faith. At this point Anselm does a disservice to his own cause.

Anselm was quite keen on insisting that the term "id quo maius cogitari non possit" precedes the concept of God at the beginning of his deliberations.[29] While he does not reject outright that the origin of the term "intelligere" is religious language, he nevertheless is convinced that the term "id quo maius cogitari non possit" is somehow understandable even to an "insipiens": "aliquo modo intelligit."[30] The term "id quo maius cogitari non possit" originates not in religious language but in thinking itself. In contrast to faith, thinking is a feature common to the whole of the human species. He argues philosophically at this stage: "intelligit quod audit ... etiam si non intelligat illud esse. Aliud est rem esse in intellectu, aliud intelligere rem esse."[31] Thereby Anselm denies the prerequisite of Gaunilo´s "intelligere." The "intelligere" is truly able to recognize "esse" and the "re ipsa existere."

It is difficult to see whether Gaunilo and Anselm agree on a common definition of "intelligere." It seems that Gaunilo stresses the difference between theology and philosophy, whereas Anselm holds that theology yields terms accessible even to non-believers.[32]

One of Gaunilo´s presuppositions was that something is only recognizable by having a comprehensive "scientia" in the background. Anselm rejects this in no uncertain terms. Recognition is not bound to a total and encompassing grasp of the object in question. He astutely observes an immanent contradiction in Gaunilo´s understanding of "intelligere." Hence the Gaunilian position cannot be sustained. On the one hand Gaunilo himself must admit that even something false/wrong can be understood. If, however, the false/wrong can in some way be apprehended, then this cannot be reconciled with Gaunilo´s definition of "scientia." The false/wrong cannot possibly be contained in the term "scientia." "quomodo inquam conveniat et falsa intelligi et intelligere esse scientia comprehendere existere aliquid: nil ad me, tu videris."[33] This established, Anselm insists all the more on his understanding of "intelligere."

---

28 P 2 : 101,8; cf. PR 9: 138,15f; PR 6: 136,9.

[29] PR 1: 130,7.

[30] PR 7: 137,5.

[31] P 2: 101,8-10.

[32] Hopkins holds that Anselm misunderstood Gaunilo´s definition of "intelligere." cf. Hopkins, "Anselm´s Debate with Gaunilo" 31ff.

[33] PR 6: 136,16f.

To Anselm "intelligere" derives at the beginning from an unordered hearing as regards its object - however concentrated it may be. This is the case even when the recoginized is not completely understood. Such is also the case when understanding the "unthinkable," or as Anselm puts it: the "ineffabile." "Sicut enim nihil prohibet dici `ineffabile,´ licet illud dici non potest quod `ineffabile´ dicitur."[34] Not only false things, or something unpronounceable can be recognized but even somehow the "unthinkable." This does not imply that the recognized must be materially understandable. On the same grounds one cannot negate the "highest being" as a term simply because one does not "know" it at the beginning.

Anselm has confounded two of Gaunilo´s arguments. "Scientia" is not the basis for every kind of "intelligere" and not every mode of "intelligere" can be verified in confrontation with reality, the "res ipsa." This does not, however, imply that Anselm holds no correlation to exist between "intelligere" and "res ipsa." But he - contrary to Gaunilo - does not reduce the "res ipsa" to the concrete and palpable realm. The relationship of "intelligere-res" requires

1. outside experience - an "auditum vel dictum"
and 2. "intelligere" does not preclude recognizing the "res" but comes to perfection precisely in the act of the "res"recognition.[35]

In the second case "intelligere" is of a higher quality than in the first, commencing stage. In the act of recognizing the "res," "intelligere" experiences its fulfillment and perfection. "Intelligere" finds its primordial origin in the "res," unfolds the same to a term and finally perfects itself in the process of recognition. Being is the necessary prerequisite of "intelligere." Without "intelligere" there is no knowledge of being: "intuere" as the grasping of the "res" comes about by way of "cogitare." A "significare" of the beheld occurs.[36]

In Gaunilo´s judgment a term must be rooted in the "res" in order to be part of a true statement. The vague term Anselm uses is for him but a mere "vox." In this vein Anselm´s thinking is a mere "significatio vocis" with no rapport with reality. Thinking in the wake of Anselm means building castles in the air according to Gaunilo´s judgment. A term gained from such a process is poetry: "effingere." To stress that something is totally unrelated to being, Anselm prefers using "habere in intellectu" to "essere in intellectu."[37] In

---

[34] PR 9: 138,6f.
[35] Cf. P 2: 101,9f. Kohlenberger, Similtudo und Ratio 156.159.
[36] P 4 : 103,18ff. cf. Kohlenberger, Similitudo und Ratio 30ff; Warnach, "Wort und Wirklichkeit" 166. The same is repeated with the terms "vox," "intellectus" and "res." Cf. Kohlenberger, Similtudo und Ratio 140ff; Warnach, "Wort und Wirklichkeit 171ff. Gaunilo appreciates merely a one dimensional relationship for "intelligere - res," while for Anselm it is dynamic.
[37] Cf. PI 3: 126,15-17. See also Kohlenberger, Similitudo und Ratio 157f; Richthammer, Die Systematik des Proslogionbeweises 21ff. Vuillemin, Le Dieu d´Anselme 98ff.

contrast, for Gaunilo true being is beyond and outside thinking. From Anselm's point of view on the other hand, by divorcing thinking and being, Gaunilo negates the inner possibility of the highest term altogether.

Anselm rejects the notion of an all-encompassing insight ("scientia comprehendo") and opposes similarly the direct correlation of the term with the "res ipsa" in the sense of univocity. The two are related but not identical, one (term) not exhausting the other. The "esse in intellectu" is grounded in the "intelligere" and follows from it: "consequitur esse in intellectu, ex eo quia intelligitur." Terms come about from within the "intelligere."[38] In principle every term is related to being. Therefore, the above definition of "esse in intellectu" applies to every possible term, even to a false one. But the being of every term does not acquire the full quality of a "re ipsa illud existere."[39] This discussion serves to illustrate the intimate connection between being and thinking. A mere thinking that reflects exclusively on the "significatio vocis" addresses being or the "res." Thus mere thinking is already more than only "mere."[40] "Res" must verify its being in thinking. The term's being must be put to the test by the "res." This process of verification occurs by "intelligere" which is cognizant of the relationship between term and subject matter. This said, truth is appreciated as the dynamic entity arising from the relationship between term and reality. In order to have truth appear, one cannot negate the "esse" in the expression "esse in intellectu." Rather it is demanded. It becomes evident then that the leap from "esse in intellectu" to "esse in re" does not necessarily come about by employing the "intelligere." However, the "intelligere" presupposes being. On the other hand "intelligere" cannot ground being. "Intelligere" merely executes being.

At this point of the discussion, Anselm merely wants to demonstrate the principal possibility of relating "esse in intellectu" to "esse in re." These considerations given, Anselm holds that the consideration of the highest term in the "esse in intellectu" is justified.[41] To illustrate this point, that the "specialis generalisve notitia" cannot be a prerequisite for every recognition, Anselm points to the example of beholding light. With no "scientia" at one's disposal, one comes to recognize light (= in its essence as light). This also holds true for the highest term. It is part of the essence of the unthinkable not to be recognized, but it can nevertheless be thought. In this case being determines the parameters. There is a foundational relationship between cognition and being which one may not tear apart. This relationship can be described as a

---

In contrast, "vox" is frequently a "vox significativa" and related to the "res." "Vox" is an expression of spoken language for a "res." Parallel to that, "cogitatio" is the "significatio vocis" representing the "res" in thinking. Cf. Kohlenberger, Similitudo und Ratio 48.155.

[38] Kohlenberger, Similitudo und Ratio 158f.

[39] PR 6: 136, 15.

[40] P 4: 103,18ff.

[41] Kohlenberger, Similitudo und Ratio 142.

convenience or a congeniality between the two. Such a convenience is only possible if cognition is in principle oriented towards being. In this sense one can also appreciate the term "esse in intellectu."

As long as one presupposes a thoroughgoing line of separation between thinking and being one might accuse Anselm of a naive understanding of the term being. However, Anselm evidently presumes a yet more fundamental relationship between the two. Depending on whether one prefers the first or second option, one sides with Gaunilo or Anselm. For Gaunilo the "res" does not appear in the term. Only a posteriori can the term then be verified in the "res." Should one favor Anselm's position, however, then the term would be thought to contain being within itself. If this is the case, still the term neither loses its independence nor does it become intellect's variable. The term contains two moments: that of thinking and that of being. The term's bonds are equally strong to both. These two moments are constitutive for the term.[42] The term acquires the conditions of the "intelligere" but does not succumb to it. Rather it posits itself in the horizon of being.

8.2.2 Being and Thing

The ontological argument inferentially moves from the "highest being" truly existing solely in the intellect to its being also in the (real) matter: "esse et in re." Anselm does not subscribe to a naive realism where reality follows the term. Rather he is cognizant of truth coming about in a multi-layered process. Terms such as "vox," "significatio vocis," "sententia," "oratio," "enuntiatio"and "prolatio" mediate this process. His subtle, highly differentiated view becomes apparent when he distinguishes between the "intelligere" that recognizes its own term and the "intelligere" that acknowledges the "esse in re."[43] When Gaunilo challenges him to produce by way of magic the most beautiful island, Anselm responds that such could be possible only with the term "God." Only if God is being thought is he also.

Gaunilo does not reject out of hand any connection between term and reality. But to him the possibility of something's existing must be contained already in its term. Only if this condition is fulfilled does a connection between the term and "re" come about: "secundum veritatem cuiusquam rei." This criterion cannot be applied to the highest term. The "esse" occurs only in thinking when the term contains the possibility of real existence or when the term can be a posteriori tested at the "res."[44]

The "esse" of the "esse in intellectu" is put into quotation marks just as something false or doubtful because this "esse" is without basis in reality's "esse." In the same vein, the "maius esse" of the highest term cannot be compared with the "esse" of an actually existing entity. The highest being's

---

[42] PI 3: 126,14ff; PR 2: 132,17; cf. Kienzler, Glauben und Denken 245f.
[43] Cf. P 2: 101, 9f.
[44] Cf. PI 5: 127, 25ff.

"esse" is but a "vox," a construction of a human mind. Actual predication does not occur. [45]

In order to render Anselm´s argument conclusive, Gaunilo argues that an additional proof must be supplied to demonstrate that the highest term can exist: "rei veritate subsistere" or that it in fact exists somewhere: "re vera esse alicubi maius ipsum."[46] Gaunilo distinguishes strictly between "rei veritate subsistere" and "esse in intellectu." He seems not to ponder the possibility of overcoming this hiatus. Only if one were to claim that the human mind participates in the highest term could one construct some sort of "esse" for that highest term. But Gaunilo readily adds that then one would be compelled to establish a connection between the spirit´s being and reality´s being. The resolution of this problem would merely be postponed.

In his statements Anselm is keen on preserving the distance but also the relationship between thinking and being. Thinking is posited under being´s overarching horizon. As Kienzler does not tire of elaborating, Anselm made two basic epistemological decisions:

1. He does not reject Gaunilo´s objection outright as regards the possibility of incorrect thinking. But he points out that incorrect or false thinking is only possible if true thinking is a priori possible. Cognition´s destiny is to address ever again the ontological issue and not the concrete and single "res" as its concretion. Thinking intends being. Even if thinking frequently fails to live up to this destiny it always retains the potentiality of actualizing its ontological destiny. Thinking not only mediates between being and thinking, it also sustains the difference between the two. [47] What gives cause to this difference ever anew?

2. Though Anselm does not extrapolate from being to thinking, for him being and experience enable and to this degree also condition thinking. The "intelligere" neither starts with itself nor with the thinking subject´s self but rather with experience: "auditum" or "dictum." Impelled by such experience, the "intelligere" commences its task. This task is not a static one but one that mirrors life and indeed is life. The task is the intellectual itinerary from external sense perception to the interior translation of a term. There it does not come to rest but proceeds through new "intelligere" to verify the acquired interior term on the outside reality: "intelligere rem esse." Cognition does not lack the qualities of adventure. It is a drama, that is to say a mental itinerary, taxing, demanding but also rewarding. The term reached is never sovereign and self-

---

[45] See PI 5: 128, 2ff; Gombocz had argued that the statement "God exists" is logically not contradictory. Cf. Wolfgang L. Gombocz, Uber E! Zur Semantik des Existenzprädikates und des ontologischen Arguments für Gottes Existenz von Anselm von Canterbury (Wien: Verband der wissenschaftlichen Gesellschaft Österreichs, 1974); Vuillemin, Le Dieu d´Anselme 50ff.

[46] PI 5: 128, 12.

[47] Kohlenberger, Similitudo und Ratio 155-163.

contained. It departs from the "intelligere" and is always subject to outside verification.[48] In this sense cognition is not merely oriented towards being but also impelled and enabled by being. Thinking never unilaterally takes hold of being. In this connection Anselm speaks of the "lux solis."[49] One cannot say that one is unable to recognize sunlight because one does not behold the full radiance of that same sunlight. The same holds true for "esse." Cognitionally one is never able to fully fathom thinking and yet, one gains insight into what it means to think. "Nicht das Denken bestimmt über das Sein, sondern das Sein gibt sich zu denken."[50] Thinking does not determine being. Being presents itself as a task to cognition. Being, therefore, demarks the limits of thinking while in relationship to thinking. Being is also always contained in thinking. Therefore, thinking could never from itself quasi construct a posteriori a relationship to being. The relationship is already established from thinkings's very beginning.[51]

8.2.3 Summary

Thinking is the place where truth occurs. It is the coincidence of "intelligere" and "res." Already in *De Veritate* Anselm holds a double congruency between thinking and being. First, every statement is fundamentally related to being. Even a false statement is oriented towards being. In accordance with this first "rectitudo" every statement must ascertain its own rectitude. In this distinction between the relationship-statement of truth and the finite execution of truth in the statement a difference becomes apparent which permeates all finite thinking. The possibility of a false statement makes one acutely aware of this inalienable difference.

While in *De Veritate* the relationship between thinking and being expresses an ethical concern, in the *Monologion* the correspondence between thinking and being is expressed in the figure of "similitudo." This "similitudo" unfolds itself on three different, but related planes. There is sensual and conceptual insight and finally an immediate grasping of the "res ipsae." This last plane seems to correspond to the "intelligere" of the *Proslogion*. In a way the controversy with Gaunilo gave Anselm the opportunity to define more exactly the nature of truth by using the term "intelligere." Thinking rests under the claim of truth and this truth in turn safeguards thinking's relationship to being. While "intelligere" actuates truth and gains insight into this actuation it

---

[48] Cf. Gäde, Eine andere Barmherzigkeit 274f; Kienzler, Glauben und Denken 247ff; Kohlenberger, Similitudo und Ratio 153ff; Schurr, Die Begründung der Philosophie 78ff.

[49] PR 1: 132,7.

[50] Kienzler, Glauben und Denken 251.

[51] Kant accused Anselm of subscribing to a mixing up of different kinds: "μεταβασις εις αλλω γενος." The above discussion of the "intelligere" and the "cogitare" not only demonstrate that the terms are of utmost importance for the ontological argument but also that there is neither a divorce nor an identification between thinking and being. Rather there is a relationship between the two which philosophy struggles to articulate. Cf. Flasch, "Zum Begriff der Wahrheit" 323ff.

does not supply the basis for truth. Thinking cannot cause the relationship between thinking and being.

If one separates thinking and being, one must necessarily conclude to the untenability of the ontological argument. This, however, runs counter to Anselm´s and Plotinus´ philosophies. A separation of the two does not allow the term to come to its own being. Thinking in the latter tradition means the highest degree of intensity of being and at the same time calls upon the thinking subject (and therefore thinking) to marvel that being offers itself to thinking. Up to this point Anselm was concerned only to refute preliminary objections.

8.3 Thinking Terms

The next question regards the "how" of the inference of the "esse et in re" from the "esse in intellectu." The "intelligere" cannot by itself illuminate the connection and can, therefore, not supply the proof for an "esse et in re." Where does the interrelationship of the two occur? This occurs in the "cogitare."

Gaunilo had proposed to substitute "intelligere" for "cogitare.[52]" Anselm had rejected this notion because the ontological argument would have lost its own characteristic feature. While "intelligere" acknowledges what is and reflects upon this, the "cogitare"strives to think being as necessary for thinking. "Intelligere" is a reflex upon the self-revealing being. "Cogitare," however, is thinking from the origin of thinking.[53] The leap from "cogitare" to "esse" is the decisive moment in the ontological argument. Wherein lies the cause for the "intelligere´s" relationship to being? Anselm responds to this question: only by thinking the highest term of the "id quo maius cogitari nequit" can thinking recognize its own causation from being. Anselm rejects Gaunilo´s suggestion that one could then bring the most beautiful and most perfect island into being merely by thinking it.

Anselm chose a precariously narrow trail to arrive, in the company of thinking, at being´s necessity. Only one term expresses this trail. This term puts to test the relationship between thinking and being. If this conclusion succeeds then the relationship´s foundation is uncovered. If, however, the conclusion suffers shipwreck, then all previously held assumptions and foundations are imperiled and no longer can one state the communicability of thinking and being as presumed in the term "intelligere." In other words, the whole of Anselm´s endeavor has arrived at a neuralgic point.[54]

---

[52] P 2: 101,8.

[53] Cf. Renate Esser, `Cogitatio´ und `Meditatio´ - Ein Beitrag zur Metaphysik des Gebetes nach Anselm von Canterbury (Würzburg: Würzburg U, 1985) 87ff; Kienzler, Glauben und Denken 255; Kohlenberger, Similitudo und Ratio 161f; Schurr, Die Begründung der Philosophie 74; Vuillemin, Le Dieu d´Anselme 38ff.

[54] It is at this crucial bifurcation in the interpretation of the ontological argument that scholars choose different paths. One group subscribes to a realistic interpretation. This group is

By being confronted with the expression "id quo maius cogitari nequit," thinking develops a dynamic ("vis prolationis"[55]) propelling it towards being. There is a chain of arguments which leads to the explaining and grounding foundation of being. In Anselm's view the thinkable hypothesis of the highest term contains as a "posse" already an "esse." "Si vel cogitari potest esse necesse est illud."[56] Even if the term is only thought as term, the term's existence is already in evidence. At least for thinking the inference that the term must exist is necessary for thinking. "Si ergo in solo intellectu est: id ipsum, scilicet, `quo maius non potest cogitari,' est quo maius cogitari non potest."[57] Thinking is subject to a dynamics which has it transcend mere thinking "ex necessitate."[58] This renders a more thorough investigation into the nature of "cogitare" as imperative, indeed as "necessary."

8.3.1 Thinking as Action

It is Gaunilo's intention to distinguish the highest term from a false term. This is not Anselm's intention and, therefore, he is quite intent on distinguishing between "cogitare" and "intelligere." It is precisely by virtue of this distinction that the necessary inference of being from thinking comes about. Gaunilo did not consider this possibility. The "insipiens" remains oblivious of the wholeness of being.

Gaunilo argues "(a)liter enim cogitatur res cum vox eam significans cogitatur, aliter cum id ipsum quod res est intelligitur. Illo itaque modo potest cogitari deus non esse, isto vero minime."[59] As a result, if one is able to consider only the term's meaning, then also the opposite could be thought, namely that God does not exist. On this level Anselm admits that there is a lack of precision in the term "cogitare." This can only be overcome if thinking is already in the vicinity of the "res" (for instance God) and its insights are in turn determined by this "res." Precisely this is not the case for the term "God." For the time being, "God" is a pure term and his existence must be evidenced.

---

perhaps best represented by Kant, Russel, Frege and Anglo-American logicians such as John Barnes, "The Ontological Argument" in; John Hick and Arthur C. McGill eds. The many-faced Argument. Recent studies on the Ontological Argument for the Existence of God (New York: Macmillan, 1967) 29-41, at 39ff; Terry L. Miethe, Does God exist?: a believer and an atheist debate (San Francisco: Harper, 1991) 164f; Heinrich Scholz, "Der anselmische Gottesbeweis," "Mathesis Universalis" Abhandlungen zur Philosophie als strenge Wissenschaft. Hans Hermes, Friedrich Kambartel, Joachim Ritter eds. (Basel/Stuttgart: Benno Schwabe, 1961) 68ff. Another group sees in the "cogitare" the hingepoint: Flasch, "Zum Begriff der Wahrheit" 323ff; Kienzler, Glauben und Denken 251; Kohlenberger, Similitudo und Ratio 15-25; Vuillemin, Le Dieu d'Anselme 19.

[55] PR 10: 138,31.
[56] PR 1: 131,6.
[57] PR 2: 132,23f.
[58] PR 1: 131,5.
[59] P 4: 103,18-20.

On the first level of thinking "cogitare" relates to the "vox significans." This renders thinking conscious of itself as thinking. It abstracts from particular entities and arrives at the term, unfolding its cognitional possibilities according to "ratio´s" laws. This is categorical thinking and Anselm is quite in agreement with Gaunilo on this point. However, Gaunilo presses the issue too much by insisting on thinking as having only the "ex-cogitatum" as its result.[60]

Anselm does not disqualify the "insipiens" outright from the beginning. A certain lack of decision and clarification must be granted at an early stage of discussion. Not every form of thinking is already confronted with the "res." "Cogitare" is at the beginning preoccupied with itself. But remaining on this level would not yield epistemological progress. Anselm distinguishes two kinds of thinking. On one level I know that I am ("scire"). But beyond that I can think that I could also not be ("cogitare"). On this level of categorical thinking possibilities can be contemplated.[61]

Gaunilo fails to consider another form of thinking. Yet the issue at hand will be decided by it.

Illa quippe omnia et sola possunt cogitari non esse, quae initium aut finem aut partium habent coniunctionem, et sicut iam dixi, quidquid alicubi aut aliquando totum non est. Illud vero solum non potest cogitari non esse, in quo nec initium nec finem nec partium coniunctionem, et quod non nisi semper et ubique totum ulla invenit cogitatio.[62]

There is a kind of thinking which ponders its possibility. Such is categorical thinking. Another kind of thinking reflects upon its "esse." This one knows neither beginning nor end. It is not composed of different parts and is always and everywhere. It constitutes a self-contained "totum." Such thinking reflects on the ontic facticity of reality and perceives this reality to be a totality ("totum"). Either thinking contemplates these dimensions or it fails to be this kind of thinking. Categorical thinking is preoccupied with multifarious entities which have a beginning and an end. One could also imagine these objects not to be. The transcendent object, however, requires a thinking that is capable of considering the totality of reality. Such transcending thinking does not think a concrete object from within its own imagination, but dares to be addressed by the object. This kind of thinking had already been presented by Anselm and is now in part being presupposed. Gaunilo is unaware of the existence of this second kind, but this second kind of thinking forms the basis for the ontological argument.[63] Such is the meaning of "cogitare."

---

[60] PI 3: 126,24.
[61] PR 4: 133,21ff.
[62] PR 4: 134,2-6.
[63] Esser, Cogitatio und Meditatio 87; Kienzler, Glauben und Denken 259ff; Kohlenberger, Similitudo und Ratio 129

8.3.2 Thinking's Abilities and Limits

In the tension between ability and inability, "cogitari's" reach becomes apparent. According to Anselm the only means to conclude from hypothetical "posse" to actual "esse" is "cogitare." "Cogitare" must perform this task from within its own self and without the assistance of something else.[64] Mindful of the potential "cogitare" of Anselm cannot permit it to be replaced or identified with "intelligere." "Intelligere" is bound to the "res" and cannot decide between "posse" and "esse." Insofar as thinking is categorical, it is hypothetical in character. Anselm distinguishes between two kinds of thinking and two cognitional capabilities. While the one is reduced to apprehending the merely palpable, the other is a transcendental thinking and is the "proprium" by which to infer from a "posse" an "esse." It also safeguards the "proprium" of the unique object in question.[65] It is Anselm's enterprise to distill both the "proprium" of "cogitare" and the "proprium" of God. As long as Gaunilo remains shackled to categorical thinking he cannot reflect upon this transcendental thinking. Categorical thinking may lead to contradictions but not to a decision.[66] This comes to a climax when Anselm observes that "proprium est deo non posse cogitari non esse" and adds "posse cogitari deus non esse."[67] The following quote from the *Proslogion* is pertinent: "Nullus quippe intelligens id quod deus est, potest cogitare quia deus non est, licet haec verba dicat in corde, aut sine ulla aut cum aliqua extranea significatione."[68] Remaining in the opinion of "posse cogitari deus non esse" is therefore identified as that of the "insipiens." A full appreciation of the meaning of the term "cogitare" must come to the negative conclusion, "non posse cogitari deus non esse." The alternatives "cogitare" faces are twofold: either affirming or negating its capability to think or not to think.

Thinking is able to think the term. It also produces the negation of the term in the sense of "nequit cogitari." The highest term sets the limits of thinking. On the one hand thinking, mindful of its limits, allows a term to arise and at the same time this very same thinking must inform the term of its own inability to grasp positively its meaning. In Vuillemin's words: "La force analytique de la preuve repose sur son charactère négative."[69] Existence cannot be the criterion with which to resolve this question. The total interrelation of thinking and being is the final ground in which the highest term has to persevere. The ontological argument rests solely on the formulation, "non potest cogitari non esse id quo maius cogitari nequit."[70] The final and necessary

---

[64] Henry, The Logic of St. Anselm 134ff; Kohlenberger, Similitudo und Ratio 66.

[65] PR 4: 133,27ff.

[66] PR 4: 134,10; Kohlenberger, Similitudo und Ratio 63.

[67] PR 4: 134,16.

[68] P 4 : 103,20-104,2.

[69] Vuillemin, Le Dieu d'Anselme 16.

[70] P 3: 103,1.

interrelation of thinking and being results only from the negative formulation of the "cogitare's" abilities "non potest cogitari non esse id quo maius cogitari nequit."[71]

Thinking can only be thinking if the term is. Would the term not exist, then thinking as "cogitare" would also not exist. The negation of the term would result in the negation of thinking, and this with cognitional necessity. This cognitional necessity is evident in "cogitare"'s self-reflecting thinking. Here, "cogitare" is confronted with Lear's question to be or not to be. Thinking can only be insofar as the term exists.

By no means is the ontological argument a victim of some kind of ontologism. Thinking is ontological due to its interrelation with being. Without the term "id quo maius cogitari nequit" thinking in its constitution would not exist. Such transcendentally reflexive thinking is cognizant of its ability and limits. This term, in order to give justice to thinking, must be both within thinking and preceding such thinking. This term must be nothing less than thinking's (as "cogitare") epitome. This is the import of Anselm's "Responsio."

> Si vero cogitat, utique cogitat aliquid quod nec cogitari possit non esse. Si enim posset cogitari non esse, cogitari posset habere principium et finem. Sed hoc non potest. Qui ergo illud cogitat, aliquid cogitat quod nec cogitari non esse possit. Hoc vero qui cogitat, non cogitat idipsum non esse. Alioquin cogitat quod cogitari non potest. Non igitur potest cogitari non esse "quo maius nequit cogitari.[72]

Either thinking thinks the term or it does not think at all: "aut cogitat aliquid quo maius cogitari non possit, aut non cogitat." Thinking itself is at stake with the term: "alioquin cogitat quod cogitari non potest."

In order for thinking to be true to itself it must arrive at an affirmation of the term's "esse" and not rest in the "posse." It must opt for the first and thereby come to its own: "ratio est princeps omnium quae sunt in homine." The last court of appeal for thinking is thinking's own transcendental necessity. Thus thinking is in its highest degree a transcendental thinking and thereby necessarily transcendent towards its highest term.

8.3.3 Confronted with The Limit

The discussion of this term takes on special urgency. Only via "id quo maius cogitari nequit" can thinking depart from an "esse in solo intellectu" to an "esse et in re".

On the one hand Gaunilo argues that the "res" of the highest term is unknown according to the "specialis generalive notitia." On the other hand the only option remaining is that of analogy: "conicere ex alia simili." But this

---

[71] P 3: 103,1.
[72] PR 3: 133,14-20.

also has to be rejected because the "res" in question cannot be buttressed by the "res alia similis." God is radically dissimilar to any other "res". Therefore, there exists in Gaunilo´s estimation no basis for arriving at the term "God." The phrase "id quo maius cogitari nequit" is not a true term.

With characteristic precision Anselm responds to these remonstrances:

> (i)tem quod dicis "quo maius cogitari nequit" secundum rem vel ex genere tibi vel ex specie notam te cogitare auditum vel in intellectu habere non posse, quoniam nec ipsam rem nosti, nec eam ex alia simili potes conicere: palam est rem aliter se habere. Quoniam namque omne minus bonum in tantum est simile maiori bono inquantum est bonum: patet cuilibet rationabili menti, quia de bonis minoribus ad maiora conscendendo ex iis quibus aliquid maius cogitari potest, multum possumus conicere illud quo nihil potest maius cogitari.[73]

Anselm also defends the possibility of analogy also for the highest term. Thinking´s "similitudo" grounds such an analogy. He reiterates the train of thought he had presented already in the *Monologion*, chapters 1-4. The "ratio" in its "iudicare" and "discernere" is able to distinguish and to relate diverse "bona": "magis bonum" and "minus bonum." This is only possible because of thinking´s possession of a transcendental term: "bonum per se." The "similitudo" guarantees a correspondence among single "bona" and the transcendental "bonum." As Anselm´s term "id quo maius cogitari nequit" is a transcendental term, it corresponds to transcendent thinking. Consequently, Gaunilo´s objection that this term has no relation to reality, "secundum rem," does not hold. The term "bonum" is gained by deduction from diverse "bona" and proceeds inductively from "minus bonum" to "magis bonum." This is categorical thinking. It is important for Anselm to note that such categorical thinking must presuppose transcendent thinking. The diverse "bona" become possible only if the transcendental term "bonum" exists. The concept of "similitudo" guarantees the unity of thinking. It vouches for the correlation of transcendental and categorical thinking. The term "id quo maius cogitari nequit" is the conditio sine qua non for finite thinking.

The "maius omnibus" proposed by Gaunilo suggests in Anselm´s judgment that the highest term is merely the terminal point of a chain of objects. The "maius omnibus" is not part of thinking but of reality. In that case thinking would be forced to verify the term. In contrast to this the "id quo maius cogitari nequit" is capable of performing this verification from within thinking itself. Anselm´s term is already a part of thinking. But the "maius omnibus" is also outside of thinking and, therefore, its existence or nonexistence is not simply verifiable by reality. In the tension between "posse" and "esse" the term

---

[73] PR 8: 137,11-18.

"quo maius cogitari nequit" thematizes thinking. At the same time it transcends thinking and thrusts forward to being.[74]

8.3.4 Concluding Remark

When comparing the description and account Anselm gives of thinking in the *Monologion* and *De Veritate* with that of the *Proslogion* we find a greater precision in the latter. The "intelligere" plays a significant role in the event of truth. In the *Proslogion* "cogitare" evidences thinking's constitution. In a subtle way the *Proslogion* echoes the connection between thinking's recognizing God and its self. Every object requires a corresponding thinking. Only transcendent thinking can correspond with the highest object or the highest term. Such thinking forms necessarily the highest term. This knowledge concerning its own necessity to formulate this term grants thinking insight into its transcendental constitution. On the one hand it discovers the highest term as its own (= thinking's) transcendental term, on the other hand this necessary term for thinking remains transcendental, which means the term's being is never dissolved into or subsumed under thinking.

---

[74] Esser, Cogitatio und Meditatio 97f; Kienzler, Glauben und Denken 171ff; Vuillemin, Le Dieu d'Anselme 21ff.

9.0 Faith and Reason - a Plotinian/Anselmian Unity

The previous deliberations served the purpose of establishing the foundations for the actual argument. One of the achieved insights is that the principle of non-contradiction prevails within thinking and the term "id quo maius cogitari nequit." In the confrontation of "intelligere" and "cogitare" with this term reservations against this term were allayed.

The *Proslogion* starts with the term in question from the beginning. The term is without prerequisites. It contains all previous considerations and all future insights. The term proves everything from within itself. The term is handed over to thinking. From such thinking all further steps must develop.[1] What is contained in the term must come into thinking. In the process one should be able to infer that God truly exists. This is only possible if the "unum argumentum" uncovers the relationship between "esse in intellectu" and "esse et in re" as necessary. Parallel to this investigation it must also probe whether the review of the relationship between "cogitare" and "esse" evidences this relationship as necessary.

These preliminary considerations have ramifications for the argument's structure and methodology. No longer can this be termed a proof in the sense of a chemical examination in a laboratory. Rather there is a demonstration or showing of what is contained from the very beginning. In connection with *Proslogion,* chapter two, scholarship has defined this approach as "apagogic." It proves something by demonstrating the contradiction in its counter-thesis: "falsum non sequitur nisi ex falso." It assumes everything to be true if the contrary is false.[2]

9.1 In the *Proslogion*

The second chapter opens with a credal statement that is, as Anselm did not tire of demonstrating, philosophical in nature: "credimus te esse aliquid quo nihil maius cogitari possit." This highest possible term is intentionally placed at the beginning of the reflections. Both the believer and non-believer are to grasp, "intelligere," this term's import. Both are only able to obtain this deeper insight into the term's dimensions if they engage "cogitare" in this endeavor.

This chapter discusses the "intelligere" and the highest term as the "id quo maius cogitari nequit."[3] The primordial comprehension of the highest term

---

[1] Schurr, Die Begründung der Philosophie 35ff.

[2] This interpretation is held by Horst Enslin, "Der ontologische Gottesbeweis bei Anselm von Canterbury und bei Karl Barth," Neue Zeitschrift für systematische Theologie und Religionswissenschaft 11 (1969): 154-177 at 157ff; Koyré, L'idée de Dieu 200ff; Schurr, Die Begründung der Philosophie 86f; Söhngen, Einheit der Theologie 43ff; Vuillemin, Le Dieu d'Anselme 15.120ff.

[3] Here the paper adopts the assumption held by Gombocz, that chapter 2 discusses primarily the "intelligere", whereas Chapter 3 of the *Proslogion* discusses the "cogitare." Cf. Wolfgang L. Gombocz, "Zur Zwei-Argumenten-Hypothese bezüglich Anselms Prosalogion," Salzburger Jahrbuch für Philosophie 20 (1975): 131-147, at 133ff.

is a mere hearing: "intelligit quod audit." The aim of such thinking is to evidence the highest term's "esse et in re." This "audire" has its correlation within the intellect: "esse in intellectu." Again the question is whether one encounters here, in the case of the highest term, a mere mirage - "esse in solo intellectu" - or whether one can illustrate a coherence and a correspondence between that term and reality and whether one can define such a being-in-reality as the term's constitutive moment. The "intelligere" alone is well capable of bringing about this correspondence with the "res" but it is ill equipped to establish the causal grounds for this relation. It is the "res" task to demonstrate to the "intelligere" that it is able to execute this congruency from within its own understanding.

Beheld from outside it is impossible to decide whether the highest term exists merely and exclusively in the intellect or whether it possesses objective and real being. In contrast to common exegesis of the *Proslogion*, a close reading of the text reveals that the highest term cannot only be thought as a mere term but already from within itself it must be greater and, therefore, eclipse the intellect: "et certe id quo maius cogitari nequit, non potest esse solo in intellectu."[4] In the unique case of the highest term the "intelligere's" relationship to the "res" is presumed to be necessary. Therefore, the argument presented is not so much an argument to prove this claim (i.e. that the highest term possible must also be), but rather to prove that this claim withstands the rigorous probing of the subsequent discussions. The majority of interpretations fails to apprehend that the discussion does not serve to prove the relationships between "intelligere" and "res" and between term and reality, but rather that the thinker is called to analyze in order to recognize these fundamental relationships. The relationships are presumed to exist already prior to the argument's inception. The thinker more fully enters into these relationships within which he/she already stands and does not contrive these relationships in the discussion's process.

The term must be able to demonstrate these relationships in order for the "intelligere" to gain insight into and to execute these relationships. Therefore, it is not the "intelligere" that is able to get this insight into the highest term from within its own capabilities, but rather the "cogitare" that considers the highest term's valency and unfolds that term's implications. It is within the scope of this second form of thinking, "cogitare," where the viability of the "id quo maius cogitari nequit" comes to a head and is decided. Here the relationship between the highest term and its reality and the "intelligere" as "intelligere" is uncovered and explained. In this sense, the so-called ontological argument is not a mere ontological discussion but with equal force from its very outset also an epistemological argument, for the "cogitare" become its all-deciding fulcrum. Only on its secondary level, when inferring being from thinking, and

---

[4] P 2: 10,2f.

when thinking is explained ontologically, does the argument take on the character of a truly "ontological argument."[5]

This discussion confirms the above stated apagogic thesis. The mode of questioning prevails within its own disciplined discourse. It belongs to the structure of an apagogic argument that the verity that should be evidenced is posited at the argument's very beginning.

9.1.1 The Line of Argument

"Intelligere" as the common feature of faith and thinking gives rise to the alternative of whether the highest term is "solo in intellectu" or "et in re." It is the term's force which decides the issue. At the beginning Anselm presents the thesis: "Et certe id quo maius cogitari nequit, non potest esse in solo intellectu." The alternative with which "intelligere" is confronted is: "vel in solo intellectu ... vel esse et in re." Thereupon, he postulates as a positive hypothesis that the highest being can develop itself as cognitionally possible from within thinking: "potest cogitari esse et in re." One cannot contradict this cognitional hypothesis as there exists no contradiction between the highest term and the "res." As a result of this it follows that as a positive statement it is higher: "maius est." This means that the positive hypothesis of the highest term is greater than the counterthesis, which negates the highest term. In order to justify this "maius" further, Anselm makes use of the contradiction which results from the confrontation of the counterthesis with the positive hypothesis: "id ipsum quo maius cogitari non potest, est quo maius cogitari potest. Sed hoc certe esse non potest." The "esse solo in intellectu" is confirmed as an impossible possibility, confirming the certitude of the "esse et in re." The positive hypothesis of the highest term is being propelled to a positive affirmation by precluding a contradiction within thinking. What remains is but the possibility of the "esse et in re." At the end of this discussion Anselm states the result of his deliberations. "Existit ergo procul dubio aliquid quo maius cogitari non valet, et in intellectu et in re."[6]

Cognition's hypotheses are not randomly arrived at. They are subject to two forms of thinkability: thinking and the object to be thought. Thinkability follows the principle of non-contradiction. The highest term can also on first glance be either only in the human mind or also in reality. This means that cognition must have the possibility of thinking that it is also in reality. The decision concerning this thinkability cannot be arrived at by the "intelligere" because "intelligere" is a corollary of the "res" and, therefore, cannot supply the

---

[5] In this context Vuillemin observes: "seule la forme négative et épistémologique est charactéristique de la preuve ontologique d'Anselme." Vuillemin, Le Dieu d'Anselme 19. Cf. Schurr, Die Begründung der Philosophie 75.

[6] P 2: 102,2f. Henry, The Logic of Saint Anselm 142f; Kienzler, Glauben und Denken 179ff; Richthammer, Die Systematik des Proslogionbeweises 58ff.127ff; Schurr, Die Begründung der Philosophie 87f; Söhngen, Die Einheit der Theologie 43ff.

explanation for this relation. It can only execute it. The decision occurs outside the "intelligere."

Anselm claims the term is "higher" when it not merely exists for the human intellect but also in reality. The criterion for the decision is whether the highest term indeed results from the word "maius." One gains insight into this not through the "intelligere" but through the "cogitare." It is the "cogitare" which is able to examine the alternatives and to determine where the predication "maius" is applicable. But what does "maius" predicate? It is not the highest possible term but rather the cognitional form which thinks the highest term. In Anselm's judgment thinking cannot extricate itself from a contradiction when reducing the highest term merely to an "esse in solo intellectu." There are two predications for thinking resulting from the term "quo maius cogitari nequit." On the one hand, thinking's affirmation of a "potest cogitari", and on the other hand an equally real inability of the same thinking: "non potest cogitari." Through the highest term, thinking becomes conscious of its own abilities and limits. The term uncovers in thinking a "maius" towards which thinking thinks but which it cannot exhaustively think or define in a comprehensive manner. Thinking contains a "maius," a greater. Cognition, by thinking the highest term, encounters a limit within itself which it is able to recognize and yet which it is not able to overcome.

Thinking as "intelligere" automatically respects one boundary, namely that of reality, of the "res." Whether the thought exists exclusively in the mind or also in reality cannot be determined by thinking. Such an indication must be given by the "res." Reality in this sense becomes a litmus test for thinking. Thinking's "posse" is kept in check by reality. Thinking does not design reality. In this "ductus," reality appears as the "maius" vis-à-vis thinking. In its sum-total, reality is greater than cognition. Yet this defines not merely the limitations but also the telos of thinking. It is conceived as a "thinking-towards" reality: "potest cogitari."[7]

This reflection brings thinking's character to the fore. Thinking knows itself under the appeal, claim and beckoning of the "maius" which is reality. This does not, however, entail that every single "res" in and of itself is already greater than thinking. Yet, as thinking is able to consider/think this "maius," which reality in a sense is unable to render, thinking is in a sense "maius." Again, a thinking capable of achieving this insight is "maius" to one who cannot supply such awareness. It becomes apparent that the Anselmian "maius" intends to connote "more" than an ontic superiority of something that is truly "esse in re" over the merely thought ("esse solo in intellectu"). There exists a "maius" within cognition. By recognizing the "esse et in re" it becomes obvious that thinking's "maius" is the greater beyond which it cannot probe: it reflects (on) the "quo maius cogitari nequit." For precisely this reason Anselm

---

[7] Richthammer, <u>Die Systematik des Proslogionbeweises</u> 89f.

concludes: "Existit ergo procul dubio aliquid quo maius cogitari non valet, et in intellectu et in re." This by no means implies a negative definition but rather indicates a positive "destiny-ation" of thinking. It is its very constitution to live from within the relationship of reality-thinking. This relationship is as a possibility pre-given to thinking. But since there is no other alternative, this thinking apprehends in the making real of this possible relationship the only and necessary actuation of itself. Vice -versa, reality must grant itself to thinking.

These deliberations illustrate Anselm's position. The highest term exists first in reality and subsequently in the human mind. Thinking is from its very beginning in (perhaps at first a vaguely definable) relationship to this reality. The highest term qua term is thinking's reality: "est in intellectu." Thinking's relationship to reality occurs nowhere else but in thinking. The intimate intertwined relationship of the terms "in intellectu", "in re", "intelligere" and "maius" becomes apparent in the event of "cogitare," when thinking in its totality sufaces as thinking transcends thinking towards being.

9.1.2 "Cogitare" and "Esse"

"Quod utique sic vere est, ut nec cogitari possit non esse." Thus the third chapter starts. It does not want to produce something radically new, but wants to follow through on the facts already established in chapter two.[8] Something like a reinforcement of the previously stated occurs. The "in re existere" of the highest term is being reproduced as "sic vere esse." In addition, there is a remarkable emphasis on the "nec" in connection with the formula "nec potest cogitari." This expression accentuates thinking's constraints.[9] Chapter three reflects upon the effects of the results of the previous discussion in chapter two and now probes thinking's negative form: "non potest cogitari."

"Cogitare" and "esse" per se figure prominently. The relationship of being and thinking thereby becomes the central theme of the chapter. "Intelligere" is concerned with something which is not part of itself and thus with something that is greater than thinking's totality. A congruency between "intelligere" and "res" is to be established in normal situations. Is this always the case? Does one deal with a special case when confronted with the highest term? Does the highest term require a special form of thinking that finds its basis in a transcendental ground ? Indeed, attention is given in this chapter not to the givenness of the "intelligere," but rather to the transcendental constitution of thinking per se: "cogitare." "Maius" and "esse et in re" have been noted in the previous chapter as "intelligere's" limits. Does the "esse" become the limit for the "cogitare"? This is the fundamental issue the third chapter addresses. It

---

[8] Barth, Fides quaerens intellectum 124-150; Gilson, Sens et Nature 12ff; Külling, Wahrheit als Richtigkeit 86ff; Richthammer, Die Systematik des Proslogionbeweises 88ff..
[9] Henry, The Logic of Saint Anselm 143ff; Vuillemin, Le Dieu d'Anselme 19.

attempts to illumine the relationship between "cogitare" and "esse" and uncover the necessity of a cause for "cogitare" in "esse".[10]

This transcendental connection between the two is not obvious because there remains a principal difference between "cogitare" and "esse" which Anselm encapsulates in the term "posse." It is this chapter's principal argument that this lack of determination does not hold in the case of the highest term and has already been decided prior to the question. This interwovenness of the two terms in the highest term becomes evident in the phrase: "Quod si vere est, ut nec cogitari possit non esse id quo maius cogitari nequit."[11]

This expresses a double negation and draws attention to an absolute necessity within the relationship of thinking and being. The "esse" asserts itself so forcefully in thinking that it is altogether unthinkable that it could not be: "non esse." The "cogitare" is subject to and dependent on the "esse's" necessity in such an intense way that it necessarily refers to that "esse" and, therefore, necessarily thinks it. In other words, the "esse's" necessity is not further deducible and inferrable. It precedes every inference and is without any presuppositions. It rests in itself as an absolute necessity. Thinking's transcendental necessity arises from this first necessity. Chapter three's argument is that this first necessity is already always connoted in the highest term.

9.1.3 The "maius"

Chapter two had established that the highest term is constitutive for thinking it. Otherwise it could not refer beyond itself to the "maius" and be transcendental thinking. Is the necessity of the relationship between thinking and being thinking's result and is the principle of being postulated with its own necessity or is this necessity an ontic one that asserts itself in thinking? This chapter's aim is to illustrate that being is necessary for thinking and that thinking when faithful to itself and penetrating to the mind's extreme recesses arrives at being. This occurs by reflecting upon the highest term, namely "id quo maius cogitari nequit."

The positive hypothesis reads, "nam potest cogitari esse aliquid, quod non possit cogitari non esse." This hypothesis thematizes thinking as thinking by reflecting upon thinking's abilities and limits. It is a thinking thinking.[12] The decision concerning the "esse" (positive hypothesis) and the "non esse" (negative hypothesis) cannot arise from a thinking that only actuates its

---

[10] Evdokimov rejects a rational interpretation of this chapter leading to the necessity of a relationship between thinking and being and opts for an apophatic, intuitive and evidential proof of divine existence. Cf. Evdokimov, "L'Aspect apophatique" 233-242.
[11] Wolfgang L. Gombocz, "Zu neueren Beiträgen zur Interpretation von Anselms Proslogion." Salzburger Jahrbuch für Philosophie 20 (1975): 85-98, at 93ff; Henry, The Logic of Saint Anselm 103.
[12] Kienzler, Glauben und Denken 290f; Kohlenberger, Similitudo und Ratio 129.

relationship with its highest term. It must be a different kind of thinking, one that is able to be conscious of its own inner necessity. Such reflexive thinking can articulate its pondering the term "quo maius cogitari nequit." Thinking must decide what kind of thinking is higher: that which consideringly thinks the highest term's being or that thinking which claims the highest term's non-being. Only thinking is able to muster the energy required for such a decision. But this thinking is confronted with the term "quo maius cogitari nequit." Face to face with this term thinking must arrive at a decision. Only by prevailing as the term's "maius" in thinking do the highest term and actual thinking become congruent. This is the requirement of Anselm's argument. On the other hand the term always co-constitutes thinking. In its final analysis the highest term must be nothing less than the very embodiment of thinking.[13] The question whether "esse" or "non esse" is greater determines which kind of thinking is greater: a thinking which presupposes an "esse" or a thinking which ultimately claims a "non esse." By playing through the alternatives, thinking uncovers in the counterthesis a contradiction to the term "maius." This contradiction renders the positive hypothesis certain. Only thus does the term remain what it is. This contradiction is double. It violates both the term and thinking. The counterthesis must contradict the thinking that articulates the term as that thinking's highest expression. That counterthesis must also contradict the term which presupposes such thinking.

The term "quo maius cogitari nequit" contains two moments of thinking. The term is not outside of thinking, but within thinking. It is the highest term of that thinking. At the same time the thinking of the highest term illustrates an ability and a limit of that very thinking. On the one hand it is able to think towards or even to reach the "maius." On the other hand it is not able to fully reach this "maius." The "maius" is at the same time within thinking and greater than this thinking. It can approach asymptotically the highest term of the "maius," but can never exhaustively think it. The "potest cogitari" is the prerequisite for the "non potest cogitari." Thinking's inability is only possible if it presumes a fundamental ability to think. "Maius" demarcates thinking's limit and at the same time illustrates the highest possible cognitional achievement of that thinking.

From where does this limit come? It is possible that thinking itself sets this limit, that there is no factor beyond this cognition which contributes to this boundary. This thinking is first and foremost a pure ability, "potest cogitari." This capacity is as regards its cognitional possibilities boundless. Nevertheless, in the phrase "non potest cogitari" it is conscious of some kind of boundary. Can this limit arise from some other source than cognition?

At this point the counterthesis' contradiction comes in place: "quare si id quo maius cogitari nequit, potest cogitari non esse: id ipsum quo maius cogitari

---

[13] Kienzler, Glauben und Denken 291f.

nequit, non est id quo maius cogitari nequit; quod convenire non potest." That thinking is greater than that which is able to gain insight into its own conditions of constitution. The two phrases "potest cogitari" and "non potest cogitari" offer thinking such indications. A thinking which does not know about the possibility of a counterthesis cannot in principle explain "non potest cogitari." Thinking as "cogitari," however, is able to think both. Therefore, a thinking that is able to think also its not-being-able is to be judged greater. The counterthesis, however, is unable to name a reason for thinking's not being able; provided it is in a position to evidence that thinking is sufficient to explain itself and to set its own limits. This thinking does not provide its own explanation and does not set its own limits.

The highest term is both thinkable and not thinkable. The counterthesis would not be able to reach this term because it would not be able to express the dialectics of this term. In contrast, the positive hypothesis determines the term as thinking's other principle to which thinking is constitutively related. For this reason the term can never be subsumed under or grasped by thinking. Only in such a way does there come about the congruency between the actually thought term and the term thinking must think.

On this level Anselm's second objection against the counterthesis becomes apparent. "Quare si id quo maius nequit cogitari, potest cogitari non esse: id ipsum quo maius cogitari nequit, non est id quo maius cogitari nequit; quod convenire non potest." The counterthesis precludes the "esse" as cognition's other principle. On this point it contradicts the term. In chapter two of the *Proslogion* and in the other principle it ("esse") is required. By precluding the counterthesis, the positive thesis takes on the character of certitude. The term of the "id quo maius cogitari non potest" is greater because caused by "esse's" principle. "Esse" becomes the prevailing force in this contest. As thinking is not able to supply the strength for deciding the issue, "esse" is called to the rescue. In confrontation with thinking being proves to be the "maius." The result of the argument is expressed in the following words: "Sic ergo vere est aliquid quo maius cogitare non potest, ut nec cogitari possit non esse." "Esse" is considered in its positive valence; "cogitare" is expressed in the negative form. In thinking's inability being's positivity becomes apparent. Though negative moments exist in the relationship between being and thinking, thinking cannot be reduced to mere non-thinking. True thinking is cognizant of its abilities and inabilities. Particularly when confronted with its inabilities, thinking acutely knows of its fundamental relationship with being. In the double negation of not being able to think non-being, thinking becomes profoundly aware of its transcendental necessity to be in relationship to being. To this degree, the "non potest cogitari" contains a self-revelatory, constitutive moment. Quite in marked contrast to thinking, being is neither subject to a limitation nor to an inability. Therefore, due to thinking's deficiencies and the positive attributes being possesses, being itself becomes transcendentally necessary to thinking. Thinking's (ponderingly) thinking of its inabilities is the true occasion for being's epiphany.

In *Proslogion*, chapter two, thinking has been evidenced as a self-transcending thinking. In *Proslogion*, chapter three, this thinking is defined in a more precise form as a transcendentally caused thinking. Self-transcending thinking finds its cause in being's transcendent reality. Exactly by virtue of this insight does thinking come to its own: it obtains its own contours.

9.1.4 Oneness

This argument sums up Anselm's thinking and defends it against all the objections brought forth. It is one argument because it is formed through thinking's highest term. All that Anselm had arduously developed in the *Monologion* and *De Veritate* as well as the discussions with Gaunilo is present in the "unum argumentum." And yet this newly found unit is greater and more powerful than all previous statements. In a unique way the highest term contains as a unit thinking's knowledge of God and the self. In this sense the "unum argumentum" is truly a new beginning without any premises. It can no longer be analized as it is absolute. All this is obtained by using the principle of "sola ratione." All previous arguments in the *Monologion* and *De Veritate* but serve as elaborations, however, not as explanations for the "unum argumentum". It is the heart piece of Anselm's thought as it yields certitude in two areas particularly dear to him: knowledge of the self and knowledge of God in thinking. This argument allowed thinking to meet the term in such a way that thinking met thinking and articulated God, as it is proper for thinking to do.

The methodology chosen was determined from the very beginning by the highest term. It is here that the necessity of the highest term became evident. Only a thinking which reflects on thinking's own constitution as thinking could grant this insight. Justifiably the principle of "sola ratione" stood at the very beginning of Anselm's scholarly deliberations. Within the course of these arguments this principle was confirmed. This "sola ratione" as thinking was first expressed under the concept of "intelligere" and subsequently under the considerations of "cogitare." Thinking persevered from the very beginning. In the "maius," self-transcending thinking beheld God as transcendence. In the "esse" transcendentally caused thinking apprehended the transcendent God as its own transcendentally necessary ground. And yet there is no gainsaying that God remains in a mysterious way concealed for thinking. Thinking could understand that such transcendence is not rooted in any kind of "res" but in a reality which is to thinking in its totality greater. Such transcendence needs to be the "summum" of reality. Finally this cause appears to thinking as the transcendent-transcendental cause of "esse." This cause is identified as the end of the third chapter expressly as the God of his faith: "et hoc est tu, domine deus noster." In this explicit identification of the highest term with Anselm's God both credal certitude and the difference between faith and reason are manifested. This God must be the "summum" of all of reality as well as the "summum esse." One has proven divine existence and yet has preserved God's ineffable omnipotence by realizing that God exists in veiled form.

The achievement of the "unum argumentum" is to grasp the unity of God and self-knowledge in one term and in one argument. [14] Such unity of thought could not come about without an inner correspondence between God and thinking. In this most concentrated form the "unum argumentum" gives form and execution to the concept of "similitudo." A "similitudo" between God and creaturely thinking as well as between "summa ratio" and "ratio" exists. Divine unity enables cognitional unity. In this one thinking God appears as one and thinking thinks - in the sense of being "mindful(l)" - its own unity as grounded in divine unity. The flavor of dissatisfaction arising from the remaining infinite difference between God and thinking expresses thinking's yet greater "dissimilitudo" found in the "similitudo." God retains a "maius" which thinking in its "similitudo" is utterly unable to grasp. Nevertheless, this divine "dissimilitudo" deigns to reveal itself as "dissimilitudo" in the mind's self-execution.

9.1.5 Tension as the Mind's "Proprium"

Anselm's Werk hat zwei Seiten: Form und Gehalt, Methode und Gegenstand, und wenn beide in Spannung zueinander stehen, so beachtet man für gewöhnlich zu wenig ihre Einheit und ihr gegenseitiges Sichbedingen. ... (aim and purpose of Anselm's writings is) ... das freie Handeln des freien Gottes mit dem frei geschaffenen und durch Christus neu in die Freiheit geführten Menschen ... [15]

Anselm's constant concern is salvation history. Human freedom and divine freedom are in tension with one another. Their unity in the human mind must be sought. Thinking and the principle of "sola ratione" serve this aim. On the one, Anselm approaches faith with the attitude of "sola ratione." On the other he takes faith's object in order to think "sola ratione." This mental pilgrimage made thinking cognizant that it is not simply delighting in a mere soliloquy. Rather it apprehends its relationship to the "greater" and therein the interwovenness of recognizing the self and God as a tension of faith and thinking. Chapter three of the *Proslogion* demonstrated that faith as salvation history is open for thinking. This permitted applying the principle of "sola ratione" also in the opposite direction: from faith to thinking. Faith became unlocked for thinking when the latter thought through its own terms. Faith put thinking to test and transformed it. Faith is at once the aim of thinking and in a second run thinking becomes the object of faith. All these considerations have

---

[14] Cf. Richthammer, Die Systematik des Proslogionbeweises 103.
[15] Balthasar, Herrlichkeit, Vol. I. 218f.

not yet reflected upon faith. The actual features of faith have not yet been addressed by reason.

The question arising is, how does faith relate to revelation and salvation history? More specifically, in what way is the tension between faith and reason (thinking) reconciled and yet maintained in a higher unity? Flasch pointed out that Johann Adam Möhler had already recognized this question as the most central of Anselm's concerns.

Möhler will Anselm vorstellen als den Protagonisten einer philosophischen Behandlung des Christentums. Bei Anselm fand er, was sein Lehrer Drey gefordert hatte: Die eigentliche Wissenschaft solle sich von der empirisch-historischen Kenntnis des Christentums zu einer Idee erheben und seinen Inhalt aus dieser Idee deduzieren. Diese Idee sei zwar durch das Christentum selbst erst gegeben und bekannt gemacht worden: "Sie ist aber in der Vernunft begründet, eine wahre Vernunftidee, die wie alle anderen erst durch den von außen anregenden Strahl der erzieherischen Offenbarung zum freien Hervortreten in der Vernunft geweckt wurde. Durch die absolute Wahrheit und Notwendigkeit, die die Idee eines Reiches Gottes vor der Vernunft hat, erlangen auch alle Erscheinungen desselben in der Geschichte der Menschheit, alle Lehren des Christentums, welche die Geheimnisse in der selben Geschichte aufdecken und erklären, den gleichen Charakter von Notwendigkeit und Wahrheit.[16]

Möhler discovered in Anselm's writings an organic view of theology and philosophy, of faith and reason which was very congenial to the organic concern expressed by the Tübingen School of his day. From diverse empirical and historical facts Christianity should be elevated and concentrated in its idea and contents. This idea is always a reasonable one, further developing and thus multiplying revelation's educational potential. Möhler found Drey's call to transform Jesus Christ's life into ideas realized in a rudimentary form in Anselm's writings. This central insight into Anselm's thought is typically considered, in twentieth century Anselm research, as an utter impossibility. One presumes a wall of separation to exist between philosophy and theology and cannot countenance in Anselm's writings a different situation. One either interprets Anselm as a theologian with no philosophical concerns or as a pure philosopher (Kant, Neoscholasticism, Anglo-Saxon language-logicians). Between the "von außen anregenden Strahl der erzieherischen Offenbarung" and the "freien Hervortreten in der Vernunft" a strict hiatus is assumed, with no prospect of reconciliation between the two.

Anselm's teaching overcomes the contradiction between reason and faith, history and God. Reason and faith are reciprocally open for impulses coming from the other side; for an osmotic exchange. Chapter two of the *Proslogion* demonstrated how thinking remains open for the always greater God. Chapter three of the *Proslogion*, alternatively, shows how faith is open for thinking.

---

[16] Kurt Flasch, "Vernunft und Geschichte. Der Beitrag Johann Adam Möhlers zum philosophischen Verständnis Anselms von Canterbury." <u>Analecta Anselmiana</u> I. Francis Salesius Schmitt ed. (Frankfurt am Main: Minerva, 1969): 165-194, at 169.

Proslogion's argument displays an independent rational logic. Within this treatise chapters two and three form the core. This becomes apparent when reading the "Prooemium"and chapters one and five. The suspicion that Anselm consciously chose chapters two and three as the stage for the core of his argument is thereby confirmed.[17] Thinking must be formed by the highest term in order to be what it is. Thereby thinking acknowledges being as the object of transcendental thinking and grasps itself as thinking. For the time being the argument remained within the possibilities set by thinking's rationality and its own transcendental reflection.

The intellectual effort demanded in the argument is neither an arbitrary one nor is the result left unreflected upon. Faith stands both at the beginning and at the end of the treatise. The "Prooemium" points to the whole work's credal intention. Chapter one provokes the question why so little light is shed upon faith. The highest term as thinking's first stimulus is also the result of faith. This highest term yearns to become luminous by virtue of going through this cognitional process. Thinking does not start from a tabula rasa but presupposes some kind of faith. Faith grows in credal contents by following reason's itinerary. Faith assents to the intellectual progress reason makes. In the process faith grows and matures. "Quid igitur es, domine deus?"[18] There is a dynamic in the mind's progression which propels faith towards God. The conclusions drawn by reason open the gates for a new beginning for faith.[19] In this sense thinking is both within and outside faith: "intellectus est medium." Finally there is agreement concerning the highest term attained among faith and thinking. In this manner thinking is faith's center and faith is its origin and aim.

While thinking serves faith, faith remains irreplaceably called to its own originality and freedom. Together faith and thinking progress faithfully to the principle "fides quaerens intellectum." This unison of the two generates an ever greater dynamic as de Lubac expresses this situation.[20]

9.1.6 Anselmian Harmony

At the very outset of his deliberations Anselm expresses his goal:

> coepi mecum quaerere, si forte posset inveniri unum argumentum, quod nullo alio ad se probandum quam se solo indigeret, et solum ad astruendum quia deus vere est, et quia est summum bonum nullo alio indigens, et quo omnia indigent ut sint et ut bene sint, et quaecumque de divina credimus substantia, sufficeret.[21]

---

[17] Cf. Barth, Fides quaerens intellectum 97ff; de Lubac, "Seigneur, je cherche to visage" 201ff. 407ff; McIntyre, St. Anselm and his Critics 95ff.

[18] P 5: 104,10.

[19] Barth recognizes this circumstance: Barth, Fides quaerens intellectum 12.

[20] de Lubac, "Seigneur, je cherche ton visage" 213ff; Söhngen, Die Einheit der Theologie 33ff.

[21] P Prooem: 93,5-10.

The aim is a confirmation of the beginning which is faith. This beginning is intended to prevail in the cognitional progression. The point is to have from thinking a confirmation for what God in revelation revealed himself to be. The "unum argumentum's" intention is to achieve a unity which allows thinking to find the one God and allows the subject of this thinking to participate therein.[22] This subject is able to agree both with thinking and with faith. This ground which can no longer be questioned or doubted explains and grounds faith. Such faith knows God to exist and to be the "summum bonum." This cause rests in itself and needs no other cause. Moreover, faith is aware that all other beings are in need of this divine unity and goodness in order to be one and good.

With its own means thinking must muster the energy to recognize God as the God faith believes in. The "unum argumentum" must be equally absolute and one, as God is absolute and one. From within itself thinking is to be lifted up to God and mirror in itself the properties which faith ascribes to God. Not unbridled arrogance but grace permits this to occur. No doubt Anselm is convinced that God's correspondence in our thinking occurs. It is in this way that the divine being prevails in thinking, while thinking from within itself recognizes that God truly exists. When this unity of thinking occurs, then it corresponds to God's unity. Thereby divine goodness shines through. Therefore, Anselm prays that God may correspond to his thoughts, that God may show himself in the "unum argumentum" and thereby may demonstrate that the human mind is merely an image of divine unity. The whole line of argumentation demonstrates that thinking rests solely and exclusively on divine thinking. This entails complete surrender to God and allows God to determine what thinking thinks. At the same time thinking is called to accept in freedom how God appears. God's divine coherence renders God as a unity present and permits the human mind to define itself as a unity (i.e. unity in the sense of inseparable unit). This is the import of the concept "similitudo." God becomes apparent as the absolute beginning, but this fact becomes known only as the human mind permits God to start with humanity this epistemological process. The human mind must start to think from God: "coepi." This "coepi" calls for the subject's (= thinker's) correspondence to the gift of insight: "coepi mecum quaerere." In freedom the human subject is called to accept the gift already intended for him or her from eternity. This requires a self-search and the recognition of always being fundamentally ordered towards the ever greater gift: the self-revelation of God as the highest term.

This existential, ethical and cognitional effort yields three kinds of unities: that of God, the unity of the human being, and the unity of thinking.

---

[22] Plotinus could not have formulated this agenda in a more concise and succinct form.

9.2 Faith and Reason in the *Proslogion*

"Fides quaerens intellectum" has been shown as the formula, indicating how faith and reason reciprocally challenge one another. Faith realizes with greater intensity and clarity what it believes. Thinking experiences itself as in itself inconclusive. This thinking is a thinking transcending towards God. Since its own ground and the way it actuates itself are presumed and moreover its own being is an indebted one, thinking is negative. In this sense thinking is aware that it is at the center of something else; that it originates in and goes forward to something else.[23] Such thinking is not accidental nor peripheral to faith but central. This centrality permits thinking to be the bridge and mediating agency within faith. It would be a gross misunderstanding to presume such thinking to fulfill merely a servile function. Precisely in its own originality and freedom it is irreplaceable for faith. Only through thinking does faith obtain self-awareness. As de Lubac observes, faith and thinking are on a common trail which is being expressed by the formula: "fides quaerens intellectum."[24] Better expressed, there is an interplay between "fides quaerens intellectum" and "intellectus quaerens fidem."

The first chapter of *Proslogion* shows the believer in front of God. It is a mixture of contemplative prayer and literary prose. It articulates what the human being experiences when placed in the presence of God. The believer experiences God as the one who begins and is at the beginning. Divine distance and proximity are felt. In this situation the believer becomes conscious of his or her powerlessness. Finally there is a yearning for light to be shed on this experience of the "Numinosum, Fascinosum et Tremendum."[25] All that hinders attunement to God should be excluded: "excludere omnia praeter deum." Only after this purgation can God appear as undiluted unity. As a second consequence "mens" and "cor" form one will.[26] Only if the human being has discovered this highest degree of unity is he or she able to apprehend intimations of divine unity. In this situation, freedom can relate to freedom. Thus oriented, "vaca aliquantulum deo,"[27] the human being from the midst of his own being and essence is able to formulate the question impinging upon the whole of reality: "dic nunc, totum `cor´ meum, dic nunc deo: quaero vultum tuum."[28]

The seeking believer supplies the answer "cur non video praesentem."[29] This diastasis is constitutive for a philosophical disposition. It leads to a search

---

[23] Söhngen, Die Einheit der Theologie 33ff.
[24] de Lubac, Seigneur, je cherche ton visage 213ff.
[25] Cf. the epochal book by Rudolf Otto, Das Heilige (München: C.H. Beck, 1997).
[26] P 1: 97,7.9; Kohlenberger, Similitudo und Ratio 113ff. 151f.
[27] P 1: 97,6.
[28] P 1: 97,9f.
[29] P 1: 98,3.

for the cause of a divine presence and absence: "lux inaccessibilis."[30] God is absolutely inaccessible "ubi et quomodo te quaerat." The believer searches for a way out of this diastasis. The "quaerere" flows over into the plea that God may be the absolute beginning and may thus overcome faith's pain. This diastasis permits existential failures to become obvious and a salvation-historical guilt breaks through as the believer realizes that the whole of humanity had alienated itself from the beginning. Because God had communicated himself "propter quod factus sum," the believer bears an indelible mark. This mark generates a longing in the believer which Anselm expresses in the terms "anhelare," "desiderare," "cuperare" and "affectare."[31] This pain is the result of being aware of one's inability to set a beginning and not to be part of a beginning. The believer did not correspond to this divinely intended beginning. The acutely sensed diastasis is also a common feeling among all human beings. From humanity's perspective it appears irreversible. The possibility of an original or primordial beginning with God is from humanity's perspective utterly impossible: " O misers sors hominis, cum hoc perdidit ad quod factus est."[32] Divine providence had planned "beatitudo," "felix" and "lux."[33] But life has turned into "miseria," "tenebrae," "exilium" and "caetitas."[34] Everything is lost and human resources are much too limited to venture a restoration of the original state. Indeed every such effort would turn into hybris. From this state of impossibility and inability Anselm asks: " Quando restitues te nobis?"[35]

The new beginning must necessarily originate from God and this "restituere" must be a repetition of the beginning of what God had intended with humanity. Therefore, Anselm implores God for this beginning and thereby to set everything new. No grand social agenda is anticipated by the monk but rather a personal encounter. "Doce me quaerere te, et ostende te quaerenti; quia nec quaerere te possum nisi tu doceas, nec invenire nisi te ostendas."[36] Divine initiative is not sufficient to overcome the deleterious effects of original sin. God must sustain, assist and illuminate my faith. From this divine action hope arises. The "cor" is arrested anew in God. Consequently, trust, hope and charity arise again: "Quaeram te desiderando, desiderem quaerendo. Inveniam amando, amem inveniendo."[37] It is from this situation as a believer that Anselm at the beginning of his treatise now asks God for "intelligere":

Non tento, domine, penetrare altitudinem tuam, quia nullatenus comparo illi intellectum meum; sed desidero aliquatenus intelligere veritatem tuam, quam credit et amat

---

30 P 1: 98,4.

31 P 1: 98, 9-12.

32 P 1: 98,16.

33 P 1: 98,18f and 99,6.

34 P 1: 98,19 and 99,2.4f.

35 P 1: 99,18.

36 P 1: 100,8-10.

37 P 1: 100,10f.

cor meum. Neque enim quaero intelligere ut credam, sed credo ut intelligam. Nam et hoc credo: quia "nisi credidero, non intelligam."[38]

The priorities are noteworthy. Faith is the basis for "intelligere" but God is the basis for faith. It is only faith that fully arrests and grounds itself in God. And it is only through God that all becomes luminous. The whole of human existence is called to faith. This is expressed with the term "cor." This sum total of human existence also contains the human mind: "mens." For God created humanity in his likeness so that it may remember, think and love him. In the "intelligere" the human being articulates what intuitively is known in the personal encounter with God. Faith receives in the "intelligere" an ascertainment. The "Prooemium" expresses faith´s dramatic ascent wherein the "intellectus" becomes the mediating agency between God and humanity.[39]

9.2.1 Faith´s access to Thinking

The first line of chapter two describes the situation in which the monk struggles with the "intellectus fidei":

Ergo, domine, qui das fidei intellectum, da mihi, ut quantum scis expedire intelligam, quia es sicut credimus, et hoc es quod credimus. Et quidem credimus te esse aliquid quo nihil maius cogitari possit.[40]

Even the "intelligere" must be a divine gift. Faith expects everything from God. For this reason we have the affirmative statement that God also gives faith. Provided that God does not withhold something of faith, God must also hand over the "intellectus"; for "intellectus" is to Anselm´s mind the inner insight and understanding of faith. Faith strives for an intellectual ascertainment so that it may mature and thereby behold the divine countenance. The unsurpassable freedom that is God´s has divine revelation yield only to human prayer. Any human contrivance to effect divine self-revelation must suffer shipwreck. Otherwise, God would not be almighty. Understanding and insight succeed only where simply one´s own understanding and insight do not prevail but where understanding and insight come from beyond the self. In this way faith beckons the human self to actuate one´s own origin and freedom. In this drama the interwovenness of divine and human beginnings becomes evident. All is entrusted to God. This seeming harmony which arises from the plea that God might come to one´s assistance, empowers the believer to his or her own autonomy and freedom which in turn is able to respond to this gift from within its own freedom and beginning.

---

[38] P 1: 100,15-19.
[39] de Lubac, "Seigneur, je cherche ton visage" 201ff.
[40] P 1: 101,3-5.

The "intelligere" demonstrates that God wants to be understood by the believer. In this sense the "unum argumentum" demonstrates what faith does not have from its own self but rather what is given to it by God as unmerited gift. This is the unreasonable demand the argument expresses. Thinking must arrive at and unfold what it thinks. God and nothing less but God should occur as form and epiphany. To think matters divine is thinking's greatest autonomy. It is called to think the highest and most audacious. From its inception such an endeavor must have been condemned to failure were God and thinking two incompatible entities. But God is present everywhere. God would be utterly unthinkable were God not to reveal himself to thinking.

It is Anselm's wish that faith may become translucent to reason. Uplifted by faith, "intelligere" then is able to understand its own paradoxical situation as oscillating between autonomy and heteronomy. The origin of the highest term from faith is not denied. The term gives thinking its own independence. Only if this autonomy as thinking's outstanding feature is established can the "unum argumentum" be a vehicle of origin and goal; can God appear to free and autonomous thinking. It is faith that liberates thinking to such freedom. Faith wants thinking to be free so that faith can come to its own. It is within this liberating event of thinking's becoming autonomous that Anselm had the intuition of the highest term: "Quo maius cogitari nequit." It is in the discovery of this term that the "unum argumentum" finds its most succinct and concrete expression. Anselm struggles to prove this term as thinking's genuine property. For this reason thinking must concentrate on what its true mission is and eliminate all alien elements. It must acquire what it hears by understanding the heard: "intelligit quod audit."[41] Simultaneously thinking understands both its possibilities and its very essence by apprehending the highest term as its very own.

The question of whether this term can be recognized by thinking's own faculty can only be answered by thinking. By acquiring the term thinking actuates its own autonomy. The affirmation and acceptance of the highest term occurs in chapters two and three through the "cogitare." Thinking is able to think the greatest and at the same time to recognize the impossibility of grasping it. In the process it comes to realize that it is the ultimate arbiter by using its freedom and originality in autonomy. Thinking is in this meaning positive, for it recognizes and makes use of its rationality. On the other hand it must admit that it is bound to presuppose a transcendence. This denotes thinking's negativity. The cognitional process never comes to a final close. Inasmuch as thinking is unable to reach existence and reality, it depends on outside, empirical experience. Though ordered towards the "maius" it is never able to overtake that term. Thinking remains bound to comparisons.[42]

---

[41] P 2: 101,8.
[42] Cf. P 2: 101,17f; 3: 102, 6f. see Barth, Fides quaerens intellectum 77f; Vuillemin, Le Dieu d'Anselme 134.

234

Thinking always shifts between its own ability and inability. From this facticity a dialectical movement appears which tries to reconcile knowledge and mystery, essence and existence, "quia es" and "quod es." Thinking is genuinely interested in every surplus which experience may produce. An appropriation of this surplus occurs insofar as it does not contradict thinking´s rationality.[43] Thinking finds the term no longer subject to its interpretation. But using its own autonomy and rationality, thinking was able to discover this very term: "et hoc es tu, domine deus noster." God has asserted himself as God. That means God has shown himself as the beginning and the sustaining cause in such a way that thinking is able to apprehend God as having begun and as sustaining thinking.

Anselm knows that faith´s certitude as well as the certitude regarding what thinking has discovered are equally strong and can never contradict one another. But the remaining difference between thinking and faith is a virulent problem. Why is the "insipiens" not compelled to believe the same things as Anselm does, since this belief arises from the "unum argumentum"? Anselm solves this dilemma by referring to thinking´s dialectics between autonomy and heteronomy. While thinking is in control of its own autonomy it is not master over its heteronomous origin. Cognizant of humanity´s fall, Anselm observes: Were thinking able to judge concerning its own origin it would claim to be above God - "ascenderet creatura supra creatorem, et iudicaret de creatore."[44] Also, when thinking the highest possible term, thinking remains autonomous. This helps Anselm explain how a non-believer in spite of following the argument can still remain non-Christian. For a transcendent thinking remains unfathomable. "Aliter enim cogitatur res, cum vox eam significans cogitatur, aliter cum id ipsum quod res est intelligitur."[45] Thinking is able to remain within the course of cognitional execution without penetrating the object. But a "bene intelligere" is accompanied by the "res" and is certain of what it apprehends. Thus, an unbridgeable difference between mere thinking and thinking from faith remains. "Nullus quippe intelligens id quod deus est, potest cogitare quia deus non est."[46] God has become luminous to thinking, nevertheless; thinking possesses its own sovereignty and independence. Thinking remains called to identify itself with its final insight. Consonant with these considerations, Anselm thanks God for what his own thinking was able to discover through the grace of God:

---

[43] Viola speaks in this context of the term´s "principe dynamique" and of "dialectique." Coloman Viola, "La dialectique de la grandeur. Une interpretation du Proslogion." Recherches de la Théologie ancienne et médiévale 37 (1970): 23-42, at 38f. see also de Lubac, "Seigneur, je cherche ton visage" 203; Evdokimov, "L´aspect apophatique" 248ff.

[44] P 3: 103,5f. Cf. de Lubac, "Seigneur, je cherche ton visage" 205ff.

[45] Vuillemin, Le Dieu d´Anselme 18. PI: 124,21f.

[46] P 4: 103,20 f.

Gratias tibi, bone domine, gratias tibi, quia quod prius credidi te donante, iam sic intelligo te illuminante, ut si te esse nolim credere, non possim non intelligere.[47]

9.2.2 "Via incomparabilis"

Is there anything beyond what is already considered thinkable concerning God? "Quid igitur es, domine, quo nil maius valet cogitari?"[48] Thus Anselm asks God. This reminds one of the introductory question: Why do I not behold thee?[49] Thinking the term God did not yet grant a comprehensive appreciation of God. Therefore, the question, "quid es?" The "quidditas Dei" is the next logical step in this investigation. With cognition´s insight, faith has not yet come to rest. The source for this inquietude is faith, for it is faith that experiences acutely the difference between the God of cogitation and the personal God of faith. The cognitively discovered God lacks some features faith knows with certitude to be proper to the highest being. "Quod ergo bonum de est summo bono, per quod est omne bonum."[50] Thinking has not discovered the "bonum" characteristic of the Divine. However, this is the foundational "credo" experience. God is overflowing "bonitas." With this question then, Anselm reveals a greater knowledge of God than his logical deliberations have yet yielded. God is not simply a metaphysically and therefore a necessarily to be believed in abstract entity, but - as faith conveys - one of goodness and infinite benevolence. The divine properties are "iustus," "verax," "beatus," "sensibilis," "omnipotens," "misericors," and "impassibilis."[51] Here, Anselm articulates his experience of God as (both present and past) have made of God as persons of faith. The divine predications resulting from this horizon are a surplus which thinking cannot surpass.

Balthasar sees in Anselm´s approach a comparative thinking at work. While thinking is unable to define the "maius," these very same properties impinge upon thinking. Thinking awaits the encounter with the greater and is, therefore, already disposed for such a comparative inclination. It is Anselm´s clear conviction that such a comparative attitude is not in conflict with thinking´s rationality. Rather rationality is founded upon thinking´s orientation to the yet other and greater.[52]

The quality of "bonum" provokes thinking to reflect upon God through comparative terms. "Tu es itaque iustus, verax, beatus, et quidquid melius est esse quam non esse. Melius namque est esse iustum quam non iustum, beatum quam non beatum."[53] Faith widens thinking not only to consider the "maius" but

---

[47] P 4: 104,5-7.

[48] P 5: 104,11.

[49] de Lubac, "Seigneur, je cherche ton visage" 209.

[50] P 5: 104,14f.

[51] P 5: 104,15; P 6: 104,20f.

[52] Balthasar, Anselm 224.231.236; Kienzler, Glauben und Denken 324ff; Vuillemin, Le Dieu d´Anselme 14-19.

[53] P 5: 104,15-17.

also the "melius." Thinking is unable to yield from within itself this new notion. Yet, the notion is not uncongenial to thinking. It is a further adumbration of the already known term "maius." Chapters 5-15 manifest this dialectics. Challenged to appropriate the "melius," thinking displays the comparative dialectics' rationality. Having recognized this, faith and reason join in addressing God. "Ergo, domine, quamvis non sis corpus, vere tamen eo modo summe sensibilis es ..."[54] Jointly faith and thinking are God's interlocutors, the possibility of experiencing and sensing God. This God is not abstract but concrete and can be addressed. God participates in the hope and suffering of his vis-à-vis. Without divine sensibility faith would be unthinkable. If God responds to this longing ("anhelare") of faith, then why does God not show his face: "Cur non video praesentem (vultum tuum)"?

Chapter seven discusses divine omnipotence. This attribute is equally pivotal for faith. As faith admits its own powerlessness, God must begin the adventure that is faith. Only then can faith fully entrust itself to God. Such faith trusts God, as the "summum bonum" beyond any caprice and arbitrariness. God will not abuse the believer's freedom. While thinking by itself is unable to reflect upon divine sensibility, it does understand that it is better (= "melius") to think God as reliable rather than as arbitrary. Moreover, such thinking is able to recognize that divine sensibility and divine omnipotence are not oxymorons. The dialectics of faith and thinking reach their climax when thinking divine mercy in diverse treatises. Anselm reflects upon this issue in chapters eight through eleven. Conspicuously much space is dedicated to this topic. There seems to be an irreconcilable contradiction between the terms "misericordia" and "impassibilitas dei."[55] Moreover, how is mercy to be reconciled with divine justice? How can God comply with justice and nevertheless forgive sinners out of mercy? Faith is unable to resolve these contradictions. Faith does, however, know of an overflowing "bonitas dei."[56] Anselm asks God in the hymn on the "bonitas dei" to impart this quality also upon the faithful: "influat in me."[57] Faith experiences overflowing divine goodness and is nevertheless not in a position to approach the source: "Cernitur unde flumen manat, et non perspicitur fons unde nascatur."[58] The "bonitas dei" reconciles all contradictions which the hymn articulates.

The "bonitas dei" is fathomless and so even thinking must "believe" in it. Thinking must muster all its energies to surrender itself to God. Comparative thinking finds its most sublime expression in this context.

---

[54] P 6: 105,4f.
[55] P 8: 106,3-14.
[56] P 9: 107,4.
[57] P 9: 108,1.
[58] P 9: 107,15f.

> An quia iustum est te sic esse bonum, ut nequeas intelligi melior, et sic potenter operari, ut non possis cogitari potentius? Quid enim hoc iustius? ... Justum quippe est te sic esse iustum, ut iustior nequeas cogitari.[59]

Thereby thinking expresses its openness for the yet greater God. Here thinking becomes a call for divine assistance: "adiuva me, ut intelligam, quod dico."[60] In the divine mercy thinking encounters the enduringly greater God. Even "bonitas" as a divine predication remains concealed in divine mystery:

> An quia bonitas tua est incomprehensibilis, latet hoc in luce inaccessibili quam inhabitas? Vere in altissimo et secretissimo bonitatis tuae latet fons, unde manat fluvius misericordiae tuae. [61]

9.3 Thinking and Beckoning

These actions are two moments of one event. Almost at the end of his treatise Anselm asks again what it was that he had sought: "An invenisti, anima mea, quod quaerebas?"[62] Anselm had sought God in his "Quidditas." His soul is in despair. True, the question at the beginning of his deliberations has been answered. Yet God seems to have withdrawn himself into inaccessible light. Yet thinking does not take exception to this situation. The "anima mea" feels itself forlorn. The diastasis has not narrowed within the course of reflection. Now fully aware of God's infinite transcendence and omnipotence, the diastasis between God and humanity has widened. For all that faith had discovered thinking postulated a "maius" or "melius." All the properties found, such as life, wisdom, light, goodness, eternal beatitude and beatific eternity, do not reveal God as person. "Nam si non invenisti deum tuum: quomodo est ille hoc quod invenisti, et quod illum tam certa veritate et vera certitudine intellixisti?"[63]

Why do feelings of forlornness and forsakenness become at the end of the *Proslogion* all the more pronounced? Faith seeks a personal God but nowhere has thinking been able to convey certitude as regards the personal appearance of God: Faith had seen something of God and recognized it but faith had not seen "Him." Yet only such a personal God as faith searches for can pacify faith.

> Si vero invenisti: quid est, quod non sentis quod invenisti? Cur non te sentit, domine deus, anima mea, si invenit te?
> An non invenit, quem invenit esse lucem et veritatem? Quomodo namque intellexit hoc, nisi videndo lucem et veritatem? Aut potuit omnino aliquid intelligere de te, nisi per "lucem et veritatem tuam?" Si ergo vidit lucem et veritatem, vidit te. Si non vidit te,

---

[59] P 9: 108,11-13; 11: 109,11.
[60] P 9: 108,8f.
[61] P 9: 107,4-6.
[62] P 14: 111,8.
[63] P 14: 111,11-13.

non vidit lucem nec veritatem. An et veritas et lux est quod vidit, et tamen nondum te vidit, quia vidit te aliquatenus, sed non vidit te sicuti es?[64]

If the reflections in the *Proslogion* do not yield a personal God, then the whole enterprise is nothing less than a cruel exercise. At the end of these reflections God should reveal himself forcefully as the center of Anselm's existence: "Formator et reformator meus."[65] Only the personal God can fulfill the longings faith has. Little wonder then that in a very concise form chapter fifteen recapitulates chapters two and three. It wishes to restate that God is not only "the greater than" but "the absolutely greater." Here thinking is able to apprehend that the dynamics of cogitation no longer propel thinking to predicate God thus. Rather, a divine property is being revealed. God is in and of himself "maius." This is the essence of God: "es quiddam maius." Thinking's vis-à-vis (thinking's addressee) acquires personal features. To thinking's perception God is not merely "maius" but "qua Deus" the "maius" for both God and faith. Every new insight reflection gained caused a sense of greater alienation because cognition's agent became aware of the distance between the thinker and the thought. The realization in chapter 15 that thinking discovers a true divine feature which exists in God "independently" from divine manifestations and rational concoctions is a source of joy. This insight into groundless freedom is given freely.[66]

At this point the question may be raised whether thinking serves any additional purpose. Is thinking, once a personal God has become thinkable, redundant? Does the cognitional epiphany of the personal God render thinking obsolete? Or does this personal evincement occasion a new quality for cognition? True, even on this new level, thinking remains aware of its contingent nature and confesses: "Vere, domine, haec est lux inaccessibilis, in qua habitas."[67] From its own faculties thinking no longer strives to overcome the difference between God and itself, for precisely in divine inaccessibility and distance, light is shed on His proximity. The experiences of distance and proximity reciprocally heighten one another. "Only since thou art so near do I sense all the more intensely the distance separating us. In the distance I experience thy propinquity." No longer does Anselm contemplate the possibility of being disowned by God. For he is in Anselm's thinking. "Ubique es tota

---

[64] P 14: 111,13-21. de Lubac considers chapters 14 and 15 of the *Proslogion* the key to understanding these deliberations. Cf. de Lubac, "Seigneur, je cherche ton visage" 420ff; Ulrich, "Cur non video" 88ff; Viola, "La Dialectique de grandeur" 46ff.

[65] P 14: 112,2.

[66] Richthammer, Die Systematik des Proslogionbeweises 116f; Ulrich, "Cur non video" 81ff. 101ff.

[67] P 16: 112,20. Borrowing from Heidegger, Ulrich uses the term "Kehre" (= sharp turn in a road, hairpin bend) to express the radical nature of thinking's new quality. Ulrich, "Cur non video" 117ff.

praesens, et non te video."[68]   No matter how far away Anselm may seek God´s countenance, his face is ever present to him: "Quam remota es a conspectu meo, qui sic praesens sum conspectui tuo."[69]   The causing and founding God sustains everything and everyone. This is thinking´s new certitude.

Such new thinking does not insist on geometric proofs nor on academic evidence. It longs to sense intimations of what God is, insofar as God grants the intuition: "intueri." The experience is one of marvel, stupefaction and awe to such a degree that distinct experiences are no longer had. One is overwhelmed by the divine plenitude. A comprehensive view with a holistic intuition of what God is occurs. Singularities are metamorphised into a whole: "Multa sunt haec, non potest angustus intellectus meus tot uno simul intuitu videre, ut omnibus simul delectetur."[70] One enjoys and delights in the fullness that is God´s. This has as its consequence a restitution of thinking to its true constitution and purpose. God is not only the one but also the "totum."[71] Although thinking is not able to recognize God in his unity, it is nevertheless able to see and admit this state of affairs. This new kind of thinking is not only a "similitudo" but aware that it is so and grateful for it. In realizing it, thinking acknowledges its being ordered towards God and that this situation in turn is divinely intended.

God contains all positive predications and is nevertheless one and unique: uncaused cause for all. Thus this new thinking is aware of its indebtedness. God reveals his "bonitas." This "bonitas" is of such a rich effulgence that it is multi-original and, therefore, trinitarian. This insight Anselm develops in greater depth in chapter three. The "bonitas dei" is an expression of and an intelligible explanation for the trinity. Yet, it would be an oversimplification to presume that this insight into the trinitarian structure of the Godhead would burst this new thinking. Rather, God brings this new thinking to a coherence, unity and necessity. With necessity God must be trinitarian. This is the new thinking´s insight. God prevails in thinking.

A Christian vision opens up. This "unum necessarium" not only reveals himself to Anselm ("anima mea") as the ultimate trinitarian coherence but as "vita," "salus," "sapientia" and "delectatio." New thinking can only conjecture ("coniectatio"[72]) these predications of divine goodness. New thinking relates to the human being something one cannot know with certitude has through clear intimations. Christian existence is a joyous anticipation of the promised. Also the heart as the human being´s center longs for its true home country and can prepare itself for this future. This heart loves the one good and is content with

---

[68] P 16: 113,2f.

[69] P 16: 113,18.

[70] P 18: 114,16f.

[71] Balthasar recognizes this all-encompassing vision of the new reason. Cf. Balthasar, Anselm 231ff.

[72] P 24: 117, 24 and 118,3-9.

240

it. This good is further predicated as simple: "ama unum bonum - et sufficit. Desidera simplex bonum - et satis est."[73] The qualities such as "iustitia," "similitudo" and "beatitudo" are reality and God's honor is fully restored, because only God's will counts. And the human being employs all its freedom to fullfill God's will. Every creature fulfills its destiny because it is divinely willed.

> Si concordia: omnibus illis erit una voluntas, quia nulla illis erit nisi sola dei voluntas. Si potestas: omnipotentes erunt suae voluntatis ut deus suae. Nam sicut poterit deus quod volet per seipsum, ita poterunt illi quod volent per illum; quia sicut illi non aliud volent quam quod ille, ita ille volet quidquid illi volent; et quod ille volet non poterit non esse.[74]

Now all human beings are to join in the newly established "rectitudo."

9.4 Theology as a Moment of Salvation History

Anselm's understanding of salvation history is expressed on a broad canvas in the *Cur Deus Homo*. Salvation is, however, not a marginal topic. Therefore, it also resonates powerfully from the *Monologion* and the *Proslogion*. In salvation history faith comes to its own. Salvation history is impossible without faith, and vice-versa, faith becomes aware of the contents of its own hope through the saving deeds of Jesus Christ. Actually salvation history starts with creation. The *Proslogion* illustrates that thinking is able to express something of faith by recurring to the experiences of salvation history. Salvation history is seen as the effort to overcome the original alienation between God and humanity.

Thinking engages historic faith and its credal contents. It asks about the positive data: "fides quaerens intellectum." Thinking's task is to mediate between faith's external form and its interior self-execution. This occurs by reflecting upon Jesus Christ's salvific deeds. Therefore, thinking is called upon as an historic effort to verify its faith through historical events. In the process the rationality of Jesus Christ's life becomes evident. Terms such as "rectitudo," "honor dei," "peccatum," "satisfactio" and "iustitia" serve to illustrate faith's and redemption's intelligibility and that Jesus Christ is indeed the incarnate Logos. This documents that the *Cur Deus Homo's* perspicacity is far greater than it appears to be at first sight.

9.5 Thinking as Participation in Salvation

The strategy Anselm pursues is documented in the preface to the *Cur Deus Homo*: in a mental itinerary from faith into the inner recesses of the mind and back from there to faith.[75] Both approaches serve to purify the "fides

---

[73] P 25: 118,16f.
[74] P 25: 119,7-12.
[75] Cf. Cu Praef 42,8ff. See also Gäde, <u>Eine andere Barmherzigkeit</u> 267ff.

Christiana" and to allow reason to become self-conscious. The underlying strategy of obtaining the two goals is the hypothetical assumption behind the "remoto Christo." In the first book reason achieves this goal of unfolding itself as reason by employing the "rationes necessariae." It strives to render faith intelligible to the "infidelis." The task common to both faith and reason becomes obvious: to render faith construable equally to the "infidelis" and to the "fidelis." For this reason such faith feels compelled to abandon itself completely to reason. In the process, faith loses its object and becomes totally unrecognizable: truly "remoto Christo." As Boso defines the "prius" of faith:

> Sicut rectus ordo exigit ut profunda Christianae fidei prius credamus, quam ea praesumamus ratione discutere, ita negligentia mihi videtur, si, postquam confirmati sumus in fide, non studemus quod credimus intelligere.[76]

Faith is able to apprehend itself only from outside. Faith does not discuss faith, but reason questions and develops faith. Reason reflects on humanity's fall ("peccatum") and on its redemption ("reddere"). The aim is "mundo vitam reddiderit" because Jesus Christ "homo factus est" through "morte sua."[77] In the process one beholds the properties of reason at first. Thereby reason is not able to overtake faith. It is utterly unable to think by itself the historical fact of incarnation and redemption. Nevertheless, it readily comes to realize the cognitive necessity of redemption.[78] But reason does not suffer superfluity. Rather, it serves to manifest the role of faith within the matrix of the mind's self-execution. Cognition's inability highlights faith's necessity as a certitude rationally verified. Thereby, faith discerns its own self-understanding. In this context cognition what precedes faith's self-apprehension.

In the second book the "fides" is no longer chosen as the point of departure, but the "natura rationalis" with its very own self-understanding: "Quasi nihil sciatur de Christo." As Boso expresses the agenda, "qua necessitate scilicet et ratione deus (naturam humanam) ... assumpserit."[79] Thinking senses a compulsion to translate redemption, sin and incarnation into a rational matrix. These historical facts find their philosophical equivalence in the terms "rectitudo," "debere," "ordo rectus" and "iustitia." Such a transformation illustrates that thinking comes to its own in confrontation with salvation history: thinking rises to the level of self-awareness. This reason knows itself destined to bliss and immortality. In felicitous contrast to Platonism the whole human being, "totus homo," is destined to beatitude in Anselm's view: "beata in corpore et anima." Here something of Aristotle's "η ευδαιμονια" resonates at a distance. Thinking evidences itself as containing a design going well beyond

---

[76] Cu I 1: 48, 16-18.
[77] Cu I 1: 48, 2-5.
[78] Cf. Gäde, Eine andere Barmherzigkeit 214-220; Kohlenberger, Similitudo und Ratio 55.
[79] Cu I 1: 48, 22f.

242

its own capacities. In this position, thinking experiences itself as foundationally given up to a referentiality to and with faith: "aperta ratione et veritate."

Reason apprehends itself as posited in a strange dialectics. On the one hand it is open with necessity towards the future. On the other hand it is neither able to construct, nor to define positively this future. Only faith is able to present the contents of this future: "atque ex necessitate omnia quae de Christo credimus fieri oportere."[80] In the confrontation with revelation reason perceives its insights, not as "thoughtless," at random mental ramblings, but as justified and necessary for both thinking and faith. In confrontation with the other, faith and reason experience self-definition.

The complex relationship of the two can thus be summarized: "fides quaerens intellectum" and at the same time and under the same consideration: "intellectus quaerens fidem." The rational structure of humanity is constitutive for both humanity and for faith. Credal contents are equally constitutive for humanity and for reason. Both reason's and faith's self-understandings are greater than what each by itself and isolated could make out. In this perspective a "preceding of understanding" is transformed into a "self-understanding" or "self-awareness" when confronted with the other. Both reason and faith contain a surplus which render apparent both the self's "impossibility" and "necessity." Thinking is ordered towards redemption and faith again is ordered towards self-ascertainment. In the process of this circular, mutually affirming and verifying movement salvation history not only becomes apparent. More precisely and more acutely, cognition becomes a part of the salvation narrative in a most real way. This insight can be gleaned from both *Cur Deus Homo* and from the *Proslogion*.[81] The thrust of both writings cannot be reduced to an exclusively philosophical or theological concern. The writings are built equally on two solid columns: thinking and faith.

Upon first consideration, the reasonableness claimed by faith seems to contradict reason. Thinking assumes it possesses principles which clearly define God. On such grounds an incarnation and redemption seem irrational. The infidel formulates his counterposition against such a background. As, however, the believer and the non-believer have a common concern, namely to discover the "ratio fidei," they decide to engage in discourse on the same level, namely that of the "ratio." As a result the argument rotates around the question of whether or not there is a harmony or disharmony between faith and reason. The non-believer seems intent on discovering even the smallest incongruency: "multa alia ... non videtur deo convenire."[82] The believer wishes to demonstrate the greatest possible degree of congruency between faith and reason: "convenienter." [83]

---

[80] Cu P: 43,2.

[81] P 3: 102, 5ff.

[82] Cu I 3: 50, 27.

[83] Cu I 3: 51,3; cf. Balthasar, The Glory of the Lord, Vol. II 231.

Boso raises three objections:

1. He does not regard the becoming human of God and thereby God is taking on of the depravity of human nature as fitting for divine essence. This seems to contradict his understanding of divinity. Anselm reacts by illustrating the yet greater harmony between the rational notion of God and the event of redemption. "Si enim diligenter considerarent quam convenienter hoc modo procurata sit humana restauratio ..."[84] The historical event results from a salvific imperative: "oportebat."[85] This inner congruency and necessity must in Anselm's judgment appear for the outside person as reasonable and therefore as a "pulchritudo." This is not enough for Boso. He cannot see a connection between a reasonable argument and the category of beauty. Instead of "beautiful arguments" he demands "soliditas rationabilis" and "necessaria ratio." [86]

2. In Boso's second argument the manner in which redemption occurred seems to contradict divine properties: "ratio repugnare videtur."[87] Why has God not chosen a less humiliating way to redeem humanity, as he is free and omnipotent? Applying the principle of non-contradiction Anselm riposits with an inherently theological argument. Divine will never contradicts reason. "Sufficere nobis debet ad rationem voluntas dei cum aliquid facit, licet non videamus cur velit."[88] Boso is not content with this information. The divine will must prove itself as not only not in contradiction with reason, but as positively reasonable.

3. The third objection treats the divine will and freedom. How can the Son of God be forced to redeem humanity if he is divine and free? How can God demand from God the same obedience that is demanded from created human beings? "deus ab omni rationali creatura exigit."[89] Anselm responds that such obedience cannot contradict reason. Anselm holds it most fitting for the Son to do whatever possible to glorify the Father and serve and redeem humanity. "Immo maxime decet talem patrem tali filio consentire, si quid vult laudabiliter ad honorem dei et utiliter ad salutem hominum, quae aliter fieri non potuit."[90]

For the time being Boso is not content with Anselm's responses. The arguments Anselm had presented remove contradictions to thinking and provide considerations for greater congruencies between faith and reason. Whatever had been presented thus far serves merely to illustrate the plausibility of credal

---

[84] Cu I 3: 51,3f.
[85] Cu I 3: 51,5.
[86] Cu I 4: 52,3.7.
[87] Cu I 8: 59,13.
[88] Cu I 8: 59,10f.
[89] Cu I 9: 61,15.
[90] Cu I 10: 66,16-18.

tenents but not to demonstrate these with necessity: "rationabilis et necessaria."[91]

For this reason Boso again points out the central question: "cur deus aliter hominem salvare non potuit; aut si potuit, cur hoc modo voluit?"[92] Reasons of mere "convenience" do not suffice. For the further proceedings Anselm and Boso agree that what is "convenient" for God is what is necessary and what is "inconvenient" for God is what is impossible.[93] Whatever is impossible for God must necessarily be impossible for reason and whatever is "convenient" for God must be appreciated as necessary by reason.[94] So the two parties to the disputation agree to eliminate whatever "inconveniencies" or impossibilities occur to the mind and to search for the necessities of reasoning. Anselm formulates the statement to which Boso gives his agreement. It is their intention to transfer terms such as "beatitudo," "peccatum," "dimittere peccata" and "salus" into philosophy.[95] The implication for Anselm is twofold. On the one hand his task is to translate theological terms such as the above into cognitional ones. On the other hand he must be able to demonstrate the criteria for the "convenience" and necessity of these new terms within the criteria cognition has at its disposal. Hence Anselm transposes: "quid sit peccare et pro peccato satisfacere."[96] Justice is the counter-term to sin. Sin is to fail in what is due, the "debitum," to God. Every rational creature owes God this obedience. If the human being fulfills what is required, then he or she is just before God. If on the other hand, however, he or she does not fulfill the "debere," then they must perform satisfaction in order to return to God the "debitum."[97]

This translation of fundamental terms into thinking discloses that justice is the criterion for the "inconveniencies" and necessities, for justice is not a criterion outside reasoning but thinking's true measure. Boso cannot object to these new terms. The question occurs whether it is fitting for God to forgive sins out of "misericordia" alone.[98] Boso on his part finds no reason why that term should not be fitting to God: "Non video cur non deceat."[99] This does not hinder Anselm from discovering in the remission of sins out of pure mercy an "inconvenientia," as this would mean that God permits injustice. Such an injustice renders "sola misericordia" unviable for God and, therefore, an "inconvenientia." Every reasonable creature, and this includes God, respects just order. Therefore, one must exclude the "misericordia dei" as the sole cause

[91] Cu I 10: 66,16-21.
[92] Cu I 10: 66,21f.
[93] Cu I 10: 67,1f.
[94] Gäde, Eine andere Barmherzigkeit 234ff; Henry, The Logic of Saint Anselm 132ff. 183ff.
[95] Cu I 10: 67,12ff.
[96] Cu I 11: 68,2.
[97] Cu I 11: 68,15f. 29ff.
[98] Cu I 12: 69,8.
[99] Cu I 12: 69,10.

for the remission of sins. [100] The other two remaining possibilities deserve consideration: satisfaction or punishment.[101]

It is not yet clear whether the hypothesis of "satisfactio aut poena" really satisfies the criterion of fittingness (= "convenientia"). "Poena" by itself only leads to an eradication of guilt but not to a restoration. It is "absurda." Moreover, such a divine action would contradict divine justice. For this simple reason punitive action alone would not be fitting for God: "non ... decet."[102] By precluding punishment alone as a means of redemption, the necessity of satisfaction comes to the fore. Only satisfaction fulfills the criterion of divine justice. One cannot think of something more just than demanding satisfaction for sins committed.[103] This permits the conclusion that salvation requires satisfaction to be rendered. Reason, not faith, achieved this insight.

Against this background one now realizes that faith is in a position to understand itself. Reasoning offers faith a possibility and a structure with which to understand the event of redemption. By supplying a rational structure, reasoning provides faith with an instrument for defending itself: "auferas mihi fidei dubitationem."[104]

The next question addressed is whether reason is also able to define salvation and to assent to it? "Quod ex necessitate per Christum salvetur homo." It cannot supply the actual event of redemption.[105] In this way the positivity of redemption and its non-deducibility are preserved. At this point reason is called upon to dare to leap into faith. Here reasoning reached a decisive watershed: either it enters faith lest reasoning remain mere ratiocination or it fails to be saved.

Hoc debes ab illis nunc exigere, qui Christum non esse credunt necessarium ad illam salutem hominis, quorum vice loqueris, ut dicant qualiter homo salvari possit sine Christo. Quod si non possunt ullo modo, desinant nos irridere, et accedant et iungant se nobis, qui non dubitamus hominem per Christum posse salvari, aut desperent hoc ullo modo fieri posse. Quod si horrent, credant nobiscum in Christum, ut possint salvari.[106]

In this regard Boso thinks an aporia would exist if one were to engage faith at this point. If reasoning is unable to agree on this point it must demonstrate another way for salvation to be accessible. Boso readily acknowlegdes that this cannot occur.[107] If reasoning cannot admit salvation to have occurred, then this

---

[100] Cu I 15: 72,31ff.
[101] Cu I 15: 74,1.
[102] Cu I 19: 84,22.
[103] Cu I 23: 91,10-29.
[104] Cu I 25: 96,6.
[105] Cu I 25: 94,25.
[106] Cu I 25: 95,1-6.
[107] Cu I 25: 95,15f.

would be, in Anselm's judgment, an expression of despair: "desperent."[108] If such is indeed the case then one must test the salvation-event and probe whether it is intelligible: "qua ratione salvetur homo per Christum."[109] Boso hesitates to take this leap because his mind did not understand the how of Jesus life and death. Anselm draws Boso's attention to this fact: "Quid respondendum est illi, qui idcirco astruit esse impossibile quod necesse, quia nescit quomodo sit."[110] In spite of this, reason's insight into redemption's rational necessity remains. Thinking is capable of demonstrating a necessity which it cannot penetrate.

There is a greater necessity underlying redemption than reason is able to articulate only a posteriori. Also divine action follows an inner logic precluding impossibilities and assuming necessities. Human logic is able to retrace "aliquatenus" the divine logic. Yet what can liberate thinking from the impossibility it recognized? The impasse is thinking's inability to recognize in Jesus Christ's concrete and tangible, historical salivific event the fulfillment of that redemption that it, reasoning itself, called for. What other way could lead out of this dilemma but an engagement with the figure of Christ?

Both human rationality and divine logic know of no contradictions and recognize necessities. Human reasoning can understand this inner logic and gain insight into it. Under this horizon thinking is able to fathom the inner logic of redemption. Divine acts and human logic are therefore not eo ipso irreconcilable contradictions. Therefore the rationality of salvation through Jesus Christ should be able to be demonstrated. Boso joins Anselm in the effort of precisely demonstrating this in the second book.

> Quapropter sicut me rationabiliter deduxisti ad hoc, ut videam peccatorem hominem hoc debere deo pro peccato quod et reddere nequit, et nisi reddiderit salvari non valet; ita me volo perducas illuc, ut rationabilis necessitate intelligam esse oportere omnia illa, quae nobis fides catholica de Christo credere praecipit, si salvari volumus; et quomodo valeant ad salutem hominis; et qualiter deus misericordia salvet hominem, cum peccatum non dimittat illi, nisi reddiderit quod propter illud debet. [111]

Boso no longer demands that reasoning be able to arrive at the necessity of the concrete redemptive event in Jesus. But the rational demonstration should be truly "rationabiliter." The "necessitas rationabilis" no longer needs to be supplied by thinking. It is thinking's task to become aware of what it is in confrontation with: its insight into the rational necessity of salvation but its own inability to demonstrate the necessity of the redemption effected by Jesus Christ. In the process thinking apprehends itself as part of both the object and subject of salvation. Thinking finds itself in self-reflection itself oriented towards salvation and indeed towards its own possible redemption.

---

[108] Cu I 25: 95,5.
[109] Cu I 25: 95,7f.
[110] Cu I 25: 95,18f.
[111] Cu I 25: 96,7-13.

Ad hoc itaque factam esse rationalem naturam certum est, ut summum bonum super omnia amaret et eligeret, non propter aliud, sed propter ipsum.[112]

Thinking is ordered towards something which is greater than reason: "beatitudo." This inner dynamics of thinking is the result of God's implanting in the human mind the concept of "iustitia." Never can reason, insofar as it is reason, fail to apprehend with certitude justice as its aim.[113] Thinking glimpses salvation from within the parameters of rationality and justice. Yet knowledge and hope remain greater and beyond thinking. In Anselm's judgment reasoning yearns and hopes for salvation and feels guilty for having failed to articulate this promise as a destination of the complete human being towards resurrection. Reasoning is faithful to itself when it articulates this call to salvation. The structure of thinking is in this manner a necessary one. The outer necessity of thinking entails thinking's own self-revelation as its being oriented towards self-awareness.

If thinking is so constituted, would it not be incumbent on God to complete the design he had implanted in the human mind? Does not salvation, as something necessary to the mind, thereby become necessary for humanity? Even more pressing, how can such a necessary salvation still be grace?[114]

Anselm attempts to solve this riddle through an example: If I promise to give someone something tomorrow, then there is a degree of necessity involved in my fulfilling this promise the next day. On the next day when I keep this promise this would be a completely new and free act requiring my fidelity and honesty. In this example, freedom and necessity are integrated into one whole. Necessity becomes the outgrowth of my fidelity. For this reason the other person is called to express gratitude for my keeping the promise.

The same applies for salvation. Creation already contains "in nuce" the promise of salvation. This entails that in creation a yearning for salvation necessarily must exist. When God offers salvation, however, it is not out of obligation but freely: "gratia aufert" and "sponte."[115] This serves to illustrate not only divine freedom, but moreover that there also exists an infinite difference between what the creaturely mind envisions as salvation and what salvation actually is. The yearning for salvation does not result in a claim on salvation. Redemption always remains a gratuitous gift.

Incarnation, Jesus' life and redemption are three steps in which Anselm demonstrates the interrelatedness of necessity and redemption. For incarnation the key-term is the notion of "satisfactio" for human sins. Its true cause lies in God's ability to send his Son. Satisfaction requires something greater than human beings are able to perform. Thinking is able to see this but remains

---

[112] Cu II 1: 97,14f.
[113] Cu II 1: 97,17f.
[114] Cu II 5: 99,21f.
[115] Cu II 5: 99,23.100,2.

unable to produce it. It requires a "maius" which only God is able to provide. But reason is able to realize this need for a "maius" and to see God as the only possible source of redemption. "Satisfactio, quam nec potest facere nisi deus nec debet nisi homo: necesse est ut eam faciat deus-homo."[116] The mind's "debere" unlocks the necessity of incarnation. If this is indeed the case, then God must have the ability to be fully human while being fully divine.[117] This has as its consequence, first, that God must become a descendant of Adam and that one person of the Trinity becomes human.[118] This "realization" has been fulfilled in faith. This results in a coherence between faith and thinking as regards the incarnation. There is a threefold "convenientius": faith knows of a "maius," confesses three persons in the Godhead and believes in the incarnation of the Son.[119]

In chapters ten through fourteen Anselm evidences the relationship of freedom and necessity in the life of Jesus Christ. How could Jesus have been forced to die on the cross and yet retain his freedom? "Sponte det et non ex debito" Christ suffered crucifixion.[120] Even God could not have demanded from Jesus what he had done. Neither God the Father nor humanity could hold title on the "magis" Christ lived. The ultimate cause for his death was his own freeedom and his love for the Father:

> Nihil autem asperius aut difficilis potest homo ad honorem dei sponte et non ex debito pati quam mortem, et nullatenus se ipsum potest homo dare magis deo, quam cum se morti tradit ad honorem illius.[121]

If human guilt had already been infinite, then the salvation effected by Jesus Christ must be infinite. The finite in itself would be incapable of the predication "necessary" for redemption.[122]

Anselm's mental itinerary proves Jesus Christ's redemptive deeds as the fulfillment of what reasoning thinks as salvation. At the same time Anselm succeeds in demonstrating that there is something to redemption which is infinitely greater than what human salvific understanding can achieve. The profundity of God's unfathomable freedom becomes visible as the measure of interior justice which eclipses any kind of human yardsticks. In the "misericordia dei" everything previously contemplated is contained. With necessity human cognition apprehends salvation's impossibility.[123] Precisely in one's own inability the necessity of the infinitely greater divine freedom

---

[116] Cu II 6: 101,17-19.
[117] Cu II 7: 102,15f.
[118] Cu II 8: 102,24f. 105,2.
[119] Cu II 9.
[120] Cu II 11: 110,10.
[121] Cu II 11: 111,16-18.
[122] Cu II 14: 114,22f.31.
[123] Henry, The Logic of Saint Anselm 134ff. 140ff.

becomes apparent: "Omnis quippe necessitas et impossibilitas eius subiacet voluntati."[124]

In this manner a "negative" human understanding of salvation postulates a necessity for a divinely effected salvation and the impossibility of doing otherwise. Yet, it also realizes that this salvation must originate completely and freely as God's divine and sovereign and thereby "unnecessitated" doing. Redemption remains freely and divinely willed. In this manner the human concepts of necessity and impossibility are but expressions of divine freedom's omnipotence and constancy: "sicut nulla necessitas sive impossibilitas praecedit eius vele aut nolle, ita nec eius facere aut non facere quamvis multa velit immutabiliter et faciat."[125]

The yet greater omnipotence and freedom of God's salvific will breaks into the "negative" understanding of salvation when God redeems. By probing the limits of this negative human understanding of salvation, reasoning experiences that the divine salvific will prevails and can never be hindered. On the other hand this same human reasoning recognizes that divine redemption cannot be coerced or obstructed. Simultaneously it must admit its own impossibility. To illustrate better what is meant Anselm differentiates between two kinds of necessities: "Necessitas praecedens ... efficiens, quae causa est ut sit res ... necessitas sequens quam res fecit."[126] The first kind is causal and exists wherever causes bring forth effects. The second kind of necessity is the feature of free actions. Wherever freedom occurs a free act cannot be deduced from something preceding freedom.[127] Divine salvation is of the second kind of necessity. It arises from unfathomable and inexplicable freedom. Such an event of divine salvation brings forth an understanding for salvation and therefore also of thinking's self-understanding.

Though divine action corresponds to the common notion of justice, such justice cannot be comprehended in human reasoning. Rather its sole correspondent is in God. Therefore, there is far more occurring in Christ's crucifixion than cognitional justice: justice between Father and Son occurs. Justice is thus beheld as an innertrinitarian event of an altogether different kind than human cognition is able to apprehend. The sole foundation and ground for such justice is divine honor.[128] In the salvation effected for humanity God's infinite benevolence and love become apparent. Boso also must recognize this without reservations: "Nihil rationabilius, nihil dulcius, nihil desirabilius mundus audire potest."[129] In the depth of divine redemption divine mercy for the human predicament finds its sublimest expression. "Quam magna et quam

---

[124] Cu II 17: 123,23. II &: 54,12.
[125] Cu II 17: 123,1-3.
[126] Cu II 17: 125,8f.
[127] Cu II 17: 125,29ff.
[128] Cf. Cu II 18: 127,10f.
[129] Cu II 19: 131,3f.

iusta sit misericordia dei."[130] For this reason *Cur Deus Homo* concludes with praise and gratitude for the divine mercy. The subject and object of reasoning blend almost to a unity of purpose:

> Misericordiam vero dei quae tibi perire videbatur, cum iustitiam dei et peccatum hominis considerabamus, tam magnam tamque concordem iustitiae invenimus, ut nec maior nec iustior cogitari possit. Nempe quid misericordius intelligi valet, quam cum peccatori tormentis aeternis damnato et unde se redimat non habenti deus pater dicit: accipe unigenitum meum et da pro te: et ipse filius tolle me et redime te? Quasi enim hoc dicunt, quando nos ad Christianam fidem vocant et trahunt. Quid etiam iustius, quam ut ille cui datur pretium maius omni debito, si debito datur affectu, dimittat omne debitum?[131]

---

[130] Cu II 20: 131,26.
[131] Cu II 20: 131,27-132,6.

CHAPTER TEN
10.0 "Concordia" and "Ordo" as "Symphonia Veritatis"

Anselm's last treatise bears the title *De concordia praescientiae et praedestinationis et gratiae dei cum libero arbitrio*. His concern is to demonstrate a synthesis of his opus by way of illustrating that his thinking breathes concord and order. How can one be so intent on illustrating the aesthetic categoriality of thinking? Why do concord and order need to be central features of reflection? Furthermore, why does the credibility of his writings depend on their fulfilling the criteria of concord and order?

10.1 "Ordo" as Structure

Throughout antiquity and the middle ages the Latin term "ordo" had been a word defining the individual's relationship to the world and God.[1] In the fortieth chapter of *De Officiis* Cicero mentions the order of things: "Deinceps de ordine rerum et de opportunitate temporum dicendum est." This expresses the relational unity which antiquity surmised to prevail in all of being. From this term a "transzendental-ontologischer Erstbegriff von Ordnung" evolved during antiquity.[2] Already Tertullian had introduced this term to Christian usage to define the priestly order in contrast to that of lay people: "sacerdotalis ordo."[3] It remained for Augustine to endow the term "ordo" with a metaphysical connotation.[4] This occurs particularly in his treatise *De ordine*. Historically and materially Anselm is indebted to Augustine.[5]

In Augustine's metaphysics "ordo" denotes the soul's self-meditation. Unity is structured by numbers, elements and order. This order appears to the beholder as "pulchritudo."

Ita enim sibi animus reditus, quae sit pulchritudo universitatis, intelligit, quae profecto ab uno cognominata est idcircoque illam videre non licet animae.[6]

---

[1] Cf. "Ordo", Thesaurus Linguae Latinae, vol. IX, pars altera (Leipzig: 1968-81) at 952-955.961-963.
[2] "Ordnung," Handbuch philosophischer Grundbegriffe, vol. II 1037.
[3] "Ordnung," Historisches Wörterbuch der Philosophie, vol. 6, 1252f.
[4] Josef Rief, Der Ordo-Begriff des jungen Augustinus (Paderborn: Schöningh, 1962). Research on Anselm's understanding of "ordo" is very limited. In all probability this is the result of the prominent role this term played during scholasticism. A multitude of publications deal with that term's use during the twelfth and thirteenth centuries. This applies also to the valuable discussions by Michaud-Quantin and Hübener: cf. Pierre Michaud-Quantin Etudes sur le vocabulaire philosophique du moyen-âge (München: Fink, 1987) 85-101 for "ordo et ordines." Wolfgang Hübener, Historisches Wörterbuch der Philosophie, vol. 6 (München: Beck, 1984) 1254-1279. The first two authors do not mention Boethius and Anselm at all. Hübener briefly refers to Anselm.
[5] Cf. Markus Endres, "Das metaphysische Ordo-Denken in Spätantike und frühem Mittelalter: Bei Augustinus, Boethius und Anselm von Canterbury," Philosophisches Jahrbuch 2 (1997) 335-361, here 339.
[6] De ordine I, 2,3 (CCSL XXIX 90, 1-3).

Perhaps this line of thinking can serve as a "summa" for aesthetics. This notion of "ordo," joined with "forma" and "species" and "pulchritudo," already contains in it the rational and ordered structure of the universe. All occurrences have therefore a profound, underlying meaning which the philosopher and theologian attempts to decipher. "Ordo" reveals God as not whimsical but the "gubernator mundi." "Ordo" is the instrument through which God steers and guides the universe: "Ordo est inquit, per quem aguntur omnia, quae deus constituit."[7] This insight also permits statements concerning the divine nature. As absolute unity God is above and beyond terrestrial order and he himself must be constituted in a similar fashion. This is corroborated by scripture. "Everyone is to obey the governing authorities, because there is no authority except from God and so whatever authorities exist have been appointed by God" (Rom 13:1).[8] From the formal character of order, Augustine and Christian antiquity in general not only deduce the universality of divine governance but also the universal nature of cosmic order. Divine charity, God's rejection of evil and love for the good, constitute the harmonious order of the cosmos. Even the saddest portions of the *Soliloquies* do not negate this underlying good order.[9] To Augustine's mind this order is the actuation and appearance of God in his divine justice "ad extra."

In the present context Augustine's use of the term "rectus ordo" is of particular relevance. In *De libertate arbitrii* this term means a proper order or the realm where bad things are subjected to good things. An ethical evaluation of created things discloses an ontic pyramid which is the "ordo." Anselm uses this very term in the first part of the *Cur Deus Homo*: " Sicut rectus ordo exigit ut profunda..."[10] In this sense the monk from Bec also speaks of "recte ordinare" within the context of penalty without satisfaction.[11] In the *De libero arbitrio* Augustine brought the "ordo universitatis" into relation with the "lex aeterna."[12] The whole of the universe is created according to measures, numbers and weights in the ancient world-view. "...sed omnia in mensura et numero et pondere disposuisti" (Wis 11:21). Every terrestial form of realization must fit into this matrix of measure, number and weight in Augustine's aesthetics. Antiquity's central notion of "ordo" implies that everything is subject to divine disposition and is being guided by divine providence. As everything without

---

[7] De ordine I, 5,14 (CCSL XXIX 103, 13f).
[8] De vera religione XLI, 77 (CCSL XXXII 237,8): "Omnis ordo a deo est."
[9] Cf. Soliloq. I, 2,3 (CSEL LXXXIX 4,13f.): "Deus, per quem universitas etiam cum sinistra parte perfecta est."
[10] Cu I 1: 48,16.
[11] Cu I 12: 69,12.
[12] De lib. arb. I 6,15 (CCSL XXIX 220,65f).

exception is ordered by God, creation in its totality must form a perfect order. Both Augustine and, later, Anselm agree that creation is "pulcherrimus ordo."[13]

The significant role the "topos" of "ordo" plays in the Boethian oeuvre has not yet been sufficiently researched. This is all the more surprising as Boethius' main metaphysical writing, *De Consolatione philosophiae,* is a systematic thematization of the "ordo" notion.[14] Boethius possessed a fair command of the Greek language. In contrast to Augustine, he knew the term "ordo" to be the Latin equivalent of the Greek term "ταξισ."[15] This allows us to establish a material link between the Latin concept of "ordo" and the Platonic principle of "μεταξισ." This carries the assumption that in the ancient world the intellectual and existential ascents to the divine "ordo" together facilitate a correction of the human situation. In the *De Consolatione Philosophiae* the allegory of philosophy consoles the despondent prisoner Boethius by reminding him of God's firm and unswerving divine guidance of the cosmic "ordo." Boethius responds with a plea that God might subject the terrestrial-human condition to his rule.[16] The lack of order in human life is the result of intellectual confusion due to humanity's being incarcerated. This occasioned humanity's losing its participation in a secure divine order: "Sic quod praecipiti via certum deserit ordinem laetos non habet exitus."[17] There is an absolute unity essential to and permeating all of being: the "summum bonum." This "summum bonum" is the common goal of all creatures' natural yearnings.[18] This relationship of the teleological givenness of life and divine providence is illustrated by Boethius by using the example of an artist. The artist at first has only an ambiguous intuition of what the piece of art should look like. But it is the divine ordering providence which allows the idea to take on concrete forms. A fittingness between what the human mind wants to express - but unaided by God, is unable to give concrete form to - and divine providence is thereby affirmed.[19] Divine initiative gives unity, order and harmonic balance, thus counteracting centrifugal cosmic forces. Thereby an "ordo rectus" comes about.[20]

Anselmian thinking is a reflection of the Augustinian and Boethian metaphysical "ordo"-concept. By and large Anselm elaborates and systematizes

---

[13] Cf. Augustine, Conf. XIII 34,49: "Omnis quippe iste ordo pulcherrimus rerum." Anselm, O 14: 59,119: "tormentorum ordine pulcherrimo subiceret se factura ... "
[14] One exception is Enders' article "Das metaphysische Ordo-Denken in Spätantike und frühem Mittelalter" 349-357.
[15] Cf. Boethius, Porphyrii Isagogen, commentorum editio prima I, 1 (CSEL 48: 4,17): "tertium, qui ordo quod (sc. Graeci) taxin vocant."
[16] Cf. Cons. I 5,11f. and Cons. I 6,4.
[17] Cons. Im. 6 (14 20-22).
[18] Cons. III 11,10-13. 30-41.
[19] Cons. IV 6,12.
[20] Cons. IV 6,34-43.

previous contributions to it.[21] Already in Anselm´s central treatise *Monologion*, proof for this thesis can be found. The "summa essentia" gives order to all things.[22] The ontic hierarchy is subject to extensive discussion in chapter 31. Created entities are to the degree of their similitude ordered towards the "summa essentia." The higher they are, the greater the degree of their goodness and of their ontological quality. The order begins with lifeless entities and leads by way of animated creatures to rational substances.[23] The Augustinian source is *De diversis questionibus,* where the degrees of varying similarities to God and different ontic degrees are used to explain the "ordo." Important Anselmian terms already occur there: "melius," "necesse," "non necesse," "particeps," "similitudo," "ordo," "similes deo" and "supra omnia bonus."[24] Anselm explicates the Augustinian graduated and storied structure of the world by applying his methodological principle of contradiction-free cognition. He defines the Augustinian levels of different similarities as conceivable and thinkable degrees of ontic intensities.[25] Augustine himself stressed that God permits nothing to remain disordered. As a consequence God´s perfect justice could not leave the ruins of sinners in disorder.[26]

Salvation is here presented already as something necessary to the divine nature. Anselm quotes Augustine verbatim, stating that God cannot possibly leave something in disorder. In the *Cur Deus Homo* Anselm writes:

> Aliter aliquatenus inordinatum maneret peccatum, quod esse non potest, si deus *nihil relinquit inordinatum* in regno suo. Sed hoc est praestitutum quia quamlibet parvum inconveniens impossibile est in deo.[27]

Earlier Augustine had stated in *De Civitate Dei*:

> qui optime et veracissime creditur et cuncta scire antequam fiant et *nihil inordinatum relinquere.*[28]

---

[21] Cf. Hübener, "Ordnung," Historisches Wörterbuch der Philosophie, 6 (1984) at 1258ff. Hübener fails to contextualize Anselm´s view of "ordo" and reduces it to a legalistic "Gehorsams-und Sühne-Ordnung" (at 1258). Hübener refers to Cu I 15:72,31-73,2 but does not entertain the idea that Anselm does not speak here of a mere order of retribution and obedience but primarily of an ontic order encompassing all of reality. Flasch also does not bear in account the influence of Augustinian Platonism on Anselm´s understanding of "ordo." Cf. Flasch, "Der philosophische Ansatz" 1-43.

[22] Cf. M 7: 22,7-10.

[23] Cf. M 31: 49,9ff.

[24] Cf. De diversis questionibus LI, n. 2 (CCSL XLIV A, 79,33-80,50). Schmitt had made this reference: Schmitt (ed.), M 31: 49,12-23.

[25] M 31: 49,29: "cogitatione auferatur."

[26] De lib. arb. III 10,29 (CCSL 293,14-16).

[27] Cu I 20: 86,21-23. Italics by author.

[28] De civ. Dei V, 8 (Dombart,Kalb I 201,18-20).

Anselm's knowledge of this passage is highly probable. Also Anselm's highly determined statements concerning humanity's subordination under the divine will, finding its place in creation's order, seems indebted to Augustine's understanding of "ordo." The same applies to Anselm's understanding of the relationship between order and beauty.[29] From this Augustinian context Anselm's central term "debere" also arises. It denotes creatures' obligation to render to God, within the divinely ordained "ordo," the commensurate "debere."[30] The same applies to the expressions "ordo rerum" and "ordo universitatis."[31] In the same vein Anselm postulates the necessity of punishment for original sin. Punishment viewed as the restitution of God's robbed honor, as well as sin viewed as a violation of creation's beauty, are Anselmian echoes of Augustine. Divinely effected salvation restores the cosmos' order and beauty.[32] Created order's beauty may not suffer lasting impairment at the hand of sin. For this reason the sinner must pay God a ransom through suffering. Augustine discusses this at great length in the third book of *De libero arbitrio*.[33] Such satisfaction or restitution is considered necessary by Augustine and likewise by Anselm, because God cannot permit something in his realm to remain in disorder. Otherwise his governance and justice would not be expressions of divine omnipotence.

... ubi perversitas rectum ordinem perturbare nititur, non adderet, fieret in ipsa universitate quam deus debet ordinare, quaedam ex violata ordinis pulchritudine deformitas, et deus debet in sua dispositione videretur deficere.[34]

God is intent on preserving his honor and dignity. For as the greatest and best God necessarily must be predicated also as the most just. It follows from this that God is best equipped to defend and restore his honor.[35] In this connection Augustine receives at the hands of Anselm further precision. It is not that God could not - as the highest just one - treat sinners and non-sinners equally by leaving sin unpunished.[36] It would be a repudiation of the very divine essence and freedom were God to leave human "debere" without a chance of realignment.

---

[29] Cf. Cu I 15: 73,3-9.
[30] Cf. Co 6: 147,16-19 and Augustine, De lib. arb. III 15,42 (CCSL XXIX 300,20-26).
[31] See Cu I 13: 71,7: "Nihil minus tolerandum in rerum ordine, quam ut creatura creatori debitum honorem aufert et non solvat quod aufert." Co 6: 147,18f.: "nec ordo congruus universitatis rerum ..."
[32] Cf. Cu I 12: 69,11-13; I 15: 73,17-74,1.
[33] Cf. De lib. arb. III (CCSL XXIX 301,59-63).
[34] Cu I 15: 73,22-25. Cf. "in eadem universitate suum tenent locum et ordinis pulchritudinem." Cu I 15: 73,22.
[35] Cf. Cu I 13: 71,15-19.
[36] Cf. Cu I 12: 69,19f; I 13: 71,25f.

Such a prospect of realignment in freedom is not only an ontic reality. As an ontic reality it would remain incomplete and therefore totally non-existent. Cosmic ordo is mirrored in the "animal rationale's"[37] mind. Salvation would be incomplete were redemption not also accessible to the human mind. Indeed, Christ would not have died for humanity if the human mind could not retrace itself in an objective, rational, accountable manner.

10.2 "Ordo" as a Philosophical Category

The multilayered nature of thinking has been reduced to but few terms: "necessitas" and "libertas." *Cur Deus Homo* gyrates around divine necessity and divine freedom as well as the mode in which these two divine qualities impinge upon human freedom and what role divine grace plays in this context. The implication of the treatise is that divine "praescientia" and divine "praedestinatio" as an outgrowth of divine necessity threaten to blot out human freedom. Moreover, how can human freedom survive when exposed to divine free grace, if the latter is not required and demanded by the former? Again and one final time Anselm puts to the test with the terms "freedom" and "necessity" the whole of his intellectual endeavors.

As God is uncaused beginning and origin, human reasoning must ascribe necessity and freedom equally to God. How can such terms coexist in the one Godhead, if freedom means spontaneity but necessity predestination? Need not freedom be diluted by necessity, or conversely necessity by freedom? The inner tension of these two reveals the dynamics inherent to reasoning when contemplating the whole. In God and in thinking an attention of these terms to one another, which dates back to their infinite origins, is revealed in their relationship. At first sight, this treatise's synopsis does not reveal profounder dimensions than Anselm's previous writings. Indeed, it seems to lack the synthetic energy to conduct discourse on a level comparable to the *Monologion* or the *Proslogion*. Explicitly it is Anselm's concern here to treat the concept of "concordia."[38] In this connection one should not fail to point out that the term "concordia" must be very central to him, as it appears already at the end of his major writings *Cur Deus Homo* and *Proslogion*.[39] Evidently he had found concord to be a conclusion to both writings. Almost in hindsight one can now appreciate again what concord may have meant to Anselm.

At the beginning of the *Proslogion's* first chapter, God and the individual's heart are confronted with one another.[40] Thereby, humanity and divinity, human existence and the personal God, are brought into dialogue. In this way two forms of freedom meet: human freedom and divine freedom. In the course of the *Proslogion* the unity of recognizing God and the self in

---

[37] Cf. M 10: 25,9. G 3: 147, 25; 13: 157,30; 21, 166,27.

[38] C 1: 245,1.

[39] Cu I 20; P 25: 119,7

[40] P 1: 97,9.98,1.

salvation history's context is established. In this way, the origin of thinking is evidenced as dual. Divine origin is always "quiddam maius." In divine gratuitous charity human freedom can freely take its origin. Human reasoning must necessarily define such a freedom. By adopting an "own" origin, human thinking and human freedom not only gain their own beginning but also their own contours. This dual beginning is an indissoluble context. However, such a context can only become apparent by thinking from one origin and thereby gaining a prospective on the whole. Both the *Proslogion* and the *Cur Deus Homo* take their points of departure from one beginning and origin, albeit different beginnings and origins.

In the *Proslogion* thinking unfolds its own necessity and originality by employing the figure of the "quo maius." The result of this argument is that necessity is necessarily transferred into freedom. The necessary compulsion of reasoning suddenly evaporates into a necessity to be free and thereby in one and the same cognitional moment there is a grasping of reasoning in its totality and a surrendering of itself utterly and completely to the other, i.e. to the absolute "maius." By reaching beyond itself, thinking comes to its own. With this insight into the necessary surrender or transferral to the "maius," this "maius" becomes present both as in thinking and as the "other" origin of thinking. Beginning with chapter five in the *Proslogion,* the God personally sought for, as the "quiddam maius," does not allow reasoning to come to rest. Rest only occurs as a correlation between the "quo maius" and the "quiddam maius" occurs.

The *Cur Deus Homo* makes a twofold approach. At the beginning it discusses divine freedom as the "quiddam maius" in the context of divine freedom. Human reasoning obtains this insight by its own effort and finds therein its own correspondence. Human reasoning is unable to imagine the "maius" and "plus" of divinity. But human freedom explicates and actuates itself with inner necessity in this process. The other entry occurs in reasoning's self-awareness. Human reasoning becomes cognizant of its own beginning and originality and of its necessarily rational structure. This necessity liberates reasoning to the "quo maius," and therefore necessity is transfigured into freedom. The bipolarity of human reasoning becomes, thereby, evident. The point of departure is always one pole - presuming for the time being that the other pole is non-existent. The complexity of both being and cognition becomes evident. This is exemplified both in the *Proslogion* and the *Cur Deus Homo* and illustrates two different moments of the one reality: faith and thinking. Faith indebted to God's free grace yearns to apprehend its inner necessity. Thinking confronted with its own necessity experiences freedom as its transcending ground. The whole of Anselmian thinking becomes apparent as an aesthetic balance of "fides quaerens intellectum" and "intellectus quaerens fidem." A beautiful symmetry comes to the fore. In the process both reasoning and faith are reciprocally structure and object for one another. In Anselm's mind, form and object constitute a synthesis by virtue of their mutual, tension-filled relationship. This tension is a constitutive part of every serious religious-philosophical discourse. Every such effort must rekindle ever anew the tension between faith and reasoning. Thereby, religious philosophy actuates salvation and reasoning becomes of salvific import for the subject of such an undertaking. Both faith and reasoning impact reciprocally one another by taking each other's origin seriously.

In these reciprocal definitions of form and object, faith and reasoning mirror the moments of freedom and necessity in faith and reasoning. Reasoning's immanent necessity, when beholding the form of faith, comes to know itself as sustained by a greater freedom. Autonomous reasoning experiences itself as underpinned by a heteronomy wholly originating in freedom and releasing freedom. Autonomous reasoning is thereby freed from the limitations of necessity and receives the gift of freedom: this is more precisely beheld as faith. Faith and reasoning reciprocally grant one another freedom and necessity.

This overarching situation is not beheld when one is immersed in a concrete text of Anselm. The interconnection becomes apparent when reflecting on the justification and viability of the principle of "sola ratione." In *De Veritate* the "intelligere" becomes apparent as the manifestation of truth, by allowing the principle of "sola ratione" to distill this insight. This writing illumines truth as the interplay and intersection of "necessitas" and "libertas." From the very onset truth is presented as the entity prevailing and resonating throughout the whole. By so doing, truth does not run the danger of becoming a mere pole in a polar relationship. It is greater than cogitation or necessity. It is evident in the praxis of necessity and freedom. Truth wants to be done for its own sake, from its own freedom and originality. In contrast the *Monologion* emphasizes the moment of "necessitas." The soteriological writings in turn tend to thematize with greater intensity the notion of "libertas" as necessary co-player with "necessitas."

The concept of "rectitudo" in *De Vertitate* encapsulates the regulatory framework of the truth event. It permits the subtle balancing of truth as it mediates between first truth and its corresponding truth in cogitation. By having first truth as its object, thinking must correspond in thinking to first truth. Such a correspondence is defined as "rectitudo." "Rectitudo" is nothing less than the aesthetic category of mental symmetry. Through the form of "rectitudo," reasoning matures into true and proper thinking. On the other hand, "rectitudo" also becomes the simile and object of concrete truth. Truth's necessity reflects "rectitudo." "Rectitudo"'s correspondence is no arbitrary necessity but the correspondence of one freedom to another freedom. To grasp "rectitudo"'s relational quality Anselm employs the term "debere." "Debere" contains the elements of freedom and necessity and the call to do what is true. And yet, "debere" must come about through fidelity to its own origin and spontaneity. The dialectics of giving, receiving, and preserving employed by Anselm serve to illustrate among others that "debere" necessarily contains the correlation of freedom to freedom so that truth may be done. In such a way, the terms "rectitudo" and "debere" are structural parameters of what verity is.

By employing "sola ratione" the *Monologion* thematizes reasoning's necessity on a broad canvas. Necessity appears as cognition's form towards the "quo maius." Cognition goes beyond itself and starts with the "bonum." Cognition reveals itself in the process as necessarily interested in its own goodness. Reasoning cannot by and of itself bring this interest to fruition. Such can only be actuated when acquiring, from outside, the "bonum." Only in this conjunction does thinking rise to the task of bringing to unity both itself and what it thinks by pursuing everything to its ultimate ground and, thereby, explaining it. Such a ground is no longer thinking itself but a transcendent cause. Nevertheless, though reasoning is able to approach the "quo maius" and to know the "maius" as its goal, it can merely asymptotically approximate it. Only by transforming itself, within the parameters of thinking's necessity, does the "maius" grant itself to thinking as its object and is thereby thinking from a necessity, which grants freedom. The greater freedom of the "maius" does not cancel cognition's necessity but rather fully restores it. Only in dialogue with this yet greater freedom does thinking realize its own necessity. Thinking in its necessity rests ultimately on this greater freedom - in the sense of both grounding and self-constituting itself.

Divine transcendentality is the *Monologion's* topic. In this approach of thinking towards God all statements of "similitudo" occasion statements of a yet greater "dissimilitudo." Here one experiences in thinking both a rupture and a definition of God from thinking's own categoriality. Thereby, the *Monologion* defines God precisely in its transcendentality. Divine freedom is threatened if it is merely thinking's necessary corollary as the greater freedom: "Si deus non potest cogitari nisi ita solus, ut nihil illi simile cogitari possit."[41]

Divine salvific will as the "quiddam maius" is Anselm's soteriological pillar. Nothing greater, better or more just can be thought, as Anselm's last treatise confirms. This "maius" vouches for God's greater freedom. This divine freedom must not be thinking's mere corollary or even subsumed under thinking's necessity. It is thinking's endemic danger to do an injustice to divine freedom by apprehending only the correlation of divine rationality with human reasoning and to deduce divine freedom from its own necessity. Such a temptation always accompanies human, post-lapsarian reasoning. Caving in to such a temptation is in Anselm's judgment the actual human transgression vis-à-vis God, and the essence of sin. This is the essence of sin: the sinner wants to be equal to God: "ille peccavit et voluit esse similis deo."[42] In this sense the "quiddam maius" threatens to become a part of presumptuous human thinking.

---

[41] Ca 4: 241,31.
[42] Ca 4: 240,15.

Yet does thinking not call inherently this simile of "quo maius" its own merely to correspond to divine freedom? Therefore, divine and human freedom must find their proper fine-tuning in human reasoning - for humanity's own sake. The discovered proper relationship must be the guiding principle for the cognitional enterprise.

Sometimes it seems as if divine redemptive action is dependent on rationality. This is a cause for some uneasiness. Rationality introduces a certain one-sidedness to both Anselm's anthropology and soteriology. Already thinking's overwhelming interest in salvation brings about a certain proclivity. But it is not Anselm's intention to construe credal contents from reasoning's necessities. Anselm exclusively wishes to demonstrate the rational correlation of faith and reasoning. Divine salvation and charity do not become evidenced so much as the abundant overflow of divine freedom and charity but rather as their correspondence to human necessity and freedom. This might be a cause for presuming that transcendentality exhausts the definition of divinity. Christian existence as participation in divine benevolence and charity - as divine plenitude - would receive short treatment.

On the other hand, Anselm's rationality opens remarkable vistas. Despite a certain relentlessness, Anselm thematizes in both the *Cur Deus Homo* and in the *Proslogion* his search for "concordia." This "concordia" constitutes the aesthetic synthesis for all of Anselm's travails. No matter whether cognition moves from thinking to faith or from faith to thinking, every cognitional movement gains a reciprocally complementing perspective of the whole. The relationality of perspectives evidences God as the "quiddam maius." The *Proslogion* actuates the thought for "concordia." Thinking necessarily probes the frontiers of the "quo maius." At the end of thinking's necessary movement stands God's "quiddam maius."

Divine freedom flows into human thinking as the infinitely greater personal ground. Thus divine freedom becomes part of thinking's necessity by having revealed itself as the genuine "quo maius." In the *Cur Deus Homo's* conclusion the immensity of God's freely giving divine mercy becomes evident. Thus, reasoning formulates in a definitive and defining manner the term "misericordia dei." Here, cognition meets its limits. It can no longer arrive at the "misericordia dei" on its own. It is endebted to the "quiddam maius" of divine freedom. Divine freedom is the source not only for the fact of "misericordia dei" but equally for the cognitional concept of the "misericordia dei." Cognition must admit its agony in humility.

We must detect Anselm's lasting and perhaps most challenging contribution to religious philosophy in the search and discovery of "concordia." This discipline attempts to bring thinking and faith, God and humanity, freedom and salvation into dialogue, and finally all these moments into one symphonic melody. Religious philosophy must measure up to Anselm's writings and endeavor to think God as God, "quiddam maius," and thereby exhaust cognition when confronted with the "quo maius cogitari nequit." Two citations perhaps express best the challenge Anselm's notion of "concordia" poses to modern philosophy: "'tam magnam tamque concordem iustitiae invenimus, ut maior nec iustior cogitari possit" [43] and "Ergo domine, non solum es quo maius cogitari nequit, sed es quiddam maius quam cogitari possit."[44]

Anselm had shown eloquently and convincingly that thinking is thinking's most appropriate and safest tool. Thinking becomes both religious philosophy's object and highest term. In this term God is put to the test and must prove Himself. On the other hand, present-day philosophy could also gain its bearings from this Anselmian highest term. Anselm's contributions are not only an eloquent expression of monastic theology, albeit tied to a particular time. Every serious intellectual endeavor, be it philosophical or theological, must confront anew Anselm's formula, "id quo maius cogitari nequit." Equally, every such mental adventure must raise the question of whether the absolute merely appears as an interlocking moment within cognition or whether in it the sovereign epiphany of the "quiddam maius" occurs.

---

[43] Cu I 20:131,28.
[44] P 15: 112,14.

CHAPTER ELEVEN
11.0 The Rediscovery of Anselm as a Moment of Christianity's "Résourcement"

11.1 The Appropriation of Anselm's Thought after World War I

The atmospherics in Continental Europe after the upheavals the Great War had brought about were unique. Centuries-old institutions had collapsed. The Hapsburg Empire as well as the German Reich had been reduced to footnotes in the history of Central Europe. The social fabric had been torn asunder. Many had to find a new role in a society yet not stabilized. It had been in no small way workers alienated from faith who had overthrown ancient regimes. In this situation of political unrest and social insecurity nobody knew whether indeed German society would be able to emulate the democratic models of the victors: France, England and the United States. Not a few favored an authoritarian form of government. Amid these social and political uncertainties the populace suffered poverty, as exorbitant reparations had to be paid, and spiralling inflation reduced wealth to a pittance within a few days' time.

The Westphalian Peace of 1648 had placed the Protestant churches under a suzerain's protection within the ages-old Holy Roman Empire. With the downfall of the Wilhelmian Reich these "Landeskirchen" had to find a new place within a secularized but of itself uncertain order. No longer did a ruler dispense laws for churches. Rather, for the first time in its history the "Evangelische Kirche" had to develop its own ecclesiastical law. For the first time these churches had to reflect in an excruciating way on their own self-definition. While not subjected to such profound changes, the Catholic Church also had to adapt to new realities. The now deposed Hapsburgs and Wittelsbachs had been columns and multipliers of church influence. Overshadowing these domestic troubles, from the east loomed the danger of a totalitarian and avowedly atheist ideology.

The European world-view had been proved hollow. The pillars upon which society had been established had collapsed within a few days. Amid these doubts and tribulations there was a wide-spread yearning for the undiluted and true, for the organic whole, for what had grown naturally and with no artificial, superfluous arabesques over centuries. It is within this context that the Church instituted the feast of Christ the King (1925), that Grabmann wrote his epochal *Die Geschichte der scholastischen Methode* (already 1909) - thereby inaugurating a departure from Neo-Scholasticism - that Guardini postulated "the awakening of the Church in the souls of the faithful," that various church youth organizations (cf. Guardini's "Quickborn") came into being and that a new, organic appreciation of liturgy set in.

Within this general intellectual climate Anselm received fresh attention. For the purpose of the present investigation two contributions seem particularly insightful. The widely acclaimed book *Fides Quaerens Intellectum* by the young Reformed theologian Karl Barth was published in 1931 but reflects research dating back to at least 1926. In this book Karl Barth establishes the foundations for his subsequent magnum opus *Church Dogmatics*. Faith can no longer be grounded in a political order for the Protestant fold. In his Anselm book Barth consciously attempts to ground faith afresh in scripture, tradition and the church. Faith is not a subjective, individualistic contrivance grounded in a personal angle or affectivity. Faith is for Barth an objective entity with its own effulgent veracity. Thereby the havoc which von Harnack and Ritschl as Protestant theology's most prominent representatives of a church-state axis had wrought would be prevented from re-occurring. Faith would no longer rest on a church-state alliance but solely on the Protestant church's "Creed." Parallel to Barth but already in 1923 Romano Guardini published a brief, but alas a little noticed essay, titled *Anselm von Canterbury und das Wesen der Theologie*. This treatise appeared in the book *Auf dem Wege*, Versuche.[1] In this book Guardini already attempts to ground faith in the organic life of the Church and to demonstrate the organic unity of theology as it existed in pre-academic Scholastic theology.

11.2 Romano Guardini

In this only thirty two pages long essay Romano Guardini introduces the reader to Anselm by characterizing him as fresh and youthful, and by not offering a merely dry repristination of Platonism.[2] By way of introduction, he contextualizes Anselm's thought in the church-state controversy over investiture. The church struggled to free herself from earthly entanglements and to retain her independence from temporal powers. Reconsidering her nature, religion strives for her own profile. Similarily and simultaneously ecclesial, religious science sets itself apart from its surrounding culture. In Guardini's judgment Anselm's agenda is theology's attempt to assert its own call and essence. The program "credo ut intelligam" serves to illustrate theology's self-sufficiency vis-à-vis a secular although by no means necessarily unchristian order.

Confronted with newly discovered ancient philosophical texts, the Christian mind in Anselm's era had to choose between a merely traditional and authoritarian method or individualistic rationalism. Guardini discerns in Anselm's oeuvre a synthesis of the two tendencies paradigmatic for and essential to every genuinely theological enterprise:

> Doch nicht in äußerlich-eklektischer Weise, sondern durch organische Verbindung, ja Durchdringung und wechselseitiger Bedingung beider Denkrichtungen.[3]

---

[1] Romano Guardini, "Anselm von Canterbury und das Wesen der Theologie," Auf dem Wege, Versuche (Mainz: Grünewald, 1923) 33-65. It is noteworthy that this essay is preceded by a meditation on the nature of Christian obedience: "Der religiöse Gehorsam" 9-32.

[2] Guardini, "Anselm von Canterbury" 33, footnote.

[3] Guardini, "Anselm von Canterbury" 35.

This synthesis lies in the super-sensual divine facts which are more concrete and tangible than the material world surrounding it. Taking "credo ut intelligam"as the point of departure, Anselm is seen as opposing rationalism. As faith contains everything, it must form the basis for science. It is faith that grants essential insight into reality. Without creed there is no possible "theologische Erkenntnismöglichkeit."[4] Reason serves to illustrate the rationality and intelligibility of faith and revelation. Guardini stresses this Anselmian claim in order to counter the "subjectively individualistic" Zeitgeist of his time. Anselm is used to illustrate faith as being organically rooted in the community of the believing Church. Much like Barth subsequently, this faith is considered bound to an authority defined as comprised of sacred scripture, tradition (the Fathers) and the magisterium.[5]

All questions of faith are to be definitively decided by this authority. This authority circumscribes revelation's scope, content and purpose. Such a faith by no means thereby becomes sterile and obsequious. "Der Glaube ist nicht bloße Zustimmung des Verstandes, sondern Hingabe des ganzen Menschen."[6] The complete human being is called to a full and living faith that has as its constitutive attitude the affirmation of divine truth. All life's labor and yearning should be directed towards this "Wahrheitsbeziehung zu Gott" (= truth-relationship to God) and should derive from him their formative principle.[7] Using *De Trinitate*,[8] Guardini calls this virtue of truth "rectitudo." This is a comprehensive sense for what is right and proper both in action and knowledge. This "rectitudo" is grounded in the believer's personal relationship to God.

Anselm's theological thinking is considered demanding and daring at the same time. It neither yields to rationalistic constructions of mysteries of faith nor does it subscribe to blind traditionalism. Faithful to the line of tradition of Augustine and Bonaventure, Guardini also apprehends in the *Proslogion* a unity of thinking and prayer. Anselm formulates an organic theory of theology. This science in turn renders faith conscious and forceful. Supernatural reality becomes a conscious part of life. The clarity gained thereby perfects life. This Anselmian approach to theology Guardini favorably contrasts with more recent abstract, closed systematizations of faith.[9] Thinking is adoration of being; as more profound realities coming to light through theology.

---

[4] Guardini, "Anselm von Canterbury" 37.
[5] Guardini, "Anselm von Canterbury" 38.
[6] Guardini, "Anselm von Canterbury" 39.
[7] Guardini, "Anselm von Canterbury" 40.
[8] This treatise has been proven by Schmitt as inauthentic. Cf. Franciscus Salesius Schmitt, "Geschichte und Beurteilung der früheren Anselmausgaben," Studien und Mitteilungen zur Geschichte des Benediktiner-Ordens und seiner Zweige. 65/4 (1955): 90-115, at 112.
[9] Guardini, "Anselm von Canterbury" 45.

Guardini considers a réssourcement by Anselm's hermeneutics helpful in demonstrating that thinking and faith are rooted firmly in the one organism that is the Church. Not the isolated subject but the organized sequence of many subjects brings forth a unified and uniform orientation which is able to breathe more than its sum-total.[10] Thus constituted theology supplies faith with supernatural certitude. In the process theology's actual subject becomes apparent. The individual is not the bearer of theology but the thinking community that is the Church Catholic. "Eigentliches Subjekt der Theologie ist die Denkgemeinschaft der Kirche."[11] Through the ecclesially legitimized magisterium the Church becomes a collective subject. In view of this nature of theology the individual is called to exercise restraint and to practice "Aszese des Glaubens" in order to realize "sentire cum Ecclesia."[12] By this constant practice the individual becomes a fuller and purer organ of the Church. This notion of unity is an essential part of the definition of Christian faith.

Denn wer im vollen anselmischen Sinne Theologe sein will, muß wissen, daß er nicht aus Ich und Gegenwart heraus, sondern aus der Kirche und ihrer, das ganze Aevum umspannenden Tradition her denken muß. Daß er nicht autonomer Gesetzgeber und persönlicher Schöpfer, sondern selbstloses Organ sein soll.[13]

Guardini made do with the uncritical Migne-Edition of Anselm. Frequently he unwittingly quoted from Pseudo-Anselmian literature. He was aware of Möhler's article on Anselm and tried to articulate the fecundity of the Anselmian approach for modernity. A bit one-sided, Guardini considers Anselm's concern to be a predominantly theological one. It is up to speculation whether Barth was at all aware of this essay. Barth's equally asymmetric reading of Anselm as propounding an exclusively theological agenda may well be due to his reading of Guardini's text. It must be considered Guardini's lasting contribution to have discovered in Anselm's thinking an ethical message which to this day still awaits broader scholarly appreciation. A thinking which reflects on God must be born out of an attitude which is commensurate to its object. This calls for ethical prerequisites. Theology is based according to Guardini on an ethics promoting an asceticism and education of proper discovery and recognition.[14]

---

[10] Guardini, "Anselm von Canterbury" 48.
[11] Guardini, "Anselm von Canterbury" 58.
[12] Guardini, "Anselm von Canterbury" 59.
[13] Guardini, "Anselm von Canterbury" 62.
[14] Guardini, "Anselm von Canterbury" 47. As above demonstrated, there is no irreconcilable rupture between philosophy and theology in Early Christianity's self-understanding. As a pre-scholastic thinker, Anselm is still in agreement with this worldview. Insofar, every attempt to predicate Anselm's thoughts as either exclusively philosophical or as exclusively theological in nature bears eloquent testimony to the critics' "Sitz im Leben," but does little justice to Anselm.

11.3 Karl Barth and Anselm

11.3.1 Introduction

The first signs of Barth´s occupation with Anselm date back to his time as professor in Münster. During the summer semester of 1926 he conducted a seminar on the treatise *Cur Deus Homo*. As Barth readily admitted to Eduard Thurneysen in a letter dated May 5, 1926, he had then been confronted with a multitude of philological, logical, and material difficulties.[15] In the next year, 1927, Barth referred emphatically to Anselm in his draft for a Christian dogmatics: *Christliche Dogmatik im Entwurf*.[16] It seems, however, that only in the ensuing discussions surrounding Anselm did Barth truly become aware of the serious implications of such a heuristic decision. These discussions concerning the proper interpretation of the Anselmian opus were intensive.[17] In spite of his claim that he does not side with Anselm for apologetic reasons, it is clear that dogmatic interests primarily motivated him to take particular issue with Anselm´s theology.[18] Prior to continuing the task of developing his own dogmatics, he was compelled to satisfactorily clarify methodological points. In all probability Barth struggled intensively for a proper understanding of Anselm´s approach during the years 1928-1929. In the summer semester of 1930 Barth conducted a second seminar on *Cur Deus Homo*. A lecture by the philosophy professor Heinrich Scholz, who also had then been teaching in Münster, proved of crucial significance for Barth´s interpretation of Anselm. On July 11 of that semester this personal friend of Barth, Scholz, gave a lecture on the proof of God in Anselm´s *Proslogion*. As a logician it was his concern to discuss the logical justifications for theological statements.[19] As a result of this presentation, Barth concentrated his Anselm research on that treatise. The results of this pursuit culminated in 1931 in the book *Fides quaerens intellectum*. In the same year Barth also published a brief article in which he attempted to show by way of his book´s summary that Anselm considers theology a necessarily exclusive

---

[15] Cf. Karl Barth/Eduard Thurneysen, Briefwechsel. Band 2: 1921-1930 (Zollikon: TVZ, 1993), at 411.

[16] Karl Barth, Die christliche Dogmatik in Entwurf, Erster Band: Die Lehre vom Worte Gottes, Prolegomena zur christlichen Dogmatik (Zollikon: TVZ, 1982) here: 97ff. 226ff.

[17] Cf. Hans Michael Müller, "Credo ut intelligam," Theologische Blätter. 7 (1929), rubrics 167-176; Karl Diem, "Credo ut intelligam. Ein Wort zu Hans Michael Müllers Kritik an Karl Barths Dogmatik," Zwischen den Zeiten. 6 (1928) 517-528; Karl Barth, "Bemerkungen zu Hans Michael Müllers Lutherbuch," Zwischen den Zeiten 7 (1929) 561-570; Karl Barth, Kirchliche Dogmatik. Vol. I,1 (Zollikon: TVZ, 1986/87) at 235.242f.

[18] Cf. Barth, Fides quaerens intellectum. introduction, 1.

[19] Bent Flemming Nielsen, Die Rationalität der Offenbarungstheologie. Die Struktur des Theologieverständnisses von Karl Barth (Aarhus: Aarhus UP, 1988) 180-203. This is perhaps the best summary discussion on this aspect of Barthian theology.

discipline.[20]   In these reflections on Anselm's proof of God Barth finds the foundations for his *Kirchliche Dogmatik*. Throughout his *Church Dogmatics* Barth makes numerous references to Anselm. These occur particularly in volumes I,1; II,1; and IV,1. In the winter semester 1942/1943 he again held a seminar on the *Cur Deus Homo*. Only much later, in the summer semester of 1959, did he also conduct a seminar on "Anselms Beweis der Existenz Gottes." The foundation for this seminar had been the second, revised edition of his Anselm book. As Torrance observes, Barth's occupation with Anselm represents "the decisive turning point in his thinking."[21] In a later work on the Swiss theologian, Torrance entitles a complete section "Help from St. Anselm". In this section he notes that Barth's "epoch-making study of the thought of St. Anselm" was "in large measure" responsible for the reconstruction of his understanding of theology after his book on the Letter to the Romans.[22]

11.3.2 The Barthian Concern

Barth does not want to grant subjective speculation a platform throughout his theology. Revelation is to take center stage and should determine the form and content of theological discourse. Christ is the measure of all things. This he wishes to spell out anew in a fresh and edifying manner for his faith community. To this kerygmatic end, he concedes that there is no hiatic irreconcilability - in the sense of an insurmountable chasm - between creator and creature. The basis for such a claim is not the "Catholic" view of "analogia entis," - at least as he understands it, but Christ's incarnation. In the second volume of his *Church Dogmatics* Barth recognizes that Christ's nature effects human nature as "causa exemplaris." Because God loved humanity he had sent his own Son.[23]   This means that in the incarnation God presumes something as a prerequisite which makes incarnation possible. Human nature is prepared for a liturgical disposition. This formal statement already contains a contents. Human nature is created towards grace and for revelation.[24] This formal situation seems already a graced one. The Augustinian definition of freedom, in the background, permits Barth to

---

[20] This is meant in the sense of not accessible to the un-churched. Karl Barth,   "Die Notwendigkeit der Theologie bei Anselm von Canterbury," Zeitschrift für Theologie und Kirche 12 (1931): 350-358.

[21] Thomas F. Torrance, Karl Barth: An introduction to his Early Theology 1910-31 (London: SCM, 1962) at 182.

[22] Cf. editors' introduction to the reprint of Karl Barth, Fides quaerens intellectum. Anselms Beweis der Existenz Gottes im Zusammenhang seines theologischen Programms. Karl Barth Gesamtausgabe. Bd. II: Akademische Werke. ed. by Eberhard Jüngel and Ingolf U. Dalferth (Zürich: TVZ, 1981) at VIIff; Torrance, Karl Barth 150.

[23] Karl Barth, Kirchliche Dogmatik V. Studienausgabe (Zollikon: TVZ, 1986/89/93) at 53f. Hans Urs Balthasar, Karl Barth. Darstellung und Deutung seiner Theologie 4th ed. (Einsiedeln: Johannes, 1989) 129.

[24] Barth, Kirchliche Dogmatik V 107.

appreciate freedom primarily as the gratuitous potentiality to partake in divine life. Such human freedom receives its actuation only through the incarnation.

This definition of the relationship between nature and grace has a gnoseological component to it. It begs for the relationship between faith and insight. As the nature of the human race becomes meaningful only through grace, likewise reason becomes rational only through faith. Barth subscibes to a radical form of christocentrism. Nature and insight rest on grace. All truth emanates from God's revelation and from his divine Word. Though God did reveal himself in an ontic and in a noetic form to nature, such revelation is by no means natural but divine. Any principle of non-contradiction must rest on God's permanence and omnipotence. This principle of non-contradiction also applies to created being and to finite truth, but is founded exclusively in God's absolute being.[25] Even a mathematical equation such as $2 \times 2 = 4$ is not grounded simply in the terms themselves, but in divine condescension and freedom. As a result Barth cannot help but see in Descartes' meditations a circular movement.

The Cartesian "cogito ergo sum" is the herald of radical scepticism. Gaunilo is identified as such a protagonist. Whatever cannot be thought must be doubted. Descartes began the era of subjectivism in intellectual history. This is developed thoroughly by Kant in his *Critique of Pure Reason*. The subject as bearer of awareness becomes the condition of the possibility of philosophy. The idea of the infinite is already contained in human consciousness. His "cognitio Dei naturalis" is the basis for self-knowledge and for natural theology which Barth combats (against v. Harnack and Ritschl).[26] Kant cannot think God. But the term "God" is to him a necessary postulate of a philosophically matured reason. The ontological argument must meet Kant's rejection as it combines postulate and reality and, therefore, does not comply with the Kantian definition of a transcendental idea.

God exists independently from his being thought as "esse in re et in esse."[27] God exists in Barth's opinion necessarily and untouched from the fact that he is being thought or not. This insight into the necessity of divine existence is arrived at primarily through revelation. Mere thinking cannot yield such a result. As this thought is revealed it cannot reasonably be thought non-existent. As a result the Barthian theological program rests on whether God does indeed reveal himself in his true being ("quidditas").

The Barthian program can be summed up as "faith rendering itself transparent." The presumption is that the believers already are in possession as churched Christians of the whole faith as Creed. Theology is therefore a positive science for Barth - as it was already for Schleiermacher - as it reflects on something concrete and pre-given. This pre-given is the faith of the church

---

[25] Karl Barth, Kirchliche Dogmatik III. Studienausgabe (Zollikon: TVZ, 1993) 600-605.

[26] Barth, Fides quaerens intellectum 156.158.

[27] Barth, Fides quaerens intellectum 77.90f.98.102f.106f.

(= "Creed"). Consequently theology is a function of the church. Theology's task is to make this ecclesially sanctioned "Creed" understandable and in the process to harmonize the individual's "creed" with the "Creed". The "Creed" consists of three moments which relate to one another in a non-contradictory manner: 1. Christ, 2. scripture and 3. ecclesial proclamation including dogma. Dogma also takes on the character of something obligatory. The effort to believe on one's own alone is in Barth's system necessarily irrational. But once the believer finds him-/herself within the church, faith becomes rationally accountable. Faith becomes the medium of insight in a rationally and even scientifically responsible way. God is "veritas" and the "causa veritatis."[28] This shows that the believer is always able to give an account of his/her faith. This giving account of faith is at the same time also part of believing, a form of the "Creed's" self-execution.

On the other hand human beings remain, due to their contingency and constitution in original sin, unable to recognize God. Only God can enable a recognition of God. Faith is therefore wholly a divine product. The formulation "Deum veritatem esse credimus" in the *De Veritate* is for Barth decisive.[29] It is completely at the disposition of divine discretion whether and how God reveals himself.[30] In this matrix theology and "intellectus fidei" become synonymous. Eo ipso faith yearns to become transparent through the "intelligere." The "fides" is thereby presumed. "Fides explicates itself in the "intellectus fidei." Theology is in this framework never apologetics but a credal act of assent.[31] True faith is the explication in an evidential manner of the "veritas."[32] Faith "rests in God."[33] Reformation theology had from its very beginning emphasized the fiducial character of faith. As God is the cause for the "cogitatio," reason is a divine gift. Thus, contrary to what deism holds, God himself is the guarantor and the pledge of the world's coherence. In such a definition God is never subject to human manipulation.[34] God has to render himself objectifiable. This is the deeper reason for praying for the Holy Spirit.

By no means can Barth support the Schleiermacherian claim that the Creed depends on the creed. God is the foundation for any kind of creed.[35] Proclamation must be such that it makes God present through scripture. The Holy Spirit is then the point of convergence between Creed and proclamation. The creed is no simple achievement but grace through the Holy Spirit. To the outside beholder the fact of revelation remains incomprehensible. The "that" (=

[28] Barth, Fides quaerens intellectum 48.
[29] Barth, Fides quaerens intellectum 9; cf. P 1: 176,4.
[30] As Barth holds such an understanding of God and insight, how can he preserve human freedom?
[31] Barth, Fides quaerens intellectum 8f.
[32] Barth, Fides quaerens intellectum 9.
[33] This is an unambiguous dig against pietism and revivalist movements during the 19th century; also against August Tholuck (1799-1877).
[34] Barth, Fides quaerens intellectum 17f.
[35] Barth, Fides quaerens intellectum 19, footnote 18.

"daß") of revelation remains undeducible. The paradox of incarnation remains standing and cannot be demonstrated ad extra. In contrast, Hegel firmly held that the incarnation is logically deducible. Barth on the other hand insisted that the way from "above to below" is non-deducible from the world in itself.[36] Nevertheless, revelation´s content is positive.

All creaturely truth presumes a noetic foundation in God. From this it results that both theology and philosophy have their common feature in the fact that they cannot "prove" - meant in an Enlightenment sense - but only evidence something. Both presume a primordial openness towards the absolute truth. Barth modifies the ontological proof by having the "esse in re" precede the "esse in intellectu." As the mode of being is separate and independent from any kind of cognitional mode, God exists independently from his being thought.[37] Thus the "intelligere" becomes a mode of revelation. This presence of the Spirit is again present within the faith of authority. Through Christ God pleases to reveal himself completely. The "noesis" of finite human beings is marred through sin. There is an irreconcilable inadequacy inherent to human knowledge and cogitation. The capital Creed ("Credo") of the church should be acquired in the personal small creed ("credo").[38]

This concord between Creed and creed, as well as between the ontic and the noetic "ratio," is brought about by a divine spark. This circumstance vouches for the pre-givenness of religion´s object. God is not imperilled by a finite subjects´ projections. On these grounds, then, Barth must hold that ontic reason is already ordered towards noetic reason. In the event of grace both become congruous with one another "je und je."[39] Prayer is the access to the "ratio veritatis" which can facilitate such congruity; provided this pleases God.[40]

Only in the divine "descensus" is human ascent thinkable and possible.[41] The teaching on predestination constitutes the core of Barth´s theology. All of II/2 of the *Church Dogmatics* is dedicated to this crucial aspect of Reformation theology. In contrast to previous teachings, which subscribed to a loose form of predestination, Barth roots predestination in a christological foundation. From eternity the God-Son had been elected to guide the created world back to God the Father and to take on all sin. In Christ election turns into "double-predestination." As the first chosen one God will attract his divine Son as the elected one to him. At the same time he will reject all sinners and have his Son take on condemnation, death, and hell. The rejected will be released for the sake of his Son and will experience mercy. Through this notion of a definitive and general salvation of all of human kind, this volume concludes on a paschally triumphal

---

[36] Barth, Fides quaerens intellectum 21f.
[37] Barth, Fides quaerens intellectum 49ff.
[38] Barth, Fides quaerens intellectum 46ff, point 3.
[39] Barth, Fides quaerens intellectum 45.
[40] Does a predestinational particularism seem at this point not too distant?
[41] Balthasar, Karl Barth 161.

note. The incarnate Son of God becomes the "causa exemplaris" and the "causa finis" of all human creatures. In this sense, philosophy is reduced to but a subordinate and ancillary discipline at the service of theology. Theology´s relevant term for nature cannot be distilled from a philosophical consideration alone. Such a term can only be defined from grace. Nature as a part of the factual world order must be subtracted a posteriori. This does not mean that all of creation is deducible from revelation or grace. It does, however, imply that grace is ordered towards nature. As Balthasar observes:

> Insofern Gnade ergeht und die Natur ergreift, ist diese auch schon begnadete und somit übersetzte Natur. Natur existiert dann konkret jeweils im übersetzten, erhobenen "Modus" der Begnadung, das Subjekt aber, das in dieser Übersetzung sich befindet, ist kein anderes (non aliter) als das der Natur, auch wenn es darin anders (aliter) geworden ist. In diesem "aliter, non aliter" liegt das ontologische fundamentum in re der noetischen Analogie im Naturbegriff.[42]

In this predestinational framework Barth seems to subscribe to a certain kind of agnosticism. The chances of gaining insight apart from revelation and theology are very limited [43]

11.3.3 The Content of Barth´s Anselm-book

It is Barth´s thesis that on the whole Anselm´s proof of divine existence in chapters two through four of the *Proslogion* is thoroughly theological in nature. No matter how much the "philosophical genealogy" dates back to Augustine, Plotinus, and Plato, Barth can make out no valid argument for intrepreting the *Proslogion* as articulating a philosophical, let alone Platonic, concern.[44] This exclusively theological interpretation is not accidental to Barth. Barth had known quite well the Catholic scholar Adolf Dyroff. Already in 1928 Dyroff had published his Anselm interpretation. The core thesis of this publication was that the intellect cannot contribute to a greater certitude as regards matters of faith.[45] In this vein, it is Barth´s avowed intention to liberate his own *Church Dogmatics* and his book on Anselm from any final philosophical or anthropological explanation.[46] There is no final anthropo-logical or philosophical foundation for theology. As it was Heidegger´s plan to rid philosophy of

---

[42] Balthasar, Karl Barth 292.
[43] Engelbert Gutwenger, "Natur and Übernatur. Gedanken zu Balthasars Werk über die Barthsche Theologie," Zeitschrift für katholische Theologie 75 (1953): 82 -97, at 88.
[44] Barth, Fides quaerens intellectum 56f.
[45] Adolf Dyroff, Der ontologische Gottesbeweis des hl. Anselmus in der Scholastik (Münster: Aschendorff, 1928) 79-176. On pages 84f. Dyroff develops the same thesis on the *Proslogion* as Barth shall present three years later in greater detail. Cf. Söhngen, Die Einheit in der Theologie 7f, footnote 7.
[46] Eberhard Busch, Karl Barth´s Lebenslauf. Nach seinen Briefen und autobiographischen Texten. 5th ed. (Gütersloh: Gütersloher, 1993) 218f.

Christian remnants, Barth's intention was simultaneously diametrically the opposite.[47] Theology should never simply be ontology and Christian dogmatics should never simply be philosophical dogmatics - as Aristotle is not its ancestor.[48] As natural theology in Barth's sense is not the proper access to God's Word, it would just lead to a logical circle and to the gospel's becoming "bourgeois."[49] Philosophy may not become a final principle for catechizing, lest subjectivism rule.[50]

Little wonder then Barth contends that Anselm's argument is not an actual proof of God's existence.[51] It is not at all philosophical in nature but theological and based solely upon faith. In his view Anselm was a believing Christian monk. For him it was a matter of faith that God exists. Therefore it cannot be that Anselm set out to prove divine existence. Rather it was his design to demonstrate how such an affirmation is true.[52] All believers know God not to exist in an analogical manner to human existence.[53] Anselm illustrates in the *Proslogion* merely that God is unthinkable. The insight into the unthinkability of God is gained not by recourse to philosophical categories or lofty speculations in a religion-free space but by purely credal means. Only within the professing context of the believing church community does such an argument gain validity. According to Barth the term "quo maius" is a revealed term which demonstrates a two-fold insight:

1. the necessity of divine existence and
2. the need of the believer to obtain essential knowledge via faith.

Anselm's intention - thus Barth - is to render the proposition "God exists" not credible but intelligible.[54] The argument presented in the *Proslogion* does not want to deduce from the idea of God his actual existence, but rather it aims at understanding divine existence. God is not the product of a human effort nor let alone à la Feuerbach a human contrivance, but is granted to the believer as the eternal one in humble prayer. As it is a part of faith, this insight is a gratuitous gift.[55] When Anselm solemnly affirms that "Certe ipse idem insipiens, cum audit hoc ipsum quod dico, aliquid quo nihil maius cogitari potest, intelligit

---

[47] Martin Heidegger, Sein und Zeit. 7th ed. (Tübingen: M. Niemeyer, 1953) § 44, p. 229.

[48] Barth, Kirchliche Dogmatik II,1. Studienausgabe (Zollikon: TVZ, 1986/87/88) 657; Karl Barth, Kirchliche Dogmatik I/2. Studienausgabe (Zollikon: TVZ, 1989/93) 918.

[49] It is not sufficiently illumined by research in what ways then yet nascent National Socialism had influenced his methodological decisions.

[50] Barth, Kirchliche Dogmatik I/2, at 867. Barth, Kirchliche Dogmatik II 1 at 182.157.

[51] Cf. Wilhelm Anz, "Was bedeutet es, daß Karl Barth sich auf Anselms Proslogion beruft? Ein Versuch, Barth und Bultmann gleichzeitig zu lesen," Existenz und Sein. Walter Schmidthals ed. (Tübingen: Mohn, 1989): 1-13.

[52] Barth, Fides quaerens intellectum 63.

[53] Barth, Fides quaerens intellectum 102f.

[54] Barth, Fides quaerens intellectum 82.

[55] Barth, Fides quaerens intellectum 101. 198.

quod audit,"[56] Barth underlines the words "audit" and "dico" to emphasize that the rebus sic stantibus in this case is a biblical one. Human rationality is utterly unable to explicate itself. It is grounded in the supreme rationality and intelligibility of God. To give the Anselmian understanding of "ratio" structure, Barth argues for certain distinctions. There is a noetic reason which corresponds to the "esse in intellectu" and which forms the basis of knowing an object. This noetic reason is dependent on the ontic reason which corresponds to the "esse et intellectu et in re." Finally, the ontic reason depends on the "summa veritatis" as the "ratio" per se. This "summa veritatis" is the source of all knowledge and insight because it gives cause for things' existence. This secures in Barth's opinion the fact that human beings cannot independently arrive at a knowledge and understanding of God. Through all of the *Church Dogmatics* it will be Barth's primary concern to rebut any kind of natural theology. Scientific insight is gained when the "ratio" of the knowing subject (noetic reason) is totally conformed to the ontic "ratio." The noetic reason is defined as the intellect's ability to formulate terms and judgments. The ontic reason reflects on the ontic reasonableness of the ontic constitution of the world and of revelation. A direct relationship of the two Barth does not consider. Only via the "ratio veritatis" can a connection between the two be established. In the event of grace and faith the "ratio veritatis" must grant this on occasion ("je und je"). Every noetic effort, however, is subordinate to the ontic "ratio". Thinking and being acquire some semblance of identity in grace.

Anselm's intuition is derived from faith and communicated by preaching and is hence (altogether) unphilosophical in nature. As an exclusively theological argument, the *Proslogion* gives testimony to the intelligibility of faith. In addition, there is not the slightest indication of doubt on Anselm's part. Thus the concept "God" is not presented as an abstract human idea arrived at through reflection from a "tabula rasa."[57] Divine illumination yielded the term "maius." This established, Barth considers it absurd to call Anselm's proof henceforth "ontological." At this point he reveals his true opponents. The Anselm book should serve to undo the supposedly deleterious effects on humankind caused by an inaccurate appropriation of the *Proslogion* - their names are Descartes, Leibniz and Kant.[58]

It is interesting to trace the arguments Barth puts forth for a theological interpretation of the *Proslogion*. He cites Anselm's opening invocation, "Ergo, domine, qui das fidei intellectum, da mihi, ut, quantum scis expedire, intelligam, quia es sicut credimus, et hoc es quod credimus."[59]

This is not a scientific research report but the report of the experience of a prophetic illumination. It must be considered Barth's merit to point to the

---

[56] P 2: 101,7, not correctly quoted by Barth, Fides quaerens intellectum 117f.
[57] Barth, Fides quaerens intellectum 117.173f.
[58] Barth, Fides quaerens intellectum 198f.
[59] P 2: 101,3f.

monastic context in which the proof in the *Proslogion* had come about. The argument commences with a prayer and is (in its final analysis) an act of worship and adoration. It is also true that Anselm seeks to prove what he believes and insofar already knows. Also it is equally true that Anselm's faith would not depend on the outcome of this argument. Anselm knew on faith that God possesses being and a specific nature. Barth understands the subtitle "fides quaerens intellectum" to convey well the spirit of the deliberations: faith seeking understanding. To confirm this Anselm admits - and Barth quotes this passage to buttress his interpretation - :

> Non tento, Domine, penetrare altitudinem tuam, quia nullatenus comparo illi intellectum meum; sed desidero aliquatenus intelligere veritatem tuam, quam credit et amat cor meum. Neque enim quaero intelligere, ut credam, sed credo, ut intelligam. Nam et hoc credo: quia, "nisi credidero, non intelligam.[60]

From these words Barth concludes that the "intelligere kommt zustande durch Nachdenken des vorgesagten und vorbejahten Credo."[61] The "intelligere" becomes a part of faith's self-articulation. It is quite natural for Barth to conclude that Anselm pursues a theological agenda, as the passage cited immediately precedes the proof for God's existence. The argument must flow from faith. Faithful to this line of argumentation he then sets out to prove that Anselm's notion of God is derived from faith. Next Barth endeavors to clarify the ambiguous term "faith." Does faith exclude employing rational faculties? If such is the case, where is the limit? In addition, does faith have a meaning communicable to the outside or is it exclusively a lightning-like event one is forced to take at face value? In no uncertain words he insists that Anselm's proposition - "Et quidem credimus te esse aliquid, quo nihil maius cogitari possit" must be a "desideratum fidei." It must be an article of faith. Anselm appeals to Gaunilo's faith in order to convince him that the term "quo maius" is not at anybody's whimsical disposition.[62] It is the term gained from faith that Anselm then uses to prove divine existence and perfection. Barth stresses that Anselm had found this term only after resigning his own efforts. As a result Barth has two arguments for his theological reading of the *Proslogion*: the prayerful tenor of the text and the hermeneutical source of the term "quo maius."

The ecclesial foundation of Barth's theology is evident.[63] Christ's word must be legimately presented in certain human words.[64] The church's creed is a

---

[60] P 1: 100,15-19.
[61] Barth, Fides quaerens intellectum 20.
[62] Barth, Fides quaerens intellectum 80. Cf. P 2: 101,5.
[63] Barth's ecclesiology seems to be perhaps the most controversial aspect in all of his systematics. Cf. Wolfgang Greive, "Die Kirche als Ort der Wahrheit" - Das Verständnis der Kirche in der Theologie Karl Barths (Göttingen:Vandenhoeck & Ruprecht, 1991).
[64] Barth, Fides quaerens intellectum 21.

historic fact and refers to the fact of revelation. The "ratio" is contained within the credal assent.

> Darum, weil die Wahrheit über alle "ratio" verfügt und nicht umgekehrt, darum muß die Offenbarung zuerst und grundlegend im Modus der Autorität, des äußeren Textes, erfolgen: die "ratio veritatis" kann zunächst gar nichts anderes sein als eben Diktat.[65]

Faced with this "Diktat" there exists but one proper attitude, namely that of awe and humble obedience. This emphasis on authority and obedience corresponds to the laws of the believed object's "Sein und Sosein", i.e. of factual being and thus being. This manifests itself in the "ratio fidei." The programatics of the "fides quaerens intellectum" - as well as Anselm's *Proslogion*-argument - are biblical and ecclesial. The "fides" envelops the "intellectus" in such a manner that the "intellectus" must be termed "churched."[66]

The publication of this book was a sensation. Here, no longer did someone agree or disagree with Anselm's "ontological argument" on simple philosophical grounds. The proof's validity was not in the foreground of attention, but the question concerning theology's methodology and the relationship between faith and reason.

11.3.4 Immediate Reactions to the Anselm Book

In 1933 the renowned Anselm scholar and critical editor of Anselm's writings, Franciscus Salesius Schmitt, OSB, reacted to Barth's book with a book-review.[67] He identifies Barth's concern as showing Anselm to pursue a theological and not a philosophical agenda. But this is in Schmitt's judgment not a valid interpretation of Anselm's concern. He notes a "einseitige Ausdeutung der Texte." He criticizes Barth for investigating earlier writings from the perspective of later ones. Also he states Anselm's fiduciary estimation of natural reason. Schmitt stresses Anselm's use of the word "ratiocinando" already in the "Prooemium" to the *Proslogion*.[68] Against Barth, Schmitt holds that Anselm does claim to prove divine existence. Schmitt makes reference to the *Monologion's* title to chapter 1: "Quod sit quiddam optimum" as well as to the concluding remark: "est igitur unum aliquid summe bonum ...." To interpret "remoto Christo" in *Cur Deus Homo* to imply merely the suspension of christological dogmas is considered by Schmitt as problematic. It does not do justice to Anselm's overall strategy. The addressees of Anselm's writings are not restricted to Benedictine monks as Barth asserts[69] but include everyone. Anselm's intention is to convince Boso, who plays the role of an "infidel" and,

[65] Barth, Fides quaerens intellectum 45.
[66] Cf. Greive, Die Kirche 19ff.249-279.
[67] Schmitt, "Der ontologische Gottesbeweis Anselms."
[68] Schmitt, "Der ontologische Gottesbeweis Anselms" 219. P Prooem: 93,4.
[69] Barth, Fides quaerens intellectum 64.

therefore, has access to faith only from the "ratio." In Schmitt's opinion, faith serves not as the norma normans for everything but as the confirming vehicle of reason's results.[70]

In 1934 Etienne Gilson's reaction to Barth's book was published. Although he readily admits that the *Proslogion* begins with a prayer and thereby takes its point of departure from God's existence, it cannot be surmised that this proof is solely theological in nature.[71] Nowhere does one read in scripture "aliquid quo maius cogitari nequit" is a divine name. He notes that only in Anselm's answer to Gaunilo does one come across this term again. If Barth quotes Anselm in the *Liber Apologeticus* -

> tantum enim vim huius probationis in se continent significatio (d.h. eben der vorausgesetzte Name Gottes) ut hoc ipsum quod dicitur, eo ipso quod intelligitur vel cogitatur, et revera probatur existere et idipsum esse quidquid de divina substantia oportet credere -[72]

- then Gilson feels compelled to point out that exactly this text endeavors to prove God's existence: "probatur existere" and not merely "how" God exists.[73] In addition, nowhere in the text is there reference to "nomen Dei." The emphasis is hence not on "nomen" but on "cogitatio." Gilson speculates whether Barth had not been misled by Thomas' interpretation of Anselm's proof: "Sed intellecto quid significat hoc nomen (sic), Deus, statim habetur, quod Deus est."[74] Gilson contends that Anselm's approach is a very special case of "intellectus fidei." Thereby he remarkably refrains from calling it theological or philosophical, but holds that it is "purely rational" knowledge.[75] It is not theological because it owes nothing to scripture. Gilson points out that there barely existed a distinction between philosophy and theology at that phase of medieval history.

Gilson holds that to Anselm's mind the concept of God expresses an "essence" in the sense of a content of thought.

> Enfin, c'est elle (la notion fonadamentale de l'être-essence) qui inspire le célèbre argument du "Proslogion." Car Dieu est essentia; tout le problème se réduit donc à savoir si

---

[70] Schmitt does chide Anselm for permitting reason to fathom even mysteries such as Trinity and incarnation and thereby accuses him of rationalism. Schmitt, "Der ontologische Gottesbeweis" 221.

[71] "Car nul n'ignore que le 'Proslogion' part de la foi en l'existences de Dieu. La notion de Dieu dont il tire sa preuve lui est fournie par la foi. Que nous faut-il d'autre pour établir que nous sommes en pleine théologique?" in: Gilson, "Sens et nature" 19.

[72] Barth, Fides quaerens intellectum 76,

[73] Barth claimed generously that "probatio" means "intellectus fidei." Barth, Fides quarens intellectum 63.

[74] S. Th. I, q. 2, a. 1, ad 2. Cf. Gilson, "Sens et nature" 26.

[75] Gilson, "Sens et nature" 20f.45-48.

l'essentia, dont c'est la définition même d'être 'ce qui existe,' peut-être conçue comme n'existant pas.[76]

The French medievalist attributes to Anselm a kind of Platonic realism in the sense of "essences" or universals, a view which was also typical for Clement of Alexandria.[77]

11.3.5 Critique

There are primarily two lines of approach which allow Barth to reject any notions of the intellect's independent functions when gaining knowledge on matters divine.

Barth defines the "intelligere" as a via media between faith's two points, namely "notitia" and "assensus." The "intelligere" describes the road from revelation to assent.[78] Here one might ask whether this movement of the intellect does not describe a dialectical "Kreislauf des Bestimmens"[79] in the Hegelian understanding of dialectics. Neither in general for his dogmatics nor in particular concerning Anselm does Barth answer the question wherein the difference lies between a faith joined by theological (rational, i.e. scientifically verifiable) reflection and one that makes do without it. It sounds a bit artificial when the notion of a primary "notitia" is being postulated but the moment of intellectual understanding simultaneous with and within this "notitia" is being rejected by implication. In this sense "intelligere" is defined as affirming the necessity of credal statements and the rejection of the viability of their negation.[80] "Intelligere," therefore, can only mean supplying evidence for the system's immanent coherence of a sentence in the creed. The term serves to clarify the reciprocal relationships of sentences within the creed in the sense of a noetic rationality. Here one might want to interject that even a system of completely absurd claims can be immanently coherent. Credal claims must convince "ad extra." Is Barth making recourse to a doctrine of double truth in establishing a difference between the "ratio fidei" and the common noetic "ratio." There exists to his mind a profound distinction between a noetic-ontic and true "ratio." Barth cannot deduce these terms directly from Anselm. Nowhere does Anselm postulate a reason whose bearer is exclusively a believer. In order to convince the infidel, Anselm uses arguments understandable to both the believer and to the non-believer. The assumption of a double truth in Anselm's oeuvre would be a grave error. "Ratio" for Anselm means the natural

---

[76] Etienne Gilson, Le Thomisme, introduction a la philosophie de Saint Thomas d'Aquin. 5th ed. (Paris: Vrin, 1945) 77f.
[77] Gilson, "Sens et nature" 50f.
[78] Barth, Fides quaerens intellectum 24.
[79] Hans J. Oesterle, "Karl Barths These über den Gottesbeweis des Anselm von Canterbury," Neue Zeitschrift für systematische Theologie und Religionsphilosophie 23 (1981): 91-107, at 102.
[80] Barth, Fides quaerens intellectum 24.

gift of reason every human being by virtue of his human nature and by virtue of his faith holds title to.[81] The modes in which these are related in the order of salvation-history is Barth's central epistemological interest when reading Anselm.

Barth defines "id, quo maius cogitari nequit" as a prohibition by revelation to think something greater or beyond God.[82] Does Barth not countenance that Anselm agrees with his partner Gaunilo on a common philosophical denominator? Anselm wants to gain access to the "fool's" (= "insipiens") philosophical rationality. Anselm does not burden the "insipiens" with an intellectual salto mortale, nor does he want him to surrender his intellect. It is in this sense that every human being can be addressed with no restrictions: "Fateor, domine, et gratias ago, quia creasti in me hanc imaginem tuam, ut tui memor te cogitem, te amen."[83] Anselm presumes the "imago dei" quality to be a feature common to every human being. There is no doubt that Anselm stands firmly in the Platonic-Augustinian "anamnesis/memoria" tradition. Already simultaneously with creation humanity had been endowed with "memoria," This "memoria" establishes the basis for knowledge of God in spite of its "statu corruptionis":

Doce me quaerere te, et ostende te quaerenti; quia nec quaerere te possum nisi te doceas, nec invenire nisi te ostendas. Quaeram te desiderando, desiderem quaerendo. Inveniam amando, amem inveniendo.[84]

This is the hinge point for Anselm's interpretation and for an adequate appreciation of Anselm's thoughts. Barth is altogether unaware of the idea's historical context from within which Anselm develops his intellectual edifice. Neither an exclusively revelation-oriented intention nor a formal-logical approach may take control of Anselm's views. Anselm implicitly presumes a harmony and reciprocal indebtedness between both philosophy and theology in all of his writings. As a result, the question whether faith holds primacy vis-à-vis reason - as one is inclined to query as modernity's child, is incorrect. As demonstrated in the previous chapters, faith and reason are "by grace" intertwined in ways that one yields the other; i.e. the one provides access to and justifies the other. Much in the vein of the password "sola gratia," one does greater justice to Anselm - and indeed to Christianity - by stating a primacy of grace in contrast to the created order. Luckily, in his day the necessary terminologies to distinguish unambiguously between these two disciplines had not yet been developed. Such was Anselm's kairos. As the renowned Anselm scholar Richard Southern aptly observes, Anselm's ontological argument

---

[81] Cf. M 4: 17, 14; M 6: 19, 12f; M 8: 22, 32; M 15: 29,28; M 18: 33, 6; M 22: 39, 26.
[82] Barth, Fides quaerens intellectum 98.
[83] P 1: 100, 12f.
[84] P 1: 100, 8-11.

thrives by virtue of its ability to remain beyond any logical proof or disproof.[85] Does Barth fail to countenance that even a worldly "revelation" can supply the basis for a truth that is not of the world? The imperishable issue of contention ever since Reformation, namely of grace and nature in post-Reformation theology, hindered Barth and numerous other theologians in both camps in appreciating Anselm's true message. The perennial question of the "Analogia Entis" and Barth's still controverted view of it is perhaps the underlying issue in a more complete study of this pivotal matter.

In Barth's judgment it would have been impossible for Anselm to write a *Summa Theologica* or a *Summa Contra Gentiles*, for he was exclusively concerned with establishing the "how" and therein the credibility of faith. As Charlesworth rightly points out this is patently incorrect.[86] Anselm's writings combine philosophy and theology in one structure, in the mind's one movement. If Barth is simply negating the possibility of a rational approach to God, then he "makes Anselm into a fideist of a very rigorous kind."[87] The *Cur Deus Homo* serves to convince the unbeliever by "sola ratione" alone of the incarnation of God. Correctly, Charlesworth notes that if Anselm were of the fideist kind Gaunilo's argument would be out of context. Given his different understanding of grace, is Barth able to recognize the ramifications the "imago Dei" teaching has on the relationship of philosophy and theology (as also Anselm used)? Finally, Charlesworth asks us to consider the fact that Anselm's immediate disciples Rodulfus and Gilbert Crispin did not subscribe to "a fideist or neo-Barthian" approach.[88] In his *Disputatio Christiani cum Gentili de Fide Christi,* Gilbert Crispin replicates Anselm and wants to prove to an unbeliever by rational means alone the credibility of Christian faith. Scripture is explicitly disregarded in this discussion. The apologetics Barth seems to reject is vehemently applied in this case. Rodulfus in turn asserts that whoever lives a decent life according to reason may experience the "visio beatifica" one day.

To do justice to Barth one should add in passing that there is no evidence that Barth had been familiar with either Möhler's or Guardini's contributions to Anselm research. In addition the critical edition of Anselm's writings had only recently been completed. His knowledge of Grabmann's seminal book on medieval theology, *Die Geschichte der scholastischen Methode,* remained sketchy. Grabmann is mentioned only in passing in the first footnote of *Fides quaerens intellectum*, and there unkindly.

---

[85] Richard W. Southern, Saint Anselm and his Biographer. A Study of Monastic Life and Thought. 1059 - c. 1130 (Cambridge: Cambridge UP, 1963) 61.

[86] Charlesworth, St. Anselm's Proslogion 40-46, at 40f.

[87] Charlesworth, St. Anselm's Proslogion 41. As above suggested, one cannot accuse Barth of pursuing a purely fideist line of argument.

[88] Charlesworth, St. Anselm's Proslogion 44f.

Also some Protestant scholarship[89] thinks that Barth did not do justice to Anselm. Jossutis states unequivocally that Barth failed ("verfehlt") to grasp the Anselm's approach.[90] The same applies to Enslin. The term "id quo maius cogitari non potest" is a rational term and not one distilled from faith.[91] From that term Anselm derives the inevitability of gaining insight into divine being. Anselm does not separate natural and supernatural faith.

The tensions in Barth's scheme between faith and reason may, on the other hand, be interpreted as a subcutaneous dualism which neither Barth nor Anselm subscribed to, even if there is no gainsaying that it has a certain Augustinian and Aristotelian tradition behind it.[92] Nevertheless, Barth was able to set up for himself and many of his collegues[93] a corrective to a falsely perceived natural theology - which found it more difficult to set itself apart from ideologies. In the final analysis, Barth perhaps would not have a quarrel with a natural theology residing firmly in revealed theology. Jüngel correctly notes that Barth's Anselm study provided the grounds for a "complete reorientation of the previous direction of his thought," which was necessary for the structure of the subsequent *Church Dogmatics*.[94]

In express opposition to the modern philosophical and theological turn to the subject and to consciousness, Barth presupposes an ontic necessity and rationality which is ontologically prior to the corresponding noetic necessity

---

[89] One is able to cite only Edmund Schlink, "Anselm und Luther: Eine Studie über den Glaubens-begriff in Anselms Proslogion," World Lutheranism Today: A Tribute to Anders Nygren (Stockholm: Svenska Kyrkans Diakonistyrelses Bokförlag, 1950): 269-293, 269ff and Heinrich Ott, "Der Gedanke der Souveränität Gottes in der Theologie Karl Barths," Theologische Zeitschrift 12 (1956): 403-428, 414f as neutral.

[90] Manfred Josuttis, Die Gegenständlichkeit der Offenbarung. Karl Barths Anselm-Buch und die Denkform seiner Theologie (Bonn: Bouvier, 1965) 3.

[91] Enslin, "Der ontologische Gottesbeweis bei Anselm von Canterbury und bei Karl Barth" 176f.

[92] Thomas F. Torrance, The Ground and Grammar of Theology (Charlottesville VA: UP of Virginia, 1980) 81.

[93] Bonhoeffer held a course during the winter semester of 1932/33 on the topic "Jüngste Theologie." Within this course he defined Barth's theology by using three principles, as derived from the Anselm book;
   a) theology is thinking bound to the church as the place of revelation,
   b) theology is thinking bound to the church's creed, and
   c) theology presupposes Credo and credo (fides quae and fides qua).
Cf. Eberhard Bethge, Dietrich Bonhoeffer. Theologe - Christ - Zeitgenosse. Eine Biographie. 6th ed. (München: Kaiser) at 263.
   Particularly in a time of vehement anti-religious tendencies, an insistence on faith as enjoying primacy vis-à-vis reason and philosophy may serve as a valuable assistance in claiming independence from a totalitarian regime. A faith-oriented reading of the *Proslogion* could have encouraged Barth in signing the "Barmer Erklärung."

[94] Cf. Jeffrey C. Pugh, The Anselmic shift: christology and method in Karl Barth (New York: Lang, 1990) esp. at 153-167.

and rationality. Furthermore, he firmly anchors this ontological priority in a truth which is identical with God.[95]

Torrance holds that this view of Anselm allowed Barth to break free from the "psychologism and dualism of St. Augustine." Form and being combine to form a unity which is truly grounded in the self-revelation of God. Somewhat differently than Barth, Torrance's point of reference is not unequivocally the incarnation but more generally "self-revelation." Perhaps less sensitive to the cultural and philosophical context of Anselm's writings than Barth, Torrance believes Anselm to have reestablished this unity of form and being and to have thereby warded off Aristotelian and Augustinian influences at that early stage of the Middle Ages.[96] As an investigation into the book *Fides Quaerens Intellectum* demonstrates, Anselm is by no means an adiaphoron to Barth's theology but its center of gravity, the still point in the (Barth's) turning world. The fourteen points Barth formulated in his Anselm book represent his theological program. The Anselmian "intelligere" leads to the interior certitude of dogma.[97] Faith becomes from this central insight God's very own unfolding, or as Barth's expresses the subject matter, faith thinks itself.[98] From the insights he had gained into the nature of faith by way of his occupation with Anselm he was able to formulate the following prayer to the Holy Spirit:

> Herr, unser Gott! Wir treten vor dein Antlitz in Anbetung, vor deiner Majestät, in Erkenntnis unserer Unwürdigkeit, mit Dank, für alle deine guten Gaben, die du uns an Leib und Seele immer wieder zuwendest. Wir danken dir insbesondere für diesen Sonntag und Festtag, an dem wir dessen gedenken dürfen, daß dein lieber Sohn, unser Herr Jesus Christus, uns nach seinem Hingang zu dir nicht Waisen werden ließ, sondern uns im Heiligen Geist, dem Tröster und Lehrer, der uns lebendig macht, gegenwärtig sein und bleiben wollte, bis er selbst wiederkommt in seiner Herrlichkeit. Und nun hilf du, daß wir dich recht erkennen und recht preisen in dieser deiner Wohltat, daß dein Wort recht verkündigt und recht gehört werde an diesem Ort und überall, wo dein Volk dich anruft. Heilige und segne du auch die Feier des Abendmahls, die wir miteinander begehen wollen. Dein Licht leuchte uns! Dein Friede sei unter uns! Amen.[99]

---

[95] Eberhard Jüngel, Karl Barth, A Theological Legacy (London: SCM, 1982) 41f.

[96] Here one might add with Charlesworth: "If Barth's interpretation of St. Anselm's position on faith and reason is correct, St. Anselm must have been out of step with the whole Augustinian tradition of his own time; he must have been misunderstood and misrepresented by his contemporaries, including his own close disciples; and finally St. Anselm himself must have been unaware of the revolutionary character of his own views." Cf. Charlesworth, St. Anselm's Proslogion 45.

[97] Barth, Fides quaerens intellectum 35ff.

[98] Barth, Fides quaerens intellectum 38f.

[99] Karl Barth, Gebete. 4th ed. (München: Kaiser, 1974) 40.

CAPTER TWELVE
12.0 Hans Urs von Balthasar: Appropriating Anselm within the Context of the Programatics of a "Theological Aesthetics"

12.1 The Background

> Anselm's work has two sides: form (Gestalt) and contents, method and subject matter; and if both exist in tension with one another, too little attention is usually paid to their unity and their mutual interdependence.[1]

The above quote illustrates well Balthasar's attraction to Anselm. During his studies in Vienna he came to know Rudolf Allers.[2] Allers, a Jewish convert, had found in Catholicism a response to the Freudian approach to psychology, and the sense of l'ennui of modernity in general then prevalent in Vienna.

Balthasar also painfully experienced the *tristesse* of Freudian circles. "Mahler's torn pantheism touched me deeply, Nietzsche, Hofmannsthal, George entered my view." The mood of impending global doom of Karl Kraus, the manifest corruption of a culture in decline" [3] were characteristics of his days in the Austrian capital. This disorder must have disturbed young Balthasar even more since he came from Switzerland, a country known for its tidiness and order and untouched by the deleterious, dehumanizing and - for the loser - humiliating effects of World War I. However, on a deeper level Vienna - and later Berlin - sensitized him to the perilous state of modernity per se. Now consciously he was being drawn back to the organic and holistic view of the Romanticism of his youth and its appreciation of the organic whole and of the dimension of beauty. On the occasion of the conferral of the "Wolfgang Amadeus Mozart Preis," he related in his address his early exposure to the influences of Romanticism during his childhood. [4] His piano-instructor had

---

[1] Balthasar, The Glory of the Lord, Vol. II. 212.

[2] John O'Donnell, Hans Urs von Balthasar (Collegeville MI: Liturgical P, 1992) does not mention Allers and Balthasar's early formative experiences. At the expense of other influences on Balthasar, this book places too much emphasis on Ignatian spirituality. The varied influences Balthasar had been exposed to are Thomas, Goethe, Dante, John, Benedict, Plotinus, Anselm, Ignatius, Allers, Przywara, Adrienne von Speyr and Barth who are, very much like truth itself, symphonic. This means these influences are in Balthasar's judgment non-contradictory and contribute to the view of the one and whole form and mirror it; they all failiate the "Schau der Gestalt" - the beholding of the form.

[3] Hans Urs von Balthasar, Prüfet alles - das Gute behaltet (Ostfildern: Schwabenverlag, 1986) 8.

[4] Cf. Innsbruck Address I, held in 1987; Walter Kasper and Karl Lehmann, Hans Urs von Balthasar, Gestalt und Werk (Köln: Communio, 1989) 36.

been an elderly lady who in turn had been the pupil of Clara Wieck Schumann.[5] The "Mass in Es-major" by Schubert greatly impressed the five-year-old. Later, in the Benedictine monastery and boarding school at Engelberg he participated in orchestral Masses.[6] The Viennese days saw him consciously appreciate the organic unity that is Romanticism's hallmark, and inaugurated a lifelong quest for the organic "form" (Gestalt) of life.[7] Only in the theology of the Thomist Matthias Joseph Scheeben (1835-1888) does Balthasar detect theological aesthetics, albeit as one among other elements. [8]

Allers showed his friend an avenue for overcoming the fin de siècle melancholy. As a trained psychologist, Allers had developed a central and sweeping notion of "love of one's fellow human being as the objective medium of existence" and impressed on the young student "that in this turn from the ego to the reality - filled with the other, full Thou, lay philosophical truth and the psychotherapeutic method."[9]

In German Idealism the Being-question leads to the concept of the absolute spirit or of absolute self-presence. The intention of German Idealism "seemed to lie in a subjectivity positing itself absolutely, identifying itself with God, continually circling about and grounded only in itself."[10] The rejection of German Idealism's view of religion allowed Balthasar to reject very early on every attempt of systematization. Due to this critical position towards systemic adventures, the accusation of integralism does not hold in his case. In its extreme form Idealism obliterates the difference between subject and object. In contrast, by recourse to Anselm and Thomas, Allers proved to his friend that Being is dynamic, relational and love. The tension generated by the difference of object and subject abides and is indeed constitutive for a healthy human being. Human experience does not find illumination in an approach - such as Idealism - that ponders the subject's self. Rather, illumination occurs by experiencing the presence of the responsorial Thou. Finally, this in turn will disclose Being as trinitarian love, as the relational love of Father, Son and Holy

---

[5] Cf. Elio Gueriero, Hans Urs von Balthasar, Eine Monographie (Einsiedeln and Freiburg i. Br.: Johannes, 1993) 36, for this section at 30-40. The original Italian text had been somewhat modified in the German edition.

[6] Hans Urs von Balthasar, Unser Auftrag. Bericht und Entwurf (Einsiedeln: Johannes, 1985) 31.

[7] Balthasar is fully aware of the lack of distinction between nature and grace during the Romantic Era. His contention, however, is that by condemning Aloys Gügler, Neo-Thomistic theology also crushed the aesthetic dimension of theology. Cf. Balthasar, The Glory of the Lord. Vol. I at. 94-104. 173.

[8] Balthasar, The Glory of the Lord. Vol. I at 104-117.

[9] Hans Urs von Balthasar, Mein Werk. Durchblicke (Einsiedeln and Freiburg i. Br.: Johannes, 1990) 70.

[10] Medard Kehl, "Hans Urs von Balthasar: A Portrait," The von Balthasar Reader, ed. by Medard Kehl and Werner Löser , trans. by Robert J. Daly and Fred Lawrence (Edinburgh: T. And T. Clark, 1982): 9-21, at 12.

Spirit. "Time will find its fulfillment in eternity."[11] In the experience of Idealism's pathological consequences in the post World War I era lies the root of Balthasar's perceiving Being as something dynamic and dramatic. In the vicissitudes of history and of the Zeitgeist, the human being is not forsaken to experience exclusively the merely superficial, palpable and material. Even and especially there the relational context into which human existence is graciously - and as a consequence inextricably - given abides.

Many years later, in his contribution to the reference work *Mysterium Salutis* Balthasar again sums up his central insight of Being as love.[12] The encounter between Allers and Balthasar had evolved into a life-long friendship. In Vienna, Allers had aroused in Balthasar a nascent interest in theology. In the preface to his doctoral dissertation, *The History of the Eschatological Problem in Modern German Language* (1930), Balthasar expressed the conviction that his "beloved friend Rudolf Allers" had opened his eyes to the Johannine notion of love Allers himself had translated Thomas and Anselm. His single-volume translation of Anselm's opus was for many years the only usable German language edition available. In his book *Anselm von Canterbury - Leben, Lehre, Werke,* Allers unfolds Anselm's metaphysical assumptions and presents in the first section a "Prinzipienlehre" of Anselmic theology. This conveys a good picture of that era's spiritual background. He also brings to bear the question of realism, nominalism and neoplatonism. By way of a luminous exegesis of the term "rectitudo," Allers lets the architecture of Anselm's world view arise. In the second volume of *The Glory of the Lord,* Anselm's term "rectitudo" is seen again as the key to developing the specifically Anselmian understanding of freedom. Like Balthasar, Allers is not guided by a merely historical or philosophical concern, but by a sense of ministry marked by extraordinary intellectual rigor and fidelity to the object. Allers expresses the wish that secularized modernity may be given a fresh heart by considering the thought of Anselm as normative. Anticipating Balthasar, Allers does not call for a repristination of Anselm or of Scholasticism but for an actualization of both the teaching and life-context of Anselm.

Anselm's balanced view with its appreciation for the unity of faith contrasted favourably to the Vienna of the late twenties and left a lasting impression on Balthasar. An important foundation of Balthasarian theology was thus laid in Vienna.[13] It seems safe to assume that his exposure to Anselm by

---

[11] O'Donnell, Hans Urs von Balthasar 7.

[12] Hans Urs von Balthasar, "Mysterium Paschale," Mysterium Salutis, vol. 2, Die Heilsgeschichte vor Christus, eds. Johannes Feiner and Magnus Löhrer (Einsiedeln: Benzinger, 1962): 15-43; cf. Hans Urs von Balthasar, Glaubhaft ist nur die Liebe. 5th ed. (Einsiedeln: Johannes, 1985); Werner Löser S.J., "Unangefochtene Kirchlichkeit - universeller Horizont," Herder Korrespondenz (Okt. 1988) 477.

[13] His abiding fondness for Anselm is further evidenced by his publishing house's printing Anselmic literature in the series Christliche Meister.

way of Allers induced him to give attention to the rule of St. Benedict and thereby to obtain familiarity with the life-context of Anselm and his thoughts.[14]

The simultaneity of exposures to a dialogical philosophy of love as manifested in John, Scholasticism and the monastic theology of Anselm by the mediation of Allers cannot be estimated too highly. Together they were the foundational impulses Allers conveyed to Balthasar. He himself readily admits: "Whatever there may be of value in the following discussions had matured in this friendship period."[15] "Here something was begun, which only later would evolve to an `umfassende Sicht'" (i.e. comprehensive vision, perhaps in the sense of an aggregating and integral vision) "and would then allow to insert in a grand mosaic all stones in their proper place."[16]

In light of Allers' "personal ontology," charity alone is seen as "credible," for it alone is rationally reconstructable ("nachvollziehbar") and unexcellable in the sense of the Anselmian "id quo maius cogitari nequit." This also delineates a fundamental line of disagreement with the Thomist notion of Being. Being is not to be seen as static and perhaps exclusively exalted beyond any actual interaction with the created order. Rather, since Being is love, it possesses an inner, inherent and dramatic dynamics.[17] It enables Balthasar to glean new insights from the incarnation, which will unfold later on in Balthasar's theology. Since charity and Being are one, the whole of theology is apprehended under the category of the beautiful. It is then only one further step to beholding the "Gestalt" of theology and to pursuing a "holistic" and aesthetic theology. God's triune love as expressed in the form of Jesus Christ will then become the field of inquiry in *The Glory of the Lord*.

When the agenda for Balthasar's future theological project was laid in Vienna, Anselm played no small role therein. The conditions in Vienna forced upon Balthasar the need to raise the same kind of questions which had motivated Anselm and every occidental philosopher since Greek antiquity. Balthasar was confronted with the question of Being. The critical and inseparable nexus between philosophy and theology lies in the very nature of existence and is apparent in the writings of both Anselm and Balthasar. One can state that Anselm is responsible for the intuition of wholeness, the oneness of Being (though Plotinus, too, deserves credit in this regard), form and aesthetics, while Thomas conveyed the four properties of this one Being, i.e.

---

[14] Most certainly he had obtained some familiarity with Benedictine life-style already early on. He had attended the Benedictine boarding-school at Engelberg in Switzerland from 1917 until 1920. Guerriero, <u>Balthasar</u> 31f.

[15] David L. Shindler ed., <u>Hans Urs von Balthasar. His Life and Work</u> (San Francisco: Ignatius P, 1991) 167, footnote 93.

[16] Shindler, <u>His Life and Work</u> 34.

[17] Here one detects Balthasar's theological affinity with Pope John Paul II. Cf. Karol Wojtyla, <u>The Acting Person. Analecta Husserliana X</u>, Anna-Teresa Tymieniecka ed. (Dordrecht: Reidel, 1979). There action is taken as the key to entering the interior of personhood.

Being as a transcendental reality with the properties "unitas," "bonitas," "veritas" and "pulchritudo." *The Glory of the Lord* then unfolds the divine nature of this beauty. In the dramatic dynamics of charity, Christ reveals in the "Mysterium Paschale" the divine glory. In *Theodramatik* Balthasar thematizes Being's goodness, and in *Theologik* the truth of Being.

However, Balthasar's justification of the claim that Christ is the concrete universal was to become more sophisticated. Later, in the article "Anspruch auf Katholizität"[18], the process appears as one of elimination: of Buddhism, Platonism, Hegelianism and Judaic faith. Only in Christ do both the One and the concrete many (multifarious) retain their respective value and does suffering receive meaning. In Christ the meaning of Being is unveiled. Jesus as the catholic par excellence originates in the Trinity. Hence, as the most singular human being, Jesus reveals the universal meaning of Being.

12.2 Balthasar's Estimation of Anselm
12.2.1 The Consonance of the Benedictine Charism with Balthasar's Johannine Perspective

It is rightful first to give some attention to Balthasar's appreciation of monasticism in general. While not mentioning it explicitly, Balthasar does discuss the points which render Anselm and his theology so central to the Swiss theologian. Balthasar's reflections on monasticism show his conviction that "religious life is, by its taking seriously the command to let go of everything, a sacramental vow so to speak of the universal Church; without `sacramentum' there would not be the `res' of the Church."[19] To him the laity and the disciples describe two different movements within the one Church. While the churched laity consistently seek the Lord, the religious move, following the Lord's bidding faithful to the mission of Christ, into the world and return along with the lay people to the Father. He views the monk as living from the cross in the radical imitation of Christ. Thus one may state:

> Every genuine reform of the original spirit of the Gospel comes forth from the counsels of Christ. The `living out and for' ("Darlebung") of which, inspite of the manifold transformations religious life underwent through the ages, remains faithful to the same eternal and untouchable identity of the fundamental form ("Grundform") as the (complete) Church.[20]

The monastic life is then the guardian of the gospel's totality. The church's vitality will be always measured by the strength of her members' commitment to live the evangelical counsels. Because it undividedly gives

---

[18] Hans Urs von Balthasar, Pneuma und Institution. Skizzen zur Theologie V (Einsiedeln: Johannes, 1974) at 61-116.

[19] Hans Urs von Balthasar ed., Die grossen Ordensregeln. 2nd rev. ed. (Einsiedeln: Benzinger, 1962) at 20.

[20] Balthasar, Die grossen Ordensregeln 20.

testimony to "the love of the cross," "the estate of orders is also the refuge of all Christian beauty."[21]   "The nexus between baptism and vows, between the charism of the whole Church and monastic office, between pure obedience to the Gospel and obedience within the order was never interrupted."[22] Such is the case because religious life is nothing less than the faithful living out of the Gospel message. Rather than being elitist and isolated, the religious live under an ecclesial office and offer the fruits of this radical love to the universal Church. From the very beginning monastic life had understood itself as an ecclesial ministry and as a charismatic gift of the Holy Spirit to the individual who is called and to the Church Catholic.

In Balthasar's perspective the monastic charism possesses a gift sanctifying the whole church body. The monastic calling is an epistemological experience, the harvest of which is no longer at the disposition of individuals or the Church as a whole to accept or reject. The living of the evangelical counsels is a "conditio sine qua non" for the Church's self-definition. It is an indispensable, church-constituting component of the mystical body.

Only well after the publication of *The Glory of the Lord* did Balthasar publish his views on Benedict.[23]   The title already intimates the proximity in which the *Rule of St. Benedict* (RB) stands to the Apostle John and in turn how significant in the author's own estimation the Benedictine spirit is to him.[24]

In *Sponsa Verbi*, one chapter discusses the topic "Philosophy, Christianity and Monasticism."[25] It was published two years prior to *The Glory of the Lord*, Vol. II, in 1960. This section reflects both Balthasar's intimate acquaintance with the Fathers and his reading of Leclercq's book *L'Amour des Lettres et le Désir de Dieu* (1957). As the title suggests, the author considers the philosopher's life as a "religious ideal" aspired to by the Fathers, who provided a synthesis of philosophical and Christian "Theoria."[26]   To them Christian life was philosophy. John Chrysostom reserves particular praise for the "philosophy of the monks."[27] For Balthasar this also applies to the Middle Ages.   "Im monastischen Mittelalter wie im Altertum besagt also `Philosophie´ nicht primär eine Theorie im modernen Sinn oder eine Erkenntnistechnik, sondern eine dargelebte Weisheit, eine vernunftgemäße Lebensart."[28]   Anselm is understood accordingly: he is called to learn the philosophy of Saint Benedict.

[21] Balthasar, Die grossen Ordensregeln 23.
[22] Balthasar, Die grossen Ordensregeln 55.
[23] Balthasar, "Les thèmes johanniques dans la régle de S. Benoît et leur actualité," Collectio Cisterciana 37 (1975): 3-14.
[24] After leaving the Jesuit order, Balthasar renewed his vows in the Benedictine monastery Maria Laach. Cf. Peter Henrici, "Erster Blick auf Hans Urs von Balthasar." Hans Urs von Balthasar, Gestalt und Werk (Köln: Communio, 1989): 45-57, at 38.
[25] Balthasar, Sponsa Verbi 349-387.
[26] Balthasar, Sponsa Verbi 349.
[27] Balthasar, Sponsa Verbi 351.
[28] Balthasar, Sponsa Verbi 352.

To be a monk is to be a philosopher in the Medieval world. This entails the task "of pouring forth lovingly the light of divine philosophy."[29] Monastic philosophy was considered of vital importance for Christian society. The early Christian monks offered this newly appearing light as an aid to guide the people(s), because it was their philosophical conviction to do so.[30] Balthasar observes: "not at all did the monks want to be `contemplatives´ in opposition to `the practical Christians in the world´; they wanted to realize the purity of the original Christian synthesis and to present it anew to the eyes of the secularized Church."[31] Quoting Evagrius, Balthasar defines theology as penetrating the forms towards God. "The science of Christ does not need a dialectical soul but a diaretic ... soul."[32] To Balthasar the monastery possesses a greater visibility than the walls alone suggest. "The strict monastic enclosure, the solemnly vowed `stabilitas loci´ endows the commitment of the chosen to God with an earthly-sacramental form of irrevocable definitiveness."[33] It is a sacramental sign that exudes from the Johannine "remaining" (μενειν); it is a "source of a new culture."

At first sight the rule seems little influenced by Johannine theology. Only eight quotes from John´s gospel exist in the RB - and these all originate from the *Rule of the Master* (RM). The latter contains many Johannine citations not taken on by Benedict.

Yet, in Balthasar´s judgment marked internal similarities between the RB and John´s gospel exist. While the RM makes monastic life appear as an ascetical achievement, Benedict places the emphasis on participation in Christ´s life. Thus a "`renversement´ occurs in Benedict´s Rule: Theology, or yet better Christ, has the primacy; asceticism is secondary and serves him."[34] Benedict makes reference to all of salvation history and scripture. This in turn implies for Balthasar that Benedict incorporates Johannine theology. This point is buttressed by Benedict´s reference to Basil (cf. *Rule* 73,5), which suggests that Scripture itself is the living rule.[35]

Further, the text exudes a Johannine atmosphere when in chapter 64, RB refers to the love of the good shepherd. "Without explicit Johannine quotes, a Johannine atmosphere nevertheless permeates the whole of the rule, particularily towards the end."[36] The explicit mention of the living tradition in chapter 73, RB, which notes that "hanc minimam inchaotionis regulam" is "initium conversationis" is taken to confirm the Johannine hypothesis.

---

[29] "das Licht der göttlichen Philosophie liebend auszuströmen", Balthasar, Sponsa Verbi 354.
[30] Balthasar, Sponsa Verbi 360.
[31] Balthasar, Sponsa Verbi 361.
[32] Balthasar, Sponsa Verbi 381; cf. Evagrius, Centuriae Gnost. IV, 90.
[33] Balthasar, Sponsa Verbi 386.
[34] Balthasar, "Les thèmes johanniques" 5f.
[35] Balthasar, "Les thèmes johanniques" 4.
[36] Balthasar, "Les thèmes johanniques" 5.

"Whoever wishes to hurry ("festinare") from there on the path of the `holy fathers,' such will then have the whole Scripture as an inexhaustible rule. `Quae enim pagina aut quis sermo divina auctoritatis Veteris ac Novi Testamenti non est rectissima norma vitae humanae?'" (chapter 73,3, RB).[37] Balthasar sums up his appreciation: "Benedict adapts his rule to the spirit of Augustine and Basil and thereby includes the spirit of John. On the other hand he keeps the rule open to the whole Gospel as a rule of life and this entails openness to the mystery of Christ. And thus Benedict necessarily is confronted with the last and deepest interpretation of this mystery: with that of John."[38]

As a consequence, Balthasar very much appreciates Benedict's understanding of taciturnity, humility and obedience. All three virtues are understood in the Johannine manner as a participation in Christ's virtues of taciturnity, obedience and humility, rather than as ascetic achievements of the individual Christian. Christian obedience "is quite definitely not an ascetic trial of strength, but rather derives its vitality from Christ's example." Balthasar also sees here a notable parallel to the *Rule of Basil* (chapter 69): "Cum definitum sit, mensuram oboedientiae usque ad mortem esse." Christ dies obediently in spite of God's demanding "the impossible" of his Son. Only the example of Christ justifies this emulation for both Benedict and Balthasar in chapter 68: "si fratri impossibilia iniungantur." Certainly, if a brother presents his reasons to the abbot without a spirit of contradiction, he follows the example of Christ in the garden of Gethsemane. If, however, an abbot insists on upholding the instructions in spite of the monks' objections, "then the brother follows Christ on the cross."[39]

Therefore, the whole of the rule of Benedict is Johannine in its shape and spirit. Balthasar further establishes the spiritual affinity between the Johannine corpus and Benedict's *Rule* by taking up four themes central to both:

1. The Johannine "μενειν" is the "stabilitas Christi." "Christ represents the goal, he is the stable element, the `stabilitas.' In this faithful constancy through his vows the monk mirrors Christ's constancy, his decision arrived at once and for all."[40]

2. A further common element to both John and Benedict is in Balthasar's judgment concerning the struggle of light against darkness. The monk is constantly a participant in this struggle. He imperfectly images Christ, who is already always the light shining in darkness (Jn 1: 4f). Success in this struggle is no merit of the monk. Rather the Lord glorifies his own name. Particularly in the section on humility (chapter seven) this virtue receives a christological dimension. To be "like a worm and no human being, humanity's disgrace and

[37] Balthasar, "Les thèmes johanniques" 5.
[38] Balthasar, "Les thèmes johanniques" 5.
[39] Balthasar, "Les thèmes johanniques" 6.
[40] Balthasar, "Les thèmes johanniques" 5.

the people's scum (chapter 7, 52) ... can only possess a meaning in the becoming of like shape with the suffering Christ."[41]

3. In this line of thought the order the abbot gives the monk becomes a two-fold gift. It is a synthesis of authority and a proof of love. As a consequence, charity in the order of obedience is the monk's response. The christological dimensions of the relationship abbot - monk have their basis in John's Gospel. "Christ appears as both Master and disciple, for he is inseparably the nomothetic legislating logos and the humiliated servant. The foundational monastic relationship represents Christ in his `dramatic' existence and in his comprehensive, all-encompassing dimension: in his divine sovereignty and in his humiliation to the very last spot (sixth and seventh levels of humility). The one is not viable without the other. It is the honor ... of monasticism and the theology it lives to persevere and remain in this `dramatic', or better, `sacramental' representation of the person and of the work of Christ."[42] Balthasar considers this synthesis of authority, obedience and charity to be the "centerpiece of the Johannine testimony." It reappears uncurtailed and unabridged in both the *Rule of Benedict* and in the *Spiritual Exercises* of Ignatius.

4. Finally, both the Johannine corpus and RB breathe a genuine trinitarian theology. Christ is at the same time savior, judge and logos and the representative of his Father. In him the Father is concrete. Simultaneously, Jesus is the spirit-filled human-being; the presence of the pneuma in the world. Everyone sacrifices to God something out of one's own volition which goes beyond the bounds of obligation. Balthasar discovered theology to be wholly trinitarian for both John and Benedict. Benedict desists from describing paradise in order "to advance to that charity `quae perfecta foris mittit timorem' (1 Jn 4:18). Whatever the monk has thus far fearlessly done, he observes with no effort ... no longer out of fear of hell, but rather out of love for Christ (chapter 7, 68f)." This is a remarkable text since the rule stresses frequently the "timor domini." Balthasar observes here: "the `caro factum est' has fulfilled itself - let us express it technically: to the end of a realized eschatology".[43]

There is in RB a Johannine element most congenial to Balthasar: an inner dynamics towards Christ encompassing the whole of life. From this characteristic of the rule Anselm formed his monastic life. His works breathe the broad christological vision laid down by Benedict. To the mind of Balthasar the Johannine writings are the profoundest and most comprehensive verbalisation of the Christ mystery. Nowhere else does one find in Scripture that God is trinitarian love and that loving obedience is humanity's most fitting response.

If Balthasar goes to great length to demonstrate the Johannine character of RB, then this serves to elucidate that it belongs to the living pre-history of his

---

[41] Balthasar, "Les thèmes johanniques" 9.
[42] Balthasar, "Les thèmes johanniques" 10.
[43] Balthasar, "Les thèmes johanniques" 13.

own work. Later foundings of orders, such as that of Ignatius of Loyola, have not simply rendered superfluous the centrality of the Johannine message and Benedict's elaborations that freedom and authority jointly find a reconciled center in Christ's person and life. All major foundations relate - in spite of their varied and different charisms - to a "deep and essential communication."

> Through different members of the mystical body the same blood flows. Whether Benedict now translates the "staying" of Christ in the will of the Father as "stabilitas" or whether Ignatius understands it as 'homelessness' (Heimatlosigkeit) in the world and as "finding God in all things" ... always the same is envisioned:

to take one's bearings by the Gospel of John.[44]

Especially in his prayers one detects a strong affinity of Anselm to John. Not by mere coincidence does Balthasar quote from one of the proofs when closing his reflections on the archbishop of Canterbury:

> Johannes, certe vides, vides me. Ergo vide me Domine, vides me noscendo, vide me miserando. Vides et scis, vide ut sciam.[45]

In the relational and communal act of con-templation with the evangelist John and the saints Benedict, Anselm and Ignatius, Balthasar apprehends the "cantus firmus" of the Christian message. This con-templation is a meditation with the complete church, unrestricted by time and space, through participation in the concrete, present church's liturgical and sacramental life. The church is "the" enduring incarnate beauty. From this form of Christ, the Church, "the purest of springs flows."

12.2.2 The central Concern of *The Glory of the Lord*

Eugen Biser, a successor to Romano Guardini's chair - one specifically concerned with sensitizing the academy to the intrinsic unity of philosophy and theology - observed that with Balthasarian theology "the theology of our days has reached a universality rarely equalled since the times of the Fathers and the Scholastic luminaries."[46] This much admired universality is no accidental feature of Balthasar's reflections, but central to his understanding of Jesus as the Christ, as the concrete universal. In turn, this explains his concern to evidence the Christian as the irrecoverably and inexcellably greatest. However, as *Schleifung der Bastionen* (1952) proves, this does not lead him easily to ecclesial domestication. "To honor tradition does not absolve one from the duty to start ever anew; not at Augustine, not at Thomas or Newman but at Christ."

---

[44] Hans Urs von Balthasar, Göttliches und Menschliches im Räteleben (Einsiedeln: Johannes, 1963) at 404f.

[45] Balthasar, The Glory of the Lord. Vol. II 259; cf. O 12: 48, 106.

[46] Eugen Biser, Glaubensprognose: Orientierung in postsäkularistischer Zeit (Graz: Styria, 1991) at 524.

Tradition does not mean passing on finished results. This would just produce "Langeweile" (= boredom).[47] Little is to be found in "the mighty stone-quarries and shops of curios" of Counterreformation Neo-Scholasticism.[48] It tends to be a schoolbook-like, supernatural rationalism which sees authority as the source of a truth divorced from its sacramental roots. The created order is deprived of its expressivity. Faith is lacking a sensorium for glory. Such a view of faith does indeed culminate in Dostoyevsky's figure of the "Grand Inquisitor" in the novel *The Brothers Karamazov*, where a rigid hierarchy virtually substitutes its beliefs for that of the faithful.[49] Even in scripture Christ is portrayed in differing ways. Nor did the Church ever attempt a reduction to one unity, nor to an exhaustive systematization of faith.[50] Since scripture is also partly a product of human finitude and perspectivity, it is deliberately loose and perspectival.

Balthasar pleads for "a return of all truth to the una Catholica. The truth of Goethe, the truth of Nietzsche, the truth of Luther and of all who gathered one broken piece of an infinte mirror."[51] Here he gives free rein "to his powerless anger against the hollow authority of a traditionalism upholding tradition for its own sake." He reacts very much indeed like the prophet Jeremiah's hammer (Jer 23:29).[52] He struggles equally against the immobility of traditionalism, with its blindness towards spiritual needs and against "the unending discussions of intellectuals who have talked mystery into nothingness, in order to flog it to death." Both extremes are to him abstract ideologies, distant and removed from the concrete Christ of the New Testament and the Fathers. In the second millenium theologians from Scholasticism onward have systematized faith and given less attention to the centrality Christ plays in faith. For this reason Balthasar uses a pictorial-metaphorical language making do without a tightly fixed terminology in order to demarcate an aesthetic theology from a theoretic, conceptual theology, so that one can address not only human reason, but the complete human person. This is consonant with the narrative and perspectival style of scripture itself.

His "Leitmotiv" - to use a term from music - is God's descent, or to be more precise, the con-descent of God.[53] Pursuing an approach one can best describe as Chalcedonian christocentrism, he does not search for the essence in

---

[47] Hans Urs von Balthasar, Schleifung der Bastionen. Von der Kirche in dieser Zeit. 5th ed. (Einsiedeln: Johannes, 1989) 22f.

[48] Balthasar, Schleifung der Bastionen 37.

[49] Balthasar, The Glory of the Lord. Vol. I 569.

[50] Balthasar, The Glory of the Lord. Vol. I 520-604; Balthasar, The Glory of the Lord. Vol. VII. Theology: The New Covenant. (San Francisco: Ignatius, 1991) 153.

[51] "eine Scherbe des unendlichen Spiegels auflesen," Balthasar, The Glory of the Lord. Vol. VI I 69.

[52] Cf. Pöhlmann, Gottesdenker 232f.

[53] In German "Kondeszendenz" has no negative flavor to it and possesses the advantage of bearing out an economic, trinitarian dimension in the descent by having a relational "con" contained in the term.

the tangible, but for the form through which the essence is disclosed for all. This "modus operandi" retains the unity of the "inchaotio visionis" and "fides." The unity of vision and faith mirrors God's unity and His Word. It permits a vision of the "forma Christi." Therefore, unlike other ways of conducting theology, Balthasar does not investigate the condition for the possibility for humanity's understanding faith. He probes Christ's aptitude to impart His light onto contingent human beings.

To convey his own intentions, Balthasar places at the beginning of his second volume Bonaventure's thought:

> Qui tantis rerum creaturam splendoribus non illustratur caecus est; qui tantis clamoribus non evigilat surdus est; qui ex omnibus his effectibus Deum non laudat mutus est; qui ex tantis iudiciis primum principium non advertit stultus est.[54]

The Son is thus the original picture, the exemplary idea of all things outside God. Christ is unique ("einmalig") for he alone is the whole, the totality ("das Ganze") in the world. Bonaventure relates - as did the Greek fathers - creation with the inner-trinitarian begetting of the Son. As Balthasar bears out on various occasions, Jesus is at the very same time the most singular of human beings and therefore, he reveals in himself the universal meaning of Being.

Taking Anselm's "id quo maius cogitari non potest" as inspiration, revelation must in Balthasar's judgment confront the believer with something "vor etwas unübertreffbar Höchstes" (= unsurpassably greatest).[55] This is revealed on the cross (Jn 15:13; Eph 5:25). In Jesus Christ the incomprehensibility of God is not annulled but duly constituted on the cross.

> Liebe ... kein Begriff holt sie ein. Erst recht ist das Warum der absoltuen, göttlichen Liebe jedem Denken uneinholbar überlegen.[56]

He criticizes Christians for reducing God to comprehensibility. Joining Augustine and Anselm, he insists that one can only comprehend God in his incomprehensibility. Modifying Augustine's observation - "Si comprehendit, non est Deus" - Anselm states more precisely: "Comprehendit incomprehensibile esse."[57] In Balthasar's own words: "the key to Christian self-understanding ... lies only in the self-glorification of God's love." This is "the intention of my work *The Glory of the Lord* ... `aesthetics' in this work is a purely theological

[54] Balthasar, The Glory of the Lord. Vol. II 8.
[55] Hans Urs von Balthasar, Spiritus Creator. Skizzen zur Theologie III. 2nd ed. (Einsiedeln: Johannes, 1988) 322.
[56] Hans Urs von Balthasar, Klarstellungen. Zur Prüfung der Geister (Freiburg i. Br.: Herder, 1971) 30.
[57] M 64: 75,11.

enterprise, namely ... the receiving, the perception possible only in faith, of the glory of God's most free love as it reveals itself to us."[58]

In the personal Thou Jesus Christ identifies himself with humanity; he has irrevocably come "into the world" (Jn 1:14) and has thus endowed the world with expressivity.[59] This justifies considering Balthasar's principle of analogy. Only against the background of life-long occupation with this aspect of theology does one arrive at an appreciation of Balthasar's central concept of "form." This in turn provides access to the Anselmian definition of freedom.

12.2.3 The Concept of "Analogy" as the Common Ground for Balthasar and Anselm

The topos of analogy of being is a life-long constant in Balthasar's opus. It enters stage already in *Die Apokalypse der deutschen Seele*. In this regard Balthasar's debt to his Jesuit confrère and collaborator in "Stimmen der Zeit" (1935-38), Erich Przywara, and to the dialogue with Barth ensuing therefrom is well-known.[60] In the post-World War I atmosphere the appreciation for the organic was rather wide-spread. Przywara lauds Balthasar's dissertation, *A History of the Eschatological Problem in German Literature,* in his book *Analogia Entis.*[61] Already for Przywara analogy meant more than mere logical symmetry or congruity. It meant typifying a relationship of opposite tendencies and tensions by way of living figures of the past. The agenda for *Herrlichkeit* was thus prepared. Przywara further establishes analogy as a "basic rhythm and over-all structure" of creation and the key to the phenomenon of living tradition.

The "analogia entis" is discussed by Balthasar but not divorced from his other theological investigations. Nor did the discussions with Przywara find him unprepared. As *Die Apokalypse der deutschen Seele* (1937-39) attests, his affinity to an analogical approach had arisen from his occupation with German idealism. His Patristic studies on Origen (1936-38), Gregory of Nyssa (1939-42)

---

[58] Balthasar, Glaubhaft ist nur die Liebe 5f.

[59] At this point one might criticize Balthasar for not distinguishing sufficiently between the expressivity of incarnation and that of creation.

[60] Jean-Marie Faux observes: Przywara "was the first contemporary thinker who furnished Balthasar the tools of his reflection." Cf. Jean-Marie Faux, "Un Théologien: Hans Urs von Balthasar," Nouvelle Révue Théologique 10 (1972): 1009-1030, here 1014.

In these dicussions Gottlieb Söhngen played an important role. However, his contributions seem - i.e. there is no written evidence to suggest this - not to have influenced Balthasar to such an extent, and therefore, need not be treated extensively here: cf. Gottlieb Söhngen, "Analogia Entis in Analogia Fidei," Antwort. FS Karl Barth. Ernst Wulf, Christiane von Kirschbaum, Rudolf Frey eds. (Zollikon: TVZ, 1956): 266-271.

[61] Erich Przywara, Analogia Entis. Metaphysik. Ur-Struktur und All-Rhythmus (München: Pustet/Kössel, 1932) at 250. Balthasar highly valued this fresh approach to an old problem and printed in his publishing house a second edition of this work in 1962, including a new preface and epilogue.

and Maximus Confessor (1941) acquainted him with the intellectual milieu and spiritual climate in which the Christian concept of "analogia entis" had been prefigured and originated. He sees in the Patristic era something contrary to German idealism. The religious experience of antiquity is wed to Christian revelation. In idealism the Christian element was subsumed under an overarching secular, philosophical concern and thereby altered beyond recognition.

While Balthasar's fundamental theology is to gain contours through Przywara and Barth, his exposure to idealism predates his collaboration with his Jesuit confrère. His dialogue with Barth runs parallel with his Patristic studies. Thus it appears justified to brieflly outline, first idealism's position as regards this "Problemfeld" - as perceived by Balthasar -then to turn one's attention to the ecumenical discourse between Przywara, Barth and Balthasar, and finally to close the study on analogy of being by bringing to bear on it Balthasar's treatment of analogy in his studies on exemplifications of theological aesthetics.

12.2.3.1 German Idealism's Influence on Balthasar's Reception of the Analogy of Being

Balthasar rejects transcendental philosophy as a post-Christian ideology. For it claims that human beings develop dynamics inherent to the human condition to transcend themselves. The assertion of a radical human autonomy is merely one step away. Balthasar, nevertheless, does concede that idealism is religious. Sharpened and sensitized by Vienna and Allers, the question to his mind is whether one defines human greatness by an ability to continuously transcend the self by obeying an inner law or rather by seeking a glory ("Herrlichkeit" conveys something of the notion of "the glory of the lord" as "Herr" means "master" or "lord").[62] Such a question is cause for Fichte to postulate the radical unconcreteness (= "Ungegenständlichkeit") of God. Seized by an absolute vigor, the human being is carried off beyond the torpid concreteness of natural opposites. This vigor to overcome fatality and blind non-identity is sought in the self. The human spirit continuously transcends the object, which is the non-I.

In Balthasar's judgment the optimism of such an enlightenment leads invariably to panentheism: the absolute grows to the extent the human being remains faithful to her/himself. In this context, Balthasar is confronted with the question of the analogy of being as a relationship of correspondence between the finite human being and the absolute. How does the congruence - as analogy - between the human will and the summons issued by God (and thereby becoming immanent) become commensurate to both parties in their beings as the analogues in the one and same analogy? "In nuce" this is already asked in

---

[62] Cf. Hans Urs von Balthasar, Cordula oder der Ernstfall. 4th ed. (Einsiedeln: Jahannes, 1966).

Die Apokalypse der deutschen Seele. In *The Glory of the Lord* firmer lineaments are gained.[63]

Balthasar accuses Fichte's secularized mysticism of postulating "a reciprocal priority of the per se and relative absolute."[64] In the evolutionary process of human self-realization the absolute is co-generated. The absolute is absorbed into the vital dynamics of the human and immanent order. After closely examing Fichte's analogy of being, Balthasar rejects the enlightenment's concept of the self-developing "homo faber." Since the human being is created, there must be a creaturely obedience - as analogy - vis-à-vis the divine will.

Confronted with the accusation of being an atheist, Fichte had revised his philosophy along lines Balthasar will appropriate in his own approach many decades later. The mystical intertwinement of the unconcrete absolute and concrete, human dynamics towards the future are present in Fichte's integration of the Plotinian world-view and Johannine theology.

"Our constituting of absolute reason ... is the absolute constituting of reason." This line of Fichte is judged by Balthasar to be open to an apophatic theology in which our knowledge of the future is purified ("geläutert") through a humble and loving surrender. Here one sees the *point d'appui* of the rich bridal imageries Balthasar is to develop in his subsequent writings. Fichte's earlier notion of vigorous freedom is transformed by the philosopher into self-surrendering devotion ("Hingabe"). No longer does the human I grasp divine life; rather, divine life embraces the human I by entering the world and allowing the human to partake in it.

> The pathos of the free act - which for Fichte's point of departure is of paramount import - is in the end transformed into the quietude of a self-effacing doing, wasting ist freedom in charity.[65]

The human being comes into its own by living a mission.[66] The image of the sovereign God becomes apparent to the degree the human I has itself - with its finite being and tasks - incorporated into the diffusing divine love.

Surprisingly, Balthasar sees idealism's ethical climax in the person of Schelling.[67] Balthasar's aesthetic concerns are in no small way indebted to Schelling. Schelling attempts to make "the aesthetic indifference between the infinite and the finite" transparent towards God. The supra-concrete (supra in the sense of beyond) as God himself becomes visible in the human being made transparent towards him.[68]

---

[63] Cf. esp. Balthasar, The Glory of the Lord. Vol. I 467-480.
[64] Hans Urs von Balthasar, Die Apokalypse der deutschen Seele. Prometheus. Studien zu einer Lehre der letzten Haltungen (Salzburg: Pustet, 1937/38) at 176.
[65] Balthasar, Die Apokalypse der deutschen Seele 200.
[66] Balthasar, Die Apokalypse der deutschen Seele 316-346.
[67] Balthasar, Die Apokalypse der deutschen Seele 205.
[68] Balthasar, The Glory of the Lord. Vol. V 567.

In the early Schelling, transcendentality is paralleled by the self-unfolding and self-developing God. God attains his all-encompassing identity through living beings as a visible and palpable entity in the created order. The essence of God requires the outer essences. Here God is not - as in Fichte's system - an elongation of the act-constituting I. Rather, God is the living unity of divine self-affirmation and the affirmed objective being (= here used as a noun). The finite affirmation is nothing less than a gradual expressivity of the divine. In this expressing process God evolves from the eternal ideal to his absoluteness.[69] In an "intellectual vision - a form of the analogy of being - the human being is transported beyond the self. In this act God grows to an immanent absoluteness, the human, created being an "indifferentia" echoing the notion of "Gelassenheit."

In Schelling's call for indifference Balthasar detects a genuine concern for a religious, ontic congruence with Being. This is the "analogia entis." Nevertheless, he objects to Schelling's evaporation of the individual, finite person into the all-effecting, "immanentizing" absolute. Schelling's view is fettered by "an aesthetic theology" never capable of moving onward towards a "theological aesthetics" equipped to thematize from a human and transparent position the glory of God in history.

The late Schelling assigns greater value to the individual. The individual who lost God now finds God present. Thereby an analogy is possible, albeit an unchristian one. "In him is the deepest abyss and the highest heaven, or both in the center."[70] Sin is to produce light. The "analogia entis" is maintained here. However, in the sinful self-withdrawal the triumph of reason's ecstasis occurs. Necessarily sin and a rejection of the good must occur so that in ecstasis the restoration of a state of congruence as analogy can come about. Here the birth of a melancholic fatedness characteristic behind the façade of the outgoing Victorian era and of the twentieth century occurs.

Due to the need for ecstatic redemption, Schelling's thought is permeated by an indelible ("unaufhebbar") melancholy. Schelling is in Balthasar's judgment the key-figure to comprehending the tragic fundamental cloud over modern philosophical and theological thought. This is the key to understanding Kierkegaard, Heidegger, Rilke, the dialectical theology of the early Barth, but also the strong, naively strong reaction to follow in the second half of the twentieth century. This tragic sense of being in the world - requiring evil for an ecstatic salvation to occur - has a precursor in the melancholy of gnostic antiquity. "This is the (cause) for the mournfulness afflicting all finitude ... the veil of dejection spread over all of nature, the deep, indelible melancholy of all life."[71]

---

[69] Cf. Balthasar, Die Apokalypse der deutschen Seele 223.
[70] Balthasar, Die Apokalypse der deutschen Seele 242.
[71] Balthasar, Die Apokalypse der deutschen Seele 249.

12.2.3.2 Przywara and the "Analogia Entis"

Amid this intellectual distress - multiplied by the effects of war - a fresh appreciation for - "one concrete order of salvation" in an organic perspective was the obvious "locus" for analogy in the 1920's and 1930's. The principal question then was how to maintain God's transcendence in the face of idealism and rationalism and, yet, how not to allow this world of suffering to be foresaken and forlorn without God. Analogy seemed to allow for transcendence in immanence. How can nature relate to supernature while remaining wholly a created nature? In marked demarcation and contrast to Baius, but consonant with the Fathers, Balthasar defines nature as the created within the order of salvation.[72]

The principal issue is whether biblical revelation and Christ can be received as revealed. Can the incarnation truly have occurred? Can Jesus Christ be, if not the central, some part of history at all? One step further, how can the church claim that humanity is capable of divinisation? This would be questioning the possibility of the Chalcedonian formula. Is Jesus the Christ? Drawing on Przywara and his discussions in this regard with Barth, Balthasar sees the tenets of Christian faith to be viable only insofar as one accepts the notion of analogy. This term is the essential key to an appreciation of Balthasar's program of a theological phenomenology - or as he is later to state it as the theme for *The Glory of the Lord* - an "aesthetic theology." Only thereby is a correlation possible between the concrete order and revelation.

The concept of analogy is utilized in Wis 13:5 to define a way of knowledge through perceiving the grandeur and beauty of creatures. Rom 12:6 employs it as the congruence between prophetic speech and faith. Biblical speech in general sees a way from creation to God's rule. Jesus' parables are understood in this sense. In Jn 14:9 Jesus makes visible in his person the reality of God. Rom 1:18ff assumes that one can deduce something of the divine nature from God's creation. Pseudo-Dionysius observed that, "as regards divine matters, negations are true (and) affirmations insufficient."[73] It is in this intellectual milieu that Anselm takes analogy for granted and can formulate the "id quo maius cogitari nequit potest" and postulates God as greater than anything that can be thought. God can become human and suffer death on the cross because he is love.[74] As Thomas is later to state succinctly: "because he is good, he communicates goodness to things."[75] Divine love, freely revealed, enables analogy as analogy to arrive from created matters at the incomparable and absolutely transcendent God. These considerations contribute to forming Balthasar's position.

---

[72] See Balthasar, <u>Karl Barth, Darstellung und Deutung seiner Theologie</u>.

[73] Ps-Dionysius, <u>De coel.hier.</u> 2,3.

[74] Balthasar, <u>The Glory of the Lord</u>. Vol. II 217f.

[75] S. Th. I 13,2.

To ward off any kind of Protestant critique - especially Barth's shrill accusation that the "analogia entis" is "the invention of the Anti-Christ" - both Przywara and later Balthasar stress that God is, in "the final analogy," "semper maior" or as the Fourth Lateran Council in 1215 solemnly decreed: "quia inter creatorem et creaturam non potest tanta similitudo notari, quin inter eos maior sit dissimilitudo notanda."[76] While the human mind can observe a similarity between God and creation, it must recognize "an even greater" mystery of the Divine. Yet, such dissimilitude requires that a prior positive analogy exists.

Reformation theology is the basis for Barth's rejection of the "analogia entis" as he understood it. Luther had stressed a "theologia crucis." In this teaching, Christ "sub contrario" has to suffer death. Luther emphasized that death is altogether alien to God. Protestant theology concludes therefore that analogy is an impossible mission, for it admits something less than divine in God. Söhngen, Przywara and Balthasar went to great extents to demonstrate that the analogy from creation to creator does not violate the "theologia crucis." The concept of analogy need not convey that the notion of God is at the disposition of human thought. It only names the reason for a relative comprehensibility of divine matters; as a creature man is seized by God and knows of his being seized.

This allows for a degree of systematization which, however, will always grant priority to the suprarational, unsystematic and dramatic when confronted with the immediate revelation of truth itself. Przywara already had detected an ontological dynamism which lives in the tension of "noesis" and "noema." Thus to him thought and prayer are intimately connected.[77] The world is thus open to the totality of reality.[78] For this reason Balthasar goes to great lengths to overcome the "diastasis" of theology as a science on the one hand and prayer on the other.[79] One senses a great similarity between Balthasar and Anselm at this point. What is unspoken, but implied through Christian and more specifically monastic existence and forms the basis for the Anselmian philosophy, comes to the fore in many bifurcations in Balthsar's writings. Both de Schrijver and Schmid demonstrate the central role the "analogia entis" plays in Balthasar's oeuvre.[80] God's glory is in the world, is a "new Light from God known visibly in the incarnate Word which cannot be equated with other kinds of aesthetic

---

[76] DH 806.

[77] Note the same distinction in Barth's treatment of Anselm: Anselm links prayer and reflection.

[78] Balthasar, The Glory of the Lord. Vol. V 141-147.

[79] Cf. Hans Urs von Balthasar, Einfaltungen. Auf Wegen christlicher Einigung (München: Kösel, 1963) 36ff.

[80] Georges de Schrijver, Le merveilleux Accord de l'Homme et de Dieu: étude de l'analogie de l'être chez Hans Urs von Balthasar (Leuven: Leuven UP, 1983); Johannes Schmid, Im Ausstrahl der Schönheit Gottes (Münsterschwarzach: Vier Türme, 1982): 167-174.

radiances." Such a mysterious splendor "is not beyond any and every comparison."

The "analogia entis" certainly does not allow a complete knowledge, for a creaturely metaphysics[81] which is free from the rules of dialectics is nevertheless bound to the principle of non-contradiction. The analogy is finally perceived as a dramatic movement, "a tending towards" and "a balance of tensions."[82] To Przywara as to scholastic thought, analogy has two properties: creaturely concreteness and intelligibility. The "rationes necessariae" must be understood in this sense. Analogy entails necessity on the part of the contingent order. In the inner-creaturely analogy, the analogy between creature and creator is perceived.[83]

There is both the "analogia attributionis," which as creaturely analogy is an ascending movement of the human mind, and the "analogia proportionalitatis," which is an analogy from above. This latter analogy is impelled towards a positive unity.[84] Thus there is dynamism to life and to human thought which encompasses the horizon of mystery. It is the living "All-Rhythmus"[85] and not only one principle among several other principles. It is interwoven with the human state to such a degree that one cannot ponder human categoriality without it.

This analogy is intensified as "primordial structure" ("Urstruktur") in the living church of Christ. It is focused in a poetically concentrated ("verdichtet") form in the clerical and lay styles, Balthasar draws on a theological aesthetics to illustrate his understanding.[86] In such a structure the human being is "tending" towards and "deriving" from God. This living and dynamic relationship means a dynamic balance of tensions. This in turn produces a serenity which cannot be confused with passivity or with a surrender to fate. It gives way to the attitude of equanimity, in the present author's judgment.

No amount of intellectual prowess can do without the cognizance of creatureliness and creation's constant referral beyond itself. Failure to recognize the ontic facticity of analogy will give rise to difficulties in extricating oneself from the extremes of univocity or equivocity, of identity or radical rupture. Either the kingdom of God collapses into the immanent realm or one subscribes to deism and even holds revelation utterly impossible.[87] For this reason

---

[81] Thus Przywara, Analogia Entis 99-141.

[82] At this point it would be helpful to investigate what connections exist between Przywara and Gabriel Marcel.

[83] Przywara, Analogia Entis 121-124.

[84] Przywara, Analogia Entis 135-139.

[85] The German term "das All" contains the word "alles," meaning in English "all," as an exhaustive summation of all things. The noun "das All" refers to the "cosmos." Hence, Przywara is able to address simultaneously the individual members of the cosmos and the organic whole of the same.

[86] Balthasar, The Glory of the Lord. Vols. I and III.

[87] Balthasar, Karl Barth 210.

Balthasar feels compelled to criticize the early Barth and welcomes his later "turn to analogy" of faith, at least.

Besides the feature of a "living" and balanced "structure," Przywara holds that "the one, concrete order" is an additional prerequisite for analogy. Given his rather foundational exposure to Plotinus in Vienna, Balthasar finds this congenial to his own inclinations and temper. Both Balthasar and Przywara see revelation as part of a contingent, creaturely reflection. Only this third (after creator and creature), last and common prerequisite for the "analogia entis" makes their writings understandable. Ultimately the concept of pure nature would be a contradiction in terms, for it would deprive creation of its analogical nature. Since the theologian is already in the concrete and one order revealed by Christ, he/she cannot but reflect upon the tension - and therefore related unrelatedness - between creator and creature and therefore secondarily between creature and creator.

12.2.3.3 "Semper Maior" and the Barth-Balthasar Exchange

For these reasons, Balthasar argues that Barth's understanding of a dialectical theology must be situated within the overarching theme of analogy.[88] While Barth called the "analogia entis" the single most important reason for not becoming Catholic, Przywara retorted that to develop a dialectical theology is nothing short of leaping over the bridge between creator and creature. Every comparison or opposition presupposes in Balthasar's view a relationship and, therefore, an analogy. One does violence unto the created order unless one affirms analogy unwittingly and/or implicitly.[89] Sin disrupts the "analogia cogitationis" (= the order of consciousness) but not the "analogia entis." In spite of all sin the creatureliness of humanity and, therefore, the "analogia entis" remain realities.[90] Since Barth strives to avoid both identity and contradiction, his mature dialectical theology is analogical.[91]

To Balthasar's mind Barth is primarily arguing against the abuses of analogical thought in theology and attempts to ensure that God cannot appear subject to manipulation by human beings. In the act of creation, however, the human being neither is "a second God" nor a mere nothing. It is, therefore, incumbant upon the created mind to think by way of analogy, lest it de facto negate its createdness.

Balthasar thus makes concessions to Barth as regards the nineteenth century Catholic notion of "natura pura." This is viewed as incorrect. Barth's insistence on a christological reconsideration ("Rückbesinnung") is considered

---

[88] Balthasar, Karl Barth 44ff. 107ff. The sections on analogy had been submitted to Przywara prior to publication. Cf. Guerriero, Hans Urs von Balthasar 108ff.

[89] Guerriero, Hans Urs von Balthasar 196ff.

[90] Guerriero, Hans Urs von Balthasar 208.

[91] Guerriero, Hans Urs von Balthasar 211.

of vital import also for Catholic theology.[92] The rekindling of analogy as a question has Balthasar realize that the creature is nothing outside its relationship to God. In the factual order of Adam's creation God freely and gratuitously reveals creation as creation. Nevertheless, such knowledge can be gleaned only in an analogous manner. The arrival at a theological analogy can only be perceived as an elaborating moment of the a priori of factual analogy.[93]

In this context the question arises: of what constitution must nature be to justify analogy? Balthasar neither shares the Reformation's negative view of nature (as that is commonly understood in Roman Catholicism) nor does he reduce theology and philosophy to a fideistic unity. He returns to the Chalcedonian notion of "physis" as an analogous concept. Only thereby are theology and philosophy held in distinction and precisely for that reason in interdependent relationship to one another. This alone avoids gnosis. Otherwise theology would no longer be the scientific knowledge and revelation of matters divine and possess relevance.

Since revelation has occurred within the world, theology must be open to the task of a phenomenology of the created order. It is the analogical nature of existence that defies a rationalistic systematization. Under the consideration of the "Deus semper maior" - upon which Barth with much verve insisted - and the analogical nature of the human condition, only "approximations" are legitimate. The difference between but also relatedness of philosophy and theology to one another perdure in a tension of unity. Anselm's "fides quaerens intellectum" does not allow discoveries in the sense of a total, exhaustive metaphysics. Within the experience of unity a yet greater unity is discovered. One may be a part of that greater unity in a way that neither grants an understanding of neither that greater unity nor of the mode of one's participation therein.

Were one to reject Anselm's programmatic "fides quaerens intellectum," then invariably the constitutive difference between nature and grace would be dissolved into mere necessity. The consequence would be the lack of a personal relationship and life would be deprived of its magic/surprise. The "analogia entis" is the admission of creatureliness as creatureliness without resigning oneself to agnosticism.[94]

---

[92] Guerriero, Hans Urs von Balthasar 335-372.
[93] Guerriero, Hans Urs von Balthasar 176f.
[94] Guerriero, Hans Urs von Balthasar 452. If Puntel argues against this by believing the logical principle of analogy does not do justice to the moment of historicity into which every thought is unquestionably given, one to has bear in mind that for Balthasar - as for all of Christianity - salvation, as the climax of an analogically unfolding process is "the" event par excellence within the categories of time and space. The difference between the known and the unknown remains by virtue of human contingence. Analogy is always more than historic givenness. It relates the similarity and dissimilarity of Being and being - thereby frequently bridging time differences. Cf. Laurencino Bruno Puntel, Analogie und Geschichtlichkeit (Freiburg i. Br.: Herder, 1969) 533-557.

Balthasar's unequivocal and yet differentiated stand on analogy rests on three assertions:

1) the unity of the created order,

2) the rejection of positivism and rationalism and

3) the living, responsorial dynamics of creator towards creature - and, therefore, also vice-versa.

These three elements summarize well his life-long concern for the problem of analogy. One also detects these three moments subcutaneously present in Anselm's writings.

Against this background Balthasar senses the need for "a phenomenology of the tradition" or as he is later to express it "an aesthetic theology." The task would be to convey intimations of the "Vollgestalt" that is revelation. Via the question of analogy and in critical distance to nineteenth-century neo-scholasticism, Balthasar introduces an indispensable corrective to an age of unparalleled scientific achievement. Understanding is not the "norma normans" of faith, but faith is the active component seeking understanding. Faith is returned to its rightful theological position as the epistemological subject.

Przywara's and to a lesser extent Balthasar's reflections on analogy succeed in maintaining the mystery of God (Barth's concern) by asserting that analogy stipulates a similarity within a yet greater dissimilarity and the critical correlation of the principle of analogy with a christocentric, i.e. incarnational corrective. The analogy here delineated is one of "con-geniality" and reciprocal congruence. More exactly, Balthasar discusses the "analogia proportionalis" in which two similar/dissimilar entities are related to one another due to their corresponding, respective harmonies. Only this enables an ontic participation granted by the creator. Finite being may in its finite acting be "God's living analogues, i.e. correspondent." As God is harmonious in himself and his actions, humanity can be harmonious in itself and in its actions and live in objective harmony before God "provided God allows the being to participate in proportionality to his (the being's) creaturely, by God constituted essence."[95] Anselm calls this harmony ("Stimmigkeit" for Balthasar) "rectitudo." It comes about within the Church and there most precisely within the confines of a monastery. In prayer, contemplative and sacramental life the monk becomes aware of it, and strives to realize it to the utmost.

Partly through his study of the fathers, Balthasar avoids the "analogia attributionis" found, for example, in Suarez and Duns Scotus. This kind of analogy is only terminological in nature. Divorced from its religious origins, such a purely abstract analogy of being invariably was fated to be reduced by secularisation to a logical exercise in dialectics involving similarities and dissimilarities (idealism, dialectic theology). Balthasar - more clearly than Przywara - avoids this peril and places analogy within the whole human

---

[95] de Schrijver, Le merveilleux accord 252.

disposition to life and to one's creator. One serves with one's "whole heart" the "God Who becomes immanent." Thus "the glory of the Lord" is poured into the created soul. This is the crowning of the human quest which asks, "How can I serve my God?" All mysteries address this question. In this openness for a response the human being allows God to grant him or her a mission - to correspond in this measure to His glory. The existential paradigm is Jesus Christ - who in his divine-human congruence ("rectitudo" as obeying and revealing the Father) gives sublime expression as the fully human and fully divine to the "analogia entis'" viability. Ignatius of Loyola and other mystics bear testimony to this.

Balthasar propounds a mystical analogy of being. This understanding goes back to Vienna and Rudolf Allers. It is confirmed and more deeply elaborated by Balthasar through an appropriation of Patristic theology. Barth's exposure to analogy had not fully encompassed the Patristic vision. Therefore, and owing to his Reformed confession, he largely argued against the (logical-conceptual) "analogia entis" without realizing the dimension of Christian interiority involved. In contrast, Balthasar's understanding of analogy is evidenced as dramatic and being-transforming. It is rooted primarily in the event of the incarnation of the divine Logos. It is both real and logical, i.e. rationally understandable and re-constructable, as well as christocentric.

The analogy of being is developed by Medieval philosophy from Christianity's belief in the image-of-God quality of human existence which is grounded in creation by God. As it is biblical, it applies to all of humanity. Tragically, due to its reduction to a mere tool for philosophical discourse, it lost its inner glow. It was no longer suitable for the concrete discipleship of Christ. In comparison, Balthasar's view of analogy, aptly described by de Schrijver's dissertation-title as "Le merveilleux Accord de l'Homme et de Dieu," breathes the freshness of early Christendom. It is one of a lesser or higher conformity with the will of God, a potential always divinely given as a gift insofar as someone is human. The primary focus is the actualization of analogy in sacramental life. This is also Anselm's understanding: the church is the "locus salutis hominum," for it enables "rectitudo."

In response to some objections raised at a conference during his visit to the United States, Balthasar responded:

My "method," in contrast to that of the Protestants, is neither dialectic, as Luther's necessarily was, nor is it Hegel's identity developed from dialectics. It is something in between: analogy. Man is essentially "God's image." Therefore he can by his own power raise his thoughts to the archetype (ton ano logon), but can approximate it only from a great distance (ana ton logon). The various biblical theologies about Christ are merely circling his unattainable image (ana ton an Christon).[96]

---

[96] Balthasar, "A response to my critics," Communio 5 (1978): 69-76, at 71.

12.3 Considerations on the Balthasarian Category of "Form"

On a broad theological and literary canvas the author discusses in seven volumes "the form of the Lord Christ." This form is important. As the New Testament attests, Jesus Christ is God's icon (Phil 2:6; Rom 8:25). This aesthetic category is presented in Volume II of *The Glory of the Lord (Studies in Theological Style: Clerical Styles)* in the rays of glory reflected by theologians.[97] The origin and the historical-theological development of the Christian idea is tied to a visible and yet elusive form. The experience of the glory and beauty of the Lord in Christian revelation, the historical modality of the aesthetic form, is exemplified in history by clerical theologians until 1300, among whom Anselm figures prominently and later by lay figures. The concern of *The Glory of the Lord* is a reintegration of nature and grace, body and spirit, theology and civilization, thought and feeling. A synthetic and comprehensive ressourcement of form is to contribute to a rebirth of Christian culture.

Looking back on his theology, Balthasar believes Rahner had chosen Kant's or Fichte's transcendental approach, whereas he, by training a "Germanist," chose "the form (Gestalt)", "the indissolubly unique, organic, developing form (Gestalt) - I am thinking of Goethe's poem "Die Metamorphose der Pflanzen" = [The Metamorphosis of Plants] "... I have attempted to see Christianity or the figure (Gestalt) of Christ as a form (Gestalt) and altogether with Christ also his Church ... This is why I do not believe in pluralism ... I believe in Catholicity."[98] The pre-supposed "analogia entis" unwittingly leads Goethe, in spite of his tendency to divinize human relations, ultimately to reverence and prayer in the sight of a cosmos perceived as sacramental. Like Heidegger, Balthasar sees truth as more than mere correspondence; the correct correlation of sentences to the reality they attempt to express.[99] Truth is the process of something emerging with clarity out of the concealment of mystery. In this regard Aquinas' notion of "esse commune" and "analogia entis" are of decisive help for Balthasar.

The interior value expresses itself in an outward form ("Gestalt") one can never fathom. Every beautiful form has this openness which enables it to express more than the sum of its components, even in a complete well-defined form. This "more" is the glory, and it means that the Beautiful as such is able to serve as form for revelation.[100]

---

[97] Balthasar, The Glory of the Lord. Vol. II 13.

[98] Balthasar, "Geist und Feuer," Herderkorrespondenz 30 (1976) 75; as translated by Michael Waldstein, "An Introduction to von Balthasar's `The Glory of the Lord,'" Communio 14 (1987): 12-33, here 15.

[99] Heidegger inspired Balthasar to embark on the multi-volume The Glory of the Lord. Cf.. Guerriero, Hans Urs von Balthasar 314.

[100] Hans Urs von Balthasar, The Glory of the Lord: A Theological Aesthetics. Vol. III. Studies in Theological Style: Lay Styles (San Francisco: Ignatius, 1986) 34.

It remains mysterious. The aesthetic form as perceived constitutes no arbitrary restriction of what is formless. It does not refer to something inaccessibly beyond itself. It manifests a "divine, infinitely determined super-form."[101] The categories "lumen" and "species" form a unity which is the actual appearance of the mystery.[102] The act of theological perception (aisthesis) experiences the hidden, yet "all-free and all-active God" in the concrete and historical dimensions of the form of human beings ("Menschengestalt").[103] Beauty is related to mystery. Nevertheless it reveals the Divine as glory.[104] Balthasar neither thinks the one experiencing such a Christian epiphany of God is a mere (Platonic) spectator who passively enjoys the event[105] nor is incarnation and revelation regarded as one among many similar events occurring at random and disparately within the general aesthetic structure of the universe. There can be no univocal application and transferral of the incarnation of Christ.

The aesthetic perception ("aisthesis" means perception) is enabled by a radiance which expresses a unified and intelligible form. Balthasar, following Goethe, sees the form overcoming the atomistic view of life to perceive a union of the parts which is greater than a mere summation of its components. The parts are unified by something interior. Hence a distinction between (in the sense of a dichotomy of the) tangible expression and the inner center exists. First the sensible appearance of a person is beheld. Only gradually does one comprehend the person through the appearance. The exterior manifestation expresses the inner. Both constitute a unity. This unity is form ("Gestalt"). Therefore, "Gestalt" refers to both the "shape" (= outline, visible components united by the principle of unity as Goethe defined "μορφη") and the inner principle of the actuality of contents. For Balthasar the "Gestalt" of Jesus, for example, refers equally to Jesus' appearance and to his being. "Form" and "content" are intertwined.

> The beautiful is above all a "form," and the light does not fall on this form from above and from outside, rather it breaks forth from within the form's interior ... Visible form not only points to an invisible, unfathomable mystery. Form is the apparition of this mystery, and reveals it while naturally, at the same time protecting and veiling it. Both natural and artistic form have an exterior which appears and an interior depth, both of which, however, are not separable in the form itself. The contents ("Gehalt") do not lie behind the form ("Gestalt") but within it. Whoever is not capable of seeing and "reading" the form will, by the same token, fail to perceive the contents. Whoever is not illumined by the form will see no light in the contents either.[106]

---

[101] Balthasar, The Glory of the Lord. Vol. I 432.
[102] Balthasar, The Glory of the Lord. Vol. I 144.
[103] Balthasar, The Glory of the Lord. Vol. I 151.
[104] Hans Urs von Balthasar, The Glory of the Lord. Vol. IV. The Realm of Metaphysics in the Modern Age (San Francisco: Ignatius, 1991) at 39f.
[105] Balthasar, The Glory of the Lord. Vol. II 11f.
[106] Balthasar, The Glory of the Lord. Vol. I 151.

This "expressity" gives tension and unity to the surface and depth.[107]

Balthasar sees in the form not a complete revelation of contents, but a revelation of the mystery as a constitutive element of the manifested form. The revealed is not accidental to the contents, but an indispensable and an inalienable part of that contents′ essence. This is seen in the tension between the interior and the exterior. Beauty is an expression of a boundless splendor, which is the interior of the exterior manifestation. Balthasar insists that God appears in the form of Christ "substantively and authoritatively"[108] For ... "the sphere of beauty is a whole, as existence, transparent to divine esse subsistens (subsistent Being), which is grasped only as a mystery. As the hidden original ground it shines forth as glory."[109]

However, would not a genuinely aesthetic theology lead to an impasse? Can this fleeting and contingent world at all contain the form of the numinous? In the context of John of the Cross, Balthasar speaks of "the full paradox" of this "mystical aesthetics."[110] The dilemma is overcome by avoiding a simply subjective understanding of aesthetics. The light illumining the form is not of human contrivance. It breaks forth from within as the divine form itself.[111] In contrast to modern aesthetics, Christian aesthetics is rooted in Being itself. It experiences the "sure light of Being" (Thomas) and thereby the aesthetic illumination of form. In agreement with Bonaventure, form′s essence lies not in its quality of being able to be subjectively perceived. Its essence is its intrinsic power to express. Bonaventure observed, "veritas declarativum esse" and "intentio veritatis est ipsa expressio."[112]

Confronted with the phenomenon of modern-day subjectivity, Balthasar echoes Heidegger when asking whether "this light does not necessarily die out where the very language of light has been forgotten and the mystery of Being is no longer allowed to express itself?"[113] Only beauty will free the "homo in se incurvatus."

Beauty is the word that shall be our first. Beauty is the last thing which the thinking intellect dares to approach, since it dances as an uncontained splendour around the double constellation of the true and the good and their inseparable relation to one another. Beauty is the disinterested one, without which the ancient world refused to understand itself, a word which both imperceptibly and yet unmistakably has bid farewell to our new world, a world of interests, leaving it to its own avarice and sadness.[114]

---

[107] Balthasar, The Glory of the Lord. Vol. I 118.151.442ff.
[108] Balthasar, The Glory of the Lord. Vol. II 33.
[109] Balthasar, Herrlichkeit, Vol. III/i 337.
[110] Balthasar, The Glory of the Lord. Vol. IV 78ff.
[111] Balthasar, The Glory of the Lord. Vol. II 30ff.
[112] Balthasar, The Glory of the Lord. Vol. II 344.
[113] Balthasar, The Glory of the Lord. Vol. I 19.
[114] Balthasar, The Glory of the Lord. Vol. I 18.

The second volume of *The Glory of the Lord* speaks of the Scholastic correlation of truth and beauty which Balthasar - as previous Christians too - embraces. The "splendor veritatis" is the manifested and attractive form of truth. The form of Christ - and through him all finite forms - does not reveal a direct resemblance to the divine in the invisible, but being as formed by the divine primordial form in the visible form.

It is in their being light and in their act of self-expression that the substances' resemblance to God lies; in this they express God, though it is rather he who expresses himself in them. This mystery of light as the creative power of revelation is broken up into the colours in their various illuminations, and into the forms, which ultimately are only various stamps of expressions.[115]

God's actual expressiveness, or perhaps better, willingness to express Himself and enter into dialogue and even relationship, is thus claimed. The divine expressiveness possesses two inherent moments: an inexhaustible and a mysterious one.

No one, nor the sum of all forms fully resembles God. At various places Balthasar refers to Bonaventure's observation that the world is but a "vestigium," a trace of God. Elsewhere Cusanus' notion of "cipher" is employed to describe the world as an image. The quality of beauty in the visible things depends on their ability to manifest the archetypal form of beauty. The aesthetics of the archetype does not eliminate the accidental, but expresses itself through the form. By expressing the expressivity of the transcendent, the visible is not deprived of its own expressivity. On the contrary, it gains its own expressivity by being an expression of the eternal expressivity. As the Logos is not a copy of the Father, neither is the created form a copy of the Son. By coming to be themselves - by their inner consistence, inner congruence or by virtue of possessing the Anselmian "rectitudo" - visible beings are beautiful.

Since this expressiveness is indiscriminate by all human standards, theology ultimately defies systematization. A theological aesthetics would otherwise close itself to the artistic and expressive dimensions of the human condition and succumb to the temptations of Baconian ratiocination. Only a beauty beyond simple systematic definition can be a transcendental attribute of Being itself.[116] The categories of beauty, unity, truth, and goodness form by their being transcendentals a unity in the totality of Being. Without the aesthetic dimension, i.e. without splendor, "verum" remains utilitarian. Without the yearning for possession ("voluptas") the "bonum" falls victim to hedonism.[117]

---

[115] Balthasar, The Glory of the Lord. Vol. I 346.
[116] Balthasar, The Glory of the Lord. Vol. I 30.
[117] Balthasar, The Glory of the Lord. Vol. I 152.

"Light" is the correlating and enabling principle of aesthetics. Since there is "a polarity within beauty between `form´ and `light,´"[118] something else must enter into existence. Balthasar describes this as ontic being and charity. Thereby, aesthetics is grounded in triune love. Being and its dynamic, expressive moment - which causes aesthetics - are "an" expression of gratuitous love. These enable us to see an analogy between the aesthetic contemplation on beauty and God´s revelation in Jesus.

Within a Johannine context, theological aesthetics is rooted in the trinitarian movement of sending and being sent, remaining transcendent and descending. In the trinitarian contemplation of the form of Christ, his claim, poverty and abandonment become apparent. The paradox of claim and poverty is resolved by seeing it as rooted in the eternal obedience of the divine Son.[119] The divine obedience of the Son is one of the three principal divine attributes of Christ. The other two are his sovereign claim to divinity and His poverty. In the majestic Jesus of the Gospel of John ("εγω ειμι"). Balthasar beholds an echo of the Old Testament in numinous characteristics ("I, I am Yahweh ... I am God, yes from eternity I am": Is 43:11,13).[120]

The second christological feature is also apprehended in the Johannine Christ: his absolute vulnerability and poverty. These two characteristics of the human and divine Christ as divinely sovereign, and yet radically abandoned constitute the "paradoxon" to Balthasar´s mind. This paradox finds its resolution only in the third christological attribute, namely in Jesus´ divine obedience and mission.[121] By way of recourse to Jn 3:31-35 Balthasar is able to establish the unity of claim and poverty as the eternal, inner trinitarian relationship of Jesus to his Father. Jesus´ obedience becomes his eternal attribute by its very divine nature.

Balthasar differentiates here between the fidelity of the Old Testament prophet to the divine order and the mission of Jesus. Jesus Christ is not a mere prophetic form of revelation ("Offenbarungsgestalt"), but is God´s form of revelation.[122] Here again, as seen above in the Balthasarian perception of the "analogia entis," Balthasar anticipates and wards off the potential prospect of interpreting the divine obedience as an anthropomorphism. The term may only analogously be applied. In this sense Christ does not merely superficially bear or assume the quality of obedience. It is a revelation of his eternal divine personhood translated into a human condition. For he is the manifestation on earth of divine glory (Heb 1:3), "the exegesis of the eternal love of the Father"

---

[118] Hans Urs von Balthasar, Theologik, Vol. I: Wahrheit der Welt. 2nd ed. (Einsiedeln. Johannes, 1985) at IX.

[119] Balthasar, The Glory of the Lord. Vol. I 186f.

[120] Balthasar, The Glory of the Lord. Vol. VII 115-161.

[121] In this context John also supplies the biblical foundation. Cf. Jn 4:34; 6:38; 14:1.

[122] Balthasar, The Glory of the Lord. Vol. I 184, 32lf, 469.

(Jn 1:18).[123] In Christ's singular abandonment to death his divine attribute of obedience becomes manifest. In the Father's generation of the Son, the paternal commands are imparted to the Son. In the very same act the Son acquires and realizes his filial identity by being obedient. Thus, when the Son reveals himself in the categories of contingent matter he reveals the Father's divine goodness as the eternal, generating moment at the very same time.[124]

This approach remains Johannine (Jn 1:29; 3:18; 4:34; 6:38; 17:5). Taking up Anselm, Balthasar sees the divine categorial "no" to the world's reaction to him revealed in the descent. This divine wrath is nothing less but his divine "justice in the covenant."[125] At another point Balthasar speaks of the necessary "unity of love and wrath" in the descent.[126]

Certainly Balthasar also holds that Jesus died "pro nobis," due to our own inability. He who was pure went beyond evil and guilt. Balthasar encapsulates in his interpretation of atonement the vicarious and juridical moments. The intensity of taking over the sins of the world means an identification of the Son with the sinners as his brothers and sisters (Jn 13:1: "Before the festival of the passover, Jesus, knowing that his hour had come to pass from this world to the Father, having loved those who were his in the world, loved them to the end.") comes about. This entails making Jesus Christ humanity's "lightening rod" of divine wrath. In this, Jesus experiences an unexcelled forsakenness. Herein God's love to humanity (Jn 3:16) and Jesus' love for his own unite with the divine justice and wrath.[127] In the tangible human form the divine kenotic form becomes manifest. "Jesus Christ is Lord, to the glory of God the Father" (Phil 2:9ff). Jesus' form is mission, bringing the Father's love to places darkened by sin.[128]

God could have reconciled the world to himself without the manifestation of the form. Yet, the revelatory moment of responsiveness in the here and now by making himself known as justice and love to the world would not have come about. Incarnation, salvation and Pentecost are the enabling moments for Christian existence's responsiveness. The form of Christ demonstrates that God's heavenly glory undoes the world's perception of the incompatibility of glory and weakness, of love and justice.[129] They emerge in Christ's form not as defeated and as opposites to be overcome, but as moments of the one Trinity.

---

[123] Hans Urs von Balthasar, Der christliche Stand (Einsiedeln: Johannes, 1977) 61.

[124] Balthasar, Der christliche Stand 27.

[125] Balthasar, The Glory of the Lord. Vol. VII 205.

[126] Hans Urs von Balthasar, Theodramatik. Vol. III: Die Handlung (Einsiedeln: Johannes, 1980) at 317.

[127] Cf. Hans Urs von Balthasar, Kennt uns Jesus - Kennen wir Ihn? 3rd rev. ed (Einsiedeln: Johannes, 1995) 37-42; Balthasar, Theodramatik. Vol. III 312ff; Balthasar, The Glory of the Lord. Vol. VII 206f.

[128] Balthasar, The Glory of the Lord. Vol. VII 147.

[129] All these elements form a non-contradictory whole; very much as with Anselm.

312

As previously indicated, "light" is the enabling principle of aesthetics. Since thus there is a "polarity within beauty between `form´ and `light´,"[130] something else must be enabling beauty. Balthasar considers this to be being and love. Thereby aesthetics is grounded in the Trinity. Indeed, Being and its dynamic expressive movement, which cause aesthetics, are "an" expression of gratuitous love. There is an analogy thus between the aesthetic contemplation of beauty and seeing God´s revelation in Jesus. Placing it in a Johannine context, theological aesthetics is rooted in the trinitarian movement of sending and being sent, remaining transcendent and descending.

In the trinitarian contemplation of the form of Christ his claim, poverty and abandonment become apparent. The paradox of claim and poverty is resolved by seeing it founded, as noted, on the eternal obedience of the divine Son.[131] Such a perspective no longer justifies seeing the crucifixion as a simple demonstration of divine wrath. Rather, in the Son´s obedience on the cross, the juxtaposition of the glory and the love of God is revealed. The cross is the ultimate revelation of God´s gratuitous and self- abandoning love. More than only reviewing justification in Jesus' sacrifice, redeemed humanity obtains the Son´s proximity to the Father.

The unifying insight of Balthasar is that the glory of God´s triune love is expressed in the form of Jesus so that humanity may partake in triune life. Created beauty images distantly the incarnate Word´s procession from the Father´s glory in the Holy Spirit. The world gains its proper place in the difference of and in the distance between Father and Son, which is kept in union by the Holy Spirit. In revealing the Divine, Christ also preserves the hidden nature of the Divine. He displays the natural expression of the relationship between the sensory and the ontological. The beautiful form manifests Being and reveals the non-manifest depth of a divine presence.[132]

To Balthasar´s mind, one can sense the implied aesthetic power of giving form, that is to say the expressivity of being - which is the condition for the possibility of transcending the merely palpable -, not only in the clear language of the seraphic doctor, Bonaventure, but also in the sober styles of Aquinas, Anselm and Albert the Great.[133] Thomas calls this "splendor formae." It draws the beholder outside her/himself.[134] The Swiss theologian approaches the form from a broad perspective - ranging from Plato and Aristotle, via major theological and literary figures, to the Old and New Testaments.

One comes to see that a "lumen fidei" implanted in faith has led to a sapiential tradition ever anew, giving witness to a spring-like "θαυμαζειν."[135]

[130] Balthasar, Theologik. Vol. I at IX.
[131] Balthasar, The Glory of the Lord. Vol. I 186f.
[132] Balthasar, The Glory of the Lord. Vol. I 443.
[133] Balthasar, The Glory of the Lord. Vol. I 78.
[134] Balthasar, The Glory of the Lord. Vol. I 118.
[135] Balthasar, The Glory of the Lord. Vol. I 70f.

313

The "whole person" responds to the beauty, truth and goodness of the manifestations of the glory of the Lord. In Balthasar's judgment the Platonic "εξαιφνης"[136] is echoed in the "subito" of Anselm.[137]

This last term calls to mind the "je und jäh" (= occasionally and abruptly) of both Karl Barth and Martin Heidegger. The uncovering (= "Entbergen") of fate (= "Geschick") occurs "je und je" for the Freiburg philosopher.[138] In the same essay, entitled "Die Frage nach der Technik," he thinks the categories of the beautiful and aesthetic impart insights into the essence of being. However, it is Heidegger's contention that manifold technological achievements and their omnipresence in daily life prevent one from perceiving and experiencing in modernity the essence of being, of transcendence and contingence, and as a consequence of the purpose of life. Religion, literature and philosophy are increasingly apprehended in a simplified chain of causality as facilitators of a way of life amid technological achievements - technology in itself is another matter - imposed upon human society. Heidegger famously thinks western philosophy suffers a "forgetfulness of being" ("Seinsvergessenheit"). Because he wants to recover the whole human being, he proposes the attitude of "Gelassenheit" (= letting things be, calmness, composure) by acquiring a worshipping heart. Heidegger had borrowed this term from German mysticism.[139] Balthasar also uses this term to develop "the metaphysics of the saints."[140] He seems to take up this suggestion as a further argument to thematize on a broad landscape the category of the beautiful in the fields of religion, philosophy and literature. *The Glory of the Lord* attempts to reawaken a sense of awe and wonder which allows a new appreciation of beauty, sublimity and glory.

Thereby, humanity should return to its primary, ontically given orientation ("vorgegeben") to the transcendentals. The beautiful is "the manner in which God's goodness gives itself and is expressed by God and understood by man as the truth (verum)."[141] Confirming Allers and the intuition of the Romantic era, Hölderlin is the decisive inspiration for the insight that "the sisterhood of truth and goodness (rests) in beauty alone."[142] The theophanous nature of the Greek cosmos is transformed into the Christian universe of glorifying divine love.[143] The beautiful ("pulchrum") is thus the mediating element of truth and goodness. The beautiful also protects the other transcendentals.[144] When beheld in the

---

[136] Balthasar, The Glory of the Lord. Vol. IV 194.
[137] Balthasar, The Glory of the Lord. Vol. II 230-234.
[138] Heidegger, VA, p. 29.
[139] Cf. Hans Urs von Balthasar, The Glory of the Lord. Vol. V. In the Realm of Metaphysics in the Modern Age (San Francisco: Ignatius, 1991) at 41.
[140] Balthasar, The Glory of the Lord. Vol. V at 48-140.
[141] Balthasar, foreword to The Glory of the Lord. Vol. I 11.
[142] Balthasar, The Glory of the Lord. Vol. V 298-338, here 299.
[143] Balthasar, The Glory of the Lord. Vol. V 311.
[144] Balthasar, The Glory of the Lord. Vol. IV 38.

light of glory, the temptation to yield either to intellectualism or aestheticism is avoided.[145]

The principal intuition of Balthasar is that in the incarnation Christ assumes human nature; the whole of human nature receives a transformation. Jesus Christ is simultaneously the perfect expression of God´s love and of the human correspondence to God. The analogy of Christ, insofar as he is human, becomes the inspiration for Christian existence as the concrete universal. This is the condition for the possibility for aesthetic theology. Theology also acquires thereby an aesthetic dimension. From God, i.e. from Bethlehem, one discerns "the divinity of the Invisible, which radiates in the visibleness of Being of the world."[146] The incarnation is nothing short of the revelation of a "super-form,"[147] albeit one neglected by Christians. In his judgment, Latin Scholasticism rendered the church too structured and overly intellectualized for it to remain a vital mirroring of the form.[148] His intention is to rejoin the "super-form" and humanity, i.e. grace and nature, by presenting a broad - though not exhaustive - analysis of major examplifications of a theology of form.[149] Thus the topic of the multi-volume work is "the divinity of the invisible, which radiates in visibleness of Being in the world."[150] By rooting form in the Divine, Balthasar rejects the subjective outlook of current art. As with Plotinus and the Greek fathers, light does not result from the perceiver´s vision, but rather breaks forth from within the form itself.[151] Beauty is seen as a central manifestation of God. This ontological root, namely beauty, Balthasar endeavors to recover.

With Thomas, he thinks human existence gains meaning by way of the transcendentals. If beauty is not contemplated, the two other transcendentals, truth and goodness, become divorced from their mediating center.[152]

As the last "transcendentale" the beautiful guards the others and sets the seal on them: there is nothing true or good, in the long term, without the light of grace of that which is freely bestowed.[153]

Ever since Scholasticism and the reaction to Romaticism,[154] Western thought has disregarded the category of the "καλον" and thus suffers a "forgetful-ness."[155]

---

[145] Balthasar, The Glory of the Lord. Vol. I 37ff.
[146] Balthasar, The Glory of the Lord. Vol. I 431.
[147] Balthasar, The Glory of the Lord. Vol. I 432.
[148] Balthasar, The Glory of the Lord. Vol. IV 494.
[149] Balthasar, The Glory of the Lord. Vol. I 11; Balthasar, The Glory of the Lord. Vol. IV 15.
[150] Balthasar, The Glory of the Lord. Vol. I 431.
[151] Balthasar, The Glory of the Lord. Vol. IV 41.
[152] Balthasar, The Glory of the Lord. Vol. I 9.
[153] Balthasar, The Glory of the Lord. Vol. IV 38.

Since according to the New Testament (cf. Jn 1:14) God became not spirit but flesh, Balthasar considers Christianity the only aesthetic religion. To him it is therefore only consistent - and by no means does one sense a note of intolerance - to assert that neither atheism, nor Buddhism, nor Islam, nor Judaism redeem and take seriously every single human being as Christianity does. As an expression of this divine "con-descendence" "Christ has taken on a body of flesh, of letter, scripture, term, picture, voice and proclamation."[156] Christianity becomes the advocate of the disinterested beauty in a world radically interested and egoistic. Again,

beauty is the disinterested one, without which the ancient world refused to understand itself, a word which both imperceptibly and yet unmistakably has bid farewell to our new world, a world of interests, leaving it to its own avarice and sadness[157]

In a world without beauty - even if people cannot dispense with the word and constantly have it on the tip of their tongues in order to abuse it - in a world which is perhaps not wholly without beauty, but which can no longer see it or reckon with it; in such a world the good also loses its attractiveness, the self-evidence why it must be carried out.[158]

Taking up the insight of Jesus as "the perfectly human being," Balthasar sees in Christ the definitive and irrevocable form of God. God does not merely play the role of one human being on the stage of history. God performs and lives the quintessentially human role. This role is played in the real and contingent world. Its aesthetics allows one through this divine acting to be prepared for God in the analogy of freedom. Here Przywara was particularly

---

[154] Balthasar readily admits Romanticism to have insuffiently distinguished between nature and grace. Cf. Balthasar, The Glory of the Lord. Vol. I 104.

[155] Balthasar, The Glory of the Lord. Vol. V 449f. With Heidegger he notes a cloud of "deep forgetfulness of Being" which obscures the radiance of the form. Philosophical reason and theological faith no longer possess the sensorium for the form, namely the category of beauty (Balthasar, The Glory of the Lord. Vol. V 18f). He is also critical of Protestantism's rejection of art. No longer is God - as Karl Jaspers held - a mere cipher - but the God who had taken on "Gestalt" - form. "Only that which has form can snatch one" (= recte who had been formed and who is in the position to know that he had been formed) "up into a state of rapture (and delight). Only through form can the lightening-bolt of eternal beauty flash." "To be transported (= electrified), moreover, belongs to the very origin of Christianity. The apostles were transported by what they saw, heard and touched - by everything manifested in the form. John especially" describes the contours of Jesus' figure (the German term "die Gestalt" means both "form" and "figure" in English) as "the ray of the Unconditional." The Apostles forsook everything when moved "by the folly of that enthusiasm which even Plato knew in his own way." Had not Paul when beholding "the highest beauty" sold all else for the sake of one pearl?" (Balthasar, The Glory of the Lord. Vol. I 32ff).

[156] Hans Urs von Balthasar, Verbum Caro. Skizzen zur Theologie I. 3rd ed. (Einsiedeln: Johannes, 1990) at 159ff.

[157] Balthasar, The Glory of the Lord. Vol. I 18.

[158] Balthasar, The Glory of the Lord. Vol. I 18.

instrumental.[159] In the sacrament of the eucharist Christ and the believer in the Church encounter each other but remain distinct. By this "tight-rope act" Balthasar achieves a balance which is comprehensive. It overcomes the dilemma wrought by a rationalistic isolation of God from the world. Christian spirituality is neither a flight from the world nor a submission to immanent reason. At the same time a nirvana-like attempt to abolish all form as price for finding unity in the divine is avoided.

Very much like the Church fathers, Balthasar continues a "form" that gives testimony to the spirit of earliest Christendom. One senses a hypostatic union between divine "sapientia" and human "theoria" in praxis. Knowledge is not sterile but personal. The fragmentation of reality is overcome. The reader cannot help being reminded of a Romantic poem bearing out precisely this appreciation for the organic whole, as a cause for delight in discovering God's and the world's goodness:

Wünschelrute
Schläft ein Lied in allen Dingen,
Die da klingen fort und fort,
Und die Welt hebt an zu singen,
findest Du nur das Zauberwort.   *Joseph v. Eichendorff (1835)*

The aesthetic theology put forth by Balthasar appreciates a part of Nietzsche's critique of Christianity. The philosopher had remarked that "Christianity negates all aesthetic values." Yet Balthasar also insists that the glory of God conceals itself.[160] Taking Anselm's inspiration, "id quo maius cogitari non potest," God and Christ's taking on of form manifests God as the most important to humanity: beyond which nothing greater can be thought. This allows Balthasar to state: "Only where God is taken seriously, can the human being as person be taken seriously."[161] It reminds Balthasar of Beethoven: "love demands everything." Divine con-descendence remains irrevocably a mystery one cannot calculate or set off against something else. The original distance within the Trinity allows the Son to penetrate the realm of creation in a way too distant for a creature to fathom let alone to follow.[162] Never is faith an "intellectual high performance." "Rather it is a matter for the simple-minded, unburdened and non-adjusted to scholarly terminology."[163] Balthasar considers

---

[159] Balthasar, Mein Werk 70; Balthasar, Prüfet alles - das Gute behaltet 9. He did not, however, follow Przywara's negative theology: cf. Balthasar, Unser Auftrag 32.

[160] Balthasar, The Glory of the Lord. Vol. I 316f; Balthasar, The Glory of the Lord. Vol. II, 11.248.

[161] Balthasar, Klarstellungen 38.

[162] Hans Urs von Balthasar, Theodramatik. Vol. IV: Das Endspiel (Einsiedeln: Johannes, 1983) 465.

[163] Balthasar, Spiritus Creator 69f.

Hopkins' contribution to be his observation that there is no "opposition between image and concept, myth and revelation, the apprehension of God in nature and the history of salvation."[164] Balthasar's hermeneutic raison d'être is to arouse wonderment, not skepsis. Plotinus similarly held that only "εκστασις" leads to truth. In his judgment metaphors and communicative imageries bring about community, while terms isolate and are causes of disagreement. In *Verbum Caro* Balthasar accordingly defines theology as reflection on the proposition: "Without ceasing to be God, the Word was made flesh." Therefore, "through the passionlessness of a theory of adoration and obedience the word that was Christ must flame, as it flames through all of the word of God, who, burning of this fire, allowed itself to be devoured."[165] To behold a "Gestalt," a form, means to find a systematic view. In the objective evidence of the world in metaphors, being reveals itself as beautiful, good and true.[166]

In Neo-Scholasticism either the competence to formulate truth propositions is delegated to an authority and/or one can arrive at them (rationalistically) deductively.[167] Yet they lack expressivity.[168] By recourse to the Plotinian notion of unity and the analogy of being, Balthasar retrieves in an almost exhaustive ressourcement beauty as rooted in the notion of the Dionysian "ens" or "esse commune,"[169] so that one might participate more clearly, in the Church, in seeing the sublimity of the form.

The theological concern can thus be summed up: "Being itself here unveils its final countenance, which for us receives the name of trinitarian love; only with this final mystery does light fall at last on the other mystery: why there is being at all and why it enters our horizon as light and truth and goodness and beauty."[170] Therefore, Balthasar concurs with Bonaventure, when the latter insists that it is proper to the essence of a form to express a hidden divine form. The form's essence does not lie in the beholder's perceiving it. When in the *Itinerarium Mentis* Bonaventure states that the beauty of the tangible world attests to an archetypal reality transcending it, this best defines Balthasar's own view. Beauty - and this includes beauty of thought - is a transcendental attribute of Being itself, occasioning an "anamnesis."[171] And yet, God is freely making himself present. To Balthasar this cannot simply be compared to the Platonic, passive notion of the radiance of divine goodness.[172] The topic of *The Glory of the Lord* is not an ascending movement to God, but

---

[164] Balthasar, The Glory of the Lord. Vol. II 19.
[165] Balthasar, Verbum Caro 163.
[166] This triad reminds one of Goethe: "Das Wahre, Gute und Schöne."
[167] Balthasar, The Glory of the Lord. Vol. V 21.
[168] Balthasar, The Glory of the Lord. Vol. IV 436f.
[169] Balthasar, The Glory of the Lord. Vol. IV 374f. 406.
[170] Balthasar, The Glory of the Lord. Vol. I 158.
[171] Balthasar, The Glory of the Lord. Vol. I 30.
[172] Balthasar, The Glory of the Lord. Vol. II 12.

rather a descending movement beholding the created order in the revealed and divine light of its creator. In the incarnation the mystery of God did not remain hidden behind the forms, but became one form that influenced all other forms.[173] Very much like his friend and teacher de Lubac, Balthasar strives to see the supernatural not as an entity removed from reality, but on the contrary as firmly established as divine immanence in the cosmos.

Faith can only be perceived as the "radiance resulting from the presence in us of `lumen increatum,´ a `gratia increata,´ without our ever being able to abstract from God´s Incarnation when considering this light and this grace."[174] Revelation establishes its own sensorium in the soul for Balthasar - as it does for Augustine.[175] "Along with the ontic that orients humankind and the form of revelation to one another, the grace of the Holy Spirit creates the faculty that can apprehend this form, the faculty ... that can relish it and find its joy in it, that can understand it and sense its interior truth and rightness."[176] In faith the soul develops a receptivity to the Christian form because it is the perfect archetype of the absolute expression. In the trinitarian obedience of the Son "appears not God alone; necessarily, there also appears the inner-trinitarian event of his procession; there appears the triune God." Beauty viewed in the light of glory permits the avoidance of - much like in Homer´s *Odyssey* - the skylla of intellectualism and the charybdis of pious practice.[177]

On this broad canvas, the treatment of Anselm is limited to a paltry forty nine pages. Bonaventure received more attention. The relatively slight treatment of Anselm is somewhat misleading. Anselm plays a major role in the correlation of the aesthetic and reason in Balthasar´s thinking. The limited space still enables Balthasar to succeed in freeing Anselm from a one-sided rationalistic appreciation, and compels a general re-reading of the monk from Aosta.[178]

---

[173] Balthasar, The Glory of the Lord. Vol. III 393.

[174] Balthasar, The Glory of the Lord. Vol. I 215.

[175] Balthasar, The Glory of the Lord. Vol. I 249.

[176] Balthasar, The Glory of the Lord. Vol. I 247.

[177] Balthasar, The Glory of the Lord. Vol. I 37ff.

[178] This by itself can already be considered a strong argument for why all of theology should accord both Balthasar and Anselm more attention. Indeed, it would take an "ideengeschicht-liche" investigation of its own to illumine to what extent modern-day research would benefit from Balthasar´s reflections on Anselm. Though written well over four decades ago, Balthasar´s interpretation of Anselm´s thought can meet the approval of current scholarship. Balthasar may also have said concerning Anselm:

"And it is not as if something good is to be effected by the theologian´s looking restlessly back and forth between the needs of his age and the apparently so uncontemporary divine truth in the Church; but just with earthly pictures, if the painter looks constantly at the archetypical form, not distracted by any visible object, nor divided at all in himself, then what is to be depicted ... is duplicated and he can show forth the truth in its likeness, the archetype in the image and each in the other, only the substances remaining different. cf. Balthasar, The Glory of the Lord. Vol. II 166f.

In Volume II the aesthetic project of seeing the form receives theological and historical concreteness. The central positive aspects of the study on Anselm by Balthasar are:

1. in similarity to Barth [179] the joy of reflecting on God's essence,
2. the contemplation on the trinity   and
3. the incarnation.[180]

The "intelligere" is completely in the service of the "credere" and cannot be divorced from the same. In Balthasar's judgment it is the greatness of Anselm thus to stress a foundational unity between philosophy and theology. Thereby his approach is consonant with his predecessors of antiquity, namely Plato, Plotinus, Augustine, Denis, Boethius, Thomas, Bonaventure and others. Only in Descartes does one experience the total rupture of philosophy and theology, which is to become characteristic of modernity.[181] Now philosophy is defined by the natural sciences. Thus the "intelligere" is separated from the "credere." Reason ponders the meaning of life and probes the extent of the knowable without the aid of revelation. Thereby a hiatus between nature and grace also occurs.[182]

12.4 The Valence of Anselm in Balthasar's Theology - Analogy as Freedom

In Anselm, as well as in the four by Balthasar subsequently treated theologians, God implanted a profound awareness of his beauty. The whole of the Anselmian corpus attests, in Balthasar's view, a harmony, order and intelligibility in the contingent world which is grounded in God. God's freedom is manifested in incarnate things so that as a full partner in the covenant with God humanity might grow in this freedom. By way of a reconstituted freedom, humankind may better perceive supreme beauty and transcend towards spontaneous, sacrificial love. What Anselm calls "necessary reasons," Balthasar explains, is no trite rationalism but the human response to God by contemplating divine beauty, freedom and love. With Anselm the "intelligere" always refers to and serves the "credere." Thereby, the "intelligere" gains space to unfold and better become itself.

Anselm is characterized as breathing a pronounced sense of unity and form. Natural science and methodological exactitude are not eclipsed and by-passed by a "hiatus infusus" from the Holy Spirit in faith.

---

[179] Cf. Karl Barth, Kirchliche Dogmatik. II/1 (Zollikon: TVZ, 1986/87/88) at 741-749.

[180] Balthasar, The Glory of the Lord. Vol. I 55.

[181] In Balthasar's estimation Descartes was prepared by John Scotus, who apprehends being as an empty concept, indifferent to creation. The rationalism of Scholasticism and Neo-Scholasticism then became inevitable. Therefore, Balthasar's emphasis on the dynamic nature of Being.

[182] Cf. Balthasar, The Glory of the Lord. Vol. I 70ff.

They would not enjoy such a shaping power if their talents had not themselves been transformed through the Spirit's shaping power: if, that is to say, these theologians were not in a Christian ecstatics, had not been caught and drawn into the unity of enthusiasm and holiness.[183]

For Balthasar the "intellectus fidei" includes "this interior completion of the philosophical act in theology"[184] for God revealed his figure in a manner comprehensible to humanity (Jn 1:18). By this divine communication of Jesus Christ's full glory, the mysteries of faith - such as incarnation, resurrection and the eucharist - come to be thought of as conforming to Anselm's axiom of the "necessity of faith."

Anselm lived in the romanesque era. This style of architecture is an uninterrupted continuation from Roman days. On the intellectual plane as well one can detect no significant rupture. As a Benedictine monk, he views contemplative reason as an "aesthetic" category. It brings about a "spiritual intuition of measure and right relationship."[185] The whole of the world as a form is the expression of God's inconceivable freedom and love. Therefore, the horizon of thought is already a priori encapsulated in a unity that is akin to an "unlimited limit." By wholly concentrating on "the inner structure and ordering of the mystery," Anselm frees his text of all personal features and attempts to faithfully mirror the divine impression. The intellectual, rational construction endeavors to explicate to the human mind what Christian faith is, fully knowing the "form" by what is apprehended in a faith which encompasses everything radically.[186] The light of faith is never seen as in contradiction to reason. God becomes impressed on the created spirit and thereby a further similarity is achieved.

In contrast to Barth,[187] Balthasar had at his disposal almost all of Anselm's corpus in the critical edition of F. S. Schmitt, O.S.B. As in all his other writings too, Balthasar heavily makes abundant use of primary sources. He also desists from engaging in polemics. He devotes forty nine short pages to Anselm and treats his theology as having three moments:

1. aesthetic reason,
2. the radiance of freeedom   and
3. the victory of prayer.

Alas, in this volume no other figure receives such a short treatment.

In the introduction Anselm is praised for being "perfectly balanced" and for realizing in the purest form the concerns of a "theological aesthetics,"

---

[183] Balthasar, The Glory of the Lord. Vol. I 78.

[184] Balthasar, The Glory of the Lord. Vol. I 146.

[185] Balthasar, The Glory of the Lord. Vol. II 18. Unless otherwise stated the subsequent references are to The Glory of the Lord. Vol. II when thus indicated Balthasar, Anselm.

[186] Cf. Augustine, De vera religione.

[187] Cf. Balthasar, Anselm 233, footnote 170.

321

contemplating "God's beauty in the freely fashioned form of the world."[188] He situates Anselm's theology already decades before Bacht, Penco and Härdlin[189] in a Benedictine, monastic context, rather than in a Scholastic one. The monastic realm is viewed by Balthasar as enabling the specifically Anselmian understanding of freedom. Freedom experiences itself as actualized by freely embracing spatial limits. Such an appreciation of freedom is thought of as central to the Benedictine charism: "manifest in the consciousness of freedom and in a form of life sealed by freedom."[190]

By his contemplation of "the highest rectitude," Anselm is seen as contemplating the dimensions of harmony, necessity, utmost freedom and absolute beauty rooted in the Godhead. Beauty and reason are even correlated - "rationis pulchritudinem" - and Balthasar is quick to point out that Anselm's monastic contemplation does not allow him to be carried away. It is neither ecstasis, nor feeling, but contemplative reason: "rationis contemplatio," albeit contemplation of a reason on a pilgrimage of longing, between earthly faith and eternal vision ("meditetur ... esuriat ... desideret tota substantia mea").[191] The monk is the utter realist for he apprehends God's beauty in the freely fashioned form of the world.[192] The beauty is beheld by the monk not only in concrete categories but equally when the mind ponders "the beauty of reason (rationis pulchritudinem)."[193] Such "speciosa ratione" is more than a light-hearted treatment by artists. The Swiss theologian stresses that cognitive problematics dominate Anselm's opus. He has little immediate concern for the expressivity of the form. A close nexus between thought and contemplation is established, allowing for thought to take on the form of meditation and even prayer. Against this background "rationes necessariae" as the foundational philosophical method become understandable. The subject of the philosophical act is also "the free dealings of the free God with a mankind freely created and brought into new freedom by Christ."[194] This does not yield to an identification or near synonymity of philosophy and theology. They are, however, reciprocally and mutually interpenetrated (in a way osmotically, and yet retaining their independence therein). The Monologion and the Proslogion are divined as primarily philosophical in intention, whereas the remaining works are theological.

---

[188] Balthasar, Anselm 211.
[189] Cf. Heinrich Bacht, "Theologie der Mönche," Christ in der Gegenwart 33 (1981) 51ff; Gregorio Penco, "Medioevio monastico," Studia Anselmiana 96 (1988) 537-548; Alf Härdlin, "Monastische Theologie: eine praktische Theologie vor der Scholastik," Zeitschrift für katholische Theologie 109 (1987): 400-415.
[190] Balthasar, Anselm 211. See also at 251.
[191] Balthasar, Anselm 212.
[192] Balthasar, Anselm 211.
[193] Balthasar, Anselm 211. Balthasar seems to have gleened this insight from a then recently discovered, but incomplete work by Anselm. Cf. also at footnote 1.
[194] Balthasar, Anselm 211.

Faithful to this vision (= "Schau"), philosophical contemplation almost inevitably receives in a Benedictine and therefore monastic context the proper experiential ambience to be also theological: the choice of experience shapes the hermeneutics: "qui non crediderit non experietur, et qui non expertus non fuerit non cognoscet."[195] Balthasar considers Anselm to be viewing "form and contents, method and subject matter" as tension-filled unities, mutually dependent within one organism.[196]

Therefore, in the first section entitled "Aesthetic Reason"[197] the consonance of philosophy and theology in Anselm's writings are stated. The monk as the perfect philosopher contemplates the divine realities. Here Balthasar dialogues primarily with the *Monologion* and the *Proslogion* as the sources for Anselm's epistemological method.

Such a Christian reason "grows organically" from the question of Being investigated by antiquity. The two strands of thought, biblical revelation and pagan philosophy, are brought to perfection in the revelation of Christ. The monk living the evangelical counsels mediates the One. He is received by Balthasar and Leclercq as "the philosopher in the Christian realm."[198] Taking up the ancient philosophical quest, the monk apprehends God in faith as a person.[199] Rightly, Balthasar justifies this assertion by calling to mind that ancient philosophy was primarily a quest for the numinous. Faith reveals this God as one, free and loving. A separation between faith and reason would deprive reason of its enabling foundation and goal. But reason cannot be severed from creation. By implication, Anselm is seen in an intellectual climate that would outright reject tendencies towards - "post festum" - fideistic reactions. Reason so constituted is a defense against unbelief and impells one towards God.

In Anselm's beauty of reasoning ("pulchritudo rationis") Balthasar discerns three moments: 1. the life liberated by truth, 2. conceptual insight and 3. the joy of the truth found ("delectatio"). These are the ingredients for an aesthetic theology.[200] Faith and prayer lead to reason's ("intellectus") unfolding which in turn results in the beholder's rejoicing over the unity of all. For this to occur one must free cogitation from subjective intentions so "'that God may

---

[195] Balthasar, Anselm 216; cf. I 1: 284,27-31:
"Nam qui non crediderit, non experietur; et qui expertus non fuerit, non cognoscet. Quantum enim rei auditum superat experientia, tantum vincit audientis cognitionem experientis scientia. Nemo ergo se temere immerget in condensa quaestionem, nisi prius in soliditate fidei conquista morum et sapientiae gravitate, ne per multiplicia sophismatum diverticula incauta levitate discurrens, aliqua tenaci illaqueetur falsitate."
[196] Balthasar, Anselm 212.
[197] Balthasar, Anselm 213-237.
[198] Balthasar, Anselm 213.
[199] Balthasar, Anselm 214.
[200] Balthasar, Anselm 215.

reveal what he had previously concealed."[201] In the Swiss theologian's judgment one must embrace truth with "life-giving love."[202] Such a life for the sake of truth calls for freedom from sin. Purity is the groundwork for epistemological progress. It also entails freeing oneself from bad inclinations. This opens the human mind to rectitude and truth. One does not experience such knowledge simply through physical, intellectual or ascetical achievements[203] but by a prayerful life. Worship and reverence are key dimensions, naturally, of the prayerful attitude.

In contrast to Roscelin, Anselm is fully aware that a cleansing of the soul and a constant struggle in faith are necessary for obtaining what antiquity terms "θεωρια."[204] Anselm does not belittle the impact sin has on the human state. Yet, given sin, the epistemological weakness it brings can be overcome by prayer, as the *Proslogion* demonstrates. Here Balthasar finds the "analogia entis" presupposed: "I do not try, O Lord, to penetrate your depths, because I do not at all compare my understanding to that; but I desire to understand in some measure ("aliquatenus") your truth, in which my heart believes and loves."[205] Seeing in the epistemological act God intervening, Anselm maintains well before the IV. Lateran Council's definition a yet "maior dissimilitudo."[206] On one's own, every sinful human being is bereft of the epistemological sensorium needed to think in a manner commensurate to the divine object. Grace ameliorates this distance by making this distance comprehensible as distance; i.e. eliminates the hiatus without doing away with the analogy. In the confrontation between "your beauty" and "your harmony" the human mind experiences its inadequacies. In spite of all effort "there are things in God that his understanding cannot penetrate."[207] Grace is necessary for epistemological advance. Precisely for this reason it cannot be something extrinsic, imposed upon nature as an alien entity. At the same time grace also shrouds.

This brings one to Anselm's specifically Christian understanding: "intelligere fidem." To understand things of faith is for Anselm a question of showing gratitude. "It seems to me negligence, if, after we have been established in the faith, we do not make the effort to understand what we believe."[208] Rightly, Balthasar argues in favor of this Anselmian understanding of reason because there is no "pure reason." Either there exists the post-lapsarian reason or the graced reason. "Tertium non datur." As Balthasar renders Anselm's position: there "is no `pure reason,' but only a reason sinful

---

[201] Balthasar, Anselm 216. Cf. Cu I 1: 49,4: "ut Deus aperiat quod prius latebat."
[202] Balthasar, Anselm 215.
[203] Cf. RB and Plotinus above.
[204] Balthasar, Anselm 216.
[205] Balthasar, Anselm 217; P 1: 100,12-17.
[206] DH 806.
[207] I 13: 31,3f.
[208] Balthasar, Anselm 219; Cu I 1: 48,18.

324

and redeemed, and colored by the historical dimensions of existence, and that it demonstrates from historical reality the conditions of its possibility and therefore, reduces to silence those who deny and scoff."[209] Balthasar adds that Anselm´s "intellectus" is neither simply related to the Patristic reason nor an anticipation of the "ratio" of later Scholasticism. It is not an autonomous human mind, but one that is being led to a spiritual seeing: "videre."

Perhaps as a result of his intensive discussions with Przywara and Barth on this topic, Balthasar stresses the significance of the "analogia entis" in Anselm´s thought. "The formula for the analogy between God and the creature so characteristic of Anselm (videt se non plus posse videre propter tenebras suas) makes the philosophical one with the theological."[210] In Balthasar´s judgment, Anselm does not merely echo Augustine, but sees original sin depri-ving humanity specifically of important Balthasarian divine "predications": namely beauty and harmony.[211] At this point the archbishop goes beyond Augustine.

To Anselm a thing´s true nature is opened in a spiritual way. To Balthasar the aesthetic moment of "videre" is a key-term with which to understand Anselm. The teacher opens a perspective and the student confesses: "Now I see clearly what up to now I had not noticed."[212] The vision thus imparted is evident, obvious, necessarily convincing and beyond contradiction. "Videre" has, as Balthasar demonstrates, a multitude of synonyms in Anselm´s vocabulary. Balthasar describes a process which allows "truth and its grounds ... to appear in its incontrovertibility." For this reason Anselm uses terms as "claritas veritatis," "ratio necessaria," "rationis necessitas" and "necessitas veritatis." Anselm cannot help but call resistance to the acceptance of the truth so evidenced an absurdity.[213]

Quite convincingly, Balthasar terms Anselm´s process of thought on one level "a spiritual demonstration" which is a protest against the "modern dialectic" of the monk´s day.[214] Insofar as it remains a dialectic it posits things of the sensible realm against one another. Bound to that realm, it can never gain the plateau to think the unity which is aesthetic reason: "a simple under-standing, not overwhelmed by the multiplicity of imaginations."[215] From such a vista one does come to realize the validity of Anselm´s notions, such as fitting-ness, necessity, etc.

---

[209] Balthasar, Anselm 219.
[210] Balthasar, Anselm 217f.
[211] Balthasar, Anselm 218; cf. P 16: 113,4ff.
[212] Balthasar, Anselm 220; cf. V 9: 189,26: "video nunc aperte quod hactenus, non animad-verti."
[213] Balthasar, Anselm 222f.
[214] Balthasar, Anselm 223; cf. I 10: 289,18.
[215] Balthasar, Anselm 223; cf. I 10: 289,18: "simplicem intellectum et non multiplicitate phantasmatum obrutum." One is reminded of Plato´s observation, "the divine is simple."

The relationship of faith and reason is complementary and harmonious. Balthasar employs on other occasions the bridal imagery to illustrate the relationship of reason and faith. Reason does not arrive at faith on its own. It is in need of faith in order to experience its own fulfillment. Here both Anselm and Balthasar successfully avoid dualism and attempt to integrate the subjective and objective. Thereby they succeed in preventing faith from dwindling into interiority and reason from becoming the sole realm of objectivity.

Balthasar further avoids the pitfalls of rationalism and fideism by placing emphasis on the concrete and historic form of Jesus Christ, a topos Anselm himself never explicitly considers, but one which nevertheless is present in his works. Only with the aid of God's grace does reason meet faith, does the object reveal itself to the subject as personal and yet shrouded. Reason obtains a greater certitude about reality and lends credibility to faith. For the Swiss theologian, this is a gradual introduction by reason to faith through under-standing the "praeambula fidei." Sometimes Balthasar speaks of the perichoretic nature of faith and reason. It is the object of faith which as form draws the subject forth. Going beyond anything Anselm stated, Balthasar sees the content of faith and the act of faith forming one aesthetic act.

Certainly, this goes well beyond what Anselm had explicitly envisioned. It is nevertheless consonant with his basic tenets, since the abbot of Bec thought of faith - in keeping with the Semitic mind-frame and the Patristic tradition - as an experience. The Middle Ages called this a "conversio ad phantasma." Ignatius further elaborates this notion by his attempt to integrate the senses in the prayerful surrender ("indiferencia").[216] Balthasar along with Anselm would never relinquish the objective evidence of faith, arrived at in an ecclesial, more specifically monastic experience.

Betraying his long occupation with Anselm, Balthasar brilliantly sums up Anselm's epistemology. He marks out as a central illustration of Anselm's teachings the tenth chapter of the *Monologion*. This is accomplished in a four-step-summary:

1. the mere ostensive naming of a significant name, such as man; 2. the inward thinking of a name (nomen cogitare); 3. the spiritual apprehension of the thing itself through a sensible image (imago); 4. the spiritual apprehension of the thing itself by reason (ratio).[217]

Here Balthasar takes up an important distinction. While the "imago" only signifies the "figura sensibilis," reason ("ratio") is capable of apprehending the

---

[216] Peter Knauer (trans.), Ignatius von Loyola, Gründungstexte der Gesellschaft Jesu (Würz-burg : Echter, 1998) 110f; cf. Retreat Book, No. 23.
[217] Balthasar, Anselm 224; cf. M 10: 25,49.

underlying and overarching "universalis essentia."[218] The "universalis essentia" can only be arrived at if one is able to derive from the sensible world general terms such as "species, man, person ..." To Anselm, Balthasar concludes, nominalist philosophy would be a "contradiction in itself."[219] Without universals, philosophy is an impossible task, for it would be unable to arrive at synthetic statements.

The conceptual vision ("simplex intellectus") is no mean feat. It demands experience and a synthetic vision (called "speculatio," "meditatio" and "consideratio") in order to arrive at a unifying judgment, which is a "iudicium animae" not a "iudicium rationis." This vision of the whole eclipses human reason, but one can perceive - Balthasar probably means this - features of it. While only fragments are beheld, they - the fragments - contain the guarantee of the whole.[220] Balthasar does not tire of stressing that it is the "analogia entis" which allows the thinker to comprehend that he/she can no longer see: " videt se non plus posse videre."[221] Or, as Anselm puts it in the *Monologion*: "It can be comprehended most evidently ... (that it) cannot be comprehended by human knowledge."[222] And he observes later on in the same treatise: one "understands rationally that it is incomprehensible (rationabiliter comprehendit incomprehensibile esse)."[223] Here again, as in *Sponsa Verbi*, the Swiss theologian does not hesitate to remind the reader that "the theological act is rooted in the philosophical."[224] Consonant with recent tendencies within scholarship to appreciate better the interrelated unity of both disciplines, Balthasar already made out in Anselm this correlation of the two. The free spiritual creature of God contrasts itself to the absolute Spirit and experiences itself as free and spiritual.

To Anselm ideas are not the result of a logical deduction from sensible matter alone. Rather, Balthasar implies they result from the central event of the incarnation. In this context Balthasar quotes the preface for the feast of Christmas:

> Through the mystery of the incarnate Word the new light of your brightness has shone onto the eyes of our mind; that knowing God visibly, we might be snatched up by this into the love of invisible things.[225]

---

[218] This beholding of the essence of matter is as old as occidental philosophy. In German since idealism this spiritual act is considered under the term "Wesensschau" and is aligned with the term "Wesenserkenntnis" (insight into the essence of matter).

[219] Balthasar, Anselm 225.

[220] Balthasar, Anselm 227.

[221] Balthasar, Anselm 227; P 14: 112,1.

[222] Balthasar, Anselm 227; M 36: 54,16-18.

[223] Balthasar, Anselm 228; M 64: 75,1-12.

[224] Balthasar, Anselm 228; cf. Balthasar, Sponsa Verbi 346ff, written two years prior to vol. II of The Glory of the Lord.

[225] Balthasar, The Glory of the Lord. Vol. I 119f.

The theological object supplies the enabling context for its being known, to Anselm, Bonaventure, Balthasar, and others. The "Gestalt's" effulgence is the condition for the possibility of rapture and knowledge. "The beautiful is above all a `form,´ and the light does not fall from above and from outside, rather it breaks forth from the form's interior."[226] The "creatrix essentia" became human and the believer becomes Christoform. This actualizes the human spirit, and makes the theology it undertakes an "imago trinitatis." In contrast to Augustine - so Balthasar - there is in Anselm's work a greater stress on the total freedom and spontaneity involved in God's self-disclosure.[227]

In the *Monologion* a philosophical path is treaded to arrive at Christian reason. The arrival is not a simple human achievement but "the free self-expression of God," Whose "generation" is a trinitarian achievement. While this reminds one of Augustine, Balthasar is quick to add that the insistence on divine freedom and the spontaneity of his self-disclosure is an Anselmian addition. Anselm was at the verge of giving up when suddenly the answer "emerged." By living the attitudes of faith, hope and charity, in Balthasar's judgment, Anselm was able to gain knowledge. Therein the "appetitus naturalis ad Deum" finds its movement and goal. The believing act becomes the ability to see matters divine. The human mind actualizes itself as "imago trinitatis" in this attitude by the strength of revelation, which Balthasar describes as "the word of eternal love."[228]

Balthasar would receive scholarship's general agreement in observing that the *Proslogion* is but a condensed form of the *Monologion*. The formula, "quiddam maius quam cogitari possit," is the equivalent to the *Monologion's* "id quo maius cogitari nequit." Both denote "a dynamic movement of thought."[229] However, this dynamism comes not from a concept, but rather from "the revelation of the mercy of the Father in the suffering son." Here a relevant formula appears: "That (mercy) can be thought neither greater nor more just."[230]

According to Balthasar, Anselm joins statements on essence and on existence. The abstract observation must find a "pendent" in reality. If this is the case, Anselm argues, the reality, which is cause for the highest thought, must exist. Therefore, one does not deduce God from a mere concept. Rather the philosophical occurs in the "theological experience of the revelation of the mercy of the Father in the suffering Son."[231] Balthasar gives Anselm's "philosophical" proof a soteriological justification. This "ut nec maior (misericordia) nec iustior cogitari possit" is for Balthasar nothing less than an

---

[226] Balthasar, The Glory of the Lord. Vol. I 151.
[227] Balthasar, Anselm 229ff.
[228] Balthasar, Anselm 231.
[229] Balthasar, Anselm 232.
[230] Balthasar, Anselm 232; cf. Cu II 20: 131,29: "ut nec maior (misericordia) nec iustior cogitari possit."
[231] Balthasar, Anselm 233.

"overwhelming of the aesthetic reason of faith by the incomprehensibility of the divine love." Balthasar thus appreciates Anselm´s Johannine view.

The realization of this dynamic structure of aesthetic reason gives cause for joy, "gaudium" and "delectatio." The hidden terrestial harmonies are likened to the experience of a discoverer who had concentrated his thought for a long time: "gaudeo invenisse - I rejoice in finding."[232] Yet, along with de Lubac, Balthasar notes a rupture in the *Proslogion* and cautions that this intellectual joy of discovering a proof for God´s existence should not be confused with the "visio beatifica": with the joy of beholding God face to face, which is still withheld. Constantly Balthasar stresses the "comprehendit incomprehensibile esse" - and its variants - and parallel to it the "sola fide" in his chapter on Anselm. This is further evidence that he wrote this chapter with Barth and the problematics surrounding the "analogia entis" in mind. The meditation leads into the joy of God and not back to the subject who conjectures. Consequently this joy of the aesthetic reason is seen to be grounded in a staurocentric attitude. In the third Meditation, Balthasar remarks as he closes the first section, Anselm finds nothing but the joy of a grace "given ... as Christ´s Easter present."[233]

The second section, titled "The Radiance of Freedom,"[234] is more dogmatic in nature. Balthasar draws heavily on the treatises *Cur Deus Homo*, *De Veritate*, *De conceptu virginali et de originali peccato*, *De libertate arbitrii*. and the *Meditatio*, dwelling on Anselm´s definition of freedom. This freedom is ultimately found only in the "unitas" and "identitas" of the Godhead. To the degree that human freedom participates in triune freedom, it becomes free. Therefore, it cannot be a part of freedom in the full sense to choose between good and bad, i.e. to be exposed to temptations. Through the two components of law and grace, divine freedom encounters "creaturely freedom." One may consider *Cur Deus Homo* as a demythologizing of the doctrine of redemption by seeing salvation history as the revelation of divine freedom. If God is freedom, Augustine´s teachings on sin and predestination need to be reconsidered, in Anselm´s judgment. Convincingly, Balthasar sees the "analogia entis" not as an abstract principle - as in later theologies - but as an "analogia libertatis" in Anselm´s thought. Absolute freedom calls to creaturely freedom. The revelation of divine freedom is the encounter of humanity with its freedom as a permit to enter into communion. In this event humanity is drawn through grace to absolute freedom. The human freedom thereby attained freely wills (intends) what God freely wills (intends) human will (intention) to will (intend). Concord between divine will and human will is the goal. This in turn excludes the ability to sin as a constitutive element in the human condition. Triune freedom knows not the ability to sin. It is viewed as germane to Anselm´s

---

[232] Balthasar, Anselm 234; cf. P Prooem: 93,20.
[233] Balthasar, Anselm 237.
[234] Balthasar, Anselm 237-253.

329

doctrine of freedom that human beings strive to attain this state of created freedom.

The term used by Anselm to define this alignment of the true and good is rectitude. Balthasar here considers the dimension of the beautiful as again implied.[235] The correspondence of something existent to the highest norm is termed true. Therefore, in Anselm's judgment, the ontic acknowledgment of truth always already contains an ethical truth. As a consequence, Anselm's definition of freedom is that "freedom of the will is the power of preserving the rectitude of the will for the sake of rectitude itself."[236] This effects a novel vista on what freedom, without the aberrations caused by original sin, truly means. Only where the opposition between autonomy and heteronomy have been overcome by a theistic view of life is true freedom beheld. By way of "rectitudo" the mind apprehends a way of participating in full, i.e. divine freedom. Again Balthasar quotes the central Anselmian line: "voluntas non est recta quia vult recte, sed recte vult quoniam recta est."[237]

Against this background Balthasar then illustrates how Anselm contrasts divine freedom with Adam's freedom. Anselm thinks of divine freedom as an identity of "being and self-being,"[238] which is necessarily free of coercion, because it is existent prior to every other thing. In the fall Adam lost his "rectitudo voluntatis." Balthasar seems to stress that unmerited grace alone can restore rectitude.

Balthasar seems to ask whether one can uphold the relational definition of truth and yet claim that God is in and of himself true. He finds an explanation in the "identity of being and self-being." Here one might ask whether a trinitarian answer would not have been better. Trinitarian life has laid down prior to time the norms of willing. Since trinitarian life is established by living the norms, necessity and freedom are one in the Godhead.

Although he had lost the original rectitude - which is the consonance of his will with the divinely ordained good - he still possesses freedom. This reduced freedom still can be utilized to preserve rectitude. Because it was God's free act which created Adam, his creature retains some form of freedom. This freedom is idled ("otiosa") and is reactivated by prevenient and subsequent "grace alone." The acquisition of divine freedom by human freedom is seen in a dialogical and hence personal way. The human being is impelled towards the same rectitude as God's. To this salvific end "memoria" and "intellectus" serve: to establish the "rectum cor."[239] Interestingly, Balthasar points out that Anselm hardly mentions the Augustinian term of "delectatio spiritualis," which was

---

[235] Balthasar, Anselm 239.
[236] Balthasar, Anselm 239.
[237] Balthasar, Anselm 240; cf. Co 3; 265, 28f. "A will is not upright because it wills rightly, but it wills rightly because it is upright."
[238] Balthasar, Anselm 240.
[239] Balthasar, Anselm 244; cf. M 68: 179, 5-9; Co 2: 265, 1-9.

later to play an important role in the controversies surrounding Jansen.[240] The "analogia entis" in Anselm's deliberations "becomes the analogia personalitatis or libertatis:"[241] it is the freest and truest obedience to submit to the will of God. In this context Balthasar dwells on the bridegroom - bride analogies used by Anselm.[242]

If such is the nature of freedom, according to Balthasar, Anselm's treatment of redemption in the *Cur Deus Homo* must follow therefrom. Not by necessity ("debere") but freely ("sponte") does Christ suffer death to save humanity. Balthasar uses the term "inner necessities" to express Anselm's understanding of the divine salvific act. One might want to ponder whether today "congruencies" would not be a more fitting term. However, if this is freely willed, how have God's plans for creation been affected by humanity? As the abundant quotes from Anselm attest, Balthasar conducts a thorough exegesis. Anselm only briefly treats, in Balthasar's judgment, Augustine's aesthetic justification of evil. Human beings were not created as a substitute for the fallen angels, but possessed their own value in God's estimation. Going beyond Augustine, Anselm develops a subtle difference. While God's honor remains untouched by virtue of divine punitive justice, God's love suffers dishonor. He is therefore grateful for the love given him: "Deus ei scit gratias."[243] Humanity's rendering this in turn originates in rectitude, a virtue given by God.[244]

In Balthasar's view Anselm's argument has "nothing of the 'juristic.'"[245] Anselm outright rejects the notion that God was in need of "the blood of the innocent." The Swiss theologian explains that the blemished pearl cannot be part of an ontological union.[246] The rectitude is restored by human beings rising up again. Balthasar interprets Anselm to mean that humanity is an effective party in salvation. Were it merely an inner-trinitarian event, salvation would not affect humanity, for God's expressivity would be missing. For this reason a God-man is needed. Only then is the covenant upheld and does humanity remain a full partner therein. Christ does not merely mediate in an Arian fashion between God and humanity. Echoing the Chalcedonian formula - fully human and fully divine -, Christ also effects a restoration of the covenant: "pacti efficacia."[247] Here again Balthasar's Chalcedonian Christocentrism comes to bear. This interpretation is consonant with Anselm. If the monk says, "I must (debeo) be wholly yours," when entering the monastery, he imitates the God-

---

[240] Balthasar, Anselm 243.
[241] Balthasar, Anselm 245.
[242] Balthasar, Anselm 244f.
[243] Balthasar, Anselm 248; cf. Eadmer, Vita Anselmi I, 41 (PL 158.73B).
[244] Balthasar, Anselm 249.
[245] Balthasar, Anselm 249.
[246] Balthasar, Anselm 243; cf. Cu I 10: 66,25.
[247] Cu II 16: 118,18.

man: "suscipe." The creaturely free act of wholly giving oneself to eternal freedom finds in Christ a model: both in its human "suscipe" and in its goal, - trinitarian freedom.

Since the fall, the Fathers knew that satan holds dominion over humanity. The Fathers perceived satan to have rights over mankind like a master holding rights of ownership over his slaves. Inevitably this held the dangerous prospect of a dualism. God and satan could be seen as opponents on an equal footing. Some arrived at the conclusion that ransom had to be paid to satan in order to free humankind. Anselm rejects the concept of satan holding any rights at all over mankind. As a consequence, Anselm cannot share the Patristic view of Christ paying a ransom to the devil. Rather, Anselm argues that this debt is owed by humanity to God. Humanity has not given the honor due to God. Owing to the deleterious effects of sin, humanity has nothing to offer to satisfy God. Christ, God's only begotten, reconciled his Father with humanity in his death. In the *Cur Deus Homo* Anselm demonstrates how Jesus Christ repays the debt humankind owes to God since the fall in a manner rising above a merely juridical act.

> When we say God exercises weakness or lowliness, we do not understand this in accordance with sublimity of his impassible nature but in accordance with the weakness of the human substance which he bore ... We show that the person of God and of man was one. Therefore, we do not understand the incarnation of God to have involved any abasement: instead, we believe the nature of man was therein exalted.[248]

Anselm reveals in his discussion with Boso that the incarnation would not have been necessary for satisfying satan's claims on humanity. This catches Balthasar's interest. He is less interested in the "rationes necessariae." What, then, is the mission of Christ? To keep his commandments, to honor and serve him, God created rational beings. Humanity finds blessedness and perfection in this service to God. Yet, simply forgiving the sins would not be just in Anselm's argument. Then sinner and non-sinner would be on an equal footing. For this reason atonement is necessary. It is important to note that God in his omnipotence, "qua Deus," is not dishonored. Rather, in his disobedience the sinner had destroyed the only order in which he can render praise and worship to God. Only insofar as humanity dishonors God does it destroy creation. The human being created by God no longer reflects the beauty of his/her maker and therefore no longer can praise the creator.[249] Since humanity cannot out of itself restore the created order, only God can atone for sin. However, since on the other hand humanity owes this satisfaction, only the Son of God, only the God-

---

[248] Glenn W. Olsen, "Hans Urs von Balthasar and the Rehabilitation of St. Anselm's Doctrine of the Atonement," Scottish Journal of Theology 34 (1981): 49-61, at 51; cf. Jasper Hopkins, A Companion to the Study of St. Anselm (Minneapolis: U of Minnesota P, 1972) 187f.

[249] Balthasar, Anselm 251; cf. above: "disorder in the divine entourage," or "disorder at the divine, royal court".

man, could bring this about. To Anselm´s mind God must fulfill "rectitudo" out of his own necessity, otherwise, the world would cease to be good.[250]

Balthasar supports Anselm in his trinitarian point of departure. Generally, Anselm´s view of salvation is rejected as "feudal" and culturally deformed. Balthasar clearly disproves of this evaluation. Quite rightly and in felicitous agreement with numerous other philosophers and theologians, Balthasar thinks that Anselm´s theory of satisfaction bears little resemblance to juridical thinking. One must go back along with Anselm to creation. By a free covenant with humanity God frees this humanity "for absolute freedom." Redemption is an outgrowth of creation. "Christ is not an (Arian) instance of mediation, but rather the effectiveness of the covenant itself ("pacti efficacia"); on him, therefore, the whole human race founded on Adam can converge as its center," Balthasar interprets Anselm.[251] Reading Anselm closely, Balthasar quotes from the *Cur Deus Homo:* "you (human being) do not possess what you give of yourself."[252] On the other hand Christ does not effect something that is merely owed. The response can be but "the impetus of ever greater love," for Balthasar.[253]

God chose to rehabilitate humanity in order to have a full covenant partner in humanity. Humankind had to be enabled to share in divine freedom. The motive of incarnation and redemption is an "analogia personalitatis." The triune God wishes to re-establish a correspondence between himself and the world. Thus, for Anselm God is content to remove the juridical consequences of Adam´s fall. Only a purified heart can perceive the harmony of creation and behold the beauty of the world as a reference to the Trinity´s immanence in the form of Christ. Only a purified soul will behold in the "figure défigurée" the beauty of theophany. What Anselm only indirectly suggests, Balthasar develops further. The "analogia entis" is ultimately the "analogia personalitatis." This is the center of Balthasar´s theological aesthetics. Perhaps Anselm served indeed

---

[250] Balthasar supports this view against some then current views: "Nowadays it has become fashionable ... to revolt against the soteriology as outlined by St. Augustine and put into a system by Anselm of Canterbury (though it was first indicated by St. Paul himself), that God the Father, in order to restore peace between God and the world wished to or was obliged to sacrifice his Son. Does this not betray a cruel God, who in order to restore his honor, as Anselm phrases it, resorts to such horrible means as the total abandonment of his Son on the cross? To think and speak thus is to forget creation and salvation are not unilateral decisions of God the Father, but - speaking humanly - the result of trinitarian communication and prayer. Son and Spirit had a share no less original than that of the Father." Cf. Hans Urs von Balthasar, "Christian Prayer," Communio 5 (1978): 15-22, at 20f.

[251] Balthasar, Anselm 250.

[252] Cu I 20: 87,23f.

[253] Balthasar, Anselm 251.

as a co-inspirer. Through the incarnation the Christian is configured towards the "τυπος Χριστου" and mediates God's being to the world.[254]

In general one sees now how a Johannine outlook assists the author in the interpretation of Anselm. At times the two are blurred. To Balthasar Anselm exemplifies Christian aesthetics almost par excellence. Since revelation is found in salvation and the created order, Anselm's theology radiates a rectitude and balance quite remarkable. Gerard Manley Hopkins is cited as a confirmation of this evaluation. The American Anselm scholar Jasper Hopkins had stated admiringly: "the systematic unfolding and almost total internal consistency of the writings of Anselm of Canterbury have long been cause for amazement." He notes "a perfect harmony" between the early and late writings.[255] This is a feature Anselm has in common with Balthasar. The Swiss theologian also unravels one consistent and coherent mosaic of faith throughout his writings.

As a Benedictine monk, Anselm is aware of the underlying perfect harmony and balance of proportions in the one universe. The primary reality is the revelation of who Christ is. The wisdom of the divine Logos was understood to be cosmological. All of the world was "vestigium dei" and therefore sacred. For this reason he cannot help but see a necessary balance and harmony between human freedom and that of God. While human freedom depends on God's freedom, both together demonstrate the unsurpassable beauty of God to the world. The "rationis pulchritudo," the beauty of reasoning, becomes an independent argument supporting Anselm's reasons for the incarnation. The "rationis pulchritudo" is paralleled by the "rationis contemplatio," the monastic contemplation.[256]

Balthasar convincingly regards "Anselm's aesthetic reason, which considers the mystery of salvation," as an "ultimately monastic reason."[257] The non-Christian contemplation of classical antiquity - seen in exemplary form in Plotinus - achieves in the revelation of Christ its "theoria." Distinct from both the Patristic "intellectus" and the still future "ratio" of High-Scholasticism, "reason is for Anselm the spirit's capacity to gain insight is quite an original approach. To think means to make something spiritually visible." Therein both the monk and his commentator agree.[258]   Contrary to dialectical theology, Anselm advances an "aesthetic reason," able to overcome a dialectics bound to

---

[254] Since both "das Sein" as being and "das Sein" as Being are written with capital letters in German and Balthasar as a consequence does not distinguish between the two in his writings, one encounters in this regard some difficulty. For the above text: Here one senses him threading a "via media" between German idealism's self-actuation and Barth's theomonism (as Balthasar understands it). Going beyond Przywara, he emphasizes divine presence in the world.
Cf. de Schrijver, Le merveilleux accord.
[255] Cf. Hopkins, A Companion 3.
[256] V 11: 191,11.
[257] Balthasar, Anselm 251.
[258] Balthasar, Anselm 220.

sensible matter. Such "an aesthetic reason" is grounded in contemplation and is able to unite all perspectives into one whole vision. This is "a simple understanding, not overwhelmed by the multiplicity of imaginations."[259]

Both creation and salvation are necessarily free acts of God. Human reason possesses the capacity to uncover an internal, consistent logic which allows one to perceive the consonances, and consequently the necessities of various components in the reciprocal roles as contributors to the whole. In the spontaneity of human freedom - as the conscious affirmation of freedom comes about through relations - lies the key to understanding Anselm's theory of salvation.

> It is loving, creaturely freedom, which wholly gives itself up to eternal freedom, and on its side finds a model in the trinitarian freedom of the Son, whose spontaneous loving obedience to the Father is necessitated by nothing, but in the splendors of his absolute freedom is that which is most acceptable to God and, to that extent, most necessary: "debuit facere, quia quod voluit fieri debuit; et non debuit facere, quia non ex debito."[260]

The *Cur Deus Homo* states: "He ought to do it, because what he wills, ought to be done; and yet he does not have to do it, because it is not required of him as a debt." [261] With no harm to him, God makes his "con-descendence" proportionate to the human condition.[262] For this reason "juridical" is in Balthasar's view not the correct adjective for Anselm's theory of salvation. Thereby, Balthasar means to state that while certainly atonement has a juridical element, it is not the heart of God's salvific intention according to Anselm. Participation in divine life is to be faciliated by the "bonitas Dei."

Unlike Christ, no human being could offer himself beyond all calculation. Anselm sees in atonement the covenant of God with his people upheld. This is the deeper cause for rejecting a purely legalistic interpretation of Anselm's theory of atonement. As an outgrowth of triune life, it occurs "spontaneously." If a legal dimension is to be conceded, it is part of a yet greater moment: God is mercy and to that degree not in contradiction to his own laws (which he himself had promulgated in divine sovereignty), which are again a part of his divine inner consistency and coherence. The necessity encountered here lies in the inner-trinitarian freedom of the Son.[263] It occurs within the context of fittingness ("rectitudo"). God cannot be less than fully himself. In this perspective necessity is nothing external or accidental. To lay the narrow

---

[259] "simplicem intellectum et non multiplicate phantasmatum obrutum" Ii 10: 289,10. Cf. Balthasar, Anselm 223 including footnote 111.

[260] Balthasar, Anselm 252.

[261] Cu II 18: 129,6-8.

[262] Olsen, "Hans Urs von Balthasar" 56.

[263] Balthasar, Anselm 252.

legalistic reading to rest, Balthasar quotes Anselm: because "it is not required of him (Christ) as a debt (quia non ex debito)."[264]

12.4.1 Balthasar's Soteriology: a Nuanced Appropriation and Further Development of Anselm's Theory of Atonement

In pursuing Anselm's soteriology an examination of Balthasar's theory of atonement must go beyond the slender essay on Anselm in *The Glory of the Lord*. Balthasar attempts to tread in this regard a via media. He wants to posit neither a radical divine "απαθεια," nor a simple, equal mutuality in effecting salvation. Both positions bring unwelcome results. If one states a simple equal mutuality between God and the contingent event of crucifixion, one cannot avoid the consequence of identifying God with the world process. History becomes a part of trinitarian life. Balthasar wants to avoid a Hegelian identification of the world with the Trinity in a process-like approach. Still, like Bulgakov he considers the generation of the Son the first divine "κενωοσις."[265] On the other hand, the model of divine immutability holds the prospect of deism.

Balthasar's interpretation of *Cur Deus Homo* can best be understood by considering volume III of *Theodramatik*. There one finds a sustained treatment of the soteriological problem. According to the biblical evidence sin touches something in God, perhaps an "outer honor" which calls forth divine wrath.[266] Balthasar points out that the Old Testament attests to this about one thousand times.[267] The New Testament affirms it as well. God's judgment is divine anger at sin (Heb 12:29; 1Cor 3:12; 1Pet 1:7). Sin is taken seriously (Jn 12:31; 16:10f). God's saving justice saves humanity by the concentration of all sin in Christ (2Cor 5:21; Gal 3:13). Scripture attests to the realism of salvation. This is the basis for Balthasar's soteriology. Lactantius' treatise *De Ira Dei* plays a significant role in demonstrating this.[268] It shows divine involvement in the world and rejects the concept of divine impassibility held by numerous Church Fathers. In this perspective - as well as in Anselm's - anger is an integral moment of divine grace. In the Godhead mercy and justice as well as anger and dishonor are not contradictions. On the cross the divine anger is revealed as divine suffering. God engages with the world. Here - in contrast to Anselm - Balthasar makes a distinction between God's outer and inner dishonor, inflicted by humanity's sin.

Of central concern for Balthasar is to demonstrate that Christ's living obedience of the Father in crucifixion is more than a symbol for God's intense love of humanity, or simply the removal of God's anger. It is God's effecting

---

[264] Balthasar, Anselm 252, footnote 277; Cu 18: 129,6-8.
[265] Balthasar, Theodramatik. Vol. III 273-299; Balthasar, Theodramatik. Vol. IV 148-155.
[266] Balthasar, Theodramatik. Vol. III 236f for Anselm, cf. also 15-63.
[267] Balthasar, Anselm 290.
[268] Balthasar, Anselm 315f

reconciliation of humanity to himself, by "substituting" his only-begotten Son for humankind. The substitution "pro nobis" and "pro me" (Gal 2:20; 1Cor 15:3) is more than a mere act of superficial solidarity. It is an ontological concentration of sin in the God-man, which is rejected by God the Father. This in turn brings forth a total "abandonment" of Christ by his Father on the cross (as regards this sin).

While the notion of divine honor is problematic today in Balthasar's understanding, Anselm's basic intuition is correct: divine justice is gracious and exigent. Therein divine love is revealed. The Swiss theologian considers the cross as a trinitarian drama and thereby he thinks he can overcome the objection that the Father is being cruel in sending his Son to such a death. All three divine persons freely conceive and execute the plan of redemption. In the extreme "diastasis" of abandonment and descent into hell by Father and Son in the Holy Spirit the divine love is revealed as overarching and annulling the sinfulness of the world. Such love is a fulfillment of God's role in the covenant and the restoration of humanity as a full covenant partner in divinely granted freedom. Anselm's theory of freedom shines through here. Within this horizon the Anselmian "juridical" theory of divine honor/dishonor and justice finds its proper place within a deeper penetration and profounder justification.[269] Yet, in comparison to Anselm, Balthasar in no uncertain terms shifts the emphasis. No longer is God's injured honor in the foreground, but divine love is.

Gerald O'Collins[270] characterizes Balthasar's position as "monstrous." This seems to amount to a misunderstanding of Balthasarian theology as a whole. But as Raymund Schwager proposes, if Balthasar were to emphasize more the divine anger as an expression of divine compassion and solidarity, such a misunderstanding could have been avoided.[271] In critical dialogue with contemporary theologians such as Küng, Galot, Schillebeeckx and Bultmann, Balthasar's position on the salvific value of Jesus' crucifixion gained its unmistakable contours. He particularly expressed disagreement with Karl Rahner's position.[272] Christ's obedience on the cross does not merely signify and express the fact that God is "always already" reconciled with sinners, but, as Balthasar never fails to insist that through and in the cross Christ effects reconciliation.[273]

Rahner contends, in a fashion faithful to Thomas, that it is impossible for a secondary cause to effect change in the divine. Therefore Rahner outright rejects the Anselmian notion that Christ's sacrifice appeased divine wrath; no

[269] Balthasar, The Glory of the Lord. Vol. VII 207ff.
[270] Gerald O'Collins, Interpreting Christ (Oxford: Oxford UP, 1983) 152-155.
[271] Raymund Schwager, "Der wunderbare Tausch" zur Geschichte und Deutung der Erlösungslehre (München: Kösel, 1986) 5-44.
[272] Karl Rahner, Schriften zur Theologie. Wissenschaft und christlicher Glaube. Vol. 15 (Zürich: Benzinger, 1983) 236-264.
[273] Balthasar, Theodramatik. Vol. III 253-262.

change occurs in God. On the other hand, Balthasar must grant that a change occurs. For this reason Jesus must be the Christ, that is to say, must be both God and man. No Arian-like subordinate identity will suffice. One might make the case that Anselm's soteriology assists Balthasar in combating what he perceives as Arian tendencies in twentieth century theology.

We must get away from a subordinationist or Arian view of the redemption: a supreme God the Father issuing orders to an inferior God (theos deuteros) or demigod or superman. No, as Christians our starting point can only be a consubstantial (homoousios) trinity, in which the freedom, dignity and spontaneity of the Son and Spirit do not just approve and execute the orders of the Father's creative and salvific plan, but conceive it at the very beginning in the most perfect unity with him. Now, in this plan of salvation, it is the Son who will have to suffer in order to justify the world, even though guilty, being judged finally `very good'; it is he who will have to bear the weight like a spiritual Atlas. So it is not enough to think of him just acquiescing in what the Father proposes. No we have to accept that the proposal proceeds originally from him, that he offers himself to the Father in order to sustain and save the work of creation. And it seems to me that this proposal of the Son touches the heart of the Father - to speak in human terms - more profoundly than even the world's sin; it opens in God a wound of love from before creation- or, if you like, it is the sign and expression of this ever-open wound in the heart of the trinity. A wound identical with the procession and circuminsession of the divine persons in their perfect beautitude. This wound comes before the fall , which is the point St. Anselm is concerned with, namely, the offence done to the Father by sin, the offence expiated by the Son, the only one capable of this work which must be supererogatory. And if the wound of which we speak comes before all this, there is no problem in accepting that. For the salvation of the world, the Father sends the Son, guided on the earth by the Spirit, who at every moment indicates to him the will of the Father and that this will is at once an infinite love of creatures and infinite respect for the offer of the Son, which has been accepted by the Father and allowed by the Spirit to be realized, to the point of that supreme diastasis of the Father and the Son on the Cross, which is in truth the ultimate revelation of the tripersonality of God.[274]

Following in Bulgakov's wake, Balthasar sees the wound inflicted on the Father as discrediting creation.[275] Creation is a trinitarian opus. The dishonor original sin had caused, is vis-à-vis almighty divine nature - and therefore secondarily also for humanity - surely superficial, i.e. not mortal, yet real. Whatever change occurs in God is effected by the inner-trinitarian initiative. On the other hand vulnerability is eternal and is addressed by the divinity. Hence, no harm is done to divine sovereignty - and adjoined to its immutability.[276] In the introduction to *Die großen Ordensregeln,* Balthasar sees in Christ not only a mission which distinguishes him as a person; he is the Father's mission. "He

---

[274] As translated by John Saward, The Mysteries of March. Hans Urs von Balthasar on the Incarnation and Easter (Washington D.C.: Catholic UP, 1990) 159f, note 15, from Balthasar, Au Coeur du mystère rédempteur 39f.

[275] Balthasar, The Glory of the Lord. Vol. VII 213ff.

[276] Cf. Balthasar, Theodramatik. Vol. III 240f.248,252-262; Balthasar, Cordula oder der Ernstfall 63-65; Balthasar, Mysterium Paschale 133-137; Balthasar, The Glory of the Lord. Vol. VII 213ff.

does not identify with it; from eternity he is identical with it. This is his truth ... he is not obedience, his (very) essence is complete obedience, and this is for him eternal freedom." The reference to eternal freedom indicates his debt to Anselm.[277]

From early on Balthasar does not separate Christology from the trinitarian doctrine. Along with the Cyrillian reception of the council of Chalcedon, he maintains that "one of the Trinity suffers for us."[278] Without the reality of the contents of this formula, soteriology is an impossible task. Also this aspect reveals the internal consistency and abundant wealth of insights characteristic of Balthasar's endeavor. If he defines the "Gestalt" as the "universale concretum et personale," i.e. God's universal truth and love in one concrete form, then he does not make a case for a vague unifying principle. His "Schau der Gestalt," his sense for the whole, navigates him successfully through the treacherous waters of soteriology. In Christ the "plerôma" of the trinity corporeally dwells.[279]

By recapitulating the central moments of Balthasar's soteriology one senses a nuanced change in the appropriation-process of Anselm's soteriology. The trinitarian dimensions are fully developed and the "wound" takes on a different quality. Yet, the wound/dishonor in the Godhead remains and is repaired by the actual crucifixion of Christ. This is integrated into the wealth of the Father's soteriology and Balthasar's own contribution.

In spite of its richness, this polychrome tableau defies systematization. Every serious critique of Balthasar's model must be cognizant of this (O'Collins, Rahner, Schwager). The salvific event - as a trinitarian event - defies a forced interpretation into a totally coherent system because of the mystery-nature of salvation.[280]

The whole of Anselm's thought reaches its culmination and "final illumination" in his prayers. "Aesthetic reason" is prayer.[281] It is neither a Patristic "intellectus" nor a Scholastic "ratio" but a "spiritual vision."[282] In every life-situation it might occur suddenly ("subito"). It is an occurrence similar to the Platonic "exaiphnes."[283] Fulfilled freedom is "freedom [grounded]

---

[277] Balthasar, Die großen Ordensleben 9f.

[278] Rahner avoids using this formula lest one confuse the two natures of Christ. Cf. Rahner, Schriften zur Theologie. Vol. 15 210-213.

[279] Cf. Col 2,9; Balthasar, Theologik. Vol. II: Wahrheit Gottes (Einsiedeln: Johannes, 1985) 20-23.

[280] Cf. Hans Urs von Balthasar, "Mysterium Paschale," Mysterium Salutis III,2 Johannes Feiner and Magnus Löhrer eds. (Einsiedeln: Benzinger, 1962): 133-153, 104; Balthasar, Au coeur du mystère Rédempteur 10ff; Balthasar, Pneuma and Institution 403f; Balthasar, Theodramatik. Vol. III 211. 218-224.236.310.

[281] Balthasar, Anselm 212.

[282] Balthasar, Anselm 220.

[283] Balthasar, Anselm 230-234.

339

in the good."[284] Anselm sees freedom fulfilled as the ability to "see nothing that lies beyond their desire and thus can no longer sin because of it."[285] The most fitting term is concord. Human freedom transcends itself and attains a quality of freedom which is concord and love. Here the church becomes most real.

The only alternative is the abyss "sine fundo ... nisi misericordia retineatur."[286] This is the consequence of the loss of rectitude. Again, Anselm is referred to: God did not have to suffer, but humanity needed a suffering God. Anselm is consistently interpreted by Balthasar in a staurocentric manner. Balthasar cites Anselm even to state that the mother of God is angry at the sins committed. After thematizing the christological, staurocentric and trinitarian dimensions of Anselm's thought, Balthasar touches briefly the Marian dimension in Anselm's works. The hope of humanity rests in the third prayer to Mary, in the fact that the Mother of God has made Jesus humanity's brother. This fact brings consolation, for therein lies salvation's certitude.

In what follows, Balthasar quotes from Anselm's Orations dealing with Christ and Peter, Paul, John and Mary Magdalene. This is done to demonstrate Anselm's broad understanding of faith as multi-dimensional. It integrates the Petrine ("gather up the sheep"), Pauline ("teaching - you ... educate in the faith of Christ"), Johannine ("love one another") and even the Magdalenian ("grief") elements of faith.[287] It serves to illustrate how "Anselm puts down his roots everywhere in the manifest almightiness of love."[288] Every state of life is open to the "analogia libertatis" which is "this concord of love." In the controversy over investiture Balthasar considers the defense of the liberty of the Church and of the Holy See as articulating his life-long care for the "concordia" of the mystical body. The unity and the holiness of the Church, the uncompelled freedom of Christ's bride, are threatened. The secular order can only defend this ecclesial freedom and never dominate it. To Anselm, freedom is an indispensable necessity.

As if to put to shame those criticizing Anselm for being rationalistic, Balthasar quotes Anselm:

as we are aware of the sun through its rays before we see it unveiled, so we are aware of God from the reflection (speculatio) of our reason: if we discover anything true in the light of truth, then we are aware at the same time of him by recognition and love in faith and hope. In the future we shall see him face to face ...[289]

---

[284] Balthasar, Anselm 253.
[285] Balthasar, Anselm 253; Ca 6: 243,20-22; 25: 273,29f.
[286] Balthasar, Anselm 254; C 8: 275,13f.
[287] Balthasar, Anselm 256f.
[288] Balthasar, Anselm 257f.
[289] Balthasar, Anselm 259.

And so, for Anselm there remains - as Balthasar observes - a "yearning longing for glory."[290]

One might object to Balthasar's overflowing wealth of citations. They hold the danger of a lost focus, structure and theme. Over long sections it is more a dialogue with the respective texts than a rigorously sustained argument. Hints are dropped, suggestions floated and vistas opened, only to be explained and developed at other places. The vision is sometimes blurred by virtue of its comprehensiveness. These are the negative consequences of a broad approach. Sometimes one is tempted to believe one should not press all of a theologian's writings under the overarching aesthetic concern. This notwithstanding, he certainly does not abuse Anselm's writings as a mere stone-quarry for a deliberate construction of his own approach to theology. He is able to demonstrate a fundamental, inner harmony which ultimately is non-contradictory. He considers the symphonic interrelatedness of theology as grounded in scripture and tradition. Like Anselm and all major theologians he struggles to join with the symphony of the Church Catholic through time and space: "sentire cum ecclesia." Balthasar avoids the rigidity of a system and even points out how scripture is deliberately unsystematic.

Balthasar writes in the style of an artist on a meandering journey of exploration. One shares in the joys of discovery the author makes. The author is quite independent from scholarly opinions on Anselm and refrains from engaging in a dialogue with such sources even in the footnotes. This has the advantage of producing yet more sharply the intellectual profile of Anselm. The result is a greater fidelity to the issues Anselm raised and the solutions he offered.

Balthasar's approach has frequently been criticized for its christomonism. Knowledge of God occurs only in Christ. The pneumatological and ecclesiological dimensions receive little attention in "clerical styles" but are treated later in volume VII. Easily one can take the last quote Balthasar has on the chapter devoted to Anselm as an indication of what his ideal of a theologian was. It is a citation from Eadmer's *Vita* II:

> He whose aim in serving is directed towards the recovery of the kingdom of eternal life strives to stick to God through thick and thin and with unshakeable perseverance to place his whole trust in him ... Strong in patience, he rejoices in all things and says with the Psalmist: Magna est gloria Domini. This glory, even in this earthen pilgrimage, he has a taste of ; and as he savours he desires it; and with great desire he salutes it while yet far off. Thus he is supported by the hope of attaining it, and consoled by it in the midst of all earthly dangers, and he sings with great joy: Magna est gloria Domini.[291]

[290] Balthasar, Anselm 259.
[291] Balthasar, Anselm 259; cf. Eadmer Vita II; 32; PL 158,93.

It is important to note the valence Balthasar attributes to the thought of Anselm he profiles. Rather Anselm´s attitude to faith and his theological conduct are central to the cognitive and existential actuation of faith (= "Vollzug des Glaubens") in the Church. The monastic unity of philosophy and theology serve this purpose.

Prayer is not a mere beautiful postlude, but central to understanding Anselm. Prayer is the fitting description of trinitarian dialogue: "What we describe anthropomorphically as trinitarian dialogue might just as rightly be called trinitarian prayer."[292] Both Anselm and Balthasar see in theology a particular form of participation in divine life. It is "pure archetypical prayer," paradigmatic for the entire attitude, form and contents of our human prayer.[293] Therefore, Balthasar believes "creation and salvation to be acts of the whole trinity."[294]

The exuberance of perspectives and citations Balthasar supplies can endanger the ability to keep the aesthetic focus. One does detect a slight tendency towards description and narration rather than argumentation. Philosophers and biblical scholars find this somewhat disconcerting at times. His ability to perceive all the figures in one sweeping perspective is a convincing argument for his aesthetic intuition. The rediscovery of Christ in the center of theology entails seeing that all facets of this discipline refer to this one form. All theologians play the one and same score. One finds, even in a theologian like Anselm, a contrapuntual blending of opposites into one symphonic concordance.

Balthasar judges Anselm to represent something of the "kairos" of his age.[295] His theology is deemed singular, harmonic and symphonic because it is oriented towards truth.[296] Flowing from this, scripture and magisterium are judged to be interrelated.[297] Anselm is seen as continuing the monastic-contemplative tradition of the first millennium with a special concern for the Benedictine emphasis on freedom, community and dialogue.

12.5 Reasons for a Non-Rationalistic Appropriation of Anselm

One may object that Balthasar has engaged in a forced and one-sided reading of Anselm. Some may make the case that by using terms such as "ratio necessaria," "rationis necessitas" and "necessitas veritatis," Anselm actually subscribes to the same necessitarian rationality Balthasar deplores, condemns and attempts to overcome for theology in *The Glory of the Lord*. On the other hand, if one treats Anselm so kindly, should not Thomas, Abelard and even

---

[292] Balthasar, "Christian Prayer" 19.
[293] Balthasar, "Christian Prayer" 20.
[294] Balthasar, "Christian Prayer" 21f.
[295] Balthasar, "Christian Prayer" 29.
[296] Balthasar, "Christian Prayer" 22f.
[297] Balthasar, The Glory of the Lord. Vol. I 555.

Neo-Scholasticism enjoy equally favorable treatment? Indeed it appears necessary to posit against pure randomness of freedom a Neoplatonic monism. The obvious conclusion would be to consider Anselm as espousing a form of Neo-platonism. More precisely, how is one to uphold freedom, the unity of reality and the necessity of reason at the very same time and under the same consideration? Is one not forced into an "aporia", into an inextricable dilemma?

The response Balthasar would give is that Anselm, along with the other theologians he discussed, displays in his thought a principal openness to the Triune God which defies systematization. Perhaps Balthasar should have made this assertion to be the central misunderstanding with which Anselm's theology is confronted. This holds true especially for those who consider Anselm exclusively from a logical and/or philosophical perspective. The contemplation of the beauty of Christ, the epiphany of the glory of God in incarnation, wards off an autonomous, rationalistic approach to theology and calls for the human mind's openness to the "intelligere" of incarnation. The "unfreedom" of logic is to lock Being into a timeless structure. The freedom of the aesthetic, however, apprehends the free integrity of a historical, particular concrete, which possesses the quality of beauty by virtue of its own inner rectitude.

Anselm is seen as an example of a theologian subscribing implicitly to a doctrine of personal, gratuitous divine illumination. Balthasar's concern is to demonstrate with Anselm that the human mind is by its very nature constituted in a way receptive to this gift. In contrast to Aristotelian rationalism - here one could ask whether such a term does justice to Aristotle - Anselmic rationality is free. Equally, the intelligibility of the order of creation cannot be commanded. The pure gift of God's self-revelation cannot be arrived at by a static Platonic contemplation of ideas, but by a trinitarian and Christocentric mind towards which human "intelligere" has been "a priori" created. Such a theological epistemology cannot but see autonomous reason as legitimate only insofar as it is able to delineate the human mind's scope to think its own limits, but incapable of transcending these limits. If it ventures beyond these limits -set by contingency and original sin - or yet more correctly if it does not perceive the limits as the limits of reality - it fails to experience the personal and gift nature of the knowledge of truth. More significantly, the putatively self-sufficient mind will or may think an insurmountable hiatus exists between the reality it can think and the reality beyond the same. A theological epistemology so defined maintains and affirms both the distinction between nature and grace and their relatedness. This finally distinguishes theology from religious studies. It is aware of its graced participation in a broad breadth which encircles, embraces and contains the subject of theology and never vice-versa.

Every systematization is prone to the danger of either identifying nature with grace or of perceiving an irreconcilable difference. Thomism enclosed the rational integrity of incarnate truth within the confines of transcendentally necessary structures of systematic thought. Such a systematic approach is to

Balthasar geometric and rationalistic and, therefore, wanting in a dramatic, personal, historically concrete point d'appui which is the form of Christ. As a consequence, the theologian is defined as one freely formed by the contents of a personal revelation of that form which is the glory of God in Christ.

Parallel to the discontinuity in architectural style - Roman/Romanesque versus Gothic - Balthasar notes a decline in theological style during Scholasticism. The self-defeating suppression of the personal moment of revelation led to Protestantism's anti-intellectualism, rejecting the "analogia entis" along with rationalism.

Departing from the previously held cosmological viewpoint, Jesus Christ is ultimately thought of by some as implied in the immanent order of rationally fathomable things. In this vein, theology had difficulties distinguishing itself sometimes from the natural sciences. Increasingly, theologians no longer considered revelation and grace as congruent, but as different from the universe. Soon Christ came to be thought of as implicit in the human spirit. This human spirit is, however, no longer seen as a part of a sacral order, but as part of a natural world. The fact of original sin is no longer considered. Christ is one component among many in a fixed world of which humanity is a part. The fault for this development is to no small degree to be sought in the enterprise of theologians who systematize faith into a coherent system under the implied imperative of logical universality. Such a view is abstract and non-historical. The concrete uniqueness of Christ is thereby disregarded.

Barth had criticized Catholic theology - and in Balthasar's judgment rightfully - precisely on these grounds: it failed to acknowledge the living God of the Gospels to be beyond the reach of the human mind. Only by divine gratuity is Christ known. In Balthasar's own language, it is not only gratuity in the sense of a "sola gratia," but of divine love. The consequences of the latter are portrayed in *The Glory of the Lord*. The theologies discussed in volume II are not systems, or methods, but rather "styles." Such a theological aesthetics does not yield to the allurements of synthesis and logical coherence, but as the opening prayer in the *Proslogion* demonstrates, is open for the Christian mystery. For this reason tensions in genuine theology shall ever remain. They defy systematization. By virtue of the personal encounter with the always one form of Christ in the event of faith, truth is to Balthasar always symphonic.

While he uses terms such as "Aristotelian," "Platonic," "Scholastic," "Augustinian," "Patristic," etc., Balthasar considers none of the styles to be a perfect examples. Each is an alloy in a dialectical sense. A pure method would contradict the theological intention. Only when blending strains of styles in a symphonic manner does an individual theologian or a school of thought realize the full Catholicity that finds its root in the mystery of Christ. Only such a culture remains receptive to Christ's beauty. If this is not the case, then Christ is relegated to second position. Then a theological a priori is posited as the guiding principle of theology, which ultimately is reducible to an immanent structure or concept of autonomous reason.

Balthasar criticizes Thomas for confusing philosophy and theology. In the long term he thereby deprived theology of the poetic freedom of revelation. Neither the cosmological view of medieval times nor the anthropological position dominant at least since Blondel do justice to the actual subject and object of theological inquiry. An immanent a priori is substituted for Christ. Obviously this in turn determines the outcome of a theological investigation. With such a substitution theology as an act of faith runs the danger of being deformed into an immanent, cosmic and human possibility. From the known order of nature one now attempts to extrapolate towards God. No longer is theology understood to be the work of Christ in the believer.[298] It then stands to reason that we should place increased emphasis on the biblical and practical aspects of theology.

Donald Keefe[299] criticizes Balthasar's approach for being "trans-rational"[300] and pleads the cause of systematic - perhaps better systematized - theology. Here he posits an opposition in principle between methodology and beauty. The latter defies a grasp by the human mind. However, the conclusions reached by both Anselm and Balthasar remain "retraceable" a posteriori. The thoughts and conclusions remain intelligible. It seems Keefe applies too much the arguments he had developed in the comparative study on Thomism and Tillich's theology to Balthasar.[301] Balthasar along with Barth rejected that kind of theology primarily because humanity is created in God's image. The analogy, therefore, abides. Nor is in Balthasar's judgment the aesthetic style merely culturally conditioned. Rather it is a graced charism not systematically deducible.

Certainly Anselm and Balthasar maintain along with Keefe that the created order is able to think the incarnation of the Word in a rational manner. While the human mind cannot encompass the simultaneity of nature and supernatural reality, it can converge towards it. The fallen mind remains the mind of an image of God and therefore, for both Balthasar and Anselm, theology can be both art and reasonable. Balthasar stressed the artistic areas, Anselm the rational aspect, of reality. However, one cannot completely disagree with Keefe if he claims Balthasar's emphasis on the beauty of incarnation leaves one "with a radical passivity of Revelation."[302] Yet, Anselm and Balthasar maintain the inseparable unity of the beauty and truth of Christ.

---

[298] Cf. Balthasar, Glaubhaft ist nur die Liebe 25ff.

[299] Donald J. Keefe, "A Methodological Critique of von Balthasar's Theological Aesthetics," Communio 5 (1978): 23-43.

[300] Keefe, "A Methodological Critique" 29.

[301] Cf. Donald J. Keefe, Thomism and the Ontological Theology of Paul Tillich, A Comparison of Systems (Leiden: Brill, 1971).

[302] Keefe, "A Methodological Critique" 34.

Confronted with the reality of the incarnation, of the vision of the form, Balthasar does advocate strongly a Marian attitude. On the other hand Keefe fails to consider adequately Balthasar´s claim that systematization tends to demonstrate all of faith´s propositions i.e the sanctifying realm of the Church and its sacraments to be rationally deducible by everyone without divine assistance.

By virtue of the personal encounter with the form of Christ in the event of faith truth is to Balthasar always symphonic. This axiom resonates powerfully throughout his work. Anselm thinks towards and in the same form. Such a notion of the integrity of the intelligible unity of truth cannot be reduced to equations of logic. He takes exception to the self-contained systematics which he thought, Karl Rahner and other contemporary theologians had attempted. The aesthetic approaches throughout Christian history display a remarkable unanimity: "In your light, we see light" (Augustine). All mediated concepts of God are eclipsed by a sensible knowledge of God grounded in im-mediate, aesthetic experience of the triune glory of God. From Irenaeus to Bonaventure, all theologians discussed in volume II give testimony to the free illumination by God as the "conditio sine qua non" for theology.

"Esse" is not "intelligere" by itself, but "videre" of a light which is directed to something other than the subject. In this the subject experiences the free illumination of the mind towards truth. This ontological dynamism or tension in turn enables freedom. To this extent Anselm is Augustinian. Beyond this, but consonant with tradition, Anselm sees the gift of wisdom manifest in the Church of Christ without using the term "forma" expressly in this context. "Esse" becomes "videre" and thereby an amplified "esse."

Since knowledge is event, Christian faith may not - as Irenaeus, Anselm and Bonaventure attest - be Platonized and simply supra-historical. These theologians affirm the historicity of Christ and his church. The Logos is historical and no mere myth. Sacraments are not mere signs but realities. For this reason Balthasar promotes the christocentrism of a theological aesthetics.

While Thomas did note the indispensability of illumination[303] - "trahi in Deo, instinctus fidei" - this occurred only late in his life and did not have consequences for Thomism. Thomist epistemology became intellectualistic. The free gift of faith was transformed into a necessary structure of the human mind. Then the historicity of the incarnation became accidental. Fideism and rationalism have, in this way, the same origin. Only by maintaining the constitutive free element of the theological aesthetics does one safeguard the transcendence of God and the historicity of divine revelation.

The concern of *The Glory of the Lord* is original in its attempt to articulate a theological aesthetics. Theology as the testimony to the one incarnate revelation herein becomes a polychrome work of art by artists with

---

[303] S.Th. IIa IIae, Qd. 2,10 in Qudl. 2 and in Comm. in Ion. V.VI.XV.

free and ardent hearts, variant tempers and differing talents. While Balthasar remained relatively close to one particular style, namely Plotinus´, he courageously addressed the dangers endemic to every systemic attempt and, like Anselm, avoids successfully the temptations of a system. He is perhaps thereby better equipped to establish a vision of a synthesis than any previous theologian. His lasting contribution lies in giving theology a new structure with which to behold the Form. Last but not least, due to his all-encompassing Christological "Schau der Gestalt," "the most cultured man of our times" - as the late Cardinal Henri de Lubac once described him[304] - was gifted to detect in Anselm´s notion of "rectitudo" the principle of analogy as freedom realized and, therefore, able to write a seminal, almost definitive essay on Anselm which surely may be considered a classic in the field of Anselm research.

Modernity´s fateful equation of freedom with autonomy is overcome. Freedom is only partially a natural condition. Full freedom is actualized in faith. In Anselm´s view, freedom only so apprehended is the yardstick for true humanity.

---

[304] Henri de Lubac, "A Witness of Christ in Church, Hans Urs von Balthasar," Communio 2 (1975): 218-235, at 230.

347

CHAPTER THIRTEEN
13.0 Cognitional Unity as Anticipation of the Heavenly Jerusalem

13.1 Anselm's Contribution to a Global Culture
The megatrend "McWorld" stands for today's globe. The simultaneity of
event and message can be experienced equally intensively by everyone everywhere. The guideline of a telecommunicative world implies: all are here and
now, and yet so far away. Everything is significant - a new auto model, a coup
d'état in Africa - and perhaps precisely for that reason not at all. The sensiti-
vities for justice and injustice globally blend into one. The figure of a gradual
step by step, of a leisurely then-and-thereafter is extinct. Ubiquity and
hankering for the immediately available and disposable thrive. Everything
occurs simultaneously - or even earlier. The event is equally real and virtual.
From mediated pictures and "signatures"[1] and not from immediate, personal
experience do the consumers of the global market derive their identities. Are
we moderns "upon this bank and shoal of time" still masters of our actions - still
persons? The "global village's" market is much like a supermarket offering the
most diverse and yet increasingly identical products disseminating "truth." It is
the truth of economic pragmatics and political utility. The emblem of the
mobile phone conveys the message "I am here and for everyone available - and
yet, not with myself and yet not on the ball." The semantics of the "McWorld" -
as the American sociologist Benjamin Barber[2] defines this universal disposabi-
lity of human beings and of goods, the globally identical patterns of
consumption and the almost equally worldwide availability of human beings is
completely and utterly unideological and what is yet more telling,
unphilosophical. As the old matrices of order and relation lose their cohesive
force in the regions and capitals of post-modernity - their atmospherics
heightened to the neurotic - the ephemeral, the trivial, and the arbitrarily and
randomly staged triumph. In view of these wide-ranging escapist movements
one is confronted anew and with heretofore unknown radicality with the
question: What constitutes the world's center, what is existence's meaning and
purpose? Does it suffice to transpose this "brave new world" into a unit held
together only by economic interdependence and telecommunicative integration?
Vice-versa, can the human being be content by complying with the summons
emanating forth from globalization: consumerism and performance, prosperity

---

[1] Abbreviating words and expressions such as "McDonald's," "egalité," "gravitas" etc.
defining the atmospherics and Zeitgeist of an epoche. Cf. Benno von Wiese, Signaturen. Zu
Heinrich Heine und seinen Werken (Frankfurt am Main: Erich Schmidt, 1976).
[2] Bejamin Barber, Jihad v. McWorld, How Globalism and Tribalism are re-shaping the
World (New York: Ballantine, 1996).

and ephemeral   pictures of deception, "that Power which erring men call Chance?"[3]

Towards the possible finale of post-modernity, thinking seems to have arrived at a blind alley. For a long time a hermeneutics of suspicion and a system of a methodological securing of every cognitional step in theory and praxis much like a bookkeeper seemed au courant and the best way to safeguard the individual's sovereignty. Only in this way did the modern temper consider it possible to be blazing, in the Enlightenment's trail, equipped with the pathos of realizing freedom in a world without Augustine's "memoria." Today, however, the consequences of such a scientific disposition are evident in every facet of modern life. Society implodes into unrelated entities and individuals fearful of and yet yearning for relationships. Disillusion is widespread: it is obvious that Cartesian suspicion cannot give birth to freedom. Reminiscent of Becket's *Waiting on Godot*, the modern Zeitgeist exudes a sense of uncomfortable - and more significantly uneasy - waiting. "Freedom" betrays itself as a euphemism for a lack of pillars and those waiting know not for what. Without history and without the experience of previous ages modernity would not know what to await.

It is Anselm's position that even "remoto Christo" the human mind is inalienably disposed to and pines for - and to that degree unrelentingly pursues - the personal revelation of divine existence. In the present era of globalism - when neither religious nor cultural "guard rails" are evident - this insight gains in significance. This human disposition for the Divine finds its orientation in "memoria."

13.2 "Memoria" as a Christian Attitude

Ist nicht vielmehr alle menschliche Existenz, auch die freieste, begrenzt und auf mannigfaltige Weise bedingt? Wenn das zutrifft, dann ist die Idee einer absoluten Vernunft überhaupt keine Möglichkeit des geschichtlichen Menschentums. Vernunft ist für uns nur als reale geschichtliche, d.h. schlechthin: sie ist nicht ihrer selbst Herr, sondern bleibt stets auf die Gegebenheiten angewiesen, an denen sie sich betätigt.[4]

Gadamer's thesis is that culture comes about only through "anamnesis." This means culture requires a cognitional and existential effort. It occurs through a remembering dialogue of the present with the past. History is not a mere stone quarry for producing historicity but a living and life-giving source. Meaning becomes apparent in the brokenness of temporal idiosyncracies. By acquiring such insights, Gadamer speaks of a psycho-historic "anamnesis."[5]

---

[3] Cf. Erzsébet v. Gaál Gyulai, Heinrich Heine - Dichter, Philosoph und Europäer (Frankfurt am Main: Lang, 1998) 30-35 and esp. 158-171. These pages contain a concise analysis of modernity's disposition.
[4] Gadamer, Wahrheit und Methode 276f.
[5] Gadamer, Wahrheit und Methode 276f.

Increasingly machines abound, the "intelligence" of which by far surpasses that of their inventors. By trial and error, i.e. by using memory, they learn to come to terms with reality. Could they possibly surpass human memory one day? Human memory records not only for pragmatic or statistic reasons. It distills from the information gathered a meaning which allows human society to give - this again is pragmatic - meaning to life. This meaning, however, does not serve an immediate purpose.

As the age-old order of ancient Rome waned, Augustine sought consolation in "memoria." By remembering, the spirit experiences itself and therein encounters God:

Ubi ergo te inveni, ut discerem te? Neque enim iam eras in memoria mea, priusquam te discerem. Ubi ergo te inveni, ut discerem te nisi in te supra me? Et nusquam locus, et recedimus et accedimus, et nusquam locus.[6]

Recurring to the past yields participation into insights previous generations have made. Yet more importantly, it grants the possibility of sensing something underlying history. "Memoria" means allowing that to become present and participation in the same. This notion is by no means alien to Anselm:

Rem enim cogitare cuius memoriam habemus, hoc est mente eam dicere; verbum vero rei est ipsa cogitatio ad eius similitudinem ex memoria formata.[7]

As this quote from the *Monologion* illustrates, insight occurs when the word of the object thought becomes reality. This is also the approach Anselm chose when reflecting upon God. Cogitation becomes far-reaching memory. The spirit is not able to reach further than when employing "memoria." When reflecting upon God the human spirit meets its inexcellable and insurmountable limit, a limit that is not yet simply beyond the reaches of the mind. It defines thinking and endows it with its character. Particularly in a monastic context this limit becomes the dominating topic. Here diverse forms of thinking converge: thinking reflecting upon itself, reflecting upon something thought, reflecting upon God and finally thinking itself. In the *Monologion* Anselm delineates how thinking rises to contemplate fundamental matters. Anselm admits that during a nightly vigil - "inter nocturnas vigilias" - his fears were allayed. The background to Anselm´s approach to thinking is the assumption that spiritual illumination is the beginning of radical cognition. This central and beatifying experience permits beholding the "idem in diversis bonis."[8] In contrast to modernity´s quest for "being" (Heidegger) or "meaning" (Rahner) Anselm

---

[6] Augustine, Confessiones, X, 26.
[7] M 48: 63,20-22.
[8] M 1: 14,17.

considers the fullness of life in its abundant diversity as worthy of pondering. Here one encounters the Augustinian notion of collecting from dispersal: "colligitur cogitur."[9] These terms occur numerous times in Anselm's writings. Through a central insight cogitation endows reality with unity. It is the task of the light metaphor to express this central insight. On the frontiers of insight the underlying paradigm breaks through: beholding.

> Quemadmodum enim se habent ad invicem lux et lucere et lucens, sic sunt ad se invicem essentia et esse et ens, hoc est existens sive subsistens.[10]

Confronted with nothing Anselm turns to speaking. Prior to establishing something there is an interior speaking - "prius illud intra se dicit mentis conceptione?"[11] Essence is being received. Therein lie speaking's greatness and limit. It corresponds to Anselm's point of departure that there are different modes and degrees of reproducing the received. In principle Anselm distinguishes between three: using sensual signs ("loquimur signis sensibilibus"), thinking these signs interiorly with no correlation to the sensible world ("intra nos insensibiliter cogitando") or speaking the things themselves ("intus in nostra mente dicendo").[12] This inner speaking is a beholding of a form. It is characteristic of Anselm's argumentation concerning the limits of speaking that he situates the pure image of the object in the sounds: "exprimit, quomodo illa similitudo, quae in acie mentis rem ipsam cogitantis exprimitur."[13] In a most radical form the mode of speaking becomes the highest Being's expression. Speaking lives from a more or less hidden picture within the interior recesses of the spirit. There is a difference between speaking and the picture spoken of, but a correspondence between the two is invariably intended. In the final approximation this speaking becomes God's image. Thus perceived the *Monologion* is a treatise concerning the identity of word and image in God. Having reached this turning point, the mind reflects upon the identity reached in the speaking process. There are always parameters when speaking, thinking, and recognizing: "rei faciendae quasi exemplum, sive aptius dicitur forma, vel similitudo aut regula."[14] The more something approaches the "exemplum," the more it recognizes it, and, therefore, the more true speaking concerning it becomes. Therefrom results an "ordo rerum." The more something corresponds to the "exemplum," the higher its degree within this order. This order of insight

---

[9] Augustine, Confessiones, X, 11.
[10] M 6: 20,15f.
[11] M 10: 24,26. Cf. Monologion 19: 34,12 = "An potius repugnandum est nihilo, ne tot structurae necessariae rationis expugnentur nihilo, ex summum bonum quod lucerna veritatis quaesitum et inventum est, amittatur pro nihilo?" Thereby Anselm wards off any possible danger that might come from nothingness.
[12] M 10: 24,31;25,2.4.
[13] M 10: 25,20.
[14] M 9: 24,30.

corresponds to the reality it conceptualizes, because cognition is a form of participation in divine order, as chapter thirty one of the *Monologion* demonstrates. In a way there is no neutral realm left outside and independent from this original speaking. This is not an accidental occurrence in Anselm's philosophy but is imbedded in tradition. Already Paul uses terms like "similitudo," "imago," "figura" and "character."[15] As Kohlenberger states, the identification of word and image demarcates also the insurmountable boundary which cannot be overcome.[16] This is what Anselm expresses in the words, "id quo maius cogitari nequit." This does not entail a negation of cogitation but defines its space. Were thinking to attempt indeed a "regressus in infinitum," then a differentiation between image and word in the highest Being would no longer be feasible. Such a position is not Anselm's.[17] Thinking's highest form is also its negation of any further expressiveness. In various chapters Anselm links creation with the highest Being's "verbum." In this connection the relationship between spirit and creation receives attention.

> nam ille cuius est verbum aut imago, nec imago nec verbum est. Constat igitur quia exprimi non potest, quid duo sint summus spiritus et verbum eius, quamvis quibusdam singulorum proprietatibus cogantur esse duo. Etenim proprium est unius esse ex altero, et proprium est alterius esse ex illo.[18]

The word that is free does not shy back from beholding. Anselm's "Memoria" feels impelled to verbalize the picture imprinted in the mind during a dream. The ability to articulate this relationship is not merely a question of intelligence but of ethics. To Anselm's judgment it is a question of intellectual veracity. The term "rectitudo" as "upright walk or stride" contains this understanding. All human conduct and, therefore, also all philosophical statements are measured by this term's valence. Truth is in a most foundational manner the point of departure for uncovering the meaning of "rectitudo." "Rectitudo" is a word. The word is the medium of memory. Hence, in a most Heideggerian turn, the word is the medium, the vehicle of truth.

> Sicut enim ignis, cum calefacit, veritatem facit, quia ab eo accepit, a quo habet esse: ita et haec oratio, scilicet "dies est," veritatem facit, cum significat diem esse, sive dies sit sive non sit; quoniam hoc naturaliter accepit facere.[19]

---

[15] M 33 with references to Col 1:15 and Hebr 1:3.

[16] Helmut Kohlenberger, "Anselm spricht zu (post)modernen Denkern," Anselm: Aosta, Bec and Canterbury. Papers in Commemoration of the Nine-hundreth Anniversary of Anselm's Enthronement as Archbishop, Sept. 25. 1093. D.E. Luscombe and G.R. Evans eds. (Sheffield: Sheffield Academic Press, 1996): 376-391, 383f.

[17] Vuillemin holds in Le Dieu d'Anselme such a "regressus in infinitum" to be Anselm's position.

[18] M 38: 56,27f.

[19] V 5: 183,3f.

352

This serves to illustrate that in an inalienable manner truth - in order to be truth - contains freedom; on the other hand there can never be truth without an unconditional affirmation of freedom. This assent contains a spiritual and ecstatic moment which brings forth a sense of friendship.[20] The "sensus rectitudinis" is the locale where justice, veracity, and divine charity meet the human being. This confluence enkindles freedom. In Anselm's writings modernity becomes aware of the fallacies the drive for a philosophical "Letztbegründung" had produced. Only by overcoming its playful indeterminedness will post-modernity behold in a Romanesque church more than a museum relic, will the edifice be part of the self.

Anselm's writings know prayer. Anselm's reflections in the *Proslogion* are sustained by prayer. Prayer is a sublime form of piloting whereby cogitation's movement urges beyond the immediate goal. This is the attempt to take up the right trail. It is *Monologion's* intention to reflect upon the experience of things and their constitution. In the process it attempts to name the ground for the "idem in diversis." Anselm withstands the temptation to render the "nihil" an object. Existentialism's abyss is avoided. But there is an intentionality to any form of articulation which Anselm terms "usus loquendi."[21] Upon the background of these considerations the highest Being's speaking takes on a quality par excellence. Here the "res" is no longer in contrast to the "nihil" but by and of itself. Speaking reveals an image that is more than a phantasm. Something absolute and unconditional shines through. Beholding and speaking, "imago" and "verbum," coincide. In this "coincidentia oppositorum," the unrecognizability of the highest Being, "maius omnibus," reaches its culmination. The statements "id quo maius cogitari nequit" and "quiddam maius quam cogitari possit" illustrate the mind's contingence. By accepting the impossibility of going beyond an identity of word and image in the highest Being, nothing is banished. This is Anselm's achievement and message for post-modernity. In the " memoria" a genealogy of reflections becomes visible which evidences the word's birth from historic "memoria." The trinitarian constitution of this testimony preserves and conserves the mystery which bestows upon life its charm. Without this tension between truth and mystery, between the recognized and the unrecognizable, modernity suffers shipwreck; it would see its own mirror in a moderately tepid puddle.

In the trinitarian resourcement of reality the underlying "rectitudo" becomes apparent. It is the foundational definition effective against trite lies. The Anselmian "rectitudo" is the absolute will to affirm life. Anselm's prayer in chapter fourteen of the *Proslogion* serves well to accentuate the monk's life-long inquisitive and prayerful disposition. The turning inward to discover God

---

[20] Richard W. Southern, Saint Anselm. Portrait of a Landscape (Cambridge: Cambridge UP, 1990) 138ff.
[21] M 22: 41,1.

at the roots of the self is a pattern of well-considered alteration[22] between thought and sentiment:

> God of truth,
> I ask that I may receive,
> so that my joy may be full.
> Meanwhile, let my mind meditate on it,
> let my tongue speak of it,
> let my heart love it,
> let my mouth preach it,
> my flesh thirst for it,
> and my whole being desire it,
> until I enter into the joy of my Lord,
> who is God one and triune, blessed forever. Amen.[23]

13.3 An Anselmian Symphony - A Synthetic Overview

As a novice in the Abbey of Bec and as Lanfranc´s pupil Anselm first acquired studiously the then common tools of the theological trade.[24] Yet the struggle between Berengar and Lanfranc had left a lasting impression on his mind. It had demonstrated beyond any doubt the inadequacy of the scientific community to come to terms with the tensions inherent to the relationships between the human mind and ecclesial faith, between human freedom and incarnation. Given this malcondition, it had become his life long quest to "reconcile" faith and reason. This elucidation had also taken on a note of urgency due to other, novel political, cultural and to Christendom "external" factors. The dissemination of scientific knowledge had accelerated throughout Europe. Moreover, Islam´s political and cultural presence could no longer be ignored, all the more as it controlled the Holy Land. This circumstance occasioned the disquieting question among many Christians throughout Europe: can Christianity indeed be the the only true religion on the face of the earth if it is not able to control the soil on which once Our Lord had walked? In addition, attendant to the Arab seizure of one half of the Mediterranean coastline, Byzantine theology´s lofty Platonism and Judaism´s intellectual vibrancy and economic acumen came increasingly to bear on a then almost monolithically Christian Europe. As a Christian monk and intellectual, Anselm felt compelled to demonstrate to the public that Christendom´s concept of God was the only

---

[22] Cf. for combination of cogitation and prayer Esser, ´Cogitatio´ und ´meditatio´ 57-104.

[23] Benedicta Ward trans. and ed., The Prayers and Meditations of St. Anselm (Harmondsworth: Penguin, 1973) 81.

[24] Günther Mensching, Das Allgemeine und das Besondere. Der Ursprung des modernen Denkens im Mittelalter (Stuttgart: Reclam, 1992) 105-128.

354

true one, because it eclipsed all other notions of the numinous.[25] Anselm's saw in Augustine's term of the highest desirable good ("summum bonum"[26]) his natural point of departure to move beyond Berengar and Lanfranc by integrating dialectics - always true to the Augustinian heuristic principle "fides quaerens intellectum" - into theological disputes. Irrefutably to all, Christianity's superior position should be demonstrated - even to non-believing Moslems and Jews - by means of employing human logic alone, in which all human beings participate, qua human beings, irrespective of their concrete religious persuasion, cultural, ethnic or geographic backgrounds. Simultaneously this should also serve to demonstrate Christian faith's reasonableness and intelligibilty ("ratio fidei").[27] He sought to prove Christian verities by rational means while not falling into the pitfalls of rationalism.

Nevertheless, one would do Anselm great injustice, were one to perceive in his oeuvre merely a reflex to the historically arising exigencies for Christianity's intellectual legitimization. Without taking recourse to Scripture or creation theology, he desired to present Christian faith "sola ratione" in its all-encompassing integrating force - as he firmly states in the dialogue with Boso: "in solvendo tamen omnibus est intelligibilis"[28] - as surpassing infinitely pagan rationalism, Judaism and Islam. This operating principle arises - and this pivotal for a proper understanding of Anselm's contribution to intellectual history and Chrisatianity's self-understanding - *from within the very midst of Christian faith.* This means, he was firmly convinced that not only the content of his theology, but also its presumptions and its methodology are genuinely Christian and a part of what that faith intrinsically is. Yet more to the point, his theology as "fides quaerens intellectum" asserts itself to the Christian as nothing less than a self-constitution of precisely that faith. Simultaneously with Christian faith's unsurpassable quality, divine suzerainty over the worldly realm should become obvious to all without doing violence unto anyone. Rather, it is his agenda to have Christain faith come in the individual's mind as the occurrence of the individual's self-constitution, i.e. the individual's coming into his/her own. The greatest truth is accessible through the most interior human recesses. The framework is genuinely Augustinian: "Noli foras ire, in te ipsum redi. In interiore homine habitat veritas."[29] The truth that encompasses all of reality is neither the consummation of external rational arguments nor the coerced product of worldly power. It appears instead as something gratuitous which grants the human mind unmediated access and seeks thereby human acceptance. In this heuristic event human freedom receives a name: Jesus Christ. This is his ultimate and most profound argument for ecclesial freedom:

---

[25] "optimum et maximum et summum omnium quae sunt." M 1: 13,3.

[26] First occurence in: M 4: 18,2.

[27] P P: 94,7: "Exemplum meditandi de ratione fidei, et sequens Fides quaerens intellectum."

[28] Cu I 1: 48, 8; cf. Co 17:159, 5.

[29] Augustine, De Vera Religione, XXXIX, 72; CCL 32, 234.

Ne putetis vobis sicut multi mali reges faciunt, ecclesiam dei quasi domino ad serviendum esse datum, sed sicut advocato et defensori esse commendatam. Nihil magis diligit deus in hoc mundo quam libertatem ecclesiae suae.[30]

Such a faith is not restricted by political constraints or social limitations. It addresses all "animales rationales" on the surface of this earth and is not bound to some particular law.

Scripture bears eloquent witness to an unshakable conviction that there is a profound and indissoluble unity between the knowledge human reason can acquire and historically revealed biblical truth. This is a central message of Scripture. Faith sharpens the human eye to discover the innermost structures of reality. Thereby, revelation comes to know neither the tense of a praeteritum nor that of a prognosticum. It is presentic. This is the intelligence of verses such as "The human heart may plan a course, but it is Yahweh who makes the steps secure" (Prov 16:9).[31] There is no reason to fear some kind of competition or incongruity between faith and reason. Each has its proper scope and is contained in the other. In the same vein one may quote in this context "To conceal a matter, this is the glory of God, to sift it thoroughly, the glory of the kings"(Prov 25:2). By no means does the biblical text wish to convey that the quest for faith's intelligibility is a royal prerogative reserved for worldly rulers. Rather, human beings act in accordance to their giftedness in the divine image by taking up the search for a rational ascertainment of this world's essence. Human beings evidence their divine - for creaturely - origin by actuating this unique relationship wihin which human beings and God are set by virtue of Divine loving magnanimity. By setting out on such an "Itinerarium mentis in Deum" - as Bonaventure is to observe one and a half centuries later - they truly live up to the divine intention of having human beings acquire royal bearing - for they alone among all creatures know of their createdness and are nevertheless able to enter into a relationship with the source of their being. It is the abiding message of monastic theology to spell out intellectual discourse in its essence as an itinerary *in* God. Breathing this same wisdom, Paul observes in Rom 1:20:

> For what can be known about God is perfectly plain to them, since God has made it plain to them: ever since the creation of the world, the invisible existence of God and his everlasting power have been clearly seen by the mind's understanding of the created order.

The effulgence of divine sublimity should appear epiphany-like to human reason - and this precisely on the grounds that the numinous already always thinks along. The latter becomes apparent to the thinking subject only in his/her thoughts' final steps. While at the beginning of his work, i.e. in the

---

[30] E 235:143,19-22.
[31] Cf. also Wis 7:17; 13:5.

Monologion, he exclusively uses reason to argue, he has in the *Proslogion*, and yet more so in the *Cur Deus Homo*, faith join forces with human intellectual faculties. However, as it turns out, from the very outset of this intellectual journey there is a subtle "pas de deux." Reason and faith clandestinely collaborate and are together unassumingly - though the thinker may be unaware of faith as reason's partner.

This may be seen on first sight as something of an anticipation of Rahner's concept of the supernatural existential. Upon closer scrutiny this assumption can only partially be upheld. Much too much did Anselm see an acute need for all of humanity to become members of the one and unique "ecclesia Dei." Certainly it constitutes a rejection of both the deistic model and - at least partially - of the theodicy question.[32]

To the degree that mental rigor is maintained - in Anselm's judgment - this turns out to be nothing like an open-ended, random rambling or vagabonding, but a pilgrimage with an invisible companion and a clear goal. The "summum bonum" is present from the very beginning of the journey. The individual human soul's creation contains from its very beginning a searching element which is constantly disquieting to the individual until the sought for is found. Faithful to this insight, Anselm is able to formulate "Denique ad te videndum factus sum, et nondum feci propter quod factus sum."[33] Not knowing it, the human being was created all along to behold God. And yet the quest to discover this purpose of his/her createdness remains the task which every human being is beckoned still to discover. This discovery does not render reason already capable of passing judgement on matters of faith. Its purpose is rather, to encounter meaning and thereby "to chance upon" the personal presence of truth. To the degree one is enthused by truth, one longs to know more. This desire spurs reason onward. Finally, it may well be that the inquisitive mind arrives at a rather strange insight but not impasse: it is rationally able to admit the utter incomprehensibility of the sought object and yet *to recognize* it precisely as incomprehensible and ineffable. This chapter 64 of the *Monologion* conveys:

> Nam si superior consideratio rationabiliter comprehendit incomprehensibile esse, quomodo eadem summa sapientia sciat ea quae fecit, de quibus tam, multa nos scire necesse est: quis explicet quomodo sciat aut dicat seipsam, de qua aut nihil aut vix aliquid ab homine scire possibile est?[34]

The certitude attained during this mental itinerary is by no means shaken by the sublime veiledness of the mystery. One assents to the recognized secret. This is the greatest challenge to the human intellect. Here reason recognizes in faith its

[32] Rahner, Hörer des Wortes 187, Balthasar, Cordula oder der Ernstfall 85-97.111-113.
[33] P 1: 98,14f.
[34] M 64:75,11-14.

true companion. Faith is need of the intellect, and likewise is the intellect endebted to faith.[35]

One is able to distinguish clearly three central stages in his life-long intellectual intinerary. Together they form one non-contradictory triptych: *Monologion, Proslogion* and *Cur Deus Homo:*

The first "act" of this intellectual drama is rightly titled *Monologion* and was written around 1074. In this treatise Anselm wishes to demonstrate - without calling to assistance scriptural arguments and "the authorities" - reason's congeniality with verity; the latter perceived as one and personal. In the process, actually three proofs of God's existence impose themselves on the human mind as natural consequences of its pure thinking.

Already in his earliest writing, the *Meditatio de redemptione humana*, the monk introduces his audience to a perplexing novelty: he meditates and prays while making reason his referential point. "Mande cogitando, suge intelligendo, gluti amando et gaudendo. Laetare mandendo, gratulare sugendo, iucundare glutiendo."[36] Though the term does not yet occur, materially the "sola ratione" becomes the declared principle already at this early stage. Perhaps this "recherche méthodologique," as Coloman Viola describes it, is the direct result of the monastic practice of "collationes" and long discussions also customary in the monastery of Bec.[37] Nevertheless, Anselm's approach represents a radical departure from what other contemporary monks held. Peter Damian, Gerhard of Csanád and Rupert of Deutz vehemently resisted the intrusion of profane tendencies - such as grammar, natural sciences and dialectics - into the study of the "lectio divina" and of faith in general. Moreover and more puzzling, his own fatherly teacher, Lanfranc, had refused to make use of dialectics for the purpose of elucidating the "sacra pagina" and certain dogmas. It remains a riddle to this day why Anselm addresses the innermost Christian truth, the mystery of the Trinity, clad with but a philosopher's armor.[38] It comes as no surprise therefore, that Anselm feels compelled to invoke the Fathers and Augustine's *De Trinitate* in particular to prove his orthodoxy to all early on in the prologue to the *Monologion*:

Quam ergo saepe retractans nihil potui invenire me in ea dixisse, qoud non catholicorum patrum et maxime beati AUGUSTINI scriptis cohaereat. Quapropter si cui videbitur, quod in eodem opusculo aliquid protulerim, quod aut nimis novum sit aut a veritate dissentiat: rogo, ne statim me aut praesumptorem novitatem aut falsitatis assertorem exclamat,

---

[35] Augustine, De Praedestinatione Sanctorum, 2,5: PL 44, 963.

[36] Me 3:84,9-12.

[37] Cf. Coloman Viola, "Anselme de Cantorbéry" Dictionnaire critique de Théologie. sous la direction de Jean-Yves Lacoste (Paris: Presses Universitaires de France, 1998): 54-58, at 54.

[38] It should be borne in mind, in that time one did not yet perceive a clear difference between philosophy and theology.

sed prius libros praefati doctoris AUGUSTINI *De trinitate* diligenter perspiciat, deinde secundum eos opusculum meum diiudicet.[39]

A purely philosophical attitude, outlined by rationality and ontology, supplies the key terms to describe his early work. This permits him to define God as the sole, ontically sovereign being and therefore everything else is little more than nothing. And yet, it would be a grave mistake were one to interpret this as a rupture, a sudden departure in his works. They all form one harmonious mosaic. There exists a subtle and intricate interlacement - "concatenatio" as Anselm himself formulates this strategy - of all arguments into one whole from the very first lines. As he explains in the introduction to the *Proslogion*:

> considerans illud esse multorum concatenatione contextum argumentorum, coepi mecum quaerere, si forte posset inveniri unum argumentum, quod nullo alio ad se probandum quam se solo indigeret, et solum ad astruendum quia deus vere est, et quia est summum bonum nullo alio indigens, et quo omnia indigent ut sint et ut bene sint, et quaecumque de divina credimus substantia, sufficeret.[40]

The basic assumption resonating throughout the *Monologion* is the Platonic notion of humanity's and creation's "participation" - "μεθεξις" - in the highest good, which is also the highest being and the largest. Materially this resonates in the observation: "pro praesenti possumus uti passivo praeterito participatio eiusdem verbi."[41] The world is "His" creation - the ineffable is therein present as Spirit - as "Summus Spiritus."[42] Here one beholds Christianity's differentiated, very critical and qualified appropriation of Plato and Plotinus. They had not been able to conceptualize the incarnation of the ineffable. Though arguing with a logician's terminology - "saltem sola ratione persuadere"[43] -, Anselm expresses confidence that human "life-worthiness" and safety are the direct result of that highest being's charity. There are gradations in reality and these are somewhat paralleled in his treatise. It is in this Platonic vein that he dares stipulate a rational explication of the triune God. The different and varying aspects of reality are perceived as one unity of things created and uncreated.

Building upon these insights, he strives to argue in his next work, the *Proslogion,* written approximately in 1075 - already as abbot, now from within the bounds of faith, how reason can join without tarrying in appreciating revelation. In this treatise itinerary reflection becomes prayerful and adorational

---

[39] M p: 8,13.

[40] P P: 93,4-10.

[41] V 12:196,12.

[42] Cf. M 29: 47,19. The Spirit's predication as the highest occurs in the Monologion at least forty four times. This suggests his assuming the Holy Spirit's presence in the world is justification for a "philosophical" approach.

[43] M 1: 13,11.

- pilgrimage-like. God reveals Himself as the one operating within the "ratio." Divine existence and divine attributes are proven irrefutably - in Anselm's view. The diverse arguments of the *Monologion* find here their logical synthesis in one argument.

It is here, therefore, that one encounters the famous ontological argument. In this book Anselm employs - revealingly for his program - Augustine's method "I believe in order to gain insight" ("credo, ut intelligam")[44] - inspired by Jer 7:9f. Prayer becomes here the hermeneutical tool to apprehend God as that which cannot be thought but as the unexcellably greatest - "id quo maius cogitari non potest."[45] The idea of God in our mind corresponds to the notion of that which one cannot possibly think of as either possibly "perfectable" or non-existent. The term "God" requires an existence independently from contingent cognition (which it could possibly not be) and must therefore necessarily be in reality. Readily does he concede that indeed some things do exist in the human mind that find no correspondents in external reality. Furthermore, there may be a difference between what the mind imagines and what can be painted on a canvas. Yet, in the case of the ontological order, what is thought of as unsurpassably perfect must also necessarily exist - otherwise thinking as such is reduced to a sad rubble - which entails that whatever is thought of as less than perfect could never acquire being - could not exist. In fact, even in the hypothetical case that all of humanity were reduced to the yet more imperfect state of a mental asylum, God would exist. Otherwise one would have to do away with the human mind's existence, and for this it is already always much too late.

Anselm does not merely affirm divine existence. He unequivocally also states something else: the logical impossibility of postulating the negation of God's existence.

But an additional perspective to the one ontological argument "id quo maius cogitari nequit" also exists. To the degree that contingent facts - such as temporality, presence, truth statements and good conditions - exist, there must be one absolute Being that is eternity, omnipresence, truth and goodness in one. Ephemeral phenomena require the one, absolute being. Imperfections demand the perfection's prior existence. For something contingent not merely to be thought as such, but also indeed to exist, requires that something absolute could not simply be only in one's consciousness without being also in reality. This insight is applied to human intelligence. It is God who wills contingent reason to be. As every finite quality mirrors a predication within the absolute, human reason also mirrors and to that degree also partakes in divine reason. This was to Anselm all the more acutely the case as he did not countenance the possibilty that there might exist other intelligent creatures in addition to humanity on the surface of the earth. The human "ratio" is the only instrument capable of

---

[44] P 1:100,18.
[45] P 2:101,5.

interaction with God in the palpable realm. Human intelligence is uniquely in dialogue with, but is at the same time also always put to shame by divine wisdom.

Anselm would counter rationalistic atheism with the observation that all thinking moves within the parameters of an inherent dynamics, which endows that endeavor with purpose. There is contained in every thought a thrust conveying the certain feeling to the thinker that he/she is not alone in his/her house, let alone its master. Reasonable thought - and Anselm would include therein dialogue - cannot fail to countenance in its final analysis this salient feature. As a result, such an enterprise can partially falter, but never fully fail. In this sense cognition is transformed into something more than a subject's archaeology. Descartes' pathological "cogito" rises above the first person singular and becomes something akin to a first person plural. Had not already in his day Anselm overcome existentialist philosophy, Husserl and Heidegger? Is not Kantian reception, claiming the philosopher from Königsberg would postulate cognition's finitude reduced to absurdity? There is the intellect's dynamic and burning desire for Being in every epistemological act. Herein something akin to an Ignatian "magis" is foreshadowed that is beheld as both existential and intellectual.[46] Precisely by negating a justification for the Aristotelian term "metaphysics" would Anselm uphold that term's consequences.[47] Does not equally Hegel's concept of a coming-to-itself of the absolute spirit suffer defeat at the hands of Anselm's understanding of "ratio" as a dialogical element between the individual and God? When confronted with monastic theology, even the most subtle forms of solipsism come into tribulations. Not only are human beings animated, they know about their animated state as their central and salient feature. This is the state of knowing something being bestowed gratuitously upon oneself. This awareness unleashes creativity and freedom. Spiritedness as an ultimately also divinely reflexive moment is always inherently and constitutively contained in every thought. This bears eloquent testimony to a distinction between thinker and thought (of a proof of God's existence), but also to a kinship between the two. In this sense the philosopher is truly of royal lineage - to remain in the biblical imagery (Prov 25:2).

In his central step, Anselm meticulously assembles all the dazzling wealth of Christian dogmas. All is focused on the one question of why God took on our flesh: *Cur Deus Homo*? This, for subsequent intellectual history truly fateful piece[48] was written in the years 1094-98 and thus also during his exile

---

[46] Retreat Book No. 151; cf. Knauer, Gründungstexte der Gesellschaft Jesu 167.

[47] In more than one way this reminds one of Karl Rahner's famous philosophical book Hörer des Wortes. Zur Grundlegung einer Religionsphilosophie (München: Kösel, 1941). Cognition contains a transcending element.

[48] His immediate pupil Gilbert Crispin was to write a similar treatise as later also Abelard and Nicolas de Cusa.

from the see of Canterbury. Redemption's importance is here demonstrated to Moslems and Jews alike. As nothing less than the "Logos"[49] became human, Anselm argues like a pedagogue and cathechist, intimating to his at times incredulous students nothing alien - as he wishes quite literally "to make believe" and indeed truly believes himself. Much like Socrates on the public squares of ancient Athens, Anselm wishes to awaken his even most exotic reader to that which he/she interiorly and subconsciously from the very first moment of his/her existence longs for, lives in and unwittingly presupposes - to the degree he/she is an "animal rationale"[50] - namely redemption. In the state of original sin, humanity is neither able to recognize its own divine justice nor to act accordingly.

As he had stated previously in *De Veritate* in fidelity to the Platonic-Augustinian tradition, God is truth. The "summa veritatis" is cause for the "veritas essentiae rerum," which in turn gives rise to the "veritas enuntiationes."[51] Only the last, however, is truth in the Aristotelian system. Counter to Boethius' translation of Aristotle's "logica vetus," Anselm insists on truth's transcendental nature. As a consequence, the notion of justice rests solely in God. In this divine justice Anselm apprehends the basis and hinge point of human freedom, as he establishes in *De casu diaboli*. Human beings are not free because theirs is the possibility of choosing between actions of differing moral qualities, but rather because they are capable of morality as quintessentially human comportment. Morality is a term Anselm does not use but materially intends, preferring instead "iustitia."[52] God could never have destined humanity to forsake its freedom, for otherwise humanity would be determined just as nature is. Humanity self-determines itself through the righteous intention in a morally sound way as it manifests itself in a single concrete act. This is conveyed in the notion of "rectitudo." Grace explicates the modalities of the morally good.

Humanity is able to recognize: God had to become human flesh necessarily in order to effect redemption for humanity. Not an undifferentiated God, but the God that is the "Logos" - "Verbum" - reason became incarnate.[53] As a result, human reason is capable of apprehending the necessity of the incarnation with purely rational means - "remoto Christo"[54] - necessarily. This is intended as a response to the non-believers' "obicere."[55] For this reason, a

---

[49] I 11: 29,19: Cum ergo, "verbum caro factum"...

[50] M 10: 25,9; G 8:152,23; G 10:157,30; G 21:166,27.

[51] V 2:179,11.

[52] Coloman Viola, "Anselme de Cantorbéry" 56.

[53] Michel Corbin, Prière et raison de la foi: introduction à l'oeuvre de saint Anselme de Cantorbéry (Paris: Cerf, 1992).
The term "logos" contains much more than reason. But it is that aspect with which the medieval mind immediately associated the term.

[54] Cu P: 42,12.

[55] Cu I 1: 48,1; Cu I 6: 55,8.

true dialogue among all members of the human race - both literate and illiterate, due to "rationem eius"[56] - can ensue. At the same time the non-believers' accusation that Christians are unsophisticated simpletons - Celsus had already belittled Christians as an "illiterate and uncouth" lot[57] - is confounded: "Quam quaestionem solent et infideles nobis simplicitatem Christianam quasi fatuam deridentes obicere, ..."[58]

Anselm argued similarly already in *De Veritate*. Truth is God, and humanity partakes in the divinely created ontic order and therefore inextricably in truth. What human beings decipher as insight into truth is merely the effect of truth, coming forth from God. He does not dwell on subordinate questions, such as whether Scripture enjoys priority vis-à-vis the Fathers etc. His great project was far more ambitious. Faith and reason are reconciled as both spring forth from the same source: Christian truth. Such a view is eloquently affirmed by the many pieces of art abounding in Anselm's Romanesque Europe - and in Moslem-held Africa and Asia as well.

In the service of orthodoxy Anselm appealed frequently also "intra muros" to faith's intelligibilty. This was the case for example when he argued against Roscelin of Compiègne's errors in *Epistola de incarnatione Verbi* [59] and again when he felt called to demonstrate to the Greek Orthodox the Spirit's procession from both the Father and the Son "rationabiliter"[60] in *De processione Spiritus Sancti* according to the Western Church's doctrine of the "filioque."

Early in the *Monologion* Anselm observes: "puto quia ea ipsa ex magna parte, si vel mediocris ingenii est, potest ipse sibi saltem sola ratione persuadere."[61] The word "saltem," in English best translated as "at least," in conjunction with the programmatic "sola ratione" is indicative of his understanding of insight. Contingency and original sin were unable to do complete harm to that homogenous hierarchy of cognition. Nevertheless, in that treatise this philosophical attitude turns into a theological one when he states: "fides quaerens intellectum"[62] - just to be confirmed with an apodictic "nisi credideritis, nisi intelligetis"[63] in the *Cur Deus Homo*. There is a certain form of credal priority present in the final work reflecting on the central mystery of incarnation. Faith enjoys a qualified priority. It is the wellspring of all wisdom and the corrective for all cognitional undertakings. As an already believing monk, Anselm has faith search for intellectual verification. Faith appeals to

---

[56] Cu I 1: 48,6.
[57] Origin, Contra Celsum, 3 55; SC 136, 130.
[58] Cu I 1: 47,10-48,1.
[59] I 136:279,4; I 136:280,24.
[60] Pr 1:177, 9.
[61] M 1:13,10-11.
[62] P P:94,7.
[63] Cu C: 40,8.

intelligence. As also Viola does not tire of pointing out, it is within the "ratio's"dialectic movement to answer philosophical questions that faith clearly enjoys preeminence. But as regards the natural realm he entrusts reason with the task to explicate completely this realm's intelligibility. For precisely this reason he is able to disregard Scripture and the magisterium in the *Monologion*. In the *Cur Deus Homo* he is likewise able to disregard Christ ("remoto Christo") to arrive at the necessary reasons for incarnation. The "rationes" are just as sound, valid and convincing to his mind as scriptoral citations.

Though one encounters the term "sola ratione" already in Augustine's writings, the method when Anselm employs that term is thoroughly his own. Anselm musters all the available philosophical equipment of his day. It is his grand design to assemble all rational arguments into one large chain - one is tempted to say phalanx - of arguments in the service of faith. All the more disconcerting and compelling must it be for the reader when confronted suddenly with the fact that God had accompanied him all along on his supposedly purely rational itinerary. Cognition leads the thinking subject without any forewarning to introspection and thereby to a clarification of matters central to the Christian mystery.

The interior intellectual élan one encounters in Anselm seems akin to the one already met in Augustine's *De Trinitate*. The term common to both men is "quaerere." It is at the same time inquisitive and daring and follows the psalmist's beckoning: "quaerite faciem eius semper." Thus Anselm asks "Deinde quibus signis, qua facie te quaeram?"[64] The appropriate and indeed only adequate means to conduct this search for the divine image are the "rationes necessariae."[65] The mind mirrors the divine. That renders dialectics, the utilization of logic, invincible arguments, the reduction ad absurdum, the use of philosophical terms and finally the "usus communis loquendi"[66] not only legitimate, but forms of active participation in that, or better in Him, whom one seeks. Here no facile or forced "reconstruction" occurs after the sought for had already been recognized within the monastic community. Rather, the monastic experience serves to verbalize what Anselm had sought for and finally found in the years of his "afoot but not lighthearted" wanderings in Europe. In this train of thought it is fitting to speak of "similitudines:"

Etenim omnia huiusmodi verba quibus res quaslibet mente dicimus, id est cogitamus: similitudines et imagines sunt rerum quarum verba sunt; et omnis similitudo vel imago tanto magis vel minus est vera, quanto magis vel minus imitatur rem cuius est similitudo. Quid igitur tenendum est de verbo, quo dicuntur et per quod facta sunt omnia? Erit aut non erit similitudo eorum, quae per ipsum facta sunt? Si enim ipsum est vera mutabilium similitudo, non est consubstantiale summae incommutabilitati; quod falsum est. Si autem non omnino vera sed qualiscumque similitudo mutabilium est, non est verbum summae veritatis omnino

---

[64] P 1:98,6.
[65] M p: 7,10.
[66] Cf. V 2:179,27.

364

verum; quod absurdum est. At si nullam mutabilium habet similitudinem: quomodo ad exemplum illius facta sunt?[67]

In the similarities of creation not merely the similarities of created things - "factorum" - become apparent but more importantly the truth of their essence - "veritas essentiae."[68] Similarities serve not only to give intelligible expression to the disquieting and harassing questions humankind raises every generation anew, but more significantly to seek and discover truth - and to retrace this process again for others.

The issue is what is it that unites faith and reason in such a manner that it is able to liberate reason to enjoy true "freedom"- which defines itself from within a relationality in which it experiences itself already always already - i.e, a priori - posited. It seems he still leaves greatly undifferentiated the connective(s) between faith and reason. Perhaps the later "fides qua" and "fides quae" is one way of getting at that, in the sense that the dynamism of faith - understood as "fides qua" - is a kind of ground which can kenotically hold itself in restraint and trust reason to move along, and even in some sense awaken reason. That the *Proslogion* is offering an argument which bases itself on the *concatenatio* of the various arguments, points to the grounding union between faith and reason. Obviously God, and Truth, are the ground, but how is that ground reflected in the human being? Does the Plotinian notion of *ratio* alone suffice? Perhaps Anselm remains undifferentiated. He stands at that point in Western history when human reason is becoming conscious of itself in a heightened way, and Anselm wants to accept this and he sees this as in no way a detour from faith but in some sense its outgrowth.[69]

Indeed, Anselm readily admits human beings are always prone to discover that yet better and more convincing arguments exist. A case in point is *Cur Deus Homo*. There he had mustered all his intellectual prowess and was still confronted with Boso's unwillingness to accept his line of argumentation. So he addressed one more time the question of divine incarnation in *De conceptu virginali*, until Boso's objections were put to rest. He trusts the opposing part to play a vital role in the epistemological process. Anselm's constant search for the best argument for every part of Christian dogma is well summarized by Viola:

D'autre part, cet élan ne recule devant aucun mystère posé par la foi; il embrasse *a priori* tout objet. "Fides quaerens intellectum" n'est pas seulement l'énoncé d'une méthode, c'est aussi un programme de recherche, un programme de vie nourri par la prière.[70]

---

[67] M 31:48,18-28.
[68] M 31:48,14.
[69] I am greatly indebted to Dr. William M. Thompson, my dissertation promoter, for the thoughts set forth in this paragraph.
[70] Coloman Viola, "Anselme de Cantorbéry" 57.

The intellectual quest is not merely a method or a program. It is sustained completely by a prayerful life. The epistemological optimism which allows him to embrace all of reality is founded on his monastic spirituality. Something of an emancipatory impetus is set free in Anselm's writings which is appreciated as a liberation by his contemporaries such as Guillaume de Malmesbury, who favorably compares Anselm's achievement with other theologians' insistance on authorities. Anselm's intention is not to apply force from outside so that the believer might accept something as creed. Rather, he "reminds" his listeners and readers of what they think and why and how they think it. Within this process of cognitional verification everyone should come to discover in his/her own interiority the same God which the community of believers, the church catholic, believes in under the inspiration of the Spirit. Thinking flows over into prayer. Such rationally purified prayer is the best proof of God's existence. In this Anselmian perspective, faith is not merely an intellectual self-ascertainment, but rather faith's self execution and as such a constant spring-like discovery.

Anselm's approach overcomes two comparatively recent (mis-)understandings of the relationship of the human being to the Divine. The first sees transcendence as a vis-à-vis situation wherein God is in the active role. God gives something from outside to the receiving believer. This understanding had been subject to criticism for the past 300 years (Kant). Equally, Anselm does away with the notion of a spatial projection from the individual human being to an imagined God (Feuerbach). Whenever revelation occurs, the human being is at the very center of it - to Anselm's mind. Neither does revelation precede nor does it pursue the believer. Here perhaps a taking up of an Augustinian *topos* - "interior intimo me" - occurs; though a direct quote never occurs in the Anselmian *corpus*. Rather he speaks of "sensus interior"[71] and of "intimo corde."[72] Anselm liberates the subject from the burdensome travail to design, or better haphazardly construe reality. There do exist phenomena which approach us and challenge our consciousness. Language depends on other factors than that of the subject. Language thus perceived, overcomes all constraining horizons. If therein God reveals himself, then Feuerbach's thesis of projection is a fallacy. Anselm implicitly holds that when God speaks to us, then in such a way that the addressee understands - though never producing the logos. There resides within the human being a "capax intimi et infiniti." The mind's synthetic achievement is greater than the subject, lies beyond its grasp and is nevertheless an essential part of it. There exist two movements in reason's pondering of divine matters and - one hesitates to observe - they merge into almost one movement, while granting - what bewildering wonder - each its full freedom. Indeed, within this process the subject's freedom is established; comes fully

---

[71] V 6:183,23.27. V 6:184,2.24.
[72] E 3:102,11. E 10:113, 18. E 269:184,9. E 337:275,20. E 380:323,3. E 402:346,6. E 462:411, 4.

into being. This is the weighty import of one of the last lines in the *Cur Deus Homo*:

accipe unigenitum et da pro te; et ipse filius: tolle me et redime te.[73]

This stated, how can one still accuse Anselm of either being an unrepentant rationalist or a short-sighted fideist?

---

[73] Cu II 20:132,2f.

CHAPTER FOURTEEN
14.0 Further Thoughts - Anselm, a Rationalist or a Fideist?

In her studies on the origins of totalitarianism, Hannah Arendt apprehends modernity's homeless human beings' inability to act genuinely together as the root for the "radically evil" - which manifested itself during National Socialism's reign. This circumstance is considered personified also in men such as Eichmann. A person disconnected from the great communication of cultures, he is the ideal executioner of the "radically evil." He makes do with no sophisticated intellectual argumentation to legitimize his actions. In face of such paucity of reasoning, Arendt speaks of evil's banality.[1] And yet she herself is a representative of her time when referring on the other hand to her own thoughts as the attempt to think "without guard rails" ("ohne Geländer denken").

Her contemporary and fellow jewess Simone Weil adds to this perspective greater profundity when speaking in the last of her writings, in *Cahiers IV* of "la connaissance surnaturelle."[2] No longer does she engage in dialogue with Hindu and other Eastern religions as in her previous writings. The pristine nature of human cognition now enjoys center stage exclusively. Waiting is perceived as the indispensable attitude and prerequisite for spiritual life. The category of temporality becomes the context for humility. Waiting becomes something like thinking's acting passivity. Herein in an exemplary way the dilemma and drama of a mystic's confinement in this world is acutely being made topical. It is by means of the mind's crystal clear logical line of argumentation that the subject - this means the thinker - is being propelled beyond this world. Common occidental, mutually excluding conceptual topologies are being overcome in favor of a Plotinian existential approximation of the One. Much like in Anselm's case the abyss between dialectics and mysticism is surmounted. They become good and loyal companions in the one common quest. It can no longer surprise the reader that Plato and John of the Cross are her best witnesses for a logically controlled access to the "mysterion." As she is not able to join the "Resistance" in German-occupied France, she voluntarily immolates her life for an ineffably unfathomable goal.

Thinking's mystical self-execution as a consistently recurring topic throughout civilization's history has been the subject of this paper. This intellectual disposition continues to be current as both Arendt and Weil ably attest. This is the case by virtue of the "conditio humana" which is inextricably

---

[1] Hannah Arendt, <u>Origins of Totalitarianism</u> (New York: Harcourt, Brace Jovanovich, 1951). In this context noteworthy: Arendt edited the English edition of her teacher's book discussing also Anselm: Karl Jaspers, <u>Anselm and Nicholas de Cusa</u> (New York: Harcourt, Brace Jovanovich, 1974). For a good presentation of her thought cf. Alois Prinz, <u>Beruf Philosophin oder Die Liebe zur Welt. Die Lebensgeschichte der Hannah Arendt</u> (Weinheim: Beltz & Gelberg, 1998).

[2] Simone Weil, <u>Cahiers. Aufzeichnungen IV</u>. ed. by Elisabeth Edl and Wolfgang Matz (München: Carl Hanser, 1998).

both philosophical and mystical by its very nature - and this with a prolific capacity and call for an aggregational "anamnesis" spanning over the generations. Within the medium of language reason becomes the expedient to acquire tradition. This cognitional process is then the enablement of insight. Beyond and aside from an indifferent understanding of history, "anamnesis" becomes the vehicle to regain a comprehensive understanding of truth. In this sense Anselm's hermeneutics is not content with being a means to interpret something historic solely for curiosity's sake. Rather it intends to acquire the principle conditions of the occurrence of meaning in history. Meaning is the agent by which diverse historic horizons blend into one. Every such acquisition must take seriously in its specific truth claim the acquired, lest it become merely a presumptuous critique and not a productive incorporation. As the enabling basis for and as the demarcation of meaning, "ratio" is in Anselm's view the final and ultimate horizon of every form of hermeneutic ontology.

Is the result of our examination of the "Corpus Anselmi" - namely reason's anamnetic constitution - already sufficient to posit Anselm or at least this interpreter in Neo-Scholasticism's vicinity? How can one claim no irreconcilable divorce between reason and faith without either succumbing to a rationalistic temptation or subscribing to a fideistic view - to which Barth's almost ingenious exegesis may be abused - and thereby departing from Catholicism? Moreover, and more relentlessly asked, how could Plotinus develop his notion of union with the One without being a cocksure rationalist? On the other hand, how could Anselm dare postulate reason's ability to fathom Trinity's mysteries without being a crypto-fideist? To allay fears of fideism or even of anticipating something remotely akin to Neo-Scholasticism on Anselm's part, it is helpful to have Anselm's use of reason pass review one more time.

True to the style of his day, Anselm at first professes distaste for logic[3] but observes in the introduction to the three dialogues *De Veritate*, *De Libero Arbitrii* and *De casu diaboli* concerning *De grammatico*: "non inutilis, ut puto, introducendis ad dialecticam."[4] Dialectics trains the thinking subject's mind for the proper use of the "ratio." Insight into a necessary connection between two statements is gained in such a way that the truth claims in both sentences are being affirmed. "Ratio" may also mean the immediate insight into a truth articulated in one sentence. "Rationes necessitatis" and "veritatis claritas" as the "modi procedendi" are prescribed by his fellow monks. They require these criteria rather than biblical authority. Human reason is an immediate manifestation of truth. The human condition is one fated to find invariably its fulfillment and culmination in Christian faith. This presumption is assisted by the then as

---

[3] "(T)u scis quia molestum mihi semper fuerit pueris declinare," he writes to his pupil Mauritius.
E 64:180,5.
[4] V P: 173,6.

yet little differentiated perception and use of the terms "ratio," "essentia" and "forma."[5] This pre-Scholastic lack of multi-furcation of terms is characteristic for monastic theology. The whole is beheld in a manner that is unmediated. Yet more than this, the monastic attitude is one unknowingly possibly taking up strains of the Platonic tradition. Monastic theology is the vessel preserving the ancient doctrine of creation as the unfolding of the divine will. (Human) ideas in such a defined creation are nothing less than structures of divine thinking. This is illustrated well in the term "God" as something etymologically identical with being ("ho On" - "ens") - defined as some immutable entity moving reflectively within itself. Monastic theology becomes something like a realized symbiosis of Platonic/Plotinian thought and Christian faith. Within monastic walls a monistic metaphysics of unity remained very much alive. This philosophical understanding of existence and of the universe as a whole constituted then the innermost core of all Christian reflection.[6] Confirming this commonly held presumption, the monks of Bec asked their abbot to continue in this tradition:

> sed quidquid per singulas investigationes finis assereret, id ita esse plano stilo et vulgaribus argumentis simplicique disputatione et rationis necessitas breviter cogeret et veritatis claritas ostenderet.[7]

Sections in Anselm's writings seem to exist where the whole of Christian faith is to be proved exclusively by recourse to the "ratio." Others again confirm faith as the indispensable epistemological prerequisite for any statement concerning divine matters. In the preface to the *Cur Deus Homo* he sets out to demonstrate the truth of the incarnation apart from revelation: "rationibus necessariis ... autem libro similiter quasi nihil sciatur de Christo."[8] After having disproved the opponents' arguments, he demonstrates the necessity of incarnation by mentioning humanity's createdness, one's being destined for supreme happiness, but also original sin as a breaking away from the divine plan as well as divine justice and mercy. Within this soberingly realistic matrix human epistemological capacities are defined. Finally, only God is capable of rendering infinite satisfaction for an infinite sin. In many ways one would today rather speak of this tractate as a demonstration of redemption's logical

---

[5] Sofia Vanni Rovighi, "Glaube und Vernunft bei Anselm von Aosta," Renovatio et Reformatio. FS Ludwig Hödl. Manfred Gerwing and Godehard Ruppert eds. (Münster: Aschendorff, 1985): 170-178, at 171.

[6] Cf. Beierwaltes, Platonismus im Christentum. There the author discovers the notion of unity as a carry-over from antiquity in the thinking of Marius Victorinus, Dionysius the Areopagite, Bonaventure, Meister Eckhart, Nicholas of Cusa and Marsilio Ficino, but not expressly in monastic theology.

[7] M P:7,8-11.

[8] Cu P: 42,13f.

consecution within the order of creation and the heavenly realm and intelligibility of the whole of reality: both eternal and created.

In the context of the Anselmic proceedings, Roques speaks of an axiomatic method.[9] The premises of his thinking are frequently revealed truths. Also in his dedication of the *Cur Deus Homo* to Pope Urban II the archbishop of Canterbury refers to faith as the prerequisite to all rational inquiry: "nullum tamen reprehendendum arbitror, si fide stabilitus in rationis eius indagine se voluerit execere."[10] This is yet more forcefully stated in the *Epistola de Incarnatione Verbi:*

> Nullus quippe Christianus debet disputare quomodo quod catholica ecclesia corde credit et ore confitetur non sit; sed semper eandem fidem indubitanter tenendo, amando et secundum illam vivendo humiliter quantum potest quaerere rationem quomodo sit. Si potest intelligere, deo gratias agat; si non potest, non immittat cornua ad ventilandum, sed submittat caput ad venerandum.[11]

Much in this vein the second part to the *Proslogion*'s title *Fides Quaerens Intellectum* conveys not only a psychological but also a logical "modus operandi" to gain insight into divine truths and the purpose and goal of human existence.

As a result of these seeming contradictions - for which even Anselm can not fully account - there exist two most extreme temptations when investigating Anselm. Either one beholds in this monastic author a pious fideist, if not quietist, or a sober rationalist.

Perhaps Karl Barth supplied the most ingenious of approximate fideistic interpretations for Anselm's approach. While by no means denying the existence of the term "ratio" in Anselm's writings, it loses in Barth's reading its free nature and becomes a tool to relate, mediate and coordinate between truths, deductions and implications of the highest possible creature beyond which nothing can be thought. Reason is a divine key given to humanity for use after having already entered Christian faith. To this exegesis reason serves to illumine and further explicate the inner coherence and consistency of faith from *within*. Reason is congruent and coincides with the concept "rationis necessitas." It does not serve as an access to the "veritatis claritas."[12]

True, it was Anselm's firmly held conviction to demonstrate by use of reason that certain aspects of reality cannot be fathomed unless a highest being did exist. This he described as the "summa essentia," from which all things are derived. After establishing the "summa essentia," he then is able to demonstrate

---

[9] Roques, Anselme de Cantorbéry. Pourquoi Dieu s'est fait homme 2ff.
[10] Cu C:40,1f.
[11] I 1:6,10-7,4.
[12] Barth, Fides Quaerens Intellectum 80.

all that is to believed "sola ratione." This is the thrust of the first Chapter of the *Monologion*:

> Si quis unam naturam, summam omnium quae sunt, solam sibi aeterna sua beatitudine sufficientem, omnibusque rebus aliis hoc ipsum quod aliquid sunt aut quod aliquomodo bene sunt, per omnipotentem bonitatem suam dantem et facientem, aliaque perplura quae de deo sive de eius creatura necessarie credimus, aut non audiendo aut non credendo ignorat: puto quia ipsa ex magna parte, si vel mediocris ingenii est potest sibi saltem sola ratione persuadere.[13]

As a consequence Anselm here intends to supply a convincing argument for those who do not believe in Christian faith - either by lack of knowledge or by not believing. Only by reason does he want to convert. In hindsight he observed in the *Proslogion* that he tried to place himself in the position of someone who seeks what he does not know: "... in persona alicuius tacite secum ratiocinando quae nesciat investigantis edidi."[14] Hardly could one reject a fideist position more unequivocally. In the *Monologion* he wishes to see how far reason's reach is. In that treatise human reason is capable of reaching far into the realm of faith. But he adds a word of caution. Incarnation is subject to pure reason's undiluted insight:

> ad hoc maxime facta sunt ut quod fide tenemus de divina natura et eius personis praeter Incarnationem necessariis rationibus sine Scripturae auctoritate probari possit.[15]

Remarkably in Anselm's estimation even the Trinity is accessible to human reason. Nevertheless he refrains from calling the *Monologion* something akin to a theological book but does not hesitate to reflect on the triune God. His point of departure is the insight that God creates intelligently ("cum intelligentia") and therefore the thus created order participates in the divine "ratio" - or "nous" as Plotinus would prefer. God speaks out what he creates. Divine speaking ("locutio") becomes creating speaking. Tradition's teaching on the "ratio" is seen within a trinitarian context. More precisely, creation is an expression of a trinitarian relationality within which the "Verbum Divinum" is the means of communication. For this reason he is able to speak of the "locutio divina" in chapter ten of the *Monologion*. Little wonder then that he demonstrates the existence of the Trinity in the same manner and using the same terminology as when proving the existence of God.[16] He claims every human being can know matters Christians believe in: "aliaque perplura quae de deo sive de eius creatura necessarie credimus, ..."[17] Only by employing reason's faculties - "sola

---

[13] M 1:13,5-11.
[14] P P:93,4.
[15] I 6:20,18-19.
[16] This had also been Abelard's claim: PL 178, 802D.
[17] M 1:13, 8f.

ratione" - is the non-Christian able to fathom what is faith. As Christians we believe these verities, for without these we would not be Christians. This presupposing of lived faith as reason's supporting gridwork the first chapter well illustrates. There the existence of the "summum bonum" is discussed.

> In quo tamen, si quid dixero quod maior non monstret auctoritas: sic volo accipi ut, quamvis ex rationibus quae mihi videbuntur, quasi necessarium concludatur, non ob hoc tamen omnino necessarium, sed tantum sic interim videri posse dicatur.[18]

The authority which he employs to demonstrate the highest good's existence is not that of Scripture - divine authority - but that of the Fathers, particularly that of Augustine.

> Gratias agit pro emendatione opusculi sui. - Defendit se quod in eo nihil dixerit, quod non s. Scripturae aut s. AUGUSTINI auctoritate confirmetur. - Exspectat adhuc iudicium de opere servando aut delendo.[19]

For his contemporarians in the eleventh century the *Monologion* must have contained something altogether novel. Epistola 77 conveys the impression that Lanfranc had for this reason some reservations - alas, his letter is lost - for Anselm goes to great length in demonstrating his fidelity to tradition. Moreover, the reader is called not to consider his writing as an unmovable apodictic statement but rather as one argument among diverse other possible arguments. Yet a word of caution is in order also here. Modesty was the style of the day and by no means did he want to subordinate reason under faith's tutelage. The assumption of Anselm's proceeding apart from divine revelation is confirmed by the circumstance that God is mentioned but once and then in the final chapter of the *Monologion*. Empirical evidence alone is mustered to prove the supreme being's existence and to demonstrate its divine properties. Anselm apprehends in reason a quality which endows it with the capacity to use empirical data to verify divine existence. This means that Anselm does not here postulate a priori God's being in order to arrive at all other facts. Vice-versa, he concludes God's existence a posteriori as being that which *already is*. [20]

While assuming a triune God provable, Anselm insists in this context on reason's limits. This he does particularly in chapter 64 of the *Monologion*:

---

[18] M 1:14,1-3.

[19] E 77:199,1-2. Capitals in the original.

[20] By so doing he fulfills Kant's requirement that philosophy should not prove God's existence but rather demonstrate something existing as being that what can serve as a predicate of God. Kant, "Der einzig mögliche Beweisgrund zu einer Demonstration des Daseins Gottes," in: Gesammelte Schriften, Ak. Ausgabe, Vol. II (Berlin: de Gruyter, 1969) 74.

373

Sufficere namque debere existimo rem incomprehensibilem indaganti, si ad hoc ratiocinando pervenerit, ut eam certissime esse cognoscat, etiam si penetrare nequeat intellectu quomodo ita sit; nec idcirco minus iis adhibendam fidei certitudinem, quae probationibus necessariis nulla alia repugnante ratione asseruntur, si suae naturalis altitudinis incomprehensibilitate explicari non patiantur.[21]

The ever in the background present presupposition is that all human terms are derived from created objects. It is difficult to project such terms unto a reality which transcends the human intellect because it transcends the contingent reality on which the human intellect bases its information. Only in similes and with similarities can one speak of such radically different reality.[22] Every object of being by virtue of its createdness is an image of the highest being. Yet there are gradations of such "similitudo." The highest degree of similarity is borne by the creature gifted with reason ("mens rationalis"): humankind. It contains the image of the triune God.[23]

Though bearer of the image of the triune God, the human intellect is clouded by guilt. As a result, while the arguments put forth in the *Monologion* are altogether sound and indeed intend to be conclusive, they are not thoroughly convincing to the human mind. Mindful of this, Anselm sets out to use another avenue to quench human desire for knowledge - for divine matters. This is done in the *Proslogion*. Not apart from faith and divine revelation, using only human faculties, but together with the precepts of Christian belief the *Proslogion* formulates a new argument:

Non tento, Domine, penetrare altitudinem tuam, quia nullatenus comparo illi intellectum meum; sed desidero aliquatenus intelligere veritatem tuam, quam credit et amat cor meum. Neque enim quaero intelligere, ut credam, sed credo ut intelligam. Nam et hoc credo: quia "nisi credidero, non intelligam."[24]

Here intelligibility of faith comes to the fore. The vehicle to achieve this aim is the formula "aliquod quo nihil maius cogitari possit."[25] Therein Barth perceives something like a typical narrative of a prophetic experience.[26] While the *Monologion* intends to demonstrate the logical implications of created givenness apart from a revelation that occured postlapsarian - which encompasses the human being with rational capacities - the *Proslogion* demonstrates the creed's implications. Here a constant oscillation between "ratio" and "fides," more precisely between "rationes fidei" and "necessariae

[21] M 64:75,1-6.
[22] M 65: 76.
[23] M 67: 77-78,27-11.
[24] P 1:100,15-19.
[25] P 2:101,5.
[26] Barth, Fides quaerens intellectum 80.

rationes" occurs in an effort to spread out wide the drama of humanity's struggle for faith in freedom.

This demonstration is an event that occured once and for all. As human reason mirrors the dynamics within the Trinity, the human being derives from such an intellectual exercise something of a foretaste of heavenly bliss.

Denique quoniam inter fidem et speciem intellectum quem in hac vita capimus esse medium intelligo: quanto aliquis ad illum proficit, tanto eum propinquare speciei, ad quam omnes anhelamus, existimo.[27]

Illuminating faith as intelligible and rational establishes the sensation of a kinship between God and the individual human being, which Anselm circumscribes with the verb "delectare."[28] This is thoroughly both Christian and Plotinian.[29]

Neither the *Proslogion* nor the *Monologion* deal with a quintessentially Christian subject, namely with the incarnation of the God-man. On the other hand, in the *Cur Deus Homo* it is quite obviously established that the "rationes fidei" can only be uncovered on the sound basis of faith as a prerequisite. If someone ignores or negates divine revelation, then he presupposes something else and drives towards another goal. Christians, however, long to apprehend and experience the rationality of faith and all of the cosmos. They are no exotic populaters of a tiny part in the universe, not aliens, but of kindred disposition with the creator and gifted with something that allows them to identify themselves with creation's purpose and finality: "ratio."

Quod petunt, non ut per rationem ad fidem accedant, sed ut eorum quae credunt intellectu et contemplatione delectentur, et ut sint, quantum possunt, "parati semper ad satisfactionem omni poscenti" se "rationem de ea quae in" nobis "est spe."[30]

Utilizing also the same faculty, namely reason, nonbelievers

Quamvis enim illi ideo rationem quaerent, quia non credunt, nos vero, quia credimus: unum idemque tamen est quod quaerimus.[31]

As Anselm does not tire stressing, one always deals with the same instrument, namely reason.

---

[27] Cu C: 40, 10-12.
[28] Cu I 1:47,8f. "Quod petunt, non ut per rationem ad fidem accedant, sed ut eorum quae credunt intellectu et contemplatione delectentur."
[29] Perhaps William Wordsworth's poem "Intimations of Immortality" (1807) may convey in modern English something of the sensation that Anselm meant with the term "delectare."
[30] Cu I 2:47,8-11.
[31] Cu I 3:50,18-20.

There is no gainsaying, there does indeed exist something like a shift within Anselm's appreciation - better yet use - of reason when comparing the *Cur Deus Homo* with the *Monologion*. At first he had hoped to quench his thirst for truth - which is to him (problematically) synonymous with the concept of the personal God - solely by using reason. Later on - in the *Epistola de Incarnatione* - he becomes acutely aware of the contingent shortcomings such an endeavor must suffer when relying solely on that part of reason which is a created human faculty and not yet illumined by faith. Created reason alone is only partially capable of recognizing credal truth. To reach the heights of the *Cur Deus Homo*, one must call to aid certain fundamental Christian verities. Nota bene: it is always reason in its pluriform manifestations: as purely created, human reason, as human reason enlighted by grace or as divine reason.

It would be all too facile a mistake to presume the *Monologion* to be a piece of rationalistic philosophy and *De Incarnatione* and *Cur Deus Homo* simply the reflections of a mature (perhaps even fideistic) theologian. The one human reason uses different tools. Using different tools, reason gains different, mutually beneficial horizons.

Certainly Anselm is acutely aware of the tensions within his writngs. The *Proslogion* mediates between the two positions. Both the Prooemium and the first chapter present head-on his case. He endeavors to gain insight ("intelligere") into what he believes in. There is no "tabula rasa" as with rationalists, yet equally there is no reduction to what faith dictates. Occasionally the reader has the impression faith is put aside in order for reason alone to be the guiding star. Here the dialectic tension between freedom and loyalty, reason and faith becomes intensely apparent:

Gratias tibi, bone domine, gratias tibi, quia quod prius credidi te donante, iam sic intelligo te illuminante, ut si te esse nolim credere, non possim non intelligere.[32]

In this case one must believe at first so that within the process of searching by the divine light the process grants us the evidence of what is already believed. Anselm's employment of human reason is not an abstract one, far removed from daily experience but one mirroring human existence. It is a part of every human being's youthful elan to trust in human faculties, to believe all of life and the universe exhaustibly accessible to the inquisitive human mind. On this pilgrimage of the mind he detects faith as an aid in fathoming life.[33] Firmly established on the grounds of faith one then is able to communicate with the non-believer.[34] Also in this regard Anselm is very current.

This oscillating use of that distinguishing feature of humankind, the "ratio," is neither playful nor by chance. It is the enlivening of tradition that

[32] P 4:104,5-7.
[33] P 4.
[34] Cu I 3.

occurs therein. Plotinus and Augustine come to life. The past no longer remains alien and foreign as inconsequential but is being reappropriated and reacquired. The human mind is inherently posited to refer to the past and to grant the past the opportunity to liberate the present from its constraints. Within this process meaning and purpose become apparent in a way not contradicting the past but quite on the contrary adding new perspectives. There is something deeply imbedded in the human mind which always strives to be (-come anew) present, to endow existence with youthful freshness - "θαυμαζειν" as a constant philosophical attitude. By employing reason in this transhistoric and transpersonal sense thinking renders life´s meaning present in ways both current - in the sense of relevant for the body politic - and intensely personal. The human mind is heightened to a level that is no longer temporal. Contingent beings receive intimations of their immortality. There occurs something of an interplay between temporal and supratemporal, of time and present. Hermeneutics thus perceived, grants thinking an experience of an overarching presence. This is attained by employing reason and beholding a qualified cognitional symmetry between that which is and that that (or most precisely: Who who) Is.[35] One is freed from defining history as an at random linear chain of points in time. More occurs than the mere technical or commercial mastering of the present.

In the *Phaidon,* Cebes and Simmias are ultimately not persuaded to accept the concept of the soul´s immortality by the logical force of Socrates´ arguments alone - however persuasive they may be - but yet more convincingly by the solemnity and zeal with which he vouches for that heretofore uncommon notion.[36] Likewise, the reader of Anselm´s writings is not only struck by the originality, rational symmetric balance and logically stringent consecutions of thoughts and arguments, but at least equally by the equanimity, the solemn sobriety and the passionate ardor with which these are presented.

---

[35] This sense of congeniality particularly Gothic architecture endeavored to expound on. Walter of Châtillon eloquently expressed this understanding:

> Creatori serviunt omnia subjecta,
> sub mensura, numero, pondere perfecta.
> Ad invisibilia, per haec intellecta,
> sursum trahit hominem ratio directa.

Cf. Otto George v. Simson, The Gothic Cathedral. Origins of Gothic Architecture and the Medieval Concept of Order (New York: Pantheon, 1956) 189.
[36] Phaedo 89C - 118.

Abbreviations

The abbreviations are cited according to The New Jerome Biblical Commentary. Raymond E. Brown, Joseph A Fitzmyer and Roland E. Murphy eds. (Englewood Cliffs N.J.: Prentice Hall, 1990): XXXI-XLVIII. The transliterations of the Greek terms are used as found on page XLVI of the same book.

List of Abbreviations used for Anselm's Writings

A	Epistola de Azimo et Fermentato
C	De Concordia
Ca	De Casu Diaboli
Co	De Conceptu Virginali et de Originali Peccato
Cu	Cur Deus Homo
E	Epistola
F	Fragmenta
G	De Grammatico
I	De Incarnatione Verbi
Ii	De Incarnatione Verbi recensio prior
L	De Libertate Arbitrii
M	Monologion
Me	Meditatio
O	Oratio
P	Proslogion
PI	The Fool's Reply
PR	Anselm's Reply to the Fool
Pr	De Processione Spiritus Sancti
S	De Sacramentis Ecclesiae
V	De Veritate
W	Waleramni Epistola ad Anselmum

Bibliography

All English-language quotations from Scripture are cited from New Jerusalem Bible. Garden City: Doubleday, 1985. Those in Greek are cited from Aland, Kurt, et al. eds., Nestle-Aland. Novum Testamentum Graece. Stuttgart: deutsche Bibelgesellschaft, 1985, 26th edtion.

Albert, Karl. Einführung in die philosophische Mystik. Darmstadt: Wissenschaftliche Buchgesellschaft, 1996.

Allers, Rudolf trans. and ed. Anselm von Canterbury - Leben, Lehre, Werke. Wien: Hegner, 1936.

Amour, Leslie. "Newman, Anselm and Proof of the Existence of God." International Journal for Philosophy of Religion 19 (1986): 87-93.

Anderson, Albert. "Anselm and the Logic of Religious Belief." Harvard Theological Review 61 (1968): 149-173.

Angelet, Benoît. "*Idem dicere in Corde, et cogitare.* or: What we still can learn from an existential Anselm." Aquinas, Rivista Internazionale di Filosofia XXX (1987): 93-102.

Anscombe, Gertrude E.M. "Truth: Anselm or Thomas?" New Blackfriars 66 (1985): 82-98.

Anstey, C.R.P. "St. Anslem De-Mythologized." Theology LXIV (1961): 17-23.

Antweiler, Anton. "Anselmus von Canterbury, Monologion und Proslogion." Scholastik VIII/4 (1933): 551-560.

Anz, Wilhelm. "Was bedeutet es, daß Karl Barth sich auf Anselms Proslogion beruft? Ein Versuch, Barth und Bultmann gleichzeitig zu lesen." Existenz und Sein. Walter Schmidthals ed. Tübingen: Mohn (1989): 1-13.

Arendt, Hannah. Origins of Totalitarianism. New York: Harcourt Brace, 1951.

Armstrong, Arthur Hilary. Plotinian and Christian Studies. London: Viviorum Reprints, 1979.

---. "St. Anselm and his critics: Further reflection on Cur Deus Homo." Downside Review 86 (1968): 354-376.

Arnou, Renatus. Le désire de dieu dans la philosophie de Plotin. 2nd ed. Rome: Gregorian UP, 1967.

Audet, Théodore A. "Problématique et structure de Cur deus Homo." Études d'histoire littéraire et doctrinale 13 (1968): 7-115.

---. "Une source augustinienne de l'argument de Saint Anselme." Recontres 30 (1949): 105-117.

"Augustinus." Lexikon des Mittelalters. Bd. I. München: Artemis, 1980.

Aulén, Gustaf. Dogmhistoria den Kristna Lärobildningens Utvecklingsgång fran den Efterapostoliska Tiden till Dagar Vara. Stockholm: Norsedt, 1917.

Aumann, Jordan. Christian Spirituality in the Catholic Tradition. London: Reed and Ward, 1985.

"A. v. Canterbury." Lexikon des Mittelalters. Vol. I. 1st. ed. München: Artemis, 1980.

Bacht, Heinrich. "Theologie der Mönche." Christ in der Gegenwart 33 (1981): 51-52.

Baeumker, Clemens. "Der Platonismus im Mittelalter." Platonismus in der Philosophie des Mittelalters. Werner Beierwaltes ed. Darmstadt: Wisssenschaftliche Buchgesellschaft, 1969. previously in: Beiträge zur Geschichte der Philosophie des Mittelalters. Vol. XXV 1/2. Münster: Aschendorff, 1927.

---. Witelo, ein Philosoph und Naturforscher des 13. Jahrhunderts. Beiträge zur Geschichte des Mittelalters 3/2. Münster: Aschendorff, 1908.

Baeumker, Franz. Die Lehre Anselms von Canterbury über den Willen und seine Wahlfreiheit. Nach den Quellen dargestellt. Beiträge zur Geschichte der Philosophie des Mittelalters 10/6. Münster: Aschendorff, 1912.

Balthasar, Hans Urs von and Engelbert Gutwenger. "Der Begriff der Natur in der Theologie - Eine Diskussion." Zeitschrift für katholische Theologie 75 (1953): 452-464.

Balthasar, Hans Urs von. Apokalypse der deutschen Seele. Prometheus. Studien zu einer Lehre von den letzten Haltungen. Salzburg: Pustet, 1937/38.

---. "A response to my critic." Communio 5 (1978): 69-76.

---. Au coeur du Mystère redempteur. Paris: Aubier, 1980.

---. "Christian Prayer." Communio 5 (1978): 15-22.

---. Cordula oder der Ernstfall. 4th ed. Einsiedeln: Johannes, 1987.

---. Das betrachtende Gebet. 4th ed. Einsiedeln: Johannes, 1976.

---. Das Ganze im Fragment. Aspekte der Geschichtstheologie. 2nd impr. ed. Einsiedeln: Johannes, 1990.

---. Der christliche Stand. Einsiedeln: Johannes, 1977.

--- ed. Die grossen Ordensregeln. 2nd rev. ed. Einsiedeln, Zürich, Köln: Benzinger, 1962.

---. Einfaltungen. Auf Wegen christlicher Einigung. München: Kösel, 1961.

---. Glaubhaft ist nur die Liebe. 5th ed. Einsiedeln: Johannes, 1985.

---. Göttliches und Menschliches im Räteleben. Einsiedeln: Johannes, 1963.

381

---. Herrlichkeit. Eine theologische Ästhetik. Bd. 1. Schau der Gestalt. Einsiedeln: Johannes, 1961.

---. Herrlichkeit. Eine theologische Ästhetik. Bd. 2. Fächer der Stile. Teil 1: Klerikale Stile. Einsiedeln: Johannes, 1962, cf. esp. 219-263 for Anselm.

---. Homo Creatus Est. Skizzen zur Theologie V. Einsiedeln: Johannes, 1986.

---. Karl Barth. Darstellung und Deutung seiner Theologie. 4th ed. Einsiedeln: Johannes, 1989.

---. Kennt uns Jesus - Kennen wir Ihn?. 3rd imp. ed. Einsiedeln: Johannes, 1995.

---. Klarstellungen. Zur Prüfung der Geister. Freiburg i. Br.: Herder, 1971.

---. "La Concordantia Libertatis chez Saint Anselme." L'Homme devant Dieu. Mélanges offerts au Père Henri de Lubac. Vol. 2. Du Moyen Age au siècle des lumières. Paris: Aubier (1964): 28-45.

---. "Les thèmes johanniques dans la régle de S. Benoît et leur actualité." Collectio Cisterciana 37 (1975): 3-14.

---. Mein Werk. Durchblicke. Einsiedeln and Freiburg i. Br.: Johannes, 1990.

---. "Mysterium Paschale." Mysterium Salutis III, 2. Johannes Feiner and Magnus Löhrer eds. Einsiedeln: Benzinger (1962): 133-153.

---. Pneuma und Institution. Skizzen zur Theologie V. Einsiedeln: Johannes, 1974.

---. Prüfet alles - das Gute behaltet. Ostfildern: Schwabenverlag, 1986.

---. Schleifung der Bastionen. Von der Kirche in dieser Zeit. 5th ed. Einsiedeln and Freiburg i. Br.: Johannes, 1989.

---. Spiritus Creator. Skizzen zur Theologie III. 2nd ed. Einsiedeln: Johannes, 1988.

---. Sponsa Verbi. Skizzen zur Theologie II. Einsiedeln: Johannes, 1961.

---. The Glory of the Lord: A Theological Aesthetics. Vol. I, Seeing the Form. trans. E. Leiva-Merikakis. San Francisco: Ignatius, 1982.

---. The Glory of the Lord: A Theological Aesthetics. Vol. II, Studies in Theological Style: Clerical Styles. A. Louth, F. McDonagh, B. McNeil trans. San Francisco: Ignatius, 1984.

---. The Glory of the Lord: A Theological Aesthetics. Vol. III. Studies in Theological Style: Lay Styles. A. Louth, J. Saward, M. Simon, R. Williams trans. San Francisco: Ignatius, 1986.

---. The Glory of the Lord: A Theological Aesthetics. Vol. IV. The Realm of Metaphysics in Antiquity. B. McNeil, A. Louth, J. Saward, R. Williams, O. Danier trans. San Francisco: Ignatius, 1989.

---. The Glory of the Lord: A Theological Aesthetics. Vol. V. In the Realm of Metaphysics in the Modern Age. O. Davies, A. Louth, B. McNeil, J. Saward, R. Williams trans. San Francisco: Ignatius, 1991.

---. The Glory of the Lord: A Theological Aesthetics. Vol. VI. The Old Covenant. B. McNeil, E. Leira-Merikakis trans. San Francisco: Ignatius, 1991.

---. The Glory of the Lord: A Theological aesthetics. Vol. VII. Theology: The New Covenant. O. Davies, A. Louth, B. McNeil, J. Saward trans. San Francisco: Ignatius, 1991.

---. Theodramatik. Vol. I: Prolegomena. Einsiedeln: Johannes, 1980.

---. Theodramatik. Vol. III: Die Handlung. Einsiedeln: Johannes, 1980.

---. Theodramatik. Vol. IV: Das Endspiel. Einsiedeln: Johannes, 1983.

---. Theologik. Vol. I: Wahrheit der Welt. 2nd ed. Einsiedeln: Johannes, 1985.

---. Theologik. Vol. II: Wahrheit Gottes. Einsiedeln: Johannes, 1985.

---. Unser Auftrag. Bericht und Entwurf. Einsiedeln: Johannes, 1984.

---. Verbum Caro. Skizzen zur Theologie I. 3rd ed. Einsiedeln: Johannes, 1990.

Bamberg, Corona. Mönchtum in einer heimatlosen Welt. Würzburg: Echter, 1984.

Bandmann, Günter. Mittelalterliche Architektur als Bedeutungsträger. 9th ed. Darmstadt: Wissenschaftliche Buchgesellschaft, 1990.

Bandry, Leon. "La Préscience Divine chez S. Anselme." Archives d'Histoire Doctrinale et Litteraire du Moyen Age 13 (1940/42): 223-237.

Barber, Benjamin. Jihad v. McWorld, How Globalism and Tribalism are reshaping the World. New York: Ballantine, 1996.

Barnes, John. "The Ontological Argument," John Hick and Arthur C. McGill eds. The Many-faced Argument for the Existence of God (New York: MacMillan, 1967): 29-41.

Barnes, Jonathan. The Ontological Argument. London: MacMillan, 1972.

Baron, René. "L'idée de liberté chez Saint Anselme et Hugues de Saint Victor." Recherches de théologie ancienne et médiévale 32 (1965): 117-124.

Barral, Mary Rose. "Truth and Justice in the Mind of Anselm." Les Mutations Socio-Culturelles au Tournant des XIe-XIIe Siècles. Colloques Internationaux du Centre National de la Recherche Scientifique. Paris: CNRS (1984): 571-582.

Barth, Karl. "Bemerkungen zu Hans Michael Müllers Lutherbuch." Zwischen den Zeiten 7 (1929): 561-570.

---. Der Römerbrief. 12th ed.1922. Zollikon: EVZ, 1978.

---. Die christliche Dogmatik in Entwurf. Erster Band: Die Lehre vom Worte Gottes. Prolegomena zur christlichen Dogmatik. 1926/27. Zollikon: TVZ, 1982.

---. "Die Notwendigkeit der Theologie bei Anselm von Canterbury." Zeitschrift für Theologie und Kirche N.F. 12 (1931): 350-358.

---. Fides quaerens intellectum. Anselms Beweis der Existenz Gottes im Zusammenhang seines theologischen Programms.1931. 2nd rev. ed. Zollikon: Evangelischer Verlag, 1958. reprint London: SCM, 1958.

---. Fides Quaerens intellectum. Anselms Beweis der Existenz Gottes im Zusammenhang seines theologischen Programms. Karl Barth Gesamtausgabe. Bd. II: Akademische Werke. intro. by Eberhard Jüngel and Ingolf U. Dalferth, critical apparatus Zürich: TVZ, 1981.

---. Gebete. 4th ed. München: Kaiser, 1974.

---. Kirchliche Dogmatik. I,1. Studienausgabe. Zollikon: TVZ, 1986/87.

---. Kirchliche Dogmatik. I,2. Studienausgabe. Zollikon: TVZ, 1989/93.

---. Kirchliche Dogmatik. II,1.Studienausgabe. Zollikon: TVZ, 1986/87/88.

---. Kirchliche Dogmatik. III. Studienausgabe. Zollikon: TVZ, 1993.

---. Kirchliche Dogmatik. V. Studienausgabe: Zollikon: TVZ, 1986/89/93.

Barth, Karl and Eduard Thurneysen. Briefwechsel. Band 2: 1921-1930. Zollikon: TVZ, 1993.

Bartmuß, Hans-Joachim. "Die `fides´ in den erzählenden Quellen des 10. und beginnenden 11. Jahrhunderts und die sogenannte `germanische Treue.´" Jahrbuch für die Geschichte des Feudalismus 3 (1979): 51-65.

Bassler, Wilhelm. Die Kritik des Thomas von Aquin am ontologischen Gottesbeweis. Diss. Cologne: Kleikamp, 1970.

Bauer, Emmanuel J. Von der Wissenschaft zur Weisheit: christliche Gotterfahrung heute. Innsbruck, Wien: Tyrolia, 1992.

Bäumer, Remigius and Leo Scheffczyk eds. Marienlexikon. Vol. I. St. Ottilen: EOS, 1988.

Bayart, Jean. "The Concept of Mystery According to St. Anselm of Canterbury." Recherches de Théologie Ancienne et Médiévale Tome IX (1937): 125-166.

Bayer, Oswald. "'Vernunft ist Sprache.' Johann Georg Hamann." Auf der Suche nach dem verborgenen Gott. Alois Halder, Klaus Kienzler and Joseph Möller eds. Düsseldorf: Patmos (1987): 55-67.

Becker, Jos. Blas. "Der Satz des hl. Anselm: *Credo, ut intelligam* in seiner Bedeutung und Tragweite." Philosophisches Jahrbuch 19 (1906): 115-127.312-326.

Bedouelle, Guy. "Das Auge und das Feuer. Die 'Reinheit des Herzens' im monastischen Leben" Internationale katholische Zeitschrift Communio 17 (1988): 402-411.

Beier, Brigitte. DieFrage nach der Technik bei Arnold Gehlen und Martin Heidegger. Frankfurt am Main: Lang, 1977.

Beierwaltes, Werner. Denken des Einen. Studien zur neuplatonischen Philosophie und ihre Wirkungsgeschichte. Frankfurt am Main: Klostermann, 1985.

---. "Hen." Reallexikon für Antike und Christentum. Vol. 14. Ernst Dassmann ed. Stuttgart: Anton Hiersemann (1985): 445-472.

---. Platonismus und Christentum. Frankfurt am Main: Vittorio Klostermann, 1998.

---. Plotin über die Ewigkeit und Zeit. 3rd ed. Frankfurt am Main: Klostermann, (1967) 1981.

---. Proclo: I fondamenti della sua metafisica. Milano: Vita e Pensiero, 1988.

Beierwaltes, Werner, Hans Urs von Balthasar and Alois Haas. Grundfragen der Mystik. Einsiedeln: Johannes, 1974.

Beinert, Wolfgang. "Die Kirche - Gottes Heil in der Welt. Die Lehre von der Kirche nach den Schriften des Rupert von Deutz, Honorius Augustodinensis und Gernoch von Reichersberg." Beiträge zur Geschichte der Philosophie und Theologie des Mittelalters N.F. 13. Habil. Münster: Aschendorff, 1973.

---. "Theologie und christliche Existenz." Catholica 30 (1976): 101-109.

Bendemann, Reinhard von. Heinrich Schlier, Eine kritische Analyse seiner Interpretationen paulinischer Texte. Gütersloh: Gütersloher Verlag, 1995.

Bergenthal, Ferdinand. Das Sein, der Ursprung und das Wort. Der Gottesgedanke des Heiligen Anselm. Augsburg: Johann Wilhelm Naumann, 1949.

---. "Ist der 'ontologische Gottesbeweis' Anselms von Canterbury ein Trugschluß?." Philosophisches Jahrbuch 59 (1949): 155-167.

Berlinger, Rudolph. "Das höchste Sein. Strukturmomente der Metaphysik des Anselm von Canterbury." Tradition und Kritik. FS Rudolf Zocher. Wilhelm Arnold and Herrmann Zeltner eds. Stuttgart: F. Frommann (1967): 43-54

---. "Zur Sprachmetaphysik des Anselm von Canterbury. Eine spekulative Explikation." Untersuchung zur Person und Werk Anselms von Canterbury. Bd. V. Helmut Kohlenberger ed. Frankfurt am Main: Minerva (1976): 99-112.

Berthold, George C. ed. Faith seeking Understanding: Learning and the Catholic Tradition. Manchester, N.H.: St. Anselm College Press, 1991.

Bertola, Ermenegildo. "I precedenti del metodo di Anselmo di Canterbury nella storia cristiana." Recherches de Théologie Ancienne et Médiévale L (1985): 99-144.

Bestul, Thomas H. "St.Anselm, the Monastic Community at Canterbury, and Devotional Writing in Late Anglo-Saxon England." Anselm Studies I. An Occasional Journal. Millwood NY: Kraus International (1983): 185-198.

---. "St. Augustine and the Orationes sive Meditationes of St. Anselm." Anselm Studies II. An Occasional Journal. Joseph C. Schaubelt e.a. eds. White Plains NY: Kraus (1988): 597-605.

Bethge, Eberhard. Dietrich Bonhoeffer. Theologe - Christ - Zeitgenosse. Eine Biographie. 6th ed. München: Kaiser, 1983.

Betzendörfer, Walter. "Glauben und Wissen bei Anselm von Canterbury." Zeitschrift für Kirchengeschichte XLVII III/IV (1929): 354-370.

Biffi, Innos. Cristo. Desiderio del Monaco. La Costruzione della Teologia. Milano: Jaca Books, 1998.

Biffi, Innos and Constante Marabelli eds. Anselmo d´Aosta, Figura europea. Convegno di Studi, Aosta. Milano: Jaca Books, 1989.

Biser, Eugen. Glaubensprognose: Orientierung in postsäkularistischer Zeit. Graz: Styria, 1991.

Blumenthal, Uta-Renate. Der Investiturstreit. Stuttgart, Berlin, Köln, Mainz: Kohlhammer, 1982.

Bourke, Vernon J. "A Millennium of Christian Platonism. Augustine, Anselm and Ficino." Anselm Studies II: an occasional Journal. Joseph C. Schaubelt e.a. ed. White Plains N.Y.: Kraus International (1988): 527-557.

Bouyer, Louis. "Die mystische Kontemplation bei den Vätern." Weisheit Gottes - Weisheit der Welt. FS Joseph Ratzinger. Vol. I. Walter Baier e.a. eds. St. Ottilien: EOS (1987): 637-666.

---. Le Sens de la Vie Monastique. Turnhout: Brepols, 1950.

Brecher, Bob. "Aquinas on Anselm." Philosophical Studies XXIII (1974): 63-66.

Brecher, Robert. Anselm's Argument. The Logic of Divine Existence. Aldershot: Gower, 1985.

Brechtken, Josef. "Das Unum Argumentum des Anselm von Canterbury. Seine Idee und Geschichte und seine Bedeutung für die Gottesfrage von heute." Freiburger Zeitschrift für Philosophie und Theologie 22 (1975): 171-203.

Bredow, Gerda von. Platonismus im Mittelalter. Freiburg i. Br.: Rombach, 1972.

Bréhier, Emile. Les idées philosophiques et religieuses chez Philon d'Alexandre. Paris: Vrin, 1950.

Brentano, Franz von. Geschichte der mittelalterlichen Philosophie. Hamburg: Felix Meiner, 1980.

Brooke, Christopher. The Monastic World 1000-1300. London: Elek, 1974.

---. Die große Zeit der Klöster 1000-1300. Die Geschichte der Klöster und Orden und ihre religions-, kunst- und kulturgeschichtliche Bedeutung für das werdende Europa. Regine Klett trans. Freiburg i. Br.: Herder, 1976.

Brown, Robert F. "Some Problems with Anselm's View of Human Will." Anselm Studies II. An Occasional Journal. Joseph C. Schaubelt e.a. eds. White Plains NY: Kraus (1988): 333-350.

Brown, Stephen F. "Key Terms in Medieval Theological Vocabulary." Méthodes et Instruments du Travail intellectuell au moyen âge. Olga Weizers ed. Turnhout: Brepols (1990): 82-96.

Busch, Eberhard. Karl Barths Lebenslauf. Nach seinen Briefen und autobiographischen Texten. 5th ed. Gütersloh: Gütersloher, 1993.

Buske, Thomas. "Existenz als Accomodatio des Seins. Der `ontologische' Gottesbeweis bei Anselm von Canterbury." Theologische Zeitschrift 28/3 (1972): 197-211.

Bütler, Anselm. Die Seinslehre des Hl. Anselm von Canterbury. Diss. U Fribourg. Ingenbohl: Theodosius, 1959.

Butterworth, Edward J. The Identity of Anselm's Proslogion Argument for the Existence of God with the Via Quarta of Thomas Aquinas. Studies in the History of Philosophy Vol. 8. Lewiston: Edwin Mellen, 1990.

Campbell, Richard. "Anselm's Background Metaphysics." Scottish Journal of Theology 33 (1980): 317-343.

---. "Anselm's Theological Method." Scottish Journal of Theology 32 (1979): 541-562.

387

---."Freedom as Keeping the Truth: The Anselmian Tradition." Anselm Studies II. An Occasional Journal. Joseph C. Schaubelt e.a. eds. White Plains NY: Kraus (1988): 297-318.

---. From Belief to Understanding. Canberra: Australian National University, 1976.

---. "On Preunderstanding St. Anselm." The New Scholasticism 54 (1980): 189-193.

---. "The systematic Character of Anselm's Thought." Les Mutations Socio-Culturelles au Tournant des XIe - XIIe Siècles. Colloques Internationaux du Centre National de la Recherche Scientifique. Paris: CNRS (1984): 549-560.

Camus, Albert. Hochzeit des Lichts. Peter Gau trans. Zürich: Arche, 1981.

Cantin, André. "L'usage de la sainte Ecriture chez S. Anselme et S. Augustin ou Le projet historique, conçu au XI siècle, d'une science sacrée rationelle, non positive." Anselm Studies II. An Occasional Journal. Joseph C. Schaubelt e.a. eds. White NY: Kraus (1988): 423-445.

de Carolis, Fausto. "Fides Quaerens Intellectum. Il linguaggio razionale di Anselmo d'Aosta." Miscellanea Francescana 93 (1993): 96-147.

Cattin, Yves. "La Prière de S. Anselme dans le Proslogion." Revue des Sciences philosophiques et théologiques 72 (1988): 373-396.

Cessario, Romanus. The godly image: Christ & salvation in Catholic thought from St. Anselm to Aquinas. Studies in historical theology: 6. Petersham: St. Bede's Publications, 1990.

Chadwick, Henry. Boethius. The Consolations of Music, Logic, Theology and Philosophy. Oxford: Clarendon P, 1981.

Charlesworth, Maxwell John, St. Anselm's Proslogion with a reply on behalf of the fool by Gaunilo and the author's reply to Gaunilo. translated and introduced by Maxwell J. Charlesworth. 1965. Oxford: Oxford UP; South Bend: Notre Dame UP, 1979.

Chenu, Marie-Dominique. La théologie au XIIième siècle. Paris: Vrin. 1957.

Christe, Wilhelm. "Sola ratione. Zur Begründung der Methode des intellectus fidei bei Anselm von Canterbury." Theologie und Philosophie 60/1 (1985): 341-375.

Chubb, Jehangir N. "Commitment and justification. A new Look at the Ontological Argument." International Philosophical Quarterly 13 (1973): 335-346.

Church, Richard William. Saint Anselm. 1870. London: MacMillan, 1937.

Clayton, John. "The Otherness of Anselm." Neue Zeitschrift für systematische Theologie 37 (1995): 125-143.

388

Clévenot, Michel. Als Gott noch ein Feudalherr war. Geschichte des Christentums im IX. - XI. Jahrhundert. Fribourg/Luzern: Edition Exodus, 1991.

Cobb, John B. "Perfection exists: A critique of Ch. Hartshorne." Religion in Life 32 (1963): 294-301.

Colish, Marcia L. "Eleventh-Century Grammar in the Thought of St. Anselm." Arts Libéraux et Philosophie au Moyen Age. Actes du Quartième Congrès international de Philosophie Mediévales. Montreal: Institut d'études médiévales (1969): 785-795.

---. "Systematic theology and theological renewal in the twelfth century." Journal of Medieval and Renaissance Studies 18/2 (1988): 135-156.

---. The Mirror of Language. 2nd rev. ed. Cheyenne NE: University of Nebraska P, 1983.

Collinge, William. "Monastic Life as a Context for Religious Understanding in St. Anselm." American Benedictine Review 35/4 (1984): 378-388.

Congar, Yves M.-J. A History of Theology. trans. and ed. Hunter Guthrie. Garden City NJ: Doubleday, 1968.

---. "Der Platz des Papsttums in der Kirchenfrömmigkeit der Reformer des 11. Jahrhunderts." Sentire Ecclesiam. FS Hugo Rahner. Jean Danielou, Herbert Vorgrimler eds. Freiburg i. Br.: Herder (1961): 196-217.

---. "L'église chez Saint Anselm." Spicilegium Beccense I. Congrès international IXe centenaire de l'arrivée d'Anselme au Bec (1959): 371- 399.

Constable, Giles. Monks, Hermits and Crusaders in Medieval Europe. London: Viviarum, 1988.

Coplesten, Frederick C. A History of Medieval Philosophy. London: Methuen, 1972.

Corbin, Michel. Prière et raison de la foi: introduction à l'oeuvre de saint Anselme de Cantorbéry. Paris: Cerf, 1992.

---. "Se Tenir dans la Verité. Lecture du chapitre 12 du dialogue de saint Anselme sur la Vérité." Les Mutations Socio-Culturelles au Tournant des XIe - XIIe Siècles. Colloques Internationaux du Centre National de la Recherche Scientifique. Paris: CNRS (1984): 649-665.

Courcelle, Pierre. "Etude critique sur les commentaires de la Consolation de Boèce (IXe-XVe siècles." Archives d'histoire doctrinale et littéraire du Moyen Age 12 (1939): 5-140.

Courtois, Stéphane. Le Livre Noir du Communisme: Crimes, terreur, répression, Paris: Robert Laffont, 1997.

Craig, William L. "St. Anselm on Divine Foreknowledge and Future Contingency." Laval théologique et philosophique 42/1 (1986): 93-104.

Cushman, Robert Earl. Faith seeking Understanding. Durham NC: Duke UP, 1981.

Dalferth, Ingolf U. "Fides Quaerens Intellectum. Theologie als Kunst der Argumentation in Anselms Proslogion." Zeitschrift für Theologie und Kirche 81 (1984): 54- 105.

---. Kombinatorische Theologie, Probleme theologischer Rationalität. Quaestiones Disputatae 130. Freiburg, Basel, Wien: Herder, 1991.

Dangelmayr, Siegfried. "Maximum und Cogitare bei Anselm und Cusanus. Zur Problematik des Proslogion-Arguments." Analecta Anselmiana IV/1 Untersuchungen über Person und Werk Anselm von Canterburys. Helmut Kohlenberger ed. Frankfurt am Main: Minerva (1975): 203-209.

Daniels, Augustinus. Quellenbeiträge und Untersuchungen zur Geschichte des Gottesbeweises im 13. Jahrhundert mit besonderer Berücksichtigung des Arguments im "Proslogion." Baeumkers Beiträge 1 vol. 8. Münster: Aschendorff, 1909.

Davie, Ian. "Anselm's Argument re-assessed." The Downside Review 112 (1994): 103-120.

Davies, Brian. "Quod Vere Sit Deus: Why Anselm Thought that God Truly Exists." New Blackfriars 72 (1991): 212-244.

Delhaye, Philippe. "Quelques aspects de la morale de Saint Anselme." Spicilegium Beccense I. Congrès International du IXe centenaire de l'arrivée d'Anselme au Bec. Paris: Cerf (1959): 401-422.

Delling, Gerhard. "Monos Theos." Theologische Literaturzeitung 77 (1952): 46-76.

de Mottoni, Faes Barbara. Il "Corpus Dionysiascum" nel Medioevo. Milano: Jaca, 1977.

De Rijk, Lambert-M. La philosophie au moyen âge. Leiden: Brill, 1985.

de Schrijver, Georges. Le merveilleux accord de l'homme et de Dieu: étude de l'analogie de l'être chez Hans Urs von Balthasar. Leuven: Leuven UP, 1983.

Diels, Herman. Die Fragmente der Vorsokratiker. Berlin: Weidemann, 1954.

Diem, Karl. "Credo ut intelligam. Ein Wort zu Hans Michael Müllers Kritik an Karl Barths Dogmatik." Zwischen den Zeiten 6 (1929): 561-570.

Dodds, Eric Robertson. "The Parmenides of Plato and the origin of the Neo-Platonic 'One'." Classical Quarterly. 22 (1928): 129-142.

Dombois, Hans. "Juristische Bemerkungen zur Satisfaktionslehre des Anselm von Canterbury." Neue Zeitschrift für Systematische Theologie 9 (1967): 339-355.

Duby, Georges. Die Kunst des Mittelalters. Das Europa der Mönche und Ritter 980-1140. Stuttgart: Klett-Cotta'sche, 1984.

---. Le Moyen Age. Paris: Hachette, 1987.

du Cange, Domino. Glossarium Mediae et Infimae Latinitatis. Favre: Niort, 1883.

Duclow, Donald F. "Anselm's Proslogion and Nicholas of Cusa's Wall of Paradise." The Downside Review 100/1 (1982): 22-30.

---. "Structure and Meaning in Anselm's De Veritate."American Benedictine Review 26/4 (1975): 406-417.

Duncan, Roger. "Analogy and the Ontological Argument." The New Scholasticism LIV (1980): 25-33.

Dunn, Ian. "The Saint's Legend as History and as Poetry." American Benedictine Review 27 (1976): 357-378.

Dyroff, Adolf. Der ontologische Gottesbeweis des hl. Anselm in der Scholastik. Probleme der Gotteserkenntnis. Münster: Aschendorff, 1925.

Eckardt, Burnell F. Jr. Anselm and Luther on Atonement. Was It "Necessary"?. San Francisco: Mellen Research UP, 1992.

Eco, Umberto. Der Name der Rose. München: DTV, 1987.

---. Il pendolino di Foucault. Milano: Bompiani, 1988.

Ehlers, Joachim. "Monastische Theologie, Historischer Sinn und Dialektik. Tradition und Neuerung in der Wissenschaft des 12. Jahrhunderts." Miscellanea Mediaevalia 9, Antqui et Moderni. Albert Zimmermann ed. Berlin: de Gruyter (1974): 58-79.

Eliade, Mircea. Le sacré et le profane. Paris: Gallimard, 1965.

Enders, Heinz Werner. "Die `quinque viae' des Thomas von Aquin und das Argument aus Anselms Proslogion. Eine beziehungstheoretische Analyse." Wissenschaft und Weisheit 40 (1977): 158-188.

Enders, Markus. "Das metaphysische Ordo-Denken in Spätantike und frühem Mittelalter: Bei Augustinus, Boethius und Anselm von Canterbury." Philosophisches Jahrbuch 2 (1997): 335-361.

---. Wahrheit und Notwendigkeit, Die Theorie der Wahrheit bei Anselm von Canterbury im Gesamtzusammenhang seines Denkens und unter besonderer Berücksichtigung seiner antiken Quellen. (Aristoteles, Cicero, Auigustinus, Boethius). Leiden: Brill, 1999.

Enslin, Horst. "Der ontologische Gottesbeweis bei Anselm von Canterbury und bei Karl Barth." Neue Zeitschrift für systematische Theologie und Religionswissenschaft 11/2 (1969): 154-177.

Ernst, Karl and Heinrich Georges. Ausführliches lateinisch-deutsches Handwörterbuch. 4 Vols. Hannover: Hahn, 1913.

Ernst, Stephan. Ethische Vernunft und christlicher Glaube. Der Prozeß ihrer wechselseitigen Freisetzung in der Zeit von Anselm von Canterbury bis Wilhelm von Auxerre. Münster: Aschendorff, 1996.

Esser, Renate. `Cogitatio´und `meditatio´ - Ein Beitrag zur Metaphysik des Gebetes nach Anselm von Canterbury. Diss. Würzburg: Würzburg U, 1985.

Evans, Gillian Rosemary. A Concordance of the Works of St. Anselm. Vols. I - IV. Millwood NY: Kraus International, 1984.

---. Anselm and a new Generation. Oxford: Oxford UP, 1980.

---. Anselm and talking about God. Oxford: Oxford UP, 1978.

---. "Argumentum and Argumentatio: The Development of a Technical Terminology up to c. 1150." Classical Folia 30 (1976): 81-93.

---. "A Theology of Change in the Writings of St. Anselm and His Contemporaries." Recherches de Théologie Ancienne et Médiévale. XLVII (1980): 53-76.

---. "Inopes Verborum sunt Latini. Technical Language and Technical terms in the Writings of St. Anselm and some Commentators of the Mid-twelfth Century." Archives d´Histoire Doctrinale et Littéraire du Moyen Age XLIII (1976): 113-134.

---. "Mens Devota: The Literary Community of the Devotional Works of John of Fécamp and St. Anselm." Medium Aevum XLIII/2 (1974): 105-115.

---. Old Arts and New Theology. The Beginnings of Theology as an Academic Discipline. Oxford: Clarendon, 1980.

---. Philosophy and Theology in the Middle Ages. London: Routledge, 1993.

---. "`Sententiola ad Aedificationem´: The `Dicta´ of St. Anselm and St. Bernard." Revue Bénédictine 92 (1982): 159-171.

---. "Similitudes and Signification-Theory in the Twelfth Century." The Downside Review 101/10 (1983): 306-311.

---. "St. Anselm´s Analogies." Vivarium XIV/2 (1976): 81-93.

---. "St. Anselm and St. Bruno of Segni: The Common Ground." Journal of Ecclesiastical History 29/2 (1978): 129-144.

---. "St. Anselm and Teaching." History of Education 5 (1976): 89-101.

---. "St. Anselm's technical Terms of Grammar." Latomus 38 (1979): 413-421.

---. "The Hereford Proslogion." Anselm Studies I. An Occasional Journal. Millwood NY: Kraus International (1983): 253-257.

---. The Language and Logic of the Bible: The Earlier Middle Ages. Cambridge: Cambridge UP, 1984.

---. "The `Secure Technician': Varieties of Paradox in the Writings of St. Anselm." Vivarium XIII/1 (1975): 1-21.

---. "The Use of Technical Terms of Mathematics in the Writings of Anselm." Studia Monastica 18 (1976): 67-75.

Evdokimov, Paul. "L'aspect apophatique de l'argument de Saint Anselme." Spicilegium Beccense. Congrès international du IXe centenaire de l'arrivée d'Anselme au Bec. (Paris: Cerf, 1959): 233- 258.

Fairweather, Eugene R. ed. trans. A Scholastic Miscellany - Anselm to Ockham. The Library of Christian Classics. Vol. X. John Baillie, John T. McNeill, Henry P. van Dusen gen. eds. Philadelphia: Westminster, 1956.

Fastiggi, Robert L. "The Divine Light within: Reflections on the Education of the Mind to God in Augustine, Anselm, Bonaventure and Newman." Faith seeking Understanding: Learning and the Catholic Tradition. George C. Berthold ed. Manchester NH: St. Anselm College P (1991): 195-206.

Faux, Jean-Marie. "Un Théologien: Hans Urs von Balthasar." Nouvelle Revue Théologique 10 (1972): 1009-1030.

Feiss, Hugh. "The God of St. Anselm's Prayers." American Benedictine Review 36/1 (1985): 1-22.

Fellermeier, Jakob. "Der ontologische Gottesbeweis - Geschichte und Schicksal." Theologie und Glaube 64/4 (1974): 249-286.

Feltrin, Paola and M. Rossini, eds. Verità in quaestione. Il problema del metodo in diritto e teologia nel XII secolo. Bergamo: Pierluigi Lubrina, 1992.

Fichte, Johann Gottlieb. Anweisung zum seligen Leben, oder auch die Religionslehre. Hansjürgen Verweyen ed. 4th rev. ed. Hamburg: Felix Meiner, 1994.

Figal, Günter. Der Sinn des Verstehens. Beiträge zur hermeneutischen Philosophie. Stuttgart: Reclam, 1996.

Findlay, John Niemeyer. "Can God's existence be disproved?." Mind 57 (1948): 176-193.

Fischer, Joseph. Die Erkenntnislehre Anselms von Canterbury. Nach den Quellen dargestellt.
   Münster i. W.: Aschendorffsche Verlagsbuchhandlung, 1911.

Fisichella, Rino. "Rileggendo Hans Urs von Balthasar." Gregorianum 71 (1993): 511-546.

Flasch, Kurt. Das philosophische Denken im Mittelalter. Stuttgart: Reclam, 1986.

---. "Der philosophische Ansatz des Anselm von Canterbury im Monologion und sein
   Verhältnis zum augustinischen Neuplatonismus." Analecta Anselmiana.
   Untersuchungen zu Person und Werk Anselms von Canterbury. II. F.S.Schmitt ed.
   Frankfurt am Main: Minerva (1970): 1- 43.

---. "Die Beurteilung des anselmianischen Arguments bei Thomas von Aquin." Analecta
   Anselmiana. Untersuchungen über Person und Werk Anselm von Canterburys. Bd.
   IV/1. Frankfurt am Main: Minerva (1975): 111-125.

---. Einführung in die Philosophie des Mittelalters. Darmstadt: Wissenschaftliche
   Buchgesellschaft, 1987.

---. "Vernunft und Geschichte. Der Beitrag Johann Adam Möhlers zum philosophischen
   Verständnis Anselms von Canterbury." Analecta Anselmiana I. Franciscus Salesius
   Schmitt ed. Frankfurt am Main: Minerva (1969): 165-194.

---. "Wozu erforschen wir die Philosophie des MA?." Die Gegenwart Ockhams. Wilhelm
   Vossenkuhl, Rolf Schönberger eds. (Weinheim: Acta Humiora, 1990): 393-409.

---. "Zum Begriff der Wahrheit bei Anselm von Canterbury." Philosophisches Jahrbuch 72
   (1965): 322-352.

Fløistad, Guttorm ed. Contemporary Philosophy. A new survey, Philosophy and Science in the
   Middle Ages, parts 1 and 2, Vol. 6. The Hague: Nijhoff, 1990.

Florenski, Pawel. Raum und Zeit. Olga Radetzkaja trans. and ed. Berlin: Ed. Kontext, 1997.

Fodor, James. Christian Hermeneutics: Paul Ricoeur and the Refiguring of Theology. New
   York: Oxford/Clarendon P, 1995.

Folghera, Jean Dominique. "La Vérité Définie par San Anselme." Revue Thomiste 8 (1900):
   414-426.

Frank, Karl Suso. Geschichte des christlichen Mönchtums: Grundzüge. Darmstadt:
   Wissenschaftliche Buchgesellschaft, 1988.

Fränkel, Hermann. Dichtung und Philosophie des frühen Christentums. 2nd ed. München:
   Beck, 1962.

Frankl, Viktor. Der Mensch vor der Frage nach dem Sinn. 3rd ed. München: Piper, 1988.

---. Im Anfang war der Sinn. Wien: Deutike, 1982.

Fries, Heinrich. "Fides quaerens intellectum." Vernunft des Glaubens. Wissenschaftliche
Theologie und kirchliche Lehre. FS 60th birthday of Wolfhart Pannenberg. Jan Rohls
and Gunther Wenz eds. Göttingen: Vandenhoeck & Ruprecht (1988): 93-108.

Fries, Heinrich and Georg Kretschmar e.a. eds. Klassiker der Theologie. Vol. 1. München:
Beck, 1981.

Fröhlich, Walter. "Anselm´s Weltbild as Conveyed in His Letters." Anselm Studies II. An
Occasional Journal. Joseph C. Schaubelt e.a. eds. White Plains NY: Kraus (1988):
483-526.

--- trans. and ed. The Letters of Anselm of Canterbury. Cistercian Studies Series Number
ninety-six. Kalamazoo MI: Cistercian, 1990.

Fromm, Erich. The Art of Loving. 2nd impr. ed. London: Allen & Unwin, 1976.

Gaál Gyulai, Erzsébet von. Heinrich Heine - Dichter, Philosoph und Europäer. Eine Studie
zum weltanschaulich-philosophischen Strukturprinzip seiner Pariser Schriften.
Frankfurt am Main: Peter Lang, 1998.

Gadamer, Hans-Georg. Der Anfang der Philosophie. trans from Italian by Joachim Schulte.
Stuttgart: Reclam, 1996.

---. Hermeneutik I, Wahrheit und Methode. Grundzüge einer philosophischen Hermeneutik.
1962. now in: Gesammelte Werke. Bd. 1, Tübingen: Mohr, 1986.

---. ed. Um die Begriffswelt der Vorsokratiker. Darmstadt: Wissenschaftliche
Buchgesellschaft, 1968.

Gäde, Gerhard. Eine andere Barmherzigkeit: zum Verständnis der Erlösungslehre Anselms
von Canterbury. Bonner dogmatische Studien. Bd. 3. Würzburg: Echter, 1989.

Gaiser, Konrad. Platons ungeschriebene Lehre. 2nd ed. Stuttgart-Bad Canstatt: Frommann,
1968.

Gale, Colin. "From Dialogue to Disputation: St Anselm and his Students on Disbelief."
Tjurunga 44 (1993): 71-86.

Gall, Ernst. Die gotische Baukunst in Deutschland und Frankreich. Vol. I. Braunschweig:
Klinkardt und Biermann, 1925.

Galonnier, Alain trans. and intro. L´oeuvre de Saint Anselme de Cantorbéry. Vol. 2. preface
by Jean Jolivet. Paris: Cerf, 1986.

Garin, Eugenio. Studi sul platonismo medievale. Quaderni di Letteratura e d´arte 17. Firenze:
Le Monnier, 1958.

Gauss, Julia."Anselm von Canterbury und die Islamfrage." Theologische Zeitschrift 19 (1963): 250-272.

---. "Anselm von Canterbury. Zur Begegnung und Auseinandersetzung der Religionen." Saeculum 17 (1966): 277-363.

---. "Die Auseinandersetzung mit Judentum und Islam bei Anselm." Analecta Anselmiana Untersuchungen zu Person und Werk Anselms von Canterbury. Helmut Kohlenberger ed. Frankfurt am Main: Minerva (1975): 101-109.

---. "Toleranz und Intoleranz zwischen Christen und Muslimen in der Zeit vor den Kreuzzügen." Saeculum 19 (1969): 362-389.

Gerke, Friedrich. Christus in der spätantiken Plastik. 3rd ed. Mainz: Kupferberg, 1948.

Gersh, Stephen. "Anselm of Canterbury." A History of Twelfth Century Western Philosophy. Cambridge: Cambridge UP (1988): 255-278.

---. "Platonism - Neoplatonism - Aristotelianism. A Twelfth-Century Metaphysical and its Sources." Renaissance and Renewal in the Twelfth Century. R. L. Benson and G. Constable eds. Cambridge: Harvard UP (1982): 512-534.

Gerwing, Manfred. "Zur Bedeutung der Mediävistik für die systematische Theologie." Freiburger Zeitschrift für Philosophie und Theologie 43 (1996): 65-83.

Gessain, Robert. "Le chemin de l´interpretation." L´Inuoui de Dieu. Six Études Christologiques. Michel Corbin ed. N.p.: Bouwer (1949): 13-57.

Geyer, Bernhard. Die patristische und scholastische Philosophie. F. Überwegs Grundriß der Geschichte der Philosophie. Vol. 2. 11th ed. Berlin: Mittler, 1923-28.

---. "Zur Deutung von Anselms Cur Deus Homo." Theologie und Glaube 34 (1942): 203-210.

Geyser, Joseph. "Die Theorie Augustins von der Selbsterkenntnis der menschlichen Seele." Aus der Geisteswelt des Mittelalters. Beiträge zur Geschichte und Theologie des Mittelalters - Supplementband III/1. Halbband. Albert Lang, Joseph Lechner, Michael Schmaus eds. Münster: Aschendorff (1935): 169-187.

Giles, Constable. Monks, Hermits and Crusaders in Medieval Europe. London: Vivarum, 1988.

Gilson, Etienne. La Philosophie au Moyen Age des origines patristiques à la fin du XIVe siècle. Paris: Payot, 1976.

---. L´Esprit de la philosophie médiévale. 2nd ed. Paris: Vrin, 1969.

---. Le Thomisme, introduction a la philosophie de Saint Thomas d´Aquin. 5th ed. Paris: Vrin, 1945.

---."Sens et Nature de l'Argument de Saint Anselme." Archives d'Histoire Doctrinale et Littéraire du Moyen Age. 7 (1934): 5- 51.

Glorieux, Palémon. "Quelques aspects de la christologie de Saint Anselme." Spicilegium Beccense I. Congrès International du IXe centenaire de l'arrivée d' Anselme au Bec. Paris: Cerf (1959): 337-347.

Gombocz, Wolfgang L. "Anselm von Canterbury. Ein Forschungsbericht über die Anselm-Renaissance seit 1960." Philosophisches Jahrbuch 87 (1980): 109-134.

---. "'Facere esse Veritatem.'" Les Mutations Socio-Culturelles au Tournant des XIe - XIIe Siècles. Colloques Internationaux du Centre National de la Recherche Scientifique. Paris: CNRS (1984): 561-569.

---. Über E! Zur Semantik des Existenzprädikates und des ontologischen Arguments für Gottes Existenz von Anselm von Canterbury. Diss. U Graz. Wien: Verband der wissenschaftlichen Gesellschaft Österreichs, 1974.

---. "Zu neueren Beiträgen zur Interpretation von Anselms Proslogion." Salzburger Jahrbuch für Philosophie 20 (1975): 85-98.

---. "Zur Zwei-Argumenten-Hypothese bezüglich Anselms Proslogion." Salzburger Jahrbuch für Philosophie 20 (1975): 131-147.

Grabmann, Martin. Die Geschichte der scholastischen Methode. Bd. 1: Die scholastische Methode von ihren ersten Anfängen in der Väterliteratur bis zum Beginn des 12. Jahrhunderts. Freiburg i. Br.: Herder, 1909

Grammont, Paul. "Sant'Anselmo: Un'Esperienza Monastica." Anselmo d'Aosta - Figura Europea. Atti del Convegno di Studi. Aosta 1o e 2o marzo 1988. a cura di Innos Biffi e Constante Mirabelli. Milano: Jaca Book (1989): 63-71.

Grant, M. Colin. "Anselm's Argument Today." Journal of the American Academy of Religion LVII/4 (1989): 791-806.

Grégoire, Réginald. Brune de Segni. Exégète mediéval et théologien monastique. 3. Spoleto: Centro italiano di studi alto medioevo, 1965.

Greive, Wolfgang. "Die Kirche als Ort der Wahrheit" - Das Verständnis der Kirche in der Theologie Karl Barths. Göttingen: Vandenhoeck & Ruprecht, 1991.

Greshake, Gisbert. "Erlöste Freiheit. Eine Neuinterpretation der Erlösungslehre Anselms von Canterbury." Bibel und Kirche (1978): 7-14.

---. "Erlösung und Freiheit. Eine Neuinterpretation der Erlösungslehre Anselms von Canterbury." Theologische Quartalschrift 153 (1973): 323-345.

Griffith, Sidney H. "'Faith seeking Understanding´ in the Thought of St. Ephraem the Syrian." Faith seeking Understanding: Learning and the Catholic Tradition. George Berthold ed. Manchester NH: St. Anselm College P (1991): 35-55.

Gross, Julius. Das Erbsündendogma in der Scholastik. München/Basel: Ernst Reinhardt, 1971.

Großmann, Ursula. "Studien zur Zahlensymbolik des Frühmittelalters." Zeitschrift für katholische Theologie 76 (1954): 19-54.

Gruber, Joachim. Kommentar zu Boethius, "De Consolatione Philosophiae." Berlin: de Gruyter, 1978.

Guardini, Romano. "Anselm von Canterbury und das Wesen der Theologie." Auf dem Wege - Versuche. Mainz: Matthias Grünewald (1923): 33-65.

---. "Das argumentum ex pietate beim hl. Bonaventura und Anselms Deszenzbeweis." Theologie und Glaube 14 (1922): 156-165.

---. "Zum Begriff der Ehre Gottes." Auf dem Wege - Versuche. Mainz: Matthias Grünewald (1923): 66-85.

Guerriero, Elio. Hans Urs von Balthasar. Eine Monographie. Einsiedeln and Freiburg i. Br.: Johannes, 1993.

Gutwenger, Engelbert. "Natur und Übernatur. Gedanken zu Balthasars Werk über die Barthsche Theologie." Zeitschrift für katholische Theologie 75 (1953): 82-97.

Hadot, Pierre. Plotin ou la simplicité du regard. Paris: Plon, 1973.

---. Porphyre et Victorinus. 1/2. Diss. Paris: Etudes Augustiniennes, 1968.

Haenchen, Ernst. "Anselm, Glaube und Vernunft." Zeitschrift für Theologie und Kirche 48 (1951): 312-342.

---. "Anselm und Barth. Zur Frage der Apologetik." Wort und Geist. Festgabe für Karl Heim. Berlin (1934): 181-197.

Hallier, Amadée. The Monastic Theology of Aelred of Rievaulx. An Experimental Theology. Shannon: Irish UP, 1969.

Hammer, Felix. Genugtuung und Heil. Absicht, Sinn und Grenzen der Erlösungslehre Anselms von Canterbury. Wien: Herder, 1967.

Härdlin, Alf. "Monastische Theologie - eine 'praktische´ Theologie vor der Scholastik." Münchener Theologische Zeitschrift 39 (1988): 108-120.

Härle, Wilfried. SystematischePhilosophie. Eine Einführung für Theologiestudenten. Göttingen: Vandenhoeck und Ruprecht, 1982.

Hartshorne, Charles. "Anselm and Aristotle´s First Law of Modality." Anselm Studies I. An

    Occasional Journal. Millwood NY: Kraus International (1983): 51-58.

---. Anselm´s Discovery: A re-examination of the ontological proof for God´s existence.

    Lasalle IL: Open Court, 1965.

---. Man´s Vision of God and the Logic of Theism. Chicago: Willett Clark, 1941.

---. The Logic of Perfection and other essays in Neoclassical Metaphysics. Lasalle IL: Open

    Court, 1962.

Hasse, Friedrich Rudolf. Anselm von Canterbury. 2 vols. Leipzig: Engelmann, 1843-52.

Haubst, Rudolf. "Anselms Satisfaktionslehre einst und heute." Analecta Anselmiana. Bd. 4/2.

    Frankfurt am Main: Minerva (1975): 141-157.

---. "Das hoch- und spätmittelalterliche `Cur deus homo.'" Münchener Theologische

    Zeitschrift 6 (1955): 302-312.

Hegel, Georg Wilhelm Friedrich. Einleitung in die Philosophie der Religion. Der Begriff der

    Religion. Walter Jaeschke ed. Hamburg: Felix Meiner, 1993.

---. Phänomenologie des Geistes. ed. by Hans Friedrich Wessels and Heinrich Clairmont.

    Hamburg: Meiner, 1988.

Heidegger, Martin. Die Technik und die Kehre. 7th ed. Pfullingen: Neske, 1988.

---. Sein und Zeit. 7th ed. Tübingen: M. Niemeyer, 1953.

---. Was ist Metaphysik? 14th ed. Frankfurt am Main: Klostermann, 1992.

Heinrichs, Ludwig. Die Genugtuungstheorie des hl. Anselmus von Canterbury, neu

    dargestellt und dogmatisch geprüft. Paderborn: Schöningh, 1909.

Heinzmann, Richard. "Anselm von Canterbury." Klassiker der Theologie vol. I. Heinrich

    Fries and Georg Kretschmar eds. Munich: Beck (1981): 165-180. 406-408.

---. "Veritas humanae naturae. Ein Beitrag zur Anthropologie Anselm´s von

    Canterbury." Wahrheit und Verkündigung. FS für Michael Schmaus. Vol. 1.

    München: Schöningh (1967): 779-798.

Heitz, Sergius. Christus in Euch: Hoffnung auf Herrlichkeit. Orthodoxes Glaubensbuch für

    erwachsene und heranwachsende Gläubige. Göttingen: Vandenhoeck und Ruprecht,

    1994.

Hendley, Brian. "Anselm´s Proslogion Argument." Miscellanea Mediaevalia. Albert

    Zimmermann ed. Bd. 13/2 Sprache und Erkenntnis im Mittelalter. Berlin/New York:

    de Gruyter (1981): 838-846.

Henrich, Dietrich. Der ontologische Gottesbeweis. Sein Problem und seine Geschichte in der Neuzeit. Tübingen: Mohr, 1960.

Henrici, Peter. "Erster Blick auf Hans Urs von Balthasar." Hans Urs von Balthasar, Gestalt und Werk. Köln: Communio (1989): 45-57.

Henry, Desmond P. "Anselmian Categorial and Canonical Language." Les Mutations Socio-Culturelles au Tournant des XIe-XIIe Siècles. Colloques Internationaux du Centre National de la Recherche Scientifique. Paris: CNRS (1984): 537-548.

---. "Saint Anselm as a Logician." Sola Ratione. FS F.S. Schmitt. Stuttgart - Bad Cannstatt: Friedrich Frommann (1970): 13- 17

---. "St. Anselm and the Linguistic Disciplines." Anselm Studies II. An Occasional Journal. Joseph C. Schaubelt e.a. eds. White Plains NY: Kraus (1988): 319-332.

---. The Logic of Saint Anselm. Oxford: Clarendon P, 1967.

Herrera, R(obert) A. "Augustine's Concept of Purification and the Fool of the Proslogion." Anselm Studies II. An Occasional Journal. Joseph C. Schaubelt ed. White Plains NY: Kraus International (1988): 253-259.

---. "St. Anselm's Proslogion: A hermeneutical Task." Analecta Anselmiana Untersuchungen über Person und Werk Anselm von Canterburys. Bd. III. F.S. Schmitt ed. Frankfurt am Main: Minerva (1975): 141-145.

Hestevold, H. Scott. "The Anselmian `Single-Divine-Attribute Doctrine'." Religious Studies 29 (1993): 63-77.

Heufelder, Emmanuel M. "St. Benedikt von Nursia und die Kirche." Sentire Ecclesiam. FS Hugo Rahner. Jean Danielou, Herbert Vorgrimler eds. Freiburg i. Br.: Herder (1961): 176-184.

Heyer, George S. Jr. "St. Anselm on the Harmony between God's Mercy and God's Justice." The Heritage of Christian Thought. Essays in Honor of Robert Lowry Calhoun. Nortbert E. Cushman, Egil Grislis eds. New York: Harper & Row (1965): 31-40.

Hick, John and Arthur C. McGill eds. The many-faced Argument. Recent Studies on the Ontological Argument for the existence of God. New York: Macmillan, 1967.

Hödl, Ludwig. "Anselm von Canterbury." Theologische Realenzyklopädie. Vol. 2. Berlin: de Gruyter (1978): 759-778.

---. "Bild und Wirklichkeit der Kirche beim Hl. Anselm." Les Mutations Socio-Culturelles au Tournant des XIe - XIIe Siècles. Colloques Internationaux du Centre National de la Recherche Scientifique. Paris: CNRS (1984): 667-688.

---. "Die `Entdivinsierung´ des menschlichen Intellekts in der mittelalterlichen Philosophie und Theologie." Zusammenhänge, Einflüsse, Wirkungen - Kongreßakten zum ersten Symposium des Mediavistenverbandes in Tübingen, 1984. Berlin: De Gruyter (1986): 57-70.

---. "Die Gottesebenbildlichkeit des Menschen und der sakramentale Charakter des Christen." Der Mensch als Bild Gottes. Wege der Forschung Bd. CXXIV. Leo Scheffczyk ed. Darmstadt: Buchgesellschaft (1963): 499-525.

---. "Die ontologische Frage im frühscholastischen Eucharistietraktat Calix Benedictionis." Sola Ratione. FS F.S. Schmitt. Stuttgart Bad Cannstatt: Friedrich Frommann (1970): 87-110.

---. "Welt-Wissen und Gottes-Glaube in der Synthese des Thomas von Aquin." Weltwissen und Gottes-Glaube in der Geschichte und Gegenwart. FS for Ludwig Hödl. Manfred Gerwing ed. St. Ottilien: EOS (1990): 11-17.

---. "Zur Entwicklung der frühscholastischen Lehre von der Gottesebenbildlichkeit des Menschen." L´Homme et son Destin. Actes des premiers Congrès international de Philosophie Médiévale. Louvain/Paris: Nauwelaerts (1960): 347-359.

Hoffmann, Ernst. Platonismus und Mittelalter. Liechtenstein: Warburg Institute, 1923/24.

Hölscher, Uvo. "Anaximander und die Anfänge der Philosophie." Um die Begriffswelt der Vorsokratiker. Darmstadt: Wissenschaftliche Buchgeseelschaft (1968): 95-176.

Hopkins, Jasper. A Companion to the Study of St. Anselm. Minneapolis: U of Minnesota P, 1972.

---. A New, Interpretive Translation of St. Anselm´s Monologion and Proslogion. four volumes. Minneapolis: Arthur J. Banning, 1986.

---. "Anselm´s debate with Gaunilo." Analecta Anselmiana. Vol. 5. Frankfurt am Main: Minerva (1976): 25- 37.

---. "Discussion Article I: On Understanding and Preunderstanding St. Anselm." The New Scholasticism LII/2 (1978): 243-260.

---. "Existence as Perfection: A Reconsideration of the Ontological Argument." Religious Studies 4 (1968): 178-193.

Hopkins, Jasper and Herbert Richardson trans. and eds. Anselm of Canterbury. Vols. 1-5. Toronto and New York: Edwin Mellen, 1974-76.

Hopkins, Jasper and Herbert Richardson trans and eds. Truth and Evil. Three Philosophical Dialogues by Anselm of Canterbury. New York: Harper & Row, 1967.

Howe, Leroy T. "Existence as a Perfection: A Reconsideration of the Ontological Argument." Religious Studies 4 (1968): 78-101.

Hufnagel, Alfons. "Anselms Wahrheitsverständnis in der Deutung Alberts d. Gr." Sola Ratione. FS F.S. Schmitt. Stuttgart - Bad Cannstatt: Friedrich Frommann (1970): 19-33.

Imbach, Ruedi. "Interesse am Mittelalter. Beobachtungen zur Histographie der mittelalterlichen Philosophie in den letzten hundertfünfzig Jahren." Freiburger Zeitschrift für Philosophie und Theologie 43 (1996): 196-207.

---. Laien in der Philosophie des Mittelalters. Amsterdam: Grüner, 1989.

---. "Notabilia V." Freiburger Zeitschrift für Philosophie und Theologie 42 (1995): 186-207.

Ivánka, Endre v. Plato Christianus. Übernahme und Umgestaltung des Platonismus durch die Väter. Einsiedeln: Benzinger, 1964.

Jacobi, Klaus. "Begründen in der Theologie. Untersuchungen zu Anselm von Canterbury." Philosophisches Jahrbuch. 99/II (1992): 225-245.

Jacquin, Alcide-Mannès. "Les `Rationes Necessariae´ de Saint Anselme." Mélanges Mandonnet. Études d'Histoire Littéraie et doctrinale du Moyen Age II. Pierre Mandonnet ed. Paris: Vrin (1930): 62-78.

Jaeger, Werner Wilhelm. The Theology of the Early Greek Philosophers. Oxford: Clarendon P, 1960.

Jaspers, Karl. Aus dem Ursprung denkende Metaphysiker. München: Piper, 1957.

Jaspert, Bernd. "Benedikts Botschaft am Ende des 20. Jahrhunderts." Regulae Benedicti Studia, Annuarium Internationale. Makarios Hebler ed. St. Ottilien: EOS (1986): 205-232.

Jauss, Hans Robert. Literaturgeschichte als Provokation. Frankfurt am Main: Suhrkamp, 1970.

Jelke, Robert. "Fides quaerens intellectum." Theologisches Literaturblatt. LX/1 (1939): 1-8.

Johnson, Harold J. "The Ontological Argument and the Languages of `Being.´" Miscellanea Mediaevalia. Albert Zimmermann ed. Sprache und Erkenntnis im Mittelalter Bd. 13/2. Berlin, New York: de Gruyter (1981): 724-737.

Jordan, Robert. "Homage to St. Anselm." Patterns of the Life-World. Essays in Honor of John Wild. James M. Edie, Francis H. Parker and Calvn O. Schrag eds. Evanston: Northwestern UP (1970): 40-61.

Josuttis, Manfred. Die Gegenständlichkeit der Offenbarung. Karl Barths Anselm-Buch und die Denkform seiner Theologie. Bonn: Bouvier, 1965.

Jüngel, Eberhard. Karl Barth. A Theological Legacy. London: SCM, 1982.

Kane, G. Stanley. "Elements of Ethical Theory in the Thought of St.Anselm." Studies in Medieval Studies XII (1978): 61-71.

Kant, Immanuel. Gesammelte Schriften. Ak. Ausgabe, Vol. II. Berlin: de Gruyter, 1969.

Karpiev, Georgi. ... Ipsa Vita et Veritas. Der "Ontologische Gottesbeweis" und die Ideenwelt Anselms von Canterbury. Leiden: Brill, 1998.

Kasper, Walter. "Dogmatik als Wissenschaft, Versuch einer Neubegründung." Theologische Quartalschrift 157 (1977): 189-203.

Kasper, Walter and Karl Lehmann eds. Hans Urs von Balthasar, Gestalt und Werk. Köln: Communio, 1989.

Kazantzakis, Nikos. Rechenschaft vor El Greco. 3rd ed. München, Berlin: Herbig, 1970.

Keefe, Donald J. "A methodological critique of von Balthasar's theological aesthetics." Communio 5 (1978): 23-43.

---. Thomism and the ontological Theology of Paul Tillich. A Comparison of Systems. Leiden: Brill, 1971.

Kehl, Medard and Werner Löser eds. The von Balthasar Reader. trans. by Robert J. Daly and Fred Lawrence. Edinburgh: T. and T. Clark, 1982.

Keller, Albert. Einführung in die philosophische Mystik. Darmstadt: Wissenschaftliche Buchgesellschaft, 1996.

Kenny, Anthony. "Anselm on the Conceivability of God." Archivo di Filosofia LVIII (1990): 71-79.

Keulman, Kenneth. The balance of consciousness: Voegelin and the mind's fate. College Park PA: The Pennsylvania State University, 1990.

Kienzler, Klaus. "Der garstige Graben zwischen Vernunft und Offenbarung - Gotthold Ephraim Lessing." Auf der Suche nach dem verborgenen Gott. Alois Halder, Klaus Kienzler and Joseph Möller eds. Düsseldorf: Patmos (1987): 35-54.

---. Glauben und Denken bei Anselm von Canterbury. Freiburg, Basel, Wien: Herder, 1981.

---. Gott ist größer. Studien zu Anselm von Canterbury. Würzburg: Echter, 1997.

---. "Zur philosophisch-theologischen Denkform bei Augustinus und bei Anselm von Canterbury." Anselm Studies II: an occasional Journal. Joseph C. Schaubelt e.a. ed. White Plains N.Y.: Kraus International (1988): 353-387.

Kilzer, Martha Clare. "The Place of Saint Benedict in the Western Philosophical Tradition." American Benedictine Review 25 (1974): 27-39.

Kimmerle, Helmut. Die Gottesbeweise Anselms von Canterbury. Ihre Voraussetzungen und ihre Bedeutung für die philosophische Theologie. Diss. Berlin: Freie Universität P, 1958.

Klaghofer-Treitler, Wolfgang. Gotteswort im Menschenwort. Inhalt und Form von Theologie nach Hans Urs von Balthasar. Innsbruck-Wien: Tyrolia, 1992.

Klibansky, Raymond. The Continuity of the Platonic tradition. London: SCM, 1939.

Klimek, Nicolaus. Der Begriff "Mystik" in der Theologie Karl Barths. Paderborn: Bonifatius, 1990.

Kline, Morris. Mathematics in Western Culture. London: Allen & Unwin, 1976.

Klotz, Reinhold. Handwörterbuch der lateinischen Sprache. 7th ed. Graz: Akademische Druck- und Verlagsanstalt, 1963.

Kluxen, Wolfgang. "Die geschichtliche Erforschung der mittelaterlichen Philosophie und die Neuscholastik." Christliche Philosophie im katholischen Denken des 19. und 20. Jahrhunderts. Vol. 2. Emmerich Coreth, Walter M. Neidl, Georg Pfligersdorffer eds. Graz, Wien, Köln: Styria (1988): 362-389.

Knauer, Peter (trans.). Ignatius von Loyola, Gründungstexte der Gesellschaft Jesu. Würzburg: Echter, 1998.

Knowles, David. Saints and Scholars, Twenty-five medieval Portraits. London: Cambridge UP, 1962.

---. The Evolution of Medieval Thought. Baltimore: Helicon Press, 1962.

---. The Monastic Order in England. A History of its development from the times of St. Dunstan to the Fourth Lateran Council 943-1216. Cambridge: Cambridge UP, 1949.

Koch, Josef. "Augustinischer und dionysischer Neuplatonismus und das Mittelalter." Kantstudien 48 (1956/57): 117-133.

---. Platonismus im Mittelalter. Ernst Hoffmann zum siebzigsten Geburtstag gewidmet. Kölner Universitätsreden 4. Krefeld: Scherpe, 1948.

Kohlenberger, Helmut. "Anselm spricht zu (post)modernen Denkern." Anselm: Aosta, Bec and Canterbury. Papers in Commemoration of the Nine-hundreth Anniversary of Anselm's Enthronement as Archbishop, Sept. 25. 1093. D.E. Luscombe and G.R. Evans eds. Sheffield: Sheffield Academic Press (1996): 376-391.

404

---. "Comptes Rendus de Congrès. VI,1 - Die internationale Anselm-Tagung in Bad Wimpfen." Societé Internationale pour l´Étude de la Philosophie Mediévale Vols. 10- 12 (1968-70): 370-376.

---. "Fides quaerens intellectum." Verkündigung und Seelsorge. 30/2 (1985): 72-76.

---. "Konsequenzen und Inkonsequenzen der Trinitätslehre in Anselms Monologion." Analecta Anselmiana V. Frankfurt am Main: Minerva (1976): 149-178.

---. "Libertas Ecclesiae und Rectitudo bei St. Anselm." Les Mutations Socio-Culturelles au Tournant des XIe - XXe Siècles. Colloques Internationaux du Centre National de la Recherche Scientifique. Paris: CNRS (1984): 689-700.

---. Similitudo und Ratio. Überlegungen zur Methode bei Anselm von Canterbury. Bonn: Bouvier, 1972.

--- ed. by in collaboration with Bernhard Geyer und Adolf Hufnagel. Sola Ratione. Anselm Studien für Dr.h.c. F.S. Schmitt zum 75. Geburtstag. Stuttgart: Kohlhammer, 1970.

---. "Sola Ratione - Teleologie - Rechtsmetaphorik. Ein anselmianisches Thema." Sola Ratione. FS F.S. Schmitt. Stuttgart - Bad Cannstatt: Friedrich Frommann (1970): 35-55.

---. "Über das Monastische in der Theologie des Heiligen Anselm." Anselm Studies II. an occasional Journal. Joseph C. Schaubelt, Thomas A. Losoncy e.a. eds. White Plains N.Y.: Kraus International (1988): 37-52.

Kolping, Adolf. Anselms Proslogion-Beweis der Existenz Gottes im Zusammenhang seines spekulativen Programms "Fides Quaerens Intellectum." Bonn: Peter Honstein, 1939.

---. "Ein Vermittlungsvorschlag auf dem Felde der Anselminterpretation." Theologische Rundschau 56 (1960): 145-150.

Konda, Jutta. Das Verhältnis von Theologie und Heiligkeit im Werk Hans Urs von Balthasars. Bonner dogmatische Studien. vol. 9. Würzburg: Echter, 1991.

Kopper, Joachim. "Kants Stellungnahme zum ontologischen Gottesbeweis in seinen Randbemerkungen zu Eberhards `Vorbereitung zur natürlichen Theologie.'" Analecta Anselmiana. Untersuchungen über Person und Werk Anselm von Canterburys. Bd. IV/1. Frankfurt am Main: Minerva (1975): 249-253.

---. Reflexion und Raisonnement im ontologischen Gottesbeweis. Köln: Kölner Universitätsverlag, 1962.

405

Koyré, Alexandre. L'idée de Dieu dans la philosophie de Saint Anselme. Paris: E. Leroux,
1923.

---. Vergnügen bei Platon. trans. with an intro. by Horst Günther. Berlin: Klaus
Wagenbach, 1997.

Krämer, Hans Joachim. Der Ursprung der Geistmetaphysik. Untersuchungen zur Geschichte
des Platonismus zwischen Platon und Plotin. Amsterdam: Schippers, 1964.

---. "Grundfragen der aristotelischen Theologie." Theologie und Philosophie 44 (1969):
363-382.

Kreimenthal, Lothar. "Zur Geschichte des ontologischen Gottesbeweises." Philosophische
Rundschau 44 (1997): 44-51.

Kremer, Klaus. Gott und Welt in der klassischen Metaphysik. Vom "Sein der Dinge" in Gott.
Stuttgart: W. Kohlhammer, 1969.

Krings, Hermann. "Das Sein und die Ordnung. Eine Skizze zur Ontologie des Mittelalters."
Deutsche Vierteljahreszeitschrift für Literaturwissenschaft XVIII/3 (1940): 233-249.

Krüger, Karl H. Die Universalchroniken.Vols. 1 and 2. Turnhout: Brepols, 1976/1985.

Kuhlmann, Gerhardt. "Zu Karl Barths Anselmbuch." Zeitschrift für Theologie und Kirche 13
(1932): 269-281.

Külling, Heinz. Wahrheit als Richtigkeit: eine Untersuchung zur Schrift "De Veritate" von
Anselm von Canterbury. Bern, Frankfurt am Main, Nancy, New York: Lang, 1984.

Küng, Hans, "Karl Barths Lehre vom Wort Gottes als Frage an die katholische Theologie."
Einsicht und Glaube. Joseph Ratzinger and Heinrich Fries eds. Freiburg i. Br.: Herder
(1962): 75-97.

---. Weltethos für Weltpolitik und Weltwirtschaft, München: Piper, 1997.

Kurtz, Waldemar. "Domus Dei - Der Kirchenbegriff des Hl. Benedikt." Regulae Benedicti
Studia. Annuarium Internationale 5. Hildesheim: Gerstenberg (1977): 119-130.

Kutschera Franz von. Vernunft und Glaube. Berlin, New York: de Gruyter, 1991.

Labbé, Yves. "Réceptions Théologiques de la `Postmodernité'." Révue des Sciences
philosophiques et théologiques 72 (1988): 397-426.

Landgraf, Arthur Michael. Dogmengeschichte der Frühscholastik. Die Gnadenlehre. Bd. I.
Regensburg: Pustet, 1952.

---. Einführung in die Geschichte der theologischen Literatur der Frühscholastik. Regensburg:
Pustet, 1948.

Langenmeyer, Bernhard Georg. "Leitideen und Zielsetzungen theologischer
  Mittelalterforschung aus der Sicht der systematischen Theologie." Renovatio et
  Reformatio. FS Ludwig Hödl. Manfred Gerwing and Godehard Ruppert eds. Münster:
  Aschendorff (1985): 3-13.

Lauffer, Otto. Die Begriffe "Mittelalter" und "Neuzeit" im Verhältnis zur deutschen
  Altertumskunde. Berlin: Deutscher Verein für Kunstwissenschaft, 1936.

Lawn, Brian. The Rise and Decline of the Scholastic "Quaestio disputata," With special
  Emphasis on its Use in the Teaching of Medicine and Science. Leiden: Brill, 1993.

Lawrence, Clifford Hugh. Medieval Monasticism. New York: Longman, 1984.

Leclercq, Jean. "A propos de `La renaissance du XIIe siècle.´ Nouveaux témoignages sur la
  `théologie monastique.´" Collecteanea Cisterciensia 40 (1970): 65-72.

---. "Essais sur l´esthetique de S. Bernard." Studi Medievali III:9 (1968): 688-728.

---. "Faith seeking Understanding through Images." Faith seeking Understanding: Learning
  and the Catholic Tradition. George C. Berthold ed. Manchester NH: St. Anselm
  College P (1991): 5-12.

---. introduction to Baudouin de Ford, Le sacrement de l´autel. Sources Chrétiennes 93 (1968):
  47-51.

---. L´amour des lettres et le désir de Dieu. Initiation aux auteurs monastiques du moyen âge.
  Paris: Cerf, 1957.

---. The Love of Learning and The Desire for God. A Study of Monastic Culture. trans. by
  Catherine Misrahi, New: Fordham UP, 1961.

Leftow, Brian. "Anselm on Omnipresence." The New Scholasticism LXIII/3 (1989): 326-357.

---. "Anselm on the Necessity of the Incarnation." Religious Studies 31 (1995): 167-185.

LeGoff, Jacques. Le Moyen Age d´aujourd´hui. Paris: Léopard d´Or, 1998.

---. L´imaginaire médiéval. Paris: Gallimard, 1985.

Lehmann, Karl and Walter Kasper eds. Hans Urs von Balthasar, Gestalt und Werk. Köln:
  Communio, 1989.

Levasti, Arrigo. S. Anselmo: vita e pensiero. Bari: G. Laterza, 1929.

Levinas, Emmanuel. "L´événement de Vérité - Lecture de `de Veritate´ d´Anselme de
  Cantorbéry." L´Innoui de Dieu. Six études christologiques. Michel Corbin ed. N.p.:
  Bouwer (1949): 59-107.

Lewis, Charlton T. and Charles Short. A Latin Dictionary. 1879. Oxford: Clarendon, 1958.

Löhrer, Magnus and Johannes Feiner eds. Mysterium Salutis. vol. 2. Die Heilsgeschichte vor
Christus. Einsiedeln, Köln: Benzinger, 1965.

Lohse, Bernhard. Mönchtum und Reformation. Göttingen: Vandenhoeck und Ruprecht, 1963.

---. "Zur theologischen Methode Anselms von Canterbury in seiner Schrift `Cur Deus
Homo.'" Vernunft des Glaubens. Wissenschaftlliche Theologie und kirchliche Lehre.
FS 60th birthday of Wolfhart Pannenberg, Jan Rohls and Gunther Wenz eds.
Göttingen: Vandenhoeck & Ruprecht (1988): 322-335.

Lonergan, Bernard J. F. Method in Theology. New York: Herder and Herder, 1972.

Löser, Werner. "Unangefochtene Kirchlichkeit - universeller Horizont." Herder
Korrespondenz 10 (1988): 477.

Losoncy, Thomas A. "Chapter 1 of St. Anselm's `Proslogion'; Its Preliminaries to Proving
God's Existence as Paradigmatic for Subsequent Proofs of God's Existence." The
European Dimensions of St. Anselm's Thinking. Josef Zumr and Vilém Herold eds.
Prague: Institute of Philosophy (1993): 95-106.

---. "The Proslogion Argument and the Anselmian Cogito." Anselm: Aosta, Bec and
Canterbury. Papers in Commemoration of the Nine-Hundreth Anniversary of
Anselm's Enthronement as Archbishop, Sept. 25 1093. D.E. Luscombe & G.R. Evans
eds. Sheffield: Sheffield Academic Press (1996): 238-246.

---. "Will in St. Anselm: an Examination of his Biblical and Augustinian Origins." Les
Mutations Socio-Culturelles au Tournant des XIe - XXe Siècles. Colloques
Internationaux du Centre National de la Recherche Scientifique. Paris: CNRS (1984):
701-710.

Löw, Reinhard. "Die Wertneutralität der Wissenschaft ist eine Chimäre." An den Grenzen der
Ratio - Conturengespräche. Theo Faulhaber and Adalbert Reif eds. München: Langen-
Müller-Herbig (1988): 341-393.

Löwith, Karl. Wissen, Glaube und Skepsis. 3rd. ed. Göttingen: Vandenhoeck und Rupprecht,
1962.

Lubac, Henri de. "A Witness of Christ in the Church, Hans Urs von Balthasar." Communio 2
(1975): 218-235.

---. Corpus Mysticum. L'Eucharistie et l'Eglise au Moyen Age. 2nd aug. ed. Paris: Aubier,
1949.

---. "Ein Zeuge in der Kirche. Hans Urs von Balthasar." Communio 4 (1975): 390-409.

408

---. "'Seigneur, je cherche ton Visage.' Sur le chapitre XIVe du Proslogion de saint Anselme" Recherches dans la Foi. Trois études sur Origène, saint Anselme et la philosophie Chrétienne. Henri de Lubac ed. Paris: Beauchesne (1979): 6-124.

---. "Sur le chapitre XIVe du Proslogion:" Spicilegium Beccense I. Congrès international du IXe centenaire de l'arrivée d'Anselme au Bec. Paris: Vrin (1959): 295-312.

Luscombe, David E. and Gillian Rosemary Evans eds. Anselm: Aosta, Bec, Canterbury. Papers in Commemoration of the Nine-hundreth Anniversary of Anselm's Enthronement as Archbishop. Sept. 25. 1093. Sheffield: Sheffield Academic P, 1996.

Magal, Otto, Eva Irblich, and István Németh. Wissenschaft im Mittelalter. Wien: Hollinck, 1975.

Malcolm, Norman. "Anselm's ontological Argument." Philosophical Review 19 (1960): 41-54.

Mandonnet, Pierre. Siger de Brabant et l'averroïsme latin au XIIIe siècle. 2nd rev. ed. Louvain: Institut de l'Université, 1908-11.

Mann, William E. "Divine Simplicity." Religious Studies 18 (1982): 451-471.

Manser, Gallus M. "Gibt es eine christliche Philosophie?." Divus Thomas. Jahrbuch für Philosophie und spekulative Theologie 14 (1936): 19-51.123-141.

Marcel, Gabriel. Werkauswahl III, Unterwegssein. Paderborn: Ferdinand Schöningh, 1992.

Maréchal, Joseph. Le point de départ de la métaphysique. Cahiers I-V. Bruxelles, Paris: Alcan, 1922-1947.

Maritain, Jacques. "De la notion de philosophie chrétienne." Revue Neo-Scholastique de Philosophie 34 (1932): 153-186.

---. Science et sagesse, suivi d'éclairissements sur la philosophie morale. Paris: Labergerie, 1935.

Martinich, Aloysius P. "Credo ut Intelligam." Studies in Medieval Studies XII (1978): 55-59.

Mascall, Eric Lionel. "Faith and Reaon: Anselm and Aquinas." The Journal of Theological Studies XIV/1 (1963): 67-90.

---. The Openness of Being. Natural Theology Today. Philadelphia: Westminster Press, 1972.

Masini, Guy. "St. Anselm, `Satisfactio´, and the `Rule´ of St. Benedict." Revue Bénédictine XCVII/1-2 (1987): 101-121.

McEnvoy, George. "La philosophie du Moyen Age, la civilisation médiévale et la culture du médiéviste." Actualité de la pensée médiévale, Receuil d'articles. Louvain-laNeuve, Paris: Ed. Peeters (1994): 69-78.

McGinn, Bernard and John Meyendorff eds. Christian Sprituality. Origins to the Twelfth Century. Volume 16 of World Spirituality: An Encyclopedic History of the Religious Quest. New York: Crossroad, 1985.

McGrath, Alister E. "Rectitude: the Moral Foundation of Anselm of Canterbury's Soteriology." Downside Review 99 (1981): 204-213.

McIntyre, John. St. Anselm and his critics. A re-interpretation of the "Cur deus homo." Edinburgh, London: Oliver and Boyd, 1954.

Menke, Christoph. Tragödie im Sittlichen. Gerechtigkeit und Freiheit nach Hegel. Frankfurt am Main: Suhrkamp, 1996.

Mensching, Günther. Das Allgemeine und das Besondere. Der Ursprung des modernen Denkens im Mittelalter. Stuttgart: Reclam, 1992.

Merlan, Philip. From Platonism to Neoplatonism. 2nd ed. The Hague: Nijhoff, 1960.

Mews, Constant J. "St. Anselm and Roscelin: some new Texts and their Implications." Archives d'Histoire Doctrinale et Littéraire du Moyen Age 58 (1991): 55-81.

Meyer, Heinz and Rudolf Suntrup. Lexikon der mittelalterlichen Zahlenbedeutungen. München: Fink, 1987.

Michaud-Quantin, Pierre. Etudes sur le vocabulaire philosophique du moyen âge. München: Fink, 1987.

Michel, Otto. "Philosophia." Theologisches Wörterbuch zum Neuen Testament. G. Kittel ed. Stuttgart: Kohlhammer, 1933-1979.

Miethe, Terry L. Does God exist?: a believer and an atheist debate. San Francisco: Harper, 1991.

Milis, Ludo J. R. Angelic Monks and Earthly Men: Monasticism ans Its Meaning to Medieval Society. Woodbridge: Boydell, 1992.

Möhler, Johann Adam. "Anselm, Erzbischof von Canterbury. Ein Beitrag zur Kenntniß des religiös-sittlichen, öffentlich-kirchlichen und wissenschaftlichen Lebens im elften und zwölften Jahrhundert." Gesammelte Schriften und Aufsätze. Vol. 1. Jgnaz Döllinger ed. Regensburg (1939): 32-176.

Mojsisch, Burkhard. "Mittelaterliche Grundlagen der neuzeitlichen Erkenntnistheorie." Renovatio et Reformatio. FS Ludwig Hödl. Manfred Gerwing and Godehard Ruppert eds. Münster: Aschendorff (1985): 155-169.

Moltmann, Jürgen. Was ist heute Theologie?. Freiburg, Basel, Wien: Herder, 1988.

Moreau, Joseph. "Logique et Dialectique dans l'Argument du `Proslogion.'" Miscellania Mediaevalia. Albert Zimmermann ed. Bd. 13/2. Sprache und Erkenntnis im Mittelalter. Berlin: de Gruyter (1981): 718-723.

Mühlenberg, Ekkehard. Die Unendlichkeit Gottes bei Gregor v. Nyssa. Gregors Kritik am Gottesbegriff der klassischen Metaphysik. Göttingen: Vandenhoeck und Ruprecht, 1966.

---. Dogma und Lehre im Abendland. Handbuch der Dogmen- und Theologiegeschichte. Bd. 1. Carl Andersen ed. Göttingen: Vandenhoeck und Ruprecht, 1982.

Müller, Hans Michael. "Credo ut intelligam." Theologische Blätter 7 (1929): 167-176.

Müller, Max. Anselm von Canterbury. Das Verhältnis seiner Spekulationen zum theologischen Begriffe des Übernatürlichen. Diss. U Augsburg, 1914. Kempten: Kösel, 1914.

"Mystik." Historisches Wörterbuch der Philosophie. Vol. 6. rubrics 268-279. 1984.

Nédoncelle, Maurice. "La notion de personne dans l'oeuvre de Saint Anselme." Spicilegium Beccense I. Congrès international du IXe centenaire de l'arrivée d'Anselme au Bec. Paris: Cerf (1959): 31-43.

Neuhaus, Gerd. Transzendentale Erfahrung als Geschichtsverlust? Der Vorwurf der Subjektlosigkeit an Rahners Begriff geschichtlicher Existenz und eine weiterführende Perspektive transzendentaler Theologie. Düsseldorf: Patmos, 1982.

Nichols, Aidan. A Grammar of Consent. Notre Dame: U of Notre Dame, 1981.

Nielson, Bent Flemming. Die Rationalität der Offenbarungstheologie. Die Struktur des Theologieverständnisses von Karl Barth. Aarhus: Aarhus UP, 1988.

Nigg, Walter. Vom Geheimnis der Mönche. Zürich and Stuttgart: Artemis, 1953.

O'Collins, Gerald. Interpreting Christ. Oxford: Oxford UP, 1983.

O'Donnell, John. Hans Urs von Balthasar. Outstanding Christian Thinkers Series. Collegeville: Liturgical Press, 1992.

Oening-Hanhoff, Ludger. "Der sogenannte ontologische Gottesbeweis bei Descartes und Bonaventura." Analecta Anselmiana IV/1 Untersuchungen über Person und Werk

Anselm von Canterburys. Helmut Kohlenberger ed. Frankfurt am Main: Minerva
(1975): 211-255.

---. Ens et verum convertuntur. Stellung und Gehalt des Grundsatzes in der Philosophie des
Hl. Thomas von Aquin. Münster: Aschendorff, 1953.

Oesterle, Hans J. "Karl Barths These über den Gottesbeweis des Anselm von Canterbury."
Neue Zeitschrift für systematische Theologie und Religionsphilosophie 23/1.2 (1981):
91-107.

O'Hanlon, Gerard F. The Immutability of God in the Theology of Hans Urs von Balthasar.
Cambridge: Cambridge UP, 1990.

Ohly, Friedrich. "Geist und Form der Hoheliedauslegung im 12. Jahrhundert." Zeitschrift für
deutsches Altertum und deutsche Literatur 84 (1954/55): 181-197.

Olivetti, Marco M. "Sich in seinem Namen versammeln: Kirche als Gottesnennung." Gott
nennen - Phänomenologische Zugänge. Bernhard Casper ed. Donauwörth: Auer
(1976): 189-217.

O'Loughlin, Thomas. "Who is Anselm's fool?" The New Scholasticism. LXII/3 (1989):
313-325.

Olsen, Glenn W. "Hans Urs von Balthasar and the Rehabilitation of St. Anselm's Doctrine of
the Atonement." Scottish Journal of Theology 34 (1981): 49-61.

---. "The Image of the first Community of Christians at Jerusalem in the Time of Lafranc and
Anselm." Les Mutations Socio-Culturelles au Tournant des XIe - XIIe Siècles.
Colloques Internationaux du Centre National de la Recherche Scientifique.
Paris: CNRS (1984): 341-353.

O'Meara, Thomas F. "Notes of Art and Theology: Hans Urs von Balthasar's Systems."
Theological Studies 42 (1981): 272-276.

O'Neill. John. "'The Same Thing therefore ought to be and ought not to be:' Anselm on
conflicting oughts." The Heythrop Journal 35 (1994): 312- 314.

Oppy, Graham. Ontological Arguments and Belief in God. Cambridge: Cambridge U P, 1985.

"Ordnung." Historisches Wörterbuch der Philosophie. Vol. 6: 1252ff.

"Ordo." Thesaurus Linguae Latinae vol. IX, pars altera. Leipzig (1968-81): 952-955. 961-963.

Osborn, Eric. The beginning of Christian Philosophy. Cambridge: Cambridge UP, 1981.

Ott, Heinrich. "Anselms Versöhnungslehre." Theologische Zeitschrift 13 (1957): 183-199.

---. "Der Gedanke der Souveränität Gottes in der Theologie Karl Barths." Theologische
Zeitschrift 12 (1956): 403-428.

---. "Theologie als Gebet und als Wissenschaft." Theologische Zeitschrift 14 (1958): 120-132.

Ottaviano, Carmelo. "Quaestioni e testi medioevali. I.: Le `rationes necessariae´ in S. Anselmo." Sophia 1 (1933): 92-98.

Otto, Rudolf. Das Heilige. Munich: C.H. Beck, 1997

Oxford Latin Dictionary. ed. by P. G. W. Glare. Oxford: Clarendon Press, 1968.

Pailin, David A. "Credo ut Intelligam." Analecta Anselmiana. Untersuchungen zu Person und Werk Anselms von Canterbury. IV/2. Helmut Kohlenberger ed. Frankfurt am Main: Minerva (1975): 111-129.

---. The anthropological Character of Theology. Cambridge: Cambridge UP, 1990.

Pannenberg, Wolfhart. "Die Rationalität der Theologie." Fides Quaerens Intellectum. Beiträge zur Fundamentaltheologie. FS. Max Seckler. Michael Keuler, Wolfhart Pannenberg and Hermann Josef Pottmeyer eds. Tübingen: Francke (1992): 533-544.

---. Grundzüge der Christologie. 6th ed. Gütersloh: Mohn, 1982.

---. Systematische Theologie. Vols. 1 and 2. Göttingen: Vandenhoeck und Ruprecht, 1988 and 1991.

---. Theologie und Philosophie: Ihr Verhältnis im Lichte ihrer gemeinsamen Geschichte. Göttingen: Vandenhoeck und Ruprecht, 1996.

Parodi, Massimo. "`Imago ad similitudinem.´ I termini di imagine e somiglianza nel Monologion di Anselmo d´Aosta." Revue des Études Augustiniennes 38 (1992): 337-354.

Payot, Roger. "L´Argument ontologique et le Fondament de la Métaphysique." Archives de Philosophie 39 (1976): 227-268.427-444.629-645.

Peirce, Charles S. The Collected Papers of Charles Sanders Peirce. Charles Hartshorne and Paul Weiss (vols. 1-6) and Arthur W. Burks (vols. 7-8) eds. Bristol: Thoemmes, 1997.

Penco, Gregorio. "Medioevo monastico." Studia Anselmiana 96 (1988): 537-548.

---. Spiritualità monastica, aspetti e momenti. Bresso di Teolo: Praglia, 1988.

Phelan, Gerald B. The Wisdom of Saint Anselm. Wimmer Lecture III. Latrobe PA: St. Vincent Archabbey Press, 1960.

"Philosophie." Historisches Wörterbuch der Philosophie. Vol. 7. rubrics 572-797. 1989.

Pieper, Josef. "Die Aktualität der Scholastik." Die Aktualität der Scholastik. Joseph Ratzinger ed. Regensburg: Pustet (1975): 106-124.

---. Scholastik. Gestalten und Probleme der mittelalterlichen Philosophie. 2nd ed. München:

Kösel, 1981.

---. "Über einen verschollenen Vorschlag zum Zweiten Vatikanum." Weisheit Gottes -
Weisheit der Welt. FS Joseph Kardinal Ratzinger zum 60. Geburtstag. Walter
Baier, Stephan Otto Horn, Vinzenz Pfnür eds. Vol. 2. St. Ottilien: EOS (1987): 971-
975.

Plagnieux, Jean. "Le binome `iustitia - potentia´ dans la sotériologie augustinienne et
anselmienne." Spicilegium Beccense I. Congrès international du IXe centenaire de
l´arrivée d´Anselme au Bec. Paris: Vrin (1959): 141-154.

Plantinga, Alvin ed. The Ontological Argument from St. Anselm to contemporary
philosophers. London: MacMillan, 1968.

Plasger, Georg. Die Not-Wendigkeit der Gerechtigkeit - Eine Interpretation zu "Cur Deus
homo" von Anselm von Canterbury. Beiträge zur Geschichte der Philosophie und
Theologie des Mittelalters Neue Folge. Bd. 38. Münster: Aschendorff, 1993.

"Platon, Platonismus." Lexikon des Mittelalters.Bd. VII. München: Artemis, 1995.

Platzeck, Erhard W. "Die Verwendung der `Via Anselmiana´ bei Bonaventura." Analecta
Anselmiana IV/1 Untersuchungen über Person und Werk Anselm von Canterburys.
Helmut Kohlenberger ed. Frankfurt am Main: Minerva (1975): 127-145.

"Plotin." Lexikon des Mittelalters. Bd. VII. München: Artemis, 1995.

"Plotino e il Neoplatonismo in Oriente e in Occidente." Accademia Nazionale dei Lincei
Anno CCCLXXI (Roma) 1974.

Plotinus. Opera: I. Enneades I-III cum Vita Porphyri. Paul Henry and Hans-Rudolf Schwyzer
eds and trans. Oxford: Oxford UP, 1964.

---. Opera: II. Enneades IV et V. Paul Henry and Hans-Rudolf Schwyzer eds. and trans.
Oxford: Oxford UP, 1977.

---. Opera: III. Enneades VI. Paul Henry and Hans-Rudolf Schwyzer eds and trans. Oxford:
Oxford UP, 1982.

---. The Enneads. Stephen MacKenna trans. London: Penguin, 1991.

Pöhlmann, Horst-Georg. Gottesdenker: prägende evangelische und katholische Theologen der
Gegenwart. 12 Portraits. Rimbek bei Hamburg: Rohwohlt, 1984.

Poole, Reginald Lane. Illustrations of the History of Medieval Thought and Learning. 2nd rev.
ed. of 1920. New York: Dover, 1960.

Potter, Vincent G. "Karl Barth and the Ontological Argument." The Journal of Religion XLV
(1965): 309-325.

Pouchet, Robert. "Existe-t-il une 'synthèse anselmienne,' Une itinéraire augustinien de l'âme à Dieu." Analecta Anselmiana I. Frankfurt am Main: Minerva (1969): 3-10.

---. La Rectitudo chez Saint Anselme. Un Intinéraire Augustinien de l'Ame à Dieu. Paris: Études Augustiniennes, 1976.

Pranger, Burcht. "Anselm's Brevitas." Anselm Studies II. An Occasional Journal. Joseph C. Schaubelt e.a. eds. White Plains NY: Kraus (1988): 447-458.

Principe, Walter H. "Some Examples of Augustine's Influence on Medieval Christology." Augustiniana 41 (1991): 955-974.

Prinz, Alois. Beruf Philosophin oder Die Liebe zur Welt. Die Lebensgeschichte der Hannah Arendt. Weinheim: Beltz & Gelberg, 1988.

Przywara, Erich. Analogia Entis. Metaphysik. Ur-Struktur und All-Rhythmus. München: Pustet/Kösel, 1932.

Pucelle, Jean. "Note sur Kant et la preuve ontologique." Analecta Anselmiana. Frankfurt am Main: Minerva (1970): 187-198.

Pugh, Jeffrey C. The Anselmic Shift: Christology and Method in Karl Barth's Theology. New York/Bern/Frankfurt am Main/Paris: Lang, 1990.

Puntel, Laurencino Bruno. Analogie und Geschichtlichkeit. Freiburg i. Br.: Herder, 1969.

Rahner, Karl. Grundkurs des Glaubens. 4th ed. Freiburg, Basel, Wien: Herder, 1976.

---. Hörer des Wortes. Zur Grundlegung einer Religionsphilosophie. München: Kösel, 1963.

---. Schriften zur Theologie. Wissenschaft und christlicher Glaube. vol. 15. Zürich: Benzinger, 1983.

Ratzinger, Joseph. Einführung in das Christentum. Vorlesungen über das Apostolische Glaubensbekenntnis. München: Kösel, 1968.

---. "Gewissen und Wahrheit." Fides Quaerens Intellectum. FS Max Seckler. ed. by Michael Keuler, Wolfhart Pannenberg, Hermann Josef Pottmeyer, Tübingen: Francke, 1992.

---. Wesen und Auftrag der Theologie, Versuche zu ihrer Ortsbestimmung im Disput der Gegenwart. Einsiedeln: Johannes, 1993.

Reale, Giovanni. Zu einer neuen Interpretation Platons. Paderborn, München: Schöningh, 1993.

Recktenwald, Engelbert. Die ethische Struktur des Denkens bei Anselm von Canterbury. Heidelberg: C. Winter, 1998.

Reiter, Josef. "Die versuchte Selbstbegründung endlichen Wissens als Wissen im Anselmianischen Argument.'" Analecta Anselmiana V. Untersuchungen über Person und Werk Anselms von Canterburys. Helmut Kohlenberger ed. Frankfurt am Main: Minerva (1976): 113-132.

---. "Phänomenologie des Nennens Gottes: Konsequenzen einer nicht nur methodologischen Verlegenheit in geschichtlich-systematischer Sicht." Gott nennen - Phänomenologische Zugänge. Bernhard Casper ed. Freiburg i. Br.: Karl Alber (1984): 125- 163.

Richthammer, Siegward. Die Systematik des Proslogionbeweises. Transzendentalphilosophische Überlegungen zu Anselms Beweis der Existenz Gottes. Diss. Regensburg U, 1996.

Ricoeur, Paul. Du texte à l'action. Paris: Ed. du Seuil, 1986.

Rief, Josef. Der Ordo-Begriff des jungen Augustinus. Paderborn: Schöningh, 1962.

---. "Die Wahrheit der Weisheit als Movens der augustinischen Wahrheitssuche." Weisheit Gottes - Weisheit der Welt. FS Joseph Ratzinger. Vol. I. Walter Baier e.a. eds. St. Ottilien: EOS (1987): 667- 688.

Rist, John M. "Theos and the One in some texts of Plotinus." Mediaeval Studies 24 (1962): 169-180.

Roberts, Victor W. "The Relation of Faith and Reason in St. Anselm of Canterbury." American Benedictine Review XXV (1974): 494-512.

Röd, Wolfgang. Der Gott der reinen Vernunft. Die Auseinandersetzung um den ontologischen Gottesbeweis von Anselm bis Hegel. München: C.H. Beck, 1992.

---. "Some Remarks on the Prehistory of the Logical Form of St. Anselm's Argument in Proslogion II." Anselm Studies II. An Occasional Journal. Joseph C. Schaubelt e.a. ed. White Plains NY: Kraus International (1988): 241-252.

Rogers, Katherin A. "Can Christianity be Proven?: St. Anselm of Canterbury on Faith and Reason." Anselm Studies II. An Occasional Journal. Joseph C. Schaubelt e.a. eds. White Plains NY: Kraus (1988): 459-479.

---. The Neoplatonic Metaphysics and Epistemology of Anselm of Canterbury. Studies in History of Philosophy Vol. 45. Lewiston: Edwin Mellen, 1997.

Rohls, Jan. Theologie und Metaphysik. Der ontologische Gottesbeweis und seine Kritiker. Gütersloh: Gütersloher/Gerd Mohn, 1987.

Rondet, Henri. "Grace et péché, l'augustinisme de Saint Anselme." Spicilegium Beccense I. Congrès international du IXe centenaire de l'arrivée d'Anselme au Bec. Paris: Vrin (1959): 155-169.

Root, Michael. "Necessity and Unfittingness in Anselm's Cur Deus Homo." Scottish Journal of Theology 40 (1987): 211-230.

Roques, René. Anselme de Cantorbéry. Pourquoi Dieu s'est fait homme. Texte latin, introduction, bibliographie, traduction et notes, de R. Roques. Sources chrétiennes 91, Série des textes monastiques d'Occident 11. Paris: Cerf, 1963.

---. "La méthode de S. Anselme dans le Cur deus home." Aquinas 5 (1962): 3-57.

---. "Les pagani dans le Cur deus homo de Saint Anselme." Miscellanea Mediaevalia 2. Die Metaphysik im Mittelalter, Berlin: de Gruyter (1963): 192-206.

---. Structures Théologiques de la Gnose à Richard de Saint-Victor. Essais et analyses critiques. Paris: Presses Universitaires de France, 1962.

Rousse, Jacques. "Lectio divina et lecture spirituelle." Dictionnaire de spiritualité ascétique et mystique Vol. 9. Paris: Beauchesne (1975): rubrics 470-487.

Rousseau, Edward L. "St. Anselm and St. Thomas - A Reconsideration." The New Scholasticism LIV (1980): 1-24.

Rousseau, Pierre. "Note sur la connaissance de Dieu selon Saint Anselme." De la connaissance de Dieu. Recherches de la philosophie 3/4. Paris: Cerf (1958): 177-185.

Ruh, Kurt. Geschichte der abendländischen Mystik. Bd. 1. München: C.H. Beck, 1990.

Salmann, Elmar. "Korreflexive Vernunft und Theonome Weisheit in der Logik von Monologion und Proslogion." L'Attualità Filosofica di Anselmo d'Aosta. à cura di Maternus Hoegen. Studia Anselmiana. Rome: Pontificio Ateneo S. Anselmo (1990): 143-228.

Sandoz, Elias ed. Eric Voegelin's Significance for the Modern Mind. Baton Rouge: Lousiana State UP, 1991.

Sartre, Jean-Paul. L'être et le néant, essai d'ontologie phénoménologique. Paris: Gallimard, 1943.

Sauter, Gerhard. "Reden von Gott im Gebet." Gott nennen -Phänomenologische Zugänge. Bernhard Casper ed. Freiburg i. Br.: Karl Alber (1984): 219-242.

Saward, John. The Mysteries of March, Hans Urs von Balthasar on the incarnation and easter. Washington D.C.: Catholic UP, 1990.

417

Schaeffler, Richard. "Spiritus sapientiae et intellectus - spiritus scientiae et pietatis -
Religionsphilosophische Überlegungen zum Verhältnis von Weisheit, Wissenschaft
und Frömmigkeit und ihrer Zuordnung zum Geiste." Weisheit Gottes - Weisheit der
Welt. FS Joseph Ratzinger. Vol. I. Walter Baier e.a. eds. St. Ottilien: EOS (1987):
15-35.

---. "Wahrheitssuche und Reinigung des Herzens - Zur Frage nach dem Zusammenhang von
Erkenntnisfortschritt und Moralität." Internationale katholische Zeitschrift Communio
17 (1988): 412-422.

Scheeben, Matthias J. Die Mysterien der Christentums. Freiburg i. Br.: Herder, 1958.

Scheffczyk, Leo. "Die Frage nach der Gottesebenbildlichkeit in der modernen Theologie."
Der Mensch als Bild Gottes. Wege der Forschung Bd. CXXIV. Leo Scheffczyk ed.
Darmstadt: Wissenschaftliche Buchgesellschaft (1969): IX-LIV.

Scheible, Helga. Die Gedichte in der Consolatione Philosophiae des Boethius. Heidelberg:
C. Winter, 1972.

Schelling, Friedrich Wilhelm Joseph. Bruno oder über das göttliche und natürliche Princip der
Dinge. Berlin: Unger, 1802.

Schlier, Heinrich. "Kurze Rechenschaft." Bekenntnis zur katholischen Kirche. Karl Hardtz ed.
4th ed. Würzburg: Echter (1956): 171-195.

Schlink, Edmund. "Anselm und Luther: Eine Studie über den Glaubensbegriff in Anselms
Proslogion." World Lutheranism Today: A Tribute to Anders Nygren. Stockholm:
Svenska Kyrkans Diakonistyrelses Bokförlag (1950): 269-293.

Schmaus, Michael. "Die metaphysisch-psychlogische Lehre über den Heiligen Geist im
Monolgion Anselms von Canterbury." Sola Ratione. FS F.S Schmitt. Stuttgart - Bad
Cannstatt: Friedrich Frommann (1970): 189-219.

---. "Die theologiegeschichtliche Tragweite der Trinitätslehre des Anselm von Canterbury."
Analecta Anselmiana. Vol. 4/1. Frankfurt am Main: Minerva (1975): 29-45.

Schmid, Johannes."Die Gemeinschaft der Lebenden und Verstorbenen in Zeugnissen des
Mittelaters." Frühmittelalterliche Studien. Bd. 1. Karl Hauck ed. Berlin: de Gruyter
(1967): 365-405.

---. Im Ausstrahl der Schönheit Gottes. Münsterschwarzach: Vier Türme, 1982.

Schmidt, Martin Anton. "Anselm von Canterbury." Nimm und Lies. Hans Freiherr von
Campenhausen ed. Stuttgart: Kohlhammer (1991): 141-170.

Schmiechen, Peter M. "Anselm and the Faithfulness of God." Scottish Journal of Theology 26 (1973): 151-168.

Schmitt, Franz Sales. "Anselm und der (Neu-)Platonismus." Analecta Anselmiana - Untersuchungen über Person und Werk Anselms von Canterbury. Franciscus Schmitt ed. Bd. I. Frankfurt am Main: Minerva (1969): 39-71.

---. Anselm von Canterbury, "Cur Deus Homo," Warum Gott Mensch geworden ist. Latin-German. 5th ed. München: Kösel, 1993.

---. "Der ontologische Gottesbeweis Anselms." Theologische Revue 32 (1933): 217-223.

---. "Die wissenschaftliche Methode bei Anselm von Canterbury und Thomas von Aquin." Analecta Anselmiana. Untersuchungen über Person und Werk Anselms von Canterbury. IV/2. Helmut Kohlenberger ed. Frankfurt am Main: Minerva (1975): 33-38.

---. "Die wissenschaftliche Methode in Anselms `Cur deus homo.'" Spicilegium Beccense I. Congrès international du IXe centenaire de l'arrivée d'Anselme au Bec. Paris: Vrin (1959): 349-370.

---. Ein neues, unvollendetes Werk des hl. Anselm von Canterbury. F.S. Schmitt ed. and trans. Beiträge zur Geschichte der Philosophie und Theologie des Mittelalters 33/3. Münster: Aschendorff, 1936.

---. "Geschichte und Beurteilung der früheren Anselmausgaben." Studien und Mitteilungen zur Geschichte des Benediktiner-Ordens und seiner Zweige. 65/4 (1955): 90-115.

---. S. Anselmi Cantuariensis Archiepiscopi Opera Omnia. confecit Franciscus Salesius Schmitt. Vols. I-VI. Edinburgh: Thomas Nelson, (1938) 1946-1961; now in 2 vols.: Stuttgart, Bad Cannstatt: Frommann, 1968.

---. "Zur Überlieferung der Korrespondenz Anselms von Canterbury." Revue Bénédictine 43 (1931): 224-238.

"Scholastik." Handbuch theologischer Grundbegriffe. Heinrich Fries ed. vol. 2. München: Kösel, 1963.

Scholz, Heinrich. "Der anselmische Gottesbeweis." "Mathesis Universalis" Abhandlung zur Philosophie als strenge Wissenschaft. Hans Hermes, Friedrich Kambartel, Joachim Ritter eds. Basel/Stuttgart: Benno Schwabe & Co. 1961.

Schönberger, Rolf. "Responsio Anselmi. Anselms Selbstinterpretation in seiner Replik auf Gaunilo." Freiburger Zeitschrift für Philosophie und Theologie 36/1 (1989): 3-46.

---. Was ist Scholastik?. Hildesheim: Bernward, 1991.

Schönborn, Christoph. "Die Autorität des Lehrers nach Thomas von Aquin." Christian Authority. Essays in Honour of Henry Chadwick. Gillian Rosemary Evans ed. Oxford: Clarendon (1988): 101-126.

Schrimpf, Gangolf. Die Axiomenschrift des Boethius (de Hebdomadibus) als Philosophisches Lehrbuch des Mittelalters. Studien zur Problemgeschichte der Antiken und Mittelalterlichen Philosophie. Vol. II. J(ohannes) Hirschberger ed. Leiden: Brill, 1966.

Schubert, Hans von. Geschichte der christlichen Kirche im Frühmittelalter. Tübingen: Mohr, 1921.

Schubert, Venanz. Plotin. Einführung in sein Philosophieren. München, Freiburg i. Br.: Alber, 1973.

Schufreider, Gregory. Confessions of a rational Mystic - Anselm´s Early Writings. Purdue University Series in the History of Philosophy. West Lafayette IN: Purdue UP, 1994.

Schurr, Adolf. Die Begründung der Philosophie durch Anselm von Canterbury. Eine Erörterung des ontologischen Gottesbeweises. Stuttgart: Kohlhammer, 1966.

---. "Philosophische Überlegungen zu Anselm von Canterbury: Cur Deus Homo." Anselm: Aosta, Bec and Canterbury. Papers in Commemoration of the Nine-Hundreth Anniversary of Anselm´s Enthronement as Archbishop, Sept. 25 1093. D.E. Luscombe & G.R. Evans eds. Sheffield: Sheffield Academic Press (1996): 264-279.

---. "Relevanz und Dimension eines erkenntnis-kritischen Philosophierens. Die Artikulation christlichen Glaubens im Gegenüber zur Position des Nicht-Glaubens bei Augustinus und Anselm." Anselm Studies II. An Occasional Journal. Joseph C. Schaubelt e.a. eds. White Plains NY: Kraus (1988): 389-321.

---. "Wissenschaftstheoretische und existentielle Relevanz des Erkenntnisbemühens Anselms von Canterbury." The European Dimensions of St. Anselm´s Thinking. Josef Zumr and Vilém Herold eds. Prague: Herold (1993): 107-136.

Schwager, Raymund. "Der wunderbare Tausch" zur Geschichte und Deutung der Erlösungslehre. München: Kösel, 1986, esp. 161-191.232-317.

Scola, Angelo. Hans Urs von Balthasar. Uno stile teologico. Milano: Jaca Books, 1991.

Seibt, Ferdinand. Glanz und Elend des Mittelalters. Berlin: Goldmann, 1991.

Seifert, Josef. Gott als Gottesbeweis. Eine phänomenologische Neubegründung des ontologischen Arguments. Heidelberg: C. Winter, 1996.

---. Sein und Wesen. Heidelberg: C. Winter, 1996.

Séjourné, Paul. "Les trois aspects du péché dans le `Cur deus homo.'" Revue des sciences
  religieuses 24 (1950): 5-27.

Sharpe, Richard. "Two contemporary Poems on Saint Anselm attributed to William of
  Chester." Revue Bénédictine XLV/3-4 (1985): 266-279.

Shindler, David L. ed. Hans Urs von Balthasar. His Life and Work. San Francisco: Ignatius P,
  1991.

Shofner, Robert D. Anselm revisited. A Study of the role of the ontological argument in the
  writings of Karl Barth and Ch. Hartshorne. Leiden: Brill, 1975.

Simson, Otto George von. The Gothic Cathedral. Origins of Gothic Architecture and the
  Medieval Concept of Order. New York: Pantheon, 1956.

---. Die gotische Kathedrale. 3rd edition. Darmstadt: Wissenschaftliche Buchgesellschaft,
  1979.

Smalley, Beryl. The Study of the Bible in the Middle Ages. New York: Philosophical Library,
  1952.

Söhngen, Gottlieb. "Analogia Entis in Analogia Fidei." Antwort. FS Karl Barth. Ernst Wulf,
  Christiane von Kirschbaum, Rudolf Frey eds. Zollikon: EVZ (1956): 266-271.

---. "Die antik-christliche Wissenschaft und Weisheit in Anselms neuer, germanischer
  Denkform." Wissenschaft und Weisheit 8/1 (1941): 14-23.

---, "Die Einheit in der Theologie" - gesammelte Abhandlungen, Aufsätze und Vorträge.
  München: Karl Zink, 1952.

---. "Die Grundaporie der Theologie `Weisheit im Geheimnis´ und Wissen durch Vernunft."
  Mysterium salutis. Vol. 1: Grundriß heilsdogmatischer Dogmatik. Johannes Feiner and
  Magnus Löhrer eds. Einsiedeln: Benzinger (1965): 907-980.

---. Grundfragen einer Rechtstheologie. München: Pustet, 1962.

---. "Rectitudo bei Anselm von Canterbury als Oberbegriff von Wahrheit und Gerechtigkeit."
  Sola Ratione. FS F.S. Schmitt. Stuttgart - Bad Cannstatt: Friedrich Frommann (1970):
  71-86.

Southern, Richard William. "Anselm at Canterbury." Anselm Studies I (1983): 7-22,

---. Medieval Humanism and other essays. Oxford: Basil Blackwell, 1970.

---. Saint Anselm and his Biographer. A Study of Monastic Life and Thought. 1059 - c.1130.
  Cambridge: Cambridge UP, 1963.

---. Saint Anselm. Portrait in a Landscape. Cambridge: Cambridge UP, 1990.

---. Scholastic Humanism and the Unification of Europe. volume I. Oxford: Blackwell, 1995.

---. The Life of Saint Anselm. Archbishop of Canterbury by Eadmer. London: Thomas
Nelson, 1962.

Speck, Johannes ed. Grundprobleme der großen Philosophen. Bd. I. Göttingen: Vandenhoeck
und Ruprecht, 1972.

Speer, Andreas. Philosophie und geistiges Erbe des Mittelalters mit Beiträgen von Jan A.
Aersten, Klaus Jacobi, Georg Wieland und Rémi Brague. Köln: U Köln, 1994.

Splett, Jörg. Denken vor Gott, Philosophie als Wahrheitsliebe. Frankfurt am Main: Knecht,
1996.

Spoerl, Johannes. Grundformen der hochmittelalterlichen Geschichtsbetrachtung. Studien
zum Ethos der Geschichtsschreiber des 12. Jahrhunderts. München: Hueber, 1935.

Stacpoole, Alberic "St. Anselm's Memorials." Downside Review 88 (1970): 160-180.

Stapert, Calvin. "Gregorian Chant and the Power of Emptiness." Faith seeking Understanding:
Learning and the Catholic Tradition. George C. Berthold ed. Manchester NH: St.
Anselm College P (1991): 107-115.

Steidle, Basilius. Die Regel St. Benedikts. Beuron: Beuroner Kunstverlag, 1952.

Steiger, Lothar. "Contextes Syllogismos. Über die Kunst und Bedeutung der Topik bei
Anselm." Analecta Anselmiana I. Franciscus Salesius Schmitt ed. Frankfurt am Main:
Minerva (1969): 107-143.

Steiger, Ludger. "Ontologisches oder kosmologisches Argument? Anselm, zwischen Kant,
Hegel und Barth." Analecta Anselmiana IV/1 Untersuchungen über Person und Werk
Anselm von Canterburys. Frankfurt am Main: Minerva (1975): 317-322.

Stock, Brian. The Implications of Literacy. Princeton: Princeton UP, 1983.

Stolz, Anselm. "Anselm's Theology in the Proslogion." The Many-Faced Argument. Recent
Studies on the Ontolgical Argument for the existence of God. John Hick, Arthur C.
McGill eds. New York: MacMillan (1967): 183-206.

---. Anselm von Canterbury. Sein Leben, seine Bedeutung, seine Hauptwerke. München:
Kösel/Pustet, 1937.

---. "Das Proslogion des Hl. Anselm." Revue Bénédictine 47 (1935): 331-347.

---. "'Vere esse' im 'Proslogion' des hl. Anselm." Revue Bénédictine 47 (1935): 331-347.

---. "Zur Theologie Anselms im Proslogion." Catholica 2 (1933): 1-24.

Synan, Edward A. "Truth: Augustine and Anselm." Anselm Studies II: an occasional Journal.
Joseph C. Schaubelt ed. White Plains N.Y.: Kraus International (1988): 275-295.

422

Taylor, Henry Orsborn. The Medieval Mind. A History of the Development of Thought and Emotion in the Middle Ages. in two volumes, Cambridge: Harvard UP, 1962.

Tester, S. Jim ed. Fides Quaerens Intellectum. Medieval philosophy from Augustine to Ockham. Bristol: Bristol Classical, 1989.

"Thomas von Aquin." Grundprobleme der großen Philosophen. Josef Speck ed, vol. I. Göttingen: Vandenhoeck und Ruprecht, 1972.

Thompson, William M. Christology and Spirituality. New York: Crossroad, 1991.

---. Fire and Light. New York: Paulist, 1987.

---. The Jesus Debate: a survey and synthesis. New York: Paulist, 1985.

---. The Struggle for Theology's Soul, Contesting Scripture in Christology. New York: Crossroad Herder, 1996.

Torrance, Thomas F. Karl Barth: An Introduction to his Early Theology 1910-31. London: SCM, 1962.

---. "The ethical implications of Anselm's `De veritate.'" Theologische Zeitschrift 24 (1968): 309-319.

---. The Ground and Grammar of Theology. Charlottesville VA: UP of Virginia, 1980.

---. "The Problem of Natural Theology in the Thought of Karl Barth." Religious Studies 6 (1969): 121-135.

Ubbelohde, Karl-Friedrich. Glaube und Vernunft bei Anselm von Canterbury. Eine Studie zur Genese systematischer Theologie und zum Verständnis von "Theologia" und "Philosophia" zwischen Patristik und Frühscholastik. Diss. Göttingen U, 1969.

Ullmann, Wolfgang. "Karl Barths zweite Wende. Ein neuer Interpretationsvorschlag zu `Fides quaerens intellectum.'" Theologie als Christologie, Zum Werk und Leben Karl Barths - Ein Symposium. Heidelore Köchert and Wolf Kröthe eds. Berlin (West): Evangelische Verlagsanstalt (1988): 71-89.

---. "Zur Auseinandersetzung Anselms von Canterbury mit der trinitätstheologischen Terminologie Augustins." Philologus. Zeitschrift für klassische Philologie. 123/1 (1979): 75-79.

Ulrich, Ferdinand. "Cur non video praesentem? Zur Implikation der `griechischen' und `lateinischen' Denkform bei Anselm und Scotus Erigena." Freiburger Zeitschrift für Philosophie und Theologie 22 (1975): 70-170.

Vagaggini, Cipriano. "La hantise des `rationes necessariae' de S. Anselme dans la théologie de processions trinitaires de S. Thomas." Spicilegium Beccense I. Congrès international du IXe centenaire de l'arrivée d'Anselme au Bec. Paris: Vrin (1959): 103-139.

van Buren, Paul M. "Anselm's Formula and the Logic of 'God'" Religious Studies 9 (1973): 279-288.

Vandenbroucke, François. "La divorce entre théologie et mystique, ses origines." Nouvelle Revue Théologique 72 (1950): 289-372.

Vanderjagt, Arjo. "Knowledge of God in Ghazali and Anselm." Mediaevalia Miscellanea. Albert Zimmermann ed. Sprache und Erkenntnis im Mittelalter. Bd. 13/2. Berlin New York: de Gruyter (1981): 852-861.

van der Meer, Frederick. Die Ursprünge christlicher Kunst. Freiburg i. Br.: Herder, 1982.

Van Fleteren, Frederick. "Augustine and Anselm: Faith and Reason." Faith seeking Understanding: Learning and the Catholic Tradition. George C. Berthold ed. Manchester NH: St. Anselm College Press (1991): 57-66.

Vanni Rovighi, Sofia. "Glaube und Vernunft bei Anselm von Aosta." Renovatio et Reformatio. FS Ludwig Hödl. Manfred Gerwing and Godehard Ruppert eds. Münster: Aschendorff (1985): 170-178.

---. "Il Problema del male in Anselmo d'Aosta." Analecta Anselmiana Bd. 5. Frankfurt am Main: Minerva (1976): 179-198.

---. "L'etica di S. Anselmo." Analecta Anselmiana. Bd. 1. Frankfurt am Main: Minerva (1969): 73-99.

---. "'Ratio' in S. Anselmo d'Aosta." Studia Anselmiana 63 (1974): 65-74.

---. Sant' Anselmo e la filosofia del secolo XI. Storia della filosofia italiana 1. Milano: Vita e Pensiero, 1949.

Vansina, Jan. Oral Tradition. A Study in oral methodology. London: Routledge, 1973.

van Steenberghen, Fernand. Introduction à l'étude de la philosophie médiévale. Louvain-Paris: Nauwelaerts, 1974.

Vaughn, Sally N. "The Monastic Sources of Anselm's Political Beliefs: St. Augustine, St. Benedict, and St. Gregory the Great." Anselm Studies II: an occasional Journal. Joseph C. Schaubelt e.a. ed. White Plains N.Y.: Kraus International (1988): 53-92.

Verweyen, Hansjürgen. Anselm von Canterbury. Freiheitsschriften. De Libertate Arbitrii. De Casu Diaboli i.a. Fontes Christiani Vol. 13. Freiburg i. Br.: Herder, 1994.

---. Anselm von Canterbury. Wahrheit und Freiheit. Über die Wahrheit. Über die Freiheit des Willens. Vom Fall des Teufels. Über die Vereinbarkeit des Vorherwissens, der

Vorherbestimmung und der Gnade Gottes mit dem freien Willen. Einsiedeln: Johannes, 1982.

---. "Anthropologische Vermittlung der Offenbarung: Anselms 'Monologion.'" Fides Quaerens Intellectum, Beiträge zur Fundamentaltheologie. FS Max Seckler. Michael Kenzler, Wolfhart Pannenberg, Hermann Josef Pottmeyer eds. Tübingen: Francke, 1992.

---. Gottes letztes Wort. Grundriß einer Fundamentaltheologie. Düsseldorf: Patmos, 1991.

Vess, Deborah. "Continuity and Conservatism in the Cathedral Schools of the Twelfth Century: The Role of Monastic Thought in the so-called Intellectual Revolution of the Twelfth Century." American Benedictine Review 45 (1994): 161-183.

---. Humanism in the Middle Ages: Peter Abailard and the Breakdown of Medieval Philosophy. Denton: U North Texas, 1991.

Vignaux, Paul. "La Méthode de Saint Anselme dans le *Monologion* et le *Proslogion*." Aquinas, Ephemerides Thomisticae VII (1965): 110-129.

---. "Necessité des raisons dans le Monologion." Revue des sciences philosophiques et théologiques 64 (1980): 3-25.

---. "Structure et sens du 'Monologion.'" Revue des sciences philosophiques et théologiques 31 (1947): 192-212.

Viola, Coloman Etienne. "Anselme de Cantorbéry." Dictionnaire critique de Théologie. sous la direction de Jean-Yves Lacoste. Paris: Presses Universitaires de France (1998): 54-58.

---. "Between Canterbury and Rome. The Greatness of God as a means of Transcending Human Limits in Saint Anselm's Thought." The European Dimension of St. Anselm's Thinking. ed. by Josef Zmur and Vilém Herold. Prague: Institute of Philosophy (1993): 41-64.

---. "Dalle filosofie ad Anselmo di Canterbury. L'itinerario teologico di Karl Barth." Doctor communis 24 (1974): 98-117.

---. "Foi et Vérité chez Saint Anselm." Les Mutations Socio-Culturelles au Tournant des XIe - XIIe Siècles. Colloques Internationaux du Centre National de la Recherche Scientifique. Paris: CNRS (1984): 583-593.

---. "La dialectique de la grandeur. Une interpretation du Proslogion." Recherches de la Théologie ancienne et médiévale 37 (1970): 23-42.

---. "L´Influence de la Méthode Anselmienne: la Méthode de Saint Anselme Jugée par les Historiens de Son Temps." Analecta Anselmiana. Untersuchungen über Person und Werk Anselms von Canterbury. IV/2. Helmut Kohlenberger ed. Frankfurt am Main: Minerva (1975): 1-32.

---. "Origine et portée du principe dialectique du `Proslogion´ de saint Anselme de l´ `argument ontologique´ à l´ `argument megalologique.´" Rivista di filosofia neoscolastica 83 (1992): 339-384.

Voegelin, Eric. The Collected Works of Eric Voegelin. Vol. 12: Published Esssays, 1966-1985. Paul Caringella e.a. ed. Baton Rouge: Lousiana State UP, 1990.

---. The Collected Works of Eric Voegelin. Vol. 28: What is history? and other late unpublished works. Paul Caringella e.a. ed. Baton Rouge: Lousiana State UP, 1990.

de Vogüé, Adalbert. Die Regula Benedicti - Theologisch-spiritueller Kommentar. Regulae Benedicti Studia - Supplementa. Vol. 16. Bernd Jaspert ed. Hildesheim: Gerstenberg, 1983.

---. "Prayer in the Rule of Saint Benedict." Monastic Studies 7 (1969): 113-140.

---. The Rule of Saint Benedict - A Doctrinal and Spiritual Commentary. John Baptist Hasbrouck trans. Cistercian Studies Series: Number Fifty-Four. Kalamazoo MI: Cistercian Publications, 1983.

von den Steinen, Wolfram. Der Kosmos des Mittelalters. Von Karl dem Grossen zu Bernhard von Clairvaux. 2nd rev. ed. Bern/München: Francke, 1967.

---. Homo Caelestis. Bd. I. Bern/München: Francke, 1965.

---. Menschen im Mittelalter. Peter Moos ed., Bern: Francke, 1967.

---. "Monastik und Scholastik." Zeitschrift für deutsches Altertum und deutsche Literatur 89 (1978): 243-256.

---. Notker der Dichter und seine geistige Welt. Darstellungsband. Bern: Francke, 1948.

---. Vom Heiligen Geist des Mittelalters. Anselm von Canterbury und Bernhard von Clairvaux. Breslau: Ferdinand Hirt, 1926.

Vossenkuhl, Wilhelm and Rolf Schönberger eds., Die Gegenwart Ockhams, Acta Humaniora, Weinheim: VCH, 1990.

Vuillemin, Jules. "Id quo maius cogitari potest. Über die innere Möglichkeit eines rationalen Gottesbegriffs." Archiv für Geschichte und Philosophie 53 (1971): 279-299.

---. Le Dieu d´Anselme et les apparences de la raison. Paris: Aubier, 1971.

Waldenfels, Hans. "Die vielen Gesichter der einen Welt. Christlicher Glaube an der Wende zur Postmoderne." Christ in der Gegenwart. (1997): 157.

Waldstein, Michael. "An introduction to von Balthasar's 'The Glory of the Lord.'" Communio 14 (1987): 12-33.

---. "Hans Urs von Balthasar's theological aesthetics." Communio 11 (1984): 13-27.

Ward, Benedicta. "II. Anselm of Canterbury and His Influence." Christian Spirituality - Origins to the Twelfth Century. Bernhard McGinn, John Meyendorff, Jean Leclercq eds. New York: Crossroad (1989): 196-205.

---. "'Inward feeling and deep thinking': The Prayers and Meditations of St. Anselm Revisited." Anselm Studies I. An Occasional Journal. Millwood NY: Kraus International (1983): 177-183.

---. "St. Anselm and the Development of Prayer." Cistercian Studies VIII/1 (1973): 72-81.

--- trans. and intro. by. The Prayers and Meditations of St. Anselm. Harmondsworth: Penguin, 1973.

Warnach, Victor. "Wort und Wirklichkeit bei Anselm von Canterbury." Salzburger Jahrbuch für Philosophie 5/6 (1961/62): 157-176.

---. "Zum Argument im Proslogion Anselms von Canterbury." Einsicht und Glaube. FS Gottlieb Söhngen. Joseph Ratzinger and Heinrich Fries eds. Freiburg i. Br.: Herder (1962): 337-357.

Watson, Gordon. "A Study in St. Anselm's Soteriology and Karl Barth's theological Method." Scottish Journal of Theology 42 (1989): 493-512.

Weber, Franz Josef. Die Fragmente der Vorsokratiker. Paderborn, München: Schöningh, 1988.

Weil, Simone. Cahiers. Aufzeichnungen IV. ed. by Elisabeth Edl and Wolfgang Matz. München: Carl Hanser, 1998.

Weizers, Olga. Méthodes et Instruments du travail intellectuell au moyen âge. Turnhout: Brepols, 1990.

Welch, Adam C. Anselm and his Work. New York: Charles Scribner, 1901.

Wells, Norman J. "The Language of Possibility - Another Reading of Anselm." Miscellanea Mediaevalia. Albert Zimmermann ed. Sprache und Erkenntnis im Mittelalter. Bd. 13/2. Berlin/New York: de Gruyter (1981): 847-851.

Welte, Bernhard. Auf der Spur des Ewigen. Philosophische Abhandlungen über verschiedene Gegenstände der Religion und Theologie. Freiburg i. Br.: Herder, 1965.

---. Heilsverständnis. Philosophische Untersuchungen zum Verständnis des Christentums. Freiburg i. Br.: Herder, 1966.

---. Religionsphilosophie. Freiburg i. Br.: Herder, 1978.

---. "Was hat die Philosophie in der Theologie zu tun.?" Theologische Quartalschrift 4 (1974): 303-323.

Werner, Hans- Joachim. "Anselm von Canterburys Dialog `De Veritate´ und das Problem der Begründung praktischer Sätze." Salzburger Jahrbuch für Philosophie XX (1975): 119-130.

Whitehead, Alfred North. Process and Reality. An essay in cosmology. New York: Humanities Press, 1955.

Wiedmann, Franz. "Wahrheit als Rechtheit." Epimelia. Die Sorge der Philosophie um den Menschen. FS H. Kuhn. München: Hueber (1964): 174-182.

Wierenga, Edward. "Anselm on Omnipresence." The New Scholasticism 62 (1988): 30-41.

Wiese, Benno von. Signaturen. Zu Heinrich Heine und seinem Werk. Frankfurt am Main: Erich Schmidt, 1976.

Wiese, Hans-Ulrich. "Die Lehre Anselms von Canterbury über den Tod Jesu in der Schrift `Cur Deus Homo.´" Wissenschaft und Weisheit 41 (1978): 149-179 and 42 (1979): 34-55.

Wigley, Stephen D. "Karl Barth on St. Anselm: The Influence of Anselm´s `Theological Scheme´ on T.F. Torrance and Eberhard Jüngel." Scottish Journal of Theology 46 (1993): 79-97.

Williams, Daniel D. "The Concept of Truth in Karl Barth´s Theology." Religious Studies 6 (1969): 137-145.

Wilmart, André. "La tradition des lettres de S. Anselme. Lettres inédites de S. Anselme et de ses correspondants." Revue Bénédictine 43 (1931): 38-54.

Winandy, André. Ambroise Autpert, moin et théologien. Paris: Vrin, 1953.

Wittgenstein, Ludwig. Philosophische Untersuchungen. Frankfurt am Main: Suhrkamp, 1967.

---. Tractatus logico-philosophicus. Schriften 1a. Frankfurt am Main: Suhrkamp, 1960.

Wojtyla, Karol. The acting Person. Analecta Husserliana X. Anna-Teresa Tymieniecka ed. Dordrecht: Reidel, 1979.

Wolf, Gunther G. "Est modus in rebus, sent certi denique fines, quos ultra citraque nequit consistere rectum (Horaz, Sat. I, 1, 106). Einige Bemerkungen zum Symbolcharakter von Maß und Kreis." Miscellanea Mediaevalia 16/2, Mensura, Maß, Zahl, Zahlensymbolik im Mittelalter. Berlin: de Gruyter (1984): 476-483.

Wollasch, Joachim. Cluny - "Licht der Welt" - Aufstieg und Niedergang der klösterlichen Gemeinschaft. Zürich: Artemis & Winkler, 1996.

Wolz, Henry G. "The empirical Basis of Anselm´s Arguments." The Philosophical Review LX/3 (1951): 341-361.

Wood, Robert E. "Philosophy, Aesthetics, and Theology: A Review of Hans Urs von Balthasar´s The Glory of the Lord." American Catholic Philosophical Quarterly LXVII (1993): 355-382.

Wyshogrod, Edith. Saints and Postmodernism: revisioning moral Philosophy. Chicago: U of Chicago P, 1990.

Zimmermann, Albert. "Die Ratio Anselmi in einem anonymen Metaphysikkommentar des 14. Jahrhundert." Analecta Anselmiana Untersuchungen über Person und Werk Anselm von Canterburys. Bd. IV/1. Helmut Kohlenberger ed. Frankfurt am Main: Minerva (1975): 195-201.

Zimmermann, Karl. "Anselm von Canterbury. Der ontologische Gottesbeweis und das Problem der metaphysischen Erkenntnis." Miscellanea Mediaevalia 2. Die Metaphysik im Mittelalter. Berlin: de Gruyter (1963): 184-191.

Zumkeller, Adolar. "Der Terminus `sola fide´ bei Augustinus." Christian Authority. Essays in Honour of Henry Chadwick. Gillian Rosemary Evans ed. Oxford: Clarendon (1988): 86-100.

Zumr, Josef and Vilém Herold eds. The European Dimensions of St. Anselm´s Thinking. Proceedings of the Conference organized by the Anselm-Society and the Institute of Philosophy of Academy of Sciences of the Czech Republic. Prague: Institute of Philosophy, 1993.